Colombia

the Bradt Travel Guide

Sarah Woods

edition
I

www.bradtguides.com

Bradt Travel Guides Ltd, UK
The Globe Pequot Press Inc, USA

CARIBBEAN SEA

VENEZUELA

PANAMA

PACIFIC OCEAN

UNESCO Seaflower Biosphere Reserve in the San Andrés Archipelago — located 700 km northwest of Colombia's Caribbean coast
page 197

San Gil and the Rio Fonce — Colombia's adventure sports Mecca
page 160

Cosmopolitan Bogotá
page 111

Nevado del Ruiz volcano in Los Nevados National Park
page 318

Punta Gallinas
Puerto Estrella
Cabo de la Vela
Península de la Guajira
Golfo de Venezuela

Puerto Carreño
Puerto Nuevo
Puerto Nariño
Rio Tomo
Maleza
Vichada
Rio Meta
Orocue
Aguaclara
Sogamoso
Rio Meta
Tame
Arauca

Maicao
Riohacha
Santa Marta
Ciénaga
Valledupar
Sierra de Perijá
El Banco
Rio Magdalena
Convención
Cúcuta
Pamplona
Bucaramanga
Floridablanca
Barrancabermeja
La Dorada
Tunja
BOGOTÁ
Girardot
Ibagué
Armenia
Cartago
Pereira
Manizales
Oriental

BARRANQUILLA
Soledad
CARTAGENA
Sincelejo
Montería
Caucasia
Turbo
Riosucio
Serranía de Baudó
Quibdó
Nuquí
Cabo Corrientes
Punta Magdalena
Bello
Itagüí
Envigado
MEDELLÍN
Occidental

Golfo de Morrosquillo
Rio Sinú
Rio Cauca
Golfo de Panamá

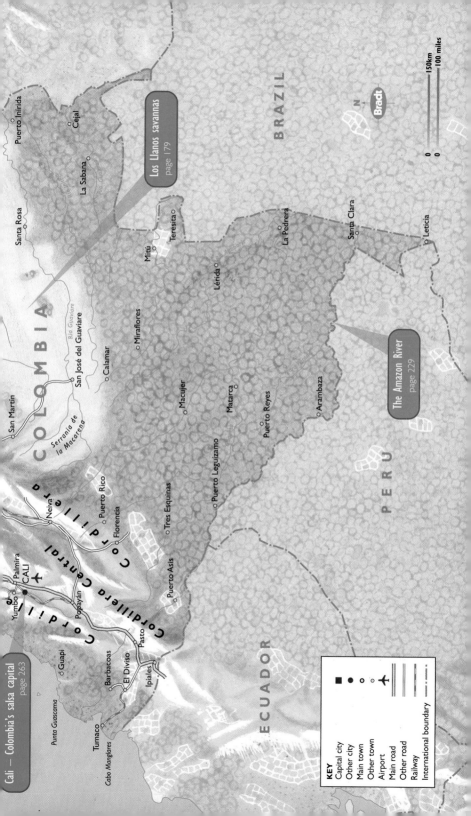

Cali – Colombia's salsa capital
page 263

Los Llanos savannas
page 179

The Amazon River
page 229

COLOMBIA

BRAZIL

PERU

ECUADOR

Serranía de
la Macarena

Cordillera Occidental

Cordillera Central

Cordillera

Río Guaviare

Río Guainía

Puerto Inírida
Santa Rosa
Cejal
La Sabana
San Martín
Mitú
Teresita
Lérida
La Pedrera
Santa Clara
Leticia
Miraflores
San José del Guaviare
Calamar
Macujer
Matarca
Puerto Reyes
Arambaza
Puerto Leguizamo
Tres Esquinas
Puerto Rico
Neiva
Florencia
Puerto Asís
Popayán
Pasto
Ipiales
El Diviso
Barbacoas
Tumaco
Guapi
Punta Guascama
Cabo Manglares
Yumbo
CALI
Palmira

Bradt

N

0
0
150km
100 miles

KEY
■ Capital city
● Other city
○ Main town
○ Other town
✈ Airport
Main road
Other road
Railway
International boundary

Colombia
Don't
miss...

Bogotá
South America's third-highest capital city — 2,630m above sea level
(SW) page 111

White-water rafting on the Rio Fonce
A mecca for adventure sports
(DITUR) page 161

Los Llanos
Ride across the
prairies with cattle-
roping cowboys
(DITUR) page 179

**San Andrés
archipelago**
First-class diving
and home to the
UNESCO seaflower
biosphere reserve

(DITUR) page 197

Amazon River
Home to
indigenous tribes
and thousands of
species of flora
and fauna
(DITUR) page 229

 top Market day on one of Medellín's sunny plazas
(DITUR) page 302

above Cathedral, Rionegro
(DITUR) page 307

right Dog statue (Botero), Plazoleta de Las Esculturas, Medellín
(SW) page 304

AUTHOR

Since first discovering her itchy feet in the mid-1980s, British-born travel writer **Sarah Woods** has barely stood still. In over 20 years of travel, she has criss-crossed the globe in several directions, clocking up almost a million kilometres and visiting around 60 countries along the way. Sarah first visited Colombia on an unscheduled flying visit and, struck by the spirited verve she encountered, made plans to return to travel the nation in depth – and has since travelled its length and breadth. Ask Sarah what makes Colombia so special and she is unequivocal, citing the country's extraordinary biodiversity, stunning scenery, friendly faces and magnificent cultural mix.

A veteran of volunteering, Sarah sponsors an SOS village for abandoned and orphaned children in central Bogotá. She writes about her experiences in Colombia for magazines and newspapers worldwide and has also contributed to film and television documentaries on Colombian themes. Sarah won the British Guild of Travel Writers' 'Travel Guidebook of the Year' in 2005 for the Bradt Guide to Panama. In 2007, she was awarded the Kenneth Westcott Jones Memorial Award for travel writing.

CONTRIBUTOR

Heloise Crowther is a specialist writer on Latin America and has travelled extensively in the region. She lives in London.

AUTHOR'S STORY

Colombia first came to my attention as a nine-year-old at junior school when, in a geography lesson, I learned about the Spanish settlement of fortified Cartagena. I studied pastel drawings of colonial streetscapes and marvelled at sketches depicting Colombia's ancient indigenous tribes. Almost 30 years later, after completing *Panama: the Bradt Travel Guide*, I journeyed to Colombia and was able to make those illustrations from my childhood come to life. For even in modern Colombia, I was able to pass through vast, open expanses of countryside gloriously free of traffic, noise and people. I savoured jaw-dropping scenery dotted with pretty, rustic towns and grazing cattle and witnessed Indian tribes practising ancient rituals as they'd done for many centuries past. I realised quickly, that Colombia is a very special country; a nation poles apart from the one so often primitively depicted in the headlines news.

Like many travellers, I was frustrated by the scant coverage offered in the back-end of regional 'South American' travel guides, so I am glad that in my own small way I am able to help redress the balance. In all honesty, I could fill an entire bookshelf describing what Colombia has to offer visitors. Thank goodness that the Bradt team were there to remind me that travel guides need to be portable and should weigh in at under a ton.

Re-reading this guide brings back memories of the many life-enriching experiences I owe to Colombia and its people. One simple, but memorable example of the Colombian hospitality I encountered was a handwritten note handed to me by a young girl in Huila welcoming me warmly to her country. I still have the note, stained purple by the freshly-picked berries we shared in the sunshine, whilst swapping stories and etching pictures in the blood-red dust of the road.

The first Bradt travel guide was written in 1974 by George and Hilary Bradt on a river barge floating down a tributary of the Amazon. It was followed by *Backpacker's Africa*, published in 1979. In the 1980s and '90s the focus shifted away from hiking to broader-based guides to new destinations – usually the first to be published on those places. In the 21st century Bradt continues to publish these ground-breaking guides, along with guides to established holiday destinations, incorporating in-depth information on culture and natural history alongside the nuts and bolts of where to stay and what to see.

Bradt authors support responsible travel, with advice not only on minimum impact but also on how to give something back through local charities. Thus a true synergy is achieved between the traveller and local communities.

* * *

Nearly 40 years ago I arrived in Barranquilla, Colombia as a nervous lone woman traveller. I spoke no Spanish, and had only the vaguest idea of where I was going and what I would find there. Within 24 hours I was staying in the home of a delightful family in Bogotá and making great strides in learning the language. But I never did understand why the three teenage boys collapsed with laughter whenever I repeated one phrase they taught me: 'No joda', 'Stop bothering me', and it stood me in good stead throughout my four-month trip. But I needed this book finally to learn what it actually means (see page 431)!

Sarah has done a wonderful job in bringing this most beguiling of South American countries to life. Reading it I remembered so well the warmth of the people – surely the most friendly in the entire continent – the scenery, birdlife, beaches and numerous eccentricities that make the place so special. I only wish I'd had it with me in 1969!

Reprinted September 2008   First published April 2008
Bradt Travel Guides Ltd, 23 High Street, Chalfont St Peter, Bucks SL9 9QE, England
www.bradtguides.com
Published in the USA by The Globe Pequot Press Inc, 246 Goose Lane,
PO Box 480, Guilford, Connecticut 06475-0480

ISBN-10: 1 84162 242 7   ISBN-13: 978 1 84162 242 2
British Library Cataloguing in Publication Data
A catalogue record for this book is available from the British Library
Photographs Dr Arthur Anker (AA), Ashley Holland (AH), Bildagentur RM/TIPS (BRM/TIPS), Colombian Tourist Board (DITUR), Francesco Tomasinelli/TIPS (FT/TIPS), Kirk Smock (KS), Oscar Robles (OR), Pete Oxford (PO), Sarah Woods (SW)
Front cover Girl at Barranquilla Carnival (OR)
Back cover Beach at Bahía (DITUR)
Title page Woman weaving straw hat (DITUR), Lorica Caldas church (DITUR), Wooden carving of Colombian woman and child (DITUR)
Illustrations Oliver Whalley **Maps** Malcolm Barnes, Terence Crump, Steve Munns (colour map)

Typeset from the author's disc by Wakewing   Printed and bound in Italy by L.E.G.O. Spa-Lavis (TN)

I was extremely pleased to learn of Sarah Woods's new travel guide to Colombia as, to me, it reflects the growing interest in my country of visitors from all over the world – at last. That more and more people are prepared to come and see Colombia for themselves is great for my country and its people. I am also convinced that anyone who comes to Colombia – be it Cartagena, San Andrés, Medellín, Cali, the Amazon or my home town of Bogotá – will leave with treasured memories. Quite simply, Colombia has some of the most beautiful colonial towns, pretty beaches and unexplored jungle on earth – no contest.

I have been lucky enough to travel the world as part of my racing career and have visited some wonderful and fascinating places. However, I have always returned home to the beautiful scenery and friendly faces of Colombia – and feel constantly blessed by what I find. So, to travellers keen to explore Colombia I say keep an open mind, open eyes and an open heart. Be sure to meet the people, enjoy the many ancient cultures and, above all, discover the real Colombia – it is truly a country like no other. A warm welcome awaits you.

Juan Pablo Montoya
Former F1 racing driver, current NASCAR professional and
a UN Goodwill Ambassador.
Born in Bogotá, 20 September 1975
(*www.jpmontoya.com*; see box *Colombia's fastest guy*, page 40)

Acknowledgements

I'd need a whole chapter in which to fully extend my gratitude to every Colombian who lent their support to this mammoth project. Each and every Colombian I met, without exception, had a special story about their homeland to share and I am deeply indebted to a host people who whole-heartedly gave it their all. That this guide is so extensive, owes a great deal to the impassioned knowhow of these 'national tourism ambassadors' – all of whom are deserving of an official post on the basis of sheer enthusiasm for their homeland alone.

A special mention must go to two schoolgirl sisters in La Guajira, Kelly and Katiara, whose warm smiles and big hugs were a joy to behold. Arriving at the end of a long, dusty journey across arid desert sands took on an Oasis-in-the-Sahara scenario. I slept soundly in the girls' simple beachside posada comforted by human kindness, and lulled by rhythmic, lapping waves.

Thank you also to the Indian men-folk who guided me deftly through the fast-rising waters of the Amazon and to the jewellery-maker in Huila who allowed me a chance to taste deep fried ants. To the roadside vendor who insisted that I sell up everything in England to start a new life with him in Colonial-era Cartagena to the flower-seller who helped me find the juiciest steak in Bogotá. Thanks also to my snake-hipped driver for switching me on to Colombia's hip-swinging *musica vallenata* and to the rugged Llanero cowboy who shared his life story with me on the cattle-clad rolling plains.

I also deeply appreciate the logistical help I received when criss-crossing Colombia – the list is a long one, but the following deserve a note of thanks: Nubia Stella Martinez, José Chehab, Diana Quiazua, Lina Rincón, General Salazar, Marta Lucía Palacío, Sandra Riaño, Milena Ramírez, Andrés Gonzalez, Diego Peláez, Alejandra Fajardo, Esperanza Valderrama, Mark Rausch and Jorge Rausch in Bogotá; Luisa Urueña, Jan Fernando Salazar and Emily Goodfellow in London; Ana María Charris and María Carolina Rico in Barranquilla; Juan Alejandro Duque and Norhara Landaño and Roberto Echeverry in the Zona Cafetería; Juan Carlos Castro; Magnola Beltrán and Juan Jaime in Cali; Lourdes Lopera, Miguel Ramírez; José Tique and Cecilia Acosta in La Guajira; Pedro Luis Mogollón and Nico Medez in Cartagena; Asturia Peña, Claudia Marcela, Claudia Delgado, Dairo Cuenta Casanova, Sussan Jane Stroemer de Saad and Humberto Mejia in San Andrés; Rosa in Providencía; Claudia Santos Carrillo, Rubén Darío Sosa, Álvaro Fernández, Dámaso Yepes, Lucy Páez Peñaloza and Jehimi Rodriguez in Santa Marta; Ángela Buitrago, Rodrigo Echeverry and Sandra Atalah in Los Llanos; Sergio Osorio, Diego Velásquez, Byron Arango, Lázaro López and Oscar Jhony in Capurgana; César Isaza Vásquez in Bahía Solano; Aurelio Velazco Mosquera in Popayán; Albeiro Castro in Neiva; Adriana Gonzalez and Santiago Ospina in Medellín; Iván Mustafa in Bucaramanga; Yusara Cruz, Antonio Cruz in The Amazon. Thanks also to Erik Rupert, Ron Behrens and Robert Giles at ProAves.

John Howard Galindo in Buga has also been generous with his time and patience in double-checking Colombia's colloquialism and linguistic quirks.

Thanks to Roger Harris and Peter Hutchison for loaning their wildlife guide from *Amazon: The Bradt Travel Guide*.

Thank you also to Emma Thomson at Bradt and to the oh-so-diligent Raichel Rickels without whom a greater number of inky embarrassments would lurk amongst these pages. Marion and John Short have been particularly wonderful in too many ways to mention, so I shall just say *muchas gracias*. Thanks also go to the sterling efforts of ultra-competent contributors Helois Crowther and Helen Ponting who, like Raichel, simply rolled their sleeves up and got stuck in.

To Alejandro Navas, I owe a special heartfelt thank you for accompanying me on the lion's share of my journey. I learned so much about the real Colombia from a man who clearly adores his country – and who readily admits he wants nothing more than the world to love it too. To explore Colombia in Alejandro's company was a true revelation and his courteous good manners and charming smile opened many doors along the way. I defy anyone not to feel enlivened by his infectious enthusiasm and honest appreciation for his beloved home nation. That Alejandro also has an ability to remain cheerful when faced with cancelled flights, mudslides and sudden mechanical failure has also been invaluable in helping my challenging cross-country itinerary run smoothly.

As usual not a chapter would have been typed without the encouragement of travel photographer David Short. His unwavering support and keen interest in this project has been a tremendous boost. Thank you, as always.

DEDICATION

From Sarah to David

FEEDBACK REQUEST

Every effort has been made to ensure that the details contained within this book are as accurate and up to date as possible. Inevitably, however, things move on. Any information regarding such changes, or relating to your experiences in Colombia – good or bad – would be very gratefully received. Such feedback is invaluable when compiling further editions. Send your comments to Bradt Travel Guides Ltd, 23 High Street, Chalfont St Peter, Bucks SL9 9QE, England; e info@bradtguides.com. Please also visit the Bradt website at www.bradtguides.com for updates on Colombia from Sarah Woods.

Contents

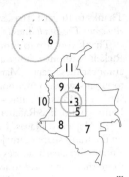

Introduction

Colombia must surely be one of the world's most bewildering paradoxes, a nation blessed with jaw-dropping natural beauty and some of the most damning headlines on the planet. Yet delve beneath the front-page drama and Colombia differs from the common perception, a country that has so much more to offer than turmoil and strife.

Spanning an area twice the size of France and about twice the size of California, Colombia is also the only South American nation with coastlines on both the Atlantic and Pacific oceans. Few countries in Latin America boast such ecological riches with an abundance of natural resources on a dramatically contrasting terrain. Rolling dusty plains edge snow-capped mountain peaks; lunar-like craterous deserts lead to lush, vine-tangled rainforests; flower-filled meadows and coffee plantations lie dotted with pretty red-and-white fincas; with palm-scattered idyllic white-sand beaches and fine colonial settlements in bubble-gum hues. Dozens of indigenous cultures speak over 60 languages in a land that is home to the greatest number of bird species on earth. Colombia is also the setting of Gabriel García Márquez's big-selling novel *One Hundred Years of Solitude* – a story as entrancing as the country itself.

Fertile waters are rich in marine life with resplendent swathes of dense jungle teeming with flora and fauna. Mighty rivers, vast canyons, magnificent waterfalls and bubbling thermal springs dot a landscape of mud-and-thatch villages with gleaming, futuristic cities that rank amongst Latin America's most progressive. Explore creeper-clad ancient civilisations dating back to 500BC, reggae-drenched Caribbean islands and flamingo-covered mangrove thickets. Discover pre-Colombian gold and sacred sites that spawned the myth of El Dorado. Delve into forests that are home to armadillo, jaguar, tapir, ocelot, monkey and spear-hunting tribes. Journey along the inky-green might of the Amazon River amongst 1,500 butterfly species, 1,800 birds, 800 insect species, 2,000 species of reptile and amphibian, 3,200 species of fish, 51,220 plant species – in a region that is home to a staggering 10% of all species found on the planet.

Yet this enigmatic nation isn't all about good news as more than 40 years of horror stories will bear out. A legacy of civil war has left Colombia with something of an image problem – despite leaving the mess of a decade ago behind. Once inextricably linked with drug lords, gang violence and guerrilla warfare, Colombia has achieved notable success in dismantling cartels and demobilising more than 30,000 left-wing and paramilitary fighters. The widespread common delinquency of the 1990s has given way to fierce national pride. Today a thriving forward-thinking society has a rising middle class with modern cities that boast some of the finest healthcare facilities and universities in the region. Peace talks have brought tranquillity to large areas of the country and today Colombia is a safer place to visit than much of the US and Mexico. Poised on the cusp of a promising future, Colombia is entering a brand-new era, bolstered by a wave of national confidence that has the country in buoyant mood. Colombian citizens and foreign and national companies alike have ploughed significant amounts of investment into the country, while much-improved infrastructure has encouraged millions of vehicles to drive across a once-deserted road system. In 2007 American magazine *BusinessWeek* named Colombia 'The Most Extreme Emerging Market on Earth' with tour operators reporting a roaring trade in ecotourism where people once feared to tread. Today, travellers in Colombia are unlikely to encounter anything more dangerous than a hungry mosquito – not bad for a country that once had the tourist appeal of a camping trip in central Baghdad.

Over 1.5 million international visitors explored Colombia in 2006, a growing sector that has increased by more than 50% since 2005. In 2006 it polled second in the Happy Planet Index. Soccer-mad Colombia even made a serious bid to host the 2014 Football World Cup – prompting a state of near-delirium and parties nationwide. Cruise ships sail into Cartagena, one of the most important colonial cities in the Americas. In 2007 Colombia attracted the third-largest market share of tourism in South America – a clear sign of things to come.

So, it just leaves me to say 'enjoy Colombia', have a great trip, *buen viaje*. I'm certain that a few myths regarding this rather fine country will be dispelled along the way. I'm also sure you'll meet some of the most friendly, genuine people in Latin America and will be dazzled by the trademark Colombian smile. One word of advice: try not to make the all-too-common mistake of spelling Colombia with a 'u' (as in Columbia). Few things are as likely to turn a smile into a scowl!

Part One

GENERAL INFORMATION

Name República de Colombia

Population 43.6 million

Location Northern South America, bordering the Caribbean Sea, between Panama and Venezuela, and bordering the North Pacific Ocean, between Ecuador and Panama

Border countries Brazil 1,644km, Ecuador 590km, Panama 225km, Peru 1,800km, Venezuela 2,050km (border total 6,309km)

Type of government Democratic Republic

Head of state President Alvaro Uribe (since 2002): Independent Liberal

Independence 20 July 1810 (from Spain)

Capital Bogotá

Climate Steamy tropical conditions along coast and eastern plains; cool with less humidity in highlands

Topography Flat coastal lowlands, central highlands, high Andes Mountains, eastern lowland plains

Coastline 3,208km (Caribbean Sea 1,760km, North Pacific Ocean 1,448km)

Lowest point Pacific Ocean (0m)

Highest point Pico Cristóbal Colón (5,775m)

Major rivers Magdalena, Cauca, Meta, Guaviare, Caquetá, Putumayo, Atrato, Vaupés, Vichada.

Currency Colombian peso (COP/$)

Rate of exchange £1 = 3,596 COP, US$1 = 1,811 COP, €1 = 2,843 COP (April 2008)

Economy GDP = US$374.4 billion (2006 est) comprising agriculture (12%), industry (35.2%), services (52.7%) with key products and industries coffee, cut flowers, bananas, rice, tobacco, corn, sugarcane, cocoa beans, oilseed, vegetables, forest products, shrimp, textiles, food processing, oil, clothing and footwear, beverages, chemicals, cement, gold, coal and emeralds.

Language Spanish, also 65 indigenous languages

Religion Catholic (90%), also Episcopal & Jewish faiths

Time GMT/UTC −5

International dialling code +57

Electricity 110V, 60Hz

Electric plug American-style plug with two parallel flat blades

Flag Three horizontal bands of yellow (top, double-width), blue and red. The yellow represents the richness of Colombian gold. The blue depicts the Pacific Ocean and Caribbean Sea. The red represents the lives lost during the fight for independence and also represents the blood of Jesús, reflecting Colombia's Christian roots.

Public holidays 1 Jan (New Year's Day), 6 Jan* (Epiphany), 19 Mar* (St Joseph's Day), 20 Mar (Maundy Thursday), 21 Mar (Good Friday), 1 May (Labour Day), 1 May* (Ascension), 22 May* (Corpus Christi), 30 Jun* (Sagrado Corazon; Sacred Heart), 3 Jul* (St Peter & St Paul), 20 Jul (Independence Day), 7 Aug (Battle of Boyacá), 15 Aug* (Assumption), 12 Oct* (Columbus Day), 1 Nov* (All Saints' Day), 11 Nov* (Independence of Cartagena City), 8 Dec (Immaculate Conception), 25 Dec (Christmas Day). (Based on 2008 calendar.) NB: *Observed the following Monday if falls on any other day.

Background Information

GEOGRAPHY

Few countries boast such striking physical variety as Colombia, a land where rugged topography combines with a location near the Equator to create an extraordinary diversity of climates, vegetation, soils and crops. Spanning 1,141,748km² (an area double the size of France or California), Colombia also boasts the distinction of being the only South American nation with coastlines on both the Pacific Ocean and Caribbean Sea. Shaped like an oversized fraying bedsheet, Colombia is South America's fourth-largest country (after Brazil, Argentina and Peru), overwhelming its many diminutive neighbours with a landmass that is as geographically complex as it is physically vast. At the Pasto Massif, near the Ecuadorian border, the mountains divide into the Cordillera Occidental (Western Range), which runs parallel to the Pacific coast, and the Cordillera Central (Central Range), which, with its numerous volcanoes, forms a dominant spine across most of the country north to south, rising to well over 5,000m. Two great river valleys – the mighty Magdalena and fast-flowing Cauca – act as dividing channels from the Atlantic coastal lowlands into the very heart of the country.

Crystalline rocks are exposed on the brooding flanks of the Cordillera Central and are home to sandstone, shale and gold and silver deposits dating back several million years. Ash and lava from more than two dozen ancient volcanoes form soaring peaks that are permanently covered in snow at over 4,600m. In contrast, Cordillera Occidental is non-volcanic and the lowest and most sparsely populated, forming a barrier between the Cauca Valley and the Pacific coast. Elevations less than 1,500m mark the lowest point between the cities of Cali and Buenaventura with higher crests reaching 3,960m at Mount Paramillo in Antioquía at the point the mountains fan into three distinct forested mountain ranges – Abibe, San Jerónimo and Ayapel. Antioquía is also the site of a magnificent weather-ravaged granite intrusion, an exposed plateau averaging 2,500m above sea level divided in two by the depths of the Porce River. This vast, irregular, deep-seated mass of intrusive igneous rock is riddled with gold-bearing quartz veins: a rich strata of lesions that once saw colonial mining prosper. The Baudó Mountains are a far less dramatic topographical attribute than the batholithic but boast one of the fastest-flowing rivers on the planet. A staggering 4,900m³ of water per second is emptied into the Caribbean Gulf by the currents of the Río Atrata. The Baudó Mountains represent a southward extension of the Isthmus of Panama where the range becomes known as Serranía del Sapo and stretches in the Darién.

Estranging the Magdalena Valley from the Llanos are the statuesque slopes of the Cordillera Oriental, a range composed of foliated metamorphic rock and marine sediments and ancient deposits of igneous matter. Rising to 5,493m with high plateaus formed by residues from nearby lakes in the Quaternary period, the Cordillera Oriental culminates in the towering Mount Cocuy before branching off into two skinny mountain ranges, one extending into Venezuela and the other creating a northern boundary.

The isolated, mystical mountains of Santa Marta boast the highest point in the country along its fault-bounded granite massif at 5,775m atop the twin peaks of Cristóbal Colón and Simón Bolívar. Rising sharply from the Caribbean littoral it sprouts up to ice-covered summits with the Atlantic lowlands behind it, forming an imposing, if compact group, surrounded by lands with elevations below 200m: an isolated array of ecosystems and the world's fifth most prominent summit.

Extending north to south almost the entire length of Colombia, the Andes Mountains dominate the central and western parts of the country, with two-fifths of the west of Colombia lying in their highlands. Lofty tablelands and fertile valleys form a dramatic contrast with steep, rugged rocks that descend into rolling coastal plains of the Pacific and Caribbean regions across the eastern interior toward the Orinoco and Amazon rivers.

Colombia's two coastlines have very distinct characteristics, from the boggy horseshoe bays, inlets and jutting marshland peninsulas that epitomise the Pacific shoreline to the Caribbean's sandy beaches, palm-fringed islands and saline lagoons.

Between the Andes and the frontiers of Venezuela, Brazil, Peru and Ecuador are some 600,000km² of very sparsely populated steamy lowlands and swamps that form catchments for the tributaries that empty into the Orinoco and Amazon rivers. To the north lies the gaping savanna of Los Llanos at roughly 250,000km², a huge open stretch in the basin of the Orinoco River. This vast semi-arid terrain of grass plains contains thick forests along the riverbanks. At more that 400,000km² the Amazon engulfs southeast Colombia, a land dominated by dense rainforest and riddled with magnificent vine-tangled rivers.

Another of Colombia's important geographic facets is its numerous outlying islands, including the photogenic cluster of white-sand palm-fringed isles located 750km northwest of the mainland in the Caribbean Sea. The islands of San Andrés and Providencía boast seven groups of coral reefs and cays in the Caribbean Sea just a few hundred miles from the Mosquito Coast of Nicaragua. Also near the Caribbean coast are San Bernardo and the Islas del Rosario, while Malpelo and Gorgona are located in the Pacific Ocean in Colombia's southwest. In the Pacific, Colombian territory encompasses Isla de Malpelo at about 430km west of Buenaventura. Nearer the coast, a former prison colony is located on Isla Gorgona. However, the combined area of all these offshore and outlying islands does not exceed 65km².

CLIMATE

Colombia lies almost entirely in the so-called Torrid Zone: a part of the earth's surface between the Tropics of Cancer and Capricorn characterised by a hot weather. However, Colombia's climate varies as a result of the differences in altitude with seasons defined by periods of lesser or greater rainfall, with little or no temperature change. Weather-wise, the country can be divided vertically into four regions with the hot country (*tierra caliente*) stretching from sea level to roughly 1,100m. In the temperate zone *(tierra templada)* elevations reach 3,000m while the remaining land is dubbed 'the cold country' *(tierra fría)* as it exceeds 3,000m. The cold zone's upper marks the tree line and roughly denotes the limit of human habitation. Adjacent to the tierra fría are Colombia's treeless regions. These can reach 4,500m and are bleak areas referred to as the *páramos*, usually with permanent snow (*nevado*). Expect an average of 24–27°C in the hot low-lying regions along the Caribbean coastline and outlying islands, but don't be surprised if they rarely exceed 22°C in lofty Bogotá. Medellín is known as 'La Ciudad de la Eterna Primavera' (or 'City of the Eternal Spring') throughout Colombia for its pleasant constant year round climate with minimal temperature variations c22°C.

Precipitation is heavy along the Pacific coast and in the Andean regions while on the leeward side of the Guajira Peninsula light rainfall is the lowest in Colombia. Rainy periods and dry weather generally alternate in three-month cycles, during April to June and October to December. However northern Colombia has one long rainy season, May to October. In Bogotá annual rainfall averages about 1,060mm per annum while in Barranquilla around 800mm is the norm. Those keen to explore Colombia's magnificent great outdoors should avoid the worst of the wet season, when many hiking trails are rendered impassable due to mudslides and flooding. Water levels in the Amazon can also be unpredictable during the raining season. Jungle expanses, islands and entire villages can be engulfed during this period when a continuous deluge can cause the river to rise by up to 13m.

For further information contact the **Colombian Meteorological Institute** (Instituto de Meteorología) (*Carrera 10 No 20–30, PO Box 3527160, Bogotá, Colombia; www.ideam.gov.co*)

HISTORY

Colombia's history is nothing short of compelling – just when you think it can't get any more dramatic, another chapter unfolds. Few countries can claim an historical account so complex and utterly haunting, with Colombia's past a colourful, if emotional, fusion of intrigue, turmoil, pain, violence and hope. Getting to grips with Colombian history isn't easy and those who seek a rounded account will need to do some serious study. Numerous sources exist – many of them conflicting. Others hone in on specific themes or eras, such as the modern-day guerrilla conflict. However, Colombia's pre-Columbian history is rich in indigenous culture while the colonial period spawned some of the finest architecture in the Americas. The following offers a starting point for those keen to learn more.

TIMELINE

1525	Rodrigo de Bastidas founds first permanent Spanish settlement in Santa Marta.
1810	Colombia declares independence from Spanish rule.
1819	After a successful campaign waged by Simón Bolívar the Republic of Gran Colombia (the present republics of Panama, Venezuela, Colombia and Ecuador) is founded.
1829	Venezuela breaks away from the Republic.
1830	Ecuador also breaks away and the Republic dissolves. Member states, except Panama, become independent countries named Nueva (New) Granada.
1836	Nueva Granada restores its name to Colombia.
1849	Conservative and Liberal parties founded.
1861–85	The country becomes divided by Liberal Party rule segmenting Colombia into nine largely autonomous entities. The Church also separates from the state.
1885	Power is recentralised ahead of 45 years of Conservative Party rule with Church influence restored.
1899–1903	Around 120,000 people are killed in the 'The War of the Thousand Days' – a violent civil war between Liberal and Conservative activists during a long period of political instability (1899–1902).

5

1903	Panama breaks away from Colombia with help from the US.
1903–mid-1940s	Colombia enjoys a period of relative calm with President Alfonso Lopez Pumarejo (1934–38) able to implement political reform.
1946	Conservatives return to power.
1948	Popular left-wing mayor Jorge Eliécer Gaitán is assassinated. Serious rioting ensues in Bogotá with thousands killed and injured.
1948–58	Political conflict between Liberal and Conservative party supporters spreads out to Colombia's rural communities, resulting in 300,000 deaths during a bloody era known as 'La Violencia'.
1957	General Rojas Pinilla, Colombia's only 20th-century military dictator, is ousted after four years at the helm.
1958	Liberal and Conservative parties agree a power-sharing deal (National Front) to run until 1974.

Recent history

mid-1960s	Colombia's guerrilla groups, the Revolutionary Armed Forces of Colombia (FARC), Maoist People's Liberation Army (EPL) and National Liberation Army (ELN), are established.
1971	The M-19 guerrilla group is formed.
1978	Liberal leader Julio César Turbay elected president. He conducts tough counter-insurgency campaign and launches an intensive fight against drug traffickers.
1982	Conservative President Belisario Betancur grants guerrillas amnesty and frees political prisoners.
1982	Drug cartels in Medellín and Cali consolidate their respective drugs trades. Paramilitary groups, hired initially for self-defence purposes, emerge as a significant force within the drug-trafficking industry.
1982	Conservative Belisario Betancur becomes president and takes the first serious steps towards a negotiated settlement of Colombia's guerrilla conflict.
1985	FARC establishes a political party, Patriotic Unión (UP). M-19 takes over Palace of Justice in Bogotá but although the military seizes back control of the building more than 100 people are killed including 11 senior judges.
1989	M-19 guerrillas demobilise and establish a democratic political movement legally after reaching a peace agreement via long and protracted negotiations with the government.
1989–90	Gunmen from the Medellín drug cartel assassinate Luis Carlos Galán – a favourite to win the 1990 Liberal Party presidential nomination. Some 200 policemen are also killed in what is a marked escalation of drug-related violence. President Barco (1986–90) appeals to the international community for support in the struggle against the narco-traffic trade.
1991	A new constitution is drafted by the Constituent Assembly with former guerrillas well represented.
1991–92	Various rounds of peace talks between government of President Gaviria (1990–94) and FARC and ELN guerrillas fail to make headway.
1993	Medellín's infamous drug cartel leader Pablo Escobar is killed by police in the city.
1994–98	The Liberal administration under President Samper Pizano is dogged by drug-related corruption scandals. He is subsequently charged and cleared of receiving drug money for his election campaign and goes on to achieve some success in dismantling the Cali cartel.

1998	Conservative Andrés Pastrana wins the presidential seat as an Independent candidate.
2000	Pastrana's 'Plan Colombia' receives almost US$1 billion in mainly military aid from America to fight drug trafficking and rebels who profit from and protect the trade.
2002	After three years of peace talks, President Pastrana breaks off negotiations with FARC and terminates their demilitarised zone. Peace talks with ELN also fail.
2002	Dissident Liberal Alvaro Uribe wins presidential elections, standing for the independent Primero Colombia Movement. The inauguration ceremony on 7 August is attacked by FARC mortar grenades. Twenty people are killed and within days a state of emergency is declared. Uribe vows to crack down hard on rebel groups.
2003	United Paramilitary Groups (AUC) announces a unilateral ceasefire, allowing formal peace talks to take place with the government. The AUC commits to demobilisation by the end of 2005, although observance of the ceasefire is very patchy.
2004	The AUC signs a further agreement to provide a 'location zone' of 360km^2 in Santa Fé de Ralito. The zone grants paramilitary leaders amnesty from arrest or extradition for the duration of the demobilisation process as verified by the Organisation of American States (OAS). More than 5,000 AUC members collectively demobilise by the end of the year.
2005	The government establishes the Justice and Peace law as a legal framework for the demobilisation process. Detractors claim it is a 'law of impunity' that makes too many concessions to rebels. Defenders of the law point to the need to eliminate armed guerrillas from the conflict, and claim it as a positive step.
2006	AUC demobilisation is complete with a reported 30,150 paramilitaries handing over some 17,000 weapons, 117 vehicles, 3 helicopters, 59 urban properties and 24,000 hectares of land under the terms of the Law of Justice and Peace. Alvaro Uribe secures a second, four-year tenure as president.

PRE-COLUMBUS Before Spanish rule, Colombia was populated by indigenous peoples. Most were hunters or nomadic agriculturists, but one part of the country, the high basins of the Eastern Cordillera, was densely occupied by Chibcha Indians who had become sedentary farmers. Numerous indigenous groups travelled through Colombia from North and Central America, using it as South America's overland gateway. Many tribes disappeared after unsuccessful migration. Others, such as the Inca, built major settlements further south. Of the enduring monuments today, Colombia's finest include San Agustín (page 277), Cuidad Perdida (page 394) and Tierradentro (page 279) although large collections of artefacts, gold and fossils can be found in museums countrywide. Colombia's first human inhabitants occupied small settlements all over the country with the main groups choosing to live along the fertile waters of the Pacific and Atlantic coasts and the Andean region. Although some inter-tribe trading existed, most of Colombia's tribes evolved independently, with vastly different cultures, languages and belief systems. Each of these hunter-gatherer communities developed its own political system with that of the Muisca people one of the most developed in South America. Other Indian groups included the Calima, Nariño, Sinú, Tolima, Tumaco, San Agustín and Quimbaya.

THE SPANISH ARRIVE From the moment the Spanish conquistadors arrived, El Dorado became an obsession – and this mythical land of untold riches was a motivating force behind many expeditions into Colombia's harsh interior regions. Although named after Christopher Columbus, the explorer never actually visited Colombia. It was his comrade, Alonso de Ojeda, who set foot on Colombian soil in 1499 – the first European to do so. In many ways, El Dorado was born out of Ojeda's awe at the Indian treasures and wealth he encountered with tales spreading (and growing in stature) over time. Although the Spanish never did discover the land of gold and emeralds, the searches they undertook with great determination were the dynamo behind Colombia's colonisation. After establishing several short-lived settlements along the coast, the Spanish founded the town of Santa Marta in 1525 with conquistador Rodrigo de Bastidas at the helm. Pedro de Heredia then went on to establish Cartagena in 1533 and this coastal trading hub soon became a principal port for shipments of supplies and slaves. In 1536, three independent advances forged towards the interior from different directions, led by Sebastián de Benalcázar, Jiménez de Quesada and Niklás Federman. Each had the goal of plundering Indian treasures after hearing tales of carpets of glittering jewels and vast piles of dazzling gold. After deserting from Francisco Pizarro's army during an assault on the Inca Empire Benalcázar launched an expedition from Ecuador reaching the newly founded Santa Fé de Bogotá in 1539 after establishing Popayán and Cali en route. Bogotá had been founded just a year prior to Benalcázar's arrival by Jiménez Quesada who had conquered two clans of Muiscas after climbing the Cordillera Oriental from Santa Marta via the Valle del Magdalena. Federman began his expedition from the Venezuelan coast and arrived in Bogotá shortly after Benalcázar, having crossed Los Llanos and the Andes. All three advances claimed supremacy and many battles ensued. In 1550, King Carlos V of Spain eventually brought the colony under single rule, establishing a court of justice in Bogotá under the leadership of the Viceroyalty of Peru.

THE COLONISATION ERA The New Kingdom of Granada (*Nuevo Reino de Granada*) comprised a collection of Spanish colonial provinces in northern South America that today correspond primarily to modern Colombia. It was established in 1564, as a new governing system, by the Spanish Crown and had military and civil power and self-ruled to a greater degree. Civil government had already been installed in the former New Granada but it was when a *presidencia* or governor was established with executive power that Nuevo Reino de Granada was born as a Captaincy General – a colony under the control of the Viceroyalty of Peru. All of Colombia (except what is known today as the Valle de Cauca, Cauca and Nariño) fell under its jurisdiction along with Panama with a mixed population of indigenous tribes, Spanish invaders and African slaves. Colombia's slave trade was concentrated on the port of Cartagena from where shipments were distributed throughout the many coastal mines and plantations along the Pacific and Caribbean coasts. Colombia's racial mix soon became more diverse once the three ethnicities began inter-breeding adding mulattos (European-African), zambos (African-Indian) and mestizos (European-Indian) to the rapidly expanding multi-racial pot. So many slaves were shipped to the colony during the 16th and 17th centuries that people of African origin or descent soon outnumbered the indigenous tribesfolk. However, it was the Spaniards who held all the power – a stronghold that would last until 1819.

FIGHT FOR INDEPENDENCE Although Spanish domination continued across the continent it stirred up strong feelings of dissent and protests became more prevalent in the early 18th century. People were angry at the throttlehold the Spanish had on land, wealth and commerce and became incensed by rising taxes – resulting in an

Despite our just resentment toward the ubiquitous Spaniards, our magnanimous heart still commands us to open to them for the last time a path to reconciliation and friendship; they are invited to live peacefully among us, if they will abjure their crimes, honestly change their ways, and cooperate with us...

15 June 1813 – Simón Bolívar (1783–1830)

Without a doubt, Simón Bolívar was one of South America's greatest generals, a leader of men who triumphed over the Spanish to win independence for Colombia, Bolivia, Panama, Ecuador, Peru and Venezuela. A wealthy orphan of rich parentage, Bolívar was born in Caracas, Venezuela. He travelled across Europe as a young man and returned home with strong ideals. Bolívar joined the group of patriots that temporarily seized Caracas in 1810 and attempted to proclaim independence from Spain. After travelling to Great Britain in an unsuccessful bid for funding, Bolívar returned to Venezuela to take command of a rebel army. In 1813, he recaptured Caracas from the Spaniards earning the name *El Libertador* – The Liberator. However, the Spaniards forced Bolívar to retreat to New Granada (now Colombia) where in 1814 he raised a Colombian force to capture Bogotá. A defeat saw Bolívar return to Venezuela after rallying up an army of skilled horsemen from the Colombian plains of Los Llanos. Strengthened by the British Legion, Bolívar marched over the Andes into New Granada in 1819. After a succession of winning battles he defeated the Spaniards in Boyacá in 1819, liberating Colombia and assuring independence. He then returned to Angostura and led the congress that organised the original republic of Colombia (now Ecuador, Colombia, Panama and Venezuela). Bolívar became its first president on 17 December 1819. However, not everything that the so-called 'George Washington of South America' did for Latin America had a positive impact and many of Simón Bolívar's actions were the cause of numerous lasting negative effects. Giving up his presidential position allowed a class structure to return to Latin American society, awarding those of Spanish and Portuguese descent to assume power and wealth. Next in the social chain came the Creole people with European ancestry with the mestizo, mulatto, African American and indigenous Indians at the bottom of the class system. The rich were also the politically strong and were able to ascend to rule. Bolívar himself said, 'We have ploughed the sea' in reference to his disappointment at the poor results achieved by revolution. Despite liberating Latin America from the Spanish, he didn't achieve quite the republic he had dreamed of – a place where no class distinctions prevailed with an equality of wealth and power. He died rejected and penniless having admitted, 'There have been three great fools in history: Jesús, Don Quixote and I.'

uprising in Socorro in 1781. The *Revolución Comunera* was sparked by new Crown-imposed levies and was the first open protest in Colombia's colonial period. In 1808, Napoleon appointed his own brother king – to the outrage of the Spanish colonies. Each refused to recognise the monarchy and a four-year wave of political infighting and chest-beating ensued. By 1812, a soon-to-be hero of the independence cause was causing ructions across the region, and eventually winning independence for Colombia in 1819 – Simón Bolívar (see box, *Hero of the Nation*, above).

INDEPENDENCE In 1819, the new state of Gran Colombia was formed in a euphoric post-independence congress in Angostura (the modern-day Ciudad Bolívar in Venezuela). The union joined Colombia, Venezuela, Panama and Ecuador, although sizeable parts of Venezuela and Ecuador remained technically ruled by the Spanish. A second assembly took place in Villa del Rosario near Cúcuta in 1821 when the strong opposing political views of each country came to the fore. These divided into two factions: federalists and centralists. Bolívar pushed for a centralist republic and got his way, gaining presidential election. However, the state of Gran Colombia was doomed to failure such was its size and political diversity. Second-in-command, Francisco de Paula Santander was a federalist at heart and struggled to govern such a large territory on a centralised basis. By 1830, Gran Colombia had disintegrated into three separate nations – the end of Bolívar's dream of unifying the countries he had liberated.

As an independent nation, Colombia got off to a troubled start. Two political parties born out of the centralist v federalist conflict were formalised in 1849 and galvanised fierce support. Bitter rivalries between the Conservatives (centralists) and Liberals (federalists) soon spawned a succession of civil wars and factions – between 1863 and 1885 alone there were more than 50 anti-government uprisings with eight 19th-century civil wars. In 1899, a federalist rebellion sparked a full-blown civil war resulting in over 120,000 deaths. It was ultimately a centralist victory but the carnage rocked the social foundations of the nation. This instability provided America with the perfect opportunity to help Panama become an independent republic. Colombia, distracted by its own affairs, reacted with considerable fury, withdrawing diplomatic ties with both nations. It eventually agreed to recognise the sovereignty of Panama in 1921 and patched things up with America, but the issue remains a sore point in the hearts and minds of Colombians nationwide.

LA VIOLENCIA In order to understand the sheer bloody brutality of La Violencia it is important to get to the heart of Colombian culture. In Colombia, religion and politics are crucial hereditary traits, defining characteristics that are upheld with considerable pride. Generations of Colombians are raised from birth with political affiliations. Politics is in their blood, in their hearts and in their minds – it's almost innate. So, when these political principles are challenged, things get incredibly heated – some of Colombia's bloodiest conflicts are testament to this. La Violencia ranks amongst the most deadly clashes in the western hemisphere, a violent struggle that broke out in Colombia in 1948 and eclipsed all other battles. On 9 April, the first of many urban revolts (known as El Bogotázo) took hold of the capital after Jorge Eliécer Gaitán was assassinated. As one of the Liberal movement's most popular leaders, Gaitán's loyal following were incensed. They took up arms and launched a vicious onslaught on the nation's Conservatives. The retaliation was brutal and during the 1940s and 1950s Colombia was engulfed by a wave of hereditary hate-crimes with thousands of atrocities that included murder, mutilation and rape. Much of the violence of this intense bipartisan conflict centred on the rural provinces with organised self-defence groups and guerrilla units fuelling the fire. A coup led by General Gustavo Rojas Pinilla in 1953 remains the only military intervention in Colombia's 20th-century history – but failed to last. In 1957, the Conservatives and Liberals signed a 16-year power-sharing agreement known as the National Front (Frente Nacional). The pact banned other parties from power thus encouraging other groups to operate outside of the official political arena. Both parties served alternating four-year terms in a system that many blame for helping to nurture Colombia's guerrilla revolutionaries.

ARMED AND DANGEROUS Colombia's political underbelly was ripe for more ideological tensions in the mid-1960s. Disillusioned components operating within the conventional political structure turned to the outer extremes. Militias were raised and security forces recruited as the political divides in Colombian society turned their back on dialogue and protest. Today, Colombia's Marxist guerrillas and right-wing paramilitaries have been at the forefront of a civil conflict spanning more than four decades. Government troops continue to wage war on these militant factions in bloody rural offensives. Over the years, many Colombians have had no option but to flee their homes to escape the violence – now Colombia has around three million internally displaced people, second only to Sudan.

More than a dozen rebel groups operate according to individual philosophies and political aims. Each has well-planned, well-organised and well-armed military strategies. Many have abandoned ideological causes for the commercial rewards of drug money to finance horrendous acts of terror. Extortion, robbery and kidnapping are other key sources of income. Military analysts suggest that FARC (Revolutionary Armed Forces of Colombia) alone earns between US$250 million and US$300 million through criminal acts, of which 65% is derived from the drugs trade. This shift in political focus has clouded the population perception that guerrillas are 'freedom fighters' with a cause. Civilian massacres, enforced enlistment at gunpoint and the banning of any form of religious spiritual expression have transformed the image of a rebel from a Che Guevara-style role model to terrorist. Nebulous political goals and involvement in drug trafficking have seen local support for guerrilla groups plummet. At their peak, Colombian guerrillas controlled up to 40% of the countryside – a region the size of Switzerland. Today membership is much diminished with guerrilla activity largely concentrated in Colombia's deep south – with the following the main groups.

Fuerzas Armadas Revolucionarias de Colombia (FARC) FARC (*www.farcep.org*) is the oldest and largest left-wing rebel group and is also one of the wealthiest and most powerful guerrilla armies on the planet. It was founded in 1964 on ideological grounds to overthrow the government and establish a communist-agrarian state. Its beliefs stem from highly nationalist and anti-capitalist rhetoric rooted in early progressive ideology. However, its political focus shifted in the 1990s and it has since become increasingly involved in the drug trade. Kidnapping and extortion are both now often ends in themselves. FARC is governed by a seven-member secretariat in an HQ in the country of Colombia, chaired by its octogenarian original founder, Manuel Marulanda Vélez. Marulanda was born Pedro Antonio Marín but is renowned throughout Colombia by his *nom de guerre*. He is also nicknamed Tirofijo by his comrades – meaning 'Sureshot' on account of his aim. Some 30% of FARC is female and most are younger than 19. FARC targets anyone suspected of conspiring with the military and paramilitaries, using explosives, landmines and bombs camouflaged as necklaces, footballs and soup cans. It also forcibly enlists people aged between 13 and 60 to work coca or poppy plantations and serve in its military battalions. After a period of relatively peaceful co-existence, FARC and the National Liberation Army (ELN) started fighting each other again in 2006 in a marked escalation of violence in southern Colombia.

Ejército de Liberación Nacional (ELN) The National Liberation Army (*www.eln-voces.com*) was inspired by the Cuban revolution and established by a group of Colombians trained in insurgent warfare in Havana in 1964. Under the leadership of Fabio Vásquez Castaño, the ELN reached the height of its power in the late 1990s with some 5,000 fighters. Today it remains Colombia's second-largest leftist guerrilla group but is much depleted after taking a hammering from right-wing paramilitary forces and the Colombian military. Today its numbers have dropped to around 3,500. The ELN pledged a ceasefire in 2007 on the basis that the government dropped a free-trade pact signed in 2006 with the United States. The ELN has so far rejected a government demand that would confine the guerrillas to a demilitarised area. Colombian President Alvaro Uribe has insisted the rebels hand over their weapons, declare a ceasefire and free some 500 hostages.

Autodefensas Unidas de Colombia (AUC) This umbrella group for a collective of small right-wing paramilitary factions was formed in 1997 and the United Self Defence Forces of Colombia (*www.colombialibre.org*) has strong links with the drugs trade. Wealthy landowners and drugs cartels form the backbone of the organisation with its roots in the paramilitary armies. AUC claims it took up arms in self-defence, in the place of a powerless state. More than 70% of its funding comes from drug lords. It is known to have carried out massacres and assassinations, targeting left-wing groups. The AUC has demobilised almost 30,000 fighters since 2004 in a process beset by endless ceasefire violations and amnesty demands.

M-19 The 19th of April Movement (Movimiento 19 de Abril) or M-19 demilitarised in 1990 to become a legal political party called the M-19 Democratic Alliance (Alianza Democrática M-19), or AD/M-19. M-19's ideology is a mixture of populism and nationalistic revolutionary socialism, with a membership that peaked during the mid-1980s to make it once the second-largest rebel group in Colombia. On giving up its weapons, the members of M-19 received pardons and publicly renounced the armed struggle.

THE COCAINE TRADE

An estimated 25,000 people die each year in Colombia due to violence relating to its cocaine industry. Today, Colombia boasts the distinction of supplying more than 80% of the cocaine on the planet – a trade that not only profits guerrilla activity but also spreads like disease through entire communities. The UN puts total cocaine

WHAT'S THE PLAN?

When President Andrés Pastrana conceived an ambitious plan to curtail Colombia's drug trade in 1999 it immediately sparked controversy. Aerial fumigation of coca crops formed a sizeable part of the plan's anti-narcotic strategy – and rather understandably, Colombia's farming communities were vehemently opposed to tonnes of poisonous chemicals being dumped on the landscape from the air. Today the success of Plan Colombia in eradicating cocaine production is questionable – reports suggest that the country's drug producers simply get their leaves from elsewhere. However, thousands of legitimate smallholdings have been wiped out by the herbicides in widespread spraying that has also damaged public health. Colombia's staggering biodiversity has also suffered with numerous species of flora and fauna falling foul of mega-strong pesticides. Critics argue that Plan Colombia does nothing to tackle the causes of the drug trade, such as global demand and the economic needs of many of Colombia's rural communities. Little evidence exists that drug cultivation has in any way been disrupted by aerial fumigation – producers have simply become more mobile, more hidden and more ingenious. Plan Colombia is an aid package agreed to during the administration of US President Bill Clinton to the tune of US$1.3-million plus 200 military troops and 300 civilian personnel. The agreement expired, but the Bush administration continued aid at a similar level – making Colombia the biggest recipient of foreign aid outside the Middle East and the third-largest recipient overall. Both the Colombian and US governments claim the Plan has had positive results with statistics from America showing a drop in coca production (see *www.state.gov*) – although officials admit replanting almost matches eradication. There has been, however, little impact on the availability of cocaine across the world – it's never been easier or cheaper to buy coke, most of it from Colombian shores.

Although cocaine may seem like a new drug, favoured by the upper-crust elite, it is, in fact, one of the oldest drugs on the planet. Cocaine hydrochloride, the pure chemical, has been an abused substance for over a century. Coca leaves have also been ingested as a stimulant for thousands of years. In the early 1900s, cocaine was used to treat a wide variety of illnesses. Chemically synthesising the coca leaves produces the white crystal powder that is commonly known as cocaine. Newer methods are continually sought to magnify its euphoric effects. This had led to the creation of the most potent and addictive form of the drug, crack. Although a relatively new drug on the scene compared with opium or heroin, crack has nonetheless been part of history and culture for nearly 150 years. Even Coca-Cola had cocaine in its list of ingredients until 1903.

The physiological effects of cocaine include constricted blood vessels and dilated pupils with increased temperature, heart rate and blood pressure. Large amounts intensify the user's high, but may also lead to bizarre, erratic and violent behaviour. Tremors, vertigo, muscle twitches, paranoia and toxic reactions are also possible effects along with feelings of restlessness, irritability and anxiety. Cocaine-related deaths are often a result of cardiac arrest or seizures followed by failure of the respiratory system. Repeated high doses may result in a full-blown paranoid psychosis, in which the individual loses touch with reality and experiences auditory hallucinations.

COCAINE FACTS

- The world's cocaine market is valued at around US$70.45 billion.
- In Europe retail prices average US$85 per gram, compared with a wholesale rate of US$43.
- In the US retail prices average US$102 per gram, compared with wholesale prices of US$25.
- In the UK street prices range between £30–60 per gram with a crack rock costing between £12–20 – and small 'clubbing rocks' retailing for about £10.
- Cocaine is known by numerous slang terms, including nose candy, snowball, tornado, wicky stick, Perico (Spanish), coke, Charlie, C, white, Percy, snow, toot and peach – with rocks, wash, stones, pebbles, base and freebase common names for crack.
- Cocaine was once sold over the counter. Until 1916 it could apparently be purchased at Harrods in a kit labelled 'A Welcome Present for Friends at the Front' containing cocaine, morphine, syringes and spare needles.
- In 2005–06, over 15,300kg of cocaine were seized in the UK with 193 trafficking groups dismantled or disrupted.
- Britain has the fastest-growing cocaine consumption in the world with almost one million users – and rising. It's now the second most widely used illegal drug in the UK after cannabis.

Further information can be obtained from the United Nations Office on Drugs and Crime (www.unodc.org), US Drug Enforcement Administration (www.dea.gov), UK Drug Strategy (www.drugs.gov.uk).

production at 640 tonnes a year, but UK law enforcement sources claim it is as high as 1,000 tonnes – that's £6 billion based on average market prices. Demand is so high that cocoa growers in Colombia are using genetically modified plants to dramatically boost cocaine yields. Dozens of routes are used by thousands of smugglers to transport the cocaine to the US and Europe – reports suggest it can be snorted in a London party in less than 24 hours after export. Yet Colombians are baffled that Europeans and North Americans fail to make any connection between their own Saturday night snort and the conflict that has blighted the nation for over 40 years. 'Don't people realise that each time they buy a bag of coke they are financing a war that is killing our country?' is a common heartfelt question.

The most infamous drug cartels include that of Medellín, run by former petty criminal and ruthless Colombian drug lord *El Patron* Pablo Escobar (1949–93) who once controlled over 80% of the cocaine trade with the United States. He continually evaded capture, despite a lengthy man-hunt by a special 1,500-strong team. He was killed in 1993 after being on the run for 499 days and amassing a small fortune, including luxurious homes, expensive cars, aeroplanes and hotels. Escobar had an effective, inescapable strategy to silence anyone who got in his way. It was referred to as *plata o plomo*, Colombian slang for 'money or bullets' intended to mean 'accept a bribe or face assassination'. In 1989 *Forbes* magazine listed him as the seventh-richest man in the world.

Yet, Colombia isn't just a cocaine supplier – Colombian police backed by US forces are now fighting the exportation of tonnes of pure heroin per year. In 2006, eight suspected traffickers were captured in Cali, a city with a lengthy association with the drugs trade. A half-tonne haul had an estimated street value of up to US$90m. There are over 13.5 million cocaine users worldwide – that's around 0.3% of the population aged 15–64 years. In 2007, two Mexicans were arrested after US$4 million was found in their carry-on bags as they arrived at a Colombian airport. Customs officials have long suspected links between Colombia and a Mexican drug cartel. Mexico receives US$40 million a year for anti-drug efforts from the United States and is thought to be a major transhipment point for narcotics bound for American shores.

GOVERNMENT AND POLITICS

When God started creating the world, he put gold into South Africa. Finding he had some left over, he gave it to Colombia. Brazil received emeralds and tropical fruits. Again, God had some left over and gave them to Colombia. He put coal into Appalachia, with Colombia getting the leftovers. The Middle East got a pot full of oil with the remainder poured into Colombia. Flowers went to the South Pacific islands but there were some of these left over too, so God gave them to Colombia, along with some surplus minerals, including iron and nickel.

'Wait a minute,' exclaimed a watching angel. 'Do you realise that you're making Colombia one of the most powerful nations on the planet?'

'Yes,' replied God, 'but don't worry. I haven't given them their politics yet.'

19th-century Colombian satire

Colombia is officially Latin America's oldest and most stable democracy although its chequered history and colourful politics boast the drama and intrigue of a Graham Greene thriller. Although fair and regular elections are the norm, Colombia's political make-up has still been contentious. Yet an ingrained respect for political and civil rights still prevails countrywide.

Traditionally, two parties – the Liberals and the Conservatives – have battled for power since the mid 19th century. Fiercely fought elections have seen the two share the role as governing party in rotation, with Colombia's armed forces seizing power on three occasions in 1830, 1854 and 1953. Since declaring its independence from Spain in 1810, Colombia has had 11 constitutions. The last was adopted in 1991 and served to strengthen the unitary republic of today. In 1821 and 1830 the statute removed significant might from Colombia's departmental governments.

However, three additional federal constitutions later awarded considerable powers to the nation's administrative subdivisions (*departamentos*) and paved the way for elected departmental assemblies. The 1886 constitution sought to resolve the great federal–unitary debate head-on, tackling the role of the Roman Catholic Church and the thorny issue of a robust central government versus a decentralised federal structure in straightforward terms. It states that sovereignty resides in the nation to ensure guaranteed civil liberties, including freedom of religion, speech, assembly, press and education along with the right to strike (unless in public service), petition the government as well as own property. Citizens over 18 years old were also granted greater legal rights (subject to owning a citizenship card and registering on the electoral roll). Exceptions include active military personnel and members of the police, both of whom are prohibited from voting and participating in political activities. Those working in an administrative capacity for the Colombian government are also barred from political involvement, although they are permitted to vote.

Colombia's constitution has undergone large-scale, frequent changes over the years, including significant amendments in 1910, 1936, 1945, 1957, 1959, 1968, 1979 and 1991. Colombia has always been a nation hungry for change and in the past student demonstrations, strikes and riots have helped effect this when government reactions have been slow. Colombia's present constitution was enacted on 4 July 1991 to bolster the administration of justice. Key reforms included civil divorce, dual nationality, the election of a vice president and departmental governors – as well as extending the basic rights of Colombia citizens to seek immediate court action (known as *tutela*) in the event of any violation of their constitutional rights.

The politics of Colombia takes place in a framework of a presidential representative democratic republic led by the President of Colombia who is both head of state and head of government. The national government has separate executive, legislative and judicial branches. Colombia's president is elected after a four-year tenure by direct popular vote and, until 2006, was constitutionally prohibited from seeking consecutive terms. President Uribe (see box, *Saying no to violence*, page 16), who was first elected in 2002, changed the constitution so he could run for a second term in office. The amendment permitted a single re-election and was ratified by Congress in December 2004 before approval by the Constitutional Court in October 2005. Mr Uribe was re-elected for a second presidential term in May 2006, becoming the first president to be consecutively re-elected in Colombia in more than a hundred years. Uribe received about 62% of the vote, consisting of about 7.3 million ballots in his favour. However, under the standard terms of the constitution, a former president may run again for the presidency only after sitting out one term. Other stipulations are that the president must be a native-born Colombian aged 55 years or over. He or she must also be in full possession of his or her political rights and should have served as a congressional or cabinet member, governor, government official or university professor (for a minimum of five years) or as a practising member of a liberal profession requiring a university degree.

Colombia's president oversees the executive branch of government as chief of state, consisting of a 13-member cabinet, a host of administrative agencies and a couple of hundred or so semi-autonomous bodies. The president has the power to elect the cabinet and is also responsible for appointing leaders to head up the many administrative agencies under his control without the approval of congress. The governors of Colombia's 23 territorial departments are also under his charge as are the heads of nine national territories. In addition to administrative powers, the chief executive has considerable legislative authority. The president is also

Until the last day of my life, I will work for this country with love for Colombians, with love for this country.

President Álvaro Uribe, 2004

When Álvaro Uribe was elected President of Colombia in May 2002 he was sworn into office amidst tight security behind closed doors with a patrol of military aircraft overhead. Thousands of soldiers were guarding the surrounding streets during a ceremony that was attacked by a guerrilla assault, killing more than a dozen and wounding 40 people. Yet this hardline independent Conservative remained resolute, citing Colombia's problems with law and order, the ills of the drug trade, and the guerrillas that support it as his key focus in the years ahead. A slim-built, rather bookish-looking man, Uribe has none of the physical attributes normally associated with a no-nonsense opponent of Colombia's four bloody decades of violence. His reputation as a tough, resolute opponent of the guerrillas, paramilitaries and drug barons has seen him declare open season on the 'scourge of his country' – delivering impassioned speeches with an aggressive wagging finger at high decibel without apology. Uribe's uncompromising stance mirrors a determination to bring about radical change within Colombia, a pledge that some say has a dubious motivation – namely, long-standing deep-rooted revenge. President Uribe's father was killed some 20 years earlier by guerrillas – the very reason behind his mission is to eradicate violence in his country at all costs.

First, Uribe set about halting drug production by arresting traffickers, spraying cocaine crops and exposing those in positions of power with links to the narcotics trade. Then he forced rebels out of Colombia's towns and cities and back into the countryside, thereby eradicating the disruption of bloodshed from everyday life. This hardline stance won him plenty of plaudits yet Uribe still attracts criticism for his disjointed approach to setting up peace talks. He is also vilified because of Colombia's growing unemployment problem while his plans to raise taxes to plug the fiscal deficit have seen protestors take to the streets several times. Civil war, drug trafficking and poverty remain Uribe's major challenges but his call to the Revolutionary Armed Forces of Colombia (FARC) to lay down their arms has so far fallen on deaf ears. FARC still control large rural areas of Colombia and the president's promise of demobilisation has yet to be fulfilled, despite some recent triumphs and high-profile arrests. Key figures in FARC may have been caught while an estimated 30,000 have laid down their weapons. Yet tens of thousands of paramilitary fighters are said to remain at large, while Uribe's efforts to stamp out Colombia's vast illegal drugs trade have also produced mixed results – despite more than US$3 billion of aid from America. Today, the president travels with dozens of bodyguards and sniffer dogs, such is his 'love-him-or-loathe-him' status. Mr Uribe is a Conservative, with deeply held Roman Catholic beliefs, who advocates a strongly centralised, militaristic state and close ties with the US. He was born in July 1952 in Medellín and is a lawyer by training. Mr Uribe was educated at Oxford and Harvard and is married to Lina María Moreno and has two sons. More information can be obtained from the presidential website (*www.presidencia.gov.co*).

obligated to maintain law and order, defend the nation, and resolve domestic unrest as commander-in-chief of the armed forces and the national police.

Yet, for a nation with a long democratic tradition, Colombia's high level of political violence is a contradictory feature and today the list of people who have lost their lives to politically motivated violence is long. President Uribe has personally made left-wing insurgency, right-wing paramilitary terrorism and the threat of narco-violence his focus while around him rural poverty is left unresolved with per capita income barely reaching half the national average. Uribe admits that these economic factors have helped spawn political violence yet direct critics argue that he has not addressed the root causes of poverty and unemployment. President Uribe's continued application of traditional trade and tax policies has been criticised by social commentators for only benefiting private and foreign investors rather than offering help to small farm owners and workers.

ECONOMY

> We toil, we struggle, we mind our manners. Our labour we enjoy. We smile like that of the true Colombian work ethic of our fathers. Our minds are quick, we need no sleep, just time to think.
>
> José Jiménez, Cuesta Mucho Trabajo (2007)

According to the World Bank, Colombia has achieved stable Gross Domestic Product (GDP) growth in recent years, with a GDP up 6.8% in 2006 – its fastest pace since 1978. Estimated at US$374.4 billion, this is an indication that Colombia's economic foundation remains firm. Unlike many countries in Latin America, Colombia has never suffered any dramatic economic collapses or periods of hyperinflation. Unemployment, which stood at 12.1% as of April 2006, is the lowest since 2001, and poverty decreased from 58% in 2002 to 49%. The Colombian economy, which experienced its first recession in nearly 70 years in 1999, is on the rebound. All these indicators, added to a reduced insecurity, have fostered greater confidence among domestic and foreign investors.

Colombia has always relied on geography for its economic fortunes in a blessed location bordering two oceans and occupying the point where the American continents meet. As a gateway for the movement of peoples and ideas long before the arrival of Europeans, Colombia's two major river valleys, the Magdalena and the Cauca, ensured a vital channel with Central America, South America and the Caribbean. Colombia has opened its economy considerably since the early 1990s. Economic liberalisation (a process known as *Apertura*) opened Colombia's economy up to international trade and inward capital investment by slashing tariff duties, ditching non-tariff barriers and negotiating free trade agreements. It also reformed foreign exchange and tax rules, labour regulations and foreign investment legislation. State enterprises, ports, railroads and banks were privatised and the sectors of telecommunications, energy and tourism reborn in a new spirit of commercial advancement.

Today, despite four decades of armed conflict, Colombia's economy has experienced positive growth and its financial position continues to improve in part because of tight government budgets and control. Yet violence has taken a high toll in Colombia – and not just in terms of human lives. If peace had been achieved in the 1980s estimates suggest the income of an average Colombian today would be 50% higher – so the economic impact has been huge. Grim determination to reduce public debt and a strong export strategy have combined with a formidable effort to improve security Colombia-wide to help the nation's GDP remain robust. However, President Uribe is faced with several economic challenges, including reforming the country's pension system and bringing down unemployment to managing a passage of fiscal reform. Petroleum ranks as the principal export, although declining oil production requires significant investment in new exploration. Colombia's annual exports earn US$13.1 billion with mechanical and electrical equipment, chemicals, food and metals Colombia's prime imports. The

US is Colombia's main trading partner with Venezuela, Germany, Japan, the Netherlands, Brazil and Peru retaining significant trade links. The Colombian government's economic policy continues to bolster growing confidence within the business sector. Apart from oil, Colombia's leading exports include coffee, vegetables, chemicals, coal, textiles, fresh-cut flowers, bananas, sugar, gold, emeralds and cattle. Illegal drugs also rank high among the country's exports with Colombia an illicit producer of coca, opium poppy and cannabis and the supplier of most of the drugs on the US market. Colombia's Bank of the Republic issues all of the nation's money and shares responsibility for monetary policy with the government. More than 25 commercial banking institutions, development banks and other financial institutions operate in Colombia with stock exchanges that serve the cities of Bogotá, Medellín and Cali. Colombia is an original member of the Andean Community (1969), an organisation that established free trade among its members and works towards regional economic and social co-operation. Colombia has been a signatory of the GATT since 1981 and a member of the World Trade Organization (WTO) since that institution's creation in 1994. Under the framework of this organisation, the country has implemented a series of reforms in the areas of trade remedies, subsidies, exchange rate controls, foreign investment, intellectual property and customs valuation, among others. Colombia also entered into two other trade associations in 1995: the Group of Three (Mexico, Venezuela and Colombia) and the Association of Caribbean States (ACS). A total of 25 nations in or along the Caribbean are members of the ACS, a group that focuses on regional co-operation and economic integration. In February 2006, Colombia agreed free trade terms with America following protracted negotiations between US representative Rob Portman and Colombian Minister of Trade, Industry and Tourism, Jorge Humberto Botero. The agreement was widely criticised by international aid agencies, including condemnation from Oxfam. Farming communities throughout Colombia also vehemently opposed the Free Trade Agreement (FTA), citing an unfair 'David and Goliath' style inability to compete with subsidised exports from the US that threatens economic disaster for the millions of people in Colombia who depend on agriculture for their livelihood. The deal is America's biggest in the western hemisphere since 1994's North American Free Trade Agreement (NAFTA) and is forecast to make more than 80% of US consumer and industrial exports to Colombia duty-free. However, critics predict the FTA will serve to institutionalise an uneven playing field between the two countries instead of establishing fair and equitable rules for trade that could promote development and reduce poverty.

Colombia draws more than half a million tourists annually, primarily from the United States and countries in South America. A government campaign to boost tourism under the banner 'Colombia is Passion' has attracted global press interest. A US$4 million budget has so far helped boost foreign visitor figures by 65% from 2002 – to just over a million in 2006. Travel and tourism in Colombia employs 1,173,000 people (5.7% of total employment) and is forecast to grow by 3.6% per annum, in real terms, between 2008 and 2017. The Colombian tourism sector is ranked 53rd in terms of absolute size worldwide, 147th in relative contribution to national economies and 138th in long-term (10-year) growth out of the World Travel & Tourism Council's 176 countries.

In addition to his domestic goals of keeping inflation and interest rates low and maintaining a stable currency, President Uribe has put a heavy emphasis on developing international trade. Colombia achieved a ranking of 91 out of 157 countries in the annual Economic Freedom in the World and Index of Economic Freedom surveys. These indices attempt to measure the degree of economic freedom in a nation using a scoring system for ten broad factors of economic

Forget coffee, plants and coconuts – one of Colombia's greatest exports is its people, with 10% of Colombians currently living abroad, according to figures from the National Administrative Department for Statistics (DANE). That's over four million Colombian migrants working overseas with most of them sending regular money back home. In fact, Colombians abroad wire more than US$3.17 billion to their families per annum – a whopping 4% of Colombia's GDP. More than 50% of this significant source of international currency is sent from Colombians living in the United States, according to the World Bank – particularly New York and Florida. International Organisation of Migration (IOM) research suggests that approximately 90% of these remittances are used to cover basic needs, education and heath with 6% repaying family loans and 2% for saving. Most Colombians living abroad are originally from the Valle del Cauca department (24.1%) and Bogotá (18.7%) with the main destination other than the US being Spain (23.4%). However, unlike two decades ago, the trend is to return to Colombia, according to statistics from the Administrative Security Department (DAS). A 2007 study of Colombian migration commissioned by national newspaper *El Tiempo* entitled 'Colombia: migrations, trans-nationalism y displacement' directed by National University anthropologist Gerardo Ardila from the Centro de Estudios Sociales shows that the number of Colombian citizens abroad has stabilised in recent years.

freedom. Statistics from organisations like the World Bank, the IMF and the Economist Intelligence Unit are just a few that are used as sources. Key points measured are Business Freedom, Trade Freedom, Fiscal Freedom, Freedom from Government, Monetary Freedom, Investment Freedom, Financial Freedom, Property Rights, Freedom from Corruption and Labour Freedom. At number 1 was Hong Kong while the Democratic Republic of Korea ranked at number 157. Colombia's border countries of Venezuela, Panama, Peru, Brazil and Ecuador scored 152, 49, 63, 81 and 107 respectively.

The Colombian government has actively sought to expand trade beyond its traditional partners of the US (Colombia's largest trading partner at 41% of its world total). Today, Colombia remains the United States' fourth-largest trading partner in Latin America, behind Mexico, Brazil and Venezuela, with more than 200 American companies operating in nearly every sector of its national economy. However, Colombia is keen to secure wider diversification in global trade terms and is looking to significantly broaden foreign direct investment flows into the country (US$27.3 billion during 1994–2004). By 2007, more than 700 multi-national companies had invested in Colombia, including Nestlé, Marks & Spencer, Du Pont and Unilever. According to the Economic Commission for Latin America and the Caribbean (ECLAC), Colombia ranks amongst the top destinations for foreign investment in Latin America – and hopes are high that government plans to further fine-tune foreign investment policy will establish the country as a financial dynamo within the region.

A key attraction for investors is Colombia's 22 million labour force. Some 22% is engaged in agriculture, forestry and fishing with 19% in industry and mining, and most of the remainder in service industries. Foreign investment is governed by Law 9 of 1991 Resolutions 51, 52, and 53 of the Council on Economic and Social Policy (CONPES) and Resolution 21 of the Board of Directors of the Central Bank. Investment is permitted in all sectors of the Colombian economy, except those related to national security and hazardous waste. Foreign and national investments are viewed as the same legally and administratively with no restrictions to the amount of foreign capital invested. Red tape has been simplified with the electronic submission of required documents to Colombian authorities now permitted. Foreign businesses in Colombia are, however, governed by labour laws that stipulate firms with more than ten employees should not allow more than 10% of the general workforce (and 20% of specialist skills) to be non-nationals. According to Pro Export, Colombia's trade agency, key reasons to invest in Colombia include:

- One of the most qualified labour markets in Latin America
- One of the highest adult literacy rates in Latin America
- Competitive labour costs and flexible working hours
- Colombia's 10 Duty Free Zones and 5 Special Economy Export Zones
- Colombia is strategically located as a middle point between North and South America
- Both Pacific and Atlantic coasts with modern port infrastructure
- Easy access to North American, European, Asian and Latin American markets
- Significant investment in high-tech telecommunications infrastructure
- Increasing investments in transportation infrastructure
- Five international airports

All foreign investments must be registered with the Central Bank's foreign exchange office within three months of the transaction date to assure the right to repatriate profits and remittances and to access official foreign exchange. All foreign investors, like domestic investors, must obtain a licence from the Superintendent of Companies and register with the local Chamber of Commerce, who can also provide practical help and guidance to a wide range of industries. Key considerations include corruption, according to CONFECAMARAS (Confederation of Colombian Chamber of Commerce) which estimates up to US$3 million of income is lost in Colombia each year. Not true, says the World Bank, which estimates that corruption in Colombia tops US$480 million annually. Joint initiatives by the Colombian government, World Bank and other non-governmental institutions have actively sought to tackle corruption since 2001, with assistance from a wide variety of trade bodies. Another point to ponder is Colombia's appetite for industrial action, although this has waned considerably since Uribe took office. The right to strike constitutionally is guaranteed to all employees not working for public utilities with the Central Unitaria de Trabajadores (CUT, Unitary Federation of Workers) and the Confederación de Trabajadores Colombianos (CTC, Confederation of Colombian Workers) Colombia's most dominant trade unions. Each year, the Colombian government, following negotiations with the main employee unions, trade groups and business associations, establishes a minimum wage for a 48-hour workweek. Colombia has no wage categories or a minimum wage for specific jobs. Employer and employee are free to agree on a different wage, provided it is no less than the minimum wage, or the wage established in collective bargaining agreements, or than the wage resulting from arbitration rulings. In 2007, the monthly minimum wage was 433.700 COP. The 48-hour workweek covers Monday to Friday or Saturday during 06.00 to 22.00. Workers on shifts between 22.00 and 06.00 earn 35% above the hourly wage. Hours worked in addition to the normal workweek are compensated as overtime at 25% per hour.

The World Competitiveness Yearbook (WCY) ranks Colombia tenth out of 60 countries for the quality of its management staff. It also placed Colombia 24th in terms of availability of information technology skills ahead of countries that included Brazil, Spain and Mexico.

Office of Commerce, Industry & Tourism (Ministerio de Comercio, Industria y Turismo) Calle 28 No 13A–15, Bogotá, Colombia; ☎ 1 606 7676; f 1 606 7521; www.mincomercio.gov.co

British–Colombian Chamber of Commerce 2 Belgrave Sq, London SW1X 8PJ; tel: 020 7235 2106; www.britishandcolombianchamber.com

British–Colombian Chamber of Commerce (Cámara de Comercio Cámara Colombo-Británica) Calle 95 No 13–55 Oficina 409, Bogotá, Colombia; ☎ 1 621 2401; f 1 621 2431; e britanica@colombobritanica.com; www.colombobritanica.co

Confederation of Colombian Chamber of Commerce (Confederación Colombiana de Cámaras de Comercio – CONFECAMARAS) Carrera 13 No 27–47 Oficina 502, Bogotá, Colombia; ☎ 346 7055; f 1 346 7026; e confecamaras@confecamaras.org.co; www.confecamaras.org.co

Colombia's Government Trade Office – UK ProExport UK, 6th Floor, 2, Conduit St, London W1S 2XB; ☎ 020 7491 3535; e london@proexport.com.co; www.proexport.com.co

Colombia's Government Trade Office – Miami ProExport Miami, 601 Brickell Key Dr, Suite 801, Miami, FL 3313, USA; ☎ 305 374 3144; e miami@proexport.com.co; www.proexport.com.co

Colombia's Government Trade Office – New York ProExport New York, 140 East 57th St 2nd Floor, New York, 10022, USA; ☎ 212 922 9114; e newyork@proexport.com.co; www.proexport.com.co

PEOPLE

'We are black, white, Indian and mixed blood. We are Colombia. We are a family. We care about our country. We believe in our homeland.'

Pedro Medina, *Yo Creo en Colombia (I Believe in Colombia)*

Colombia is the most populous nation of Spanish-speaking South America with 43,593,035 people and a population density of 42 persons per km². Colombia now boasts the distinction of being the third most populous country in Latin America, after Brazil and Mexico. Its people are a diverse mix of ethnicity derided from Colombia's three main groups, namely its indigenous Indians and those of Spanish and African descent. This multi-culturalism mirrors Colombia's colourful history and today more than 58% of its population claim mestizo heritage (mixed white and indigenous). Whites represent 20% of the population, 14% are mixed white and black, 4% black and 3% mixed black and indigenous. Scholars estimate that the Indian population at the time of the Spanish conquest numbered between 1.5 million and 2 million yet today indigenous peoples account for just 1% of Colombia's modern population. Recent studies also indicate an increased number of immigrants in Colombia, especially from the Caribbean, other Latin American countries (especially Peru) and Turkey.

Colombia is divided into four distinct regions, each with a major city at its core. More than three-quarters of Colombians live in urban congregations. Principal centres are located in the Magdalena and Cauca river valleys and along the Caribbean coastal region. With a population of 7.5 million, the capital Bogotá forms the heart of the centre of the country. The nation's 'Second City' is Medellín, the hub of the northwest of Colombia with a population of 2.5 million. In the southwest, the city of Cali is only a smidgen smaller than Medellín at 2.4 million. On the Caribbean coast the capital Barranquilla (population 1.3 million) is the nucleus of this region, seconded by the popular tourist town of Cartagena.

Colombians are generous, gregarious and friendly people whose acts of kindness and compassion form a sharp contrast to the mean, vicious and violent stereotypes their homeland's troubled history has popularised across the world. Expect high levels of courtesy, good manners and a considerable pride for all things Colombian – characteristics that are truly refreshing for travellers worn down by the indifferent welcome favoured by so many so-called more civilised nations. What's more, travellers will find that the average Colombian is keen to interact with international tourists and is openly thrilled when asked for tips on what to see

COLOMBIANS 'SECOND HAPPIEST PEOPLE ON THE PLANET'

Happiness needn't cost the earth, according to the 2007 New Economics Foundation's Happy Planet Index (HPI) (*www.happyplanetindex.org*), with Colombians having plenty to smile about. Using a barometer that measures the relative efficiency with which nations convert the planet's natural resources into long and happy lives for their citizens, the HPI incorporates three separate indicators: ecological footprint, life satisfaction and life expectancy. It also takes into account the goals of a country in regards to providing long-term well-being for the population, without exceeding the limits of equitable resource consumption.

Out of the 178 countries assessed, the UK ranked 108th with Spain 87th. Panama came in fifth and Costa Rica third. Vanuatu came out tops at number one, whilst the USA ranked 150th.

The Happy Planet Manifesto includes the following:

- To eradicate extreme poverty and hunger
- Improve healthcare
- Relieve debt
- Shift values from material consumption to community initiatives
- Support meaningful lives to recognise the contribution of individuals to economic, social, cultural and civic life
- Empower people and promote good governance
- Identify environmental limits to work with the earth's bio capacity
- Design systems for sustainable consumption and production
- Address the issues of climate change
- Measure what matters to help people worldwide to lead happy and complete lives

and do. They are also extremely proficient at networking and this natural skill for putting people together will almost certainly mean introductions to family, friends and contacts throughout the country, from the address of a kindly uncle who owns a flower-filled *pensionado* in Cali to the telephone number of a former colleague in Mompóx with fabulous tales to tell. This big-heartedness forms a sharp contrast with the headline-grabbing news of tragedy and brutality that blights the reputation of ordinary people of Colombia – and this can be a surprise to first-time visitors who arrive with preconceptions of a nation of gun-toting drug *banditos*. Those visitors prepared to abandon themselves to the irrepressible passion for life demonstrated by Colombians will be greatly rewarded, learning much about the indomitable spirit and considerable warmth of a national psyche that is deserving of celebration.

FAMILY LIFE Regardless of class, Colombia's family structures tend to be authoritarian, patriarchal and patrilineal with strong ties to relatives and considerable importance applied to respect. Even modern families view the Roman Catholic Church as a dynamo behind marriage and the family unit and for the vast majority of Colombians Catholic marriage remains the ideal and preferred legal, social and sexual family foundation. In recent decades, the patriarchal extended family structure has declined in urban societies largely because of increased geographic and social mobility and the greater independence this affords younger members. However, these weakened kinship ties haven't diminished the importance of the family in Colombian society and it is still commonplace for teenage children, parents, grandparents, uncles and cousins to socialise several times a week. However, surveys suggest that today 58% of Colombian families are nuclear, 30% extended, 5.5% compound and 6.5% one-person households. The family also takes centre stage in other ways and is often a prime source of support and advice. Great loyalty is shown to other family members, especially the elder members who are revered. In 2007, it remains common for children to live at home until they marry. In 1964 the average family had 6.8 children, by 1985 the average was five. Since the 1990s, contraceptive use had risen dramatically throughout Latin America, and in Colombia this is reflected in households of 3–4 children instead of 6–8. However, almost 20% of Colombian children have no birth certificate, which makes it difficult for the state to care for them. The under-five mortality rate is 21 per 1,000, while more than 20,000 babies die under the age of one from preventable causes according to UNICEF figures.

For further information contact PROFAMILIA (*Calle 34 No 14–52, Bogotá;* ℷ *1 339 0900;* f *1 287 5530; email: info@profamila.org.co; www.profamilia.org.co*).

MEN IN SOCIETY Colombia's male citizens aged 18 and over must complete one to two years of military service. Some 207,000 people served in the Colombian armed forces in 2004, although the popular (if illegal) option of 'buying out' of the obligation remains commonplace in the middle and upper classes. Like many Latin American societies, Colombia is accepting of the traditional machismo attitudes of its men. Masculinity in Colombia is generally viewed as a positive characteristic and few men, even those in the lower socioeconomic bracket, help with housework or child rearing. Colombian males also typically subscribe to the sexual attitudes characterised by double standards, where men are permitted sexual freedom while 'decent' women are limited to sexual activities largely within the confines of marriage for reproductive purposes. This view is likely to be affected by Colombia's religious beliefs although this view of sexual conduct is at odds with the teachings of the Catholic Church. Although many of these societal values have changed and the status of women improved considerably, 80% of men surveyed in 2006 admitted that they viewed a man's infidelity as less serious than a woman's because he is biologically driven, whereas women's infidelity is not. According to UN figures, a Colombian man can expect to live on average for 69 years.

ALL JOKING APART

Colombian's have an irrepressible love of humour and joking – a sense of fun that bubbles up in all aspects of everyday life. Although Colombian television doesn't boast a comedy tradition like Mexico or Spain, joking around is very part of the national psyche. Expect strangers to share their witticisms, jokes to be scrawled on walls and serious amounts of silliness. Dubbed American comedies known locally as *enlatados* (meaning canned as in canned food) satisfy the Colombian need for a giggle. During the late 1990s Colombian comedian José Ordoñez became a national celebrity by setting a world record for spending the longest time telling jokes on the radio. Other popular comedic talents include Andrés López Forero, Martín de Francisco and Santiago Moure along with Jaime Garzon who died in 1999. The following joke cropped up in a menu in a rainforest watering hole:

Man: My love, why don't you learn to cook like the maid? It will save on the cost of a housekeeper.
Woman: My dear, why don't you learn to make love better – it will save on the cost of a chauffeur.

WOMEN IN SOCIETY

Today the Court fulfilled its duty in recognising the rights of Colombian women.
Monica Roa, lawyer and abortion campaigner (2006)

Until a change in the constitution in the 1950s, Colombian women, at least in theory, stayed at home. Without political rights and governed by her spouse under law, a woman in Colombian society had little power, status or authority. In this subordinate role women often had limited access to education or money and lived the life of second-class citizens. Since being awarded suffrage, however, some marked changes have ensued. Today, women are evident throughout corporate entities, government bodies and grassroots movements. Colombia has one of the highest numbers of female politicians in South America with almost a quarter of all cabinet, congress and mayoralty posts filled by women. Powerful role models also exist in Colombia such as pop star Shakira, who at 26 became the youngest official Goodwill Ambassador to UNICEF, the world's leading organisation for children. President Uribe has also appointed an unprecedented number of women to his cabinet during his tenures, including positions with defence and foreign affairs portfolios. In fact, a law passed in 2000 set quotas for the executive branch of the Colombian government, stating that 30% of appointment positions be filled by women.

Women do, however, continue to take prime responsibility for the lives and care of their children. These family obligations certainly challenge the pursuit of a career, especially in Colombia's infamous world of late-night, back-room dealings. However, many Colombian women see no conflict in using their attractiveness to further their status – a strategy often encouraged by the mother from an early age via modelling and beauty pageants. Indeed a number of Colombian catwalk queens have made it in the hardnosed world of public office, including a minister of culture and a minister of defence. In Cali and Medellín, women are particularly keen on plastic surgery to enhance their God-given assets, while Colombia-wide there's an overriding sense of female sexual confidence from females of every age.

However, despite considerable progress, few would argue that machismo and its discrimination against woman have been eradicated from Colombian life. Year on year, the number of single mothers continues to increase within the poorer classes (in 2006, 200,000 girls and adolescents between 15 and 19 became mothers), while divorce has only been possible since 1992. Abortion is still ostensibly illegal in Colombia although an estimated 300,000 backstreet terminations are performed each year. However, in 2006 Colombia's highest court ruled that abortion is permissible in certain circumstances, such as when a pregnancy threatens a woman's life or health, in cases of rape, and in cases where the foetus has abnormalities incompatible with life outside the womb. Bungled abortions account for a significant number of maternal mortalities, especially in the lower classes. Wealthier women have the option of leaving the country to seek a termination in the US. The average life expectancy for a woman is 75 years, according to UN figures, although UNICEF studies reveal 900 die from childbirth-related causes each year.

CHILDREN IN SOCIETY Colombia's children enjoy vastly contrasting fortunes, depending on the economic situation of their family. Those in the lower classes often experience extreme poverty in family structures that have broken down. Some suffer at the hands of their parents or other family members due to alcoholism, drug taking and mental illness. In 2005, 184 children committed suicide with 680 murders perpetrated against children under 18. In 2004, 25,000 cases of sexual exploitation were reported along with 18,000 cases of sexual abuse with Colombia's

national forensic medicine authority registering 10,170 abused children, although the true figure is thought to be as many as 200,000. Poorer children suffer from a lack of housing, food, clothes and sanitation, so it is unsurprising that at least 750,000 drop out of basic education each year. In 1999, aid organisations estimated that about 2.5 million children in Colombia were forced to work by their families, despite a law prohibiting child labour under the age of 14.

In middle class and upper class families, children are generally cared for considerably better, with low reported levels of child abuse. Many children from middle and upper class homes enjoy private, coeducational air-conditioned classrooms complete with IT facilities, laboratories, libraries, gym, swimming pool and auditorium. They are also encouraged to study to university level to achieve the status and profession of their class. In rural areas, it is not uncommon for middle and upper class families to 'adopt' a child of a local farmer. This is usually a girl, who may serve as a maid in their home. In return, the child will be given a salary, full schooling, room and board, and will become, in essence, a member of the family. This arrangement usually ends at the age 17, but can sometimes last into middle age and beyond.

Conservative estimates suggest Colombia has almost one million orphans aged under 17 – many of them in the care of organisations such as SOS Children's Villages in Bogotá. The Colombian government recognises the rights of the nation's 18 million children under a 1989 convention. However its controversial 2006 Child and Adolescent Code has been denounced by aid agencies worldwide that see it as a step backwards in children's rights and an act that offers no practical help. The legislation, which criminalises and penalises children coerced into working in armed groups or the drug trade, affects those aged 14 to 18. Jail terms of five to eight years apply in accordance with Colombia's penal code. In 2001, Movimiento de los Niños por la Paz (Children's Peace Movement) received the World's Children's Honorary Award for success in promoting children's rights. Members total more than 100,000 children from 400 different youth organisations Colombia-wide. In 2007, Bogotá authorities launched a poster campaign in a bid to tackle child abuse, erecting 40 6m x 2m billboards city-wide. Each displays the photos and personal details of convicted paedophiles along with their crime and sentence. The age and sex of their victims is also displayed. Lawyers for the prisoners had argued that the campaign violated the men's constitutional rights. When it was first announced, the campaign was the subject of more than 30 unsuccessful legal challenges.

GAY RIGHTS

Laws are not enough; an important cultural shift is needed ... for discrimination to end.

Marcela Sanchez, Colombia Diversa (2007)

Colombia has a relatively small gay scene confined to its major cities but has witnessed significant improvements in gay and lesbian rights in recent years. However, discrimination remains rife, despite Colombia's increasingly liberal social attitudes. Today, it may be easier to be openly homosexual in major cities but in rural areas the attitude towards gays and lesbians shows little sign of softening. Dozens of groups in Colombia have conducted anti-gay campaigns under such names as 'Death to Homosexuals'. Even a human rights ombudsman once described homosexuals in a television interview as 'abnormal faggots' that should be subject to 'social control'.

However, Colombia does have openly gay politicians, an active Gay and Lesbian Information Network and an active gay rights group in Bogotá-based Colombia

Diversa, founded in 2004. Consensual homosexual activity was decriminalised in 1980 with amendments to the Criminal Code so there is a single age of consent of 14. In 2003, following strong opposition from the Catholic Church, an extremely progressive bill to give legal recognition to lesbian and gay partnerships was shelved. However, in February 2007 the Colombian Constitutional Court ruled that same-sex couples are entitled to the same inheritance rights as heterosexuals in common-law marriages. It marked a giant step forward for gay rights. Even Colombia's powerful Catholic Church hierarchy backed the bill on the basis that it didn't include same-sex marriage or adoption. According to gay rights group Colombia Diversa at least 100,000 couples will benefit from the new legislation, which is one of the most progressive gay rights reforms in Latin America.

Colombia Diversa \ 1 483 1237; e info@colombiadiversa.org; www.colombiadiversa.org. This non-profit organisation promotes the rights of lesbians, gays, bisexuals & transgendered (LGBT) persons in Colombia. It was founded in Bogotá in 2004.

Centro Comunitario LGTB Calle 66 No 9A–28 Bogotá; \ 1 249 0049; www.guiagaycolombia.com. This gay support group has an excellent online guide to the Colombian gay & lesbian scene. A city by city search facility covers most of the country & lists everything from cafes & bars to nightclubs & porn shops.

LANGUAGE

Spanish is the official language of Colombia and is spoken by everyone apart from some isolated Indian communities. English is the second language but is a rarity away from Colombia's main cities. Mastering a few Spanish basics is essential for those heading to the interior provinces where anything else will be as alien as an intergalactic tongue. However, English is being increasingly taught in schools and colleges as a mandatory subject across the country and is the primary language on the island of Providencía and commonly found in San Andrés. The average Colombian is receptive to anyone willing to have a decent stab at Spanish, offering much encouragement and attempts at Spanglish – and politely ignoring all grammatical faux pas. Colombian Spanish is relaxed, informal and generally easy to understand although even accomplished linguists will find numerous inventive *Colombianismos*, words and phrases that are wholly unique. Latin American Spanish is also littered with American influences, rather than Spain's formal European style. The most obvious difference is the absence of the 'th' lisping used in European Spanish for a 'z' and a 'c'. This is pronounced as a soft 's' in Colombian, as in much of Latin America. Greetings also tend to be much more elaborate in Colombian style, comprising a long exchange of incalculable pleasantries rather than the perfunctory '*hola*'. Slang has also infiltrated the Colombian language to a large extent and *Streetwise Spanish*, a guide to Latin American Spanish, is especially useful countrywide. Some Indian tribes in remote areas still speak their own languages. The current constitution, adopted in 1991, recognises the languages of ethnic groups and provides for bilingual education. *Cundiboyacences* (those from Cundinamarca and Boyacá) are distinctive in linguistic terms as they use the second-person pronoun sumercé. See also *Appendix 2, Language*, page 427.

RELIGION

Colombia is often referred to as 'the most Roman Catholic of all South American countries' – and in terms of its out-and-out religious devotion it remains very much a colony of Spain. Although modern Colombia's immigrant Lebanese, Turkish and Jewish populations each have their own places of worship, more than 90% of Colombia's population is Roman Catholic. A ratio of priests to inhabitants of 1:4,000 is one of Latin America's highest with such primary rites of the church as baptism, first communion and marriage viewed as key turning points in life. Small Protestant communities can be found on the former English colonies of San Andrés and Providencía where gospel-singing congregations rub shoulders with those practising ancient slave rituals and African beliefs.

EDUCATION

> So far we have created 750,000 new school places, especially for the poorest. If you look at the universities, for the poor people you will see that we have created a huge number of places in the system.
>
> President Álvaro Uribe (2005)

In the past 30 years the Colombian government has made great inroads in improving accessibility to primary and secondary education, but the gaps in the country's schooling are still immense. In 2001, the ratio of pupils to teachers in primary school was 26:1 and in secondary school 19:2 but as recently as 1994 just five of every ten children aged 12 to 17 years of age were in regular attendance. Colombia's poorest people have always received the least education. In urban areas children are schooled for an average of seven years, double that in the rural communities. The quality of education in public primary and secondary schools is also substandard in rural areas due to a lack of materials prescribed in the curriculum. In three decades, public expenditure on education as a percentage of gross domestic product (GDP) hasn't changed a great deal: 2.85% in the 1970s, 2.99% in the 1980s and 3.03% in the 1990s. Since President Uribe came to power in 2002 he has cut the education budget in order to pump more capital into his military campaigns. Access to higher education by Colombia's youth population is also lagging behind by international and regional standards. The country's 22% enrolment rate does not meet the country's needs in terms of technological and economic development. In Colombia, 70% of education is private, and there are 900 private higher education institutions compared with 32 public ones. Instruction in Roman Catholicism is standard in all public schools, most of which are controlled by the Roman Catholic Church. In 2000 some 5.2 million pupils annually attended primary schools with 3.6 million students at secondary school. Among the largest universities are the National University of Colombia in Bogotá, the University of Cartagena, the University of Antioquía in Medellín, and the University of Nariño in Pasto. Since 2003, Colombia's national programme for literacy and basic education for young people and adults has benefited 275,000 people with several specialised adult education methods winning UNESCO literacy prizes. International Literary Day is celebrated on an annual basis. Considerable effort has been devoted to eliminating illiteracy in Colombia since the 1970s, and today 93% of all citizens over the age 15 can read and write. In recent years Bill Gates has been instrumental in helping raise IT skills in Colombia through his foundation and company Microsoft Corp. Gates has set up computer learning centres in areas where demobilised paramilitary fighters are in dire need of job training, at a cost of US$1 million. Another deal has helped put 15,000 more computers in Colombian schools. The nation has one computer per 40 students and Gates wants that to drop to 25.

SOCIAL STRUCTURE

Colombian society exhibits strong class divisions and regional distinctions with people often referred to in terms of the administrative departments in which they live, such as Antioqueños, Nariñenses, Bogotános, Santandereanos, Tolimenses and Boyacanses. There is also a tradition of identifying Colombians by their colour, dress, diet and speech, and class structure remains based on a combination of occupation, wealth and ethnicity. Colombian society is split into six numerical socioeconomic strata (*estrato*). This grouping is of great importance to Colombians, so much so that even the most modest person will allude to their stratum – should it be sufficiently high. However, above all else, strata is about location.

1 poor
2 lower working class
3 working class
4 upper working class
5 more affluent working class
6 upper class

According to the World Bank, Colombia's rate of inequality is one of the highest in Latin America. Colombians from the top quintile retain 60% of the national income, in strong contrast to Sweden, for example, where the top quintile retains 34% of the national income.

However, the majority of Colombia's 43.6 million population belong to the so-called 'marginal' classes, a sector of society without regular employment that tends to eke out a living by any possible means. This lower class relies on manual labour for a sporadic income and largely comprises those of African, Indian or mixed race who are politically powerless, poorly educated and living below the poverty line. Few of the benefits of economic growth have reached Colombia's poorest members of society who put up with a standard of sanitation, housing and healthcare that is inadequate at best.

Colombia's middle classes tend to be skilled professionals who lack the wealth, connections and pure European heritage of their upper-class compatriots. In order to infiltrate the upper echelons of society, middle-class people must transform aspiration into *real* connections. As a relatively small and politically passive group, Colombia's middle classes have traditionally settled in their comfort zone, although during President Uribe's tenure a greater number of small business owners and merchants have felt the confidence to rise through the ranks.

In the upper echelons of Colombian society, professional occupations aren't that dissimilar to the middle classes. However, this social segment is dominated by a relatively small group of wealthy families of mainly pure Spanish background who control most of the country's land and property. Many of Colombia's rich elite can trace their lineage to the aristocracy of the colonial era, although the wealth of this privileged group also includes those that have made their money in more recent times through entrepreneurial wheeler-dealing. Colombia's exclusive wealthy cliques are preoccupied with the protection of family pride, name and assets (*abolengo*) and these family links are key to the business and political life of every member of the upper classes.

Colombia's chasm between rich and poor was described by the United Nations in 2004 as 'the worst humanitarian crisis in the Western hemisphere'. Despite pockets of considerable wealth Colombia's average daily income remains at about £4, less than a tenth of the UK's with an annual per capita gross income of US$2,500, according to the UN (June 2006). However, a US$4 billion wealth tax imposed on Colombia's 6,000 richest citizens and biggest companies in 2007 by the Uribe administration is seen as a positive step in attempting to redress the imbalance.

Colombia has a lengthy arts tradition born out of the nation's innate compulsion to seek out new creative outlets. Colombian artists have been renowned for their energy and spirit throughout history, from great literary and musical movements to the modern mediums of photography, cinema and television. Today, a genuine desire to retain Colombia's artistic heritage prevails throughout the country along with a considerable commitment to furthering a wide range of contemporary arts across numerous ethnic and mixed-race groups. Colombians remain hugely proud of their Nobel Prize winners and make much of the fact that more celebrated home-grown poets (men of the pen) than military men (men of the sword) have made it to the presidency role.

MUSIC AND DANCE

Voy a beber del veneno malevo de tu amor
(I drank from the malevolent poison that was your love)
yo quedé moribundo y lleno de dolor
(I remain a dying man and full of pain)
respiré de ese humo amargo de tu adios
(I breathe in that bitter second of your goodbye)'

Juanes, *La Camisa Negra* (The Black Shirt, 2005)

Colombia's most deeply rooted musical tradition, the folkloric tunes and melodies of the indigenous peoples, is found in distinct geographic pockets in both its pure and modern forms. Spanish elements blend with native rhythms and a hybrid of American, Trinidadian, Cuban and Jamaican styles. Broadly speaking, Colombian music falls into four musical geographic zones: the Andean region, the Atlantic coast, the Pacific coast and Los Llanos (the plains). Andean melodies boast strong Spanish influences. Instruments used include the *tiple guitarra* and piano in genres such as the *bambuco, pasillo guabina* and *torbellino*. Music in the Caribbean (Atlantic) is a pulsating mix of hot, steamy rhythms, such as the *cumbia, porros* and *mapalé*. On the Pacific coast the *currulao* uses heavy pounding drumbeats tinged with some telltale Spanish inflections while the music of Los Llanos (*música llanera*) is usually accompanied by a harp, *cuatro* (a sort of four-string guitar) and maracas. These older musical styles have been joined by two important newer additions that now dominate Colombia's music scene countrywide. Because of its popularity, 'la salsa' seems endemic to Colombia, yet it didn't arrive until the late 1960s when it spread like wildfire and is now a music-and-dance mainstay. Sexy, sassy and fluid, new style salsa has become a symbol of pride and cultural identity for Latinos and is found on every street corner in salsa epicentres of Cali and Barranquilla. Another omnipresent musical form is the infectious *vallenato*, a celebrated genre from the northern tip of Colombia that fuses European-style accordion riffs with traditional folkloric themes. Reggae, calypso and *socca* are the most popular music styles on the islands of San Andrés and Providencía, where dozens of waterfront bars and restaurants sway to hypnotic rhythms 24 hours a day. *Reggaetón* has also been prevalent throughout San Andrés since gaining popularity in the mid-1990s. This oh-so-cool fusion of hip hop and Jamaican dancehall with Latino beat has its own unique rhythm, a hybrid of various musical genres from the Caribbean, Latin America and the United States. Reggaetón has attracted criticism for its sexually explicit lyrics that allegedly exploit women, although fans insist the message is non-violent, albeit a little risqué. Further controversy surrounds *perreo*, a bump-and-grind dance with explicit sexual overtones associated with Colombia's reggaetón scene. Some **ancient musical forms** from the colonial period have survived in Colombia, according to the Academy of American Franciscan History. Numerous folkloric festivals celebrate these ancient traditions nationwide.

Vallenato According to historian Tomás D Gutiérrez Hinojosa, *vallenato* music is traditionally played with *un acordeón vallenato* (accordion), *una caja Vallenato* (large bongo) and *una guacharaca* (bamboo guiro) with commercial groups adding a singer (*un cantante*), two harmony singers (*coros*), a conga player (*un conguero*), a bass player (*un bajista*), a guitarist (*un guitarrista*) as well as a timbales player (*un timbalero*). Traditionally, vallenato has been inextricably linked with the songwriter Rafael Escalona, a pioneering recording artist in the 1950s and 1960s. Other well-known songwriters of the same era are Leandro Díaz, Emiliano Zuleta, and Tobías E. Pumarejo, to name just a few. Today, a modern form of so-called techno *vallenato* is popular throughout Colombia, with big-selling artists that include Carlos Vives.

Colombia stages a number of vallenato folkloric festivals and competitions with highly coveted awards for categories such as 'professional accordion player', 'amateur accordion player', 'young accordion player', 'best new vallenato song' and '*piquerías*' (verse singers).

Vallenato festivals include the 41st Annual Festival de la Leyenda Vallenato (*Valledupar, César; www.festivalvallenato.com*), Festival Cuna de Acordeones (*Villanueva, Guajira; www.elvallenato.com*), Festival National de Compositores de Música Vallenato (*San Juan del César, Guajira;* www.fundacionbat.com.co), Festival Tierra de Compositores (*Patillal, César; www.folklorvallenato.com*), Festival Folclórico del Fique (*La Junta, Guajira; www.miriohacha.com*), Festival de Acordeoneros y Compositores de Chinú (*Chinú, Córdoba; www.parrandaVallenato.com*), Festival Sabanero (*Sincelejo, Sucre; www.teatrosucre.com*).

Cumbia This complex mix of African rhythms was popularised on Colombia's Caribbean coast with primal percussive drums, simple vocals and a tit-for-tat-style dance. Courtship rituals are depicted through a flirtatious performance with shuffling footwork said to portray slavery in ankle chains. In the 1940s, many of Colombia's urban communities discovered Cumbia, which soon evolved from its rural form to a more refined style. The so-called Golden Age of Cumbia was the 1950s when Colombians nationwide embraced the rhythmic performances with gusto, often in large groups of male and female couples. Cumbia is characterised by women playfully swirling long skirts whilst holding a candle, while each man, wearing a red handkerchief around the neck, dances behind with one hand on his back. The remaining hand pulls his hat on and off and waves it flamboyantly. Until the mid 20th century, cumbia suffered from a poor reputation and was considered a vulgar dance, practised only by peasants. Today it remains a stalwart of Colombia's working classes with drums and claves giving an instantly recognisable backbeat. Today, modern cumbia is fused with other genres, such as vallenato, pop and rock music, and has been popularised by Grammy Award-winning artists (see *www.grammy.com/latin*) such as Colombia's dreadlocked heartthrob, Carlos Vives. A former soap opera star, Vives has become a national hero for championing vallenato, cumbia and porro for a new, young audience. He has worked with English producer Richard Blair as well as a repertoire of veteran Latino musicians on the albums *Los Clásicos De La Provincia*, *La Tierro del Olvido* and *Tengo Fe*.

Música llanera This harp-led music originates from the Colombian plains but has become part of a national tradition renowned for its verbal contests *contrapunteo*, a form of sung poetry performed head to head. *Joropo* musical style resembles the waltz with an accompanying dance that mixes African and European influences with its roots in Venezuelan and Colombian folklore. Música Llanera (*www.musicallanera.net*) also features a *cuatro* (a type of four-string guitar) and maracas with lyrics redolent of the rural cattle-farming life of the *llanos* region.

Colombian salsa Although originally born among Puerto Ricans and Cubans, salsa soon spread to a receptive audience in Colombia and during the late 1960s it truly captured the hearts and souls of music lovers nationwide. By 1970, salsa was fast becoming an epidemic as Colombia took the reins of Latin America salsa music, with its irrepressible, sexy, sultry rhythms popularised by Fruko y sus Tesos. This Cali-based crowd-pleasing band of musicians led by Ernesto Fruko Estrada enjoyed huge popularity throughout Latin America with big-selling albums that include *Pura candela*, *El preso*, *Cali de rumba*, *Son de la loma*, *El patillero*, and *Charanga campesina*. Today Fruko and his boys still rank among the best Colombian salsa bands, famed for their hardcore, swing-inspired music of the highest quality. Joe Arroyo began singing in Fruko y sus Tesos in 1971, wooing the salsa world with his vibrant vocal style and mischievous dance moves. He finally started his own band, La Verdad (The Truth), in 1981, with a talented orchestra of musicians. He was born in Cartagena, and his father had 40 sons with many different women, a story that he famously tells during his set. A versatile singer of many Caribbean rhythms, Joe Arroyo is a vivacious performer of sones and boleros as well as the cumbias and fandangos of his native region. Today he remains highly popular and much revered within Colombia, and regularly invents new rhythms and styles with roots in his local salsa traditions. Santiago de Cali (better known as simply Cali) is Colombia's undisputed 'Capital de la Salsa' with hundreds of clubs, festivals, dance schools and concerts that pay homage to the city's infatuation. An annual week-long Summer Salsa Festival takes place in Cali in early July, attracting many of the world's greatest salsa bands and devotees to a host of dance shows and 'melomano' competitions. The competition is fierce between salsa connoisseurs and aficionados, who try to out-do each other with fancy moves to vintage long-lost salsa tunes. January 2008 also heralded the 50th anniversary of the Feria de Cali, the largest salsa festival in the world. More than three million salseras and salseros descend on the city for the mother of all Cali's famous parties. The event includes the World Salsa Championship and World Salsa Congress and accounts for a massive hike in the sales of rum and aguardiente.

Pop music

> No puedo pedir que el invierno perdone a un rosal
> (I can't ask winter to spare a rose bush)
> No puedo pedir a los olmos que entreguen peras
> (I can't ask an elm tree to bear pears)
> No puedo pedirle lo eterno a un simple mortal
> (I can't ask the eternal of a mere mortal)
>
> Shakira, *La Tortura* (The Torture, 2007)

Think Colombian pop music and Shakira is bound to spring to mind, yet on domestic soil artists like Fonseca (*www.fonseca.net*), Juanes (*www.juanes.net*), Carlos Vives (*www.carlosvives.com*) and Mauricio y Palo de Agua (*mauricioypalodeagua.blogspot.com*) are headline-grabbing musical icons. Bogotá-born heart-throb Fonseca's acclaimed double-platinum album *Corazon* blends vallenato, bullerengue, tambora and African drums with a hint of classic salsa and features the heart-warming 'Te Mando Flores', a big-selling single in 2006. Triple-Grammy Award-winner Medellín-born Juanes launched his solo career in 1998. His sophomore album, *Un Día Normal*, was certified platinum throughout much of the Spanish-speaking world, and its lead single 'A Dios le Pido' topped singles charts in 12 countries. Juanes is also renowned for his extensive humanitarian work, especially with aid for Colombian victims of anti-personnel

COLOMBIAN MUSIC GLOSSARY

baile	meaning *dance*
bambuco	an Andean style of dance music or Andean lyric
balada	Spanish romantic popular music, as in ballad
bandola	used in llanera, stringed musical instrument similar to a mandolin
bandolin	larger style of *bandola*
bombo	drum used in folklore music on the Caribbean coast, traditionally used in cumbia
bullerengue	traditional flute-and-drum music
caja Vallenato	a goatskin drum used in vallenato
campana	traditional cowbell
capachos	traditional maracas
champeta	gutsy Atlantic coastal music, Afro-Colombian in origins
contrapunteo	an improvised, verbal duel to music
cuatro	small guitar used in llanera music
guache	seed-filled rattles used in vallenato
joropo	courtship dance endemic to cattle-ranching culture
llamador	traditional drum used in cumbia
melómano	a true music lover
parrandero	a person who loves to party – a lot
pasillo	Andean lyrical song
porro	brass band flute-and-drum music
salsoteca	a salsa venue
tiple	small stringed instrument used in llanera
zarzuela	traditional Colombian operetta

mines. Yet it is undoubtedly two-time Latin Grammy Award-winner Shakira (*www.shakira.com*) that remains Colombia's biggest musical celebrity, selling 50 million albums and establishing herself in history as the only Colombian artist to reach number one on the Billboard Hot 100 and UK Singles Chart. In July 2006, she earned the distinction of performing the last-ever song on legendary British music programme *Top of the Pops*, with 'Hips Don't Lie', after seven weeks in the charts. A number of free concerts play host to some of Latin America's most popular rock, R&B and pop acts each year in Bogotá's Simón Bolívar Park.

Classical music

It's as if he is conjoined to the music, he is one with its energy.

Música Clássica article (2006)

Colombia is justifiably proud of its shining classical star Andrés Orozco-Estrada, a handsome 30-something with incredible musical pedigree and flair. Born in 1977 in Medellín, he started playing the violin at the age of five and by 15 was conducting an orchestra. Today this darling of the orchestral circuit is fast emerging as one of the most creative conductors. 'He is dazzling, a master. A genius,' said one critic in 2007.

In 1992 Orozco-Estrada began studying conducting and the violin at the Universidad Javeriana in Bogotá, followed by a master class during 1997–2003 at Vienna Music University. During this time Orozco-Estrada participated in the International Lovro von Matacic Conducting Competition in Zagreb. He was also a semi-finalist in the Hungarian Television 10th International Conductors' Competition in Budapest. In 2000 he was selected to represent Austria at the

Festival of Contemporary Music Biennale Internazionale di Torino. He also participated in several concerts with the Anti Dogma Orchestra while with the Austrian Society of Contemporary Music in May 2003 he debuted with the Tonkünstler-Orchester Niederösterreich. In Vienna he also premiered the operas *Die Geschichte des Picando* by Gernot Schedlberger and *Der gestiefelte Kater* by Perikles Liakakis (with the ProArte Orchestra Vienna). In Germany he conducted performances of *Orfeo ed Euridice* by Gluck in Munich (Orpheus Ensemble Munich) as well as *Il Campanello* by Donizetti at the Court Theatre of Schönbrunn (Solisti del Teatro Bratislava).

Andrés Orozco-Estrada has conducted the Colombian National Orchestra and the Philharmonic Orchestra of Bogotá. Today he frequently works with the most prestigious orchestras in Colombia, including the Orquesta Filarmónica de Medellín, Orquesta Filarmonica del Valle, Orquesta Sinfonica Universidad Eafit, Coral Tomás Luis de Victoria in Medellín and Coro Polifónico de Medellín.

THEATRE Each of Colombia's main cities boasts a wide range of theatres and venues that stage an array of performances spanning the conventional and classic to the bizarre. Colombia's theatre tradition was born in the mid 19th century, but it wasn't until the emergence of its National Theatre almost a century later that the arts benefited from a firmer footing and significantly higher profile nationwide. Today, Bogotá, Cali and Medellín remain the main centres for theatre groups with more than 150 amateur, semi-professional and professional troupes countrywide. A growing number of theatrical academies are feeding the future development of Colombia's national theatre, from social projects in deprived communities via the Amateur Dramatic Association and programmes at the Escuela Nacional de Arte Dramático in Bogotá. A ballet school in Bogotá has a growing international reputation, while a male voice choir in Medellín has put the city's choral societies on the map. Every two years Bogotá plays host to the Iberoamerican Theater Festival, when the best of scenic arts from five continents, 33 countries, 45 international companies and 140 guest Colombian groups fill 12 theatre halls, six coliseums, 20 parks, the Bullfighting Arena and Bogotá Fair venue to deliver 556 shows and over 1,200 performers. Concerts range from classical music, dance, avant-garde performances, circus troupes and plays to street theatre in every auditorium, public park, coliseum and street space throughout the capital, attracting upwards of 30,000 visitors from all corners of the globe.

For further information contact the Colombian Amateur Dramatic Association (Corporation Cultural Nuestra Gente) (*Calle 99 No 50 c38, Barrio Santa Cruz, Medellín, Colombia;* ✆ *4 258 0348;* e *nuestragente@epm.net.co; www.nuestragente.org*), Iberoamerican Theater Festival (*www.festivaldeteatro.com.co*), **Fundación Teatro Nacional** (✆ *4 211 1741;* e *teatronacional@teatronacional.com.co; www.teatronacional.com.co*).

LITERATURE Since independence from Spain, Colombia has enjoyed a long and glorious literary tradition. Numerous authors of note have achieved international acclaim, including one Nobel Prize in Literature winner,.

Gabriel García Márquez (b 1928)

> In my ninetieth year, I decided to give myself the gift of a night of love with a young virgin.
>
> Gabriel García Márquez, *Memoria de Mis Putas Tristes*
> (Memories of My Melancholy Whores) (2004)

Because of his strong political views, Colombia's most famous novelist, journalist, publisher, political activist and celebrity García Márquez has lived much of his life in exile in Mexico City. He began his career at a local newspaper working on regional giants such as *El Heraldo* (Barranquilla) and *El Universal* (Cartagena) when he joined forces with other writers and journalists to form what became known as the Barranquilla Group. These creative, influential compatriots became a strong source of inspiration for Márquez who went on to work in Paris, Barcelona, Caracas and New York City as a foreign correspondent. He openly criticised Colombia's political situation which provoked accusations from the government regarding his support of guerrilla groups, such as the FARC and ELN, although there has never been any evidence to back up these claims. García Márquez is noted for his friendship with Cuban President Fidel Castro and in 2006 he joined other international figures to demand sovereignty for Puerto Rico. He also joined the Latin American and Caribbean Congress for the Independence of Puerto Rico to push for the island-nation's right to independence, at the behest of the Puerto Rican Independence Party. His first novel, *La hojarasca* was published in 1955 (translated in 1972 as *Leaf Storm and Other Stories*) but it was *Cien Años de Soledad* in 1967 that thrust García Márquez into the international limelight, gaining him acclaim worldwide (published in English in 1970 as *One Hundred Years of Solitude*). Affectionately known as Gabo, García Márquez is a master of the literary style known as magic realism. In 1982 he became the first Colombian to date to win the Nobel Prize in Literature, just one of 104 winners worldwide since 1901.

Today, García Márquez ranks as one of South America's greatest 20th-century authors. Born in the town of Aracataca in the department of Magdalena on 6 March 1928, Márquez is the father of television and film director Rodrigo Garciá. Since being diagnosed with cancer in 1999, García Márquez has started work on his memoirs, an event that in 2000, prompted premature reports of his death in Peruvian newspaper *La República*. Plans by British film director Mike Newell (*Four Weddings and a Funeral*) to produce a film based on García Márquez's *Love in the Time of Cholera* are under way in Cartagena (see page 363). The screenplay has been written by García Márquez himself.

Jorge Isaacs (1837–95)
Isaacs studied for a medical career before becoming a journalist, poet and writer, drawing on his childhood, growing up in a small Jewish community in Cali. In 1987 his only novel *María* (published in English in 1890 as *María: A South American Romance*) became one of the most notable works of the Romantic Movement in Spanish literature. Many of his poems portray the Valley of the Cauca. Isaacs also lived in Popayán before moving to Bogotá in 1848.

Porfirio Barba Jacob (1883–1942)
Miguel Ángel Osorio Benítez was better known by his pseudonym Porfirio Barba Jacob and was also dubbed 'The Poet of Death' for his avant-garde writing style. Born in Santa Rosa de Osos in Antioquía, Jacob founded the literary magazine *El cancionero antioqueño* (*The Antioquian Songbook*) in Bogotá under the pseudonym Marín Jiménez. He also wrote a novel *Virginia* that remains unpublished because the original manuscript was seized by authorities due to its alleged immoral themes. In 1906, he moved to Barranquilla under the name Ricardo Arenales, a name he would use until 1922. For the rest of his life, he lived as Porfirio Barba-Jacob, enjoying the success of poems 'Árbol viejo', 'Campiña florida', and his most famous work – *Parábola de la vida profunda* (*Parable of the deep life*). Jacob died in 1942 of tuberculosis in Mexico City where he had became famous for his poetic style known as *nueva sensibilidad*.

José Asunción Silva (1865–96)
The poems of Bogotá-born José Asunción Silva are renowned as some of the most beautiful in the Spanish language, marked by haunting angst and a brooding spirit of pessimism. The best known is *Nocturno III*,

an elegy for his sister, *Crepúsculo*, and *Día de difuntos* (Day of the Dead). Silva also wrote a novel, *De Sobremesa*, notable for its rejection of realist conventions and its intense emotional themes.

Unfortunately José Asunción Silva's life was overshadowed by periods of deep depression, caused by the loss of a crucial manuscript, family debt and the death of a beloved sister. In 1896, he committed suicide, leaving a debt of US$210,000. The lasting legacy of this most gifted writer is a collection of poetry called *Los Nocturnos* in which Silva displays extraordinary genius. Baldomero Sanín Cano subsequently published many of his works in Paris in 1913.

John Jairo Junieles (1970–present day) This young Colombian poet has won considerable acclaim since winning the prestigious 2006 II 'Ciudad Alajuela' International Poetry Award in Costa Rica with his book *Passenger With a Ticket to a Strange Land*. Junieles, who received US$5,000 and the publication of his book, was born in Sincelejo, Sucre, Colombia in 1970. He currently resides in Bogotá

CINEMA, TELEVISION AND RADIO

I'm going to get Daniel a new horse to ride… That didn't sound as dirty in my head.
Betty Suárez, *Ugly Betty* (Yo Soy Betty la Fea), ABC (2006)

Colombian television programmes appear to move seamlessly from light and fluffy escapist trash to the harsh reality of the nation's social discourse. Cinema tends to be harder hitting, exploiting these themes to much acclaim as in films such as *Rosaria Tijeras* in 2005 and 2004's *Sumas y Restas*. Although widely ignored anywhere outside of Colombia, these gritty celluloid triumphs achieved sizeable success on home soil with their dark tales of narco-traffickers and contract killing. Colombians, like most Latin Americans, adore *telenovelas* (soap operas) and no self-respecting household isn't a slave to at least one each night. These kitsch mishmashes of drama, comedy and topical themes regularly fight it out for national ratings via increasingly bizarre and outrageous storylines. A favourite at the time of writing is RCN's *Los Reyes*, a mix of controversy, woes and hardship with just the right hint of drama and glamour. Another RCN show, *Yo Soy Betty la Fea*, inspired ABC's hugely popular American prime time hit *Ugly Betty*, the tale of a bespectacled, bushy-browed, braces-wearing heroine played with aplomb by América Ferrera (*Real Women Have Curves* and *The Sisterhood of the Traveling Pants*). American imports are also popular in Colombia, especially reality television shows. Expect to find *X Factor* re-runs and lots of shows portraying teen angst, such as *Dawson Creek* and *The OC*.

Colombia has hundreds of great radio stations that broadcast everything from religious classics and political talk shows to pumping rock and salsa. Stations come and go but the following are currently worth a listen:

• La Vallenato (97.4)	vallenato
• Tropicana FM (102.9)	salsa
• La Z – Bogotá (92.9)	salsa
• Los 40 Principales (89.9)	reggaetón
• La Mega (90.9)	reggaetón
• SuperEstación (88.9)	rock
• RadioActiva (97.9)	rock
• Vibra Bogotá (104.9)	rock & pop, retro 80's music, news
• CaracolRadio (94.9)	news & pop
• WRadio (99.9)	news & retro pop
• UNRADIO (Universidad Nacional de Colombia) (98.5)	all genres

- Javeriana Estéreo (Pontificia Universidad
  Javeriana) (91.5)   jazz, rock, pop
- Javeriana Estéreo Cali (107.5)   salsa
- Amor Estéreo (93.9)   retro 70s, 80s & 90s pop
- RCN (104.4)   news
- La X (103.9)   retro pop & news

ARCHITECTURE Those that dismiss Colombia as an architectural wasteland are guilty of overlooking some of South America's most handsome buildings. For Colombia has a wealth of incredible good-looking structures, from the gleaming Miami-esque skyline of Cartagena's shoreline and the ramshackle faded colonial façades of Bogotá's La Candelaria district to some of the finest preserved 16th- and 17th-century architecture in Latin America in Villa de Leyva and the walled city of Getsemaní. Cali, Medellín and Bogotá each boast plenty of futuristic, needle-thin spires, while Barranquilla's white stucco and red tiled buildings in the historic El Prado district and Popayán's resplendent aged streets and churches are truly deserving of acclaim. Styles that dominated the 16th and 17th centuries were the elaborate Plateresque (as seen at the Tunja Cathedral), Mannerism (exemplified by Bogotá's San Ignacio church) and the extravagant, ornate Baroque (epitomised by the Palace of the Inquisition, Cartagena). In 2006, the prestigious Golden Lion Award for Architecture recognised Colombia in its tenth International Architectural Awards, rewarding Bogotá for its positive stance in applying Mies van der Rohe's dictum 'less is more' to its civic space. Judges were impressed by the city's widespread redesign that saw its streets improve aesthetically as well as in economic and social terms. In 2007 the Biblioteca Pública Piloto de Medellín para América Latina (Medellín Pilot Public Library for Latin America) staged an exhibition entitled '100 years of Architecture in Colombia', a photographic journey through Colombia's architectural heritage in conjunction with UNESCO and the Memory of the World Programme. Numerous books have been published on the subject, including *Casa Republicana: Colombia's Belle Epoque* in which author Benjamin Villegas takes a look at Republican architecture and examines the era of ornate design. *Country Houses in Colombia* sees authors Alberto Saldarriaga and Antonio Castenda Buragua explore how indigenous plants (such as guadua, a local bamboo) have influenced the Colombian architectural form. Similarly, *Casa De Hacienda: Architecture in the Colombian Countryside* by German Tellez showcases some of the finest old rural properties in the Colombia's rural provinces. And see *Appendix 3, Further information*, page 433.

PAINTING AND SCULPTURE Religious themes dominated much of Colombia's artistic scene prior to independence, with Bogotá-based Gregorio Vásquez de Arce y Ceballos (1638–1711) one of the colonial era's finest. On his death he bequeathed more than 500 pieces of his work to the nation. These are now found in an array of museums and churches across the country, including some particularly fine paintings in the cathedrals of Bogotá. Colombia's artists became considerably more experimental after independence when European influences began to permeate traditional outlets, leading to more creative, rave and expressive original art. Distinct styles and themes began to emerge during the 1930s and 1940s, heralding a defining moment in Colombia's artistic history. At the forefront of this exciting creative explosion were a host of masters, including painter and sculptor Luis Alberto Acuña; watercolour, oil and mural artist Pedro Nel Gómez; Alejandro Obregón, a fine abstract painter; Eduardo Ramírez Villamizar, an artist renowned for his geometric style in three-dimensional space; Guillermo Wiedemann, a German-born painter who made Colombia his artistic home; and

...by the time you come to create art yourself you're spoilt – you're tired of beauty as such and want to do something else. With me it was quite different. I wasn't tired of beauty; I was hungering for it.

When Medellín-born Fernando Botero came into the world on 19 April 1932 he immediately began to look at it through unique eyes, according to his parents. This creative early bloomer had his own exhibition at the Leo Matiz Gallery in Bogotá whilst still in his teens, developing an instantly recognisable style of painting and sculpture characterised by the use of distorted proportions. The following year he was awarded a Second Prize at the National Salón, using the money he earned to travel to Spain, France and Italy to study the work of the old masters. Botero's neo-figurative works are often described as fat – but this is a gross oversimplification of the subject matter. Situational portraiture is his trademark, using exaggerated elements and shifts of scale. Botero also plays with the corpulence of the figures in his art with proportion manipulated to distort colour, shape and size.

Many paintings depict influences from a traditional Colombian upbringing. Botero describes himself as 'the most Colombian of Colombian artists' and some astute social commentary is also woven throughout his work. Paintings of small-town Colombian life centre on themes that range from political figures and military men to criminals, prostitutes and nudes. Many possess comic qualities that satirise power and excess, while family portraits depict greater affection and restraint. Those that dwell on the death of his son are particularly touching.

Botero moved to New York in 1960 but left in 1973 for Paris. Today he divides his time between Paris, New York, Tuscany and his homeland. In 2004, he donated a series of 23 oil paintings and 27 drawings to the National Museum of Colombia, depicting the country's long-lasting violence. In early 2005, Botero also unveiled a series of 50 controversial paintings graphically representing his anger at prisoner abuse at the Abu Ghraib jail. After exhibiting at the Palazzo Venezia in Rome, and later in Germany and Greece, Botero took this headline-grabbing collection to New York in October 2006, where they were shown at the Marlborough Gallery to great critical acclaim.

Rodrigo Arenas Betancur, Colombia's most celebrated monument creator. In the footsteps of these artistic forefathers came Colombia's most international renowned artist, Fernando Botero (see box above) as well as a painter famed for his erotic, nude work, Leonel Góngora. Today, Colombia is at the heart of Latin America's fine arts scene and boasts numerous exhibitions of international repute in galleries nationwide. Genres range from pre-Columbian to modern contemporary and include art, design, photography and cutting-edge high-tech visual mediums. Many of the nation's finest galleries are free to the public, including the magnificent El Museo Botero de Bogotá.

For further information contact the Colombian Fine Arts portal (*www.manzanazeta.com*).

HANDICRAFTS Colombian handicrafts are easily found in markets, street stalls and shops throughout the country, from the woven shoulder bags of the Arhuaco Indians of the Sierra Nevada de Santa Marta to the exquisite *sombrero vueltiao* made by the people of Córdoba. Other beautifully crafted items include hammocks of San Jacinto in Bolívar, decorated figures of Pasto, Nariño, and cheerful pottery of Ráquira in Boyacá – not to mention the Paez people's wonderfully thick, homespun triangular shawls (*ruanas*). In Bogotá, in the cloister of Las Aquas, a neighbourhood just off La Candelaria, Artesanías de Colombia (*Las Aguas Cra 2, 18A–58, Bogotá; ℩ 091 286 1766; www.artesaniasdecolombia.com.co*) stocks everything from straw umbrellas to hand-woven ponchos. Atop Cerro Nutibara in Medellín in the recreated typical Paisa village plaza an impressive range of artesanias sell bags and jewellery, while on the basis of choice alone, the colourful array of handicraft stores in the old dungeons in walls of Cartagena is difficult to beat.

SPORT

FOOTBALL

> Every defeat is a victory in itself.
>
> Francisco 'Pacho' Maturana, defender in 1982 Colombian World Cup squad

Colombians are passionate about football (soccer) with fierce regional competitiveness that leads to highly emotional matches between rivals. The Colombia Football Federation (*Federación Colombiana de Fútbol*) is the national game's governing body, dating back to 1924. It has been affiliated to FIFA since 1936 and is a member of CONMEBOL (Confederación Sudamericana de Fútbol). Professional football in Colombia was established in 1948 by DIMAYOR, now the Asociación de Clubes del Fútbol Profesional Colombiano. Today football is a national pastime with high levels of support from fans on a local and national level. Known as Los *Cafeteros,* Colombia's home-grown football talent includes the skilful past heroes of Willington Ortiz and René Higuita, who shone in the 1970s and '80s. Other great idols include Jorge Bermúdez, Iván Valenciano, Freddy Rincón and the wild-haired Carlos Alberto Valderrama Palacío. In 2007, a five-year-old boy from Barranquilla was hailed a football genius. Juan David Torres was spotted exhibiting extraordinary skill on a scrap of wasteland in his home town and is already rumoured to be the subject of a bidding war between Colombia's biggest clubs. *Futbolred.com*, Colombia's dedicated soccer website attracts over 17 million hits per month – 75% from home-based fans and the balance from the rest of Latin America and the wider world. It is even possible for Colombian soccer fans that live for their team to wear club colours in the afterlife too. Medellín funeral director San Vicente makes caskets for soccer-crazed fans in green for Atletico Nacional and red for Independiente Medellín. Club emblems are also embroidered on the inside lining of the casket lid – all for around 150,000 COP.

Colombia's greatest international achievements include the America Cup of 2001 (which it hosted), Central America Cup (1946 and 1970), second place in the America championship in 1975, winning the South American Youth Championship in 1987 and the South American Under-17 in 1993 – as well as qualifying for the World Cup in 1962, 1990, 1994 and 1998. However, Colombia's cavalier approach cost them dearly in their early qualifying games for Germany 2006. In the same year, Colombia joined the race to host the World Cup in 2014, challenging CONMEBOL's nomination of Brazil as the sole applicant from South America. Colombia was awarded the 1986 event but withdrew for financial and safety reasons. Mexico stepped in as a replacement host.

Colombia's national squad has also been involved in some of the greatest personal tragedies to hit football in recent years. In 1994, defender Andrés Escobar was murdered after scoring an own goal in a World Cup against the US. In 2003, spectators watched in horror as Cameroon midfielder Marc-Vivien Foé died on the pitch from a heart condition at a Confederations Cup semi-final. In 2004, striker Albeiro Usuriaga (nicknamed 'Palomo') was gunned down in a nightclub in Cali. In 2006, Elson Becerra was also shot and killed in his home town of Cartagena.

Becerra played in four games in qualifiers for the 2006 World Cup and was hailed a hero for his attempts to revive Marc-Vivien Foé after his collapse.

Colombia's performance on the world stage has since been disappointing, despite fielding some of the most exciting players on the planet. However, Colombia did supply the vinyl-coated fabrics used to cover the VIP seats at the 2006 World Cup stadium in Frankfurt; some 9,000m of Colombian-made fabric.

CYCLING Colombia has a strong cycling tradition with up-and-coming cyclists benefiting from some of the world's most inhospitable mountain ranges as their personal training ground. Fierce peaks in the area surrounding Armenia and the Andean cordilleras have both helped create some of the greatest climbing cyclists in the world. Many have competed internationally in events such as the Tour de France.

Colombia has several hundred thousand ardent cyclists and the areas that surround cities like Bogotá, Cali and Medellín are deluged with two-wheels each Sunday when enthusiasts take to the hills. In 2006, three Colombians left Bogotá to bicycle to Ushuaia in Argentina, in a bid to support the Colombian Campaign to Ban Landmines and to draw international attention to their country's extensive landmine problem. Colombia's capital also boasts 300km of cycle paths, known as the Ciclovia. This cycle-friendly initiative costs US$1.5 million a year to run, but is part–funded by Colombia's many cycle-mad corporate sponsors. The annual Tour of Colombia takes place in March and April. El Vuelta de Colombia covers 2,000km in 12 days.

Yet Colombia's professional cycling scene is not without controversy. In 2006, the Colombian Cycling Federation (**Federación Colombiana de Ciclismo**) (✆ *1 211.6659;* ✉ *contacto@ciclismodecolombia.com; www.ciclismodecolombia.com*) cleared Santiago Botero of doping charges, following investigations that forced him to withdraw from the Tour de France. Among those arrested included Dr Eufamiano Fuentes, who was Botero's team doctor when the Colombian rode with the Kelme team from 1996–2002. In the 2004 Athens Olympics, Colombian cyclist María Luisa Calle was stripped of her bronze medal after testing positive for the banned substance Heptaminol. She was third in the women's points race in the velodrome, giving Colombia its first medal of any colour in the short history of women's Olympic track cycling.

In 2007, the 39 year old Colombian cyclist Hernán Buenahora defied his critics to win an overall victory in the 42nd Vuelta al Táchira in Venezuela. The evergreen Colombian (nicknamed *escarabajo* or cockroach) triumphed after 14 stages over a 15-day period. He joins a long list of illustrious winners of the race inaugurated in 1966. It is the first Colombian victory in the race since Hernán Muñoz in 2003 with Buenahora the 17th Colombian to claim the crown. Like many Colombians, he is a natural climber whose hard graft in the mountains of his homeland paid dividends when he turned professional in 1990. In 1995 he put on a scintillating display in the Tour de France, gaining a very respectable tenth place. Yet for most Colombians, the 1985 Tour de France is an emblematic moment, for this is when working-class hero Luis 'Lucho' Herrera won a mountain stage after crashing and opening a deep gash on his temple. In a true display of grit, Herrera got back into the saddle and pounded on up the mountain, even as a medic tried to stem the bleeding from a car speeding alongside. Television images of a blood-soaked Herrera crossing the finish line provoked considerable displays of patriotism within Colombia. *El Tiempo* newspaper declared: 'We came, we suffered, we won.'

For further information, Matt Rendel's excellent book *Kings of the Mountains: How Colombia's Cycling Héroes Changed Their Nation's History* is recommended. See *Appendix 3*, page 438.

He was so little when he started racing that he learned to drive by looking through the hole in the steering wheel.

Juan Pablo Montoya's father, Pablo

When Juan Pablo Montoya Roldán was born in Bogotá in September 1975, his father had a feeling he'd be a star. After mortgaging the family home, his father Pablo helped his five year-old son begin karting, winning both local and national titles in the Children's Kart Championship and Kart Komet Division. But money was often a struggle and Montoya couldn't even afford to travel by public transport, so he used roller blades to go from one place to another. He secured a scholarship at the famous Skip Barber School in the US before moving to Britain to race in the Formula Vauxhall series with Paul Stewart Racing. He then made a move to the Copa Formula Renault Series in Colombia, capturing five poles and four wins in eight races. He spent a year in F3, notching two wins, one pole position and five fastest laps, before moving on to the International F3000 series – a long-awaited break that came in 1997.

Landing a drive with the crack Super Nova outfit for 1998, he duly took the title with four wins and seven pole positions. He tested for Williams' F1 squad and He was then summoned to participate in his first Formula One test before getting signed to a multi-year testing contract in 1998. In addition to his testing duties, Montoya competed again in the Formula 3000 series and grabbed the FIA International Formula 3000 Championship. The young Colombian would soon find himself heading to the United States in 1999 as part of a driver swap between Williams and Ganassi. The team owner exchange resulted in Montoya taking over for two-time CART Champion Alex Zanardi at Ganassi's Indianapolis-based open-wheel shop, while Zanardi returned to Formula One.

Immediately, Montoya made his presence known in the CART Series, and all across the United States. At the age of 24, the rookie driver proceeded to set several series records en route to claiming his first and Ganassi's fourth-consecutive CART Championship. Altogether, he collected more wins, pole positions, laps led and earnings than any other driver during the 1999 CART season. In 2000, as the defending series champion, Montoya added three additional wins to his CART resume. In addition to the

RUGBY An international sevens tournament is held every November in Bogotá, following the introduction of rugby to Colombia in 1986. Initially played solely by groups of European expats, the game started to generate wider interest in the early 1990s, attracting local participation in 1992. Today, there are over 25 clubs in six Colombian cities, the two main ones being Bogotá and Medellín. Colombia's home-grown players are showing lots of raw potential. However as a minority sport rugby suffers from a lack of funds and proper organisation, despite being enjoyed by a growing number of people keen to reach the top of their top game. For further information contact the National Union of Colombian Rugby (*www.rugby7.com/Colombia*).

GOLF Colombia is home to a growing number of golf courses, especially in and around the major cities and Caribbean coast. The popularity of golf has been helped by the success of golfers such as Camilo Villegas, who finished second in the FBR Open behind John Holmes from the United States in 2006. Villegas hails from Antioquía and achieved the best performance ever by a native Colombian golfer in the PGA Tour. The Colombian Golf Federation (Federación Colombiana de Golf) (*Carrera 7a No 72–64 int 26, Santafé de Bogotá;* ✆ *1 310 7664;* e *olgagolf@ federacioncolumbianadegolf.com; www.federacioncolombianadegolf.com*) stages a packed regular CART season, Ganassi decided to enter his teams in the Indy Racing League's Indianapolis 500 for the first time since 1995. After just missing the pole and starting second on the grid, Montoya set a rookie record by leading 167 out of 200 laps on his way to an Indy 500 victory. That same weekend, Williams announced Montoya had signed a two-year deal to drive for them in the Formula One Series.

Montoya made his debut with BMW Williams in the premiere open-wheel series at the Australian Grand Prix in 2001, and then captured his first F1 victory at the Italian Grand Prix at Monza. The rookie racer also tallied three pole positions and four podium finishes during his freshman season to finished sixth in the Drivers' Championship standings. In 2002, Montoya fared even better, even though Ferrari dominated the season. He finished third, turning the fastest qualifying laps in seven out of the 17 races and earning four runner-up finishes. During this season he lit up the track at Monza by posting a record-fast qualifying lap with an average speed of 259.844682 km/h. In 2003, Montoya finished third in the Drivers' Championship with 82 points, and captured two victories. He also had six additional podium finishes - four second and two third places. He announced his departure from BMW Williams at the end of the 2004 season to move over to the McLaren Mercedes team – but not before finishing fifth in the 2004 F1 Drivers' Championship, taking the chequered flag in Brazil. Juan Pablo Montoya wasted no time making his presence known in the NASCAR world after transitioning from open-wheel cars to the 2007 NASCAR Sprint Cup Series. Not only did he become the first Latino to win in NASCAR's premier Series and capture the 2007 Sprint Cup Rookie of the Year title, but he earned the respect of his team, his competitors and fans as well, adding his name to an elite list of drivers who have achieved top-level racing success across the Sprint Cup Series, IndyCar Series, Grand-Am Prototype cars, stock cars and Formula One. The only other driver to accomplish such a feat is Mario Andretti. Montoya is also the only driver to have competed in all three major events at Indianapolis, the Indianapolis 500, the US Grand Prix, and the Brickyard 400.

Today, Juan Pablo Montoya continues to chalk up racing success in the Sprint Cup Series. With his wife Connie he also runs the charitable foundation, 'Formula Smiles' for underprivileged children with ambition. For more information visit: www.formulasmiles.com.

year-round calendar of events across the country, including those in the Coffee Zone. Cristóbal von Rothkirch's first-class book *Campos de golf en Colombia* (Villegas Editores, 2005) takes a look at more than 50 of the nation's finest golfing establishments and includes blueprints, maps of the greens and signature holes.

CONSERVATION

> We are in danger of losing our natural heritage if we don't dedicate ourselves to protecting it. This is critical, given all that is at stake.
>
> Fabio Arjona, Conservation International, Colombia (2007)

Modern Colombia has struggled to manage its environmental issues during its most turbulent chapters in history and today deforestation, soil erosion and poor water quality are serious concerns. Excessive pesticide usage has caused damage to agricultural land while air pollution is sparking widespread unease, especially in Bogotá where vehicle emissions are high. Other urban environmental issues include health disorders linked to inadequate refuse disposal and contaminated food.

Colombia's diminishing forests are another key concern. More than 700,000ha of forests are cut down each year for wood and paper and to create farmland for crops and cattle. This is in part the consequence of continued poverty in the countryside and a legacy of the prejudiced land distribution policies that date back to colonial times.

At this rate, Colombia's forests will be almost completely wiped out by 2050, creating a major environmental catastrophe and destroying many of its wildlife species, plants and marine life. Such large-scale deforestation has already caused widespread soil destabilisation in Colombia's rural heartlands, annihilating the natural habitat of dozens of species of birdlife, while increasing the propensity of flooding and causing rivers to fill with silt.

Another large ecological conundrum for Colombia relates to its drive to bolster a global, market-based economy and the pressure that brings on the environment when it comes to developing land. Sizeable swathes of countryside in Boyacá and along the Caribbean coastline have already been eaten up by large-scale construction projects such is the demand for swish designer condominiums, new hotels and gated golf resort complexes. Mineral extraction on the Pacific side continues to forge ahead as part of an ambitious plan to strengthen the fragile economy of this often marginalised community. Poverty is rife in many of the Afro-Caribbean coastal towns along the Pacific stretch and few local inhabitants have the heart for ecological conscience when it comes to trying to feed their families. Environmentalists continue to attempt to spark serious debate about the dilemma caused by Colombia's wealth imbalance.

Another pressing conservation concern is the loss of forest to Colombia's drugs trade. More than 50,000ha are chopped down each year in order to plant coca, opium and marijuana, primarily deep in virgin rainforests of the Amazon region and the Andes. As you'd expect, Colombia's cocaine producers care little for ecology, dumping the noxious by-products of cultivation and production into streams and poisoning water supplies with toxic waste.

Many of Colombia's biggest urban concentrations have benefited from city-funded environmental initiatives such as Bogotá's 300km of cycle paths that have encouraged millions of Bogotános to trade their car for two wheels. In 2000, Bogotá was honoured with the Stockholm Challenge Award for making the city car-free once a month on a Sunday. More than 120km of Bogotá's main arteries are closed to vehicles for seven hours, allowing the city's 7.5 million population to walk the streets, ride bicycles, jog and appropriate their city without traffic fumes or tooting horns. In 2008, traffic-free Sunday remains the largest and most successful car free initiative of its kind in the world today.

Bogotá is also home to a UN-sponsored tree-planting project in partnership with the city's schoolchildren. Some 50 pupils plant 275 native trees provided by the city's Botanical Garden (Colombian laws do not allow the planting of non-native species). In Cali, a similar replanting programme funded by the Botanical Gardens is part of a large-scale ecological restoration process, designed to promote the growth of native vegetation in the degraded hillsides at the edge of the city.

Rubbish, waste disposal and recycling are hot topics with Colombian environmentalists, despite a concerted effort by government ministers to promote recycling since the early 1980s. However, to date, no legally imposed recycling restrictions or programmes have been developed or implemented. Waste laws remain extremely complex and full of loopholes. There are also numerous ongoing disputes between the Ministry of Economic Development (MINDESA), the Ministry of Health (Minsalud) and the Environment Ministry (MinAmbiente) regarding the exact scope of their jurisdiction and control. In late December 2006, the Colombian Senate announced a bill that would repeal the existing hazardous waste framework law (Law 430/1998), banning all imports of hazardous wastes into the country. In 2007, Colombia had an estimated 20 non-government household

WHAT A WASTE!

Colombia's major cities are home to an estimated 50,000 scavenger families (*recicladores*) that earn a livelihood collecting rubbish from local tips. Conditions are grim and the work hard for these professional scavengers with many hours spent trawling Colombia's piles of waste. Many recicladores work within family groups to run a non-stop dawn-to-dusk shift. Ages range from pre-school children to the elderly. Many scavengers suffer from serious health conditions because of ongoing exposure to contaminated waste and hazardous materials.

A programme launched in 1986 has helped to better organise Colombia's unofficial recyclers. First, the Asociación Nacional de Recicladores (ANR) was formed using local NGO assistance. Improving working conditions was high on the list of priorities. The ANR also realised that the recicladores would better understand the value of the rubbish collected via education relating to markets, products and quality control. NGO advisers helped implement facilities for storing collected waste properly. They also developed simple waste management systems and trained communities of scavengers in stock control. Educational programmes equipped the recicladores with supply-and-demand market information. It also helped train them in selective rubbish harvesting and identified items to avoid.

So far, more than 125,000 individuals from Colombia's garbage-picking families have benefited from such NGO projects, many as a result of help from Fundación Social. The upshot has been a 30% increase in revenue stream for the recicladores with a greater level of productivity and improved medical care and social security support. The ANR has also opened so-called Scavengers' Houses in Colombia's main cities, including Bogotá, Medellín, Cali, Barranquilla, Cartagena, Neiva, Pasto, Popayán, Buga, Armenia, Manizales, Pereira, Soledad and Sincelejo. Some ANR branches have successfully negotiated contracts and joint ventures with many of the nation's largest private companies. On the north coast, 14 co-operatives of recicladores are represented by ARCON (Association of Recyclers and Collectors).

rubbish recycling programmes in its major cities. Five recycling plants countrywide also supply schools and libraries with refurbished computers as part of the 'Computadores para Educar' programme. Other items that are recycled successfully to lower income communities via Colombia's rubbish tip *recicladores* (see box, *What a Waste!*, above) include batteries, electrical parts, telecommunication products and televisions. One of Colombia's finest citizen-run recycling schemes can be found in the tiny village of Puerto Nariño in the Colombian Amazon, where waste is managed by a network of community volunteers. Its pristine neighbourhoods and 6,000 ecologically aware house-proud residents have been hailed an environmental beacon by green campaigners in Colombia. Ironically, Puerto Nariño is also fast becoming a centre for conservationists studying the impact of untreated sewage, illegal pesticides and industrial waste on the Amazon's eco-system.

Colombia is party to the following international agreements: Antarctic Treaty, Biodiversity, Climate Change, Climate Change-Kyoto Protocol, Desertification, Endangered Species, Hazardous Wastes, Marine Life Conservation, Ozone Layer Protection, Ship Pollution, Tropical Timber 83, Tropical Timber 94, Wetlands signed, but not ratified: Law of the Sea.

NATURAL DISASTERS

Colombia is susceptible to volcanic eruptions, earthquakes, periodic droughts and flooding and is located in an active seismic zone. In 1979, an earthquake and tsunami destroyed six fishing villages along the Pacific coast. Hundreds of people died in the state of Nariño in Colombia with tremors felt in Bogotá, Cali, Popayán, Buenaventura and other major cities and villages in Colombia as well as Guayaquil, Esmeraldas, Quito and other parts of Ecuador. In 1985, four towns in the Andes region were buried under ash spewed from the Nevado del Ruiz volcano, causing a horrific mudslide that claimed 23,000 lives. Worst affected was Armero, the province of Tolima's second-largest city, about 50 miles from Bogotá. Fatalities were particularly high because the eruption occurred at night when most of the town's 27,000 residents were asleep. Nevado del Ruiz, known locally as 'the Sleeping Lion', had not erupted for nearly 150 years. In 1999, at least 1,000 people were killed and more than 4,000 injured when an earthquake measuring six on the Richter scale struck the heart of the country's coffee-growing region. The most powerful quake to hit Colombia for 16 years destroyed large sections of the cities of Armenia and Pereira, trapping people in the rubble and in landslides and leaving 200,000 homeless. In November 2004, a state of emergency was declared across eight states, as torrential downpours caused dangerous floodwaters and landslides. Hundreds died and many were injured in the districts of Atlántico, Bolívar (particularly in the cities of Cartagena, Achí and San Jacinto del Cauca), Guajira, César, Cordoba, Magdalena, Sucre and Santander, affecting 49,660 families and 251,717 people. In 2005, the Galeras Volcano erupted in the Nariño department sparking a mass evacuation of more than 9,000 people living on its slopes near the border with Ecuador. The threat to life was complicated by hundreds of people who refused to leave their smallholdings, despite a pledge by the Colombian government to pay evacuees US$40 a month to help with temporary accommodation. In January 2006, heavy rains deluged much of Colombia causing severe flooding across the country, particularly in the northeast. In the same year, eight boy scouts and their guide were killed by a mudslide at the foot of Nevado del Ruiz volcano. Bad weather took the group by surprise as a huge flow of water carried them into rocks. The expedition was swept away while bathing in a canyon known as La Gruta when heavy rains upstream caused the Chinchiná River to swell.

NATURAL HISTORY

Colombia is one of the most biologically diverse countries in the world. Within its borders you'll find hot and sticky humidity, chilly high altitude temperatures, both Caribbean and Pacific coastlines, palm-laden islands, mountains reaching 5,000m, dry scrub, volcanic hills and a chunk of thick subtropical Amazon basin that hosts extraordinary, untamed ecosystems. This eco excess is remarkable considering Colombia's size, and makes the country an extremely attractive destination for wildlife enthusiasts. Colombia supports more species of birds than any other country and the second-largest number of amphibians in the world. To date, over 1,880 species of bird and 700 amphibians have been recorded there. Most excitingly, since 2005, two new bird species have been recorded: in 2005, two tapaculos (scytalopus) were discovered in the central Cordillera and in October 2006, the Yariguies brush finch (*Atlapetes latinuchus yariguierum*) was discovered in the Serranía de los Yariguíes. The brush finch, a vibrant-coloured finch with a scarlet head, gold chest and dark wings and tail, has impressed wildlife enthusiasts on a global scale.

Mammals number over 400 and range from jaguars and pumas to spectacled bears. Not surprisingly, plant life is abundant; around 130,000 species have been recorded, of which a third are endemic. Colombia is renowned for its orchids, but there are endless exotic plants from the wax palm (*Ceroxylon quindiuense*; the country's national tree) to giant water lilies so vast they can hold a child.

Sadly, rapid deforestation in Colombia is threatening a growing number of species; a staggering 10,000 plant species are believed to be facing extinction as well as around 10% of the country's mammal species. Deforestation is wiping out depleting forests annually, due to logging, industrial corporations, commercial crops and locally produced charcoal (see above, *Conservation*). In addition, strong pesticides deployed in aerial coca crop spraying further threaten the country's flora with extinction. Numerous zones in the country are pinpointed by the Alliance for Zero Extinction (AZE) (*www.zeroextinction.org*) and a number of environmental groups are now actively involved in conservation such as Proyecto Tití (Project Tamarin) (*http://proyectotiti.com*) and the Wildlife Conservation Society (*www.wcs.org/international/latinamerica/northernandes/colombia*).

SPOTTING WILDLIFE Most wildlife is concentrated on the spine of the Andean chain, the Western Cordillera, the Central Cordillera and the Eastern Cordillera, three mountain ranges that cross the country. However, due to deforestation, the region is fragmented and now many areas are stripped of their previous habitat. In new urban expanses a lot of wildlife has been shot or simply frightened out of town. Monkeys, mammals and birds are easiest to find in national parks that can provide maps and guides to what you can expect to see.

ORCHIDS Parts of Colombia are festooned with orchids, and in some areas the flowers literally blanket the trees. The flowers are spectacular and attract people on a global scale. Some 15% of the world's orchid species are found here and it is claimed that up to 53,000 plants have been recorded per acre in the Nariño region. So valuable are these ornate flowers that horticulturist Tom Hart Dyke was kidnapped on the Panama side of the border with Colombia whilst searching for plants in 2000 (he was released after nine months). Indeed, the country is so enamoured with orchids they have made the *Cattleya trianae* their national flower. It is indigenous to Colombia and named after Colombian botanist, José J. Triana and English botanist William Cattley (1788–1835). The flower grows without soil in 15 different colours in the central departments of Tolima, Huila and Cundinamarca, and is sadly now threatened due to loss of its natural habitat.

There are now around 3,500 orchid varieties found in Colombia and orchid fever has spread throughout the country. Regional orchid societies in Bogotá, Pereira, Cali, Manizales and Medellín are respected by enthusiasts all over the world and hold regular local shows. There is also huge national pride in the annual Exposición Internacional de Orquídeas de Colombia (Colombian International Orchid Show), which is hosted by a different city each year. Colombia even has its own award system designated by the Comité Colombiana de Orquideología; it awards only Colombian species.

The Sociedad Colombiana de Orquideología, the oldest society in the country, hosted the seventh World Orchid Conference in 1972, in Medellín. The society was founded 40 years ago, and promotes cultivation and conservation. Another group, the Orchid Foundation of Tolima, an NGO in central Colombia, maintains an 'orchidary' where visitors can enjoy 150 species that are under threat.

Where to spot an orchid Orchids grow best between 1,800–2,500m above sea level. However, Colombia's countless species vary in requirements and can be found almost anywhere, from jungle to mountain, even by the beach. The Zona Cafetera is probably the best area to find orchids, but those looking for a more organised display should head to the Botanical Gardens of Bogotá. Tour operators are generally accustomed to visitors wanting to find orchids and should have well-informed guides available. De Una Colombia (see *Chapter 2, Practical information,*

Founded in 2001 ProAves charity (*www.proaves.org*) is Colombia's largest conservation NGO. It aims to protect around 50 of the country's 88 threatened bird species, as well as endangered amphibians and some mammals. The organisation owns and maintains ten forest reserves, which serve as effective protection areas for birds. In addition, ProAves is actively involved in ongoing, extensive research programmes and runs environmental education programmes for children. These local programmes are taken to local communities around the country in the 'Loro Bus' (Parrot Bus) and the project is highly respected in Colombia. ProAves Reserves include:

PAUJIL The reserve covers 3,000 acres at an altitude of just 300m so the climate is tropical and very humid. It's located close to Puerto Pinzón, Boyacá, an eight-hour drive from Bogotá, the last 40km of which is unpaved so it is not easy to reach. However, there is accommodation with both private and shared rooms, air conditioning and internet. More importantly you'll get the chance to see a blue-billed curassow, saffron-headed parrot and variegated spider monkey. Rubber boots are advised.

ARRIERITO ANTIOQUEÑO Situated close to Anori, Antioquía, the 610ha reserve is a four-hour drive from Medillín. Accommodation is basic, but has electricity. Set at an altitude of 1,500m the temperature is subtropical and humidity is high. The main bird species to look for is the chestnut-capped piha.

LORO OREJIAMARILLO This subtropical 120ha specialist reserve, set at 2,200m, consists of dry forest and is named after the yellow-eared parrot that inhabits it. Accommodation is basic with electricity, but there is a selection of good hotels in the local area to choose from. Situated close to Jardín Antioquía, a three-hour drive from Medillín.

EL DORADO One of the most accessible of ProAves reserves, this subtropical park covers 245ha, at an altitude of 2,000m, and is situated close to Minca Magdalena, outside Santa Marta. Popular with students, teachers and biologists the accommodation is superb and the park offers a chance to see 17 endemic bird species, such as the Santa Marta parakeet and the Santa Marta sabrewing hummingbird, and three endangered frogs, two of which (*Atelopus laetissimus* and *Atelopus nahumae*) were once presumed extinct until they were rediscovered in 2006. The reserve is a 2½-hour drive from Santa Marta, 1½ of which is unpaved. However, EcoTurs (*www.ecotours.com.co*) will organise a jeep to collect you from Santa Marta.

EL MIRADOR Mirador reserve covers 1,950ha of mountain habitat high up in the 'paramo' at an altitude of 3,500m. Perfect for adventurers, the ascent is tough and you'll need to

page 61, for contact information) is in contact with orchid organisations and therefore can arrange trips with professional guides for those looking for 433 flowers. See also *Appendix 3, Further information*, page 432.

Using a guide will ensure you get the most from a trip in the more remote national parks. Most offer full-inclusive packages that allow plenty of time to watch for birds and wildlife. For details of local tour operators see *Chapter 2, Practical information*, page 57.

NATIONAL PARKS Over the last few decades the government has promoted Colombia's eco-diversity and, impressively, there are 52 designated national parks and protected areas in Colombia that cover around 8.5% of the country. These include travel 2½ hours by horse. EcoTours (*www.ecotours.com.co*) will organise horses and a guide to stay with you throughout your trip. Accommodation however, is basic with hydro-electricity, but there is cell phone reception. The environment of lichenous forests and valleys feels fresh but the temperature drops sharply at night so warm clothing is essential. You can observe endangered parrots here such as the fuertes parrot, as well as the brown-banded, bicoloured and crescent-faced antipitta, rufous-fronted parakeet and mirador parrot. Situated close to Génova, Quindío it's a two-hour drive from Armenia, 20k of which is unpaved.

EL PANGAN At an altitude of just 800m, the wet subtropical reserve of El Pangan covers 810ha and is located a two-hour walk from Junín, Nariño, 2½ hours from Tumaco. The accommodation is basic with hydro-electricity. Look for the long-wattled umbrella bird, chocó vireo, banded ground-cuckoo and Pangan poison-arrow frog. Rubber boots are advised.

COLIBRI DE SOL In a similar location to El Dorado, Colibri de Sol covers 2,800ha at an altitude of 3,500m and is only accessible by a two-hour horse ride from Urrao, Antioquía (four hours' drive from Medellín). Accommodation is basic but does have hydro-electricity. Spectacled bears inhabit the park, and although it is highly unlikely you will catch a glimpse of one, the chance is exciting. You should get to see dusky starfrontlets, rusty-faced parrots and the chestnut-bellied flower-piercer.

REINITA CERÚLEA (CERULEAN WARBLING RESERVE) The 205ha reserve is popular with many Americans who are concerned about the endangered Cerulean warbler's future. This tiny, blue-grey bird migrates from the US to Colombia during winter and now faces extinction due to deforestation in Colombia. At the reserve, ProAves has established a hillside coffee plantation, where coffee beans grow in the shade, providing an ideal environment for the warblers who love such a habitat in forest environs. The coffee itself is harvested and sold within the local co-operative. The park, set at 2,000m altitude, is humid and subtropical; look out for gorgeted wood-quail, black inca and the white-mantled barbet as well as the warblers. Accommodation is good and provides internet access. Located close to San Vicente in Santander, a two-hour taxi drive from Bucaramanga.

HORMIGUERO DE TORCORMAMA A smaller tropical reserve, with 120ha set at just 600m altitude and situated close to Ocaña (15 minutes by taxi), Norte de Santander. There's no onsite accommodation, but there are several good local hotels. The climate here is dry, and not as humid as some parks; look for recurve-billed bushbird and Todd's parakeet.

nine Sanctuarios de Flora y Fauna (Sanctuaries of Fauna and Flora), two natural reserves Nukak and Puinawai, the Vía Parque Isla de Salamanca and Los Estoraques, Área Natural Única (Unique Natural Area). Colombians are extremely proud of their environment; even FARC claim to protect the jungle and forest in areas it inhabits. However, national park status hasn't meant that these areas are fully protected; aerial coca spraying, which is carried out in some parks, is reputed to be a particular threat. There has also been some cultural dispute over the recent development of luxury five-star accommodation within some national parks, which has created backlash among locals who feel they are priced out of enjoying the areas themselves.

Many national parks are off-limits due to paramilitary and guerrilla activity. Furthermore, some of the most spectacular are those that remain almost untouched by human life, making them almost impossible to reach. Visitors attempting to reach remote parks must check their safety before their trip and must get permission and advice from the relevant park warden. It is vital to check that a park is safe to visit when planning a trip as some occasionally attract guerrillas. Contact the park authorities and discuss the full itinerary, including all routes and trails. Up-to-date advice should also be sought on onsite facilities to establish exactly what gear to take. The System of Natural National Parks in Bogotá can also be contacted for information (` 243 3095/1634; ` e ` ecoturismo@parquesnacionales.gov.co; www.parquesnacionales.gov.co `).

A full spectrum of climate zones ranges from coral fringed islands, glacial mountain ranges and dry scrub to steaming jungle and sticky Amazonian bogs in the parks that are accessible and much safer to visit. It is possible to witness, and occasionally interact with, indigenous communities living in some parks, but it is vital to respect any regulations that require visitors to stay away from particular tribes. Several national parks are currently open to tourists and offer good, basic facilities, such as restaurants, information centres (some with language translations), and advice on footpaths and trails. Accommodation ranges from basic camping and hammocks to luxurious 'eco-habs'. Travellers planning to camp in a park should bring equipment, including ropes and tent pegs, and be prepared for all eventualities. It is also important to check with the relevant authorities (see Parque Nacional contact details below) regarding the rules for each park as some prohibit campfires or cooking outside designated zones. All specify that non-biodegradable rubbish should be removed from the park and it is illegal to take home any flora or fauna. Admission to Colombia's national parks is relatively inexpensive with concessions available for children. In 2007 the Colombian government announced the creation of a new national park to protect one of the greatest areas of biodiversity in the country, inhabited by such rare and endangered animals as the Andean bear, jaguar, puma and tapir. The new park – **Serranía de los Churumbelos Auka Wasi** – stretches from the lowlands of the Amazon Basin to the slopes of the Andean Mountains over 97,180ha. Some 461 species of birds have been registered in the region, equivalent to 26% of the birds in all of Colombia. The mountainous Churumbelos area is recognised for its incredible biodiversity and contains 30 species of amphibians, 16 species of reptiles, more than 140 species of butterflies and 825 species of plants.

Amacayacú (Hammock River, Quechua) (est 1975) (e dtao@ parquesnacionales.gov.co)

Covering 293,500ha Amacayacú is perhaps one of the country's most interesting parks, located deep in the jungle basin, a half-hour boat ride from Leticia, Colombia's most southern point. Few tourists venture so far south, but the park is very popular with Colombians and is by far the best way to experience the Colombian Amazon. You may see pink river dolphins (botos) in the rivers and black-mantle tamarins in the forests.

The park is also home to around 500 bird species and 150 mammal species; look for the golden lion tamarin, the jabuti tortoise (the world's largest freshwater tortoise) and macaws. The observatory platforms provide a fantastic vista of untouched forest for creature spotting. The terrain offers both dry vegetation and the thick humid jungles typical of the Amazon. There is also a visitors' centre with renovated accommodation facilities that sleep 40 people, as well as a museum, auditorium and research centre.

Cahuinarí (est 1987)

Some 575,000ha of dense tropical rainforest, lagoons and piranha-filled rivers are situated in the regions of Caquetá and Putumayo in Colombia's south-central Amazon. During the 19th century many trees here were felled for rubber, much of the park was destroyed and indigenous people exploited. The area, and the indigenous Cahuinarí, hunter-gatherers that live within the park, is now protected. Endangered species here include the jaguar, giant river otter, puma, black caiman and the now extremely rare charapa (giant river turtle). Parks in Peril (PIP) (*www.parksinperil.org*) are currently supporting the park and have carried out training of the Cahuinarí people to work as park wardens as well as launching the Charapa Conservation Plan. In 2001 a Co-operative Agreement enabled joint management between the local community and Unidad de Parques, Colombia.

Farallones of Cali (Cali Headlands) (est 1968) (e *mmambiente@emcali.net.co*)
Located on the Occidental Mountain Range, in the region of Valle del Cauca, the Cali Headlands cover 205,266ha of subtropical forest overlooking the Pacific Ocean. As you ascend the temperature drops from around 25°C (77°F) to 5°C (41°F). The spectacled bear roams here, as do pumas and five species of monkey. Emberá Indians inhabit some of the lower regions on the park.

Catatumbo-Bari (est 1989) (e *norandina@col1.telecom.com.co*) This park covers
158,125ha of humid tropical forests and mountain terrain, located in the Oriental mountain range in Norte de Santander, close to the Venezuelan border. There are an estimated 114 species of mammal here and 616 species of birds. Several indigenous communities live here, including the Yuko-Yukpas, Dobokubis and Barí, whose numbers have been decimated since the area was ravaged for oil during the early 20th century.

Chingaza (est 1977–78) (e *amazonia@parquesnacionales.gov.co*) Chingaza spans
76,600ha and rises to over 4,000m above sea level. The park is situated close to Bogotá in the Cordillera Oriental in the regions of Cundinamarca and Meta. The tropical mountain forests contain spectacled bears and pumas, deer, coati, and monkey as well as the Andean condor and toucans among many others.

Serranía de Chiribiquete (est 1989) (e *amazonia@parquesnacionales.gov.co*) Humid
Amazonian mountain range, covering 1,280,000ha located in the regions of Caquetá and Guaviare. Currently closed to tourists.

Corales del Rosario y San Bernardo (Rosario and San Bernardo Corals) (est
1977) (e *ecoturismo@parquesnacionales.gov.co* or *a@parquesnacionales.gov.co*) A total 120,000ha of water and islands. Spectacular archipelago located 45km from the Bay of Cartagena, the park is host to 52 species of coral, 45 species of sponge, hundreds of species of molluscs and crustaceans and numerous multi-coloured fish that bask in the clear tropical waters of the Caribbean Sea. There are also important mangrove networks on Barú Island. The park is geared towards tourism and there's a popular aquarium at the Oceanario Islans del Rosario as well as the Museum of Marine Life.

Cordillera Los Picachos (Mountain Range Picachos) (est 1977) Some 447,740ha
of humid subtropical jungle mountain situated between the Orinoco and Amazon rivers, to the west of the Meta region. The park is closed to tourists.

Cueva de los Guácharos (Cave of the Oilbird) (est 1960) South of Picachos, in
the Oriental mountain range in the region of Caquetá, Guácharos occupies 700ha. Guácharo birds (small, thin relatives of the nightjar) are protected here and nest in fascinatingly formed caves carved out along the Suazas River. The park has been

sited as a UNESCO Biosphere Reserve along with the Puracé National Park and the Nevado del Huila National Park. There are basic tourist facilities here including a restaurant and camping area with an outdoor kitchen setup.

El Cocuy (est 1977) Around 306,000ha of subtropical forest, mountain lakes and glacial peaks in the Cordillera Oriental in the regions of Boyacá, Arauca and Casanare, northeast from Bogotá. The park offers breathtaking climbing and trekking opportunities (see *Hiking*, page 54) and visitors can camp with guides on the mountain. There are reputedly plans for cable cars in the future here.

El Tuparro (est 1970) (e amazonia@parquesnacionales.gov.co) Around 548,000ha of dry savannah, woodland and swamp along the Orinoco River in the region of Vichada inhabited by jaguar, tapir and otter. Indigenous communities live within the park but they remain isolated from outside contact.

Gorgona Island (est 1984) (e *minambiente@emcali.net.co*) Named by conquistador Francisco Pizarro, after the Greek Gorgon, due to the islands many snakes and located in the Pacific, off Cauca on Colombia's west coast, Gorgona and neighbouring Gorgonilla islets cover around 62,000ha of rich, vibrant jungle on volcanic islands. Surrounded by coral reef, the islands are home to white-faced monkeys and the three-toed sloth as well as numerous bird species such as the blue honeycreeper. The wet season here is September/October; however, it is worth noting that humpback and finback whales mate offshore from September–December. Accommodation is currently being renovated. Note – you may need proof that you have had a vaccination against yellow fever.

Parque Nacional Natural Alto Fragua Indi-Wasi (est 2002) (e *amazonia@ parquesnacionales.gov.co*) An interesting part of Colombia's cultural heritage as well as precious Amazonian flora and fauna, Indi-Wasi spans 68,000ha and is inhabited by a wide ethnic mix of South American indigenous peoples. Some have migrated from Ecuador and Peru, but others, who live in the south of Putumayo, are reputed to descend from groups who refused to bow down to the conquistadors. Sadly, the park has no facilities and is currently closed to tourists.

La Paya (est 1984) (e *amazonia@parquesnacionales.gov.co*) This remote park covers 422,000ha of thick, humid tropical jungle along the Putumayo River close to the Peruvian border in Colombia's western Amazon region. Spectacular and remote, and now protected by PIP the park is home to the giant anteater, woolly monkey, red howler monkey, pygmy marmoset, red brocket deer, jaguar and manatee not to mention macaws, toucans and hawks. It is currently closed to tourists.

Las Hermosas (Beautiful) (est 1977) (e *mmambiente@emcali.net.co*) Some 125,000ha of fog-smothered, rugged mountain range in Colombia central cordillera, in the regions of Cauca and Tolima are inhabited by tapir, the spectacled bear, puma and deer. There are reportedly 500 lagoons here that have come from the mountain glaciers and run down to supply the surrounding towns and villages. There are currently no tourist facilities here.

Las Orquídeas (The Orchids) (est 1973/77) (e *uniparquesnoro@epm.net.co*) Around 32,000ha located in the Occidental mountain range in the region of Antioquía, northwest of Bogotá. Around 300 species of orchid have been recorded here. The park is currently closed to tourists.

Los Katíos (est 1973) (e *uniparquesnoro@epm.net.co*) Located in the Chocó, in northwest Colombia, the lush swampy jungle of Los Katíos forms part of the Darién National Park in Panama. Rich in eco-diversity, endemic flora and wildlife, the park was designated a UNESCO World Heritage Site in 1994. The park covers 72,000ha of tropical forest and hillside, the thick swamps of Tumaradó and is home to jaguars, tapirs, crocodiles and rare orchids. Due to the park's location, anyone wishing to visit *must* check with authorities *before* they plan a trip. The area can be frequently used by paramilitary and guerrillas. The area steams with heat and humidity and accommodation is basic.

Los Nevados (est 1973) (e *uniparquesnoro@epm.net.co*) This 58,300ha park in the central Andean mountain range crosses Caldas, Risaralda and Quindío, and is popular with hikers due to its snow-capped volcanic peaks, palm forests, Ruiz and Rancho hot springs and Lake Otún and Guali Falls. In addition there's a chance you'll glimpse bear, tapir and deer. At 8,500–17,000ft above sea level it is cold and the temperatures average 3–14°C. Accommodation is currently being renovated here.

Macuira (est 1977) (e *ecoturismo@parquesnacionales.gov.co*) The tropical forest here is warm and dry; Macuira covers 25,000ha on a mountainous peninsula that juts into the Atlantic. Various indigenous groups as well as cloudforests and an abundance of wildlife inhabit the area. There's no entrance fee and although there are no government constructed tourist facilities, the indigenous Wayúu rent hammocks in their ranchos to visitors. Check the area's safety before visiting.

Munchique (est 1977) (e *surandin@emtel.net.co*) Spanning 44,000ha, Munchique is located in the Cordillera Occidental, northwest of Popayán. The park is formed by several peaks and tropical rainforest and has been noted for the recent discovery of the Munchique wood-wren (*Henicorhina negreti*, named after the Colombian ornithologist, Alvaro José Negret). Visitors are currently restricted.

Nevado del Huila (est 1977) (e surandin@emtel.net.co) Around 158,000ha of rocky terrain, snow covered peaks and active volcano, set in Colombia's central mountain range that reaches to 5,780m above sea level. The park straddles the departments of Cauca, Huila and Tolima and is currently not open to visitors.

Old Providence McBean Lagoon Nature Park (est 1995) (e *caribe@ telesantamarta.net.co*) Some 890ha of the 9,90ha park are under water; the land part covers the 500ft-high Iron Wood Hill on the northeastern end of the volcanic island of Providencía. The area is notable for intricate ecosystems of the McBean mangrove, which includes red mangrove (*Rhizophora mangle*), yellow mangrove (*Avicennia germinans*) and white mangrove (*Laguncularia racemosa*). Along the shore are the palm-laden lagoons Crab Key and Three Brothers Key that are protected by substantial reef. Look out for the large black, dramatic man-of-war or frigate bird. You can stay in huts provided by the local community. Park tickets cost US$7.69, concessions US$1.23.

Paramillo (est 1977) (e *ecoturismo@parquesnacionales.gov.co* or *dtca@ parquesnacionales.gov.co*) Mountainous terrain and humid subtropical forest across 460,000ha, including the Paramillo Massif, situated to the north of the central Andes to the south of Cordoba.

Pisba (est 1977) (e *norandina@col1.telecom.com.co*) Some 45,000ha rising 2,000m above sea level in the Oriental mountain range in Bocayá, northeast of Bogotá. The forests attract spectacled bears and deer, but are currently closed to tourists.

Puracé (est 1961) (e *surandin@emtel.net.co*) Located in the central mountain range, close to Popayán, the park spans 83,000ha and includes the Andean Almaguer Massif and Volcán Puracé, an active volcano that's a four-hour hike from the visitors' centre. Laguna de San Rafael is situated 8km from Pilimbalá, and the waterfall, Cascada del Bedón, is a further 5km from the lagoon. There are a number of other rivers and waterfalls, as well as an orchid area, and walks here can be beautiful. There are currently three cabañas that sleep up to six people in each and four camping spaces.

Río Puré (Puré River) (est 2002) (e *amazonia@parquesnacionales.gov.co*) Dense Amazonian forest covers one million hectares of lush jungle and river networks (including the Río Puré) between the Caquetá River and Putumayo River basins. A previously unknown fish, the Batman (*Otocinclus batmani*, named after the fictional character), was recently discovered in the Río Puré. The Carabayo-Aroje, an 'uncontacted people', inhabit the park.

Sanquianga (est 1977) (e *mmambiente@emcali.net.co*) This cluster of islands and a chunk of mainland covers 80,000ha on the southwest pacific coast, north of the Nariño region. Mangroves and sandy beaches attract an abundance of tropical flora and fauna. The park is currently closed to tourists.

Serranía de los Yaraguies (est 2005) (e *norandina@col1.telecom.com.co*) Warm, dry terrain on the Oriental mountain range in Santander, spanning 78,837ha and set between 1,700m–2,300m above sea level. Both dry and humid forests cover the páramo attracting the spectacled bear among other mountain creatures.

Sierra de la Macarena (est 1971) (e *amazonia@parquesnacionales.gov.co*) Dense tropical jungle across 629,280ha in the department of Meta. Tourism is restricted here.

Sierra Nevada de Santa Marta (est 1964) (e *ecoturismo@parquesnacionales.gov.co* or *dtca@parquesnacionales.gov.co*) Colombia's highest peaks and the world's highest coastal mountain peaks, the Sierra Nevada's highest point reaches 5,775m. The mountain sits just 26 miles from the Caribbean ocean and is not connected with the country's central Andean chain. It now supplies the water to 1.5 million Colombians and the country's largest indigenous groups live in the region. Located to the north of Colombia, the park itself covers 383,000ha of tropical lowlands, cloudforest, snowy ledges and glaciers. All of the reptiles and amphibians above 3,000ft are reported endemic as well as numerous species of mammals and birds below that level, including the white-tipped quetzal.

Tourism is growing here, accommodation is available and a cable car system is planned that will carry people to Ciudad Perdida and Pueblito.

Sumapaz (est 1977) (e *amazonia@col1telecom.com.co*) Around 178,634ha of mountain terrain that rises to an altitude of 4,000m above sea level. The park includes rivers and cloudforests and is situated in the Oriental range just south of Bogotá, in the Meta region. There are some trails in the park, but visitors must first apply to the warden.

Tamá (est 1977) (e *norandina@col1.telecom.com.co*) The park spans 48,000ha and is located to the north of the Cordillera Oriental, in Norte de Santander. It meets the Parque Nacional El Tamá de Venezuela, over the border. The climate zones range from tropical jungle to rough terrain and snowy peaks. Some 172 bird species have been recorded here, as well as the spectacled bear, puma, armadillo and otter.

Tatamá (est 1987) (e *uniparquesnoro@epm.net.co* or *parquetatama@hotmail.com*) Located south of the Chocó in the Pacific region, the park covers 51,900ha and rises to 4,000m above sea level. A visitors' centre (Centro de Visitantes 'Planes de San Rafael'), can accommodate 40 people in shared dorms and offers a restaurant and park information.

Tayrona (est 1964) (e *caribe@telesantamarta.net.co*) It is not difficult to see why Tayrona is Colombia's most popular national park. Occupying a strip of land and sea on the north coast's Magdalena region, the jagged shore is lined with golden beaches, caves and lagoons whilst inland the tropical jungle is humid and verdant, reaching an altitude of 3,200ft above sea level. Around 49,000ha of the park is mainland jungle and forest and 1,200ha is ocean, reef and Caribbean marine life. Accommodation comprises eco-habs which have recently been updated from basic to luxury cabins offering cable television, airconditioning and a high-season price tag of almost US$200 per night. The renovations have been successful and are very attractive to tourists, but some local people are now unable to afford the park themselves. Close to cruise ship ports and the holiday areas of Cartagena, Santa Marta and Barranquilla, the park offers opportunities to spot toucans and monkeys.

Tinigua (est 1989) Some 208,000,ha of humid jungle and forest in the Amazonian region, in the department of Meta. The park has no facilities for tourists.

Utría (est 1987) (e *uniparquesnoro@epm.net.co*) Around 54,300ha of tropical jungle, mangrove swamps, estuaries and coral reefs in the departamento del Chocó in the Pacific region of northern Colombia. Emberá communities utilise the jungle lakes for fishing and trading by boat. There are numerous reptiles and poison arrow frogs and it is possible to see migratory whales and dolphins. There is some lodging in the park.

SANCTUARIES OF FAUNA AND FLORA
Ciénaga Grande de Santa Marta (est 1977) (e *ecoturismo@parquesnacionales.gov.co*)
Around 23,000ha of land and ocean situated in the Caribbean Magdalena region and easily reachable from Santa Marta or Barranquilla. The park hosts fishing eagles, coloured corals, reptiles, iguanas, caimans, turtles and manatee.

El Corchal 'El Mono Hernandez' (The Monkey Hernandez) (est 2002)
(e *ecoturismo@parquesnacionales.gov.co* or *dtca@parquesnacionales.gov.co*) Named in memory of scientist Jorge Ignacio Hernandez Camacho (1935–2001), who was known by his peers as 'the Monkey or Wise person Hernandez'. An important reserve, covering 3,850ha, located on the Caribbean coast. Flooded plains support five species of mangrove, marsh and swamp ecosystems and fine, organic clay sediment. Inland there are acres of cork forests that are home to howler monkeys among other tropical creatures. There are currently no facilities for tourists here.

Galeras (named after the Galeras Volcano) (est 1985) (e *surandina@ emtel.net.com*)
This volcanic park spans 18,800ha and reaches an altitude of 16,000ft. Water from the park supplies the surrounding towns and the mountainous region feels invigorating, vibrant and overflowing with life. There's an abundance of canyons, lakes and crystal- clear waters pouring from rocky fissures. Overlooking the city of Pasto, the high páramo is a popular climb and the views are spectacular. Temperatures range from 3–15°C and the cloud-

reaching heights of the Andean forests are often swirling in mist. The Consacá hot springs are an attraction as well as the lakes Laguna Negra, Laguna Mejía, Laguna Telpis and Laguna Verde and the Galeras Volcano crater. There are also 16 species of hummingbird to spot here.

You need to fill in an application before you can embark on this climb, which can be done in Pasto.

Guanentá Alto Río Fonce (est 1993) (e *norandina@col1.telecom.com.co*) A 10,429ha stretch of cold Andean forests and deserts along the Oriental mountain range in southern Santander that is home to threatened species of deer, bear and wild cat. There's no lodging here but Virolín ecological school, in Encino, and Hacienda Cachalú can provide shelter.

Iguaque (est 1977) (e *norandin@col1.telecom.com.co*) The sanctuary covers 6,750ha along the páramo of the Oriental mountain range in Boyacá, which rises over 10,000ft above sea level. The area is important to the locals who inhabit the surrounding area, not least because their water supply comes from the forest springs, but also, according to Muisca legend, Lake Iguaque is believed to be the source of human life. These sacred waters are a three-hour walk into the park, but there are also some interesting rock paintings to see. There is a restaurant, some accommodation and a camping area. Locals recently blocked a proposed development for more upmarket tourist facilities.

HIKING IN COLOMBIA

Colombia offers some of the best trails in Latin America and trekking is a top requirement for tourists visiting the country. The mountain peaks of the **Sierra Nevada del Cocuy** (see page 50) are perhaps the most popular choice as they offer several routes that vary from enjoyable one-day climbs to a challenging seven-day mission. The views from the Nevada's 20 snow-topped peaks are breathtaking and visitors will find the glass-like lakes and rocky plateaux a euphoric reward to the climb. **Los Nevados National Park** offers dry scrub plains, remote cactus-clad hills, waterfalls and hot springs (El Rancho). However, it is hard to believe you're still in Colombia when you hit the glaciers at the summit of **volcano Tolima**, which stands at 5,215m above sea level. For those on a stopover, or just wishing to stay closer to Bogotá, there are several superb hiking possibilities. Colombia's multi-faceted environment oozes diversity; on a day trek, the plants alone offer a firework display of vibrant colours and shapes ranging from alien-like lumpinas plants to tiny, ghostly white orchids. As an alternative to the high altitude hikes of Cocuy and Los Nevados national parks, a gruelling six-day hike to **Ciudad Perdida** in the Sierra Nevada offers a very different experience. The vegetation is tropical and the climb highly rewarding – the highest point on Ciudad Perdida is 1,200m. Instead of tucking up in a tent in thermals, you can sleep in outdoor hammocks or cabins, and your food is carried by porters. Remember, long treks can be incredibly tough so it is imperative you seek professional advice before embarking, and for these types of hikes a guide is essential. Dutch company, De Una Colombia, are hiking aficionados and provide a wealth of information on trekking in Colombia. Specialist guides at De Una say the possibilities for custom-made tours are endless – and they themselves want to explore more of hidden Colombia. The company's most popular trek is a five-day hike to **Púlpito de Diablo** (the Devil's Altar) at the top of Pan de Azúcar in Cocuy National Park. The campsite is located next to Laguna de la Plaza, one of Colombia's most stunning lakes. The hike starts at 3,800m above sea level and ascends 200m on the first day and 1,100m on the second day with 200m climbed with crampons. The trek provides a

La Corota (est 1977) (e *surandina@emtel.net.com*) Located in the Andean region of Nariño in the south of Colombia, La Corota is an island of wild grasses, paloerosa, myrtle and ferns on the ancient high plateau lake of La Laguna de La Cocha. The forests, which can be cloaked in clouds, were once the place of worship by the now extinct Quillacinga, an ancient indigenous culture. The island, of volcanic origin, spans just 8ha, rises 2,830m above sea level and can be extremely cold.

Los Colorados (est 1977) (e *ecoturismo@parquesnacionales.gov.co* or *dtca@parquesnacionales.gov.co*) A thousand hectares of both dry and tropical forest situated near the Caribbean coast in the department of Bolívar. Some 288 bird species have been recorded here and the mammals present include Colorado monkeys, tamarin, coral snakes and boa constrictors. There are no tourist facilities onsite, but in the nearby town of San Juan de Nepomuceno there are hotels, restaurants and camping areas.

Los Flamencos Sanctuary (Flamingos Sanctuary) (est 1977) (e *caribe@ telesantamarta.net.co*) Located in La Guajira on the Caribbean, Los Flamencos offers a breathtaking view of striking pink flamingos. The birds strut about in shallow lagoons formed in the coastal marshes of Manzanilla, Laguna Grande, Navío Quebrado and Tocoromanes. There are other birds here such as pelicans and herons, as well as many migratory birds, but the flamingos are the most spectacular. Flamingos come to shore between March–June and September–November, but

chance to climb the glaciers of Cerro's de la Plaza and experience a De Una custom of diving into a freezing cold lake.

PARQUE NACIONAL EL COCUY This 306,000ha national park was founded in 1997, stretching from temperate forests to snow-capped peaks and arid, desert land. Wooden lower plains rise to glacial terrain with alpine lakes. Lush valleys are home to waterfalls and rocky crags. Dominated by the Cordillera Oriental's highest peak, Ritacumba Blanco's 5,330m tip, Parque Nacional El Cocuy is regarded as one of Colombia's most resplendent reserves. Indigenous Indian tribes occupy the western flank of the park environs and mountain trails are relatively easy to navigate with an experienced guide. Access points are the towns of Guicán and El Cocoy located approximately 230km of Bogotá where it's possible to stock up on basic essentials ahead of an overnight stay in the park. Pack warm weather clothing and a thermal sleeping bag for camping as temperatures can drop to 0°C. An absence of on-site facilities means that you'll need to bring all food and equipment. Hikers also need to stick to official trails and engage the services of an authorised guide – solo treks are not allowed. Age restrictions also apply, so unless you are under 60 and over ten it is unlikely you'll be allowed in.

Several tour companies offer trips into Parque Nacional El Cocuy, including many with a strong ecological focus – an important consideration given the park's fragile status. According to the Colombian Institute of Hydrology, five major glaciers in the park that were expected to last at least 300 years in 1983 are now under serious threat. Measurements taken in 2006 suggest that they may all disappear within 25 years. Dwindling numbers of several species of the park's rich abundance of wildlife are also a cause for concern, including eagles, spectacled bears and mountain tapirs. Items that pose a threat to the frailty of the ecosystem are also prohibited, so leave non-biodegradable plastic bags and aerosols behind. For further information contact Parques Nacionales de Colombia (✆ 76 349418/423; e *norandina@col1.telecom.com.co; www.parquesnacionales.gov.co*).

by Erik Rupert at DE UNA Colombia Tours (☎ +57 312 3510753; www.deunacolombia.com). Erik is a seasoned adventurer and specialist tour operator who offers several hiking itineraries for visitors keen to explore Colombia's most enjoyable climbs.

NATIONAL PARK LOS NEVADOS Although many exhilarating trekking and climbing opportunities exist within this magnificent national park, only a few are well marked. The northern part of the park is well organised with a visitor's centre at 4,050m and a small refugio at 4,800m close to the glacier of Nevado del Ruiz (5,321m). Both are reachable by car from Manizales. However the southern section of the park is less organised with fewer signed trails and no other accommodation possibilities other than camping. A concern for hikers is poor visibility. Incoming clouds can suddenly restrict visibility to just a few metres to leave hikers prone to disorientation, so that they are likely to become lost.

Popular treks include the following:

* 3 day climb to the summit of Nevado del Tolima from Ibagué. Lowest point: 2,400m (El Silencio); highest point: 5,215m (summit of Tolima) – 275,000 COP.
* 4 day trek from Pereira to Manizales passing by the lakes of Laguna del Otún & Laguna Verde Encantada. Lowest point: 2,100m (El Cedral); highest point: 4,600m (pass between Ruiz & Olleta) – 425,000 COP
* 5 day trek from Valle de Cocora to Manizales passing by the lakes of Laguna El Encanto, Laguna La Leona, Laguna del Otún & Laguna Verde Encantada. Lowest point: 2,400m (Valle de Cocora); highest point: 4,600m (pass between Ruiz & Olleta) – 500,000 COP
* 5 day trek from Valle de Cocora to Ibagué with climbing Nevado del Tolima. Lowest point: 2,400m (Valle de Cocora); highest point: 5,215m (summit of Tolima) – 450,000 COP

this is also rainy season so come prepared. The park spans 17,000ha and the climate is hot and humid.

Malpelo (est 1985) (e *mmambiente@emcali.net.co*) The tiny island of Malpelo – 350ha – lies in the Pacific Ocean 506km from the southwest Colombian mainland. However, Malpelo National Park also covers a staggering 860,000ha of surrounding ocean and has now become known as one of the best diving locations on the globe. The marine park's inhabitants are varied and include hammerheads, giant manta rays, and many endangered and rare species such as the short-nosed ragged-toothed shark. The park is a designated no-fishing zone – the largest in the Eastern Tropical Pacific and was added to UNESCO's World Heritage List in 2006.

Otún Quimbaya (est 1986) (e *uniparquesnoro@epm.net.co*) Joining the Los Nevados National Park, Otún Quimbaya is a 485ha forested region in the central Andes. As the park ascends from 6000–8000ft above sea level, the climate is a mix of tropical warmth during the day and cold mountain air at night, with temperatures averaging 16°C (60.8°F). Spectacled bears are present in the park, although it is extremely rare to spot them. A research and information centre is available for public use.

Reservas Nacionales (national reserves to protect indigenous communities)
(e *amazonia@parquesnacionales.gov.co*) The park spans 855,000ha and is located in

Prices are per person (minimum of 4 persons, ask for prices for smaller groups). Price includes necessary transport, park fees, camping fees, cooking equipment and a bilingual DE UNA guide. A good physical condition is required for all the above treks and climbs.

NATIONAL PARK EL COCUY The Sierra Nevada de Güican, El Cocuy and Chitá is a hiker's paradise with endless possibilities for hiking, trekking, climbing and camping. It is home to 20 snow-capped mountains, as well as glacier lakes, waterfalls, beautiful valleys and extraordinary fauna and flora and is my favourite park in Colombia with the 6 day itinerary my preferred trail.

Popular treks include the following:

- 5 day trekking and climbing: Valle de Lagunillas – Púlpito del Diablo & Pan de Azúcar – Laguna de la Plaza. Lowest point: 3,850m (Valle de Lagunillas); highest point: 5,100m (summit of Pan de Azúcar) – 500,000 COP
- 6 day round trek: Valle de Lagunillas – Laguna de la Plaza – Laguna del Pañuelo – Valle de Cojines – Laguna La Isla – Laguna Grande de los Verdes. Lowest point: 3,850m (Valle de Lagunillas); highest point: 4,700m (Paso de la Sierra) – 600,000 COP
- 4 day trekking and climbing: Laguna Grande de la Sierra – Cóncavo – Toti. Lowest point: 4,000m (Finca La Esperanza); highest point: 5,200m (Summit Cóncavo) – 500,000 COP
- 5 day climb: Ritacuba Blanco and Pan de Azúcar. Lowest point: 3,850m (Valle de Lagunillas); highest point: 5,300m (Summit Ritacuba Blanco) –550,000 COP

Prices are per person (minimum of 4 persons, ask for prices for smaller groups). Price includes necessary transport from and to Cocuy/Güican, park fees, camping fees, cooking equipment and bilingual guide DE UNA. A good physical condition is required for all the above treks and climbs.

the department of Guaviare in the Amazon region. The Makús (from the Piaroa linguistic family) inhabit the mountain range of Tunahí, and the area between Papanauá and Inírida. Their communities live on subsistence farming within the Amazon forest. There are no facilities for tourists.

Puinawai (est 1989) (e *amazonia@parquesnacionales.gov.co*) Puinaves, Kurripacos and Cubeos peoples inhabit the 1.1 million-hectare park in the department of Guainía, in the Amazon region to the east of Colombia on the Brazilian border. There are no facilities for tourists.

Vía Parque Isla de Salamanca (est 1964) (e *ecoturismo@parquesnacionales.gov.co* or *dtca@parquesnacionales.gov.co*) The park covers 56,200ha and is located in the department of Magdalena, on the northern Caribbean shores. It incorporates the shoreline, estuaries, lagoons and dunes as well as the Magdalene River's overflows, swamps, bogs and marshes and mangroves. There's an abundance of flora and fauna here, including 98 species of invertebrate; 35 reptile species, such as caiman, both marine and fresh water turtles; more than 140 species of fish; 199 species of birds; and 33 species of mammal, including the manatee. There are public footpaths between some mangrove sites and it is also possible to tour the 'bogs' in a local boat; however, you must go with a guide. There's no lodging onsite, but in nearby Barranquilla you can find good hotels that offer excursions to the park.

Área Natural Única, Los Estoraques Natural Area (est 1988) (e *norandina@ col1.telecom.com.co*) A haunting rise of ancient geological rock formations that has been shaped over millennia due to weather erosion. Located in the Oriental mountain range in the region of Norte del Santander, the park spans 640ha and is open to tourists. A public footpath winds through the rocks. Various formations have been named such as El Rey (the King), El Barco (the Boat) and Ciudad Perdida (the Lost City). There are no lodging facilities onsite, but you can find hotels in nearby Ocaña and make day trips to the park.

2

Practical Information

WHEN TO VISIT

Colombia's *verano* (summer) is from December to March. These months and those from mid-June to mid-August are the best times to visit, with the exception of the northern plains where the wet season continues. Some 90% of Colombia's territory is below 915m, tropical and warm with temperatures averaging around 25°C. The Caribbean coast and the Amazon are extremely humid and rain is sporadic and unpredictable even in the dry season. As you ascend Colombia's Andes the temperature will drop around 6% per 1,000m. And, at an altitude of 1,980m, you'll find yourself amongst glaciers, where temperatures can be as low as −17°C.

This choice of climate and scenery is one of Colombia's best assets and the country offers visitors the full spectrum of travel opportunities. Adventurous travellers can hop between the snow-capped peaks of the Colombian Andes and the Caribbean's tropical turquoise waters and golden sands. Those looking for a more relaxed break can simply pick their preferred holiday – mountain hike, Caribbean beach, city jaunt or jungle trek are just some of the many, many choices available.

High season in Colombia can be busy with hordes of domestic vacationers. Visit during the celebratory months of Carnaval (in Barranquilla, Feb/Mar), Semana Santa (Holy Week, Mar/Apr) or Navidad (Christmas) and plans should be made well in advance with hotels and transport booked. In addition, check for regional celebrations, when towns, villages and even roads close entirely to enable locals to enjoy the fiesta. Unless you dislike big or lively crowds, these regional and national festivals are a great way to become immersed in Colombia's many different cultures. Witness colourful rituals, dancing and the relaxed side of local life, as businesses close for the holiday and people revel in a party atmosphere that can last several days – at least.

HIGHLIGHTS

RAFT THE FAST-FLOWING RAPIDS ON THE RÍO FONCE Colombia's adventure sports Mecca, San Gil, is home to kayaking, climbing, rappelling, paragliding and potholing on a dramatic mountainous terrain dotted with rocky, gushing streams. Less radical pursuits include horseback riding and fishing with craggy ravines, canyons and gorges crossed by a riddle of fine hiking trails.

HEAD TO THE UNESCO SEAFLOWER BIOSPHERE RESERVE Located in the reggae-drenched San Andrés Archipelagos to dive amidst sunken galleons home to 57 species of coral, 24 species of sponge and over 270 fish species. Octopus, dolphin, nurse shark and spotted eagle ray are commonly sighted in warm, tropical waters frequented by migrating whales.

CYCLE OR ROLLERBLADE Bogotá has 121km car-free roads and 300km ciclovías (cycle paths) open on Sundays and public holidays or you can stroll through over 4,500 leafy public parks in South America's third-highest capital city, a dizzying 2,630m above sea level and edged by rivers and mountain peaks.

JOURNEY ALONG THE VINE-TANGLED INKY-GREEN DEPTHS OF THE AMAZON RIVER It's home to at least 7,500 species of butterfly, 1,800 birds, 800 insect species, almost 2,000 species of reptile and amphibian, 3,200 species of fish – a staggering 10% of all species found on the planet. The watershed is also home to several hundred indigenous tribes who speak more than 100 languages and dialects with thick swathes of impenetrable jungle covering almost one-third of the Colombian territory.

EXPLORE THE ROLLING SAVANNAHS OF LOS LLANOS (THE PLAINS) ON HORSEBACK Ride with cattle-roping cowboys across undulating prairies dotted with ranches and corals. Learn lassoing skills from the gaucho-like Llaneros (plainspeople) in a hard-working region rich in provincial culture that is home to folklore, legends and heartfelt música llanera – lilting cowboy music played with *a cuatro* guitar or harp.

CLIMB THE SNOW-CAPPED NEVADO DEL RUIZ The 5,400m (17,717ft) peak is one of five permanently white-tipped volcanoes in Los Nevados National Park (*www.parquesnacionales.gov.co*). Guided treks are available from Manizales.

TRY OUT SOME NEW MOVES IN CALI Colombia's sultry salsa capital (*www.cali.gov.co*), a haven of dirty dancing.

STAY ON A COFFEE FARM Over 300 haciendas offer lodging to tourists and can arrange walks through the coffee fields as well as horse riding, fishing, mountain biking and trips to local villages.

TOUR OPERATORS

UK

Colombia 57 ☏ Freephone 0800 0789157; Colombia office: 57 313 401 5691; www.colombia57.com

GAP Adventures Matrix Studios, 91 Peterborough Rd, Fulham, London, SW6 3BU; ☏ 0870 999 0144; f 0870 080 1757; www.gapadventures.com

Journey Latin America 12 & 13 Heathfield Terr, London W4 4JE; ☏ 020 8747 8315; www.journeylatinamerica.co.uk

Last Frontiers Fleet Marston Farm, Aylesbury, Bucks HP18 0QT; ☏ 01296 653 000; www.lastfrontiers.com

South American Experience Ltd 38–44 Gillingham St, London SW1V 1HU; ☏ 0870 499 0683; f 020 7821 4001; www.southamericanexperience.co.uk

The Traveller & Palanquin 10 Bury Place, London WC1A 2JL; ☏ 020 7436 9343; f 0207 269 2770; e info@the-traveller.co.uk; www.the-traveller.co.uk

Tucan Travel 316 Uxbridge Rd, Acton, London W3 9QP; ☏ 020 8896 1600; f 020 8896 1400; www.tucantravel.com

World Gate Travel 362 Goswell Rd, London EC1V 7LQ; ☏ 020 7278 2999; f 020 7278 9905; e enquiries@worldgatetravel.com; www.worldgatetravel.com

EUROPE

Aternum Viaggi Vía Mazzini, 162/164 65122 Pescara, Italy; ☏ 085 4210557; f 085 4210765; e info@aternum.com; www.aternum.com

Tagus Madrid C/ Buen Suceso, 14 28008 Madrid, Spain; ☏ 34 91 547 1044; f 34 91 559 4756;

e tagus-madrid@tagusviajes.com; www.tagusviajes.com

Voyages Wasteels 5 Rue de la Banque, 75002 Paris, France; ☏ 33 1 42 61 6987; f 33 1 49 27 0999; www.wasteels.fr

US

GAP Adventures 225 Franklin St, 26th Floor, Boston MA 02110; ☎ 1 800 676 4941; www.gapadventures.com
Latour 233 Park Av South, New York, NY 10003; ☎ 800 243 7460; f 212 370 1477; www.isram.com

CANADA

GAP Adventures 19 Charlotte Stt, Toronto, Ontario M5V 2H5; ☎ 1 800 708 7761 (North America), 416 260

AUSTRALIA

Adventure Associates Level 7, 12–14 O'Connell St, Sydney, NSW 2000; ☎ 61 2 8916 3000; f 61 2 8916 3090, toll free 1 800 222 141; www.adventureassociates.com
BFirst Travel Suite 203, 74 Pitt St, Sydney, NSW 2000; ☎ 61 2 9232 0048; f 61 2 8569 0573, toll free: 1300 763 338; www.bfirsttravel.com
GAP Adventures ☎ 1300 85 33 25; www.gapadventures.com

NEW ZEALAND

GAP Adventures ☎ 0800 33 3307; www.gapadventures.com

COLOMBIA

Agroecotur Los Abedules 21, Circasia, Quindío; ☎ 315 585 7937/ 310 421 5250; e info@agroecotur.org; www.agroecotur.org. This Bogotá-based network of ecotourism specialists offer made-to-measure tours in the Amazon, Eastern Plains (Orinoco Region), the Andes & the Caribbean coast, including home-stay accommodation with local farming families, lodging on nature reserves & educational programmes relating to biodiversity conservation.
Aviatur Avenida 19, No 4–62 Bogotá; ☎ (1) 234 7333/381 7111; f (1) 283 0141; Central de Reservas: 382 1616, e aviatur.com@aviatur.com.co; www.aviatur.com
Bluefields Carrera 13A, No 87-81, Bogotá, ☎ 662 0660; www.blue-fields.org. One of Colombia's most impressive tour operators, Bluefields offer plenty of new dimensions to standard options as well as numerous tailored alternatives off the beaten track. Established in 1997, the company is renowned for its first-class service that comes supported by state-of-the-art equipment, including GPS. All tour guides have a certificate in first aid, as well as advanced courses in management of emergencies in wild areas certified by the Colombian Red Cross. The company covers all areas of Colombia & is one of the only outfits to include Los Llanos & the Pacific coast as well as the Amazon, the Guajira & the Caribbean. Reliable & enthusiastic tour leader Andrés González speaks good English & has a passion for Colombian flora and fauna.

Miller South America 3003 Van Ness St NW Ste S-823, Washington, DC 20008; ☎ 202 250 6004; f 202 318 1260; www.miller.travel

0999 (UK & outside North America); f 416 260 1888; www.gapadventures.com

South America Tourism Level 1, 178 Collins St, Melbourne, 3000, Victoria; ☎ 61 3 9654 7977; f 61 3 9650 8177; toll free: 1300 857 805; www.southamericatourism.com
Tucan Travel 217 Alison Rd, Randwick, NSW 2031; ☎ 61 02 9326 6633; f 61 02 9326 5993, toll free: 1300 769 249; www.tucantravel.com

Colombia Ecoturística Carrera 3, No 21–46, Apt No 802b, Bogotá; ☎ (1) 241 0065/366 3059
Colombia Paragliding ☎ (312) 432 6266/(301) 352 8839; e richifly@colombiaparagliding.com; www.colombiaparagliding.com
Colombia Unlimited www.colombiaunlimited.com. Run by a professional bunch of former British Airways employees, Colombia Unlimited mixes efficiency with tour precision – expect excellent service from this Bogotá-based independent operator where no detail is overlooked. Tour leaders are particularly well versed in Colombian political & social history and specialise in Bogotá, the Caribbean & regions north of Bogotá.
De Una Colombia Tours Calle 39, No 28–49, La Soledad, Bogotá DC; ☎/f (1) 369 0112; m (312) 450 6178; (312) 351 0753; e info@deunacolombia.com; www.deunacolombia.com. Run by Erik & Thomas, two Dutchmen who emigrated to Colombia several years ago after falling in love with the country, De Una combines adventure with respect for both the local environment & culture. De Una promotes local tourism & ecotourism.
Ecoguías Carrera 7, No 57–39, Oficina 501, Bogotá; ☎ (1) 347 5736/212 1423; www.ecoguias.com (English/Spanish/German)
EcoTurs Carrera 20, No 36–61 Bogotá; ☎ (1) 287 6592; ☎ 020 8543 2083 (London), 1 540 3410191 (US); e info@ecoturs.org; www.ecoturs.com.co. ProAves are now making their reserves more accessible to tourists &

have set up EcoTurs Colombia to organise scheduled & customised tours. Currently 9 reserves are safe to visit but visitors must book at least a week in advance to ensure accommodation & food are available. EcoTurs can also give visitors up-to-date advice on safety in other national parks & reserves & give advice on travel arrangements. **Educamos Viajando** Calle 108A, No 18–64, Bogotá; ☏ (1) 620 5359; f (1) 215 7024; e tiquetes@eduvi.com; www.eduvi.com

Mantaraya Expeditions Calle 93, No 13–32 of 101 (Chicó), Bogotá; ☏ (1) 877 260 8632 (toll free); (1) 257 5541; f (1) 282 5728; www.mantarayakayak.com
Sal Si Puedes Carrera 7, No 17–01, Oficina 639, Bogotá; www.salsipuedes.org (Spanish)
Viajar y Vivir Carrera 13, No 61–47, Local 104, Bogotá; ☏ (1) 368 6139/211 1368; www.viajarvivir.com (Spanish)
Viajes Celtour Avenida 15, No 106–50 Mz 01 Bogotá; ☏ (1) 612 7020; f (1) 215 8602; www.viajes-celtour.com

RED TAPE

Citizens from most western European countries, including the UK, Australia, New Zealand, the USA and Canada only need a valid passport to enter Colombia. They will issue either a 30-, 60- or 90-day tourist visa on entry without the need to apply for any other visa in advance. Those planning to stay for up to 90 days should notify immigration officials as they tend to issue 30 or 60 days as standard. Once in the country, extended stays of over 90 days should be arranged by visiting the Office of Immigration Affairs (Calle 100, No11–27) in Bogotá to submit an application. Those planning to work or study in Colombia will need to apply for the relevant visa from the Colombian consulate in their home country before they leave. Citizens from restricted countries need to apply for a tourist visa in the Colombian consulate in their country of origin.

Whether arriving by plane or land, visitors must hold a return or onward ticket to prove an intention to leave the country. Furthermore, the ticket out of the country should be dated within 90 days to avoid difficulties at immigration. It is also entirely possible that proof may be required to show sufficient funds exist to cover your stay. Passport and visa requirements can change without much notice, so check with the Colombian embassy in advance of your trip.

Don't forget to allow for the airport tax on departure, which is currently 53,000 COP for a 90-day stay but less for a 60-day stay. Make sure your passport is stamped on both arrival and exit, whether you enter by air, land or sea, or you may be liable for a fine. Individuals entering or leaving Colombia are only entitled to carry up to US$10,000 in cash. Anything in excess of this may be confiscated. Recently, a British national carrying US$14,000 had US$4,000 confiscated by the authorities at the airport, despite his argument that the money belonged to both him and his wife, who was travelling with him

Those entering by sea must report to the port's local immigration office for a passport entry stamp within one day of arrival.

E EMBASSIES

COLOMBIAN EMBASSIES ABROAD
Australia Suite 2, Level 12, 100 Walker St, North Sydney NSW 2060 (PO Box 6133); ☏ 61 2 9955 0311, f 61 2 9922 5597; e ConsulateofColombia@tpg.com.au; www.consuladodecolombiasydney.org.au
Austria Consulate, Stadiongasse 6-8/15, A–1010 Wien; ☏ 43 1 408 4132; f 43 1 408 83 03; www.embcol.or.at; ⏰09.00–13.00 Mon–Fri
Belgium Embassy: Av F Roosevelt 96a, 1050 Brussels; ☏ 00 32 2 649 5679; f 00 32 2 646 5491; e colombia@emcolbru.org; www.emcolbru.org;

Consulate: Rue Van Eyck 44, B–10 00 Brussels; ☏ 02 649 0768; f 02 649 2404; e consulado.colombia@tiscali.be; ⏰09.00–13.00 Mon–Fri
Canada 1010 Sherbrooke St West, Suite 420, Montreal, Quebec H3A 2R7
Denmark & Sweden Embajada de Colombia, Östermalmsgaten 46, Box 5627 S-114 86 Stockholm, Sweden; ☏ 46 821 4320; f 46 821 8490; e eestocolmo@minrelext.gov.co; www.colombia.dk

France 22 Rue de L'elysee, Paris 75008; ☎ 33 1 4265 4608; f 33 1 4266 1860; www.embcolfrancia.com; ⊕09.00–13.00 & 14.30–18.00 Mon–Fri
Germany Kurfürstenstr. 84, 10787 Berlin; ☎ 49 30 263 9610; f 49 30 2639 6125; e l.huebner@botschaft-kolumbien.de; ⊕08.30–12.30 & 14.30–17.00 Mon–Fri; Wed by appointment only
Holland Embassy of Colombia in Holland, Groot Hertoginnelaan 14 2517EG, The Hague; ☎ 31 70 361 4545; f 31 70 361 4636; e info@colombiaemb.nl; ⊕09.00–17.00 Mon–Fri
Panama Embassy of Colombia in Panama City, World Trade Centre Building, Office 1802, St 53 Urbanizacion,

Marbella, Panama City; ☎ 507 264 9266; f 507 223 1134; www.embajadadecolombia.org.pa
UK 3 Hans Cres, London SWIX OLN; ☎ 020 7589 9177/5037; f 020 7581 1829/4718; e mail@colombianembassy.co.uk; www.colombianembassy.co.uk; ⊕09.00–18.00 Mon–Fri
USA 2118 Leroy Place, NW, Washington, DC 20008; ☎ 202 387 8338/232 8643; e emwas@ colombiaemb.org; www.colombiaemb.org; 280 Aragon Av, Coral Gables, Miami, FL 33134; ☎ 305 441 1235; www.consuladodecolombia.com

EMBASSIES IN COLOMBIA

Australia Carrera 18, No 90–38, Inter-Lingua Center, Bogotá; ☎ (1) 636 5247
Canada Carrera 7, No 115–33, Piso 14, Bogotá; ☎ (1) 657 9800
France Carrera 11, No 93–12, Bogotá; ☎ (1) 638 1400
Germany Carrera. 69, No 43 B–44, piso 7, Edificio World Business Port, Bogotá; ☎ (1) 423 2600; f (1) 429 3145/423 2628; e embajalemana@andinet.com
Israel Calle 35, No 7–25, Piso 14, Bogotá; ☎ (1) 327 7500
Italy Calle 93B, 9–92, Bogotá; ☎ (1) 218 6680; f (1) 610 5886; e ambbogo.mail@esteri.it; www.ambBogotá.esteri.it
Netherlands Carrera 13, No 93–40, Piso 5, Bogotá; ☎ (1) 618 4299
Panama Bogotá: Calle 92, No 7–70; Bogotá; ☎ (1) 257 4452; Cali: Calle 11 No 4–42, Oficina 316, Cali; ☎ (2) 880 9590; Medellín: Carrera 43A No 7–50, Oficina 1607, Medellín; ☎ (4) 268 1358
Spain Calle 92, No 12–68, Bogotá; ☎ (1) 622 0090

Sweden Calle 72 Bis No 5–83, Piso 9, Edificio Av Chile, Bogotá; ☎ (1) 325 6180; f (1) 325 6181; e embsueca@cable.net.co; www.swedenabroad.com
Switzerland Carrera 9A, No 74–08, Oficina 1101, Bogotá; ☎ (1) 255 3945
UK Carrera 9, No 76–49 Pisos 8 y 9; PBX: (1) 326 8300; f (1) 326 8302; e ppa.Bogotá@fco.gov.uk; www.britishembassy.gov.uk; Consulates outside Bogotá (Cali): Calle 22 Norte No 6–42; ☎ (2) 661 7745/1031; f (2) 667 7725; e britishcali@uniweb.net.co; ⊕09.00–12.30 Mon–Fri
USA Calle 22D Bis No 47-1, Bogotá; ☎ (1) 315 0811; Consular section ☎ (1) 315 1566, USAID ☎ (1) 423 6880; Embassy f (1) 315 2197; http://Bogotá.usembassy.gov; Consular section ⊕08.30–12.00 Mon–Thu, closed US & Colombian holidays. Consular Agency in Barranquilla: Calle 77B, No 57–141, Piso 5, Centro Empresarial Las Américas, Barranquilla, Atlántico; ☎ (5) 353 2001; f (5) 353 5216
Venezuela Carrera 13, No 87–51, Bogotá; ☎ (1) 640 1213; Calle 32B, No 69–59, Medellín; ☎ (4) 351 1614

GETTING THERE AND AWAY

✈ **BY AIR** Colombia's major international airports are El Dorado (*www.Bogotá-dc.com/trans/aviones.htm*), Bogotá (BOG), Alfonso Bonilla Aragón, Cali (CLO), José María Codova, Medellín (MDE), and Rafael Nuñez, Cartagena (CTG). Other popular international airports include Barranquilla (BAQ) and Bucaramanga (BGA). National airline Avianca (*www.avianca.com*) serves all international airports from most Latin American destinations as well as some cities in North America and Spain. The Avianca VIP lounge at El Dorado International Airport won the 'Priority Pass Airport Lounge of the Year' award in 2006.

Air France (*www.airfrance.com*) operates from most western European destinations with stopovers on some routes. Iberia flies from Madrid to all the above airports, via Bogotá. American Airlines (*www.aa.com*), Northwest (*www.nwa.com*), Continental (*www.continentalairlines.com*) and Delta (*www.delta.com*) are the major airlines between the US and most of Colombia's international airports. Copa (*www.copaair.com*) also provides services to New York, Miami and Orlando from Barranquilla, Bogotá and Cali.

From Bogotá, LAN Airlines (*www.lan.com*) connects to Miami, Quito, Ecuador and other South American destinations via stopovers. LACSA and TACA (*www.taca.com*) both connect between Bogotá and Latin American and some US destinations. Flying time is around 10½ hours from Madrid, 12 from Paris and 13 from London (excluding stopover). Flying from New York takes 4¼ hours and from Los Angeles 8 hours.

At the time of writing the Colombian government has announced the abolition of minimum air fares for national flights, prompting rumours that low-cost carriers will soon enter the market. In December 2007, American Airlines increased its flights to Colombia with daily flights from Miami to Barranquilla – an excellent option for travellers heading to Cartagena. In addition AA will increase its flights to Medellín, Bogotá and Cali on a daily schedule. At present the following international connections apply:

Aruba (from Bogotá, Medellín and Barranquilla), Alicante (from Bogotá), Barcelona (from Bogotá), Buenos Aires (from Bogotá), Caracas (from Bogotá), Curaçao (from Bogotá), Fort Lauderdale (from Bogotá), Guayaquil (from Bogotá), Lima (from Bogotá), Los Angeles (from Bogotá), Madrid (from Bogotá and Cali), Mexico City (from Bogotá), Miami (from Bogotá, Medellín, Cali, Barranquilla, Cartagena and Pereira), New York (JFK) (from Bogotá, Medellín, Cali, Barranquilla and Pereira), Panama City (from Bogotá), Punta Caña (from Bogotá), Quito (from Bogotá), Río de Janeiro (from Bogotá via São Paulo), Santiago (from Bogotá), São Paulo (from Bogotá), Valencia (Venezuela) (from Bogotá).

OVERLAND Arrival overland from Panama can be hazardous and anyone thinking of attempting it should first contact the Foreign and Commonwealth Office (*www.fco.gov.uk*) for advice. There is no road between the countries; instead you'll have to skirt around the edges of the vast Darién rainforest – known as the Darién Gap – by boat (between Puerto Obaldía in Panama and Sapzurro in Colombia) and bus along the Caribbean coast. Although, at the time of writing, this area is safer than it was – a risk remains due to guerrilla activity. In January 2006, two Spanish nationals were kidnapped in the Darién region, close to the Colombian–Panamanian border.

Immigration officers staff the borders of Ecuador and Venezuela and these are serviced by both national and international buses. At Ipiales, the border town that crosses to Tulcán in Ecuador, the office is open between 06.00–17.00 daily and there is no charge for leaving (or entering) the country. The Venezuelan crossing at Cúcuta is used by guerrillas, paramilitary groups and coca cultivators and can be dangerous, volatile and unsafe. The British Foreign and Commonwealth Office advice is not to travel in this area but should you decide to cross to San Antonio, Venezuela, using this route extreme caution should be employed. A tourist visa (US$30) can be purchased from the Venezuelan consulate in Cúcuta (*Avenida 0 y Calle 8,* \713 983/781 034; ⊕08.00–12.00 & 13.00–16.00 Mon–Fri). Travellers will need a valid passport, recent photograph, sufficient funds to cover your trip, and a return or onward ticket. National buses leave regularly from the border.

BY SEA Most tourists entering by sea do so on cruise lines (see *Cruise itineraries,* page 99), where all necessary entrance formalities are taken care of by cruise staff. Several shipping companies dock on the Caribbean coast and it is possible to take a boat tour from both Colón and Kuna Yala (San Blas) in Panama to Colombia's Cartagena. Those that do arrive in Cartagena by boat must visit the immigration office on the day of arrival for a Colombian entry stamp in your passport – fail to do so and you will be illegal in the country after 24 hours.

✚ HEALTH with Dr Felicity Nicholson & Dr Ron Behrens, Hospital for Tropical Diseases

Healthcare in Colombia is reasonably good, especially in cities where getting modern medical treatment fairly fast poses little problem. In rural areas however, don't rely on finding any medical care. Arrive prepared with any medicines that might be needed and a first-aid kit and plan for unforeseen emergencies.

Health centres in most towns should be able to treat minor ailments and costs are usually very low. However, treatment is paid for at the time it is administered so it is important to have access to cash. Ask for a receipt if you intend to claim on your health insurance and be prepared to pay upfront if an ambulance is required. Medical staff in towns or rural areas may not speak English, so it may pay to look up some useful Spanish phrases beforehand, such as the names of allergies to medicines or words about pregnancy, etc. Take out health insurance before your visit to Colombia and if you intend to trek or hike – a policy should cover every eventuality, including being evacuated for more advanced hospital care.

IMMUNISATION Visitors who intend to travel away from the city areas of Bogotá, Cali or Medellín are advised to have a yellow fever vaccination, especially those travelling through rural areas and any national parks. All travellers should ensure they are up to date with the combined polio/tetanus/diphtheria (Revaxis) vaccination. The hepatitis A vaccine, which may require a booster after six months for long-term coverage, is advised. Depending on the length of your stay, it may also be worth considering a hepatitis B and rabies vaccination although these are not necessary for holidays of two weeks or so. These vaccines are recommended for longer stays and trekking and hiking trips. Travellers who may have intimate contact with the locals are advised to have a hepatitis B vaccine. Make sure you plan

Before travelling to Colombia it is worth checking all pre-existing travel insurances to ensure they adequately cover your trip. White-water rafting in the Coffee Zone, jet skiing in San Andrés and trekking through the wilds of the Amazon may all be activities that are exempt from a standard policy. There may also be some stipulations in regards to the length of stay. **IAMAT** is a good source of advice on insurance topics and should also be able to provide a list of recommended doctors in Colombia (see *Travel clinics* below for details). Those planning to scuba dive should consider the specialist insurance plan offered by the **Divers Alert Network** (DAN) (*Peter B Bennett Center, 6 West Colony Pl, Durham NC 27705, USA;* ☎ *1 800 443 2671;* e *dan@diversnetwork.org; www.diversalertnetwork.org*). This non-profit organisation was founded in 1990 and now has 200,000 members, providing medical R&D services and health and safety support to recreational scuba divers in association with Duke University Medical Center. The organisation offers two plans that cover emergency air evacuation to hyperbaric chamber treatment, plus a wide range of equipment and medical safety aspects.

your immunisations well in advance, at least one month but preferably longer, to make sure you are completely covered. The rabies vaccine consists of three injections taken over one month, and will provide complete protection for the duration of your trip.

TRAVEL CLINICS AND HEALTH INFORMATION A full list of current travel clinic websites worldwide is available from the International Society of Travel Medicine on www.istm.org. For other journey preparation information, consult www.tripprep.com. Information about various medications may be found on www.emedicine.com. For information on malaria prevention, see www.preventingmalaria.info.

UK

Berkeley Travel Clinic 32 Berkeley St, London W1J 8EL (near Green Park tube station); ☎ 020 7629 6233
Cambridge Travel Clinic 48a Mill Rd, Cambridge CB1 2AS; ☎ 01223 367362; e enquiries@travelcliniccambridge.co.uk; www.travelcliniccambridge.co.uk. ⏰12.00–19.00 Tue–Fri, 10.00–16.00 Sat.
Edinburgh Travel Clinic Regional Infectious Diseases Unit, Ward 41 OPD, Western General Hospital, Crewe Rd South, Edinburgh EH4 2UX; ☎ 0131 537 2822; www.mvm.ed.ac.uk. Travel helpline (0906 589 0380) ⏰09.00–12.00 weekdays. Provides inoculations & antimalarial prophylaxis, & advises on travel-related health risks.
Expedition Advisory Centre Royal Geographic Centre, 1 Kensington Gore, London SW7 2AR; ☎ 0207 591 3030; f 0207 591 3031; e eac@rgs.org; www.rgs.org
Expedition Medicine Jubilee Hse, Fore St, Thorncombe, Nr Chard, Somerset TA20 4PP; ☎ 01460 30456; e events@acrossthedivide.com; www.expeditionmedicine.co.uk

Fleet Street Travel Clinic 29 Fleet St, London EC4Y 1AA; ☎ 020 7353 5678; www.fleetstreetclinic.com. Vaccinations, travel products & latest advice.
Hospital for Tropical Diseases Travel Clinic Mortimer Market Bldg, Capper St (off Tottenham Ct Rd), London WC1E 6AU; ☎ 020 7388 9600; www.thehtd.org. Offers consultations & advice, & is able to provide all necessary drugs & vaccines for travellers. Runs a healthline (☎ 0906 133 7733) for country-specific information & health hazards. Also stocks mosquito nets, water purification equipment & personal protection measures.
Interhealth Worldwide Partnership Hse, 157 Waterloo Rd, London SE1 8US; ☎ 020 7902 9000; www.interhealth.org.uk. Competitively priced, one-stop travel health service. All profits go to their affiliated company, InterHealth, which provides health care for overseas workers on Christian projects.
Liverpool School of Medicine Pembroke Pl, Liverpool L3 5QA; ☎ 0151 708 9393; f 0151 705 3370; www.liv.ac.uk/lstm

MASTA (Medical Advisory Service for Travellers Abroad) Moorfield Rd, Yeadon, Leeds, West Yorks LS19 7BN; ☎ 0113 238 7500; www.masta-travel-health.com. Provides travel health advice, anti-malarials & vaccinations. There are over 25 MASTA pre-travel clinics in Britain; call or check online for the nearest. Clinics also sell mosquito nets, medical kits, insect protection & travel hygiene products.

NHS travel website www.fitfortravel.scot.nhs.uk. Provides country-by-country advice on immunisation & malaria, plus details of recent developments, & a list of relevant health organisations.

Nomad Travel Store/Clinic 3–4 Wellington Terr, Turnpike La, London N8 0PX; ☎ 020 8889 7014; travel-health line (office hours only) ☎ 0906 863 3414; e sales@nomadtravel.co.uk; www.nomadtravel.co.uk.

Also at 40 Bernard St, London WC1N 1LJ; ☎ 020 7833 4114; 52 Grosvenor Gdns, London SW1W 0AG; ☎ 020 7823 5823; and 43 Queens Rd, Bristol BS8 1QH; ☎ 0117 922 6567. For health advice, equipment such as mosquito nets & other anti-bug devices, & an excellent range of adventure travel gear. Clinic also in Southhampton.

Trailfinders Travel Clinic 194 Kensington High St, London W8 7RG; ☎ 020 7938 3999; http://www.trailfinders.com/travelessentials/travelclinic.htm

Travelpharm The Travelpharm website, www.travelpharm.com, offers up-to-date guidance on travel-related health and has a range of medications available through their online mini-pharmacy.

Irish Republic

Tropical Medical Bureau Grafton Street Medical Centre, Grafton Bldgs, 34 Grafton St, Dublin 2; ☎ 1 671 9200; www.tmb.ie. A useful website specific to tropical

destinations. Also check website for other bureaux locations throughout Ireland.

USA

Centers for Disease Control 1600 Clifton Rd, Atlanta, GA 30333; ☎ 800 311 3435; travellers' health hotline (fax service) 888 232 3299; www.cdc.gov/travel. The central source of travel information in the USA. The invaluable *Health Information for International Travel*, published annually, is available from the Division of Quarantine at this address.

Connaught Laboratories Pasteur Merieux Connaught, Route 611, PO Box 187, Swiftwater, PA 18370; ☎ 800 822 2463. They will send a free list of specialist tropical-medicine physicians in your state.

IAMAT (International Association for Medical Assistance to Travelers) 1623 Military Rd, 279, Niagara Falls, NY14304-1745; ☎ 716 754 4883; e info@iamat.org; www.iamat.org. A non-profit organisation that provides lists of English-speaking doctors abroad.

International Medicine Center 915 Gessner Rd, Suite 525, Houston, TX 77024; ☎ 713 550 2000; www.traveldoc.com

Canada

IAMAT Suite 1, 1287 St Clair Av W, Toronto, Ontario M6E 1B8; ☎ 416 652 0137; www.iamat.org

TMVC Suite 314, 1030 W Georgia St, Vancouver, BC V6E 2Y3; ☎ 1 888 288 8682; www.tmvc.com. Private clinic with several outlets in Canada.

Australia, New Zealand, Singapore

IAMAT PO Box 5049, Christchurch 5, New Zealand; www.iamat.org

TMVC ☎ 1300 65 88 44; www.tmvc.com.au. Clinics in Australia, New Zealand & Singapore, including: *Auckland* Canterbury Arcade, 170 Queen St, Auckland; ☎ 9 373 3531

Brisbane 75a, Astor Terr, Spring Hill, QLD 4000; ☎ 7 3815 6900

Melbourne 393 Little Bourke St, 2nd Floor, Melbourne, VIC 3000; ☎ 3 9602 5788

Sydney Dymocks Bldg, 7th Floor, 428 George St, Sydney, NSW 2000; ☎ 2 9221 7133

South Africa and Namibia

SAA-Netcare Travel Clinics Sanlam Bldg, 19, Fredman Dr, Sandton, P Bag X34, Benmore, JHB, Gauteng, 2010; www.travelclinic.co.za. Clinics throughout South Africa.

TMVC NHC Health Centre, cnr. Beyers Naude and

Waugh Northcliff; PO Box 48499, Roosevelt Pk, 2129 (postal address); ☎ 011 888 7488; www.tmvc.com.au. Consult website for details of other clinics in South Africa & Namibia.

Switzerland

IAMAT 57 Chemin des Voirets, 1212 Grand Lancy, Geneva; www.iamat.org

FIRST-AID KIT No visitor to Colombia planning to spend time out of the main cities should arrive without a decent first-aid kit, especially those travelling to islands or the Amazon region. While Cali, Bogotá, Medellín and Barranquilla boast top-notch medical facilities, many with English-speaking doctors, elsewhere, the standard of healthcare is unlikely to be so reliable, or easy to access. Large stretches of rainforest remain only accessible by boat or on foot, so all it takes is a spell of poor weather or engine trouble to put medical help out of reach. On the islands, health facilities tend to be rudimentary and clinic-based. Mainland hospitals in some rural communities are often also woefully under-funded, relying on NGO assistance to provide the most basic service, without any frills.

A good first-aid kit for Colombia will vary depending on where you plan to travel. Contents should reflect the weather conditions and availability of replacement items, eg: pack as much mosquito repellent as you can for the Amazon but swap this for blister treatments if you're hiking across the Coffee Zone. If you suffer from altitude sickness then ask your doctor about a course of acetazolamide (Diamox). Other suggestions as follows:

- Antiseptic wash
- Blister patches
- Bandages and plasters
- Sachets of re-hydration mix
- Painkillers
- Anti-fungal cream
- Travel sickness tablets
- Lots of mosquito repellent
- Antibiotics
- Cold cure sachets
- Throat lozenges
- Eye and ear drops
- Indigestion tablets
- Iodine or alcohol wipes
- Your own prescription medicine

DRINKING WATER Colombia's bottled Agua Manantial comes from a natural spring 3,330m above sea level near Bogotá. Not only is it cheap, it's delicious – and widely available. As a result many travellers opt for the bottled stuff rather than risk the tap. However, Colombia is one of the few Latin American nations where tap water is good enough to drink without worry – with just a few exceptions. In the Guajira region travellers are advised to avoid the local water and to refrain from ordering drinks with ice. In contrast, the water in Manizales is of optimum quality as it comes straight from a pristine natural source near a *nevado* (snow-covered spring). Order bottled water in this Colombia city and the locals will think you're loco – or are sure to be mightily offended. Travellers venturing out to the wilds of the Amazon region should pack water purification tablets just in case. Some of the rivers in the Andes are showing signs of pollution from the coca crop-spraying programme – an initiative that made water unsafe for drinking or bathing and which has destroyed local fishing stocks.

MEDICAL PROBLEMS

Deep vein thrombosis (DVT) Although relatively rare, there is an increased risk of deep vein thrombosis if you fly for longer than eight hours. If you have a long-haul flight ahead, consider taking medical advice from your GP before you leave to check you are not in a high-risk category. DVT occurs when blood clots that form naturally in an immobilised body get stuck in the lungs. Travellers should not be alarmed as clots form regularly in the body without causing a problem. However, some people, such as cancer and heart disease sufferers and the elderly, are considered a higher risk of DVT than others. If you think you are high-risk make sure you get your doctor's permission to fly. In general anyone on a long-haul flight should move about the plane regularly throughout the flight, stretch their legs at regular intervals and rotate their ankles frequently, avoid heavy sedation, such as alcohol or sleeping pills and drink plenty of water and/or fruit juice. You can also try socks that have been designed to reduce the risk of DVT (*www.legshealth.com*, *www.donttravelwithoutit.com*).

Malaria areas The most dangerous form of malaria, plasmodium falciparum, occurs in low-lying (below 800m) tropical areas of Colombia, in particular Chocó and northwest Antioquía. Malaria is contracted by a bite from an infected female *Anopheles* mosquito and it multiplies in the oxygen-carrying red blood corpuscles (cells). The incubation period varies from ten days to three months. Signs of malaria range from fever, shaking and shivering, a temperature of >38°C rising and falling, flu-like symptoms, headaches, nausea and vomiting and diarrhoea. Falciparum is an extremely dangerous form of malaria and if you think you may have it, it is vital to seek medical attention immediately. In the unlikely chance you get malaria whilst taking antimalarials, make sure you tell any doctor treating you exactly what antimalarials you are taking. Remember symptoms of malaria may not appear until after your return.

There are various antimalarials on the market, but falciparum malaria in Colombia is resistant to the weaker varieties and therefore you will be prescribed one of the strongest three available, Malarone (Atovaquone Proguanil), Lariam (Mefloquine), Doxycycline. Discuss your needs with your GP as treatment differs and one antimalarial may suit some people more than others.

Antimalarials should be taken well before a trip, but how long before depends on whether they have been taken previously; your GP will advise you. Travellers planning to spend only part of their trip in malarial areas can wait until just before you embark on travel to that area. However, in malarial high-risk areas it is imperative you do not forget to take a tablet, and will need to keep taking them for some time after you leave the area, or return home; your GP will advise. Antimalarials do not offer 100% protection so make sure you remember all antimalarial measures:

- Cover up your arms and legs, especially at dusk, by lakes and in rural areas. Tuck your trousers into your boots, and use elastic or hair bands around your wrists to keep mosquitoes out of your sleeves.
- Choose a strong insect repellent, with a high amount of DEET (at least 50–55%), and remember to keep reapplying.
- Sleep under an insect repellent impregnated mosquito net in high risk areas – ask in rural hotels if you are unsure.
- Avoid areas with stagnant water.

Dengue fever This is carried by the infected *Aedes aegypti* mosquito, a day-biting mosquito and therefore much harder to avoid. Dengue occurs on the north

Caribbean coast, Chocó, Antioquía, Cordoba, Sucre, Bolívar and Atlántico. The World Health Organisation verified a dengue outbreak in Colombia in March 2007 that resulted in two deaths. Symptoms of dengue involve flu-like shivering and fever accompanied by aching bones, from which it takes its nickname '*rompa hueso*' (breakbone fever). Symptoms are extremely unpleasant and there is currently no effective treatment. However, do seek advice from a doctor, as some strains of dengue can be dangerous (dengue haemorrhagic fever). In general, lots of bed-rest and plenty of fluids and painkillers (but not aspirin) should eventually treat it. It is worth noting that depression can accompany dengue fever.

Cutaneous leishmaniasis Spread by the bite of an infected phlebotomine sand fly, leishmaniasis causes skin sores to erupt, usually within a week of being bitten, but sometimes symptoms don't appear for some months. Sores can be severe, swell up to 2.5cm in diameter and may weep or form a crusty surface. They heal by themselves, but they may leave scars and on very rare occasions the infection can spread to the nose and mouth (mucosal leishmaniasis). Visit a GP for advice as it can often be treated with a series of injections. Leishmaniasis is not very common, so taking precautions should be enough to protect you. It is difficult to avoid bites as sand flies are extremely tiny, about a third of the size of a mosquito, and can slip through regular mosquito nets. However, follow the bite prevention measures – see above – and use lots of insect repellent at dusk and night.

Chagas' disease (American trypanosomiasis) Chagas' is transmitted by contact with the faeces of the reduviid bug, which lives in cracks and holes of poor-quality housing, in particular mud and thatched accommodation. The disease can cause acute symptoms of diarrhoea and vomiting; however, this is seen in only 1% of cases. An untreated infection can live in the body for years without detection, but will weaken the immune system and can lower life expectancy by an average of nine years. Chagastic heart disease can develop in some cases and can be fatal. Chagas' is quite rare and unless you are staying in a poor rural area, you should not be at risk. There is currently no vaccine or treatment available for this disease.

Rabies is a quick acting fatal disease that is carried in mammals, mainly dogs, cats, monkeys and squirrels. It is transmitted through their saliva; therefore you should prevent any animal licking or biting you, especially where your skin is already broken. Travellers should not go near stray dogs or wild animals, to avoid any chance of catching rabies. Any bite, scratch or lick over an open wound from a warm-blooded animal in Colombia should be thoroughly cleaned immediately, using soap and hot water to scrub the area before wiping it with an alcohol or iodine solution. This can stop the rabies virus entering the body and will protect against secondary infections, such as tetanus. If you think you have been exposed to rabies, seek medical attention immediately. Travellers without immunisation who are bitten will need both RIG (rabies immunoglobulin) and a full course of injections. This will prevent the onset of rabies symptoms but can be expensive (RIG alone can cost around US$800 a dose excluding the cost of six or seven doses of vaccine needed). Playing it safe is sensible and vaccination, a series of three injections over one month, is available before you go. In addition, this will prevent the need for expensive RIG after the event and the number of post-exposure doses of vaccine will be reduced.

Traveller's diarrhoea (TD) Around 60% of travellers get TD at some point on their journey, so do not be shocked if it happens to you. Opinion is divided about TD: some argue it comes from contaminated food and water, others believe it is caused by a change in diet. It's wise to stick to bottled (or boiled) water, to avoid eating from dirty-looking street stalls, to avoid cooked food that has been sitting around for a while and salads that might not have been washed. TD is unpleasant, with symptoms that vary in severity from person to person. In general, symptoms settle within 48 hours but it is imperative you replace lost fluids, salts and sugars, as dehydration can be quick, and very serious. Take re-hydration sachets mixed with bottled or cool boiled water and avoid food for 24–48 hours. Don't drink alcohol or caffeine for several days as these can dehydrate you and cause cramping. If you experience diarrhoea for longer than 48 hours seek medical attention, just in case you have something more serious. Some travel clinics –eg: the Hospital for Tropical Diseases (*www.thehtd.org*) – sell very effective antibiotic treatments for TD.

Sun and heat It is tempting to lie in the sun, especially in the tropics where you might picture yourself lying under a palm tree sipping something exotic. However, the incidence of skin cancer due to sun exposure is rising. UV rays from sunlight trigger DNA cell change which can initiate melanoma, a malignant skin tumour now responsible for around three-quarters of all skin cancer deaths. Fair skinned people are more susceptible than dark skinned, but everyone should take precautions and avoid excessive sun exposure. It is advisable to avoid the midday sun, apply a sunscreen with sun protection factor (SPF) of 15 or higher with both ultraviolet A (UVA; wavelength 315–400 nm) and ultraviolet B (UVB; wavelength 280–315 nm) protection as well as wearing a wide-brimmed hat and sunglasses. Re-apply cream regularly, and especially after swimming. Babies and children are at great risk from the sun and should be covered with long sleeved swim suits, high factor sun cream and wide-brimmed hats, whenever they are outside.

Heatstroke is caused by excessive sun exposure; drinking alcohol or taking strenuous exercise in the sun are also factors. Symptoms include dizziness, nausea, headache, unclear vision, confusion and unreasonable behaviour. If you suffer heatstroke get out of the sun immediately. Drinking plenty of fluids, keeping cool with wet towels and resting for at least 24 hours can treat mild cases. You may also find after-sun creams or aloe vera gel a soothing comfort to burned skin. For severe sunstroke seek medical attention immediately as you will need re-hydration.

Remember, it is just as crucial to wear sunscreen at high altitude (mountain) or on rivers and at sea, where snow and water reflect ultraviolet light despite the air temperature.

Fungal infections Fungal infections are common in hot, humid climates where they thrive on moisture. They usually flare up in crevices of the body that sweat in the heat, in particular the groin area and between the toes. However, fungal infections are not serious and respond well to antifungal creams. Wear loose-fitting clothing in natural fabrics and if possible expose the area as much as possible.

WOMEN'S HEALTH Cystitis and other urinary tract and bladder infections are extremely common in female travellers, especially those on long-haul trips and/or on a budget. Spending hours on old buses, sleeping in less than sanitary conditions and not getting the chance to wash properly for long periods all help to raise the risk. Such infections can be extremely uncomfortable and cause a painful burning sensation whilst urinating. To make things worse, it will make you feel as though you constantly need the toilet, even when you do not. It is vital to drink plenty of water, which will help wash out the infection. Over-the-counter medicines can help. If symptoms persist, seek medical attention, as the infection can be dangerous if it spreads to the kidneys.

Like fungal infections, vaginal yeast infections such as thrush are also common, but react well to over-the-counter treatment. Buy creams or pessaries before you leave and have them in your first-aid kit just in case. Some people recommend applying fresh yoghurt to the area; it could help with the itchiness. In rural areas it may be difficult to buy tampons, so if these are your preferred method of period care, bring some from home.

USEFUL CONTACTS
Bogotá
Ambulance
Suma Emergencias ✎ (1) 621 0630 or (1) 310 229 9696
Ambulancias Medicas ✎ (1) 214 8304, (1) 620 5107/5105
Ambulancias Tras Medica ✎ (1) 625 6910, (1) 258 6669, tell them to take you to Servicio de Urgencias

Fundación Santa Fé, Calle 119 No 9–10; ✎ (1) 629 0477
Colombian Air Ambulance Aeromedicos – Ambulancia Aerea, El Dorado International Airport, Entrance 2, Int I, Of. 105; ✎ (1) 413 9160/8915

Hospitals
The Red Cross – La Cruz Roja Colombiana y el Departamento de Sanidad Portuaria del Aeropuerto El Dorado, Muelle Internacional, Bogotá; www.cruzrojacolombiana.org. Can give vaccinations such as yellow fever.

Hospital Universitario Clinica San Rafael Cra 8a.No 17–45 Sur Bogotá; ✎ (1) 328 2300; www.clinicasanrafael.com.co
Fundación Santa Fé de Bogotá Calle 116 No 9–02; ✎ (1) 603 0303; www.eng.fsfb.org.co (English/Spanish)
Hospital El Tunal Santa Fé de Bogotá, Carrera 20 No 47B–35 Sur; www.hospitaleltunal.gov.co/web/ (Spanish)

Pharmacies
Cafam ✎ (1) 646 8000, ext 1240
Colsubsidio ✎ (1) 343 0080

Olímpica Carrera 40, No 22 C–10; ✎ (1) 368 9246
Sideral Calle 22 D Bis No 42B–11; ✎ (1) 244 8757

Cali
Fundación Clínica Valle del Lili Cali, Carrera 98 No 18–49; ✎ (2) 331 7474; www.cardiolili.org (Spanish)

Medellín

Clínica Las Américas Diaginal 75B No 2 A 120 oficina
309, Centro Comerical Plazoleta Las Américas; ☎ (4)
341 6060; www.pmamericas.com

Hospital Universitario San Vicente de Paul HSVP
Medellín, Calle 67 (Barranquilla); www.elhospital.org.co
(English/Spanish)

Cartagena

Cruz Roja de Bolívar Barrio España Cl. 30 No 44 D–71;
☎ (5) 662 5267/5311/5514; f (5) 662 5388

ALTERNATIVE MEDICINE *information not from Bradt medical advisers*

NATURAL HEALTH Using medicinal plants in the everyday treatment of illnesses is common practice in rural Colombia. Medicinal herbs are widely available at public markets, many cultivated for centuries by Colombia's many indigenous tribes. Rural communities seek treatment from healers or shamans (also called *sinchis*, *curacas*, *payés* and *taitas*) and each ethnic group has its own medicinal knowledge and beliefs. There are numerous shamans in Colombia, despite the use of traditional medicines being discouraged by law. Because of the prevalence of ancient remedies in Colombian society there have been moves to incorporate some elements into modern primary healthcare. However, at the time of writing using medicinal plants in curative treatment isn't common amongst Colombia's health professionals, although more are fusing complementary therapies into mainstream medical care. In Yurayaco, Caquetá, in the foothills of the Amazon, the Ingano people have been particularly active in campaigning for their rights as indigenous healers. They consider *yage* (a potent drink, see page 235), medicinal plants and curative wisdom to be gifts from God, awarded for the benefit of the health of humanity. The Ingano have also been instrumental in promoting the benefits of traditional healing and sacred plants to Colombia's non-indigenous population, forming a coalition of Indian tribes in 1999 to protect the rights of shaman.

COMPLEMENTARY MEDICINE Practitioners of non-native holistic and complementary medicine are common in Colombia's main cities where traditional Chinese practitioners, acupuncturists and reflexologists can be easily found. Homeopathy in Colombia dates back to 1837. Although the Instituto Homeopatico de Colombia wasn't founded until 1865 there were a staggering 107 homeopathic doctors listed by 1931. The Instituto still exists, although it has no regulatory powers. However most of Colombia's homeopaths train through the institute's academy with all coming from allopathic practice. Today, in Bogotá, almost 100 homeopaths are listed in the city's *Yellow Pages*. Officially, only qualified doctors are allowed to practice homeopathy but in reality non-qualified practitioners are tolerated, especially if they are registered with the Asociación Medica Homeopatica de Colombia (ASMHOC). In 2007 there were over 40 homeopathic pharmacies in Bogotá, 10 in Medellín and at least 20 in Cali. Further information can be obtained from the following:

Instituto Homeopático de Colombia Carrera 18, No 86
A–14, Bogotá; ☎ (1) 638 6438;
e info@homeopatiacolombia.com;
www.homeopatiacolombia.com
Asociación de Terapeutas de Medicina Tradicional
Carrera 63, No 24–07, Bogotá; ☎ (1) 290 1006
Asociación Medica Homeopatica de Colombia Carrera
46, No 26–59, Bogotá; ☎ (1) 244 7156

Fundación Homeopatica de Colombia Carrera 6, No
45–29, Bogotá; ☎ (1) 285 3115
Fundación Colegio Nacional de Medicina Homeopatica
Carrera 4, No 58–58, Bogotá; ☎ (1) 249 0075
Escuela de Medicina Juan N Corpas
www.juanncorpas.edu.co

Although conflicting stories abound about safety in Colombia, the issue of travelling without incident in Colombia remains an important consideration. Those planning to criss-cross the country should do plenty of thorough research – whilst remaining mindful that Colombia thrives on urban myth and is prone to circulating safety information that is out of date. Colombia remains a place where there is danger, although the present security situation is much improved. Today, it offers the safest travel conditions for many decades and visitors who apply common sense should expect an incident-free stay. Take safety warnings extremely seriously and stay away from regions that are totally out of bounds. Several Red Zones remain under the control of warring factions, while some city slum areas are highly dangerous no-go zones where violence is rife.

On a positive note, Colombia is no longer the 'Most Dangerous Place on the Planet' according to international specialist iJet Intelligent Risk Systems. In its 'Dangerous Destinations 2007' list it awarded the Democratic Republic of Congo the highest risk rating, with Somalia, Iraq, Afghanistan, Côte d'Ivoire, Pakistan, Burundi, Liberia, Haiti, Sri Lanka, Chad and Lebanon next. Another misconception is that Colombia is the 'World's Murder Capital' but in fact Colombia ranks third highest in the world for homicide. In 2005, 18,111 murders were reported – a rate of 39 per 100,000 inhabitants – a figure below both South Africa and Jamaica. This is a dramatic fall from just five years ago when the homicide rate in Colombia was 61 per 100,000 people.

KIDNAPPING Although once the so-called 'Kidnap Capital of the World', Colombia now ranks fourth, below Iraq (where more than 20,000 people were kidnapped in 2006), Mexico (where a kidnap occurred every six hours on average in 2006) and Haiti (where around 160 abductions per month were reported in 2006). President Uribe's hardline stance has achieved a 78% drop in kidnappings since 2002. However, due to the continued struggles amongst FARC, right-wing paramilitary group (AUC), left-wing paramilitary (ELN) and the cocaine trade, Colombia still suffers from a high number of kidnappings – despite a fall of 63% in 2007 on the previous year. Kidnap figures in the first six months of 2007 were the lowest for more than a decade, according to the National Foundation for the Defense of Personal Liberty (FONDELIBERTDAD) while according to Amnesty International abductions fell from 800 in 2005 to 687 in 2006. Military and police intelligence indicates that up to 28 professional kidnapping gangs are operating in Colombia, according to the Overseas Security Advisory Council (OSAC). Reports suggest that FARC were responsible for 23.5% of cases, the ELN for 10% and common criminals for 27%. In a third of cases it was not possible to establish who the kidnappers were. At the time of writing, Bogotá has fewer reported kidnaps than Buenos Aires and Mexico City.

The British Foreign and Commonwealth Office (FCO) (*www.fco.gov.uk*) offers up to date information on which areas are dangerous and currently advises against all travel as follows: 'the departments of Putumayo, Arauca, Nariño (excluding Pasto), and Norte de Santander; to the towns of Buenaventura and San José del Guaviare and the areas surrounding them; and to the Parque Nacional de La Macarena in the department of Meta'. It also advises 'against all but essential travel to the rural areas of Cauca, Huila (including San Agustín and the Parque Arqueológico San Agustín), Caquetá, Guaviare, southern and western Valle de Cauca, southern Tolima, southern parts of Meta, Chocó, north western Antioquía, north-eastern Boyacá, Cordoba, Sucre, southern Bolívar and southern César departments. Sierra Nevada de Santa Marta (including Ciudad Perdida/Lost City)'.

To lower the risk of abduction, avoid all Red Zones and don't travel after dark in the countryside. Flying is the safest form of travel and would keep you well away from any remote rural guerrilla or paramilitary roadblocks. Take daytime buses whenever possible and only travel at night with a reputable company on safe routes. Never take a night bus on unpaved roads. Avoid unofficial tours and be wary of anyone who approaches you without good reason. In short, don't be over-trusting and keep your wits about you. Take heed of the popular Colombian saying *'no se puede dar papaya'* ('don't give papaya'), meaning don't let your guard down.

ROBBERY Robberies are probably no worse in Colombia than in any other Latin American country; however, there are basic precautions that every traveller should take – wherever they are.

For evenings out, shopping or day tours, allocate some money for the outing. Leave your passport behind with credit cards and travellers' cheques – preferably locked securely in the hotel safe. Don't take out anything other than what you'll need; just carry a photocopy of your passport as ID – a Colombian requirement.

Use a money belt and try not to carry bags and purses that are easy to grab hanging off your shoulder. Don't flaunt wealth, jewellery or Walkmans/MP3, camcorder or cameras. Put an extra note in your shoes, or somewhere discreet, so if the worst happens you can still get back to your hotel. Never walk around after dark on your own – male or female. Avoid difficult neighbourhoods (ask your hotel for the best routes before you leave) and only use licensed taxis. Be extremely careful in downtown areas at night, such as La Candelaria in Bogotá.

The US press has reported that drugging travellers has become a disturbing trend, although there have been few confirmed reports. A derivative of the drug scopolamine known as *burundanga* is thought to be administered via drinks or even cigarettes – it is colourless, odourless and tasteless and can easily be sprinkled onto food. Victims become so docile that they have been known to hand over belongings without batting an eyelid. Others awake in a state of grogginess having been robbed of all possessions. To avoid becoming an unsuspecting victim, don't accept anything from strangers – even a cookie or a cigarette. Travellers thinking of using prostitutes (male or female) should also remember that the drug can be put on parts of the body and be licked.

Drugs Whatever you hear about Colombian cocaine it is unwise to seek it out – most pushers are part of a dangerous underworld criminal element and you will be placed in immediate danger of robbery, contaminants, violence or worse. Drug-taking in Colombia is illegal and travellers caught in possession are likely to receive a prison sentence. To date, the only two foreigner arrests since 1997 in the tourist resort of Cartagena have been drug-related.

LANDMINES Despite widespread efforts to address the problem, landmines remain a threat to civilians and travellers in rural Colombia. According to the Colombian army and independent landmine monitors, the total number of landmines in Colombia was 130,000 in 2002. During 2005, Columbia's Landmine Observatory recorded 799 injuries or fatalities in 31 of Columbia's 32 states. The FCO offers the following advice, 'In 2005, more people were killed or injured in Colombia by landmines than in any other country in the world. When travelling in rural areas you should always follow local warnings about the presence of landmines.' Colombia signed the Mine Ban Treaty on 3 December 1997, ratified on 6 September 2000, and became a State Party on 1 March 2001. Of Colombia's departments, only one – the Caribbean Archipelago Department of San Andrés, Providencía and Santa Catalina – is not affected. The worst area, as of June 2006, was Antioquía, accounting for 22.6% of incidents registered since 1990, followed by Meta and Santander. Between 1990 to 1 June 2006 the Observatory recorded 8,439 landmine and (Explosive Remnants of War) ERW-related incidents in Colombia, including 1,236 people killed and 3,916 injured.

WOMEN TRAVELLERS Colombian women are highly politically active and appear extremely confident in social situations. However, machismo still plays a large role in Colombia and female travellers may feel less vulnerable in a group. Those travelling alone should be prepared for the occasional come-on, flirty comment and wolf-whistle from Colombian men – it is part of the culture and something that is best accepted with good grace. Expect it to happen wherever you are, be it a city or rural village – react without hostility but firmly ignore the attention. Avoid acting coy, shy or giggly as this may be misinterpreted as interest. Dressing in short skirts or revealing tops will only exacerbate the situation so stick to conservative clothing – even if the local girls are flaunting their bodies. Some travellers resort to wearing a wedding ring in order to put off male advances – it may work but will rarely stop a persistent suitor. Women that plan to party, or drink in bars should remember that dancing with men or accepting drinks may also be construed as interest. Avoid drinking to excess as this will make you vulnerable and when leaving a bar or party make sure you are in a group. Never accept a lift, or walk home, with someone you don't know, or have just met. In addition, if anyone you don't know approaches you on the street or on the beach, offering tours (or anything else) don't wait to hear his patter – walk away.

Safe Travel 4 Women (*www.safetravel4women.com*) offers information on female-friendly hotels, accessories, travel tours and tips on a web directory for discerning women travellers.

WHAT TO TAKE

All visitors arriving in Colombia by plane are blessed with the opportunity to make the most of Bogotá's plentiful shopping. Malls, retail zones and department stores can be found in abundance in a city where almost anything is available for cash. Need a pair of designer shoes for a night in the hottest club downtown? No problem – nor is finding tent pegs, pharmacy supplies and a Gortex jacket for that jungle trek. That supplies are so widely available is a real boon for travellers as it dispenses with the need for squeezing everything (plus the kitchen sink) into a backpack ahead of a trip. However, it is worth remembering that some essential items are likely to be more expensive in Colombia. Others may have limited availability year round.

The old travel adage 'pack half the clothes you think you need and at least twice the money' is pretty apt for Colombia. It is rarely cold, so unless you plan to ski in the Andes or camp in the Cerro Monserrate, it is worth keeping clothing pretty light.

Choose items that can cope with the climate, the terrain and activities such as watersports, trekking and hopping in and out of a boat around the islands. There are endless benefits of a single rucksack in Colombia, including avoiding charges for excess baggage on many of its domestic flights. Buses and taxis can also be pretty tight on space. A smaller pack also makes it more practical to keep your luggage with you at all times, rather than be forced to stash it out of sight in a boot.

JUNGLE EQUIPMENT Spending a significant amount of time in Colombia's jungle or remote rural areas will make the following items a worthy consideration:

- Strong boots with drainage holes
- Lightweight hiking boots
- 2 pairs of cotton-polypropylene/nylon socks
- 2 pairs of wool-blend socks
- A pair of washable pumps
- Waterproof air-inflated sleeping mattress
- Plenty of mosquito repellent (pump-spray and lotion, 50% DEET minimum)
- Waterproof poncho/jacket
- Lightweight trousers (specialist quick-dry ventilated make, eg: Rohan)
- Lightweight shorts (specialist quick-dry ventilated make, eg: Rohan)
- Quick-dry blanket (specialist make, eg: Rohan), thick for highland/light for lowland

CLOTHING Colombia's altitude plays a crucial part in planning what clothes to pack. Some of its coolest parts are found in the Nevado del Ruiz Natural Park where the air is crisp, cool and can chill at times. On its upper slopes it is common to find snow year-round, while even on the Pacific coast the Baudó Mountains are often shrouded in cloud cover and damp mists. Visitors that plan to climb or camp in the peaks of Iguaque National Park should be sure to pack a fleece jacket, waterproofs and warm clothing. At Cordillera Oriental the peaks are renowned for unpredictable, cold temperatures and hypothermia is a real risk to climbers who tackle them unprepared. Even in Bogotá some silk micro-knit underwear can prove invaluable on a chilly day. However, broadly speaking most travellers should get by on a pair of jeans, a couple of pairs of shorts, two or three T-shirts, a hat, swimming gear, a long-sleeved shirt and trousers, and a lightweight waterproof jacket. Rubber-soled shoes are great for hopping on and off boats. Some hiking boots are essential for Colombia's tougher treks with a pair of trainers for walking ideal in bigger cities.

CAMPING EQUIPMENT Pack a sleeping bag designed for tropical conditions, a sheet or sarong and a lightweight hammock. High-altitude camping will necessitate blankets and a heavy-duty sleeping bag. A lightweight tent with plenty of ventilation and a separate rain fly is ideal for Colombia. A length of strong nylon cord makes an invaluable clothesline with other essential items a nest of aluminium cooking pots, a lighter and a box of waterproof matches, a small multi-fuel stove, compass, a first-aid kit, torch, sunscreen, insect repellent, spare batteries, 3-in-1 camping utensils, bottled water, toilet paper, a small container of soap and a scouring pad.

MISCELLANEOUS It is essential to have photo ID at hand wherever you travel in Colombia and for a wide variety of practical reasons it may not be wise to solely rely on your passport for this. Pack a driving licence (if it has a photograph) or anything else that clearly identifies you. This will not only help your passport stay in good nick for longer it will also make it less likely to go astray at yet another of Colombia's many checkpoints. Outside of the major cities, a torch is essential as most streets are unlit and electricity can cease as early as 21.00. Pack a spare stock of batteries, sunglasses, a candle and a box of good-quality waterproof matches as well as a tiny MW/FM radio to make the most of Colombia's several hundred great local music channels. Spare camera film and memory cards, a handful of safety pins, a travel sewing kit, spare plastic carrier bag and cotton buds (great for all manner of things) are also useful. Bring a spare pair of contact lenses or glasses (and a spare prescription), a travel plug (Colombia uses the US-style 2-pin 110v, 60AC) and a healthy supply of plasters. A Spanish phrase book is essential outside of the major cities and English-language reading material is also thin on the ground countrywide. Women will also discover that tampons are harder to find than press-on towels in Colombia so squeezing a decent supply in your backpack is more than worthwhile.

$ MONEY

Carrying anything other than small amounts of cash is not recommended in Colombia, so most travellers rely on an ATM machine for daily needs and settle everything else on a credit or debit card. Colombia's national currency is the peso, which is expressed as COP or a $ but shouldn't be confused with the US$. It comprises 50, 100, 200, 500 and 1000 coins with paper notes in denominations of 1,000, 2,000, 5,000, 10,000, 20,000 and 50,000 pesos. Although US dollars aren't widely accepted they can come in useful as they offer the best rate of exchange with the peso, unlike the British pound or the euro. However, a large number of homemade counterfeit US dollars circulate in Colombia. In fact, more than 25% of the fake notes on the planet are thought to have originated from counterfeiters in Cali. These are often US$20 bills and are so good they are indistinguishable from the genuine article, so it is advisable not to purchase these from a money changer on the street. Fake 1,000 peso coins also exist, so these are best to avoid and they are often difficult to offload. Fast, safe money-changing services are offered by Colombia's *casas de cambio* – authorised bureaux located in most big towns and major cities. Business hours vary, but expect to find them open from early until 18.00 Monday to Friday. Most close at noon on a Saturday. Rates may be lower than the banks but changing cash is quick and easy, taking less than ten minutes for a US dollar-to-peso transaction. Numerous companies operate as casas de cambio and rates and services vary – so for the very best deal to stretch a budget further it really does pay to shop around.

Credit cards (especially Visa and MasterCard) are welcomed pretty much everywhere in Colombia, from the side-street stationery stores in Bogotá to almost every hotel across the country. Most visitors make their first withdrawal on arrival at Bogotá Airport, to cover transfer costs, bellboy tips and that all-important first night *cerveza*. ATMs are found in plentiful supply in major towns and cities, although care should be taken when withdrawing cash from machines right on the street. Opt for an ATM in a mall, hotel lobby or city supermarket to be on the safe side – and much like any place on earth be sure not to wave the cash around. Both banks and ATMs can be used for credit card cash transfers. However, to prevent any hiccups it pays to notify the bank in writing well ahead of boarding the plane – as sorting out a frozen account from Colombian soil can be highly problematic.

Some banks change currency and travellers' cheques, but many don't – and this can vary from branch to branch of the same institution. Travellers' cheques are changed at up to 5% lower than the official rate with cash exchanged at up to 3% less. Be sure to take along your passport and muster up as much patience as possible, as even the simplest transaction involves dozens of forms in triplicate and can easily take up to an hour. Banking times also differ but are generally Monday–Thursday 08.00–11.30 and 14.00–16.00, and Friday 08.00–11.30 and 14.00–16.30. The exception is the banks in Bogotá which close an hour earlier each day. Many of Colombia's banks only provide currency exchange services for a limited period each morning, so it pays to get there early – especially as every branch in the country closes at 12 noon on the last working day of the month.

BUDGETING

KEEPING COSTS DOWN Those with a meagre purse will discover that Colombia isn't a dirt-cheap option for travellers. However, food costs are minimal – unless

SOME AVERAGE PRICES

	COP	US$	£
Three-course meal (in restaurant)	20,833.33	10.43	5.26
Fast-food meal	12,000.00	6.01	3.03
Cup of coffee (in café)	1,333.33	0.67	0.34
Beer (in bar)	3,500.00	1.75	0.88
Car hire (up to 1,800cc) per day	120,000.00	60.09	30.30
Private doctor GP (30 minutes)	65,000.00	32.55	16.41
Milk Iltr	1,666.67	0.83	0.42
Butter 500g	3,020.00	1.51	0.76
Cheese 500g	6,733.33	3.37	1.70
Bread (white loaf)	3,143.33	1.57	0.79
Sugar (white) 1kg	1,346.67	0.67	0.34
Cornflakes (packet) 375g	6,166.67	3.09	1.56
Coffee (instant) 125g	5,120.00	2.56	1.29
Tea bags (pack 25)	3,166.67	1.59	0.80
Coca-Cola Iltr	1,500.00	0.75	0.38
Mineral water (still) Iltr	1,273.33	0.64	0.32
Mineral water (sparkling) Iltr	1,500.00	0.75	0.38
Orange juice Iltr	2,696.67	1.35	0.68
Beer (local, can) 0.33ltr	1,300.00	0.65	0.33
Beer (imported, can) 0.33ltr	3,890.00	1.95	0.98
Table wine 0.75ltr	10,000.00	5.01	2.52
Scotch whisky 0.75ltr	61,000.00	30.55	15.40
Cigarettes (20 pack, imported)	3,666.67	1.84	0.93

you simply can't survive without dining on top-notch à la carte each day. This is especially true in the major cities, where an excellent array of low-priced tasty food represents great value for those on a shoestring. Expect to pay 8,000 pesos for an excellent bowl of ceviche, 3,500 COP for a beer and 1,400 for a café con leche. Finding somewhere low-cost to stay isn't difficult, but many of the budget joints throw up the issue of safety so are often best avoided. Although backpacker hostels have rooms for less than 20,000 COP per night many international backpackers opt for a more comfy mid-range hotel. Allow 120,000 for a double room in Bogotá and 100,000 in Cali, while an all-inclusive stay at a beach resort in Cartagena will set you back 600,000 for three nights.

Travel Colombia relies on a mix of ground transportation, internal flights and boats out to the islands. Overland travel is often impacted by Colombia's latest security concerns of the moment, so visitors should check this out thoroughly before booking anything from Bogotá to the country. Another factor to consider when planning how to get from A to B is Colombia's sheer size, especially if spending 20 hours on a crowded bus with poor suspension is your idea of hell. On the plus side, the nation's bus companies are famously aggressive when it comes to price wars, so fares are often negotiable for those with the patience (and Spanish) to haggle. Expect to pay 1,200 COP for a cross-city *buseta* trip in Bogotá and around 50,000 COP for a ten-hour overland slog to Medellín. A more comfortable option is to hire a driver and car at about 150,000 COP a day – an appealing transfer option for groups of four when faced with any measure of personal safety risk. Domestic airfares also needn't bust the budget if purchased well in advance. In Bogotá, navigating the city's 300km of pristine cycle paths makes an excellent alternative to doing battle with the traffic. Another way to stretch the budget further is to visit museums on the 'free day' – usually the last Sunday in the month. Students should also wave their student ID at every opportunity as this often produces a discount when booking air, cinema and gallery tickets.

NO NEED TO BUDGET Colombia boasts many of the finest gastronomic haunts in Latin America with 5-star French bistros, stylish chi-chi cafes and award-winning Pan-Asian fusion cuisine. Foodies keen to join Colombia's elite nouveau riche will find plenty of high-class dining hangouts complete with menus where the prices aren't listed and where fine wines start at 15,000 COP a glass.

The best hotels in Colombia tend to be concentrated around the major cities, although some of the all-inclusive resorts on the Caribbean coastline pander to a luxury clientele. Expect to pay 300,000 COP for a 5-star suite in Bogotá and 280,000 COP in Medellín, while a night in one of Cartagena's most chic boutique hotels costs from 600,000 COP per person.

Exploring Colombia with little regard for budgetary constraints allows for cross-country journeys by private plane. Book direct with the airline or even better engage a reputable tour operator, who will almost certainly organise a ground transfer in an air-conditioned car as part of the charter package. Private jets, helicopters, chartered yachts and chauffeured limousines are some of Colombia's more upscale modes of travel – expect to pay US$5,000 for executive cross-country flights and US$350–500 per hour for helicopter charter.

GETTING AROUND

BY RAIL/METRO Colombia has over 3,000km of working railroad. However, as yet there are no real services for passengers available. The city of Medellín operates the country's only metro system. It's connected to an aerial cable car that transports passengers from Acevedo station to the hilltop district of Santo Domingo Savio. Over 90 cars offer a service every 12 seconds between four stations.

BY BOAT There are an estimated 18,000km of waterways in the country. Both the Río Magdalena (Magdalena River) that intersects the country to the north of Bogotá and the Río Cauca (Cauca River) are navigable in parts (some 1,500km). However, you should thoroughly research any such project first. Wide rivers and jungle canals sound intriguing, but they can lead you to some extremely remote destinations, which could be dangerous in the light of the current guerrilla and paramilitary situation. Jungle canals around Leticia provide a safer option, and tour operators can supply advice.

There are a number of ports on both the Caribbean and Pacific. The main ones are Buenaventura, Tumaco, Santa Marta, Barranquilla, Cartagena, Muelles El Bosque, Puerto Bolívar, Santa Marta and Turbo. Those planning to visit Isla Gorgona in the Pacific will need to go by boat – see *Chapter 10*, page 347.

BY BUS Flying is the safest form of travel in Colombia. However, if you want to bus it, there's a good service that will take you around the country (excluding the Amazon) and on to other parts of Latin America. Each city has a central bus station – *terminal de pasajeros* – although some are located out of town a short taxi or local bus journey away. Unless you are travelling during a public holiday bookings aren't essential and it is easy to purchase tickets on arrival at the terminal. It is advisable to take daytime buses wherever possible with travelling by night bus on unpaved roads best avoided.

For those travelling relatively short distances, *corriente* or *sencillo* are cheap buses that cover a vast network of villages and towns. These basic rust-buckets, like local town buses, tend to pick up passengers that flag them down on the roadside. They can be cramped and crowded so be prepared for a tight squeeze. Pullmans travel in roughly the same area but are much more respectable and offer a smoother ride.

Buses that serve long-distance routes tend to be much more comfortable and usually have air conditioning, toilets and movies (most of which are in Spanish). These *ejecutivos* are professionally run by private firms from major bus terminals. They may travel longer distances at night and often stop a couple of times *en route* at roadside cafés. Travellers planning long-distance bus journeys should pack plenty of books, music and snacks. Air-conditioned buses can also get chilly so some warm clothes are advisable. Bogotá to Cali takes 20 hours (US$45); Bogotá to Bucaramanga takes ten hours (US$25); Bogotá to Medellín takes nine hours (US$20); Medellín to Cali takes nine hours (US$16); Medellín to Cartagena takes 14 hours (US$40); Cali to Bogotá takes 12 hours (US$24) and Cartagena to Santa Marta takes three hours (US$5). Be certain to pre-book bus travel during public holidays, such as Christmas, Easter or regional holidays, like Carnaval Barranquilla, when crowded bus terminals and vehicles make reservations essential to guarantee a seat.

Urban buses All Colombia's main cities have a good bus network so getting around cheaply (no journey should cost more than 1,000 COP) isn't hard. A variety of buses suit all tastes, from the rowdy *busetas* to the very respectable TransMilenio in Bogotá. One set price applies to each journey, no matter how far you are going, although it can vary depending on the style of bus. Official bus stops – or *paradas* – are not abundant outside of the major cities so those that want to board simply stick their arms out and wave their hands – a system that works well and should be seen as a bonus, as there is rarely the need to run for a bus.

Busetas are the cheapest and liveliest mode of public transport but are not for the faint-hearted, especially if you don't like scary cruising speeds or deafening salsa music. Many areas use ex-American school buses, sometimes deemed unroadworthy in the US. They honk and growl as they career around the city spewing out fumes and rattling alarmingly. Lots have been lovingly decorated by their drivers in a rainbow of spray-can colours, motifs and slogans. Pay the driver on entry and try to find a seat to avoid being swung about on corners. Getting off is as haphazard as getting on; you'll need to let the driver, or conductor, know where you want to stop, or call out '*por aqui, por favor*' (please stop here) above the din.

Colectivos are small buses, or large people-carriers, that operate in both small towns and major cities. They provide a comfier ride than regular buses, although they are slightly more expensive. The better, newer ones can be quite plush with soft padded seats and air conditioning, especially on the most popular routes and longer trips from town to town. Although colectivos may have roughly scheduled times (hourly or every half hour for example) most will only depart once full.

TransMilenio, Bogotá The Bus Rapid Transit system was introduced in Bogotá in 2001, and has contributed to Colombia's renown as an internationally leading model for sustainable urban design. The system was put in place after plans for a metro system were abandoned and now works like an overland metro system. The TransMilenio buses that operate on the system run on exclusive bus lanes. Buses will take up to 160 passengers, although only 42 can be seated. Buses can also get very crowded during rush hour periods. However, they are clean and comfortable and there's just one price for all routes of 1,200 COP. Included in the price is a transfer onto *alimentadores* – buses that go further out of the city than the TransMilenio currently can. Main TransMilenio stations (*cabeceras*) are called *portales* and located at the beginning and end of each route. In between, *intermedias*

2

Colombia's railway system got off to a promising start in the early 1900's, guided by Europe's most skilful engineers. Projects were lavished with generous amounts of funding with components shipped in from the developed world. John Charles Gibney, an Englishman, was awarded the Government contract to connect Bogotá with the coast. Building a railroad wasn't easy on Colombia's challenging mix of terrains and the work was hard and slow-going. Progress was hindered by disease and heavy downpours, often in stifling heat.

However, once completed, the long-awaited railroad received rough treatment. Poor investment sent them into disrepair while warring guerrilla and paramilitary factions took turns to blow stretches to smithereens. As a result, Colombia's railways were already in steady decline by the late 1960s. Today, the ageing, decrepit tracks that still remain are few and far between – and testament to transportation from a bygone age. Apart from Medellín's state-of-the-art new metro system, Colombia has no passenger-carrying railway system. Of 3,380 kilometres of track just 1,746 kilometres are in use, most of which is narrow gauge. Shuttle trains connect Colombia's main coal mines to the country's maritime port, Puerto Bolívar. A rolling stock of 30 battered engines form part of a fleet of around 1,500 obsolete passenger and freight wagons.

In 2008, Colombia's National Development Plan included plans to centralize the country's railway system with the construction of railroads for both touristic and cargo-carrying use. Priority has been awarded to the departments of Magdalena, in the north coast of Colombia, and Cauca in the central-pacific region of Colombia, where goods and mined minerals require shipment.

Today, a sightseeing steam train connects Bogotá with savannah districts north of the capital on Saturday, Sundays and public holidays, at a cost of 27,000 COP per person (children 17,000 COP). Contact Turistren Ltda, Estación de la Sabana, Calle 13 No. 18-24, Bogotá on ☎ (57) (1) 3750557 & (57) (1) 3750558 & (57) (1) 3750559, www.turistren.com.co

Similarly, the Tren Turistico Café y Azuca offers steam train journeys to day-trippers from Cali to Buga, La Tebaida and Cumbre while a rum-fuelled "rumbero" option offers a party trip from 20.00 to 03.00 at weekends. Pick up a time-table from the Central Station in Cali or contact the reservations office at Avenida Vásquez Cobo No. 23N – 47, Piso 2, ☎ 666 6899 & 620 2324, e trenturistico@ert.com.co, web: www.trenturisticocafeyazucar.com.

stops serve major intersections and simple stops *(sencillas)* around each 500m. At the time of writing a number of cities are planning their own Bogotá-style mass-transportation systems, including Cartagena, Barranquilla and Cali.

BY CAR Driving a car in Colombia is not recommended. It can be risky, especially if the vehicle carries foreign licence plates, as it could attract attention from guerrillas or paramilitaries. Road quality also varies dramatically across the country and many routes also remain unsafe. Travelling by air is considered far safer but those that decide to drive should be sure to avoid Red Zones – a prime consideration on a major road trip. Colombians drive on the right and all passengers are required to wear a seat belt. Police or military roadblocks are common and stopping is mandatory. Other than this, don't stop for anyone on the road, no matter how innocent the situation looks.

Aside from the large chunk of land that forms the southeast country, the road network is relatively good. However, the landscape is rough and uneven and in

Colombia's most humid areas paving doesn't last long. Pot-holes can develop over relatively short periods of time and there are still many unpaved roads to contend with – a real challenge, even in a 4x4. The main driving roads in the country are the Pan-American Highway that runs from Cartagena to Bogotá and the Simón Bolívar Highway that connects Bogotá with Caracas, Venezuela, and Quito, Ecuador.

Driving can be extremely stressful in Colombia's main cities where roads are highly congested. More than one million cars use Bogotá's city centre alone and drivers can be reckless and quick to cut you up. Travellers that do decide to take to the wheel should find the right balance between assertion (not hesitating) and alert quick-thinking. Keep doors locked at all times, especially at traffic lights or intersections, and avoid driving after dark.

Drivers heading from Central to South America are faced with a decision – to import their car by sea or air around the impenetrable Darién Gap (between Panama and Colombia) or to simply buy another vehicle in Colombia. Paperwork and transport to bring in a car can be extremely costly, although there are companies that are prepared to entertain haggling. Colón to Cartagena is the main Panama to Colombia route; check www.shipmyvehicle.com for professional advice.

Rental cars Hiring a car offers drivers a Colombian licence plate but is still a potentially risky transport choice. It can also be a burden of responsibility in congested cities with few safe places to park. However, hiring a car in Colombia is relatively easy and there are a variety of reputable companies to choose from. Rates can be high however and it is also important to check the fine print regarding insurance clauses – if necessary pay the extra for complete insurance security. Travellers staying in the main cities or visiting popular destinations will probably find it works out much cheaper to fly or take the bus. Taxis can also often be booked by the hour, or per day – another alternative option.

You'll find a list of car rental offices in Bogotá at www.Bogotáturismo.gov.co/directorios/alquiler_vehiculos and www.Bogotá-dc.com/dir/cars.html. It is best to go for a well-known company such as Hertz (main office: *Cra.14 No 27–21, Bogotá; www.hertz.com*) or Budget, which has an office at Bogotá airport (*www.budget.com*). You'll need a valid driving licence and a credit card with suitable funds to cover an insurance deposit (can be up to US$1,000).

Driving rules In Bogotá there are rigorous laws regarding when and where you can drive a car. Driving is forbidden on Sunday in the city centre and parking in public places is restricted. In addition, the *Pico y Placa* law, introduced to reduce traffic congestion, means you can only drive your vehicle on certain days of the week. Days are arranged according to the letters on your vehicle licence plate, but the schedule changes periodically. To be certain, check with your car rental company for details or visit www.Bogotá-dc.com/trans/bog-tra.htm.

BY TAXI Most travellers arrive at Bogotá and take a taxi into the city centre. Look for the signs pointing to the taxi rank outside of the airport building – a small official taxi booth will point you in the right direction. A taxi official will issue a slip of paper confirming the price, which you then take to one of the taxis waiting.

SEEING THE LIGHT

Green traffic lights differ in colour across Colombia. Shades in the cities are markedly brighter (emerald green) than those in towns and villages (green-tinged yellow). Why – who knows?

This constitutes an order and sets the price as per the piece of paper. Should the driver ask for more, don't buy it – a common ruse is to claim that it is just a base price and that some sort of premium or surcharge applies. This is nonsense, as any surcharge would be clearly stated on the price slip.

Elsewhere, taxis are easy to find, day and night in every main city. They are also cheap even though there is a tendency by some drivers to hike up prices for tourists. Agree on a price before entering the car or insist the driver uses the meter – in Bogotá, a taxi's meter fare is priced in units per 100m at 0.55 COP. An average rate per kilometre is 750 COP, although charges to and from airports tend to be higher. In rural areas taxis with meters are non-existent so ask around town for the usual rate – and be prepared to negotiate with the driver.

Don't get into a taxi if there is anyone else in the car. Also, don't be tempted to hail a taxi off the street – get your hotel or restaurant to call one to order. Avoid taxis that appear to be unlicensed – check the front window or dashboard for an official badge.

BY BIKE Cycling the length of Latin America is becoming more popular and cyclists are no longer giving Colombia a wide berth. Crossing the country on two wheels is fast-becoming a real phenomenon fuelled, in part, by the Colombian passion for cycling as a national pastime. Bogotá now boasts a 300km network of *ciclo-rutas* (bicycle routes), the largest in Latin America, constructed under the instruction of the ex-Mayor of Bogotá, Enrique Peñalosa. The mayor also restricted car parking in public spaces and introduced the Ciclovia policy – an initiative that banned cars from the inner 120km of the city centre on Sundays and holidays. This has allowed Bogotá's 7.5 million population to cycle, jog, walk or rollerblade as they please. Bogotá now has one of the world's longest pedestrian-only streets at 17km and over 5% of the city's population cycle on a regular basis.

Peñalosa has been awarded the Stockholm Challenge Prize for his efforts – quite an achievement given Latin America's reputation for over-polluted cities. But even outside the city cycling is a highly popular pastime and visiting cyclists will find that they are well respected on the roads. The trip along the Pan-American Highway from Cartagena to the Ecuador border offers spectacular views and it is also possible to ride along the Caribbean coast to Venezuela. Cycling is also popular in the Llanos Orientales region and Boyacá – although not all roads in the country are safe for cyclists and safety precautions (combined with thorough research) should be undertaken before a trip. Seek professional advice on the roads from a specialist tour operator (see Eco Turs, page 61) – it may pay you to hire a cycling guide to help plan the journey. Vehemently stick to your route, stay on the road and don't be tempted to stray into unknown areas that may be dangerous. Never cycle after dark and allow plenty of time to hit a town before daylight dwindles.

Bogotá has some excellent cycle shops that sell repair kits and helmets – items that may be impossible to find in provincial areas.

✈ **BY AIR** Flying is by far the safest, easiest and most convenient way of getting around the country, with around 984 airports (although only around 100 have paved runways). Most domestic flights take less than 60 minutes' flying time. Some offer business class and economy tickets and serve a snack and a drink.

Avianca, Latin America's first airline (est 1919; ℩ *1 404 7862; www.avianca.com*), Aires (℩ *1 336 6039; www.aires.com.co*), AeroRepublica (℩ *1 320 9090; www.aerorepublica.com*) and Satena (℩ *1 281 7071; www.satena.com*) are some of the large domestic carriers, although there are others (for a comprehensive list of Colombian airlines visit *www.comunidadandina.org/INGLES/tourism/colombia/how.htm*).

The following towns are served at the time of writing, although routes are prone to change: Armenia (from Bogotá), Barrancabermeja (from Bogotá), Barranquilla (from Bogotá and Medellín), Bucaramanga (from Bogotá), Cali (from Bogotá, Medellín, Cartagena, San Andrés, Pasto and Tumaco), Cartagena (from Bogotá, Medellín, Pereira and Cali), Cúcuta (from Bogotá), Ibagué (from Bogotá), Manizales (from Bogotá), Medellín (from Bogotá, Cali, Cartagena, Barranquilla and Santa Marta), Montería (from Bogotá), Neiva (from Bogotá), Pasto (from Bogotá and Cali), Pereira (from Bogotá, Cartagena and Barranquilla), Riohacha (from Bogotá), San Andrés Island (from Bogotá and Cali), Santa Marta (from Bogotá and Medellín), Tumaco (from Cali), Valledupar (from Bogotá).

Flights can be reserved and tickets paid for with some carriers online or by telephone. Another option is to book with a tour operator (see *Tour operators*, page 60). Always book in advance where possible as seats are usually in demand. Return journeys should be re-confirmed, especially when departing San Andrés. Some areas of Colombia are served by small turbo planes that seat between 35–56 passengers – a bumpier ride than on a regular aircraft but often with better views.

🏠 **ACCOMMODATION**

Colombia's hotels range from simple, sparse, cut-price rooms to grand, city, no-expense hotels. Backpackers will find plenty of cheap options in the most touristy areas of the country with plenty of hotels in the major towns, resorts and cities to suit most budgets and tastes. However, most visitors to Colombia balance their personal preference with a need for good security, and this is generally the key deciding factor when it comes to finding a decent place to stay. Costs vary, but expect to pay around 28,000 COP for a double room in a budget hotel, less in many backpacker hostels. Mid-range options generally range from 32,000–60,000 COP with anything costing more categorised as high end.

CAMPING A growing number of camp sites are springing up across the country – although most Colombian's fail to appreciate why anyone sane would want to sleep under canvas outdoors. The sites that do exist usually offer basic washroom facilities but little else, although some are based within the gardens of small hotels or private homes where meals can be purchased. Although it is more than possible to camp almost anywhere other than Colombia's designated campsites, on the basis of safety very few people do. Those that decide to try it should seek permission from neighbouring *campesinos* to benefit from a few basic facilities and a watchful eye. Expect to pay 5,000–8,000 COP per night.

BUDGET Colombians use a variety of terms for accommodation, including *pensión*, hosteria, hotel and *residencia*, although in many areas of the country there are very few obvious distinctions in standards or price. Location is a giveaway when it comes to finding something dirt cheap, as most budget options are found in the noisiest part of town. Expect a basic room without a private bathroom, although it will probably be fitted with a ceiling fan but almost certainly without air conditioning. This type of shoestring accommodation often comes without hot water in the hottest parts of Colombia, but it's a necessity in the hostels in cooler Bogotá. A sheet, blanket and towel often come as part of the deal. Some also provide door locks for added security and may offer a deposit system for guarding belongings against theft. Prices vary, but range from 8,000–20,000 COP for a single and 16,000–28,000 COP for a double. Bogotá also has Colombia's only youth hostel, a member of the International Youth Hostel Association. Accommodation starts at around 8,000 COP per person, but these are rock-bottom prices, and like all budget options this will almost certainly need to be paid in cash – and settled upfront.

MID-RANGE Typically, Colombia's mid-range hotels are centred on or around the Plaza de Bolívar making it ideal for visitors keen to explore on foot. Though these functional buildings tend to be soulless affairs without any real creature comforts, they benefit from the buzz of being in the thick of it, with bars, restaurants and attractions within easy reach. Facilities include private bathrooms and rooms are generally equipped with a fan or air conditioning. However, standards in this mid-range bracket vary enormously. Some entrepreneurial owners charge astronomical prices for a room that's one step up from a cupboard. Others offer extraordinary value with prices at just 60,000 COP for plenty of space and striking city views.

HIGH END Those looking for a range of facilities that often include restaurants, bars, internet, room service, cable television, concierge services and 24-hour security will find plenty of upscale hotels in Colombia that fit the bill. Unlike many mid-range options, rooms tend to be fitted with a safe, a phone and industrial-standard door locks. There is also a good likelihood that the hotel will offer luggage storage, a round-the-clock reception desk and safety deposit boxes. However, prices aren't always a good indication of quality – and before forking out upwards of 90,000 COP it is advisable to ask to see a room. Check the area out too, as not all 5-star options are blessed with the nicest of locations, especially in Bogotá where traffic noise can be a issue.

✖ EATING AND DRINKING

In the last decade Colombia has experienced a gastronomic explosion, attracting world-class chefs to its thousands of restaurants to create a culinary scene that is one of Latin America's best-kept secrets. **(See inside front cover for restaurant price bands.)** Much of this modern gastronomic ID is found in Bogotá's uber-cosmopolitan restaurant districts, where Colombian Creole classics and champagne and oyster bars rub shoulders with pan-Asian fusion diners and stylish French brasseries. Yet, Colombia's sophisticated international culinary triumphs aren't just confined to the swish bistros of the capital city. Mini-gastronomic circles are springing up in cities such as Cali and Medellín and the resort areas in Cartagena, creating an exciting alternative to Colombia's traditional culinary staples. Yet, fear not – typical Colombian fare (*comida criolla*) remains very much in evidence on every street corner, from the sidewalk vendors selling paper-wrapped tamales to the hearty plates of chicken, rice, fried plantains and red beans served as *comida corriente* (set meal) in cantinas nationwide.

Expect to find plenty of variations in *comida criolla* during a journey across Colombia, each with its own distinct twist. On the Caribbean coastline the focus is seafood, especially lobster, while in the Andes a guinea pig dish is a regional delicacy. In Bogotá, *ajiaco* (a stew of chicken and potatoes) promises to keep city-dwellers warm during seasonal frosts, while generous helpings of *sancocho* soup are

QUENCHING A THIRST IN COLOMBIA

At the heart of every Latin American nation is a beer of the people. In Colombia, they have five. Much of Colombia's beer tradition revolves around the Cervecería Bavaria (Bavaria Brewery) (*Calle 94, 7–47, Bogotá;* \ *l 638 9000;* e *servicioalcliente@grupobavaria.com; www.bavaria.com.co*), a Colombian brewing institution founded in 1889 by German immigrant Leo S Kopp. Today 'Bavaria' is a byword for thirst-quenching *cerveza* nectar, thanks to its best-selling *cerveza* that Colombians hold so dear. To many people Aguila (A-gee-la) (*www.cervezaaguila.com*), the country's top-selling beer, is Colombia, such is its distinctive oh-so Colombian taste. Drive along any highway and you're sure to see the perfect, rounded butt-cheeks of Aguila's bikini-clad chicas on the billboards. It's also the beer of choice at thousands of events, festivals and parties countrywide. Aguila is perfect in Colombia's tropical regions as it's a crisp, clear pilsner with a sweet, mild taste. Served with lemon it's a refreshing way to ingest an alcohol content of 4% – as is its brother beer, Aguila Light. Brava, is much more of a macho sup, made for those who enjoy a beefy beer with an intense taste and high alcohol content. This deep, lager beer is 6.5% alcohol. It's another pilsner variety but is characterised by a hoppy flavour and a slightly bitter residual content. Few would deny that Club Colombia (*www.cervezaclubcolombia.com*) is the country's premier lager, Colombia's so-called perfect beer, which is extra dry and carefully crafted as a classy brand with an alcohol content of 4.7%. Costeña (*www.cervezacostena.com*) is geared towards Colombia's youth market and has been skilfully targeted at university students aged 18–25. This medium-bodied, golden pilsner is Bavaria's third-largest seller nationally. It contains 4% alcohol, so is perfect for those big nights out before a thesis beckons. In rural Colombia, Leona is the second-largest-selling lager. People describe it as the drink that's ideal for people who don't need an excuse to enjoy a beer. Antioquians favour Pilsen, a brewing tradition since 1909. The locals defy anyone not to want to sink a second bottle of this clear, gold festive beer. OK, Póker may sound like a dumb name for a drink, but this smooth beer is a big hit with Paisas in Colombia's southwest. Beer is viewed as the right of every Colombiano/a – and is priced accordingly. Even in a hotel minibar it'll rarely cost more than 48p for a 330ml bottle, to ensure no sector of Colombian society is excluded from a decent swig.

Colombia's rich regional culinary diversity may not be immediately obvious from a menu, as many dishes are found nationwide. However, ingredients and seasoning differ greatly from village to village and city to city. The result is a national gastronomic tradition that offers a vast array of recipes and flavours. Order a bowl of *sancocho* in Cali and it will taste wholly different to that in Cabo de la Vela while the Caribbean-style La fritanga bears little resemblance to that on the Pacific coast.

CUNDINAMARCA

El ajiaco Chicken soup with three varieties of potatoes (sabanera, criolla, pastusa) and *hojas de guascas* (wild leaves) served with corn, cream and avocado.

El piquete de la Sabana A variety of meats with fried or broiled giblets served with yellow potatoes, fried green slices of bananas and corn.

El puchero Soup of manioc, green bananas, *arracacha* (mountain tubercul) and pork, beef and chicken meat is served with '*el aji*' (hot sauce), boiled egg and avocado pulp.

La mazamorra Cooked corn mixed with milk and water.

El cuchuco con espinazo Wheat soup thickened with vegetables and pork loin.

ANTIOQUIA

Los frijoles con garra Red beans thickened with fried pigs' trotters.

La bandeja paisa A hearty plate of red beans, chopped meat, spicy sausages, rice, fried egg, avocado and slices of fried sweet bananas.

Los chicharrones Fried, crispy pork rind.

La mazamorra White corn cooked plain and natural.

Los buñuelos A corn puff with cheese and egg.

La natilla A thick pudding of sweet maize.

Las arepas Colombia's omnipresent corn pancake.

CARIBBEAN COAST

Las arepas con huevo A corn pancake topped with a fried egg.

El sancocho A soup of boiled meat with manioc, yam and sweet banana.

El bollo limpio Mashed young corn in a corn leaf wrap.

El bollo de yucca Mashed manioc in a corn leaf wrap.

Los patacones Fried mashed green plantain.

La cazuela de mariscos A delicious seafood soup.

La fritanga Fried meat and giblets.

PACIFIC COAST

El sancocho A soup of boiled chicken and other meats with manioc, green banana and potatoes.

Los envueltos Steamed corn pastry in a corn leaf wrap.

served using at least a hundred different recipes in every town from Leticia to El Cabo. See also *Appendix 3*, page 433.

VEGETARIAN FOOD Colombia has a growing number of good vegetarian restaurants although these are confined to the larger cities. Most are in Bogotá, Cali and Medellín, but there are a few surprises in Buenaventura, Meta and Barranquilla – to name just a few. Juice bars, organic food shops, health stores and delicatessens are also found throughout the capital. Some of Colombia's vegetarian diners are listed on

La fritanga Fried beef, pork and giblets served with manioc and fried bananas.
El cuy Roasted guinea pig.
Las empanadas de pipian Yellow potato fritter with meat.

SANTANDER
Los tamales Cornflour pastry with pieces of pork and sausages steamed in a corn leaf.
El cabrito Spicy meat with fried manioc and arepa (corn pancake).
La hormiga culona Fried ants.
El moute Whole corn soup with tripe in sauce.
La pipitoria Blood sausage (similar to black pudding).

TOLIMA
El viudo de pescado Freshwater fish served with green bananas and manioc
El tamal Rice, corn pastry, chicken, pork and bacon steamed in a corn leaf wrap.
La lechona Suckling pig stuffed with rice and peas, cooked in a clay oven.

AMAZONIA
La charapa Stewed tortoise meat.
La gamitana An Amazonian fish.

LLANOS ORIENTALES
La ternera a la llanera Venison cooked over a wooden fire.

COLOMBIAN DESSERTS
Los turrones Sweet, white nougat.
La cuajada con melao Thickened milk dish served with sugarcane syrup.
El postre de natas Milk skin cooked with sugar, cinnamon and raisins.
Melcochas Sugar cane worked until tender with butter like a soft caramel.
El manjar blanco A thick, sweet milky pudding.
Las cicadas Grated coconut with golden syrup.

DRINKS
El tinto Popular light, sweet coffee.
El guarapo Old Colombian Indian drink of *ananas* skin fermented in water.
Aguardiente Fiery aniseed liquor made from distilled sugar cane (see box, *The Nation's favourite tipple*, page 91).
La chuchuguaza Firewater of the Indians of the Llanos region.
El masato Fermented rice and corn with cinnamon, served cold.
El jugo Fresh tropical fruit juices.
La colombiana The nation's favourite soda of tamarindo.
Cerveza (see box, *Quenching a thirst in Colombia*, page 87)

international listing www.happycow.net. Entries also state if the menu is vegan-friendly, lacto, organic and eat-in or take-away. Further information can also be obtained from the Colombian Vegetarian Society (*www.ColombiaVeg.com*).

PUBLIC HOLIDAYS

1 January	Año Nuevo (New Year's Day)
6 January	Día de los Reyes Magos (Epiphany)★

19 March	Día de San José (St Joseph's Day)★
March/April	Jueves Santo (Holy Thursday) and Viernes Santo (Holy Friday)
1 May	Primero de Mayo (Día del Trabajo/Labour Day)
20 May	La Ascensión del Señor★
10 June	Corpus Christi★
18 June	Sagrado Corazón (Sacred Heart)★
29 June	San Pedro y San Pablo (Saint Peter and Saint Paul)★
20 July	Día de la Independencia (Independence Day)
7 August	Batalla de Boyacá (Battle of Boyacá)
15 August	La Asunción de Nuestra Señora (Assumption)★
12 October	Día de la Raza (Columbus Day)★
1 November	Todos los Santos (All Saints' Day)★
11 November	Independencia de Cartagena (Independence of Cartagena)★
8 December	La Inmaculada Concepción (Immaculate Conception)
25 December	Navidad (Christmas Day)

★ These holidays are moved to the following Monday to ensure a long weekend, if the date does not fall on a Monday.

FESTIVALS

FERIA DE CALI (*25 Dec–1 Jan*) The Cali 'town' fair, which some think an odd label for a city of two million, is a long- established event presenting the region's cultural ID. Great processions feature horseriders and impressive masked and costumed dancers. Music and revelry is passionate and continues until the early hours throughout the event. True to Latin tradition, there's a spectacular beauty pageant, but the bullfighting, which takes place in the Plaza de Cañaveralejo, is almost as popular. A highlight is watching the dancers in the salsa marathon on the banks of the Cali River; the buzz is infectious and you'll find it hard not to join in. The event has been criticised in the past, mainly for the gold-clad horseriders in the 'Cabalgata' parade; some have suggested these are in fact prosperous drug dealers flaunting their wealth. However the fair is renowned across the country and witnessing it is a great way to experience Cali-style fiestas, which range here from classical performances to late-night salsa.

CARNAVAL DE BARRANQUILLA (*Feb/Mar*) Travellers in the country during the four days preceding Lent who like a party, shouldn't miss the chance to do the Mardi Gras Colombian style. Colombia is extremely proud of this highly traditional event, proclaimed one of the 'Masterpieces of the Oral and Intangible Heritage of Humanity' by UNESCO (November 2003).

The carnaval's heritage reaches back to the late 19th century and combines a diverse mix of ethnicity, from the indigenous to European to Caribbean, apparent in the elaborate costumes and dances. Colombians take months planning the carnaval. Throughout the four-day event, celebrations take over Barranquilla; everything closes down while residents enjoy the party. Decorated floats, rows of traditionally dressed street dancers and orchestral festivals fill the streets; cumbia music floats in the air and crowds are fuelled with aguardiente over ice. Those who can see past the liquor-infused merriment of the hour can observe a wide range of cultural dances such as traditional Spanish paloteo and African congo. A must-see is the Gran Parada, a display of Afro-Indian Colombian dancers following the opening battle of flowers procession. The crowning of the Carnaval Queen is of course highly popular, but Colombians

What am I without Aguardiente? I'm a nation without people, a tree without roots.

The lament of a Colombian émigré

This patriotic tipple is much like whisky is to the Scots. It's fiery, harsh and extremely potent, yet Colombians swear that aguardiente is hangover-free. It has also led to many late-night tearful ramblings by misty-eyed bards. What does it taste like? Well, the name is a bit of a giveaway, meaning 'burning water'. In the mid 1600s the King of Spain tried to ban aguardiente but to no avail. Colombia fought tooth and nail for their beloved tipple right up until independence in 1810. Today, Colombia's beloved booze is at least 50% alcohol and this aniseed-flavoured national drink is enjoyed countrywide.

Served cold in shot-sized glasses, this sugar cane liquor is usually downed in one by Colombians. Tastes vary, so the amount of aniseed differs from region to region. Key brands include Antioqueño (Antioquía), Líder (Boyacá), Cristal (Caldas), Nectar (Cundinamarca), Doble Anís (Huila), Llanero (Meta), Quindiano (Quindío), Superior (Santander), Tapa Roja (Tolima) and Blanco (Valle del Cauca). Aguardiente knows no class barriers and is a communal experience. With dramatic aplomb, bottles are slammed onto the centre of the table. Glasses are then filled, toasts are made and proclamations declared. Then in one, single synchronised movement, glasses are emptied in unison in a single gulp. Businessmen enjoy aguardiente in swanky wood-panelled lounges as much as the farmers that drink it from plastic cups in the fields. More than 6.6 million cases of aguardiente are sold in Colombia each year. The Caldas distillery, at the base of a thickly forested mountain outside Manizales, now makes sugar-free Cristal – at just one calorie per glass. Billboards across the region proclaim 'Aguardiente Cristal. No sugar. No regrets'. But after a bottle or so it still inadvisable to make any significant plans for the morning.

here also crown a children's King and Queen as well as a Popular Queen, reflecting the festival's family focus.

The event ends with a somewhat tongue-in-cheek re-enactment of the funeral of Joselito, an age-old carnaval character, and an impressive firework display.

CARNAVAL DE BLACOS Y NEGROS, PASTO (*4–6 Jan*) One of the oldest festivals in Latin America, this event takes place in the southern town of Pasto in the Atriz Valley. Its history stems from the early Spanish colonial practice of giving black slaves a day off during which they were, ironically, supposed to revel in happiness. It is reflected today in the Pasto carnival where on the 5 January everyone paints themselves black and on the 6 January everyone paints themselves white. The festivities are now seen as a reflection of both integration and racial diversity and the event was declared part of the nation's National Cultural Heritage by Colombian congress April 2002.

A pre-carnival water-fest takes place on 28 December, which is Colombia's national All Fools day – known as the Day of Innocent Saints. On 4 January, elaborate floats parade the streets heralding the arrival of the Castañeda family and the start of the carnaval. The Castañeda characters are a sight to behold, based on a large family, believed to have migrated into the Pasto Valley in 1928. They arrive on a festival float surrounded by mountains of luggage, old mattresses, pots and pans, naughty children, a pregnant daughter and eccentric granny. However, as with most carnavals it is the fun that takes precedence rather than the real story

Practical Information FESTIVALS

2

behind the festivities. The following two days see lots of black paint and white talc, processions, shows and street celebrations.

CARNIVAL OF THE DEVIL, RIOSUCIO (*Jan, every other year – odd numbers, ie: 2007, 2009, 2011*) This lively bohemian festival takes place around January once every two years. It attracts poets, songwriters, artists and musicians. Known as the Devil's Carnival it originates from the mid-19th-century festival of the King's Magicians which celebrated the union of two feuding neighbouring towns, one native, one Spanish, to create the Riosucio district in northwest Colombia. A fascinating array of colourful masks and 'diablada' costumes – some more than a little scary – adorn locals parading the streets.

COLOMBIAN FESTIVAL OF FOLKLORE, IBAGUÉ (*last week in Jun*) Known as the Music Capital of Colombia, Ibagué throws a great fiesta of traditional Colombian folk music such as the bunde, bambuco and pasillo. The **National Bambuco Folklore Festival and Beauty Pageant** in **Neiva** is also an important musical event, and takes place around the same time.

FERIA DE MANIZALES (*second week in Jan*) Colombia's second-biggest celebration, after Barranquilla Carnaval, Manizales Fair, is extremely popular. The fair oozes history and costumed and masked locals parade in 'manola' processions along the streets. The city attracts Colombian musicians and artists from other parts of Latin America and there's an interesting variety of local crafts and coffees, as well as an impressive firework display during the opening event. The show has become renowned for bullfights, a custom here since the founding fair in 1951 marked the city's first centenary. However, it's perhaps most famous for its International Coffee Beauty Pageant that elects a Reinado Internacional del Café (Miss Coffee Queen). Manizales also hosts the **Manizales Jazz Festival** and the **International Theater Festival** each September.

INTERNATIONAL THEATER FESTIVAL OF BOGOTÁ (*Easter, every other year, even numbers ie: 2008, 2010, etc*) This fantastic event has run since 1988 and now attracts international interest. It offers a great chance to experience Colombian theatre, as well as work from many other Latin American nations. In addition there are lots of events for children and families. See www.festivaldeteatro.com.co

FESTIVAL DE LA LEYENDA VALLENATA, VALLEDUPAR, CÉSAR (*Apr*) In 1968 former Colombian president, Alfonso López Michelsen, vallenato composer and governor of César, Rafael Escalona, and journalist then minister of culture, Consuelo Araújonoguera created the Leyenda Vallenata Festival. It combines the Rosario Virgin festival with a regional love of Colombian vallenato music. The colonial legend – which could only have come from the Spanish camp – tells of the Tupes and Chimilas, two indigenous tribes from Tayrona. They fought against the Spanish colonies after an indigenous woman was publicly whipped. During the attack the 'Virgin of the Rosario' rose from the temple, her cloak blocking the arrows and thereby saving the building. Later the natives tried to poison the drinking water in the 'Sicarare lake', but were foiled again by the Rosario Virgin who revived the poisoned Spaniards. The Indians were finally defeated.

The event has become an historic icon and the Fundación Festival de la Leyenda Vallenata (Vallenato Legend Festival Foundation), a non-profit foundation, was set up to promote and run it. The main attraction is the contest for greatest accordion player; the players are passionate and it's all taken very seriously. Musicians are also judged on paseo, son, puya and merengue rhythms – a great chance to sample some excellent Colombian riffs. If you do attend, don't miss the chance to watch the musicians battling with each other with spontaneous lyrics, much like the recent Western hip hop trend.

SAN MARTÍN CUADRILLAS, META *(7–11 Nov)* Actors perform the historic clash between Moors, Christians, Indians and 'Negroes', showing how the contemporary blend of ethnicities was formed. The event is also popular for the *coleo*, a local-style rodeo, where Colombians ride horses to round up cattle.

SHOPPING

Colombians love to shop and the centre of every city, town and rural community has some retail opportunity at its heart. In Bogotá, you'll find several so-called shopping zones as well as numerous designer stores, malls and department stores. It's much the same in Cali and Medellín. In Cartagena and Santa Marta there are dozens of handicraft stalls selling baskets and ceramics. Visitors to the Guajira region will find it almost impossible not to leave without buying a *mochila* (handbag), while in the Andes it is Colombia's handmade woollen poncho *(ruana)* that is de rigueur. Bucaramanga's fragrant flower markets are a true delight and matched only in colour by the brilliant array of handmade jewellery stalls on Isla San Andrés. Pasto abounds in carvings and varnished tableware with gold jewellery sold in every city nationwide. Although Colombia is famous for its first-grade emeralds there are few true, great deals. However, the same can't be said about its wonderful, rich home-grown coffee, so be sure to pick up a decent-sized bag if you pass through the Coffee Zone. Smart shoppers compare the government-sponsored Artesanas de Colombia prices with those of private vendors. Shopping hours tend to be Monday–Saturday 09.00–20.00, but in Bogotá many stores don't open until 11.00.

A growing number of international retailers are entering Colombia's sector. In 2006, the Chilean department stores Casa & Ideas and Falabella opened stores for the first time as did Zara, the Spanish clothing store. In Bogotá, Starbucks promises to create strong competition for a range of well-positioned domestic companies, including the Juan Valdez and Oma coffee shops. Locatel, the Venezuelan chain of drugstores, and French supermarket Carrefour both plan to increase their presence nationwide.

Further information can be obtained from the Federación Nacional de Comerciantes (National Retail Federation, FENALCO) *(Carrera 4, No 19–85 Piso 7, Bogotá;* ⤫ *1 336 7800;* f *1 350 9424;* e *sabas@fundecomercio.com.co; www.fenalco.com.co).*

PHOTOGRAPHY

Unlike the Kuna Indians in neighbouring Panama, none of Colombia's indigenous groups places charges on photography within their communities, although some do place restrictions. The Ministerio de Cultura (Colombian Ministry of Culture) *(Carrera 8, No 8–09, Palachio Echeverry, Bogotá;* ⤫ *1 342 4100;* f *1 336 1007; www.mincultura.gov.co)* recommends that all visitors seek permission before snapping away at indigenous peoples. In Minca, for example, the Indians believe photography robs them of their soul. In the Amazon, photographing tribal rituals and ceremonies without consent is wholly unacceptable. Be mindful that openly carrying a camera may provoke considerable suspicion in some of Colombia's more remote regions because of a continued culture of distrust. Any unauthorised filming is also likely to be viewed by most indigenous groups as a serious lack of respect. Some Indians may even fear that a camera is a weapon, accordingly reacting with aggression.

INTERNET In 2006, the number of Spanish-speaking internet users in the world topped 78 million, according to Internet World Stats. Located in 20 countries in the Americas and Spain, this group represents the fourth-largest language group of internet users, after English, Chinese and Japanese. In recent years, the number of internet users in Latin America has increased at a rate of 100% per month. More than 6.7 million people use the internet in Colombia, according to the Colombian Telecommunications Regulating Commission (CRT) – almost 16% of the nation's population, ranking Colombia in joint fifth place in the region at the same level as Peru but behind Chile, Argentina, Uruguay and Brazil. This is a massive jump since 2000 when the figure was 878,000 and is a staggering two million up since 2005. Much of this increase is due to a surge in broadband subscribers, up 97% in 2007 alone. Dial-up usage in Colombia has declined by almost 12% since 2005 and currently represents fewer than 300,000 subscribers. Broadband has been available in Colombia since 1997 and represents the fastest growth rate in Latin America.

There are numerous internet cafés in all Colombian cities, and more and more are springing up in many of its smaller, rural towns. Most open early, usually at 07.00. Closing time can be as late as midnight but is generally around 22.00. Many are now open seven days a week, but Sundays can't be taken as read. Almost all of Colombia's internet joints offer printing, scanning and faxing. Some also sell computer peripherals, such as ink, discs and paper. Costs vary from place to place around the country but expect to pay between 1,500 COP and 2,500 COP per hour on average. Larger hotels almost always have an internet facility for guests that is more pricey, but convenient. An hour in a 5-star in Bogotá will cost around US$6 per hour while it could reach US$10 in one of Cartagena's top-notch hotels. Wireless internet is also becoming increasingly more accessible in Colombia's urban centres, including some of the main shopping malls. Every *Yellow Pages* region-wide contains a list of local cybercafés with many public libraries also housing internet services. NB. For the @ symbol use ALT 64

TELEPHONE AND FAX Colombia's telecommunications infrastructure has been public since 1943, when congress nationalised private telecom interests. The year 2006 proved key to the Colombian telecom market. Competition intensified as the country experienced continued fixed-to-mobile substitution and increasing convergence. It also signed a Free Trade Agreement (FTA) with the USA that signified an open and competitive telecom market with no preferential treatment given to local firms. The same year also saw the government finally sell a controlling stake in Colombia Telecom to Spain's Telefónica.

Today, Colombia's relatively modern telecommunications infrastructure has helped it remain one of Latin America's highest teledensity nations at 17%, although there remains steep disparity between rural and metropolitan areas. However Colombia still lags way behind Argentina, Mexico and Brazil with many regions falling below 10%, with over 30% in the major cities. Figures suggest the number of mainline phones in Colombia amount to 7.7 million.

The international dialling code for Colombia is +57. The outgoing code depends on which network is used to dial out on (eg: 005 for Orbitel) followed by the relevant country code (eg: 00544 for the United Kingdom). For calls to other Colombian cities, use the blue-and-yellow or red long-distance booths marked *larga distancia*. They only accept 500-peso coins. To make credit card and collect calls through an AT&T operator, dial 980 11 0011. For MCI, dial 980 16 0001. For Sprint, dial 980 13 0010.

Making a regional call is on a par with using the American phone system, but is more complicated than the UK. The access code to make a call within the country from another area depends on what network is used. For example, the area code for Bogotá is 1 but using Orbitel it would be dialled as (05)1 and for Telecom (09)1. Within Colombia, the 3-digit city code prefix is dropped when making local calls. Regular coin-operated street pay phones accept 200- and 500-peso denominations. For directory assistance within Colombia, dial 113

Colombia's healthy mobile phone market has numerous roaming agreements with international network operators. In 2005, the number of mobile phone lines in Colombia more than doubled. A year later, the total rose to 27.7 million – up 26.5% on 2005's figure of 21.9 million. COMCEL, the Colombian arm of Mexico-based America Movil, is Colombia's primary network provider with 17.80 million lines (64% of the market). Spain's Telefónica is second (with 7.75 million) with Colombia Movil SA third with 2.15 million lines – a combined market that is valued at more than 7.24 trillion COP, according to CRT statistics. Colombia is blessed with large numbers of international pay phones with well-staffed COMCEL telephone offices in most towns and cities countrywide.

Hiring a cell phone is a wise investment in Colombia as it is almost impossible to co-ordinate travel plans without one. On a safety basis, carrying a mobile is also a worthwhile precaution. Network coverage is generally pretty good although rural and mountainous areas can be patchy. In the Amazon, the roaming function goes into overdrive given the proximity to Brazil and Peru. Thousands of enterprising Colombians actively sell airtime on their cell phones to the general public at 200,000–300,000 Colombian pesos a minute. All manner of roadside signs, sandwich boards and posters in windows advertise this service all over the country, from streetside fruit stalls in Boyacá to the plazas of Medellín. Buying a cheap 'pay as you go' cell phone is another option. Expect to pay around US$50 for a decent model with phone cards sold everywhere in Colombia in 2,000, 5,000 and 10,000 values.

POST Colombia's postal system was originally established as a state-run concern in 1963 but in 2006, President Uribe dissolved the Administración Postal Nacional (National Postal Administration, ADPOSTAL). Since 1994 ADPOSTAL had shared the market with more than 800 postal service companies as a consequence of privatisation. At the time of its closure it dealt with just 20% of Colombia's mail. Today, ADPOSTAL's workload has been taken over by Servicios Postales Nacionales (National Postal Services, SPN) with the Colombian postal system a complicated jigsaw of domestic and international services delivered by a number of suppliers. All international airmail is handled by Avianca, Colombia's largest airline. Airmail post offices are normally next to the airline's offices and are open weekdays 07.30–18.00, Saturday 08.00–noon. Colombia's regular post offices are generally open weekdays 09.00–15.00 but offer a domestic service only. Sending a letter by airmail to Europe costs 8,000 pesos (7,500 pesos to the US) via a reliable service that takes between 7–14 days. Postcards are cheaper at 2,000 pesos to anywhere outside of Colombia.

Avianca also operates the poste restante system and will hold letters for up to 30 days. Be sure to take a passport along when collecting letters from Avianca's offices. Some understand the concept of poste restante far better than others, so also prepare to be patient. The main office in Bogotá is by far the most organised of the bunch. Post should be addressed as follows:

YOUR NAME
C/o Lista de Correos Avianca
Edifico Avianca
Carrera 7 No 16–36
Bogotá
Colombia

NEWSPAPERS, MAGAZINES & NEWS AGENCIES News is an important part of Colombian culture as historically communication between the regions has been sparse. This is partly due to the country being so divided geographically and also because the roads were once so difficult to travel that people rarely journeyed far from home. Therefore, Colombians have always regarded news and information as highly important and have respected reliability and accuracy. Journalism in Colombia is a skilled profession with newspapers quality-written and well edited. They are still depended on and trusted and widely available nationwide.

Colombia's news sources include seven broadcast outlets with 15 internet news media, nine news magazines (including the English-language *Economist*) and five press agencies in English, Spanish and German. Colombia's three daily newspapers (all Spanish-language) wield considerable power but are just a small part of the nation's many regional titles – at last count 37 and rising. Bogotá's leading newspaper is *El Tiempo* (*www.eltiempo.com*) with *El Mundo* (*www.elmundo.com*) and *El Colombiano* (*www.elcolombiano.com*) in Medellín, and *El Occidente* (*www.diariooccidente.com.co*) and *El Pais* (*www.elpais.com*) in Cali. *El Espectador* (*www.elespectador.com*) is another popular Bogotá-based newspaper, while *Cambio* (*www.cambio.com.co*) is another of Colombia's important news titles, published in magazine form.

SOLO TRAVELLERS

Travelling alone in Colombia is more than possible, although fair-haired solo females (ie: those obviously non-national) may find this hard going (see *Women travellers*, page 76). Women do get hassled in Colombia, ranging from some fairly harmless sexual innuendo to being doggedly pursued and intimidated. This tends to be worse along the Caribbean coast. Other travellers have found that the service they receive in hotels, bar and restaurants significantly improves when they have a friend in tow. A companion will certainly help save on single room supplements. It can also help spread the cost of charter travel arrangements, such as hiring a boat to island hop in Cartagena. Long car journeys can also be more fun as a shared experience, unless you're a traveller who really enjoys their own space. Outside of the cities, a Spanish-speaking travel buddy can be very useful. Other incentives to pair-up include improved security on the basis that there is often safety in numbers, wherever you are in the world.

Keen to hook up with like-minded travellers? Then check out the following websites:

http://community.iexplore.com/travelbuddy Sign up & post a listing to find your ideal travel partner in more than 60 countries, including Colombia.

www.wayn.com Log details of your upcoming trip to find others in the same place at the same time. A user search helps find people by location. There's also WAYN instant messenger to contact millions of members across the world.

www.companions2travel.co.uk Since establishing in July 2004 to bring like-minded travellers together, Companions2Travel has attracted over 14,00 members looking for new friends to travel with worldwide.

www.gumtree.com This UK-based, classified ads & community site has expanded significantly since its launch in 2000 & it now includes a travel-buddy bulletin board.

www.travbuddy.com TravBuddy contains several thousand travel blogs about Colombia posted by travellers &Colombian nationals. It also has an excellent travel-buddy search facility using country or region.

www.yoursafeplanet.com Puts subscribers in touch with local people with insider knowledge – a great way to gain insight on where to visit & what not to miss.

♿ DISABLED TRAVELLERS

Colombia isn't the easiest place for travellers with a disability, especially those keen to leave the major cities behind. Provincial roads tend to be unpaved, pot-holed and are often little more than dirt tracks. Although wheelchairs and mobility aids are available in large malls and shopping centres, they are rare in rural areas. However, Colombia's National Institute for the Blind (Instituto Nacional para Ciegos, INCI) (*Grupo de Desarrollo Tecnológico, Carrera 13, No 34–91, Bogotá;* e *inci@ presidencia.gov.co; www.inci.gov.co*) has made considerable inroads in campaigning for public information to be available in Braille. There are just over two million deaf people in Colombia, according to Federación Nacional de Sordos de Colombia (Colombia's National Deaf Association FENASCOL) (*Avenida 13 (Autopista Norte) No 80–60, Off 202, Bogotá;* ☏ *256 1467/68;* e *contacto@fenascol.org.co; www.fenascol.org.co*), an organisation established to promote sign language (known as LSC) in 1984. Two constitutional laws for deaf people passed in 1996 recognise Colombian sign language and requires captioning or sign language on television.

Wheelchair ramps are also mandatory in new public buildings, although compliance is poor in this respect outside of urban centres. The Murillo Toro post office building in Bogotá has an entrance ramp, as does the Ministry of Education, but older buildings are rarely modified for disabled access and usually contain steep flights of steps. Much of Colombia's public transportation system is also inaccessible, impairing the free movement of people with disabilities countrywide. The exception to this is the TransMilenio in Bogotá and Medellín's Metro system, both of which have special facilities for disabled passengers and wheelchair users.

However, Colombia is playing an increasingly active role in the preparation of a Convention on the Human Rights of Persons with Disabilities as promoted by the United Nations. As a nation it defines disability on World Health Organization (WHO) guidelines and has been responsive to change. Although there are no firm figures, the WHO estimate that up to 12% of the Colombian population are likely to have some kind of disability – that's roughly 5.5 million people.

If you need assistance from airport or airline staff at any stage of your journey, contact the airline at least 48 hours before you fly. Travellers who require a companion may be offered a reduced fare for a second ticket. Passengers with a sensory, physical or learning disability can also take advantage of the following services free of charge:

- Assistance to reach check-in
- Help with registration at check-in
- Orientation of the layout of the cabin and briefing in emergency procedures
- Assistance with embarking/disembarking
- Help with luggage
- On-board wheelchair when available
- Transport around the airport

Airline staff may ask you to complete an Incapacitated Passengers Handling Advice (INCAD) form and/or a Medical Information Form (MEDIF). You can fill in the INCAD yourself, but your doctor needs to complete the MEDIF form. Each airline has a different policy in place regarding disabled passengers and people with medical

Colombia's press and regional radio in zones of conflict are the most exposed. This phenomenon of impunity is the major threat to press freedom in Colombia and in Latin America.

Journalist Enrique Santos Calderon, *El Tiempo* (2005)

Despite both national and international press freedom organisations in Colombia reporting a significant decrease in the number of journalists murdered in relation to their work, journalism remained one of the most dangerous professions in Colombia in 2007 according to the Committee to Protect Journalists (CPJ). Twenty-eight journalists were murdered, while five others disappeared, in eight Latin American countries in 2006, according to the Commission to Investigate Attacks Against Journalists (Comisión Investigadora de Atentados a Periodistas, CIAP), affiliated with the Latin American Federation of Journalists (Federación Latinoamericana de Periodistas, FELAP). Since 1976 some 800 journalists have been slain in Latin America with 83 killed in Colombia between 1996 and 2006, according to the Organization of American States' Office of the Special Rapporteur for Freedom of Expression. In 2005 the World Press Freedom Index (*www.ifex.org*) ranked Colombia 128th out of 168 countries, placing it second to last among American continent countries but above Mexico at 135th.

Media for Peace, an NGO of journalists, has members in Bogotá, Medellín, Cali, Monteria, Sincelejo, Pasto, Florencia, Valledupar and Barrancabermeja. In 2006, three Colombian journalists were murdered (Gustavo Rojas Gabalo, Mariano Pérez Murga and Francisco Bonilla Romero) while seven others were forced to flee their homes after receiving death threats. Prayers are said for the 100-plus journalists killed in Colombia since 1980 on World Press Freedom Day each year (*http://portal.unesco.org*). This United Nations initiative is designed to raise awareness of the importance of worldwide press freedom. It was established in 1993 and is held on 3 May.

Since 1997, the UNESCO/Guillermo Cano World Press Freedom Prize has been awarded on this day to a deserving individual, organisation or institution that has made an outstanding contribution to the defence and promotion of press freedom. The prize is named in honour of Colombian journalist Guillermo Cano Isaza who was assassinated in front of the offices of his newspaper, *El Espectador*, in Bogotá in 1986.

For further information: **Reporters Without Borders** (*www.rsf.org*); **International Federation of Journalists** (*www.ifj.org*).

conditions. It should be able to supply you with a copy of its provisions in this respect or may have its disabled persons policy online. A Department of Transport code of practice 'Access to air travel for disabled people' aims to make air travel more accessible to disabled people, but only relates to the UK air travel industry including travel agents, tour operators, airlines and airports. The code sets out the good practice needed to make sure disabled and less mobile passengers enjoy trouble-free journeys by air. It includes information for airport operators who are legally bound by the Disability Discrimination Act 1995 (DDA). It also advises airlines on how to provide better services to disabled people on a voluntary basis. At present, it is a voluntary code for UK companies only, however much of its content is reflected in similar European and international best practice codes.

For more information on the services available for disabled travellers (and to download a copy of the Access to Air Travel for Disable People code in PDF format, visit www.direct.gov.uk/en/DisabledPeople. The website also includes details of the facilities for disabled people at UK airports, such as transfer arrangements, parking and wheel chair accessible toilets.

OLDER TRAVELLERS

Colombians are extremely respectful of older people, defining this by bestowing reverence on those aged 50 and over. Subsequently, older travellers will find themselves well treated in Colombia's bars and restaurants where they are often seated as priority. Hotels also tend to look after their older guests with staff more prepared to go that 'extra mile'. Many theatres, cinemas, attractions and museums offer generous senior discounts, so older travellers should be sure to always have their ID close at hand. Cheap travel is also offered to senior citizens in Colombia with a 10% discount on some domestic airlines and reduced fares on pubic transport nationwide. A significant number of foreign volunteer workers in Colombia are aged between 50–65. However, some of the country's high-altitude regions present older people with some medical challenges. The sheer physical demands of the Amazon can also make this a tough region to explore. Retired Backpackers (*www.retiredbackpackers.com*), started by Jonathan Peace after his father said he wanted to visit South America, has a number of members keen to travel to Colombia. It comprises a mix of solo travellers and married couples that are independent in spirit.

See also *Appendix 3, Further information*, page 433.

CRUISE PASSENGERS

The number of cruise ships docking in Colombia is slowly growing and it is estimated over 23,000 passengers will visit Colombia during 2007. On 2 December 2006 the *Queen Elizabeth II* arrived into Cartagena for the first time, a high spot in Colombian tourist history.

The main operators to include Colombia on their itineraries are the Royal Caribbean, Princess and Celebrity. The Colombian cruise ship destinations are Santa Marta, Cartagena, and Isla de San Andrés and Isla de Providencía, two small islands nestled in the turquoise waters off the east coast of Nicaragua. Cartagena remains the most popular stop-off, but Santa Marta, San Andrés and Providencía are now being added to more cruise itineraries.

WHAT TO EXPECT ON A CRUISE VISIT Cruise ships usually dock for a full day (excluding evenings) in each location, so you should have several hours to explore. Santa Marta is great for those seeking sunshine and Caribbean waters, whilst the islands of San Andrés and Providencía offer tiny, deserted beaches and spectacular reef snorkelling.

Cartagena excursions The excursions offered in Cartagena are professionally guided and may vary slightly. There are a variety of choices. For a mix of contemporary city life and historic culture, the **City Drive and La Popa Monastery** tour is a good option. Set on a 150m-high hill, Convento de la Popa has spectacular views overlooking the city plus an ornate 22-carat gold-foil altar and a relaxing flower-festooned courtyard. The tour continues down to the 18th-century Spanish dungeons, Las Bovédas, which were constructed in the thick city walls and are now used for handcrafted souvenir shops. You'll also be driven through the residential area of Bocagrande with the chance to browse the emeralds and handicrafts in the shops. The trip takes around 3½ hours and costs start from 69.15COP adult; 54.93COP; infants free.

Those interested in architecture should try the **Deluxe Cartagena and Fortress** tour, which starts with a browse around the Manga residential area, noted for its Republican architecture and beautifully restored houses. Afterwards, you'll visit Convento de la Popa and the 17th-century fort, San Félipe de Barajas, which was one of the strongest forts ever built by the Spanish in colonial Latin America. Next, you'll be taken to Las Bóvedas for shopping, and then will pass through Simón Bolívar Square to the spectacular Inquisition Palace that now houses an interesting museum. Finally, you'll visit the Church of San Pedro Claver – the patron saint of slaves – and finish with a shopping expedition at Bocagrande. The trip lasts 4¹/₂ hours, and prices start from 91.53COP, adult; 69.15COP, child; infants free. For a more strenuous tour outside the city, try the **Mangroves & Swamp Ecological Tour**. This is a 3³/₄-hour guided canoe ride through the Swamp of the Virgin, an important sanctuary in Cartagena for tropical birds, fish and crustaceans as well as the ornate and intricate mangrove system that oxygenates the water. Prices start from 91.53COP, adult; 69.15COP, child; infants free.

For a chance to observe the city from afar, try the two-hour **Hovercraft Experience**, which takes you on a tour of the bay of Cartagena. You'll float past several important forts including Fort of Santa Cruz de Castillogrande, Fort of Manzanillo, San Sebastian del Pastelillo Fort and the 18th-century San José de Bocachica Military Fort where you can disembark and nose around. Prices start from 105.77COP, adult or child; infants free.

For a colonial reminder and an overview of the history of Cartagena, take the **Panoramic Tour Around the Bay.** You'll sail on a replica of a Spanish galleon, past the private port of Muelles El Bosque and the statue of the Virgin and the site of the Fort of Manzanillo that guards the eastern entrance to the Inner Bay. The boat makes a loop between the island of Tierra Bomba and the peninsula of Castillo Grande. To enhance the experience, a traditional show based on local folklore takes place on board. The trip lasts two hours. Prices start from 85.43COP, adult; 65.09COP, child; infants free, and includes complimentary refreshments.

You can visit the national park area of Rosario Islands on the **Rosario Island Tour**, some 35km to the south of Cartagena. The tour stops first at Isla del Sol, for a drink and exotic fruit, after which you can take the boat around 27 islands and visit the local aquarium at Isla de San Martín. Lunch on Isla del Sol, where you can snorkel (equipment not included in price), swim, or lounge by the swimming pool. Prices for the six-hour trip start from 181.07COP adult or child; infants free, including complimentary refreshments.

Best of Cartagena is a fairly flighty overview of the city's sites. You'll visit the Manga residential area, Convento de la Popa, the Fort of San Félipe de Barajas, Las Bóvedas (The Dungeons) for handicraft shopping, the Church of San Pedro Claver, the Navy Museum for refreshments followed by a short shopping spree at Pierino Gallo Mall and return to the ship via Bocagrande and Castillogrande residential areas. For the 3¹/₂-hour tour, prices start from 85.43COP, adult; 65.09COP, child; infants free, including complimentary refreshments.

Colombian cruise packages

All cruises that dock in Colombia offer the country in combination with other destinations in the region.

Celebrity Cruises ☎ 0845 456 1520; www.celebritycruises.co.uk. Offer a 12-night cruise on the *Celebrity Quest*, leaving from Miami, Florida, calling at Port Antonio (Jamaica), Santa Marta & Cartagena (Colombia), Colón (Panama), Puerto Limón (Costa Rica), San Andrés Island (Colombia) & Playa Del Carmen (Mexico). A 14-night cruise on the same ship, also leaving from Miami, stops at Port Antonio, Santa Marta, Cartagena, Puerto Limón, Panama Canal (cruising), Fuerte Amador (Panama), Puerto Caldera (Costa Rica), San Juan Del Sur (Nicaragua), Huatulco & Acapulco (Mexico). Prices start from £932.56 pp, based on dbl occupancy (£1,621.56 sgl occupancy); prices can rise during the high-season months of Dec & Jan.

Crystal Cruises ↘ 1 800 554 0011 (US); www.crystalcruising.com. Also inc Colombia in their Panama Canal transit trip: their 14-day itinerary leaves from Miami calling at Cartagena, Panama, Acapulco, Cabo San Lucas & Los Angeles. Prices start from US$2,695 pp based on dbl occupancy.

Princess Cruises ↘ 1 800 PRINCESS (US); www.princess.com; www.princesscruises.co.uk. Include Colombia in their Panama Canal trips with a 10-night itinerary inc Aruba, Cartagena, Panama Canal partial transit, Cristóbal, Limón (Costa Rica) & Ocho Rios. They offer 2 full Grand Canal 15- & 17-day transits between Fort Lauderdale & San Francisco or Vancouver with calls at Cabo San Lucas, Acapulco, Huatulco, Puntarenas (Costa Rica), Panama Canal, Cartagena & Aruba. Prices start from US$1,199 pp, based on dbl occupancy.

BUSINESS

Colombian business executives tend to like certainty, conservatism and conformity, much like many of their Latin American counterparts. Although there is a certain regard for those prepared to bend the rules, Colombia's business world also retains a respect for regulations. It also likes controls and is slow to accept change so decisions are made slowly. Most business people would readily admit to being risk-adverse with little desire to put everything on black without good reason. Red tape makes effecting change a sluggish process.

Relationships are everything in Colombian business circles, with a high emphasis placed on close ties with individuals. Most people are tolerant of Colombia's vast inequalities of wealth and power. They are also accepting of the country's masculine business clans, despite recognising the growing number of high-powered female business leaders.

Colombia's Catholic faith plays a large part in many people's belief that there is an absolute 'truth' – and this conviction is a strong and powerful force in the nation's commercial world. There is a desire by many business people to 'get to the bottom of a problem'. Colombians tend to be astute, wise and detail orientated. However, despite good intellect, many often remain ultimately ruled by emotions and their heart.

How you dress when doing business in Colombia depends on location, as formality increases the more inland you are. On the Caribbean, a short-sleeved shirt and shorts can be OK for a meeting but elsewhere more conservative attire is a sensible option, with suits in dark colours preferred. Don't be surprised by the

COLOMBIAN TIME

To enjoy travelling through Colombia it is worth being mindful of the relaxed Colombia approach to timekeeping as this helps keep blood pressure problems at bay. 'Colombian time' is a fluid concept, open to interpretation, so if you need to be somewhere that is time-critical be sure to use the phrase 'en punto' (meaning 'on the dot').

Otherwise, travellers should factor in at least half an hour to a schedule as a contingency – and have a Plan B (and Plan C) up their sleeves for good measure. It helps to work on the basis that everything will be delayed – because it probably will. So expect breakfast to be late; planes to be rescheduled; journeys to take twice the specified time; timetables to count for little; and appointments to be kept in only the loosest possible sense. In Colombia, buses depart early without reason and often never show up at all, while boats set sail seemingly at whim with little regard for even the strictest schedule. Expect 20 minutes to mean at least an hour and don't be too surprised if 2km is actually 10.

proximity of Colombian face-to-face discussions. Personal space is not being invaded; it is just the Colombian way to stand closer together than Europeans or North Americans. Business appointments should be scheduled in advance, but once made punctuality is an altogether more relaxed affair. Foreign business people should have their business cards printed in English on one side and Spanish on the other. At a business lunch, let the host make the first toast and expect a fight over the bill. Handshaking is the customary greeting in business, while amongst friends an *abrazo* (embrace) is the norm. In Colombia, titles are important so address a person correctly by profession, such as arquitecto (architect), professo (teacher), ingeniero (engineer) or abogado (lawyer). Persons without a professional title should be addressed as Mr (senor), Mrs (senora), or Miss (senorita), plus their surnames. To be polite, stick to conversations about history, football and the weather and be sure to avoid topics that relate to politics, drugs and religion. Colombians will also be keen to ask you, as a foreigner, about your favourite experiences of their homeland, so it pays to have a few chosen anecdotes up your sleeve.

Most Colombian cities have a chamber of commerce office, as do some smaller rural towns:

Barranquilla Chamber of Commerce Antiguo Edificio de la Aduana, Vía 40 No. 36–135, Barranquilla; ↘ (5) 330 3700; f (5) 330 3700; e comunica@camarabaq.org.co;

Buenaventura Chamber of Commerce Calle 1 No. 1A – 88, Buenaventura; ↘ (2) 242 4508 & 242 3623; f (2) 243 4202; e ccbuvpresidencia@correopeopleonline.com.co; www.ccbun.org

Buga Chamber of Commerce Carrera 14 No. 5–53, Buga; ↘ (2) 228 00 88; f (2) 228 00 93; e camara@ccbuga.org; Wwww.ccbuga.org

Cartagena Chamber of Commerce Calle Santa Teresa No 32–41 A.A. 16, Cartagena; ↘ (5) 6600795 & 6600793 & 6600763; f (5) 660 08 02; e camaradecomercio@cccartagena.org.co

Cauca Chamber of Commerce Carrera 7 No. 4–36, Cauca; ↘ (2) 824 3625; f (2) 824 3625; e cccauca@cccauca.org.co; www.cccauca.org.co

Ipiales Chamber of Commerce Carrera 11 No. 15–28, Ipiales; ↘ (2) 773 2465 & (2) 773 3926; f (2) 773 4047; e ccipia@telecom.com.co

Manizales Chamber of Commerce Carrera 23 No 26–60, Manizales; ↘ (6) 884 18 40 & 884 09 19; f (6) 884 09 19; e infoccm@ccm.org.co; www.ccm.org.co

Neiva Chamber of Commerce Carrera 5 No 10–36 Piso 3, Neiva; ↘ (8) 871 37 40 & 871 3666; f (8) 871 3730; e info@ccneiva.org; www.ccneiva.org

Pereira Chamber of Commerce Carrera 8 No 23–09 Local 10, Pereira; ↘ (6) 338 7800; e información@camarapereira.org.co; www.camarapereira.org.co

Tunja Chamber of Commerce Calle 21 No 10–52, Tunja; ↘ 740 20 00; f 742 79 28; www.ccomerciotunja.org.co

Valledupar Chamber of Commerce Calle 15 No 4–33, Valledupar; ↘ (5) 574 9021 & 574 4448; e camaravalledupar@telecom.com.co; www.ccvalledupar.org.co

Villavicencio Chamber of Commerce Calle 39 No 31–47, Villavicencio; ↘ (8) 6713737; f (8) 6719220; e informacion@ccv.org.co; www.ccv.org.co

BUYING PROPERTY

In Colombia, under law a foreigner has the right to buy, own, register, sell and rent real estate. They can also repatriate all proceeds from the sale of property to their country of origin on equal terms to Colombia citizens. Although most analysts agree that a real estate boom is unlikely to happen until Colombia achieves countrywide peace, this hasn't stopped prime cities and coastal resorts experiencing significant rises in the value of property. Individual foreign investors from the US, Europe and other Latin American countries are injecting some serious money into the Colombian economy. In 2007, the world witnessed a whole new era of confidence in Colombia's real estate market, with an unprecedented number of non-nationals snapping up property 'ahead of the crowd' to take advantage of low prices. Prime hotspots include all of Colombia's major cities, including Bogotá, Medellín, Cali and

Barranquilla. Yet it is Cartagena and Santa Marta on the Caribbean coast that boast the largest density of foreign property owners. Most have invested in colonial-era homes in the centre of town or swish, new high-rise apartments along the coast. Expect to pay an average cost per square metre of approximately 1,000,000 pesos for a property in a nice location in good condition. Variables that impact on price include bathrooms, kitchens, swimming pools, dedicated parking spaces, gardens, etc. Additional fees to consider include monthly administration fees for an apartment. Construction quality is high in Colombia as there is often a tendency to 'over-design' and 'over-spec' a property because they are obligated under law to guarantee their work personally for five years. To reduce or eliminate potential structural problems, most building companies add more steel and concrete than commonly used. Labour costs are also much lower in Colombia, having a direct effect on price.

In Cartagena, the annual rate of property tax is 0.65% (in 2007) of the assessed value as determined by the local government office. Market values are usually higher than assessed value, eg: for an apartment that cost 180,000,000 COP but which is assessed at 120,000,000 COP the amount due in tax is 780,000 COP (0.65%) per year. Medellín, as in other major cities in Colombia, is undergoing a housing boom. New apartment projects are springing up all over the city, with re-sale properties enjoying a brisk demand. El Poblado is considered the most desirable area in the city. Other prime areas are Laureles, Estadio, Conquistadores, Velodromo, Floresta, Belén La Palma and Santa Monica. House-hunt here and an apartment will start at 682,500,000 COP – at least. In Barranquilla, some neighbourhoods have seen housing increase in value by 20% since 2005 with average price tags of 400,000,000 COP for a luxury two-bedroom flat. Another boomtown is Cali where numerous luxurious apartment blocks are under construction. Expect to pay upwards of 500,000,000 COP for a swish apartment that could benefit from 40% capital appreciation within a couple of years.

Many expats seek the familiar names of their homeland, and in Colombia there's always a little taste of home close at hand in the major cities. Expect to find McDonald's, Dunkin Donuts, Coca-Cola and Domino's in Cali, Bogotá, Medllín and Barranquilla. In fact, in the capital, there are arguably more global food influences than true Colombian gastronomic traditions, from crowded Irish bars selling pints of Murphy's and fish 'n' chip suppers to KFC.

Further information can be obtained from Cartagena Real Estate (*www.cartagenacolombiarealestate.com*), Colliers International (*www.colliersmn.com*) and Medellín Real Estate (*www.medellininfo.com/realestate*).

CULTURAL ETIQUETTE

Like many Latin nations, Colombians are extremely hard-working but timing (see box, *Colombian time*, page 101) is not their strongpoint. Meetings can be relaxed and it is not uncommon for Colombians to be a little late on arrival, but this is not always the case. Timings for events, buses, trains and tours can range from punctual to seriously random – but it pays to arrive on time with the attitude that waiting a little isn't a problem.

Colombians are glad to receive foreign visitors and will often go out of their way to help them. Close friends will usually share an *abrazo* (embrace) and a kiss on the right cheek – and physical exchanges, such as a touch on the arm or a pat on the shoulder, are common even between acquaintances. Colombians are often happy to offer directions and recommendations and will happily add their own opinion on the best places to eat or stay. They have a tendency to exaggerate; you may, for example, receive ambiguous directions, but this is purely because they would rather please you than let you down. The term 'Locombia' was coined by a

2

No hablas en español? Well, it's not an insurmountable problem. However, things are considerably easier if you pick up more than just a smattering of tourist Spanish. Fluency in the language is essential for those keen to stay more than a few weeks. Both the Universidad Santiago de Cali Institute of Languages and the Pontifica Universitaria Javeriana in Cali offer affordable Spanish language tuition for foreigners with Berlitz classes in Bogotá – plus an endless list of Spanish language schools. Hiring a private tutor is an easy and inexpensive option. The British Council also has an extensive database of English–Spanish tutors nationwide.

International House www.ihes.com. Spanish-language courses in Bogotá, inc intensive studies, one-to-one courses & group tuition. From US$350.

Nueva Lengua www.nuevalengua.com. Courses in Bogotá, Cartagena & Medellín in numerous shapes & sizes with prices from 20 hrs a week at US$200 per week plus a range of accommodation options. University-affiliated.

PEPE Colombia www.nativeenglishcenter.com/PEPE/. Offers Spanish lessons to foreign students with private lessons & group tuition (max 12 people). From US$347 for 4 weeks, including accommodation & all meals.

columnist of the Bogotá daily newspaper *El Espectador* to reflect Colombia's blessed (or cursed) touch of madness-cum-gusto – and the enthusiastic language they use mirrors this zest for life.

I feel fantastic!	*Me siento fenomena!*
That was delicious!	*Estaba buenisimo!*
I think I've had one too many!	*Creo que he tomado una de más!*
This is insane!	*Esto es una locura!*
Is this a local custom?	*Esto es una costumbre local o nacional?*
That was amazing!	*Eso fue incredíble!*
That's great!	*Eso, eso!*
Come on!	*Venga vamos!*
This place is great!	*Es un lugar bárbaro!*
It's been great meeting you!	*Me ha encantado conocerte!*
That's beautiful, isn't it!	*Qué precuiso, no?*
I love it here!	*Me encanta esto!*
How cool!	*Qué bárbaro!*

Although different customs apply throughout Colombia some important generalisations can be made. Colombians tend to have expectations regarding the manners of visitors to their country. This will vary from person to person so it is impossible to avoid every faux pas. However, ignoring some ingrained beliefs and behaviours is a sure way to upset someone somehow. The following may help in avoiding looking rude, foolish, or worse.

- Colombians tend to use exaggerated gestures. They also engage in physical contact and will be openly 'touchy feely' even with strangers.
- Many Colombians use smaller dimensions of personal space than people from English-speaking cultures. Avoid the temptation to step away as it sends out negative signals.
- Using a gesture of an upwards palm with the fingers curled back is considered a romantic solicitation in Colombia.

- Gifts are never opened in public unless the giver insists.
- Older people are treated with considerable respect. Men are often referred to as Don and women as Doña, followed by their first names.
- Small talk is an essential preamble to every discussion in Colombia. Don't rush it, for this seemingly trivial exchange is considered important. 'Getting to the point' straight away is viewed as pushy and impolite.
- Unless it is raised by a Colombian, shy away from talking about politics. It is also important to avoid criticising the Catholic Church or discussing Colombia's drug trade, as these are both delicate topics.

LIVING IN COLOMBIA

Many English-language expatriates in Colombia work as English teachers as native English tutors are in considerable demand. Teaching jobs usually require a university degree and applicants with a teaching certificate are highly sought after. Other expat job options include those at major hotels or with multi-national corporations. Several major global companies have a presence in Colombia, including Michelin, Mobil, DHL, Fuller, Xerox, Microsoft, Coca-Cola, Sony and Mazda. Medical care, nursery schooling, child care and domestic help are all widely available and reasonably priced.

Key lifestyle benefits for expatriates include Colombia's low cost of living, excellent infrastructure and high standard of restaurants, spas, hotels and leisure facilities. Most cities are close to either the mountains or the coastline in a country that embraces fresh air, exercise and enjoying quality family time. British and American schools offer a high educational standard. Colombia is also just a 3-hour jaunt to Florida or the Caribbean with daily flights into the UK. Of course, all this needs to be weighed against the continued safety concerns within a country still struggling towards peacetime. Yet, Colombia's growing number of foreign residents is testament to the nation's potential as a haven for expatriates.

Further information from the British Council Colombia (*www.britishcouncil.org/colombia*) and Colombia Relocation Consultancy (*www.colombiaunlimited.com*).

GIVING SOMETHING BACK

Friends of Colombia for Social Aid (FOSCA) 72 Humber Rd, Blackheath, London SE3 7LU; e friendsofcol@aol.com; www.friendsofcolombia.co.uk. This UK-based charity is devoted to improving the lives of some of Colombia's most disadvantaged children by supplying much-needed medical & educational equipment. Each year, it is inundated with requests for help from children's hospitals & charities & is looking for funding & sponsors in a bid to fulfil the demand. FOSCA is currently working with the Hospital de la Misericordia in Bogotá, the Guardería Hogar Infantil La Esmeralda in Popayán, Liga contra la Epilepsia Capítulo Valle in Cali, the Asociación Benéfica Cristiana ABC Prodein in Bogotá, the Liga Colombiana de Hemofílicos y otras Deficiencies Sanguineas in Bogotá, Guardería Infantil Niña María in Cazucá, the Hospital San José in Samaná, the Fundación CRAN in Bogotá & the Hospital Club Noel, Cali.

Fundación Caminos de Identidad (FUCAI) Calle 54, No 10–81 Oficina 301, Bogotá; www.fucai.org.co or www.bernardvanleer.org. In support of the indigenous people of Colombia, the Fundación Caminos de Identidad has a strong family focus, working with a number of tribal groups, including the Uitoto of La Chorrera in the midst of the Colombian Amazon region. Mothers with young children in some of Colombia's most remote riverside village communities are given help with child rearing. FUCAI also supports those encountering domestic violence. Local people are given training in promoting education in close collaboration with teachers & volunteers. The Foundation is a charity established in 1949 in the Netherlands by Bernard van Leer, a Dutch industrialist & philanthropist who died in 1958. Today the Foundation supports more than 140 major projects in 21 countries worldwide & has been working in Colombia since 1998 with a large international volunteer force. FUCAI desperately needs volunteer workers, funding & specialist social workers (Spanish-speaking).

Fundación Carvajal Carrera 25, No 2–01, Cali; ☎ 2 554 2949; f 2 554 2892; e comunica@ fundacioncarvajal.org.co; www.fundacioncarvajal.org.co. Since 1981, The Carvajal Foundation's primary area of activity has been the district of Aguablanca, a very poor area of Cali with 350,000 inhabitants in an area of less than 6 square miles. Most of the Aguablanca community earns a living from scavenging the local rubbish dumps. Fundación Carvajal has helped to organise these efforts in more commercial terms. Waste materials of industrial use are now sold by the community to finance basic services, such as water supplies, sewer systems, electricity & street paving. The charity provides three centres in each of Aguablanca's 3 neighbourhoods. It also runs a 'materials bank' depot for housing construction companies in the area. Volunteer workers are in short supply but are very welcome as are funds & donations. Spanish-speaking travellers with specialist skills are particularly welcome.

Healing Colombia: Family Care e healing@ cable.net.co; www.healingcolombia.org. This small, Bogotá charity is totally youth focused, working in inner city areas where Colombia's problems with poverty, drug-taking & gang crime are most prevalent. In partnership with government institutions, the therapeutic community & other NGOs in Bogotá, it runs programmes for the underprivileged. It also delivers humanitarian aid to Colombia's poorest communities. Projects include a drug prevention programme in Bogotá's slums, a drug rehab programme in the Colombian prison system, health & lifestyle counselling, music therapy sessions, sports programmes & other recreational activities & English-language courses. Healing Colombia is actively seeking a wide range of volunteer workers & is fundraising for donations via the Family Care Foundation in America (☎ 1 800 992 2383). Managers Mario Torres & Sophia Dow are also in desperate need of teaching materials & Spanish-speaking counsellors & rehab specialists. They also require musicians to help implement their highly successful Music Therapy programme.

Moi Pour Toit Foundation Rue de la Délèze 27, 1920 Martigny, Switzerland; ☎ 41 27 722 6246; f 41 27 722 0013; m 41 79 221 0246; www.fundacioncolombia.com. This non-governmental Swiss-Colombian organisation supports mistreated & abandoned children in the Pereira region, providing a refuge for 'gamines' (homeless kids) to ensure they

have warmth, shelter, legal protection, education & hope for the future. Launched in 1991 from a head office in Martigny, Switzerland, by journalist Christian Michellod, Moi Pour Toit is managed by director Juan Pablo Bedoya Florez in Colombia. Comprising 3 major sectors: an emergency centre for boys, a farm in the country, & a house for girls, the foundation can house 70 children aged 5–18. The foundation functions on the principle of direct aid with every donated Swiss franc reaching its intended destination intact. All administrative expenses are covered by the sale of clothes, handicrafts & Colombian coffee but Moi Pour Toit Foundation relies on donations to provide for its 70 children & 30 employees. Volunteers, donations & equipment (especially white goods) are particularly welcome.

Peoples of the World Foundation www.peoplesoftheworld.org. The US-based Peoples of the World Foundation is looking for additional people to join its Board of Directors as well as Forum Moderators to manage its indigenous peoples discussion board. Translators are also in demand to work on multi-language materials, especially those that can translate into any of the many native tongues. Peoples of the World champions the rights of indigenous peoples to gain access to education & as well as its work in Colombia it also campaigns against marginalisation throughout the world. Online application forms offer a wide range of volunteer opportunities.

SOS Children's Villages www.sos-childrensvillages.org. SOS has had a presence in Colombia since 1968, & 1971 saw the first arrivals in its Children's Village in Bogotá. The capital attracts large number of displaced persons from the country's rural areas & has a sizeable poor community. As a consequence, the number of orphans in Bogotá is particularly large. Today SOS Children's Villages has 5 centres across the country, including those in Bogotá, Ibagué, Rionegro & Bucaramanga. However in a country where over one million children between the ages of 5–17 are working & more than one million have been displaced in the last 15 years, the challenges are tough. As well as providing long-term care for orphaned & abandoned children in Colombia, SOS Children is involved in caring for street children in Bogotá. In the San Vitorino district many children find that stealing & drug dealing are their only means of survival. SOS provides food, shelter & education for these abandoned children, many of whom have never had an education or the support of a family unit. The oldest Bogotá Village is run by the inspirational Fabio Curtidor Argüello and contains 12–18 homes for 'families' of 10 children in close-knit settings. They are desperate for musical instruments, sports equipment and art materials for the children. They also need funding and sponsors and are keen to attract volunteers for project work, preferably Spanish speakers. Contact Fabio Curtidor Argüello directly at

SOS Children in Colombia (Aldeas Infantiles SOS Colombia), Carrera 28 No. 94 A-49, Barrio La Castellana on ☎ +57 (1) 25 64 208 & +57 (1) 63 48 049; f +57/1/53 36 825; e aldeassoscol@cable.net.co, www.aldeasinfantilessos.org.co

Colombia, the only risk is wanting to stay.

Welcome to the country of Passion, a land complete with surprises and contrasts, a land that encompasses every tropical environment, from the snow-capped peaks of the Andes Mountains to the warm beaches of the Caribbean Sea, and from the exhuberant Amazon rainforest to the arid deserts of La Guajira. Colombia is also a modern and dynamic country that preserves invaluable treasures from its aboriginal and colonial past and whose jovial, hard-working, hospitable people are its main strength.

Colombia
www.colombiaespasion.com

PROEXPORT
COLOMBIA
www.proexport.com.co

www.visitcolombia.com

Part Two

THE GUIDE

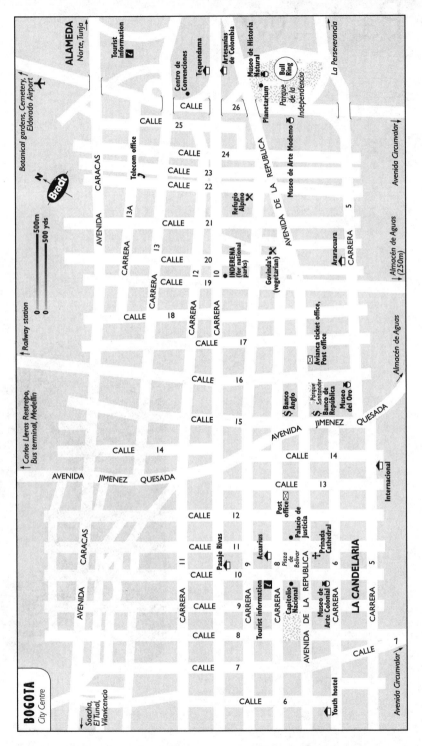

BOGOTA
City Centre

ALAMEDA
Norte, Tunja

Botanical gardens, Cemetery, / Eldorado Airport ✈

Tourist information ℹ

Soacha, El Tunal, Villavicencio

↑ Railway station

↑ Carlos Lleras Restrepo, Bus terminal, Medellin

N
Bradt

500m
500 yds
0
0

Centro de Convenciones ●
Tequendama ⊡

Artesanías de Colombia ⊡
Museo de Historia Natural ●

Planetarium ●
Bull Ring

Parque de la Independencia

La Perseverancia

Museo de Arte Moderno ◎

Avenida Circunvalar ↓

AVENIDA CARACAS

Telecom office ✆

AVENIDA DE LA REPUBLICA

CARRERA 13A

CARRERA 13

CARRERA 12

Refugio Alpino ✕

INDERENA (for national parks) ●
Govinda's (vegetarian) ✕

Araracuara ●
CARRERA 5

Almacén de Aguas ↓ (250m)

CARRERA CARRERA

Avianca ticket office, Post office ✉

Parque Santander ●
Banco de Republica $
Museo del Oro ◎

$ Banco Anglo

Almacén de Aguas ↘

AVENIDA JIMENEZ QUESADA

AVENIDA JIMENEZ QUESADA

CALLE 26
CALLE 25
CALLE 24
CALLE 23
CALLE 22
CALLE 21
CALLE 20
CALLE 19
CALLE 18
CALLE 17
CALLE 16
CALLE 15
CALLE 14
CALLE 14
CALLE 13

Post office ✉
Palacio de Justicia ●

Pasaje Rivas
Acuarius ●
Plaza de Bolivar

Prinada Cathedral ✝

LA CANDELARIA

Internacional ⊡

CALLE 12
CALLE 11
CALLE 10
CALLE 9
CALLE 8
CALLE 7
CALLE 6

CARRERA 11

AVENIDA CARACAS

CARRERA

Tourist information ℹ
Capitolio Nacional ●
Museo de Arte Colonial ◎

AVENIDA DE LA REPUBLICA

CARRERA 6

CARRERA 5

CALLE 1

Youth hostel ⊡

Avenida Circunvalar ↓

110

3

Bogotá

Telephone code: 1

> *En la patria no hay otra ni habrá*
> (There isn't another in the nation, neither will there be)
> *Nuestra voz la repiten los siglos: Bogotá... Bogotá... Bogotá!*
> (Our voice is repeated over the centuries: Bogotá...Bogotá...Bogotá!)
> Bogotá anthem, Pedro Medina Avendaño

Once a byword for danger, the city of Bogotá has undergone a significant clean-up act in recent years, following a passionate campaign aimed at nurturing societal change. Visionary leaderships have ignited fresh fire into the belly of Bogotá's 7.5 million inhabitants via a host of pioneering strategies that have helped change the mindset and behaviours of a once unruly urban sprawl. Today, Bogotá is a cosmopolitan city on the up – a metropolis that bears the signs of modern self-improvement. Sleek skyscrapers and a futuristic transit system are symbols of an (almost) transformed city that boasts 4,594 public parks. Thousands of cyclists of all ages criss-cross Bogotá's wide, green expanses on Latin America's largest bike-path network. Car use is restricted to lessen congestion. Vehicles no longer park on sidewalks and basic traffic laws such as stopping at a red light, giving priority to pedestrians and taking the bus only at bus stops are largely obeyed. Citizenship is no longer a laughable concept in the city and today the mood is one of highly charged optimism. Designer stores, swanky cafés, lounge bars and fine restaurants are testament to Bogotá's desire to become one of the most desirable cities on radar. Sundays in the city are a family day when the streets take on a party atmosphere of street clowns, music and picnics in the parks. Food vendors, churchgoers and mothers with pushchairs converge on the plazas and compete for space with armies of pigeons. Jugglers take centre stage on empty roundabouts while old women on flower stalls sit amongst a fragrant kaleidoscope of varicoloured blooms. Paths are freshly swept and roads free of rubbish in a place where choking smog once dominated the cityscape. Today the people of Bogotá love and respect their city – it is now oh-so *chévere* (cool) to be Bogotáno, a far cry from the sentiment of a decade ago when it was a place that was truly loathed.

Yet modern-day Bogotá still has its many problems, some of which are born out of a rapidly expanding refugee population displaced from Colombia's rural provinces. Constant streams of migrants arrive in the capital full of high hopes, only to find the city's streets aren't paved with gold. Most of these poor peasants end up in the makeshift shanty towns that sprawl along Bogotá's fast-decaying southern nub. Conditions are nothing short of horrendous with sanitation and fresh water scarce. Piles of rotting rubbish are scavenged for a glimmer of hope in sewage-swamped streets that are as lawless as they are vile. Pickpockets plague the shopping malls and all sorts of evils roam the streets after dark yet, despite this, Colombia's 'first city' refuses to be a necropolis in the doldrums. Bogotános are largely a morally responsive, socially conscious and fashionably introspective

Bogotá

3

111

bunch – so the mood within vast swathes of the city is upbeat. Big hotels are also expressing confidence in Bogotá's promising future – that Hilton is returning to open a swank US$27 million hotel in 2009 is a clear show of faith. However, the vast disparities that exist between the affluent north and poverty-stricken south are nothing short of shocking – two very different faces of Bogotá, wrapped around the bubblegum-coloured colonial core of the old quarter of the city.

HISTORY

Called Bacatá by the Muiscas long before the Spanish colonised the area, the fertile highland plateau on which Bogotá sprawls was once an advanced pre-Columbian ancient civilisation composed of numerous small villages. Although no historical documents exist, it is widely accepted that the Spanish settlement was founded on 6 August 1538 by Gonzalo Jiménez de Quesada. He named it 'Santa Fé de Bacatá' after his birthplace Santa Fé in Spain, affixing it to the local 'Bacatá'. At the time of its foundation, Bogotá (known as Santa Fé) consisted of a dozen wooden huts and a small chapel. The Muisca built up large collections of gold, manufacturing a diverse range of pieces, including small anthropomorphic or zoomorphic figures (*tunjos*) that were offered to the gods as funerary and sacred gifts. They also made necklaces, bracelets, earrings, pectorals, nose rings and other pieces used for self-adornment – and were also excellent at weaving and outstanding potters. The Spanish razed all of the Muisca's sacred sites to the ground to make way for churches. Communities were plundered and an indigenous population of more than half a million ultimately destroyed.

In 1810, the citizens revolted against Spanish rule but this fragile government was plagued with internal discourse. Spanish military loyalists reassumed control of the city temporarily from 1816 to 1819. After Colombia gained independence from the Spanish, Bogotá was affirmed as the capital of Gran Colombia, a federation combining the territories of modern Panama, Colombia, Venezuela and Ecuador. When that republic was dissolved, Bogotá remained the capital of New Granada, later to become the Republic of Colombia, and by the middle of the 19th century the city had grown considerably in stature and size. A 1789 census recorded 18,161 inhabitants and by 1819 the city population amounted to 30,000 distributed in 195 blocks. More than 30 churches and at least a dozen schools served the city with a mule-powered tramway built in 1884. Railway access to the trading ports on the mighty Río Magdalena signified boom time ahead of a period of industrialisation that prompted Bogotá's further growth. In 1832, a census recorded 36,465 inhabitants. In 1881, the city's population was 84,723, reaching nearly 100,000 by the end of the century. Yet, Bogotá still had very little industry with an economy that relied on artisan work grouped in the city's struggling commercial sectors. Slowly, retail outlets began to open around the Plaza de Bolívar, a popular centre of hat stores and women's fashion. Several shops selling imported goods began to spring up around Calle Ocho with four main banks opening offices in the city between 1870 and 1883. When the Bavaria Brewery established a base in Bogotá in 1889 it became one of the city's major industries. In 1923, a US compensatory pay-off in relation to Panama brought increased prosperity to the capital, attracting foreign investment and improving infrastructure and expanding the urban economy. However, violence began to erupt countrywide in the mid 1940s, drawing a steady stream of migrants to the city – yet with assassinations, kidnappings, hostage-takings and murders, Bogotá wasn't quite the safe haven many hoped it would be. Social disorder wreaked havoc in the makeshift shanty towns that began to spring up around the city – expanding it to over 33,000ha. This influx of peasants fleeing the violence of rural Colombia tripled the population, from 700,000 in 1951 to 1.6 million in 1964 and 2.5 million in 1973. By 1985, the number of inhabitants in the capital had increased to 4.1 million – by 1993 almost six million people called Bogotá home.

By the mid 1990s, Bogotá was one of the world's most dangerous cities with a homicide rate of 80 per 100,000. In the last decade, however, Bogotá has gone to great lengths to change both its crime rate and its image. By 2005, Bogotá had a murder rate of 23 persons per 100,000 inhabitants – a 71% drop in ten years. Today in terms of homicides, it ranks well below Washington DC, Caracas, Sao Paulo, Mexico City and Río de Janeiro. Bogotá is now known as the 'Athens of Latin America' on account of the city residents' education (16% of its 7.5 million population are students) and cultural appreciation. Every two years it plays host to the Iberoamerican Theater Festival – the biggest theatre festival on the planet. In 2007 Bogotá was named 'Book Capital of the World' on account of the Luis Arango Angel Library receiving a staggering 7,000 daily visits (2.2 million in total in 2006). Since 1999, it has been the most attended library on earth, with more annual visitors than the New York Public Library, the British Library and the Pompidou Centre in Paris.

CLIMATE

As South America's third-highest capital city after La Paz and Quito, Bogotá is often crisp and cooler than many visitors expect. The city's average temperature is 14°C year-round, plummeting to around 9°C at night – although as Bogotá is climatically variant, highs of 25°C can suddenly catch you out. Generally, expect it to hit around 19°C each day and pack a light sweater as a just-in-case measure. Be prepared for showers and plan for clear skies and dizzying altitude. The main dry season runs from December to March with a second in July to August. Bogotá's annual rainfall averages about 1,020mm with April and October the wettest months.

GEOGRAPHY

Bogotá is a difficult city to truly explore on account of its sprawl with an urban perimeter that continues to expand. Four large zones attempt to make sense of the structure of the metropolis – a city split into 20 sectors, each governed by a local mayor and administrative board under the control of the main mayoral office. Located on tableland in the eastern mountain chain of the Andes 2,630m above sea level, Bogotá is bounded by the Río Bogotá to the west, the Sumapaz páramo to the south and the agricultural plains of the Sabana to the north. It is also surrounded by the Arzobispo, San Cristóbal, San Francisco and Tunjuelito rivers and zoned as follows:

- **Central Zone** Including La Candelaria and the neighbourhoods around the International Center where most of the city's political and administrative offices are located.
- **North Zone** Home to the city's key financial centres, main museums, churches and cultural attractions – and also its more affluent suburbs.
- **South Zone** Primarily an industrial and working class sector with large shanty towns on its outer edges.
- **Western Zone** Including many large-scale industrial parks, athletic installations, retail outlets and the El Dorado International Airport

Carrera 14 (Avenida 14) is the city's major artery, connecting the centre with the north and south. Bogotá's urban plan is based around calles that run east-to-west with carreras that run north-south in direction. In simple terms, the city is divided into two, with around 200 blocks north and 100 blocks south.

ARCHITECTURE

Bogotá won the prestigious Golden Lion Award in 2006 at the 10th International Architecture Exhibition, forcing detractors to see the city in a different light. It is not a stunning, flawless urban centre – far from it. However, there is undoubtedly something rather pleasing about Bogotá's eclectic mishmash of architectural styles, many featuring Rogelio Salmona's (1929–2007) distinctive designs. Perfect pavements meet crumbling concrete slabs on wonky sidewalks edged by multi-coloured, pebble-dashed apartment blocks and fairy-tale gabled buildings. Faded colonial façades stand dominated by futuristic high-rise towers amidst an urban jigsaw of red brick, chrome, graffiti and mirrored glass. Painted shutters and ornate balconies look out on patches of manicured lawns. Ritzy bars and centuries-old monuments sit behind rubbish-strewn alleyways aside topiary and blooms. Golden Lion judges decided that Bogotá is a beacon of hope for other cities, whether rich or poor – and its ultra-smart commercial and financial districts seem to signify a city poised for further growth.

GETTING THERE AND AROUND

BY AIR All international flights to Bogotá land at El Dorado International Airport, located about 20 minutes' drive from the downtown area. One of the largest cargo airports in Latin America, El Dorado is the fifth busiest in the region in terms of passenger traffic, handling nine million passengers in 2006 – over six million to domestic destinations with almost three million international travellers. El Dorado lies about 15km west of the city centre, connected to Calle 26. At the time of writing, construction of a TransMilenio link looks likely to join the airport with the transportation system of the city. The Colombian government has also earmarked at least US$650 million for the airport's expansion, to include a new international terminal that will enable El Dorado to handle a capacity of 16 million passengers a year.

Two passenger terminals – El Dorado (✆ 413 9053) and Puente Aéreo (✆ 413 9511) – are distinctly separate. The first handles a mix of international flights and the second purely serves Avianca. In El Dorado, check-in counters, ticket booths, immigration officials and customs are located on the lower level. Flight information screens, seating, emigration, duty-free stores, food outlets, news-stands, three casa de cambios, and an ATM are located on the upper level. There is also a Telecom office offering international and national calls, as well as fax and internet service, between 07.00–19.00.

The newer Puente Aéreo terminal handles more than 120 daily flights – both international and domestic – but solely those of Avianca and its subsidiary SAM. It has a good range of shopping facilities, national and international telephone services, taxi booths, ATM machines, restaurants and fast-food outlets, book shops and news-stands. As Avianca also operates out of El Dorado terminal it is important to check the departure point for each flight. The turn-off for Puente Aéreo is 1km before the bigger terminal on a different approach road.

Information for both can be found online at www.elnuevodorado.com. At the time of writing an increase of 63,400 COP (or US$32) in the departure tax has been announced. Travellers departing Colombia may apply for a special tax waiver at El Dorado Airport – join the queue before you check-in and allow waiting time.

The following airlines have offices in Bogotá: Air Canada (✆ 618 600), Air France (✆ 650 600), Aires (✆ 336 6039), Aero Lineas Argentinas (✆ 313 2853),

Aeropostal ($\searrow$ 317 2850), AeroRepública ($\searrow$ 342 2850), American Airlines ($\searrow$ 343 2424), Avianca ($\searrow$ 342 6077), Avianca/SAM ($\searrow$ 404 7862), Continental ($\searrow$ 800 944 0219), COPA ($\searrow$ 800 550 7700), Iberia ($\searrow$ 610 5066), Lan Chile/Lan Peru ($\searrow$ 611 1533), Satena ($\searrow$ 281 7071), TACA ($\searrow$ 629 5507).

Getting to/from the airport All buses marked 'Aeropuerto' serve both airport terminals, including the *busetas* and *colectivos* that depart from Calle 19 and Carrera 10. At the airport, the departure point is next to the terminal entrances, although this service only runs until about 21.00. A taxi to the airport is subject to a surcharge of 2,500 COP – bringing the total cost to around 15,000 COP from the centre of town. At the airport, be sure to pick up a print-out from the official taxi booth by the baggage claim area – it confirms the price and prevents attempts to over-charge.

BY BUS AND BUSETA Bogotá's large bus terminal ($\searrow$ 428 2424) is a major hub for national and international routes across Colombia and to Ecuador and Venezuela. Located out of town to the west of the city, the terminal has three well-organised departure halls that each handles a different part of the country. Rather conveniently, these are simply called Norte (North), Oriente y Occidente (East and West) and Sur (South) – all very orderly and straightforward. Reaching the terminal requires taking a taxi (around 10,000 COP) or grabbing a seat on the shuttle marked 'Terminal' from Carrera 10.

Long-distance buses to Colombia's main cities run with slick efficiency throughout the day, often departing every 20 minutes or half-hour. Most have air conditioning and some have a video player – fares vary depending on the operator, so it pays to ask a few. Bartering for a decent ticket price is also normal behaviour as competition is fierce on the longer routes, so don't be afraid to chance your luck.

Smaller buses (busetas) are the lifeblood of Bogotá's public transport, hurling passengers around the city at breakneck speed. Simply hail one down as it passes (wherever you happen to be) and pay the driver on boarding. When you're ready to get off, ding the bell – or shout loud instructions. Each vehicle displays a sign stating its destination with fares that range from 500–1,000 COP, depending on the route.

Getting to/from the bus terminal Frequent buses and colectivos nip back and forth between the terminal and the city centre, but the service doesn't run much later than 21.00. Traffic congestion out of the city can make the journey rather torturous with the route taking anything up to an hour at peak times. Look out for a vehicle displaying a sign for 'Terminal' from Carrera 10, Calle 13 and the streets

Bogotá GETTING THERE AND AROUND

3

Destination	Distance (km)	Fare (approx)	Time (hr)
Barranquilla	1,000	85,000 COP	18
Bucaramanga	430	50,000 COP	10
Cali	480	50,000 COP	12
Cartagena	1,130	95,000 COP	20
Cúcuta	630	65,000 COP	16
Manizales	290	35,000 COP	8
Medellín	440	40,000 COP	10
Neiva	310	20,000 COP	6
Pereira	340	30,000 COP	9
Popayán	615	60,000 COP	15
San Agustín	530	35,000 COP	12
Santa Marta	970	90,000 COP	16
Tunja	150	10,000 COP	3

between Calle 19 and Calle 26 heading north – but if you're stuck for time choose a taxi (8,000 COP).

BY TAXI In Bogotá, the phone numbers of the city's dirt-cheap official taxi companies trip off the tongue with ease – choose from Taxi Libres (↘*311 1111*), Taxi Express (↘*411 1111*), Radio Taxi (↘*288 8888*) and Taxi Real (↘*333 3333*). Vast numbers of Korean-made custard-coloured taxis whiz around the city at speed, each is metered with rates that are clearly on display.

Unfortunately, despite a government crackdown, around 25,000 of Bogotá's 55,000 taxis are unregistered – however tempting the offer, these should be avoided at all costs. Look out for drivers with a companion and a vehicle that displays irregular markings. Never get into a taxi that already has one or more passengers – to be sure, get your restaurant or hotel to book a cab on your behalf rather than hail one on the street. Passengers should also be aware that many taxi drivers are armed (for good and bad reasons). Many are also affiliated in some way with a city hotel, so be wary of recommendations – it almost certainly isn't an objective critique when commission is up for grabs.

For longer trips or to keep a driver at hand, private hire might be an option. A highly dependable driver who knows the city core inside and out is Pedro Nieto. His car may not be the latest model but Pedro is reliable, trustworthy and kind-hearted. Expect to pay around 50,000 COP for five or so hours. Use him to nip to shopping malls to find those last-minute essentials or to whizz you off to a restaurant in the far north of the city – Pedro will happily wait around until you're done (↘*310 809 8843*).

BY CAR Although there have been huge improvements in safety on Bogotá's roads, it has been difficult to totally rid the city of a culture of disrespect to traffic laws. More than 50,000 road accidents per year result in about 900 deaths – with more than 18,000 speeding buses, 55,000 madcap taxis and one million private cars making driving in Bogotá only for the very brave. Those prepared to chance the city's congested streets and choked freeways will find numerous car hire options with **Abc Rent-a-Car** (↘*6918113*), **AVIS** (↘*6104455*), **Budget** (↘*2134721*) and **Dollar Rent-a-Car** (↘*6914700*), just a few of the 30 or so rental agencies with offices in Bogotá. However, a key consideration should also be the city's traffic-management programmes that restrict vehicular movement between 06.30–09.00

and from 17.00–19.00, depending on the licence-plate number. Another confusion is that roads such as Carrera 7 also change the direction of traffic flow, with cars in the south lane only running east–west from 17.00–20.00.

BY BICYCLE On a Sunday and on public holidays Bogotá becomes a cycling paradise between 07.00–14.00 when the city's 121km of streets become traffic free. Over three million cycling Bogotános make the most of the peace and quiet in what has become a model programme in South America, if not the world. Bogotá also has one of the most extensive cycleways (*ciclorutas*) on the planet, with over 300km of paths exclusively for people riding bikes. Since the construction of the ciclorutas, bicycle use has increased five-fold in the city and today an estimated 300,000–400,000 trips are made daily in Bogotá by bicycle. The ciclorutas are an ongoing project with plans to extend the cycleways highly popular as the network doesn't currently serve the whole city. Key cycle routes built since 1998 include Calle 170, Calle 127, North-Downtown South, Avenida Ciudad de Villavicencio, Avenida Ciudad de Quito, Avenida Boyacá, Fontibón-Dorado UniAndes, Bosa-Américas-Centro, Avenida Ciudad de Cali, Park Simón Bolívar, Avenida Carrera 68-Calle100, Avenida Centenario, North-Usme Highway, Calle 80, Avenida Mariscal Sucre, Calle 63, South Railroad Corridor, Calle 53, Calle 134, Franja Seca, El Porvenir, La Toscana, Florida-Juan Amarillo and Avenida Suba, Avenida 1º de Mayo and Homecenter. Cycling Bogotános are incredibly respectful of other people in the saddle. One of the best places to pick up cycle gear, spare parts and cycling tips is at **Bicicletas Castillo** on the corner of Carrera 30 and Calle 68.

TRANSMILENIO Few transit initiatives have transformed a city like Bogotá's TransMilenio (*www.transmilenio.gov.co*), a massive public bus transportation system that took over three decades to design. Sleek, fast and efficient, a network of buses provides a system very much like an above-ground metro using self-contained stations equipped with route maps, libraries and art exhibitions. For just 1,200 COP, passengers can hop aboard a bus that is clean, safe and running to schedule. Vehicles operate on their own line well away from vehicular congestion on routes that range from standard to super-express. At the time of writing, the TransMilenio carries a million people per day using more than 600 buses. Although there are plans to extend the service to the airport, current TransMilenio service routes cover Avenida Caracas to the northern and southern suburbs with lines on Carrera 30, Avenida 81, Avenida de Las Américas and Avenida Jiménez to Carrera 3.

BY FOOT Part of Bogotá's 'Mobility Master Plan' has been to encourage pedestrian use of the city, after an era when fear restricted walking – even during daylight. Pedestrian pathways were built to connect key parts of Bogotá's urban landscape, such as the University Network linking the Nacional, Javeriana, Piloto, Gran Colombia and other universities located between Calle 45 and Calle 39. Others include the Athletic Network, a route that links the Botanical Garden with the Salitre Park and Simón Bolívar Park. The Cultural Network runs from the historical centre of La Candelaria out to residential neighbourhoods. Getting more people to travel around Bogotá on foot has played a large part in improving safety, although it is still unwise to walk through the city after dark. Pedestrians should always stick to popular routes, even during daylight. A highly visible police presence makes street mugging and theft less likely in modern-day Bogotá, unless you stroll around the backstreets wearing obvious jewellery with a bulging wallet stuffed in your pocket and a mobile phone plugged to your ear.

3

TOURIST INFORMATION

Seven Tourist Information Points (Turiscade) can be found throughout the city, including a tourist police booth at the El Dorado Airport (✆ *295 4460/428 2424 ext 698*). Specialist tourist advisers are located on the Plaza de Bolívar in LA Candelaria (see below) and the Terminal De Transportes (✆ *295 4460*) as well as the domestic (✆ *425 1000 ext 2155*) and international (✆ *425 1000 ext 2156*) terminals of the El Dorado Airport. At the Teatro Jorge Eliécer Gaitán on Carrera 7 and the Recinto Ferial De Corferias on Carrera 40, tourist offices operate during key events. Most are open from 08.00–18.00, except the airport offices which close at 20.00.

The main tourist office, **Instituto Distrital de Cultura y Turismo** (*Carrera 8, No 9–83;* ✆ *327 4916; www.culturayturismo.gov.co*), is located right on the Plaza de Bolívar and is open daily 08.00–18.00.

Other useful sources of information include the official Bogotá Tourism Bureau website (*www.Bogotáturismo.gov.co*), the Bogotá local government website (*www.Bogotá.gov.co*) and the website of the city of Bogotá (*www.Bogotá-dc.com*).

TOUR OPERATORS

Agencia Parkway ✆ 338 0829/323 2676. Highlights include a walking tour on the hills of Bogotá, cultural tours around museums, galleries & theatres & day & night city tours.

Blue Fields Carrera 13A No 87-81, Bogotá; ✆ (571) 622 0660; www.blue-fields.org

Colombia Unlimited e info@colombiaunlimited.com; www.colombiaunlimited.com

Coches y Carruajes Plaza de Bolívar; ✆ 233 0440/289 1519. Specialist tour company offering sightseeing trips in horse-drawn carriages around the historic streets of La Candelaria.

De Una Colombia Tours Calle 39, No 28–49, Le Soledad; ✆/f 1 369 0112; e info@deunacolombia.com; www.deunacolombia.com.

Empresa Turística y Cultural Candelaria Carrera 8, No 11–39; ✆ 281 5569/283 2319. A specialist in romantic evening walking & sightseeing tours around Bogotá's historic quarter.

Skape Tours Calle 76, No 18–19, Oficina 206; ✆ 491 0769/490 9848. Offers a wide variety of options, including historic city tours, night tours, general sightseeing, tours of the parks, cultural & scientific-themed tours, religious tours, guided walks around La Candelaria & the Salt Cathedral tour (Zipaquirá).

Viajes Chapinero L' Alianxa Carrera 10, No 26–33; ✆ 596 0160. As well as the standard sightseeing tours this company offers shopping & gastronomic trips around the city – during the day & after dark.

WHERE TO STAY

Bogotá has an excellent array of accommodation options, including some budget hostels. However, on the basis of safety most foreign visitors choose to stay at something mid–upper range. Most consider the extra cost worth it for 24-hour security, access-controlled lifts and in-room safety deposit boxes. They also tend to be in the nicer areas of the city close to bars, restaurants and nightlife. Travellers simply looking for a couch on which to kip for the night should check out www.globalfreeloaders.com – at the time of writing more than 20 Bogotá-based people are offering free accommodation, many in the city's central neighbourhoods.

TOP END

🏠 **Casa Medina** (60 rooms/suites) Carrera 7, No 69 A–22; ✆ 217 0288/312 0299; f 312 3769; www.hoteles-charleston.com. Casa Medina was declared a National Historical Conservation Monument in 1985 & the building, which was built in 1945, combines Spanish & French design to very good effect.

Wrought-iron railings & banisters, stone walls & pillars, hand-carved wood ceilings & veneers; decorated with classic & antique furniture with rooms of classical style (14 standard dbls, 18 superior dbls & 28 suites). There's also an onsite restaurant, bar & business centre. $$$$

🏠 **Hotel de la Opera** Calle 10, No 5–72; ☎ 336 2066/5285; e sales@hotelopera.com.co; www.hotelopera.com.co. Suites are the standard accommodation at this truly gorgeous grand historic property. A bright, light, leafy courtyard bar & restaurant attract Bogotá's wealthy elite with a nice fresh juice bar & coffee bar, sumptuous spa & beautifully restored colonial exterior. $$$$

🏠 **Abadia Colonial** Calle 11, No 2–32; ☎ 341 1884; f 342 2672; e abadiacolonial@gmail.com; www.abadiacolonial.com. This charming boutique hotel is set in a beautiful colonial house with clean rooms, private bathrooms & a heater in each room — a real boon if you feel the cold in chilly Bogotá. There's also a tea room & a nice communal area. $$$

🏠 **Hotel La Bohéme** (66 rooms) Calle 82, No 12–35; ☎ 644 7132; www.hotelesroyal.com. A favourite resting place with a jet-setting business clientele, this swish 5-star option is located in the Zona Rosa close to theatres, coffee shops, boutiques, shopping malls & restaurants. The recently refurbished rooms are equipped with high-speed internet access. Comfy queen or large twin beds are standard. Onsite amenities include a business centre, dining room & cocktail bar. $$$

🏠 **Hotel La Fontana Estelar** Avenida 127, No 21–10; ☎ 615 4400; f 216 0449; e ventas@hotelesestelar.com; www.hotelesestelar.com. This rather fine 5-star city hotel employs a high percentage of English- & German-speakers & has a cosmopolitan feel. A range of very nice accommodation options include twins, dbls & vari-sized suites, all with

MID-RANGE

🏠 **Hotel Ambala** Carrera 5, No 13–46; ☎ 342 6384/341 2376; www.hotelambala.net. Another perfectly acceptable option for those looking for mid-range accommodation. Rooms have a private, hot-water bathroom & TV. $$

🏠 **Hotel San Sebastian** Avenida Jiménez, No 3–97; ☎ 334 6041. This place won't win any awards for décor or style, but is a decent enough mid-range option — another hotel favoured by bland businessmen on a budget. Large, clean rooms are perfectly adequate with a private bathroom & a TV. $$

🏠 **Hotel Villa Karina** Calle 30, No 17–47; ☎ 287 1445/5309/1298 & 285 6547. Visitors keen to hang out in the ultra-avant-garde Macarena area will find this middle-sized option appealing. It's close-ish to the bohemian arts district & attracts Colombian business

BUDGET

🏠 **Centro Plaza** Carrera 4, No 13–12; ☎ 243 3818/286 1580; e hotelcentroplaza@gmail.com; www.hotelcentroplaza.com. This Israeli-run budget

minibar, fridge, cable TV, internet, safety deposit boxes & twin phone lines as standard. There's also an excellent coffee bar, pub & restaurant onsite with a large shopping mall just across the road. Expect friendly co-operative staff who are prepared to do their utmost to make your day. $$$

🏠 **Hotel Los Urapanes** Carrera 13, No 83–19; ☎ 218 5065; e Reservas@hotellosurapanes.com.co; www.hotellosurapanes.com.co. This super little boutique hotel overlooking the Zona Rosa offers some nice views. Pick a room on the 2nd or 3rd storey to gaze out over the mountains & take in a cityscape that overlooks Bogotá's party zone. Large rooms are safe, secure & spacious — expect a doorman to check you're OK after dark. $$$

🏠 **Hotel Tequendama Crowne Plaza** (578 rooms + suites) Carrera 10, No 26–21; ☎ 382 0300; f 282 2860; e Bogotá@ihg.com; www.crowneplaza.com. This 5-star hotel in the downtown district boasts a sterling reputation as one of Bogotá's oldest establishments. The 239 dbl, 339 sgl & 103 suites are well appointed with 24-hr room service, cable TV, minibar, safety deposit boxes & voice mail. Guests can use a business centre with high-speed internet access & there is also a laundry & valet service as well as an onsite *casa de cambio*, gym & ATM. A café, restaurant, lobby bar, tour operator & English-style pub are all located around the foyer where there are also jewellery stores, boutiques & handicraft stalls. Ask for a room at the back of the building to avoid the worst of the traffic noise. $$$

executives keen to economise on their expenses. Friendly service, a decent cheap restaurant (all-day meals rarely exceed 5,000 COP for 2 courses) & good-value room rates are all good reasons to book here — there's a dirt-cheap laundry across the road. $$

🏠 **La Casona del Patio Amarillo** Carrera 8, No 69–24; ☎ 212 8805/1991; f 212 3507; e casona@telecom.com.co; www.lacasonadelpatio.net. This lovely ochre-coloured L-shaped building has been recently renovated & offers gardens, patios & a tiled terrace & some very nice rooms. It's a great budget option, in the northern suburbs of the city just 2 blocks west of Carrera 7 & served by 24-hr public transport with a straight connection to La Candelaria a 15-min bus ride away. Bright-painted rooms are adorned with modern art. $$

hotel has rave reviews from cost-conscious travellers. There's also a very nice kosher restaurant & internet cafe onsite. $$

⌂ **Hostal Sue** Calle 16, No 2–55; ☎ 334 8894; e reservations@hostalsue.com; www.hostalsue.com. This brand-new budget hotel is located next door to the Platypus but lacks the charm of its neighbour. However, it's a perfectly acceptable option with dorm beds, sgl rooms & dbls. $$

⌂ **Hotel Avenida Jiménez** Av Jiménez, No 4–71; ☎ 243 6685 & 286 7303. Expect teeny-weeny rooms at this comfortable small hotel with en-suite dbls, quadruple-bed rooms & a room with 3 dbls. $$

⌂ **Hotel Dorantes** Calle 13 (between Carrera 5 & Carrera 6). This tired-looking hotel used to be a fine building but is now in need of some serious TLC. Rundown rooms have crumbling ceilings & faded paintwork. $$

⌂ **Hotel El Dorado** Carrera 4, No 15–00; ☎ 334 399 88/281 7271. Although this nice Colonial hotel is cheap & in a good location, the rooms are often rented out by the hour when occupancy is low. However, the rooms are clean & large & come with private bathroom. $$

⌂ **Hotel Internacional** Carrera 5, No 14–45; ☎ 341 3151/8731 & 342 3768; e hotelinternacionalBogotá@hotmail.com; www.es.geocities.com/hotelinternacionalBogotá. This very decent cheapie is popular with Canadian & American budget travellers & has a kitchen for communal use. Accommodation ranges from dorm beds to family rooms. $$

⌂ **Hotel Santa Fé** Calle 14, No 4–48; ☎ 342 0560. This deliciously rundown hotel in La Candelaría has big rooms with high ceilings and looks like it hasn't been renovated since the early 1920s, which in this instance is a good thing. It's not super clean but has lots of wooden features and old-school charm. $$

⌂ **Platypus** Calle 16, No 2–43; ☎ 341 3104/341 2874; f 352 0127; e platypushotel@yahoo.com; www.platypusbogotá.com. One of La Candelaria's finest places for shoestring travellers is also one of Colombia's nicest, so be sure to make a reservation as it's a highly popular option. If not, show up in the morning at check-out time around 09.30 – & be prepared to take what's available; there's a choice of dorm beds & dbl rooms. The owner of Platypus, German (pronounced Herman) is a genuinely nice guy who loves what he does. He's installed some lovely communal areas with tables, kitchen, a book exchange, free coffee & free Wi-Fi & internet access. Rooms are simple but clean with dorm beds available. If it's full, German will ring around to find alternative options, including home-stays. A linguistic champion, German speaks a dozen languages & is very well travelled himself, with a good knowledge of his own country. Choose this place if you're keen to interact & be social – Platypus is how every small-budget place should be. $$

YOUTH HOSTELS Hostels squarely aimed at backpackers travelling on a shoestring budget tend to come & go. For an up-to-date list visit www.hostelBogotá.com – the site also includes some rather telling reviews.

⌂ **Hostel Bogotá Real** Calle 103, No 29–63. Although this hostel only opened in 2007, it already looks pretty tired. Mattresses are old & the staff indifferent to guest requests or complaints. An airport pick-up costs US$9 with room rates from US$32 per night – a steep option, despite the fact that the price includes b/fast. I'd choose the Platypus in La Candelaria over this place anytime. $$

⌂ **Hostel Anandamayi** Calle 9, No 2–81; ☎ 341 7208; e anandamayihostel@yahoo.com. This comfortable, inexpensive backpacker hostel is housed in a lovely colonial house in La Candelaria & is blessed with a pretty garden with patios, hammocks, geranium bushes, waterfalls, fish ponds & hummingbirds. Guests can use the internet & enjoy sunrise views over the Monserrate in a relaxed place popular with writers, painters & poets – the owners allow long stays & can accommodate up to 40 guests. Rates include linen, towels, safe box, luggage storage, & pizza on Fridays. Rooms are clean & comfortable with a range of mixed dorms, twin & dbl options. $

⌂ **Hostelling International Bogotá DC** Carrera 7, No 6–10; ☎ 280 3318; f 280 3460. There have been mixed reports about this backpacker hostel, so ask to have a look around. It's located in an old colonial building in La Candelaria & has a café/bar, games/TV room, restaurant, BBQ, cooking facilities & a wide variety of rooms. Stays of up to 14 nights are permitted in accommodation that caters for groups of 6, 8, 10 & 16 people. There are also separate dorms for men & women with individual lockers & linen & towels included. Communal shower rooms are equipped with hot water from 06.00–09.00. Family rooms sleep 4–6 people & have private bathrooms. La Candelaria plaza is a couple of minutes walk away, although key bars & restaurants are a longer trek or a short taxi ride. Critics say it lacks atmosphere. $

LONGER STAYS Visitors planning to stay a few weeks or months in Bogotá will find that it's relatively easy to find an apartment to share or rent – just ask the guys at the Platypus or post a message at some of the other traveller hangouts around La Candelaria. Some, but not all, of the hostels offer long-stay discounts. Almost every hotel in town is open to negotiation for longer stays, so don't be afraid to barter. Another good option is an apart-hotel. Viaggio Apartentos (*www.viaggiosuites.com*) have a wide range and are happy to haggle.

For further information see www.bedandbreakfastBogotá.com, www.apartmentsinBogotá.com, www.Bogotácolombialodging.com, www.Bogotá-apartments.com.

✗ WHERE TO EAT

Bogotá is filled with almost 20,000 truly exciting places to wine and dine, from the rustic Colombian eateries serving hearty bowls of *Santafereño sancocho* (a typical Bogotá soup) to numerous bistros, cafés, restaurants and diners specialising in Italian, Middle Eastern, Greek, Mexican and Asian cuisines. *Condé Nast Traveller* ranked the city as one of the finest culinary centres on the planet and as a gastronomic capital Bogotá rarely disappoints. The city has over 300 quality carbon-grill joints, 200 seafood restaurants, 250 oriental eateries, dozens of fast-food outlets and umpteen elegant French à la carte options. Plenty of budget places offer price tags that cater for shoestring diners with numerous mid-range restaurants and those that offer the ultimate in culinary excess. For an updated list of restaurants and dining reviews check out www.Bogotá.gov.co – click onto 'leisure' and follow the gastronomy link.

TOP END $$$–$$$$

✗ **Astrid y Gastón** Carrera 7A, No 67– 64; ☎ 211 1400/1143; www.astridygaston.com. This ultra-fancy Peruvian restaurant housed in a converted mansion also has branches in Peru, Chile & Venezuela & serves upscale dishes at lunch & dinner, Tue to Sat. Expect lots of seafood in rich Peruvian spices, such as blue crab angolotti, octopus with mango & peanut sauce, & grouper with pink peppercorns.

✗ **Carbon de Palo Parrilla** Avenida 19, No 106–112; ☎ 214 5452. This much-loved grilled-meat joint serves legendary man-sized plates of beef, pork, rabbit & chicken in a traditional atmosphere of gastronomic gusto. Expect the conversation to flow as fast as the wine – even in the so-called quiet hours between lunchtime & dinner – with tables of families, couples & co-workers squeezed into every nook & cranny. Choose a grande *punta anca* (steak) with all the trimmings and add a bottle of decent Spanish red wine & be pleasantly surprised by the final bill. Dress up, or down – it doesn't matter one iota.

✗ **Circa Cocina Fusion** Calle 69A, No 5–09; ☎ 217 1123/217 4955; e circacocinafusion@hotmail.com. An elegant European décor mixes with exquisite Mediterranean-oriental cooking styles in one of Bogotá's most relaxed yet uber-cool eateries. Choose from funky cocktails, fine wines & delicious Pan-Asian fusion food in this celebrated diner where the lounge music is as cool as the menu. It's light, bright, airy & elegant – & worth every penny.

✗ **Criterion** Calle 69, No 5–75; ☎ 310 1377/1538. Keen to splurge? Then head to this award-winning restaurant as it could give any fine Parisian kitchen a run for its money. Owners Jorge & Mark Rausch whip up only the finest French-inspired dishes with an ever-changing menu that includes lamb gigot & crab en croute. Expect a fancy clientele that comprises high-flying wheeler-dealer executives, CEOs, ladies that lunch, TV moguls & starlets who enjoy a rather fine wine cellar containing 300 European vintages with no-expense-spared taster menus at a very reasonable price pp.

✗ **Gostinos 69** Calle 28, No 6–77; ☎ 313 0612/0601. Expect to be able to feast on fine seafood, choosing from dozens & dozens of delicious recipes for ceviche, including Thai-style, red hot chilli, lemon garlic & zingy lime. Swish service & chill-out music in a contemporary-modern décor.

✗ **Leo Cocina y Cava** Calle 27B, No 6–75; ☎ 286 7095/281 6267. Ranked by *Condé Naste Traveller* in 2006 as one of the 80 best restaurants in the world, this chic Colombian-Asian fusion specialist is still the talk of the city. Day or night, expect its stark white dining room to be packed to the rafters whilst chef-owner Thorny Leonor mixes coastal Colombian traditions with French-Asian haute cuisine. Menu highlights include snail carpaccio with lemon & olive oil, stuffed carimañolas of rabbit, white fish sashimi served in coconut sauce, mango puree & mint granite & green salad with giant Santander ants.

MID-RANGE $$

✘ **Al Wadi** Calle 27, No 4A–14; ☎ 334 1434. Nestled in the bohemian district of La Macarana amidst artists' studios & bookshops, the Al Wadi restaurant is every inch the atmospheric Lebanese hideaway. Choose from a handful of tables surrounded by Arabian scenes & shisha pipes with a small menu of shish kebabs, breads, hummus & falafel.

✘ **Alina** Calle 9, No 2–81; ☎ 341 7208. Colombian-American patron Mario serves up some of the best pizza in the city. Choose from a dozen toppings & a menu of pasta dishes.

✘ **Asados Patagonia del Sur** Calle 117, No 7–54; ☎ 215 6525; www.patagoniaasadosdelsur.com; ⏰07.00–late. Weekly tango shows are just some of the entertainment staged at this lively Argentine meat restaurant where tables, chairs, posters & bric-a-brac are inspired by Argentinian traditions. Scenes depict horseriding gauchos in the rolling Argentine plains with much use of wood & brick throughout. Find it in the Usaquén neighbourhood.

✘ **Candela Café** Calle 9, No 4–93; ☎ 283 1780. This popular lunch venue serves a super menu & is also open for dinner when the lights are dimmed. Expect salmon gratins, creamy pasta dishes, grilled chicken salads & spicy meatballs.

✘ **Denostia** Calle 29, No 5–84; ☎ 287 3943; ⏰lunch only Mon–Fri & dinner Wed–Sat. The Mediterranean-Colombian menu at this trendy hangout has an army of fans, with traditional dishes subtly infused with some rather nice European touches. Diners can expect plenty of hip music with live bands on a Wed night.

✘ **Restaurante La Pola** Calle 1, No 1–85; ☎ 566 5654; ⏰11.00–17.00 Mon–Sun. This great little local food joint serves up big portions of Bogotá specialities, from grilled plates of meat, bowls of *ajiaco* (chicken soup with cream & potatoes) & *puchero sabanero* (a hearty mixed soup).

BUDGET $$–$

✘ **Autoservicio Luna Nueva** Carrera 7, No 13–55; ☎ 342 6806; ⏰08.00–20.00. This simple little Colombian café opens for breakfast each day & serves good-value dishes until evening. Set lunches are particularly good for shoestring diners.

✘ **Café Sharzab** Carrera 16, No 48–79; ☎ 285 5716; ⏰noon–22.00. Choose from a mouth-watering menu of Persian meals, snacks & desserts at this delightful little find – it's open for lunch (*nahar*) & dinner (*shahm*). Expect super-soft breads, rice, yoghurt drinks & meats cooked with nuts, dried fruit & pulses.

✘ **Comida Mexican al Pastor** Carrera 12, No 83–47; ☎ 300 561 2021; ⏰noon–late. You can't miss this canary-coloured Mexican cantina where budget-priced quesadillas, tacos, enchiladas & nachos come served in generous portions.

✘ **Restaurante Corporación Prodicom** Calle 15A, No 2–21; ☎ 2836737. Tables are at a premium in this fuss-free eatery where low-cost set meals are served from b/fast until mid-afternoon – arrive before 15.30.

✘ **Restaurante Vegetariano El Integral Natural** Carrera 11, No 95–10; ☎ 256 0899; ⏰09.00–18.00 Mon–Fri, noon–18.00 Sat. Set veggie lunches are the main draw at this dirt-cheap café with simple rice dishes, soups & sandwiches.

✘ **Sopas de Mama y Postres de la Abuela** Carrera 9, No 10–59; ☎ 243 4432/342 3973. Literally meaning 'mum's soups & granny's puddings' this restaurant, as its name suggests, offers simple, homely Colombian fare. Several branches have cropped up across the city, all boasting reasonable prices.

AROUND BOGOTÁ

✘ **Andrés Carne de Res** Calle 3, No 11A–56; ☎ 863 7880; e acr@andrescarnederes.com; www.andrescarnederes.com. Ask every Bogotáno about Andrés Carne de Res & the response will be a glowing reference, for this fast-paced party restaurant is a firm favourite with city-dwellers of all ages. Located in Chía in the far north of Bogotá's city limits (a 30,000 COP taxi ride from the centre), this legendary fun-fest is always packed, be it lunchtime or after dark. Steak is the order of the day, served big & tasty. Expect loud music, dancing waiters, raucous sing-songs & wooden menus that retract into the rafters on bungee cords. Dress up, or down – it really doesn't matter. Budget for a splurge & be prepared to queue for a table – or better still, pre-book. $$$

ENTERTAINMENT AND NIGHTLIFE

Bogotá offers all manner of fun and frolics for every conceivable taste, from cinema, theatre and salsa dancing to numerous restaurants, bars, cafés and clubs. The city's nightlife sectors are generally referred to as the M Zone (Macarena), G

Zone (the Gourmet sector), T Zone (where the main roads meet in a 'T'), Zona Rosa (around and including Carrera 13), the V Zone (referring to Usaquen, the area above the T Zone) and Parque de la 93 (around and including Calle 93). Bars, in particular, tend to be clustered around the pedestrianised district of T Zone in the heart of the Zona Rosa, where tourists and Bogotános alike party in their droves. Other key nightspot venues can be found in the city's Chapinero neighbourhood, the gay hub of Bogotá. For the definitive guide to Bogotá's nightlife and entertainment pick up a copy of local newspaper *El Tiempo* (*http://eskpe.eltiempo.terra.com.co*) on a Friday – it has a fine 'what's on' section listing events, exhibitions and concerts and includes details of new places opening up. Another option is the comprehensive monthly magazine *Informativo Cultural de Altiplano Quira* – it costs around 1,300 COP and includes detailed reviews.

NIGHTCLUBS Partying night-owls are spoilt for choice in Bogotá, where hundreds of nightclubs offer every musical style from techno and trance to reggae, tango, rumba, rap and salsa. La Candalería's bars and clubs are clustered along Calle 15 and Carrera 4 with most of the dirt-cheap student hangouts around Carrera 7 and Calle 51. Things are a little bit more upmarket in the uber-cool Zona Rosa where the mood ranges from pretentious designer beats to ultra-chic downright moody – head to the streets between Carrera 11 and Carrera 15 and Calle 81, Calle 84 and Calle 82 to be in the thick of it. Highlights include the mega-spacious **El Sito** (*Carrera 11a, No 93–52;* ☎ *530 5050*), the eclectic **Mister Babilla** (*Calle 82, No 12–15;* ☎ *617 1110*) and the pulsating **Barbar** (*Calle 82, No 12–22;* ☎ *218 1813*). Warm up with one of 50 cocktails at the neon-lit **Tropical Cocktails** (*Calle 93A, No 13A–31;* ☎ *257 1333*). Travellers keen to seek out a British-style pub should check out t**he Red Lion** (*Carrera 12, No 93–64;* ☎ *691 7938*), **Lloyd's** (*Carrera 14, No 94–26;* ☎ *616 0499*) and the **Eight Bells Inn** (*Calle 120A, No 6–23;* ☎ *213 7669*). The **Bogotá Beer Company** is the city's very own micro brewery with a branch seemingly on every corner. Some of the best are the lively Parque de Usaquén, el Park de la 93, Zona T, and where Calle 122 meets Avenida 19 – be sure to try the signature 'Jirafa' (giraffe), a yard-long glass full of the beer of your choice.

SOUNDS AND RHYTHMS OF LATIN AMERICA Bogotános love to sing along to music from the region and dance to classics from Mexico, Argentina and Cuba – as well as melodies from their homeland. Although Cali is Colombia's true salsa city (see page 263), the capital has some decent up-tempo salsatecas where the pace is fast and furious. Check out the latest threads at http://salsaBogotá.blogspot.com for details of where's hot and not.

Salsa
☆ **Club del Caribe** Carrera 28, No 52–36; ☎ 211 1554
☆ **Lázaro** Calle 108, No 15–80; ☎ 213 8811
☆ **Salsa Cámara** Carrera 14, No 82–45, piso 2; ☎ 256 4869
☆ **Salome Pagana** Carrera 14, No 82-16; ☎ 218 4076
☆ **Taberna Bávara** Centro Comercial Atlantis Plaza; ☎ 530 7519

Mexican music
☆ **Chamois** Calle 85, No 11–69; ☎ 218 3285
☆ **Houston's** Carrera 17, No 93–17; ☎ 236 4722
☆ **Ícaro Café** Carrera 13, No 93–60; ☎ 623 3223
☆ **La Cuadra** Carrera 12A, No 83–29; ☎ 616 367
☆ **Plaza México** Transversal 26, No 117–26; ☎ 214 2846
☆ **Villa Margarita** Carrera 15, No 93B; ☎ 610 2982

Cuban music
☆ **Habana Club** Avenida Calle 68, No 73–68; ☎ 252 8231
☆ **Nick Havana** Calle 122, No 25–59; ☎ 214 2083

As homosexuality becomes slowly more accepted in Colombia, the city of Bogotá is at the forefront of pushing the boundaries of convention. A popular leading character in a soap opera is openly also a transvestite in real life, while earlier this year a novel depicting gay love between two fighters in Colombia's internal conflict won a prestigious literary prize. Even the Colombian military is considering accepting a proposal by the national ombudsman for a minimum 1% quota for gays in the army. In 1996, Colombia's first Gay Pride parade attracted just 32 participants, but a decade later more than 140,000 people joined in the parade. Expulsions of gay high school students have become a rarity with reports of 'gay bashing' much reduced. Newspapers no longer use lurid headlines to report gay issues. The downfall of Catholic morals is no longer singularly blamed on homosexuals. Even the Bogotá mayor has championed gay rights and denounced Colombia's culture of machismo – joining Gay Pride revellers on the city's parade route. A decade ago, Bogotá's gay community lived life in fearful anonymity. Today, the city's Chapinero neighbourhood resembles Greenwich Village with a centre specialising in health, legal and psychological services for gays and lesbians. More than 100 bars, nightclubs, saunas, clothes shops and video stores are aimed at a gay clientele. All the best places are listed on www.guiagaycolombia.com/Bogotá – with the following some of the city's finest gay haunts:

☆ **Theatron Club** Calle 58, No 10–32; ☏ 249 2092/235 6879; www.theatrondepelicula.com
☆ **Metro** Calle 61, No 13–81; ☏ 248 0388
☆ **Lottus Bar** Calle 58, No 10–42; ☏ 249 2092/235 6879
☆ **Chase** Calle 67, No 4A–91; ☏ 249 3090
☆ **Ra Bar & Lounge** Calle 64, No 13–52; ☏ 235 6308
☆ **Mistik Bar MK** Carrera 9, No 57–76; ☏ 217 9409/310 563 9686
☆ **Zamburu** Calle 67, No 9-41; ☏ 610 2262
☆ **Música Y Buen Trago** Calle 59, No 9–36; ☏ 310 3552
☆ **Visceversa Bar** Calle 68, No 21–07; ☏ 235 7767
☆ **Ego Disco Bar** Calle 45, No 16–25; ☏ 245 2531
☆ **Kiotho** Calle 66, No 10–75; ☏ 211 4068
☆ **Village Café** Carrera 8, No 64–29; ☏ 346 6592
☆ **El Café** Calle 59, No 13–32; ☏ 249 6512
☆ **El Clóset Lounge & Club** Vía La Calera; ☏ 254 5230; www.elclosetBogotá.com
☆ **Jinetes Club** Vía La Calera; ☏ 648 6009/292 7456/520 1091
☆ **Kiotho** Calle 66, No 10–75; ☏ 211 4068
☆ **Village Café** Carrera 8, No 64–29; ☏ 346 6592
☆ **Blues Bar** Calle 86A, No 13A–30; ☏ 616 7126
☆ **Cavu Bar** Carrera 15, No 88–71; ☏ 530 2356
☆ **Bar Frances La Rue Quatre Vingts** Calle 79, No 11–42; ☏ 317 6539
☆ **Bianca Disco Club** Calle 72, No 16–48; ☏ 314 5187/217 1983

CINEMA Bogotá has almost 50 cinemas, ranging from tiny little art houses showing retro movies in French to sprawling multi-screen complexes where blockbuster films are all the rage. Some of the most interesting screenings are found at the various university *cinematecas* and art cinemas where cutting-edge documentaries and foreign films tend to be the order of the day.

🎞 **Cinematic Distrital** Carrera 7, No 22–79; ☏ 283 5598; www.cinemetecadistrital.gov.co. This rather nice art theatre shows foreign & national films in the Jorge Eliécer Gaitán Theater.

Museo de Arte Moderno Calle 24, No 6–00; 286 0466; f 281 7710; e cine@mamBogotá.com; www.mamBogotá.com. Check out the regular schedule of cine art screenings at this exciting in-house art house as it favours the unusual.

THEATRE AND CONCERTS Bogotá's highly developed theatrical scene offers plenty to choose from year-round, from small independent avant-garde productions and amateur dramatics to large-scale Broadway adaptations.

Teatro de la Candelaria Calle 12, No 2–59; 281 4814. This small repertory company stages a wide range of performances, some of them on controversial themes & is a leading force in progressive theatre in Bogotá.

William Shakespeare Theater Avenida 19, No 152–48; 614 9747. This small independent theatre within the Anglo-Colombiano High School stages British classics & Shakespeare festivals.

Fundación Teatro Nacional La Castellana Calle 95, No 30–13; 257 0893. Expect a range of shows, from light entertainment to serious, weighty theatre from this group of actors, who stage regular shows of varying styles.

Tetro Colón Calle 10, No 5–32; 341 0475. This beautiful, aged auditorium lends considerable grandeur to the backdrop & attracts numerous visiting international touring groups staging large-scale musicals & drama.

Teatro Experimental La Mama Calle 63, No 9–60; 211 2709. Edgy, experimental theatre is the speciality of this venue where local amateur groups perform year-round alternative shows.

♪ **Media Torta** Cnr of Calle 18 & Carretera Circunvalación; 281 7704. Free Sun concerts are popular with a student crowd who flock to this stage behind La Candelaria, from noon–16.00 each week.

♪ **Auditorio León de Greiff** Cnr Carrera 30 & Calle 45; 316 5562. Sat concerts feature orchestras from all over Colombia and Latin America at this university auditorium with tickets for less than 4,000 COP.

♪ **Biblioteca Luis Ángel Arango** Calle 11, No 4–14; 343 1212. Mid-week concerts by international artists attract a wealthy highbrow crowd with local acts performing each Mon appealing to a more grass-roots audience.

SHOPPING

Bogotá has more than 70 large shopping centres with a great variety of boutiques, craft shops, chain stores and malls all over the city. Prime shopping areas are located in the north and northwestern areas, as shown below: Alhambra Plaza (*Calle 114A, No 33–54*), Aquarium (*Calle 60, No 9–83*), Atlantis Plaza (*Calle 81, Carrera 14*), BIMA (*Autopista Norte, No 232–35*), Bulevar Niza (*Carrera 52, No 125A–59*), Cedritos 151 (*Diagonal 151, No 32–19*), Centro 93 (*Calle 93, No 14–20*), Centro Andino (*Carrera 11, No 82–71*), Cosmos 64 (*Calle 64, No 11–37*), El Castillo (*Carrera 7, No 72–64;* 211 4321), Galerías (*Calle 54, No 26–41*), Granahorrar (*Calle 72, No 10–34;* 312 7077), Hacienda Santa Bárbara (*Carrera 7, No 115–60*), Iserra 100 (*Calle 100 Avenida Suba*), Los Héroes (*Transversal 18, No 78–99;* 257 0459), Mazurén (*Autopista Norte, No 150–46*), Metropolis (*Carrera 68, No 75A–50*), Palatino (*Calle 139, Carrera 7*), Portal de la 80 (*Transversal 100A, No 80A–20*), Portoalegre (*Carrera 52, No 137–27*), Salitre Plaza (*Carrera 68B, No 40–39;* 416 9737), Santa Ana (*110 Av 9*), Santafé Shopping Center (*Calle 185, No 45–03; Autopista Norte*), Subazar (*Calle 140, No 91–34*), Unicentro (*Av 15, No 123–30*), Unicentro de Occidente (*Carrera 111C, No 86–05;* 434 8797), Unilago (*Carrera 15, No 78–33*).

STRICTLY LEGAL

In Colombia, the legal driving age is 18, the same age at which citizens can drink, get married, vote and become legally responsible for their own criminal actions. The age for sexual consent is 14. Bizarrely, however, children under 18 must be accompanied by both parents when travelling..

HANDICRAFTS AND SOUVENIRS Bogotá has way too many craft shops, flea markets and souvenir stores to mention all of them, but some of the best are clustered around Carrera 7, Carrera 15 (between Calles 72 and 85) and Calle (on the corner of Carrera 10). Check out the **Mecardo Artesanal Plaza Bolívar** on Carrera 9, No 12–52; the **Centro Artesanías de Colombia** on Carrera 3, No 18–60; the **Galería Artsenal de Colombia** on Calle 16, No 5–70; and the **Artesanías El Balay** on Carrera 15, No 75–63. The Mercado de San Alejo on Carrera 7 between Calles 24 and 26 is probably the best flea market – it's held every Sunday between 09.00–17.00.

EMERALDS AND JEWELLERY Every parade of shops in Bogotá contains at least a couple of *joyerías* (jewellery stores) although the main centre for emerald shopping is in and around Carrera 6 between Calle 12 and Calle 13 and in the Centro Internacional where at least 90 outlets cater specifically for this market. There's also an emerald traders street market on the corner of Avenida Jiménez and Carrera 7 and most hotel boutiques stock a small range of Colombian gold.

SPORT

Bogotá's fanatical football (soccer) scene is highly charged, with matches at the Estadio El Campín (✎ *315 8726*) on a Wednesday and Saturday night often played to maximum crowds. The 46,018-seater stadium opened in 1946 and is the home ground of the Independiente Sante Fe and Millonarios club teams as well as the Colombian national squad – although, at the time of writing, it is one of the many football grounds that are affected by the FIFA decision to ban international football at over 2,500m above sea level. The ruling was greeted with great dismay in Latin America, notably in Ecuador, Peru, Bolivia and Colombia – where Bogotá's stadium sits at 2,640m. For tickets for local games call the Millonarios (✎ *347 7080*) and Santa Fé (✎ *544 6670*) box offices. Tickets for international games are available from the Federación Colombia de Fútbol (✎ *288 9838; www.colfutbol.org*).

OTHER PRACTICALITIES

ALTITUDE SICKNESS A former motto of Bogotá was that it was '2,600 metres closer to the stars' – a direct reference to its altitude above sea level. Some travellers may find that the rapid ascent into Bogotá can lead to altitude sickness with dizziness, sweating and breathlessness the most common effects. Should these symptoms persist seek medical attention or contact Bogotá's 24-hour healthline by dialling 125. Alternatively medicine can help alleviate symptoms.

BOOKSTORES, NEWSPAPERS AND LIBRARIES Bogotá was appointed the 'World Capital of the Book' for 2007 by UNESCO in recognition of its role in promoting reading initiatives. Unlike many Latin American cities, Bogotá has a large number of bookstores, although very few stock English-language publications. One of the best range of imported titles can be found at **Gaviot @ Libros** (*Carrera 15, No 82–54;* ✎ *256 5621*). Non-Spanish-language newspapers, such as the *Sunday Times, Herald Tribune, Le Monde, New York Times, Süddeutsche Zeitung, Jerusalem Post, Financial Times* and *Mainichi Shimbun*, are stocked by a newsagent on the retail level at El Dorado Airport – although these can be up to two weeks out of date. Of Colombia's 400 public libraries, Bogotá has 33 of which the city's **Biblioteca Nacional** (*Calle 24;* ✎ *243 5969*) is the backbone. A collection of more than 800,000 books and manuscripts can be enjoyed in numerous reading rooms – tourists need to apply for a library card to visit but it's worth the red tape. Another recommendation is the **Biblioteca Luis Angel Arango** (*Calle 11;* ✎ *343 1212*) in the heart of the historic district of la Candelaria– without a doubt one of the best-equipped libraries in Latin America. Large reading rooms lead to magnificent art galleries and auditoriums that are home to a dazzling array of year-round temporary exhibitions. Other libraries include the **Biblioteca Virgilio Barco** (*adjacent to Simón Bolívar Park*) where a collection of 25,000 books and 64 reading areas is open to the public free of charge. **Biblioteca El Tunal**, in south Bogotá, has over 110,000 titles – find it on Carrera 48.

EMERGENCY/USEFUL NUMBERS

Police (emergency)	✎ 156
Police	✎ 112 (✎ *428 0677*)
Fire	✎ 119 (✎ *217 5300*)
Red Cross ER	✎ 132 (✎ *428 0111*)
Civil Defence	✎ 144 (✎ *640 0090*)
GAULA (Anti-kidnapping)	✎ 165
Citizens' Information Line	✎ 195
Tourist police	✎ 337 (✎ 4413/243 1175)
Traffic police	✎ 127 (✎ *360 0111*)
24-hour Healthcare line	✎ 125
Department of Immigration	✎ 153

LAUNDRIES AND DRY CLEANERS Hotel laundry services in Bogotá are generally fast and cheap – some charge by the weight of a bundle of garments, others on an item-by-item basis. Some of the best include **Bollé Lavandería** (*Calle 79, No 64–26;* ✎ *231 1026*), **Lavatapetes América** (*Carrera 75-7-F-51;* ✎ *411 7845*) and **Lavandería Espumas** (*Calle 19, No 3A–37*). Expect to pay around 6,500 COP for a wash-and-dry service. Travellers that decide to wash their own stuff can pick up clothes detergent at 6,000 COP for a 2kg pack.

MEDICAL SERVICES A high level of medical care comparable to that in industrialised countries is available in Bogotá and the city has many hundreds of clinics, medical centres and hospitals, both private and state-funded. Having medical insurance will allow you to visit a private doctor where facilities tend to be better and English more widely spoken. Bogotá's ophthalmology clinics already enjoy a good reputation for their pioneering use of new technology, and the city also has world-class facilities in areas such as fertility treatment, prosthetics, cancer treatment, transplantations, cardiovascular medicine and plastic surgery. Latin America's first baby born after in vitro fertilisation was born in Bogotá. The city also has the region's most advanced blood bank and transfusion centre. In 2002, city authorities in Bogotá launched a medical tourism initiative, promoting the capital as a place that is 'good for your health'. Particularly good facilities can be found at **Clínica de Marly** (✎ *343 6600*) on Calle 50 where a number of doctors cover most specialities, with a wide range of travel-related medical services offered at the **Centro de Atención al Viajero** – including vacations and laboratory tests. For a list of hospitals and private clinics visit: www.Bogotá-dc.com/dir/clinicas. Bogotá is also blessed with some excellent dentists, including **Antonio José Hurtado Soto** (*Calle 134;* ✎ *627 2684/258 1281*), **Centro Odontopediatrico** (*Calle 12;* ✎ *312 3739/211 3484*) and **Flórez Antonio** (*Calle 134;* ✎ *520 0108*). For a list of more than 50 orthodontists visit www.Bogotá-dc.com/profesiones/odontologos.

MONEY AND CURRENCY Hundreds of money-exchange specialists operate in Bogotá with 24-hour booths at the airport, outlets in most major hotels and offices

3

on almost every street corner citywide. A large concentration of casa de cambios can be found downtown at Jiménez Avenue, around El Rosario Square and the International Center and between Calle 90 and Calle 95. Most buy and sell foreign currency, travellers' cheques and handle international drafts. Four of the largest chains are **Cambios Country** (*www.cambioscountry.com.co*), **ABC Cambios Okura** (*www.cambiosokura.com*), **Giro América** (*www.giroamerica.com.co*) and **Money Gram** (*www.moneygram.com*). Rates can vary enormously so if this matters, be prepared to shop around. Credit cards are widely accepted in Bogotá's larger hotels and restaurants but expect to pay cash (often in advance) in the cheaper hostels and pensionados.

Unlike the rest of Colombia, banks in Bogotá close at 15.00 Monday to Thursday, 15.30 on Friday but stay open over the lunch period – a quirk that catches many first-time visitors out. Not all handle foreign currency or offer cash advances on credit cards, but most have an ATM, including the **Banco Popular** on Calle 24 and the **Bancoclombia** and **Banco Unión Colombiano** on Carrera 8. For a list of ATM locations visit www.Bogotá-dc.com/dir/cajeros – there are dozens citywide.

SHOWERS, EQUIPMENT AND LUGGAGE El Dorado Airport has showers with towels, disposable slippers, soap and shampoo – find them at module 4. There are also luggage lockers at modules 1, 2 and 3 – great for those keen to explore Colombia without lugging the entire contents of their backpack around, and a way to beat luggage-weight restrictions on smaller planes. Bogotá has several very good camping supply stores that stock a decent array of tents, trekking equipment, gas canisters, sleeping bags and backpacks. Two of the best are **Almacén Aventura** (*Carrera 13, No 67–26;* ✆ *248 1679*) and **Montaña Accesorios** (*Carrera 13A, No 79–46;* ✆ 530 6103) .

SOLO TRAVELLERS AND MEETING FRIENDS Lone travellers in Bogotá who fancy meeting up with like-minded people have plenty of options. Scour the notice boards in backpacker hostels in the city and you'll spot plenty of 'solo traveller seeks similar postings, usually from European and Americans seeking company on the next leg of their trip. Another option is to post details of your travel plans on **WAYN.com** (Where Are You Now), a website aimed at helping travellers keep touch that has members in Bogotá. **Sal Si Puedes** (✆ *283 3765*) is a group of outdoor-minded people who enjoy walks in the countryside on the outskirts of the city. **Ecoguías** also arrange weekly group walks for each Sunday (✆ *347 5736*). Cyclists should look up **Bici Bogotá** (e *biciBogotá@yahoo.com; www.biciBogotá.com*) – a community of two-wheeling adventurous types that head north out of Bogotá each weekend en masse.

TELEPHONE, POST AND INTERNET Most of Bogotá's major hotels offer internet access to guests, some for a nominal charge. If yours doesn't, don't despair – the city is jam-packed with internet cafés. Rates range from around 1,500–3,000 COP per hour and some are open 24 hours. **Café Internet** (*Carrera 27A, No 53a–65–Galerias;* ✆ *544 4675*) never closes and offers lightning-fast connections with **Antipasto e Internet** (*Carrera 4A, No 25c–24*) open from 06.00 until late. For a list of more than 30 internet cafes visit: www.bogota-dc.com/dir/cyber. Wi-Fi access is available at the Alta Technologia on Carrera 15 and the Atlantis Plaza on Calle 81 – for technical know-how contact **Colombia Wireless** (✆ *210 1033*) or **@.CABITEL** (✆ *363 7994*).

Most of Bogotá's internet cafes also offer international phone calls at rates of around 1,000 COP per minute. **Telecom** (✆ *561 1111*) has offices throughout the city, including a large base on Calle 23, No 13–49. Services include domestic and international phone calls and faxes with branches open 07.00–19.00 each day.

Colombia's **Adpostal** has offices in La Candelaria (*cnr Carrera 7 and Calle 13;* ↘ *353 5666*) and the Centro Internacional (*Carrera 7, No 27–54*) with **DHL** (↘ *212 9727*) on Calle 72, No 10–70, and **FedEx** (↘ *291 0100*) on Carrera 7, No 16–50. **Avianca**'s city centre branch (↘ *342 7513*) has a post restante on Carrera 7, No 16–36, with a branch at the Centro Internacional (↘ *342 6077*).

WHAT TO SEE AND DO

MUSEUMS Bogotá has over 80 public and private museums – all of which are well managed and well funded. Collections range from archaeological and colonial exhibits to modern art, sculpture and religious artefacts – and are well worth a visit. Sundays can be busy, as some museums offer free admission. Avoid the last Sunday of the month when every collection can be visited free of charge – the crowds are vast. The following are just some of the highlights.

Museo del Oro (Gold Museum) (*Calle 16, No 5–41;* ↘ *284 7450; www.banrep.gov.co/museo;* ⊕*09.30–16.30 Tue–Sat, 10.00–16.30 Sun & public holidays; admission 2,000 COP*) More than 34,000 gold pieces from most of Colombia's major pre-Hispanic cultures (Calima, Quimbaya, Muisca, Tairona, Sinú and Tolima amongst others) are contained in this innocuous modern building – making it one of the most important collections of its type worldwide. A sign states that 'birds are fundamental symbols of the shaman. Like them, he can fly, see a long way, link the earth to the sky, and take part in reproducing nature' – and throughout the exhibition the natural world is represented at every turn. Parrots, macaws, fish and iguanas feature in resplendent magnificence on this vast collection of 'ofrendas alos dioses' ('offerings to the gods') comprising masks, necklaces, bracelets and hundreds of figurines. At the heart of this collection is a circular exhibition pod with automated illumination in sections – don't miss the atmospheric display that starts off dark and culminates in a dazzling array of gold. Although most of the exhibits are signed in Spanish there are English-language tours each day (at 11.00 and 15.00 at the time of writing). The collection spans two floors and is just a small, handpicked selection of a vast collection held in the museum's guarded vault. Part of this national monument is a display of 20,000 bone and ceramic objects.

Museo Botero (*Calle 11, No 4–41;* ↘ *343 1331;* ⊕*09.00–19.00 Mon–Sat (closed Tue), 10.00–17.00 Sun; free admission*) This magnificent 208-piece collection was donated by Colombia's most famous artist Fernando Botero (see box, *Fernando Botero, Chapter 1*, page 37) and contains 123 of his own works along with 85 by an impressive range of European masters – including pieces by Picasso, Chagall, Dalí, Renoir, Matisse and Monet to name just a few. Housed in a beautifully restored colonial mansion (Casa Luis López de Mesa), the Botero collection is catalogued as the most important art exhibition in the country and comprises drawings, paintings, sculpture using some fine aquarelle, oleo and pastel techniques.

Casa de la Moneda (*Calle 11, No 4–93;* ↘ *343 1212;* ⊕*09.00–19.00 Mon, Wed & Sat, 10.00–17.00 Sun; free admission*) As the immediate neighbour of Donación Botero, this fine historic building is often visited as part of a walking tour around the area. The city's former mint boasts a succession of rooms containing several permanent exhibitions and collections, including coins, bills, printing presses and artefacts relating to the strongroom.

God made us walking animals – pedestrians. As a fish needs to swim, a bird to fly, a deer to run, we need to walk, not in order to survive, but to be happy.

Enrique Penalosa, former Mayor of Bogotá

Vast, sprawling Bogotá continues to grow at an alarming pace and offers far too much ground to cover in a single visit. However, getting to grips with the neighbourhoods of La Candelaria and Plaza de Bolívar is more than achievable in a day or two – you won't have time to see everything but it'll be a decent introduction to the city's heart and soul. The distance between the pigeon-scattered Plaza de Bolívar and the Parque Santander is less than 2km but as the route is jam-packed with museums, churches, craft shops, cafés, bars and markets allow at least a day if you plan to break for lunch.

Set off from the steps of the vast **Catedral Primada,** one of Bogotá's finest colonial structures and head to the commemorative collection in honour of the 1810 Creole Rebellion at the **Museo del 20 de Julio**. Next it's on to the beautiful **Casa de la Moneda** and the fascinating art works at **Donación Botero** – an exhibition that is practically a review of late 19th-century art history and includes original pieces by Corot, Monet, Matisse, Picasso, Dalí, Chagall, Bacon and de Kooning. Take Calle 10 downhill from the corner of Calle 4 past the quirky roof-mounted sculptures that adorn some of the bubblegum-coloured houses to the **Palacío de San Carlos**, the former government HQ before it was moved to the Palacío de Nariño. It was from this fine old palace that Bolívar fled through a window to escape a murder attempt, leaping half-naked from a bathtub, covered in soap. At Carrera 6, turn left to view the rather magnificent religious art collection at **Museo de Arte Colonial** before heading on to the ancient Iglesia de San Ignacio and the Iglesia Museo de Santa Clara. Push on up Carrera 7 from the grand **Central Plaza** to discover shops, boutiques and outlets galore before crossing Avenida Jimenéz to the handicraft stalls, buskers and food vendors at **Parque Santander.** A visit to the resplendent **Museo del Oro** provides a fitting finale to touring Bogotá on foot. Despite the extensive pillaging of pre-Columbian art by the conquistadores and the mass exportation of South American gold, the museum boasts the finest collection of pre-Columbian gold on the continent. It contains 33,000 individual pieces, from simple bangles to some of the most beautifully crafted masks and figures in the world.

Museo Nacional (National Museum) (*Carrera 7, No 28–66;* ℡ *334 8366; www.museonacional.gov.co;* ◎ *10.00–17.30 Tue–Sun; admission 3,000 COP*) Colombia's oldest museum is housed in a British-designed old stone-and-brick building, dating back to 1823. Thomas Reed created the Panóptico as the city's prison, using fortress-style architecture that includes arches, domes and columns in the shape of a Greek cross. More than 100 prison cells were constructed behind a solid façade housing both male and female prisoners up until 1946. In 1948, the building was adapted significantly to house the National Museum. It underwent further restoration in 1975 to add extra rooms and modern services and today contains a collection of over 20,000 pieces, including archaeological artefacts, indigenous and Afro-Colombian art, paintings, documents and cultural objects. There are also 57 paintings by Fernando Botero, Alejandro Obregón and Guillermo Wiedemann in this three-storey collection that spans Colombia's history from the pre-Hispanic era.

Museo Histórico Policía (Museum of Police History) (*Calle 9, No 9–27;* ☎ *233 5911/281 3284;* ⊕*08.00–17.00 Mon–Fri (closed noon–13.00), 08.00–14.00 Sat; admission free*) Most people visit this exhibition to see the blood-stained jacked of Colombia's most notorious drug baron, Pablo Escobar. The jacket was worn by Escobar on the day he was shot dead by police gunmen after a high-profile (and controversial) 499-day manhunt. Museum rooms are organised chronologically to allow running history of the Colombian police force from its inception in a building that became the national police HQ in 1923. The museum has lots of exhibits that focus on laws, penalties and punishments, containing guns, radios, uniforms and insignia.

Museo Arqueológico (Archaeological Museum) (*Carrera 6, No 7–43;* ☎ *243 1048;* ⊕*08.30–17.00 Tue–Fri, 09.30–17.00 Sat, 10.00–16.00 Sun; admission 3,000 COP*) This extensive collection of archaeological relics is housed in the beautifully restored Casa del Marqués de San Jorge, a fine 17th-century Colonial building that is museum piece in itself. Expect lots of fine ceramic pieces from Colombia's main pre-Columbian Indian groups, many of which are some of the most magnificent artistically ever found in the region.

Museo de Arte Colonial (Museum of Colonial Art) (*Carrera 6, No 9–77;* ☎ *341 6017;* ⊕*09.00–17.00 Mon–Fri, 10.00–16.00 Sat/Sun; admission 2,000 COP*) Originally a Jesuit college, this grand 17th-century building was inaugurated as a museum in 1942 and contains an impressive array of paintings, silverware, books, furniture and carvings from the colonial era. A collection of words by painter Gregorio Vásquez de Arce y Ceballos is the largest in the world and comprises 76 oils and 106 drawings – all of them truly memorable.

Museo del 20 de Julio (Museum of Independence) (*Calle 11, No 6–94;* ☎ *282 6647;* ⊕*09.00–17.00 Tue–Fri, 10.00–16.00 Sat/Sun; admission 4,000 COP*) Located on the site of the Creole revolution against Spanish rule on 20 July 1810, the Museum of Independence looks over the Plaza de Bolívar and is housed in the Casa del Florero. A rather sterile collection of papers and paintings relate to the Colombian fight for independence – it's nothing mind-blowing but it does a decent job of telling the tale.

Museo de Arte Moderno (*Carrera 24, No 6–00;* ☎ *286 0466; www.mambogotá.com;* ⊕*10.00–18.00 Tues–Sat, 12.00–17.00 Sun; admission 3,000COP*) This large collection of temporary displays of 20th-century visual arts changes frequently. It opened in the mid 1980s and contains painting, photography and sculpture by national and international artists – although home-grown talent is the focus.

Museo Quinta de Bolívar (*Calle 20, No 2–91;* ☎ *336 6410/6419;* e *quintadebolivar@ excite.com; www.quintadebolivar.gov.co;* ⊕*9.00–16.30 Tue–Fri, 10.00–15.30 Sat/Sun; admission 3,000 COP*) Built in 1880 and given to Simón Bolívar in 1820, this grand mansion was restored in 1998 and declared a National Monument as a testament to Bolívar's era. A fine example of rural colony architecture, the museum contains furniture, garments, armoury, documents and objects belonging to the Liberator and is set in splendid gardens in the foothills of the Cerro de Monserrate.

Iglesia Museo de Santa Clara (*Carrera 8, No 8–91;* ☎ *341 1009;* ⊕*09.00–17.00 Tue–Fri, 10.00–16.00 Sat/Sun; admission 2,000 COP*) This fine colonial church no longer opens for worship but as a museum it is still very much worth a visit. Built between 1629 and 1674 as part of the Poor Clare convent, it typifies Bogotá's single-nave church structures and has a stunning interior with over 100 wall paintings, ornate altarpieces and statues dating from the 17th and 18th centuries.

Museo de Francisco José Caldas *(Carrera 8, No 6–87; ⊙10.00–17.30 Tue–Fri, 10.00–15.00 Sat/Sun; admission 3,000 COP)* Located in the premises of Presidential Guard Infantry Battalion, this fascinating museum contains a range of exhibits of scientific instruments, writings and books belonging to Sabio Caldas, Colombia's most famous naturalist. Browse through documents of scientific-historical interest, including expedition plans, cartographic maps and surveys of Colombia's geographic areas. Displays also feature all manner of engineering instruments consisting of telescopes, hypsometry, metal detectors and microscopes.

CHURCHES Although only a handful of Bogotá's many churches look anything much from the outside, don't let this fool you – a great number offer plenty of surprises. Many have inwardly ornate décor and elaborate furnishings despite a dull exterior. Most date back to the 17th and 18th centuries and some contain paintings by Gregorio Vásquez de Arce Y Ceballos, one of Colombia's most famous colonial painters and a Bogotá legend. There are too many fine and interesting churches to list them all individually. Some of the highlights include the following.

Catedral Primada *(Plaza de Bolívar; ↘ 341 1954; ⊙09.00–10.00 Mon–Sat, 09.00–14.00 Sun)* This hulking great neo-Classical building stands on the site where the first mass was celebrated on the founding of Bogotá in 1538. At that time, there was just a simple thatched chapel although several larger replacement structures have been constructed over years. The first in 1556–65 collapsed in a pile of rubble due to poor workmanship and the second, built in 1572, was reduced to ruins by an earthquake in 1785. The present building dates back to 1807 but wasn't fully completed until 1823 and is by far Bogotá's largest church. The body of the city's founder Jiménez de Quesada is entombed in a chapel off the right-hand aisle away from a vast array of pews in echoing spaciousness.

Iglesia de San Francisco *(Cnr Av Jiménez & Carrera 7; ↘ 341 2357; ⊙07.00–19.00 Mon–Fri, 07.00–13.00 & 18.00–19.00 Sat/Sun)* Bogotá's oldest surviving church has a beautifully elaborate interior that includes some fine Mudejar ceiling ornamentation and a magnificent 17th-century gilded altarpiece – so don't let the rather austere exterior put you off. The building dates back to 1556 and has a loyal and flourishing congregation – so expect packed pews.

Iglesia de San Ignacio *(Calle 10, No 6–35; ↘ 342 1639; ⊙09.00–18.00 Mon–Fri (closed noon–15.00), 09.00–noon Sat/Sun)* Originally founded in 1610 by the Jesuits the building remained unfinished until their expulsion in 1767 but has been a place of worship since 1635. Today it remains one of Bogotá's most lavishly decorated churches and as befitting a large colonial relic it contains a wealth of magnificent art.

Iglesia de la Veracruz *(Calle 16, No 7–19; ↘ 342 1343; ⊙for mass only at 08.00, noon & 18.00)* An important burial place for the heroes of independence, the tomb of the martyrs of the Veracruz Church is known as the National Pantheon throughout Bogotá. Between 1810 and 1819, some 80 patriots who were killed by the Spanish came to rest in the church's catacombs. Although it has a simplistic interior, the Iglesia de la Veracruz has some fine altarpieces and an impressive panelled vault.

OTHER SIGHTS

Cerro de Monserrate (*Quinta de Bolívar;* ↘ *284 5700;* ⊕ *10.00–midnight Mon–Sat, 10.00–16.00 Sun; cost 11,200 pesos (day) & 14,200 pesos (eve)*) This dominant mountain peak shapes Bogotá's cityscape and has a handsome white church built on its summit at 3,200m. Devotees of the Señor Caído inside the church (a statue of Christ) make Sunday pilgrimages to the mountaintop, where some of the best panoramic views of Bogotá can be enjoyed unless a build-up of smog gets in the way. Looking down on the chaos of the city from Monserrate Hill on a clear day is nothing short of breathtaking with incredible views that extend from the banks of the Río Bogotá to La Candelaria's red-tiled roofs. There's a handicrafts market, cafés and a couple of excellent restaurants – all of which stay open until midnight. A half-hourly *teleférico* (cable car) or tram departs from Monserrate station near Quinta de Bolívar for the 15-minute journey to the peak.

Mirador Torre Colpatria (*Carrera 7, No 24–89, Piso 50;* ↘ *283 6665;* ⊕ *10.00–17.00 Sat/Sun & public holidays*) More stunning 360° views abound from the top of Torre Colpatria, home to the highest building in Colombia at 180m. Look out across the city's western hills, Parque de la Independencia and Torres del Parque over criss-crossing streets, rooftops and bridges. Take a lift to the top at a cost of 2,000 COP where there are numerous telescopes and a coffee shop on the 50th floor.

Jardín Botánico José Celestino Mutis (*Calle 57, No 61–13;* ↘ *437 7060; www.jbb.gov.co;* ⊕ *09.00–17.00 Tue–Sun (closed noon–14.00)*) This botanical park and centre of scientific investigation is named in honour of botanist José Celestino Mutis (see box, *Colombia's First Botanist*, page 340). Climate-controlled exhibits of flora boast staggering temperature differences and reflect the varied regions of Colombia. There is also an exhibit of 5,000 indigenous orchids – one of the most exquisite collections in the nation. Beautiful grounds offer a comprehensive selection of plants and shrubs with gardens stocked with a huge diversity of flora. A good-quality restaurant serves pan-Colombian fare.

Maloka (*Carrera 68D, 40A–51;* ↘ *427 2707; www.maloka.org;* ⊕ *08.00–18.00 Mon–Thu, 09.00–19.00 Fri–Sun; admission 9,000 COP*) One of the most impressive science and technology centres in South America, Maloka has become a byword for high-tech fun. An interactive museum with a thematic structure, it allows visitors to play science-related games and view documentaries in a giant domed-roof cinema on physics, chemistry, maths, biology and geography. The name of the museum derives from the Indian word *maloca* – a meeting house that indigenous communities believe is the centre of the universe and life, a symbol of family integration and a place to share ideas and solve problems.

La Candelaria Bogotá's old historic quarter has some magical, captivating qualities – with gorgeous blue, pink, gold, turquoise, magenta, ochre and canary-yellow colonial buildings adorned with balconies painted crimson, white and deep blue. Pretty cobbled streets cluttered with bohemian shops, craft stalls and galleries climb up towards a hazy mountain peak. Eccentric rooftop sculptures draw the gaze skywards while a cacophony of street musicians, chattering students and food vendors rises from parks and plazas. Handsome boulevards open up on the Plaza de Bolívar, a handsome and crowded meeting point with the people and pigeons of La Candelaria. Visit swish hotel courtyard cafés or trendy student juice bars in a fine aged city centre that is wonderful to explore on foot.

FESTIVALS AND EVENTS

Feria Taurina (*Jan/Feb;* \ *334 1482*) After the official launch of the bullfighting season in mid-December, regular fixtures at the Plaza de Toros de Santamaría begin in earnest each new year. Events are typically staged on a Sunday and feature the finest Spanish, Mexican and Colombian matadors in a truly resplendent 14,500-seater bullring built in 1931. Tickets range in price from 55,000 COP for a seat in the sun to 330,000 COP in the shade.

Festival Iberoamericano de Teatro (*Mar/Apr; www.festivaldeteatro.com.co*) This vast theatrical extravaganza takes place every year with an even number, celebrating its 10th anniversary in 2006. Over 200 theatre groups comprising 2,400 artists from five continents and 42 countries stage performances across dozens of Bogotá's most iconic venues, attracting an audience of over 2.5 million people to a host of plays, dramas, musicals and comedy in one of Latin America's most elaborate theatrical events.

Feria de Libro de Bogotá (*Apr/May; www.feriadellibro.com*) Since the first book fair was launched in 1988 the event has gone from strength to strength with more than 95% of Colombia's editorial industries participants in 2007. Expect 300,000 visitors from across the globe during the 13-day event where over 100,000 titles and 500 exhibitors occupy 15,000m² of space.

Carnaval de Bogotá (*Aug*) This citywide celebration of its Hispanic foundation includes masquerades, dances, processions and parades culminating in an array of activities, concerts and sports events centred on the Parque Simón Bolívar. A host of warm-up pre-carnival festivities begin each year in July with beauty pageants, folkloric shows and live music.

Jazz al Parque (*Sep*) This two-day open-air jazz concert in the Parque de los Novios attracts a high-calibre international line-up with class acts taking stage from 21.00–midnight each night. It's free and a highlight in Bogotá's crowded festival calendar, and was established in the city in 1996.

Hip-Hop al Parque (*Oct*) Hip-Hop in the Park brings beats and rhymes to the city's Parque Simón Bolívar with two-days of the finest hip-hop music. An eight-hour set starts at 13.00 each day. Since launching in 1998, this mega rap event has attracted a strong international line-up and attracts an enviable crowd of international DJs.

The distribution of knowledge is the key contemporary task. Knowledge empowers people. If people know the rules, and are sensitised by art, humour, and creativity, they are much more likely to accept change.

Antanas Mockus, Bogotá mayor 1993–2003

Mathematician, philosopher and political novice Antanas Mockus traded a top job at the Colombian National University to run as mayor of Bogotá. He won, so using his skills as an educator, Mockus set about turning Bogotá into one of the most ambitious social experiments on the planet – a ground-breaking social change project.

At the time, Bogotá was choked with violence, lawlessness and corruption – a metropolis on the cusp of chaos. People tossed garbage on the street whilst drivers showed little regard for pedestrians, actually speeding up as people attempted to cross the street. People were desperate for a change and for moral leadership – Mockus, the only son of a Lithuanian artist and an intelligent eccentric, fitted the bill. He donned a Superman costume to promote being a heroic 'Supercitizen' – softening the extreme scepticism of the city through humour and community pride. He focused on changing hearts and minds by empowering Bogotá's citizens as individuals – not through preaching. He got people to think about good and bad behaviour and to approve or disapprove. He also spoke openly with partial self-mockery of his own failings, admitting that he wasn't any more moral than anyone else. Mockus had already gained notoriety for the use of some rather unconventional teaching techniques, once dropping his pants and mooning a class of rowdy art students to gain their attention. As a leader, Mockus was equally avant-garde, hiring 420 mime artists to control the traffic in Bogotá's rush-hour chaos. They shadowed pedestrians who didn't follow crossing rules and poked fun at reckless drivers, as Mockus believed that Bogotános were more afraid of being ridiculed than of being fined. He also launched a 'Night for Women' decreeing that the city's men should stay home. On the first night alone of this three-day event, more than 700,000 women enjoyed the freedom of free concerts, bars, clubs and restaurants – walking without fear around the city's safer streets. Many women marched through Bogotá in celebration, applauding men that stayed at home or who were seen taking care of children. The police commander on duty that night was a woman. All 1,500 police officers in charge of Bogotá's security were also female.

He also appeared naked on television during a water shortage, taking a shower but soaping without water – asking his fellow citizens to do the same. Within weeks, the city's water consumption dropped by 40% once people realised how much money they were saving by conserving water use. Mockus also distributed 350,000 'thumbs-up' and 'thumbs-down' signs to the populace for citizens to use to approve or disapprove of the behaviour of fellow citizens. He also asked for volunteers to pay 10% in extra taxes – an initiative that 63,000 people agreed to. In 2002, Mockus collected more than three times the taxes that had been gathered in 1990. His leadership also saw 7,000 community security groups formed; a 70% fall in the homicide rate; drinking water provided to all homes (up from 79% in 1993); and sewerage provided to 95% of homes (up from 71%). When Mockus asked people to report kind and honest taxi drivers 150 names were submitted to his office. This prompted a meeting to set up an advisory panel of good taxi drivers – named 'Knights of the Zebra' – to work out ways of improving the drivers that were bad. He had stars painted on the streets where 1,500 pedestrians had been killed in traffic accidents – prompting a 50% drop in fatalities. 'Saving a single life justifies the effort,' he said.

For further information visit Bogotá's mayoral website (*www.idrd.gov.co*).

Bogotá **WHAT TO SEE AND DO**

3

Rock al Parque (*Oct*) Rock in the Park is the biggest annual rock festival in Latin America, attracting 300,000 rock fans to Parque Simón Bolívar with a wide variety of international, national and local bands since 1995 – all of which perform for free. In the weeks leading up to the event, local up-and-coming groups take part in a battle of the bands for the privilege of performing.

Festival de Cine de Bogotá (*Oct*; *www.bogocine.com*) Since establishing 25 years ago, Bogotá's annual film festival has become one of the most respected in Latin America, attracting films from all around the world and providing a showcase for Colombian film-making and cinema well beyond the mainstream. The festival awards its 'Pre-Colombia Circle Awards' for Best Film, Best New Director and Best Colombia Film – with numerous star-studded events across the city.

AROUND BOGOTÁ

Once you've left the city behind the topography determines the climate, and such is the variety of landscape surrounding Bogotá that this can offer significant temperature changes. Expect steamy lowlands in the west and chilly open highlands in the east – all within a couple of hours or so from the swish boutiques of urban Bogotá. Beautiful forests, lakes, streams and mountains hide hundreds of small towns and settlements on a landscape that was an important sacred site for the Muisca Indians.

PARQUE NATURAL CHICAQUE (✆ *368 3118*; e *info@chicaque.com*; *www.chicaque.com*) You'll find this private nature reserve just a half-hour outside the centre of Bogotá, 20km to the west. It contains more than 15km of maintained paths that weave through 300ha of spectacular cloudforest packed with flora and fauna, at a height exceeding 2,700m. Muggy and damp, the forest averages 74% humidity with October and November the most humid at around 80%. The reserve has gorges, creeks and rocky crags with gradual slopes and inclines and hundreds of species of plant and 200 species of birds. Temperatures fluctuate between 11°C and 17°C in the reserve where it is possible to stay overnight at 45,000 COP in a cabin (including all meals) or camp at 5,000 COP per person.

Getting there and away Hop aboard a buseta or colectivo in Bogotá's centre to the town of Soacha and haggle with a local taxi driver to get a good deal to the reserve. The administration is about 4km off the Soacha–La Mesa road, so budget for about 15,000 COP for the trip.

ZIPAQUIRÁ (*Telephone code: 1*) More than 70,000 people live in this mountain town 49km north of Bogotá where salt mines (salinas) are the main employers. Huge reserves of salt make Zipaquirá famous throughout Colombia and the town's **Salt Cathedral** has been a popular tourist attraction since 1954 (✆ *852 4035*; ◷*09.00–16.40, closed Mon; admission 8,000 COP*). It can accommodate a staggering 8,400 people and is 75m long and 18m high. There's also a **Salt Museum** (◷*10.00–16.00 Tue–Sun; 2,000 COP*) and a **Museum of Archaeology** (✆ *852 3499*; ◷*09.30–16.30 daily; 3,000 COP*) where a number of collections feature Muisca art and ceramics. Zipaquirá was founded in 1606 and named after the Chibcha word meaning the 'Land of the Zipa' – Zipa being the territorial king. A large plaza still boasts some fine colonial architecture, including the imposing green-and-white town hall building.

Getting there and away Every ten minutes a bus departs from Bogotá's TransMilenio northern terminus for Zipaquirá. It's a 1½-hour journey (*1,600*

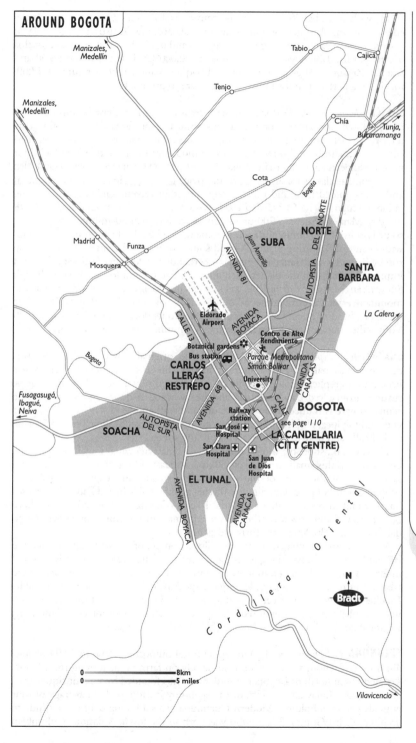

AROUND BOGOTA

Manizales, Medellín

Tabio

Cajicá

Tenjo

Manizales, Medellín

Chía

Tunja, Bucaramanga

Cota

Bogota

Madrid

Funza

Mosquera

SUBA

NORTE

AVENIDA 81

Juan Amarillo

SANTA BARBARA

AUTOPISTA DEL NORTE

CALLE 13

Eldorado Airport

La Calera

AVENIDA BOYACA

Botanical gardens

Centro de Alto Rendimiento

Bus station

Bogota

CARLOS LLERAS RESTREPO

Parque Metropolitano Simón Bolívar

AVENIDA CARACAS

University

Fusagasugá, Ibagué, Neiva

AVENIDA 68

Railway station

CALLE 26

BOGOTA

AUTOPISTA DEL SUR

SOACHA

San José Hospital

see page 110

LA CANDELARIA (CITY CENTRE)

San Clara Hospital

San Juan de Dios Hospital

EL TUNAL

AVENIDA BOYACA

AVENIDA CARACAS

Cordillera Oriental

N

Bradt

0 _____ 8km
0 _____ 5 miles

Vilavicencio

COP) with an added 20-minute walk from central Zipaquirá to the mines on the edge of town. Another option is to hop aboard the Turistren (↘ *375 0556; www.turistren.com.co*) from Bogotá on Sundays and public holidays – a ticket for this quaint puffing Billy-style steam train costs 20,000 COP. It departs at 08.30 and reaches Zipaquirá after a brief stop at Usaquen station with a return at 14.00, making it a perfect trip for lunch – but be sure to pre-book.

SUESCA (*Telephone code: 1*) Rock climbers across the world are fast-becoming aware of this town of 14,000 people as it sits amidst some fantastic mountaineering terrain. A small climbing school, Campo Base (e *deaventuraporcolombia@yahoo.com*) runs guided climbs and offers basic accommodation for around 10,000 COP per person. Expert guide Hernán Wilke (↘ *310 216 8119; www.monodedo.com*) also offers popular classes for all levels, from novice to expert. He rents out equipment and offers guided half- and full-day trips. Another recommended rock-climbing guide is Hugo Rocha (↘ *315 826 2051*) who can be hired at around 80,000 COP per day. Many of Suesca's 200 or so climbs are less than 20-minutes from town, some within a five-minute walk along some railroad tracks. Expect sandstone crags with beautiful flowering plants. A good source of info is the small climbing shop run by Fernando and Tatiana Gonzolas – Fernando is a veteran of some of the most impressive climbs on the planet, including K2, Everest and Joshua Tree. Although Suesca can be quiet during the week it springs to life at weekends, when the mountaineering fraternity descend on the town, 65km north of Bogotá. By public transport, head to Suesca on the TransMilenio to its northern terminus and catch a bus – they depart with some frequency (40 minutes, 4,000 COP).

GUATAVITA (*Telephone code: 1*) Although the original town of Guatavita was demolished to make way for a reservoir in 1967, the so-called 'New Guatavita' has been built to replicate colonial style. It's been beautifully done with white façades, rustic masonry, red clay roof tiles and heavy wooden doors and shutters. The central square is framed by a necklace of handicraft and food stalls and is popular with milling local children. Sunday is a good time to visit as the church bells ring melodically and best-dressed locals take to the streets.

However, most people think of the Laguna Guatavita when they hear the name Guatavita – as this small circular lake 50km northeast of Bogotá is a famous Muisca sacred site. At the heart of the mythical El Dorado, the Laguna Guatavita is supposedly full of gold. Certainly, 500 years ago the gold-dusted Zipa (the Muisca king) would throw gold items into the lake as offerings to the gods. Many have been retrieved and now form the basis for the magnificent collection at the Museo del Oro, where 30,000 pieces form a dazzling display.

Visitors to the Laguna Guatavita can enjoy a number of pleasant walks around the lake and into the forests along well-maintained trails that were extensively restored in 2006. Paths reach an elevation of 3,000m and offer spectacular views across the lake and surrounding countryside. English-speaking guides are sometimes available. Facilities include a visitor centre and a café. Permits are required to visit the park with numbers strictly monitored. To apply contact the Corporacion Autonoma Regional de Cundinamarca in Bogotá (↘ *320 900; www.car.gov.co*).

CUCUNUNA (*Telephone code: 1*) This agricultural outpost is home to 1,699 people, almost all of whom work on the land or rely on farming or mining for a living. Located 88km north of Bogotá the settlement was founded by Luis Enriquez on 2 August 1600. Today almost 15% of the economy is cattle with an average of four animals per smallholding. Modern Cucununa owes a lasting debt of gratitude to architect Pedro Gómez Potter, who was born in the town. A famous Colombian

Although Colombians on the steamy Atlantic coast swear that people are as warm as their environs, Bogotáno's aren't anywhere near as cool, stoic and aloof as the rest of the nation likes to think. Like most city-dwellers they have a savvy street sense born out of urban living, but visitors (especially those from overseas) will find the people in Bogotá friendly and curious. However, conversations tend to follow a similar basic pattern, whoever you speak with and where, so it pays to have a few stock answers ready to help chit-chat flow.

Question 1: Hello, introductions and why are you in Bogotá?
Question 2: What do you think of Bogotá?
Question 3: The women of Bogotá are beautiful, no? The most beautiful in Colombia…
Question 4: What is your favourite thing/place in Colombia?
Question 5: When are you coming back to Bogotá?

Ask a Bogotáno what's happening to the weather on a dull day and they'll reply '*Está haciendo invierno*' 'it's making winter'. Making winter means, simply, that it is overcast and raining – a rather charming way to conceptualise the season as a transient. Generally speaking, the weather is a welcome topic of chit-chat in Bogotá, much like it is in the UK.

exponent of progressive urban architecture across the country, he built the first commercial centre of Bogotá and won awards across the whole of Latin America. However, his success didn't distract him from improving his shabby, humble home town. Gómez Potter set about redesigning and investing in Cucunana, building a well-planned town to better serve its residents whilst being incredibly pleasing on the eye. Part of his urban layout featured workshops for local wool-knitters whom he organised into a co-operative. He then set about selling their wares to many of Bogotá's swankiest clothing boutiques. Today Cucununa has hotels, shopping malls and neighbourhoods of residential housing – a triumphant testament to a home-grown talent prepared to give something back.

UBATÉ (*Telephone code: 1*) This rural town of around 7,000 people has dairy products coursing through its veins with streets of shops and food stalls selling cheap eats on a milk or cheese theme. Named after the Muisca Indian word meaning 'Bloodied Land' the town was founded in 1592 and has been the site of many ancient battles. Renowned as the 'Milk Capital of Colombia', Ubaté has a rather fine Gothic-style cathedral and is also famed for its San Luis Convent. Construction of the church began in 1927 with modifications done by the Dutch architect Antonio Staufe. It was inaugurated on 27 October 1939, and finally blessed by Monsignor Carlos Serna in 1941.

At an altitude of 2,556m Ubaté boasts average temperatures of 14°C. It tends to be overlooked by tourists, but if you're passing through be sure to stop at one of the roadside cheese stalls – there's also a permanent seven-days-a-week market where you can feast on a whole roast chicken and all the trimmings for 25,000 COP. Don't miss a chance to try one of the finest-tasting cheeses in all Colombia, the oh-so creamy San Carlos Queso Tipo Holandes. It's sold in slabs and has a golden rind and is gooey and delicious. All-in-all, Ubaté is a great place to chow-down just 97 km outside central Bogotá.

Bogotá **AROUND BOGOTÁ**

3

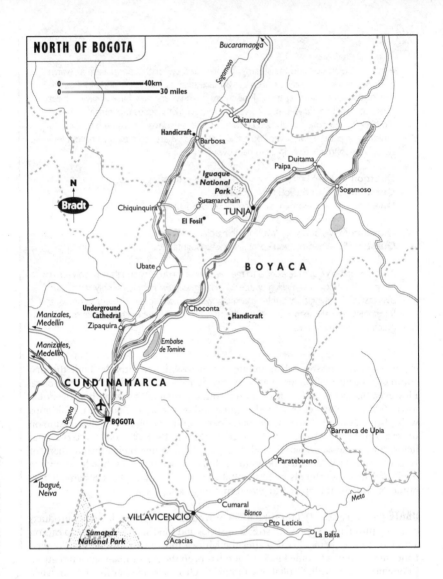

0   40km
0   30 miles

Bucaramanga

Sogamoso

Chitaraque

Handicraft Barbosa

Duitama
Paipa

Iguaque National Park

Sogamoso

N

Bradt

Chiquinquira   Sutamarchain

TUNJA

El Fosil

BOYACA

Ubate

Underground Cathedral   Choconta   **Handicraft**
Zipaquira

Embalse de Tomine

Manizales, Medellín

Manizales, Medellín

CUNDINAMARCA

Bogota

BOGOTA

Barranca de Upia

Paratebueno

Ibagué, Neiva

Cumaral
Blanco

VILLAVICENCIO
Pto Leticia
La Balsa

Meta

Sumapaz National Park   Acacias

4

North of Bogotá

Commonly referred to collectively as 'north of Bogotá,' the departments of Boyacá (*www.deboyaca.com*), Santander and Norte de Santander form a teardrop-shaped land bridge between the capital and the Caribbean coast. This breadbasket of Colombia is a picturesque farmland region, boasting magnificent countryside that is so resplendent in colour the locals call it *el tapiz* (the tapestry). Rolling pasture lies dotted with pretty red-roofed *fincas* and *campesino* shacks. Well-maintained roads weave through a lush landscape of flower fields edged by stalls weighted with slabs of cheese and churns of cream. Sombrero-wearing herdsmen usher goats through pocket-sized villages. Scrub-clad peaks overlook gushing rivers and deep rocky gorges. Machete-holding farmers tend to vast maize crops littered with broken-down farm machinery. Chickens peck at scraps of corn under apple, pear and peach trees home to tethered horses. Chubby sheep scramble up steep grassy banks navigating large piles of pumpkins and potatoes. Children run through bloom-filled meadows. Grain stores are guarded by weathered old women in ponchos woven from cheap grey wool. Proud rural traditions thrive in Colombia's crop-growing communities in a heartland region renowned for its revolutionary spirit.

As one of the Colombian mainland's safest areas, the region north of Bogotá is easily navigable with good, paved main routes and well-lit roads. Military checkpoints are less frequent than in many provinces of Colombia although it is wise to avoid travelling off the beaten track after dark.

Changing altitudes affect the climate in the undulating region with Tunja at 2,820m averaging a cool 13°C. Low-lying areas such as Cúcuta average a hot and sticky 28°C. Pack a fleece and a cold-weather sleeping bag if you plan to camp or spend time in the mountainous areas. In muggy Bucaramanga it pays to keep clothing light.

HISTORY

Colombian patriots nationwide hold this region in high regard as it is a hotbed of nationalistic passion. It stoked the flames of independence and stood up to Spanish rule and it was here that Simón Bolívar rallied a makeshift army of proud separatists to do battle with the Spanish infantry. Fierce, conclusive wars were fought at Puente de Boyacá and Pantano de Vargas. Colombia's first constitution was also drawn up here in the Villa del Rosario. However, this historic region is also an important site of Indian occupation. Large numbers of Muisca and Guane tribes once had their homes here trading with Spanish conquistadors and spawning the mythical legend of El Dorado (see box, *Going for gold*, page 151).

GETTING THERE AND AROUND

From the south, roads out of Bogotá offer spectacular scenery atop leafy mountains but can get congested with hordes of fanatical cyclists – especially on Sunday morning and holiday *ciclovias*. If you enjoy two-wheeled challenges then there are few better places in Colombia to hill-climb on a bicycle. A number of companies offer bike hire. Another option is to pick up cheap a Colombian or Chinese-made bike in stores such as Carrefour or Exito. Nicer bikes of questionable provenance can be found in the pawn shops along Avenida Caracas. By bus, Tunja is a 2½-hour journey from the capital (8,000 COP) with good connections with Bucaramanga and Medellín.

Although the region's transportation network suffers from poor development a major railroad and highway pass through the Boyacá department's capital Tunja, and other major centres. Various bus companies run services across the region. Minivans also connect cities to small towns with a frequent timetable every 30 minutes. Taxis are in good supply in larger conurbations with bike and horse hire available in the more touristy towns of Villa de Leyva and Bucaramanga.

THE ROAD FROM BOGOTÁ Travelling north out of Bogotá makes a pleasant change from doing battle with the congested traffic in the city. Picturesque roads wind through the mountains out into green countryside in a drive that offers stunning views. Wire-fenced small holdings, roaming goats and chickens, and greenhouses full of flowers sit on a landscape of potato fields and maize crops. Patches of grass become wide rolling hills the closer you get to entering Boyacá. The roadside towns of Gachancipá, Chocontá and Villapinzón are popular stop-offs with travellers heading north of Bogotá. Although technically still in the department of Cundimamarca these are listed here.

Gachancipá Lying 25km south of the important Muisca site of Guatavita this tiny cattle-ranching town is a useful stop-off on the road north out of Bogotá (Autopista Norte). Expect a string of inexpensive restaurants, hardware stores, car repair shops and gas stations with plenty of street stalls selling hot snacks, fruit and cold drinks.

Chocontá Further north, 45km from Bogotá, the refuelling spot of Chocontá is another bustling truck-stop town. Expect lorry parks, street vendors, tyre shops, hardware stores, coach parks, gas stations, oil stalls and dozens of cheap food outlets. A couple of small *supermercados* stock a good range of essentials, such as water and batteries. Cows graze on grassy verges amidst clouds of lorry fumes.

Villapinzón Yet another popular pit-stop, Villapinzón is notable for its stretch of unused railway, built by Europeans but now in disrepair and clearly visible at the northern tip of the town. Travellers can benefit from a good range of roadside services, including a Texaco fuel station, car workshops, hardware stalls, bars, restaurants, tyre shops, supermarkets and a laundry.

BOYACÁ

As you enter the department via the charming country roads a brightly coloured sign proclaims Bienvenido Boyacà Su Merced (Welcome Boyacá Its Mercy) – a courteous Colombian salutation almost lost in time. In some ways this sums up the agricultural communities of Boyacá where time is immaterial and aged traditions all important. Should there ever be a referendum regarding autonomous rule in Boyacá the locals would rush to the poll in their droves such is their fierce sense of independence. Another part of the region's psyche is a penchant for Cundiboyacences (those from Cundinamarca and Boyacá) to use a second-person pronoun *sumercé*, a source of some confusion for travellers already struggling with Colombian Spanish.

Boyacá lies in east-central Colombia, spanning over 23,000km² of fertile terrain, from the cool Andean uplands in the west and forested basins to the undulating llanos (plains) in the east. The department's agrarian economy largely relies on coffee, tobacco, cereal crops and fruits. Emeralds, iron ore and coal are also mined in the region and Boyacá produces most of Colombia's steel. The Chivor Dam, one of the highest rock-filled dams in the world, on the Batá River, is a source of hydro-electric power. People from Boyacá are known as Boyacense – and it is not uncommon to spot red-haired blue-eyed locals that are a legacy of inter-breeding with European settlers.

TUNJA Telephone code: 8

One in five residents in Tunja (*www.tunja.gov.co*) is a student and Boyacá's historical capital is very much the funky university town. The founding of the Pedagogical and Technological University of Colombia in Tunja in 1953 redefined the city. Today, along with its fine colonial churches, handsome mansions and imposing central plaza there are internet cafés, bookshops and CD stalls. Burger restaurants and coffee bars rub shoulders with statues and monuments. On street corners, undergraduates gather to swap notes and gossip. Posters advertise the arrival of a hot new DJ in town amidst magnificent examples of Hispano-American Baroque art.

Tunja was founded on 6 August 1539 by the Spanish captain Gonzalo Suárez Rendón on the site of Hunza in the domain of 'El Zaque', one of the chiefs of the Muisca tribe. Sadly very little evidence of this pre-Hispanic Muisca settlement remains in the city. The legacy of Colombia's indigenous Indians was effectively erased once the town was built. Tunja was historically known as 'The Loyal and Noble City of Santiago de Tunja' and served as an operating base for Simón Bolívar in 1819 ahead of his victory over the Spanish at the Battle of Boyacá, 8km to the south. Today it is famous for its architectural riches and is also home to some of the most unique artwork in South America – Mudejar works that are Islamic in style dating back to the 12th century.

Tunja lies in the high valley of the Río Teatinos (or Boyacá River) and as well as its academic centre the city is a communications, commercial and agricultural hub. Cattle from the rolling plains of Llanos region to the east are traded in Tunja and the area is also rich in gold and emerald mines. At an elevation of 2,820m above sea level, Tunja is Colombia's highest and coldest departmental capital. An alpine climate prevails year-round with an average temperature of 13°C. Tunja is a celebrated cultural centre and stages three notable festivals with great gusto, including the Cold Festival in October, the International Festival of Culture and Expressions and Aguinaldo Boyacense in December – one of the most important celebrations in the region.

GETTING THERE AND AROUND Tunja is situated on the Pan-American Highway linking Cúcuta with Bogotá – it's a straightforward drive or there's a frequent bus service linking the two. The 147km journey takes about three hours and costs around 9,000 COP with buses departing every 15 minutes or so. Tunja's bus terminal is located on Avenida Oriental to the southeast of Plaza de Bolívar. An hourly bus to Bucaramanga costs 30,000 COP and takes seven hours while Villa de Leyva takes 45 minutes by minibus at a cost of 3,000 COP.

WHERE TO STAY

Hotel Boyacá Plaza 740 1116; e hotelboyacaplaza@hotmail.com. Service is brisk at this mega-efficient hotel to satisfy the demands of the business executives it attracts. Private parking makes

Colombia has over 50,000 known species of flower – an estimated 10% of the world's total –although many species remain uncatalogued and many thousands unidentified. As a major exporter of blooms, Colombia's flower trade blossomed out of the Andean Trade Preference Act (ATPA) of 1991, renewed and expanded by the United States' Trade Act of 2002. The second-largest exporter of flowers in the world, behind the Netherlands, Colombia's flower exporters boast annual sales of around US$900 million in export sales. At least 65% of those flowers end up in the US. Consumers with an estimated 75% of all roses sold in America on Mother's Day have originated from Colombia. More than two billion stems of Colombian flowers are sold for Valentine's Day alone with 98% of the chrysanthemums and 90% of the carnations bought in the US and Canada coming from Colombian soil. As many as 35 flower-packed planes a day do the three-hour flight to Miami. The flower industry creates 83,300 direct jobs and 75,000 indirect jobs, making its concentration of employees per hectare the highest in Colombia's agricultural sector. Some 65% of flower workers are women.

Further information: Tierra de Flores (*www.colombianflowers.com*), Asociación Colombiana de Exportadores de Flores (*www.asocolflores.org*), ProFlora Fundación (*www.proflora.org*).

this an easy option for travellers with a vehicle. The room rate includes a generous b/fast. $$
🏠 **Hosteria San Carlos** (5 rooms) Carrera 11, No 20–12; ☎ 742 3716. This is another of Tunja's most pleasant budget hotels where 5 simple rooms offer sgl, dbl and family (5 persons) accommodation in a cosy old home. Ask to see a couple of rooms, as they vary in size. $
🏠 **Hotel Oseta** Carrera 19, No 7–64; ☎ 742 2886. Choose from sgl, dbl & trpl rooms at this popular shoestring option. Bright, clean rooms come with a private bathroom & TV. $

✕ **WHERE TO EAT** For big plates of cheap local grub head to **El Maizal** on Carrera 9 where packed tables are testament to the popularity of this shabby-looking place. What it lacks in glamour El Maizal makes up for in good value with simple chicken-and-rice dishes priced at less than 8,000 COP. Around the plaza and beyond you'll find a cluster of fried-food joints and fast-food outlets, including the **Pizza Nostra** (☎ 740 2040) where a man-sized margarita will set you back just 6,000 COP. Numerous cafés by the plaza offer pastries, doughnuts and coffee with dozens of street vendors selling *arepas, tinto* and juice.

OTHER PRACTICALITIES Tunja has a large number of internet cafés due to the demands of its student population. Most are clustered around Calle 10 and Calle 20, including the Internet Cibertienda (☎ 310 563 5665) and Internet Orbitel (☎ 743 0955). Most offer CD burning and international telephone services. Opening hours generally correlate with university hours with prices around 1,500 COP per hour.

WHAT TO SEE AND DO The city of Tunja has a significant number of 16th-century churches, some of which are considerably finer than others. One of the most notable is the **Iglesia y Convento de Santa Clara Real** (*Carrera 7;* ☎ *742 5659;* ⊕*08.00–18.00 daily, closed noon–14.00; admission 2,000 COP*), – founded in 1571 and thought to be the first convent in Nueva Granada. It was the home of Colombia's Mother Teresa figure, Madre Francisca Josefa del Castillo (see box, *Colombia's madre figure*, page 146) from 1689 to 1742. In 1863, the nuns were evicted and the convent was used as a hospital although the church itself remained a place of worship. Today, it contains a magnificent collection of religious art from the

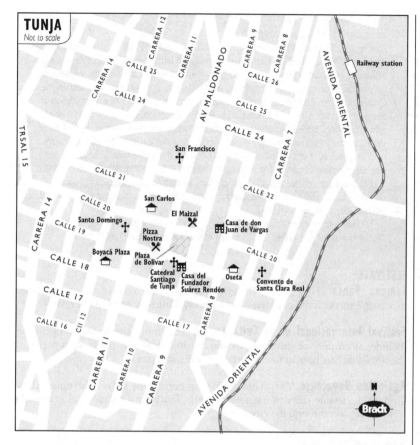

16th, 17th and 18th centuries some of which depict themes relating to the Muisca belief system – a ploy to encourage the Indians to convert to Catholicism.

Other churches worth a look include the **Catedral Santiago de Tunja** on Carrera 9 – the city's most elaborate and largest, built in 1554. Although it doesn't look much from the outside, the **Iglesia de Santo Domingo** on Carrera 11 is a myriad of colour and ornate décor with a sumptuous interior of gilded carved wood and Baroque art. An altar statue of the Virgen de Rosario is layered in mother-of-pearl and reflecting glass. A fine Capilla del Rosario has been dubbed the Sistine Chapel of New Granada's Art (*la Capilla Sixtina del Arte Neogranadino*) and is the showpiece of this stunning interior decoration design by Quito's Fray Pedro Bedón. The **Iglesia de San Francisco** on Calle 10 was built between 1550 and 1572 and contains gilded archways, a handsome presbytery and a sculpture of Christ, *Cristo de los Mártires*.

Some of Tunja's historic buildings are open to the public and the **Casa del Fundador Suárez Rendón** (*Carrera 9;* ☏ *742 3272;* ⊕ *08.00–18.00 daily, closed noon–14.00; admission 1,200 COP*) is definitely one not to be missed. Originally the home of the founder of the city, this grand mansion is every bit the resplendent residence of nobility. It was built in the mid 16th century and has numerous swanky aristocratic touches. Another fine example of Tunja's architectural splendour can be found at the **Casa de Don Juan de Vargas** (☏ *742 6611*) where beautifully painted ceilings and colonial artwork are stunningly displayed.

FESTIVALS

Semana Santa (*Holy Week*) Religious celebrations revolve around a large procession through the city streets on Maundy Thursday and Good Friday.

Festival Internacional de la Cultura (*Sep*) This multi-site festival programme includes all manner of artistic shows and musical performances, from concerts in the Iglesia de San Ignacio to exhibitions in the main plaza.

Aguinaldo Boyacense (*Dec*) This week-long event runs up to Christmas when Tunja stages a wide range of religious concerts, fancy dress parades and a carnival-style procession through the city.

AROUND TUNJA

TURMEQUE This tiny unassuming town is little more than a couple of rustic eateries and a string of fincas but it enjoys a countrywide reputation as being the birthplace of the game of Tejo (see box, *Beer and bangs: Tejo*, opposite). Turmeque's dedicated Camp de Tejo is a social focal point. Passers-by will also find some rather nice ceramic stalls along the roadside with plenty of kiosks and vendors selling fresh peaches and pumpkins.

PUENTE DE BOYACÁ Set on the Río Teatinos, the Puente de Boyacá was the scene of Simón Bolívar's last battle on 7 August 1819. Despite having no soldiers or weapons, Bolívar was determined to defeat the Spanish on the bridge, so he mustered up an upstart army from the surrounding fields and villages. Against all the odds Bolívar and his 3,000 peasant troops were victorious – a crucial battle in the wars for Latin American independence. Spanish forces were cut off at the bridge resulting in 1,800 prisoners being captured. Bolívar proceeded to take control of Bogotá on 10 August where he was hailed the liberator of New Granada. After establishing a provisional government Bolívar journeyed to Angostura in Venezuela where he announced his plan to establish the Republic of Gran Colombia.

Today Simón Bolívar is honoured in fitting style at the Puente de Boyacá. Pristine, manicured lawns sweep down to the river's edge. A succession of magnificent paved plazas encircle a grassy hillock on which a bronze monument to Bolívar towers. The bridge itself is small and white and almost unnoticeable on such a dramatic canvas. A perpetual flame burns in tribute to Latin America's revered hero and his makeshift army.

SAMACA This typical Boyacense town is reputedly Colombia's biggest beer-swilling community, quite a feat for such a small place. It is also dedicated to the pursuit of Tejo and regularly attracts crowds of players from all over the country. A 15km unmade pot-holed dusty road leads directly into town and although this is prone to flooding it is easily passable (albeit in bone-rattling style) in the dry season. To the left an abandoned stretch of railway track disappears into the distance. Beyond, the fields are dotted with tiny white fincas as the rocky shrub-lined road rolls slowly into town.

Samaca is a charming place blessed with friendly people and all the basic essentials – including plenty of places to buy beer. Since 2002, the town has more than quadrupled in size to 23,000 people from what was once a pinprick-sized hamlet. Today, an attractive plaza is edged by a bank (with ATM), church, photo shop, pharmacy and a handful of decent chicken-and-rice joints. On the edge of town there's an Esso garage, car wash and mechanic. Travellers looking for plenty of small-town character will find it in Samaca. Expect poncho-wearing campesinos selling fruit, onions, peas, red beans and potatoes and butchers stringing up loops of homemade sausages. Samaca is also famous for its cheese bread, a traditional delicacy that is baked at 16.00 each day. Arrive at 15.45 to join the growing queues before stocks run out – some of the finest is produced by Alberto Whittingham whose English name is testament to his European heritage. His forefathers moved from England five generations ago to supply iron to the nation's railway industry (see box, *Colombia's railway*, page 82). Today, Alberto runs a charming bakery just off Calle 5. Everyone knows him – especially Samaca's womenfolk who swear his bread and flaky pastries are Colombia's finest.

Driving out of Samaca towards Tunja is another journey jam-packed with stunning views. A stretch of craterous, dusty road crosses small bridges and sheep fields. Cows feed on the roadside on a backdrop of mountains and honey-coloured rocks. Fieldworkers hack at cactus scrubland and hedgerows by religious icons set

BEER AND BANGS: TEJO

Colombians, especially Boyacense, are passionate about the game of Tejo – so much so that in June 2000 it was declared a national sport. Originating in Turmeque over 500 years ago, today this humble farming community has a Campo de Tejo at its heart. Once known simply as Turmeque by the Chibcha Indians, this spirited throwing sport has evolved over time. In the past it was played using stones and pieces of wood. Today, things are different. A small 2kg metal disk is chucked at a gunpowder detonator on a clay-filled target – all in the name of good fun.

Tejo takes place in a small circular area usually behind a local bar. The goal is to make the disk strike triangle-shaped *mechas* (gunpowder) in the middle of the target. Many professional Tejo teams compete nationwide. Most are sponsored by beer companies because drinking is a vital part of the game. Even the Indians used to consume vast quantities of *chicha* (a potent drink made from corn) on match days. Today Boyacá's many Tejo players drink *cerveza* – and LOTS of it. Beer-swigging contests take place before, during and after the game. Tejo is played to nine or 21 points – or until players pass out. The person who makes the most explosions is the winner – at which time the losers must buy the next round.

in stone. Eventually, at a T-junction opposite a Texaco garage, a sign points left to Villa de Leyva and right to Tunja. At this point the landscape alters dramatically to palms and parched, hardy shrubs. Dramatic, time-sculpted orange rock forms magnificent contoured towers. Vast peaks change colour from grey-to-black-to-pink-to-gold marred only by the occasional carefully painted political slogan. On a spiralling road the sheer enormity of the terrain can be overwhelming – prepare to feel like an ant crawling over an intergalactic land.

VILLA DE LEYVA Telephone code: 8

Lying about 60km from Tunja and about 207km from Bogotá, few entire towns in Colombia have been as beautifully preserved as Villa de Leyva (*www.villadeleyva.gov.co*). Bordered by Arcabuco and Gachantivá to the north, Sáchica to the south, Chíquiza to the east and Sutamarchán to the west, Villa de Leyva was declared a national monument in 1954. Gloriously free from any ugly modern buildings, Villa de Leyva is a triumph of architectural conservation, a stunning whitewashed colonial town with cobbled streets. Octogenarians snooze on benches in an expansive plaza edged by bottle-green shuttered buildings adorned with flower-filled window boxes. Tiny little mews-style shops sell handicrafts and fresh vegetable in a town once renowned for its abundant olive crops. Pretty backstreets hide some charming boutique hotels and cafés. Although the olive groves have long gone many of Villa de Leyva's businesses and buildings still bear the names of the industry. At 2,144m in altitude, the town is also notable for its numerous fossils from the Mesozoic and Cretaceous periods. Stroll through the Plaza Mayor at dusk to join tourists, locals and famous faces alike as they congregate at the steps of the cathedral. Grab a table under flower-filled balconies to enjoy a glass of freshly squeezed *fejoa* (pineapple guava) juice to the sound of strolling musicians and *cuenteros* (storytellers). Choose from an array of fine restaurants or nibble on *besos de novia* (girlfriend kisses), a local meringue-cake sold in every *panaderia* (bakery) in town. In 2007 Colombian production company RTI shot a Spanish-language *telenovela* (soap opera) of the Zorro story in Villa de Leyva (see *La Espada y la Rosa*, page 155). Part of the Werner Herzog film *Cobra Verde* was also filmed here.

HISTORY

...that he marked ... all the land between a bright red gorge and some oak trees
found in the water of the ravine at the foot of the mountain range of the new Villa, to
the edge of the mountain, passing through a small hill made of stones, and below
Juan Barrera's mill; continuing down the hill from the ravine...

Don Juan de Otálora (19 December 1572)

Villa de Leyva was founded in 1572 by Captain Hernán Suárez de Villalobos after being charged by President Andrés Díaz Venero de Leyva with finding suitable land in the region to house the region's military upper echelons. His sidekick, Don Juan de Otálora, travelled far and wide before reporting back to Villalobos – he had discovered the perfect spot. On Thursday 12 June 1572 a group of Tunja's most prominent top-brass headed to the fertile, forested valley known as Saquencipá by the Chibcha Indians. Recording the legal foundation (*acta*) of the 'Villa de Nuestra Señora de Santa María de Leyva' they appointed San Antonio de Padua as patron of the new settlement, declaring '*bienaventurado San Antonio de Padua* (Blessed San Anthony of Padua)'.

In 1573, the *caciques* (Indian chiefs) of neighbouring villages began work on the construction of the first church in Villa de Leyva. In 1642, the King of Spain Don

Félipe IV, signed a *Real Cédula* (Royal Decree) creating a Carmelite convent in Villa de Leyva. It took three years to build but in April 1645 the convent welcomed its six founding nuns. Today, Villa de Leyva with its 14,000m² plaza and fine colonial streets is one of Boyacá's most popular tourist centres. That it has survived intact throughout Colombia's most turbulent years is nothing short of a miracle – and is testament to how Villa de Leyva is held dear in the hearts and minds of Colombians nationwide.

GETTING THERE AND AROUND Only two direct daily buses link Villa de Leyva with Bogotá (4 hours, 12,000 COP) – another option is to take one of the frequent departures to Tunja and change. Minibuses run back and forth between Tunja and Villa de Leyva every half-hour until late afternoon. Expect the journey to take around 45 minutes and to cost about 3,500 COP.

TOURIST INFORMATION

 Oficina de Turismo Cnr Carrera 9 & Calle 13; 732 0232; 08.00–18.00 daily, closed noon–15.00). Free maps, tour bookings & an abundance of local leaflets & brochures.

 www.villadeleyva.net Local tourism website.

TOUR OPERATORS Taxi drivers offer standard local tours that usually include a trip out to El Fósil, the Convento del Santo Ecce Homo and El Infiernito (at around 40,000 COP). Trips further afield tend to take in Ráquira and La Candeleria (at around 65,000 COP). Specialist tour operators offer a much more sophisticated set of services and numerous off-the-beaten track options, such as night hikes, rappelling, horseback tours, bike trips/hire, camping and walking tours. Two of the best are **Guías & Travesías** (732 0742) on Calle 12 and **Colombian Highlands** (732 1379) on Calle 9. Guías & Travesías offer bike rental by the hour, half-day or day at 3,000 COP, 10,000 COP and 20,000 COP. Umpteen hiking trails around the town offer a variety of different degrees of difficulty. Horseriding is easy to arrange with a number of local rental agencies. Expect to pay about 5,000 COP per hour.

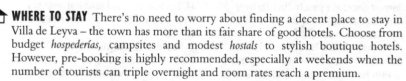

WHERE TO STAY There's no need to worry about finding a decent place to stay in Villa de Leyva – the town has more than its fair share of good hotels. Choose from budget *hospederías,* campsites and modest *hostals* to stylish boutique hotels. However, pre-booking is highly recommended, especially at weekends when the number of tourists can triple overnight and room rates reach a premium.

 Hotel Plaza Mayor (32 rooms) Carrera 10, No 12–31; 732 0425. This pricey option is worth every penny for the wonderful attention to detail it offers to ensure guests are truly rested. Expect friendly service & plenty of added-value extras on this prime location hotel. Room sizes available inc king-size & a large family-sized suite. $$$

 Hotel Plazuela de San Agustín (20 rooms) 310 299 6221; e info@plazueladesanagustin.com; www.plazueladesanagustin.com. Step over floors inlaid with thousands of fossils to enter this stylish hotel opposite the park. The very pleasant rooms overlook a courtyard & really nice tiled-floor restaurant & range from sgl to larger suites. Each is decorated to a high standard & some have exposed beams. $$$

 Hostería del Molino La Mesopotamia Carrera 8, No 15A–265; 732 0235; www.hosterialamesopotamia.addr.com. This swish restored former flour mill dates back to 1568 & many of its old original features are still on show. It's a stunning building with pretty gardens & a large freshwater swimming pool reputed to have therapeutic qualities. Rooms are split between the old part of the house & the newer section – so if you want max 440-year agedness be sure to put in a request. $$$

 La Posada de San Antonio Hotel y Restaurante (30 rooms) Carrera 8, No 11–61; 310 280 7326; e padelgo@hotmail.com. This handsome colonial-era building has been decorated to an exceptional

4

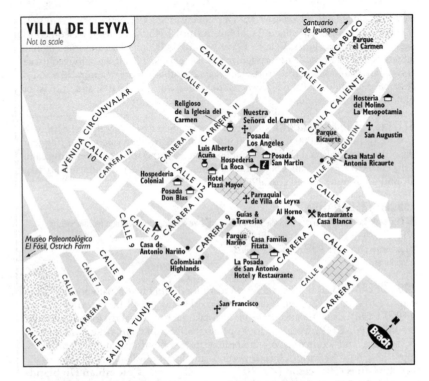

VILLA DE LEYVA
Not to scale

Santuario de Iguaque →

Parque el Carmen

CALLE 15

CALLE 14

CALLE 16

VIA ARCABUCO

CALLA CALIENTE

AVENIDA CIRCUNVALAR

CALLE 10

CARRERA 12

CARRERA 11A

CARRERA 11

Religioso de la Iglesia del Carmen

Nuestra Señora del Carmen

Posada Los Angeles

Luis Alberto Acuña

Hospederia La Roca

Posada San Martin

Hospederia Colonial

Posada Don Blas

Hotel Plaza Mayor

Parraquial de Villa de Leyva

Guías & Travesías

Al Horno

Restaurante Casa Blanca

Museo Paleontológico El Fósil, Ostrich Farm

CALLE 12

CALLE 10

CARRERA 10

CALLE 9

Casa de Antonio Nariño

Colombian Highlands

Parque Nariño

Casa Familia Fitata

La Posada de San Antonio Hotel y Restaurante

CARRERA 9

CARRERA 8

CALLE 8

CALLE 7

SALIDA A TUNJA

CARRERA 10

CALLE 9

San Francisco

Hosteria del Molino La Mesopotamia

Parque Ricaurte

San Augustin

CALLE SAN AGUSTIN

Casa Natal de Antonia Ricaurte

CALLE 14

CARRERA 7

CALLE 13

CARRERA 6

CARRERA 5

CALLE 5

CALLE 6

Bradt

standard with exquisite antiques, rich fabrics & delightful exposed stone & woodwork. A tiled-floor library leads to a private chapel & onto a charming restaurant where wooden tables look out onto a courtyard centred on a stone fountain. The lovely rooms range from sgls to king size and vary in price depending on the season. **$$$**

⌂ **Hospedería La Roca** Plaza Mayor; ☏ 732 0331. This former dirt-cheap budget option has significantly raised its game – with prices to match & b/fast is not inc. However, it is difficult to knock its great location & its plentiful supply of pleasant rooms with TV & private bathrooms. **$$**

⌂ **Posada de Los Angeles** Carrera 10, No 13–94; ☏ 987 320 562. This step up from low-budget option has a range of various sized rooms with private bathrooms that start at 35,000 COP pp inc b/fast – but has been known to hike its rates up at busier times of the year. However, it remains a very nice mid-range choice on the basis of location overlooking the Iglesia del Carmen. **$$**

⌂ **Posada San Martín** Calle 14, No 9–43. This charming historic home is run by a friendly couple who are naturally hospitable & who have earned a deserved good reputation for their b/fasts as they run beyond the standard menu of eggs & eggs. Room price

includes a private bathroom and b/fast. Rooms are spotlessly clean & the whole place has a very nice feel. **$$**

⌂ **Casa Familia Fitata** Calle 12, No 7–31; ☏ 7320 574. This home-stay has a handful of rooms at a very negotiable 15,000 COP pp – just turn up & haggle. **$**

⌂ **Hospederia Colonial** (20 rooms) Calle 12, No 10–81; ☏ 732 1364. Not all of the rooms at this perfectly acceptable cheapie have private bathrooms. Expect to pay 15,000 COP pp or 30,000 COP per room, just a block from the main square. **$**

⌂ **Posada Don Blas** Calle 12, No 10–61; ☏ 987 320 406. Don't expect any frills or fuss at this basic budget joint. **$**

⌂ **Renacer Guesthouse** ☏ 732 1379. This pleasant out-of-town option is run by the owner of tour company Colombian Highlands (see Tour operators, above) and rooms can be booked directly with Oscar Gilede by heading to the office in town. It's one of the only true backpacker-y places in Villa de Leyva – and aimed squarely at this market. Expect to pay between 12,000–18,000 COP for a bed in a dorm room. There is also a large family-sized room for 24,000 COP pp – b/fast is an extra at 5,000 COP. It's also possible to camp here at 7,000 COP per night. **$**

Camping There's an unmarked 'camping zone' on the corner of Calle 10 and Carrera 10 – it's basically just a large patch of half-decent grass with a wall around it. Stick up a tent and the patron will pop over for the money. Rates vary but expect to pay between 5,000–7,000 COP per person per night for a spot with an OK shower and some basic bathrooms. It's a similar set up at the **Casa Molina del Balcón** on Carrera 12 although this time there is a sign. Parkland style gardens offer trees for shade and privacy. Head to the house and pull the bell-cord to signify your arrival – rates are 5,000 COP per person and there's a shower block and bathrooms. Although **EL Solar** is fairly new it's already become a firm favourite with shoestring travellers. Friendly owner Martha offers camping at 8,000 COP per tent and also has dorm-room beds at 15,000 COP per night with an outside shower in the garden just beyond the plaza. It's also possible to camp in the

GOING FOR GOLD

> At this time they stripped the heir to his skin, and anointed him with a sticky earth on which they placed gold dust so that he was completely covered with this metal. They placed him on the raft ... and at his feet they placed a great heap of gold and emeralds for him to offer to his god.
>
> Eye-witness report from Juan Rodriguez Freyle (1636)

The story of El Dorado was one of the most influential myths born out of the New World. Stemming from reports from conquistador Gonzalo Jiménez de Quesada in the 1530s, tales of a gilded man of untold riches began to ignite the curiosity of every traveller on the planet. Quesada had discovered the Muisca Indians in the Andes of present-day Colombia in what are now the highlands of Boyacá, in 1537. Rituals were observed that involved offering gold to the gods and soon rumours became mixed with exaggeration.

The myth was spawned by a Muisca ritual that sees an Indian chief plaster his naked body with gold dust before plunging into the depths of Lake Guatavita. After this ceremony, his subjects threw jewels and gold into the water as gifts to the gods. As the story was retold, the legend of 'El Dorado' was soon imaged as a place – an empire, a kingdom and a city with a golden king. A succession of conquistadors sought to locate this realm of riches over two centuries, during which time the myth continued to feed on itself. The resulting El Dorado enticed explorers but was always just beyond reach.

One of the most famous doomed searches was undertaken by Francisco de Orellano in 1541 (see *Amazonia* chapter, page 229). It was a disaster but allowed Orellana the distinction of being the first exploration to journey the Amazon River all the way to its delta. Other expeditions to El Dorado include that of Phillip von Hutten in 1541 and Sir Walter Raleigh in 1595. In 1531 a man claimed to have been rescued from a shipwreck by El Dorado himself.

Today the landscape around Lake Guatavita bears a curious scar carved by Antonio de Sepulveda, a Bogotán merchant who attempted to drain the lake in the 1580s to uncover its wealth. Gold was discovered but the project abandoned when the hillsides collapsed killing many of the workers. Later excavation has uncovered numerous treasures that are now in Bogotá's magnificent Gold Museum (see *Bogotá* chapter, page 129). Today, El Dorado has become a byword for a place where wealth can be made quickly. It is also used as a metaphor to represent an ultimate prize or holy grail. Towns across Latin America bear the name El Dorado as do many in the United States. The El Dorado story is also immortalised in an array of films and literature, including Milton's *Paradise Lost* and Voltaire's *Candide* and two Walt Disney comic books, *The Gilded Man* and *The Last Lord of Eldorado*.

grounds of the **Renacer Guesthouse** (↘ *732 1379*) at 7,000 COP – it's run by a local tour guide and located 1km out of town but makes a good option if you want a cheap 'all-in' package. $.

✘ WHERE TO EAT

✘ **Al Horno** Calle 13, No 7–95; ↘ 732 1640; ☉lunch & dinner. There's something really pleasant about simply hanging out in this popular bistro where bright artwork & a cheerful décor combine to give it a funky feel. An international menu contains a dozen different pizzas along with salads, pasta dishes, sandwiches & crêpes.

✘ **Restaurante Casa Blanca** Calle 13, No 7–16; ↘ 732 0821; ☉lunch & dinner. Simple set meals offer some of the best value food in town with á la carte options not likely to break the budget at 12,000 COP. $$

✘ **Sazón y Sabor** Plaza Mayor; ☉lunch & dinner This place serves a changing menu of delicious cut-price dishes. Travellers on a budget will find it difficult to find a reason not to eat here each day at 5,000 COP.

✘ **Xirrus** Casa Quintero, Plaza Mayor; ☉lunch & dinner. For bohemian ambience & an enigmatic menu of healthy, organic food be sure to check out Xirrus – dishes range from pan-Indian lentil wraps to Morocco-inspired dips. There's also a really unusual bar popular with backpackers where the barman 'El Pote' lives up to his reputation as Villa de Leyva's real character. Script-clad walls, oddball artefacts & walls sprinkled with eucalyptus leaves make this place a real must.

ENTERTAINMENT AND NIGHTLIFE Rather surprisingly, Villa de Leyva has some lively nightspots, including a bar established and owned by the ageing former drummer with Elvis Presley's backing band. Bogotá-born Bill Lynn's joint is called the **Don D'Bill** (↘ *311 483 9757*) and until his death in January 2006 at the age of 73, this country music fanatic still performed almost every night (see box, *Drummer to the King*, page 154).

Another pumping venue is the **Latin Dreams Disco Bar** (↘ *732 1042*) – a decorative homage to the Beatles but every inch the Colombian *salsoteca*. It opens early evening but doesn't hit full throttle until midnight when the speakers are cranked up to maximum and the atmosphere is highly charged.

SHOPPING There are dozens of handicraft shops in Villa de Leyva as well as a number of artisan vendors. Most sell some rather fine basketry, jewellery, bags and ponchos (*ruanas*) as well as fossils, woven blankets and rugs. Villa de Leyva's popular Saturday market is famous throughout Colombia and often attracts visitors from miles around. It starts up bright and early and is busiest in the morning – find it southeast of the Plaza Mayor. On the Plaza itself three beautifully restored colonial buildings contain various artisan shops and crafts. Casa Quintero, Casona La Guaca and Casa de Juan de Castellanos each have gorgeous patio areas with seating and cafés that serve snacks and cold drinks.

OTHER PRACTICALITIES Head to the Plaza Mayor for a bank with an ATM, a money changer, photocopy shop and telecom office for international and regional calls. Of the internet cafés in town, the **Movistar** on Calle 14 is probably the best – the machines are new and reasonably speedy but a tad pricey at 3,000 COP per hour. For maps head to **Guias y Travesías** (↘ *732 0742*; e *guiadevilladeleyva@yahoo.com*) where owner Enrique Maldonado has a decent stock at 6,000 COP.

WHAT TO SEE AND DO To escape the dust and heat of the summer streets head to the **Hostería del Molino La Mesopotamia** (*Carrera 8*; ☉*during daylight hours*) where it's possible to swim in a beautiful spring-fed swimming pool for 4,000 COP – there's an old wooden pool house for changing but no towels.

Only two of the town's handsome churches are open to the public although the Iglesia de San Francisco and the Iglesia de San Agustín are worth a look from the outside.

Iglesia Parroquial de Villa de Leyva Built in 1608, the *Iglesia de Nuestra Señora del Rosario* (Church of Our Lady of the Rosary), is known as simply 'la catedral' by the locals although nobody is quite sure why. The most likely explanation is that its plaza location is reminiscent of the cathedral in Bogotá, which also has an atrium over the square.

Iglesia de Nuestra Señora del Carmen (*Calle 14; ☉subject to volunteer staff.*) With its adjacent cloister, this striking building belongs to a Carmelite monastic order and contains some beautiful paintings, including an image of the *Virgen del Carmelo* (Virgin of Carmelo).

Casa de Antonio Nariño General Antonio Nariño, the precursor of Colombian independence, lived out his last days in this house until his death in 1823. He suffered from poor health following long periods of imprisonment by the Spanish and diseases caught in the battlefields and so moved to Villa de Leyva in a bid to restore his health. Nariño was a staunch defender of human rights and the building has numerous artefacts relating to the work of this revered activist. The day before his death, he asked that an epithet be placed on his tombstone. It reads: *I loved my Country. How deep was that love, one day history will tell. I have nothing to leave to my children but my memories; to my Country I leave my ashes.* Nariño won acclaim for translating Thomas Paine's *Rights of Man* into Spanish and is revered throughout Colombia for his commitment to fostering socioeconomic justice.

Casa-Museo de Luis Alberto Acuña (*☉10.00–17.00 Tue–Sun, closed 13.00–15.00; admission 1,500 COP*) This fascinating museum honours the life and works of Luis Alberto Acuña (1904–93), one of Colombia's great painters, writers and sculptors. One of the founders of the radical Bachué art movement 1930–40 (so named after the mother of the human race according to Chibcha mythology), Acuña is renowned for creating beautiful oil murals on wood with one of his most famous – *Teogonía de los dioses chibchas*, (Theogony of the Chibcha Gods) – on display in the Hotel Tequendama in Bogotá. Located on the northwest side of the *Plaza Mayor*, this beautiful old colonial house was painstakingly restored by Acuña himself during the last 15 years of his life. A *galería de pinturas* contains numerous original works while the *sala de antigüedades* exhibits artefacts from the colonial era. Sculptures are displayed along with three large murals including one that depicts the region of the *Valle de Saquencipá* (Valley of Saquencipá) where Villa de Leyva is located during the Cretaceous period. Others include a beautiful interpretation of the Chibcha deities. A *colección de tapices* includes indigenous artefacts from different regions of the country with the ceiling of the old dining room decorated with stunning Baroque motifs.

Casa Natal de Antonio Ricaurte (*☉09.00–17.00 Wed–Fri, 09.00–18.00 Sat/Sun, closed noon–14.00; admission 1,500 COP*) This great hero of Colombian independence was born in this magnificent colonial building in June 1786 and it has since been beautifully restored. Located in front of a park bearing his name and a statue in honour of his heroic death in San Mateo, Venezuela, the museum contains a large collection of artefacts relating to his act of self-sacrifice to defeat Spanish aggressors. Ricaurte fought under Simón Bolívar and whilst encircled by the Spaniards he defended an armoury under attack. After letting them approach he ignited gunpowder kegs to cause a mighty explosion that killed everyone – including himself.

Casa sede del Primer Congreso de las Provincias Unidas de la Nueva Granada

This colonial building was where the *Primer Congreso de las Provincias Unidas de la*

After his father's untimely death in Bogotá at the young age of 33, Bill Lynn's mother moved with her six-year-old son to start a new life in Miami. Even as a boy, he would drum on pots and pans along to Chuck Berry, Duane Eddy, Buddy Holly and Little Richard records. By the time he was a teen, Lynn had raised enough money by delivering newspapers and shining shoes for a second-hand drum set at a cost of US$20. To practise he'd play along to the radio in the garage that adjoined his home, forming a country & western band. At 16 he added two years to his age to work in bars around America and began to earn a reputation as 'The Drummatic Bill Lynn' on account of his frenzied style. In 1960 he signed a contract with ABC Paramount Records in Nashville as a session player and Lynn was playing with Ray Charles and Bobby Vee. He was introduced to Elvis Presley during a recording session in a neighbouring studio. The King's drummer had popped out for coffee so Bill Lynn stepped in – playing drums on 'It's Now or Never'. A year later, Elvis sent Lynn a golden record to thank him for his collaboration – and a lasting partnership began. Lynn worked for Elvis Presley on his films and recordings until 1970 – the year that Priscilla demanded that Presley's hand-picked team be dismissed. Lynn went on to launch an Elvis bar in Bogotá called Legends and Superstars. He also ran an Elvis-inspired bar Don D'Bill in Villa de Leyva and specialised in music vacations and tours to Graceland. Lynn died at his home in Villa de Leyva after developing breathing difficulties following a serious bout of flu. Even in his latter years, he always wore his staff T.C.B. pin on a chain around his neck. The letters are an acronym of 'Taking Care of Business' – a nickname for the Elvis crew and a prized memento of their 17-year friendship. In 2007, Lynn's road-worn nine-piece Power Remo drum set was auctioned on eBay for US$2,499.95.

Nueva Granada (First Congress of the United Provinces of New Granada) was installed on 4 October 1812. Today there are a few documents displayed to denote the significance of this Plaza Mayor house, including details of the various representatives from each region of Colombia and how the charter was ratified.

Museo Religioso de la Iglesia del Carmen Located in the Plazuela del Carmen, this well-stocked museum of religious artefacts is adjacent to the *Iglesia de Nuestra Señora del Carmen*. A sizeable collection of religious objects includes altarpieces, carvings, paintings and communion vessels from the 16th century onwards.

FESTIVALS
Fiesta de las Cometas (*Aug*) Crowds of kite-fliers descend on Villa de Leyva in Boyacá's windiest month, including many from other nations. It's a really colourful display with a variety of different competitions as well as numerous stalls, music and food to boot.

Fiesta de Luces (*Dec*) This impressive firework spectacular is an exciting prelude to Christmas festivities. It takes place in the first or second week of the month and illuminates the whole of town.

OUTSKIRTS OF VILLA DE LEYVA The area around the town is rich in natural splendour with petroglyphs, caverns, ruins, waterfalls, lakes and creeks to explore. Some of the sights are within walking distance with gorgeous leafy trails that wind out of town. Others can be reached on horseback or by bike and taxi – all of which are in plentiful supply.

Museo Paleontológico (⊕*09.00–17.00 Tue–Sat, closed noon–14.00, 09.00–15.00 Sun; admission 1,500 COP*) This out-of-town fossil-fest is about 1km from the centre of Villa de Leyva but is worth the trip for those not planning to visit El Fósil (see below). Find it on the road to Arcabuco to the northwest of town – it contains a large collection of locally found fossils that date back to the Cretaceous era.

El Fósil (✎ *311 269 4067; 6km west of Villa de Leyva on the road to Chiquinquiá. The bus to Ráquira doesn't pass right by but can drop-off about 1km away. Otherwise it's a 15,000 COP taxi ride or an hour-long walk; ⊕08.00–18.00 daily; admission 2,000 COP*) This 120 million-year-old prehistoric marine reptile is a 7m baby kronosaurus that has been left in the exact spot where it was found in 1977. Although it has lost its tail (the fully complete fossil would have been around 12m in size) this carnivorous plesiosaur reptile is pretty impressive nonetheless. The kronosaurus lived in open oceans and breathed air. They caught prey with massive jaws and rows of sharp teeth up to 25cm long. A huge head had a large mouth and big eyes with an offset pair of nostrils that gave it directional 'water-sniffing' ability. Although other kronosaurus fossils have been discovered in Australia, the specimen in Villa de Leyva remains the world's most complete.

Ostrich farm (*5km southwest of Villa de Leyva in the direction of El Fósil; ✎ 315 233 5877; ⊕09.00–17.00 daily; admission 3,500 COP*) Although it's known as the 'ostrich farm' this place also has llamas, horses and sheep but it is a field of 120

LA ESPADA Y LA ROSA

> At heart, Zorro is not different from other men in his need to love and to be loved, his desire to fall in love and form a family, and his ambition to find the ideal woman. Will he obtain them?
>
> TV station Telemundo's promotional copy, 2007

Villa de Leyva was an obvious choice as a film set for the Spanish-language telenova, *Zorro: La Espada y la Rosa* (The Sword and the Rose), its colonial plazas, cobbled streets and bloom-filled balconies the perfect backdrop for swashbuckling dare. Based on Johnston McCulley's characters, it premiered on Telemundo in February 2007, wowing audiences across America with tales of the masked crusader's fight for justice and love for a beautiful woman. Described by Telemundo president Dan Browne as 'without doubt the best production offered on Hispanic television in the United States today' the soap opera loosely follows the 2005 novel by Isabel Allende whilst using the characters from the 1950s television series. Played by swarthy Christian Meier, the hero, Don Diego de la Vega, adopts the secret identity of masked avenger Zorro, with much of the melodrama focusing on romantic tragedy. Beautiful young widow, Esmeralda Sánchez de Moncada captures the heart of the masked crusader. Her father is the villain Fernando Sánchez de Moncada and Zorro is faced with the challenge of outwitting a host of evil-doers to brand them with his trademark 'Z' in three swift scratches. According to Telemundo, Zorro averaged 635,000 core viewers during March 2007, up 28% on the previous month. Most were Hispanic adults aged between 18 and 49. The series has been sold to almost 100 countries. The show started airing in Colombia in March 2007 on Caracol TV. During filming in Villa de Leyva the production company painted the town's white colonial buildings various shades of grey and green to add authenticity, restoring them when the film was wrapped. See http://tv.telemundo.yahoo.com/zorro for further Zorro facts.

massive, strutting birds that pulls in the crowds. A small kiosk sells a variety of ostrich-related paraphernalia, including ostrich leather shoes, smoked ostrich meat, ostrich feathers and giant ostrich eggs. An onsite restaurant also has plenty of ostrich-inspired dishes from about 18,000 COP, but this is usually open just at the weekend. Guided tours involve demonstrations of how strong ostrich eggs are – usually by a member of staff standing on one.

El Infiernito (*2km north of El Fósil, about a half-hour walk; ⊕09.00–17.00 Tue–Sun, closed noon–14.00; admission 2,000 COP*) This ancient Muisca Indian observatory dates back to the early centuries AD and contains ancient phallic stones. La Estacíon Astronómica Muisca was used to identify the seasons by determining the distances of shadows cast by the stones at different times of the year. These three dozen stone monoliths have been sunk into the ground in a meticulous pattern exactly 1m apart in two parallel formations separated by a 9m gap. By measuring the shadows the Muisca were able to gauge when to plant and harvest. The site also became a sacred place of rituals – much to the annoyance of the Catholic colonialists. In a bid to prevent the God-fearing Spanish from stepping on their land, the Indians named the spot El Infiernito, meaning 'little hell' in Spanish, to imply association with the devil.

Convento de Santo Ecce Homo (*Catch a bus to Santa Sofia and ask to be dropped off at the turn and you'll only need to walk for 15 minutes to the convent. Otherwise it's a taxi at around 15,000 COP for a car that'll take four; ⊕09.00–17.00 daily; admission 2,000 COP*) This large stone convent is about 13km from Villa de Leyva and is notable for its magnificent chapel, founded by the Dominican fathers in 1620. A small image of Ecce Homo can be found on a stunning gilded retable reached via a beautiful courtyard of whitewashed archways and old tiled paths. Cobble-flanked gardens are full of brightly coloured flowers with wooden benches and wrought ironwork. Walls are inlaid with fossilised seeds and flowers with clusters of fossils around the base of a statue and in the garden. A picture of Christ in the west cloister offers an optical illusion with eyes opening and closing depending on the angle from which it is viewed.

AROUND VILLA DE LEYVA

SANTUARIO DE IGUAQUE This beautiful expanse of wilderness offers some fine hikes up to a group of eight alpine lakes. Spanning more than 67km^2 of mountainous terrain the cool, leafy trails reach an altitude of 3,700m along the highest point of the mountain spine that stretches up to Arcabuco. Located to the northeast of Villa de Leyva, the reserve played an important role in aged Muisca beliefs, with the Laguna de Iguaque considered the sacred cradle of humankind in ancient culture. According to Muisca legend, a beautiful woman named Bachué rose from the waters of the lake with a baby in her arms. Once the boy became an adult, they married and had children together and populated the planet. In old age, the couple transformed themselves into serpents before diving back into the hallowed waters of the lake. Such is the importance of the lagoon that it gave the whole reserve its name. More than 400 species of trees, large swathes of highland shrubs and craggy peaks make this a pleasant place to hike and camp. A walk from the entrance of the reserve uphill to the lagoon takes about three hours at full pelt. Add in some additional sightseeing and it could easily be a six-hour trek.

Practicalities Temperatures drop dramatically in the Santuario de Iguaque so it is important to pack plenty of warm clothing and cold-weather camping gear. It's also pretty wet, so waterproofs and boots are recommended. Some trails can become impassable in the rainiest months so stick to January and February or July and August. Entrance to the park is 18,000 COP per person.

🏠 **Where to stay** The visitors' centre at the entrance of the reserve has beds in shabby-looking dorm rooms for 18,000 COP per person and also offers meals at a very reasonable 16,000 COP for breakfast, lunch and dinner. Pre-booking is required via the National Park office in Bogotá. $

Getting there and around Four buses a day leave Villa de Leyva for Arcabuco – at 07.00, 10.00, 13.30 and 16.00. Ask the driver to drop you at a place called Los Naranjos – it's about 11km from Villa de Leyva. From here it's a 3km walk uphill along an unmade track to the entrance of the reserve.

SUTAMARCHÁN This busy little pit-stop 25km west of Villa de Leyva is famous for its long, skinny *chorizo* sausage *longaniza*. Bogotános make a special journey to dine on Sutamarchán's spicy delicacy, especially men who eat it on man-sized plates with piles of *papas Criollas* (Creole potatoes) and fried plantain with a chuck of greasy black pudding on the side. Numerous small bars and a handful of restaurants sit right on the crossroads. To locate a *longaniza* vendor simply follow your nose.

🏠 **Where to stay** Sutamarchán's only decent accommodation option is the **Hotel Cabañas**, a roadside lodge run by a guy called Pedro (☎ *0987 251447*. $$).

TINJACÁ There are some useful shops in this little town between Chinquinquira and Sutamarchán, including a couple of small supermarkets, a drinks stall, kiosk, bakery and an arts and crafts centre. A gas station opens early until late on the road to Chinquinquira with a small Campo de Tejo nearby.

RÁQUIRA (*Telephone code: 8*) Bubblegum-coloured colonial buildings and a pretty central square make Ráquira a popular place for tourists to spend an hour or two. Cross over a narrow yellow bridge past a terracotta pot factory and a couple of roadside ceramic vendors to enter the town on a winding road. With a population of a little over 1,600 Ráquira is no metropolis, but it does have an impressive number of art shops, craft stalls and souvenir outlets. Specialities include jewellery, pottery, woven bags, baskets, beads and carvings – much of which adorns the façades of the many colourful buildings in Ráquira's beautiful centre. There are also a handful of mediocre restaurants that deserve overlooking – so unless you're really hungry head to Sutamarchán instead.

🏠 **Where to stay** At the time of writing, none of the hotels in Ráquira would win any awards for opulence and some are best described as unkempt. The following two options are by far the nicest

🏠 **Hostería Nemqueteba** ☎ 735 7083. Ráquira's most cheerful option offers bright dbl & trpl rooms. Each has a private bathroom & a TV & the hotel has a restaurant & a pleasant patio & pool. $

🏠 **Hotel Suaya** (10 rooms) ☎ 735 7029. This shabby wooden boarding house has reasonable bedrooms of varying sizes – some sleep up to 6 at 18,000 COP pp. There's also a restaurant onsite. $

Getting there and away Just a handful of buses each day travel through Rácquira along the Tunja–Chiquinquiá road to and from Bogotá. To get back and forth from Villa de Leyva hop aboard a minibus for 3,000 COP – there are four departures and the trip takes about 45 minutes.

LA CANDELARIA (*Telephone code: 8*) Almost everyone heading to this tiny community 6km beyond Ráquira is in La Candelaria to visit its monastery, founded by Augustine monks in 1597. The **Monasterio de la Candelaria** (⊕*09.00–17.00 Mon–Sat*) is an impressive place, set on a backdrop of dry, dusty hills at the end of a slippery mud road. Arrive on foot from Ráquira's main plaza along an uphill path that drops down into La Candelaria, taking about an hour. Only part of the building is open to the general public, but this includes the chapel, a library and a small museum. Monks guide visitors around the cloisters and are very knowledgeable about the many fine 16th- and 17th-century artworks on display. A leafy courtyard and magnificent gardens are a wonderful place to relax, contemplate and soak up the spiritual ambience.

CHIQUINQUIRA *Telephone code: 8*

Frayed palms line the streets of this busy town, which is renowned across Colombia as a religious centre for devout Catholics. Faith-based tourism is big business here with dozens of shops, stalls and vendors selling a vast array of holy icons in every conceivable form. Located 115km north of Bogotá, Chiquinquirá is known as the 'religious capital of Colombia' because of a mid-16th-century miracle involving a painting called the *Virgin of the Rosary*.

In 1562, the Spanish painter Alonso de Narvaez created a portrait of the Virgin Mary using pigments and dye from soil and flowers on woven cloth. The 1m image of Mary is holding baby Jesús and smiling sweetly wearing a white toque, a rose-coloured robe and a light blue headdress. A rosary hangs from the little finger of her left hand and in her other hand she is holding a sceptre. Mary is looking towards the baby cradled in her left arm. He has a small rosary hanging from his left hand with a little bird tied to his thumb. Mary is flanked by Saint Anthony of Padua and Saint Andrew the Apostle. Narvaez left the painting in a hut with a leaky roof where it was ruined by humidity. In 1577, the portrait was discarded in Chiquinquirá and propped in an unused room of the chapel. Nine years later it was rediscovered by a woman called María Ramos who, despite the painting's dreadful state, felt drawn to it. Ramos would often sit in contemplation in front of the canvas and long for its repair.

A further nine years later, a miracle occurred. Chiquinquirá was stunned to discover that the painting had been inexplicably restored to its former glory overnight. Today, Friday 26 December 1586 is honoured for this extraordinary event. The miracle had transformed the portrait from a shabby, faded wreck to a bright, vivid canvas. Tears and holes had also self-healed.

Pope Pius VII declared Our Lady of Chiquinquirá patroness of Colombia in 1829, granting a special liturgy. In 1915, 'La Chinita', as her people call her, was canonically crowned. The chapel was declared a basilica in 1927 and renamed Basilico de Nuestra Señora del Rosario de Chiquinquirá. The city was visited by Pope John Paul II in 1986.

Aside from religious tourism, Chiquinquirá has some nice architecture and a rather lovely plaza. It also has a photocopy shop, drugstore, pharmacy, banks (with ATM), hardware stores, barber shops, shoe repair stalls, supermarkets, a post office and laundry. A market has numerous vendors plying training shoes, T-shirts and fast food. Around the town there are plenty of food joints serving *tinto* (coffee) and *comida Criolla*. Several street stalls also sell Chiquinquirá's famous sweet, pink candy *(cañitas)*.

SUSA This small cattle- and horse-trading town on the road from Chiquinquirá to Ubaté is a hive of activity, hosting cattle shows and horse fairs year-round. A number of local vendors sell all sorts of associated paraphernalia, from saddles and stirrups to ropes and sombreros. Hungry travellers will also find a couple of hot-food stalls selling tamales and *arepas*. There are also a couple of *aguardiente* and *tinto* joints and a kiosk selling water, soda and beer.

PARQUE NACIONAL EL COCUY (*Parques Nacionales de Colombia;* ✆ *76 349418/423;* e *norandina@col1.telecom.com.co; www.parquesnacionales.gov.co*) This 306,000ha national park was founded in 1997, stretching from temperate forests to snow-capped peaks and arid, desert land. Wooden lower plains rise to glacial terrain with alpine lakes. Lush valleys are home to waterfalls and rocky crags. Dominated by the Cordillera Oriental's highest peak, Ritacumba Blanco's 5,330m tip, Parque Nacional El Cocuy is regarded as one of Colombia's most resplendent reserves. Indigenous Indian tribes occupy the western flank of the park environs and mountain trails are relatively easy to navigate with an experienced guide. Access points are the towns of Guicán and El Cocuy located approximately 230km from Bogotá where it's possible to stock up on basic essentials ahead of an overnight stay in the park. Pack warm-weather clothing and a thermal sleeping bag for camping as temperatures can drop to 0°C. An absence of onsite facilities means that you'll need to bring all food and equipment. Hikers also need to stick to official trails and engage the services of an authorised guide – solo treks are not allowed. Age restrictions also apply, so unless you are under 60 and over ten it is unlikely you'll be allowed in.

Several tour companies offer trips into Parque Nacional El Cocuy, including many with a strong ecological focus – an important consideration given the park's fragile status. According to the Colombian Institute of Hydrology, five major glaciers in the park that were expected to last at least 300 years in 1983 are now under serious threat. Measurements taken in 2006 suggest that they may all disappear within 25 years. Dwindling numbers of several species of the park's rich abundance of wildlife are also a cause for concern, including eagles, spectacled bears and mountain tapirs. Items that pose a threat to the frailty of the ecosystem are also prohibited, so don't bring non-biodegradable plastic bags and aerosols.

SANTANDER

This central-northern department lies east of the mighty Río Magdalena bordered to the south and east by Boyacá and to the north by Norte de Santander. Magnificent gushing rivers, craggy ravines, canyons, gorges and mountain peaks make Santander a popular region for adventure-sport enthusiasts. Thrill-seekers can enjoy kayaking, climbing, rappelling, rafting and potholing on a dramatic rugged terrain. Spiralling mountainous trails rise and fall amidst rocks and trickling streams. Santander has carved out quite a name for itself as an eco-tour centre around the fast-flowing Río Fonce. Inheriting its name of one of the nine original states of the United States of Colombia, Santander also has some delights for those seeking a more genteel pace. Several fine museums can be found in the capital city of Bucaramanga with the architecture of San Gil, Barichara and Girón a genuine treat.

HISTORY Prior to the arrival of the Spanish conquistadors, the mountainous territory now known as Santander was inhabited by numerous indigenous Indian tribes, including the Muiscas, Guanes, Chitareros, Laches, Opón, Yariguí and Carare. They honed farming skills to exploit the rugged terrain and developed terrace-style agricultural plots and irrigation systems, planting yucca, maize, beans, arracacha, cotton, tomatoes, guava, tobacco and pineapple crops. The first Spanish arrived in 1529 led by Antonio de Lebrija, but it was the aggressive stance of German explorer Ambosius Ehinger that wiped out most of the ethnic groups via a bloody campaign. Colonisation began in earnest in 1539 when the village of Vélez was founded by Martín Galeano. The remaining Indian tribes were enslaved and forced to labour on the land and work in the mines. Today the Guane are the only Indian group in Santander not to have been fully subjugated by Colombia's colonial past.

SAN GIL *Telephone code: 7*

Modern-day San Gil (*www.sangil.com.co/tourism*) has firmly established itself as Colombia's 'White-water Rafting Capital' and is without a doubt the nation's premier adventure-sport hub. Alongside a host of extreme-sport options and madcap thrills, San Gil has numerous less radical pursuits, including horseback riding, fishing and mountain hikes. Most visitors arrive in San Gil clad in outdoor garb in preparation for some serious interaction with the surrounding countryside. Much of this centres on the rapids of Rio Suarez and the tributaries of the Río Fonce, the 1,867 trees of Parque El Gallineral, and the trails that riddle surrounding mountain peaks.

However, San Gil is more than just a place for adventure nuts to gather – the town's streetscape of unspoilt colonial buildings is divine. Stroll through the town's 18th-century plaza – the Parque La Libertad – amidst balconied buildings seemingly untroubled by time. Giant ceiba trees and flower-filled planters lead to a fine cathedral while the foliage in Parque El Gallineral is truly spectacular year-round.

GETTING THERE AND AROUND San Gil is on the road between Bucaramanga and Bogotá and is therefore blessed with an efficient and frequent bus service to both cities. Bucaramanga takes about 2½ hours and Bogotá a little over six hours. The bus terminal is 2km west of the city centre – it's a 2,000 COP trip by taxi or flag down a busetas on the corner of Carrera 10 and Calle 15. Buses that pass also frequently serve the nearby village of Barichara – a very rewarding day trip just 20 minutes or so away.

TOUR OPERATORS A number of specialist eco-adventure tour agencies offer full-day and multi-day packages. The most popular centre on river rafting on Rio Suarez (class 4 and 5) and on Rio Fonce (class 2 and 3), including an 11km rapid-strewn stretch. After some basic instruction in the art of rafting survival etiquette, small groups of rafters are guided to the rapids for a water-born adrenalin rush. The river is also used by experienced kayakers and is renowned for its whirlpool undertow and tumultuous cascades. The 11km trip takes about 1½ hours and costs around 25,000 COP. Most of San Gil's tour companies are clustered around the entrance of park El Gallineral. Almost all offer short and long rafting trips (grade 1 to 3), caving, hiking, kayaking, climbing, paragliding and rappelling. Other excursions include the Río Chicamocha (grade 1 to 4) and all tour prices in San Gil are regulated so costs rarely vary by much. The main adventure tour operators include:

Aventura Total ☎ 723 8888; www.aventuratotal.com.co
Brujula ☎ 723 7000
Colombian Rafting Expeditions ☎ 311 283 8647;
e colombiakayak@hotmail.com

Ríos y Canoas ☎ 724 7220;
e riosycanoas@hotmail.com

WHERE TO STAY
The number of hotels in San Gil is growing rapidly and a host of budget options are springing up all over town. Most are clustered around the centre of town and are simple, no-fuss affairs.

Hotel Abril Cnr Calle 8 & Carrera 10; ☎ 724 8794. There's nothing special about this mid-range option but it is perfectly comfortable. Fan-cooled rooms are simply furnished. $$

Hotel Agualuna Calle 9, No 8–75; ☎ 724 4363/7220. A range of different sized rooms offer various bed configurations in this simple family-run hotel – & some are better than others. $$

Hotel Capri Calle 10, No 9–31; ☎ 724 3767/1992; e hotelcaprisangil@yahoo.es. This is one of San Gil's better mid-range options with clean, sparsely furnished rooms that are bright & comfortable – each seems to have a different price so ask to see a couple. $$

Centro Real (20 rooms) Calle 10, No 10–41; ☎ 724 0387. Each of the rooms at this bright & modern hotel is different with a range of sgls, dbls & trpls. As one of San Gil's nicer options it tends to get booked solid so it pays to pre-book. $

Hotel Viajero Carrera 11, No 11–07; ☎ 724 1965. A collection of matchbox-sized rooms make this quaint little place a disappointment but if you're prepared to compromise on space then this is worth checking out for its river views & friendly staff. $

Macondo Guesthouse Calle 12 No 7–26 ; ☎ 724 5646; e macondohostal@hotmail.com. If you've ever stayed in an Antipodean backpacker hostel you'll feel right at home here – the Aussie owner runs it just like one of Darwin's finest. Expect lots of laid-back home comforts & plenty of adventurous spirit. Rooms share a bathroom. $

Posada del Conde This simple budget option is right on the main square & offers rooms with a bed, TV & fan in a clean, friendly & comfortable family-run place. $

Hotel Cacique Guanenta Carrera 17, No 23–74; ☎ 724 2402. Reports have been mixed about this town-centre hotel where rooms vary in price depending on what's going on in town. On this basis alone, it may pay to fix a firm price ahead of arrival – rooms are nice enough & come equipped with a fridge & fan.

WHERE TO EAT
Cafeteria Donde Betty Cnr Carrera 9 & Calle 12; ⊕ daybreak–midnight. This simple little local eatery serves a hearty b/fast, fruit juices, lunches, snacks & dinner throughout the day for under 7,000 COP.

El Mana Calle 10 No 9–10. Locals in the know rave about the food at this charming restaurant where the quality is reliable, the portions generous & the ambience truly convivial.

El Turista Calle 10, No 10–27; ☎ 724 7029; ⊕ 07.00–21.00. All-day food joint; generous b/fasts. Typical lunch & dinner menus include grilled goat dishes.

SHOPPING There's a handful of handicraft vendors strung along the road that leads to the Parque El Gallineral. Expect to find ceramics, scarves, bags, jewellery and basketry.

OTHER PRACTICALITIES There's a Bancolombia on Calle 12 with a 24-hour ATM. On Calle 10 Foxnet internet café (☎ 724 6659) offers connections at 1,800 COP per hour daily 07.00–20.00, closing for lunch 12.30–14.00.

WHAT TO SEE AND DO
Parque El Gallineral (*corner of Malecón and Calle 6;* ⊕ *08.00–18.00 daily; admission 4,000 COP*) Without a doubt, this is San Gil's premier attraction. Edged by the

waters of the Quebrada Curití and the Río Fonce, this wedge-shaped 4ha island contains over 1,800 trees covered with strands of silver-grey bromeliads that give it a mystical, fairy-tale feel. An inviting freshwater pool is edged by creeper-clad bushes making it a very pleasant place for a stroll and a dip just ten minutes from the town centre. A 1km trail to Sendero Guane weaves through the trees and down to the river. Here, the Playa del Río Fonce is really just a muddy strip, but its grassy banks are a nice spot for a picnic.

Las Cascadas de Juan Curi Bike the 22km from San Gil on the road to Charalá or catch the bus from the main bridge in central San Gil to these magnificent 180m-high waterfalls. They can be reached by a little path by a small house – ask to leave your bike with the woman who owns it and she may well make you some fresh lemonade for the 15-minute hike. Some kind soul has fixed some wooden ladders at the base of the waterfalls so access to a large pool underneath and the rock face higher up the hills is easy. It's a superb place to take a dip in the heat of the day, so pack a picnic – during the week you're likely to have the place to yourself. The abseiling and rappelling here is some of the best in the area down the sheer 50m face.

AROUND SAN GIL

BARICHARA (*Telephone code:* 7) Resplendent colonial architecture abounds in this truly gorgeous little town 20km northwest of San Gil, and most people agree that Barichara is one of the most beautiful settlements in Colombia. Movie-set good looks give it an almost dreamlike ambience with immaculate streets of stunning whitewashed buildings and brightly painted shutters. Sympathetic restoration has painstakingly conserved the characteristics of Old Spain with pretty stone roads and fine churches dominated by a magnificent cathedral. In 1702, a field worker discovered a rock with an image of the Virgin Mary on it. Three years later, in recognition of this religious significance, Don Francisco Pradilla y Ayerbe erected a church at the scene of the miracle. It was named Villa de San Lorenzo de Barichara after the Guane word meaning 'place to relax' on account of its lofty views, year-round 22°C temperature and cooling afternoon breezes. Barichara was declared a National Monument in 1978 to protect its unique architecture and historical significance. Modern construction is outlawed as are neon signs and billboards. Even posters and shop window displays have to conform to strict municipal codes. Located high above the Río Suárez, Barichara offers superb views across some striking mountainous terrain. As a centre for stone masons, painters and artisans, it deserves to be crawling with tourists but you're likely to be the only sightseeing gringo in this handsome slow-paced town.

Getting there and around Buses go to and fro every 45 minutes between San Gil and Barichara but only until 19.00 each evening – catch one from the main plaza. The trip costs about 3,000 COP and takes about 35 minutes. A taxi will set you back around 15,000 COP.

Where to stay Barichara has around half a dozen hotels, plus some home-stay options – all of which tend to get booked to capacity during public holidays. If the hotels are full, many enterprising locals often rent out rooms to visitors at very reasonable rates – simply ask around town.

Hostal Misión Santa Bárbara Calle 5, No 9–12; ☏ 726 7163; www.hostalmisionsantabarbara.info. A range of comfortable sgl, dbl & trpl rooms in this grand colonial *hospedaje* can accommodate 80 people, with careful restoration ensuring plenty of character remains. All have large wooden beds, rugs, tiled floors

& private hot-water bathrooms. Some also have patios & terraces. A fine restaurant serves good local food & there is also a laundry service onsite. Rooms aren't cheap but the rate does inc a buffet b/fast. $$$

⌂ **Hospederira Aposentas** (5 rooms) Carrera 6, No 6–40; ✆ 726 7294. This quaint little family-run hotel sits right on the central plaza & comes highly recommended by travellers on a budget. Patron Miguel Bermúdez Ruiz enjoys chatting to foreign visitors & can also organise tours & guides. The rooms each have private bathrooms & a TV & are set around a pleasant courtyard. $$

⌂ **Hotel Coratá** Carrera 7, No 4–8; ✆ 726 7110. Baríchara's finest hotel is a magnificent architectural gem with a fine exterior & interior décor deserving of *Homes & Gardens* magazine. This prized historical

building dates back more than 280 years. Expect wooden balconies, vaulted ceilings, carved furnishings & numerous antiques. A charming garden centres on a large weeping willow with plenty of surrounding leafy blooms. Rooms are in demand so pre-booking is highly recommended, especially at w/ends. Each has a TV & a private bathroom & a beautiful décor. $$

⌂ **Posada de Pablo** Prices at this basic, clean family-run boarding house don't include b/fast, but an amiable patron offers guests a cup of *tinto* in the morning & is a good source of local insight. $

⌂ **Rosari García** Carrera 10, No 7–46; ✆ 726 225. This simple *casa de familia* offers home-stays at around 10,000 COP pp inc meals. Ask the patron to recommend a local guide to truly explore the local countryside's hidden trails. $

✖ Where to eat

Some of Baríchara's hotels have restaurants that stay open for dinner – and these are pretty much your only option for dining after dark, unless you've burgers and fried chicken in mind. Fast food is served with handy plastic gloves at the Boqueros fast-food joint near the plaza. Otherwise, head to the **Plenilunio Café** (✆ 726 7485) for some Italian comfort food at around 10,000 COP or the **Restaurante La Casona** for cheap grilled meats. Both are on Calle 6. The **Restaurante La Braza** on Carrera 6 serves many of Santander's traditional local delicacies at lunchtime, such as grilled goat. Baríchara's finest *arequipe* (see box, *Sweet treats*, page 165) can be sampled at **Arequipes Glorida** on Calle 6 and Arequipes Baríchara on Carrera 8.

Entertainment and nightlife

If Baríchara has any nightlife it is carefully hidden from view. The place appears totally deserted after 20.00 when even the restaurants shut up shop. A couple of kiosks sell cold beers and *aguardiente*. For a cracking hangover try the chichi de maíz – a potent cornmeal homebrew (see box, *Maize haze*, page 166).

Other practicalities

A small post office opens at 08.00 on Carrera 6 and doesn't close until 20.00 (shut for lunch noon–14.00). Baríchara has a small hospital on Carrera 2 (✆ 726 7133) and a police station on Calle 5 (✆ 726 7173).

What to see and do

Baríchara's main attraction is the Parque Principal – a beautiful central plaza that leads to sandstone churches and pretty streets. Be sure to take a look at the grandiose 18th-century **Catedral de la Immaculada** with its ten fluted 5m columns. The cemetery chapel, the **Capilla de Jesús Resucitado,** and its fascinating tombstones are also worth a visit as is the restored **Iglesia de Santa Bárbara** and the **Capilla de San Antonio.** The colonial house of the former president, the **Casa de Aquileo Parra Gómez,** has been opened up to the public on Carrera 2. A small Guane Indian pottery exhibition and fossil display is housed at the Casa de Cultura on Calle 5 (✆ 726 7002) – admission is just 500 COP.

GUANE (*Telephone code:* 7) Guane may be a tiny little one-horse town but it offers visitors expansive views, lying 10km northwest of Baríchara. A rather handsome plaza centres on a very pretty church – the Santa Lucía Iglesia – which dates back to 1720. Guane is also notable for its marvellous collection of fossils and artefacts at the **Museum of Paleontology & Archaeology.** A curator offers guided tours

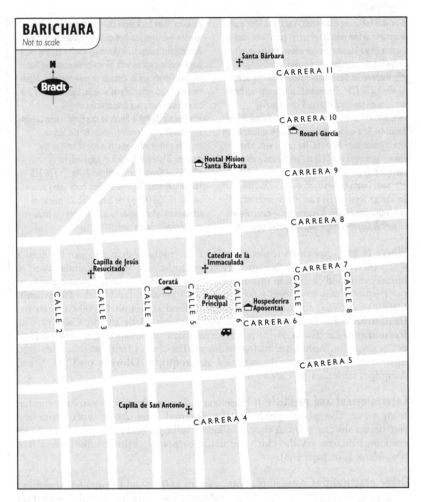

Santa Bárbara

CARRERA 11

CARRERA 10

Rosari García

Hostal Misión
Santa Bárbara

CARRERA 9

CARRERA 8

Capilla de Jesús
Resucitado

Catedral de la
Immaculada

CARRERA 7

Coratá

Parque
Principal

Hospederíra
Aposentas

CALLE 2

CALLE 3

CALLE 4

CALLE 5

CALLE 6

CALLE 7

CALLE 8

CARRERA 6

CARRERA 5

Capilla de San Antonio

CARRERA 4

seven days a week from 08.00–17.00 (closed noon–14.00). The town has a peaceful almost sleepy air and is a nice place to simply shoot the breeze. A couple of rustic restaurants serve homemade *sabajón* – a sweet non-alcoholic drink that tastes just like Bailey's Irish Cream. Good, inexpensive lunch menus offer soup, goat meat, rice and yucca. Guane is an important site of Indian heritage and was first discovered by Martín Galeano in 1540.

Getting there and around Just a couple of buses a day connect Guane with Barichara – one leaves at 11.30 and the other leaves at 17.00 and both only stay 15 minutes, Monday to Friday and Sunday only. A rather nice trail out of Barichara dates back to the conquistador era. It's been well maintained since being declared a National Monument in 1997 and is easily navigable year-round. Those that do decide to walk this 'Camino Real' will find it takes around 1½ hours – to avoid the trek back simply tout for a lift in town. It's common practice and costs around 1,000 or 2,000 COP.

Where to stay Although local residents sometimes open up their houses to bed and breakfast guests, Guane only has one official place to stay. The brightly coloured **Hostal Santa Lucía de Mucuruva** (✆ *315 294 2532*) is nothing special but offers clean, basic rooms in an old colonial home.

BUCARAMANGA *Telephone code: 7*

As a major commercial hub in the northeast of Colombia, Bucaramanga plays a significant role in trade with Venezuela. As the capital of Santander, the city is expanding rapidly with very little evidence of its colonial past amongst modern buildings and commercial districts. Bucaramanga was founded in 1622 and was used by Simón Bolívar as a strategic stopping-off point *en route* to Caracas during his campaigns. The original part of the city is today the Parque García Rovira where Bucaramanga's first church can still be seen. An ideal base for exploring, Bucaramanga offers easy access to surrounding mountains and colonial villages. It is also close to seven rivers and creeks rich in fish. Although it isn't brimming with tourist attractions, the city does have a handful of museums and a small botanical garden – along with a good stock of decent hotels and plenty of great places to shop and eat.

GETTING THERE AND AROUND Arrivals by air benefit from marvellous views on the approach to Bucaramanga's Palonegro Airport. Frequent flights connect the city with many of Colombia's main hubs, including Bogotá, Medellín, Cúcuta and Yopal. Bucaramanga's modern bus station (La Terminal de Transportes de Bucaramanga) in the southwest of the town links to a large number of cities across country as well as Venezuela, Peru and Ecuador. Locally, several public and private transit companies cover almost all of the metropolitan area (Bucaramanga, Girón, Floridablanca and Piedecuesta) with hourly buses connecting the airport to the city centre. Numerous *colectivo*s (shared taxis) also nip back and forth across Bucaramanga all day long (2,000 COP). Taxis (✆ *633 0781*) to the airport cost around 5,000 COP with the largest taxi rank stretching along the Parque de Santander. The city's brand-new Metrelinea public transit system remains under construction at the time of writing but is slated to open in the summer of 2009.

TOURIST INFORMATION AND TOUR OPERATORS Bucaramanga's central tourist information booth is located on the Parque de Santander where there is also a tourist police office stocked with free city maps and brochures. Chatty local guide Gilberto Camargo Amcrocho (✆ *311 854 2983;* e *futem2@yahoo.es*) can talk the hind legs off a donkey and can spin a yarn a mile long – but don't let this put you off. When he pauses for breath, Gilberto is a keen walker and regularly organises some serious full-day stomps across the mountains. His family also run the very nice Hotel Valle Real (see *Where to stay*) and if you like a natter Gilberto comes highly recommended.

WHERE TO STAY As a major regional hub of commerce and a tourist base, Bucaramanga has numerous hotels and places to stay. Signs for cabañas for rent can be seen by the roadside less than ten minutes from the airport on the road into the city centre, including the **Mirador Cabañas** at 20,000 COP per person. The city's cheapest accommodation is centred on the Parque Centenario although some places double as brothels so these aren't the safest or most salubrious choices.

⌂ **Hotel Dann Carlton** (133 rooms) Calle 47, No 28–83; ☎ 643 1919; e reservas@ dannbucaramanga.com.co; www.dannbucaramanga.com.co. In an atmosphere of plush grandeur, guests enjoy stunning views from a rooftop terrace at the 5-star Hotel Dann Carlton where waiters attend to their every whim beside a kidney-shaped pool. The gorgeous air-conditioned suites contain a minibar, security safe, fax, cable TV & internet connections. Onsite amenities inc a jacuzzi, sauna & gym as well as a very good restaurant & bar. This place is very popular with international visitors & tends to get packed out when there's a conference in town. $$$

⌂ **Hotel La Triada** (67 rooms) Carrera 20, No 34–22; ☎ 642 2410; www.hotellatriada.com. Choose from elegant rooms & 7 suites in this classy 5-star option where in-room facilities include free internet use, telephone, cable TV, fax, security safe & minibar. A mainly business clientele enjoy 24-hr room service & a speedy laundry service in a nice, central location. Rates inc a buffet b/fast. Other amenities inc a sauna & gym. $$$

⌂ **Hotel Chicamocha** (200 rooms) Calle 34, No 31–24; ☎ 634 3000; e reservas@solarhoteles.com;

www.solarhoteles.com. This hotel is part of a Colombian chain and offers 48 sgl, 35 twin, 24 dbl, 20 trpl & 58 family rooms that sleep between 4 & 6 guests as well as a handful of suites. Rooms are bright, clean & pleasant but vary considerably in size & style. Each comes with AC, cable TV, a minibar, safe, telephone. Amenities inc a swimming pool, steam bath, sauna, gym, bar & restaurant. $$

⌂ **Hotel Ruitoque** Carrera 19 No 37–26; ☎ 633 4567. Although this place is pretty basic, it is meticulously clean & excellent value for a room with AC, fridge, TV & minibar. It's also conveniently central & staffed by an efficient friendly bunch. $$

⌂ **Hotel Valle Real** Carrera 22, No 28–72; ☎ 645 2922/3179; e Hotelmivallereal@hotmail.com; www.hotelmivallereal.com. This uninspiring sludge-brown building may look like a 1970s office block, but it houses a very nice set of rooms that can accommodate up to 50 guests. Onsite facilities inc a small pool & a couple of meeting rooms. Rooms for 5 & 6 people cost 55,000 COP & 65,000 COP respectively. There's also a tariff for large group bookings of between 12–50 people. $$

WHERE TO EAT Umpteen local eateries, fast-food outlets and different ethnic foods can be found in Bucaramanga. Many are located in the city's various Zona Rosas and along the airport road.

Expect standard local fare and grills at the **Restaurante Club Deportivo Kumana** and the **Carbonado Restaurante y Bar** on the Vía Aeropuerto with a similar menu available at **Casa Roble** on Calle 31. Numerous street vendors sell *arepas* and drinks around the Centro Comercial with vegetarian restaurants, health food shops and juice bars along Calle 36. Santander's famous fried ants (see *Fat-assed ant any one?*, page 170). Aare sold in bags in delicatessens and shops during March–May. On Calle 33, **Restaurante El Viejo Chiflas** (632 0640) serves particularly good grilled meat with the *parrillada viejo chiflas* (a mixed meat platter) a delicious signature dish at 18,000 COP. For something a little more upmarket head to the **Restaurante La Carreta** (643 6680) on Carrera 27. Gastronomes rave about this 45-year culinary tradition and the menu in this lovely old Bucaramanga building is deserving of the hype with fine food at well under 20,000 COP a head.

ENTERTAINMENT AND NIGHTLIFE For a medium-sized city of 600,000 people Bucaramanga boasts a lot of places to eat, drink and be merry. Most after-dark nightlife is concentrated in the Zona Rosa de la Aurora in the northeast of the city but there is another string of lively bars and restaurants in the Centro Commercial and Zona Oriental in the east and in the west by the airport. For salsa music head to **Calison** in the Zona Rosa de la Aurora in front of the Chicamocha Hotel where Betos specialises in Vallenatos and New York old classics. **Mi País** in the Centro Commercial district is popular with a young and lively party crowd while **Babilonia**, **Candelaria** and **Africa** are all happening bars on the Vía al Aeropuerto. Two of Bucaramanga's most famous venues are live music joints **El Guitarrón** and **El Sombrero**. Both have mariachi bands every night from 22.00–02.00 – find them on Carrera 33 but be prepared to queue.

SHOPPING Bucaramanga's downtown shopping district and Cabecera retail zone fill with crowds at weekends – and the city is renowned as one of the best in Colombia to buy shoes. Numerous shoe factories are based around the outskirts of the city, so the range is vast and prices inexpensive with Bucaramanga synonymous with good leather and high-quality manufacturing. Several roadside stalls sell ceramics on the way into town from the airport with other vendors selling *dulces* (sweets) and desserts every mile or so.

OTHER PRACTICALITIES Banks (with ATMs) can be found around the Parque de Santander with a couple of money changers located along Calle 34 near the Centro Comercial La Triada. International phone calls can be made from Click & Play (642 2882) also on Calle 34 with numerous internet cafés throughout the city, including Telenet (670 5850) on Calle 36.

WHAT TO SEE AND DO Bucaramanga has a number of churches. The oldest in service is **Catedral San Laureano** on **Parque García Rovira** and the **Catedral de la Sagrada Familia** facing the Parque de Santander is the largest and most impressive. It took nearly 100 years to complete, between 1770 and 1865 and the result is a vast piece of religious architecture with statuesque twin towers and fine stained glass. The **Capilla de los Dolores** on the Parque García Rovira is the oldest surviving church in the city. It was built in 1748 but is no longer serving as a place of worship.

The rather nice gardens at **Jardín Bontánico Elo Valenzuela** (⊕*08.00–17.00 daily; admission 500 COP*) are located on the old road to Floridablanca in

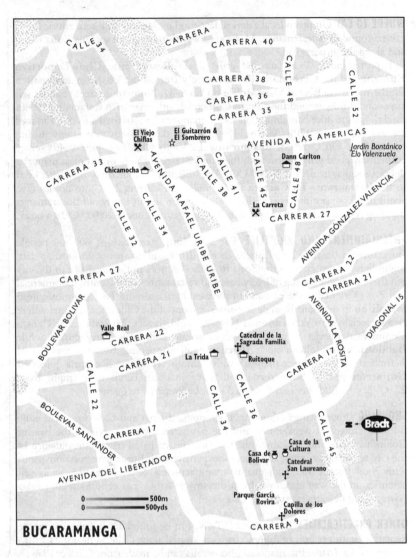

BUCARAMANGA

Map labels:

CALLE 34 · CARRERA · CARRERA 40 · CARRERA 38 · CARRERA 36 · CARRERA 35 · CALLE 48 · CALLE 52 · El Viejo Chiflas · El Guitarrón & El Sombrero · AVENIDA LAS AMERICAS · Jardín Bontánico 'Elo Valenzuela · CARRERA 33 · Chicamocha · AVENIDA RAFAEL URIBE URIBE · CALLE 41 · CALLE 38 · Dann Carlton · CALLE 48 · CALLE 45 · AVENIDA GÓNZALEZ VALENCIA · La Carreta · CARRERA 27 · CALLE 34 · CALLE 32 · CARRERA 27 · AVENIDA GONZALEZ VALENCIA · CARRERA 22 · CARRERA 21 · AVENIDA LA ROSITA · DIAGONAL 15 · BOULEVAR BOLIVAR · Valle Real · CARRERA 22 · CARRERA 21 · La Trida · Catedral de la Sagrada Familia · Ruitoque · CARRERA 17 · CALLE 22 · CALLE 36 · CALLE 34 · CALLE 45 · Bradt · BOULEVAR SANTANDER · CARRERA 17 · Casa de la Cultura · Casa de Bolivar · Catedral San Laureano · AVENIDA DEL LIBERTADOR · 0 500m · 0 500yds · Parque García Rovira · Capilla de los Dolores · CARRERA 9

Bucaramanga's Bucarica suburb. They were created by Luis Arango Restrepo – an avid orchid collector – who was keen to design a space in which he could exhibit regional flora. Shaded terraces, vibrant blooms, a small pool and a Japanese tea garden make for a pleasant afternoon stroll. It's a nice place to escape the heat with a book and there's a frequent bus from Carrera 15.

Bucaramanga's **Casa de la Cultura** (*Calle 37; ☏ 642 0163; ⊕08.00–18.00 Mon–Fri, closed noon–14.00, 08.00–noon Sat; free admission*) is housed in a character-packed old building and contains plenty of collections of paintings and crafts by local artists. It also houses exhibitions of indigenous history and Colombian art.

Of the city's many fine museums the **Museo Casa de Bolívar** (*Calle 37; ⊕08.00–18.00 (closed noon–14.00) Mon–Fri, 08.00–12.00 Sat; admission 1,000 COP*) is probably the most significant as it is housed in a building where Bolívar stayed for eight weeks in 1828. As a strategic planning point during journeys to Venezuela, he would replenish supplies and plot campaigns from this colonial mansion. Today the museum contains lots of historical displays depicting the era along with a large number of Guane artefacts, including weapons, utensils and crafts.

AROUND BUCARAMANGA

THE ROAD TO THE PARQUE NACIONAL DEL CHICAMOCHA The 54km drive from Bucaramanga to the Chicamocha National Park offers some of the most outstanding views in Colombia. As it cuts through the mountains and begins to slowly climb, silver-pink rocks take on a golden tinge and are tufted with green scrub. Woodlands and palm thickets covered with purple and red flowers lie in the valleys below. Needle-thin cacti form a line along the roadside as the gradual 600m ascent begins. The route takes in coffee fields and truly fearsome drops down to distant rivers. Travelling along this road is one of those genuinely memorable experiences when the backdrop becomes so breathtaking you almost want to drink it in.

The route also passes a lot of places to stop and eat *en route*. Grilled-meat restaurants start flanking the roadside just 10km out of Bucaramanga and continue pretty much to within 5km or so of the park – look out for the British-style blue and white signs bearing a knife and fork. A road toll approximately 40km from Bucaramanga is alive with fried-ant vendors touting bags of *hormiga culona* to passing traffic. Look out for a scattering of camping and cabaña signs – it means you're almost there.

PARQUE NACIONAL DEL CHICAMOCHA (*www.parquenacionaldelchicamocha.com;* ⊕*until 20.00 daily*) This magnificent 264ha expanse of mountains and canyons a little over 50km from Bucaramanga opened to the public in December 2006. Although a cable car is still under construction and an ambitious Mount Rushmore-style project won't be completed until 2057, most of the tourism infrastructure, hiking trails and attractions are in place. Costing US$20million the park currently includes a typical Santandereano village, viewpoints, footpaths and picnic areas. Piped *guanvinas* music adds an ethereal ambience to some of the Parque Nacional del Chicamocha's most atmospheric lookout points. In its first week of opening, the park attracted 15 walking clubs and 12 mountain biking clubs with more than 800 people walking the mountain paths from one club alone each Sunday. Eight well-maintained trails vary in difficulty and total 55km across spectacular honey-coloured rocky peaks. Contoured grassy rolls, trees and cacti are home to bears, snakes and iguanas while park rangers plan to restock rivers left depleted from centuries of over-fishing.

Morning paragliding sessions cost 130,000 COP with horseriding at 6,500 COP per person, guided walks at 30,000 COP, chiva rides at 2,000 COP per person and

FACES IN THE MOUNTAINS

It's an ambitious project that is rumoured to take over 50 years to complete, but Colombia's own Mount Rushmore-style monument is well under way. Unlike the US and its four rock-carved presidents, Colombia's mountain landmark will feature ten heroic Latin American figureheads, including Simón Bolívar, José Antonio Galán (Colombia), José Antonio Paez (Venezuela) and Fidel Castro (Cuba). Each will take five years to carve and will form part of a large hotel complex in an elevated position in the mountains between Bucaramanga and San Gil in the Parque Nacional del Chicamocha.

buggy hire from 17,000 COP. Camping is included in the 6,000 COP entry fee (2,000 COP for children) with plans to open 50 cabins for overnight stays in late 2007.

GIRÓN (*Telephone code:* 7) Much like San Gil and Guane, the town of Girón (*www.giron.gov.co*) is full of picturesque cobbled streets and colonial buildings that are seemingly stuck in time. Founded in 1631 as San Juan de Girón on the banks of the Río de Oro it was declared a National Monument in 1963. Significant restoration work has centred on the central plaza and a lot of Girón looks much as it did more than 350 years ago. The town's laid-back character makes it a popular centre for authors, academics and intellectuals and Girón has an established avant-garde arts scene. At just 9km from Bucaramanga, the town has become popular with weekending urbanites and is emerging as a popular second-home destination.

Getting there and around From Bucaramanga, pick up one of the frequent buses to Girón from Calle 15 and Calle 33 – it'll drop you half an hour later at the back of the main plaza. Girón itself can be easily explored on foot although taxis can be found around the Parque Principal.

Tourist information
Tourist Police Cnr Calle 30 & Carrera 27; ☎ 630 2046

Secretaría de Cultura y Turismo Calle 30, No 26–64; ☎ 646 1337; ⊕08.00–18.00, closed noon–14.00

Where to stay
Hotel Las Nieves Calle 30, No 25–71; ☎ 646 8968; ⊕12.00–19.00. A range of simple courtyard rooms offer sgl, dbl & trpl accommodation with private bathrooms. For views across the plaza ask for a balconied room at the front of the building – they're large with a TV. An onsite restaurant serves some of the nicest budget food in town with simple meat-&-rice dishes from 7,000 COP. $$

Where to eat
Food vendors congregate along the river at weekends while many of Girón's finer dining establishments can be found around the plaza. Two of the best are listed below.

Restaurante la Casona Calle 28, No 28–09; ☎ 646 7195; ⊕noon–18.00. Generous helpings & charming surroundings are trademarks of this local eatery. Expect hearty meals of grilled goat, chicken & *carne á la plancha*. $

✕ **Restaurante Mansión del Fraile** Calle 30, No 25–27; ☎ 646 5408; ⊕ lunch & dinner. This grand colonial mansion house is one of the finest buildings in Girón with a restaurant & craft shop that opens from noon–18.00. A small but promising menu offers plenty of local flavour with soups & grilled-meat dishes. $$

Other practicalities There's a bank with an ATM on Carrera 25 with an internet café called el port@l.net (☎ 646 9878) nearby that's open 08.00–23.00 weekdays only. In the centre of town there are a number of pharmacies and small supermarkets.

What to see and do Most visitors head to Girón to explore its tiny cobbled streets and the most striking sight-seeing attractions are the town's beautiful whitewashed colonial homes. Small stone bridges lead to shaded leafy gardens and grand mansions. Some of Girón's most notable fine architecture includes the **Mansión del Fraille** on Calle 30 and the **Catedral del Señor de los Millagros** on the main plaza. Two smaller plazas – Plazuela Peralta and Plazuela de las Nieves – are equally pleasing on the eye.

NORTE DE SANTANDER

This region on the Venezuelan border offers a varied geography with rugged, mountainous areas, patches of desert, cool plateaus, muggy plains and gently sloping hills. The department's municipalities sit at varying altitudes surrounded and divided by a criss-crossing of rivers, streams and lagoons. The magnificent peaks of the Cordillera Oriental meet the steamy savannas that roll lazily into Venezuela with three great river basins, the Río Catatumbo, Río Magdalena and the Orinoco. Due to its frontier location, Norte de Santander boasts a large number of Venezuelan influences that are evident in its dialects, culture and gastronomic tradition. The capital city of Cúcuta has a sizeable number of émigrés from Venezuela and its strategic position has ensured its status as a hotbed of contraband activity.

HISTORY The land that constitutes modern-day Norte de Santander played an important role in Colombia's independence from Spain. The department was created by the expedition of Law 25 July 1910 by territorial division at which time the Norte de Santander was born.

PAMPLONA *Telephone code: 7*

The snow ceased quickly, like music.
Birds and green come across the cold.
… but I just want to burn like a red sun in your white body.

From *Quiero Apenas* (I Just Want)
by Pamplona-born poet Jorge Gaitán Durán (1925–62)

Despite a major earthquake in 1875, this delightful colonial town in the deep Valle del Espíritu Santo in the Cordillera Oriental still contains some exceptionally old buildings in its narrow streets. Restoration projects conserved what wasn't totally razed but a great deal of modern construction was required to meet the city's needs. Today Pamplona is a key centre for commerce and political administration and has a number of important religious buildings. It is also an academic hub and is home to a growing number of schools and colleges as well as the Universidad de Pamplona. A sizeable student population gives Pamplona a laid-back campus feel and the city has a developed culture scene. It earned the nickname 'Patriotic City' as described by Simón Bolívar on account of its staunch support of the New Granada revolution. The city was founded in 1549 by Pedro de Orsúa and Ortún Velasco, making it the oldest in the region. Pamplona is the birthplace of one of Colombia's greatest poets, Jorge Gaitán.

GETTING THERE AND AROUND Numerous buses pass through Pamplona as it's on the main Bucaramanga–Cúcuta route – the trip takes about 1½ hours to Cúcuta (8,000 COP) and 4½ hours to Bucaramanga (16,000 COP). Pamplona's modern bus terminal is a very short walk southwest of the main square. However, those with luggage can grab a taxi for the 600m journey for 2,000 COP.

WHERE TO STAY AND EAT

Hotel Cariongo Cnr Calle 9 & Carrera 5; 568 1515. This tired-looking hotel at the back of the main plaza needs a lick of paint & some TLC with shabby rooms that are comfortable but could do with a face-lift. Each comes with a TV & a cold-water bathroom. $$

Hotel El Alamo Calle 5, No 6–68; 568 2137. Every room has a private bathroom in one of Pamplona's best budget options where pocket-sized rooms are basic but clean – & b/fast is just 2,000 COP. $

Hotel Orsúa Calle 5, No 5–67; 568 2571. There's a 2,000 COP premium for a room with a TV at this pokey little cheapie on the main plaza. $

El Palacio Chino Calle 6, No 7–32; 568 1666; noon–19.00. This functional oriental diner serves up a fusion of Colombian-Chinese dishes at pleasing prices, including sweet-&-sour veg-&-rice & seafood noodles. $$

OTHER PRACTICALITIES Find the post office on Calle 6 – it's open weekdays only between 08.00–18.00 (closed noon–14.00). Most of the banks with ATMs are clustered around Calle 6 and there are at least half a dozen internet cafes around Calle 5.

WHAT TO SEE AND DO Pamplona has a number of museums and the **Museo de Arte Moderno Ramírez Villamizar** (*Calle 5; 568 2999; 09.00–18.00 Tue–Fri, closed noon–14.00, 09.00–18.00 Sat/Sun; admission 1,000 COP*) is one of the finest, containing extensive works by Eduardo Ramírez Villamizar. He was born in the town in 1923 and this beautifully restored 16th-century home offers considerable insight into this great artist's career from his expressionist era to his geometric abstract sculpture. Others in Pamplona include the quirky old photograph collection at the **Museo Fotográfico** on Carrera 7 and the **Museo Arquidiocesano de Arte Religioso** (*Calle 4, Carrera 5; 568 1814*) where a rather fine collection of religious objects can be found.

Many of the town's old historic mansion houses and ten churches are also open to the public. Check out the 19th-century **Casa de Mercado** on the corner of Carrera 5 and Calle 6 and the **Iglesia del Humilladero** by the cemetery. **Casa Anzoátegui** on Carrera 6 is the former home of heroic Venezuelan general, José Antonio Anzoátegui, who fought in the Battle of Boyacá and died in Pamplona three months later at the age of 30. One of the town's oldest buildings now houses

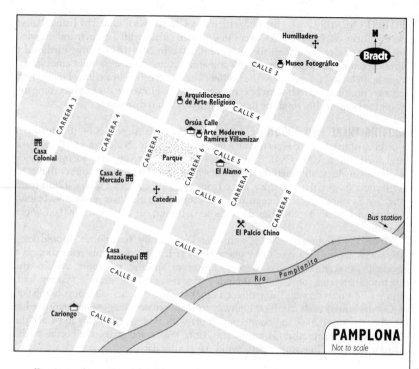

PAMPLONA
Not to scale

a collection of pre-Spanish objects. **Casa Colonial** is on Calle 6 and is open 08.00–17.00, closed noon–14.00.

FESTIVALS
Fiestas del Grito de Independenia *(June/July)* The city plans all year ahead of the 'Fiestas de Pamplona' and the result is a jam-packed two-week calendar of musical concerts, street processions, marching bands, bullfighting, beauty pageants and general merriment in a wide variety of venues across Pamplona.

CÚCUTA *Telephone code: 7*

The most populous city in the region is the capital Cúcuta, a bustling trading point bordered to the east by Venezuela. Rapid population growth has seen the city sprawl since the 1960s and today the so-called City Without Borders has a burgeoning mix of Venezuelan and Colombian inhabitants. More than a million people reside within the metropolitan area, with 600,000 living within Cúcuta's inner core. Vast temperature disparities separate the wet and dry seasons with 28°C when the rains come and highs of 35°C in the summer. December, January, February and March are the driest months. The wettest are April, May, September, October and November with August's wind attracting kite-fliers to Cúcuta in their droves. More than 300 neighbourhoods form the city's urban network with the wealthier suburbs of the north and northeast leading to the less affluent communities in the south and the slums in the southeast. Although the city has a reputation as a rather uninspiring grubby hubbub Cúcuta proudly proclaims that it has more green zones than many other cities in the nation. In fact, this urban lung benefits from less pollution than many would expect due to its proliferation of trees. These were planted by Francisco de Paula Andrade Troconis after an earthquake partially destroyed the city in 1875.

HISTORY Originally a pre-Hispanic settlement, Cúcuta was founded by Juana Rangel de Cuellarby on 17 June 1733, becoming a small village with a church and growing to a modern-day population in excess of 45,000. In May 1875 a large earthquake almost completely wiped out the city and also seriously damaged other cities in the region, including several across the border. The construction of a railroad in the 19th century prompted a fresh spurt of economic growth. However, the railroad company went bankrupt in 1960 and the line closed and fell into disrepair.

GETTING THERE AND AROUND Cúcuta's Camilo Daza Airport is on the northern outskirts of the city and is served by a regular bus service. Numerous taxis nip back and forth for a 6,000 COP fare. Flights from the city connect to most major Colombian cities, although do not always go direct. There are no direct flights to Venezuela from Cúcuta – these leave from San Antonio del Táchira, 12km from the city. Avianca has an office in the centre of town (see *Other practicalities* below) and frequent shared minibuses and taxis serve the airport at around 1,000 COP per person.

Travellers heading to Cúcuta's chaotic 'Terminal de Transportes' should keep their wits about them (see *Other practicalities*) as it has a notorious reputation as a hotbed of scamming and deceit. However, public transport within the metropolitan area of Cúcuta includes a massive public transit system with numerous buses serving Bucaramanga (25,000 COP, 6 hours) and Bogotá (65,000 COP, 16 hours) each day. The highway to Bucaramanga was greatly improved at the beginning of 2007 and connects Cúcuta with Bogotá, Medellín and Cali; the highway to Barranquilla, Cartagena and Santa Marta; and across the border to the road to Caracas. To ensure safety, avoid travel after dark.

WHERE TO STAY Like most big cities, Cúcuta has its fair share of hellhole hotels, especially around the red light district in the five or so blocks surrounding the Terminal de Transportes. Most of these double as brothels and are not considered safe.

⌂ **Hotel Tonchala** Cnr Avenida 0 & Calle 10; ☎ 571 2005; e tonchala@telecom.com.co; www.hoteltonchala.com. Choose from a variety of room styles & sizes in this upmarket casino hotel, from sgls to large suites. Amenities include a restaurant, sauna, pool & gym with rates inc buffet b/fast. $$$

⌂ **Arizona Hotel** Avenida 0, No 7–62; ☎ 571 884. Room rates include b/fast at this pleasant contemporary hotel set behind a distinctive dark-glass façade. Conveniently located in the heart of the city, the Arizona has a bar, restaurant & a pool with each room equipped with AC, minibar, safe, cable TV & telephone. Choose from sgls, dbls & trpls – each has a private hot-water bathroom. $$

⌂ **Hotel Amaruc** Avenida 5 No 9–73; ☎ 571 7652. This mid-range hotel has a range of sgl & dbl rooms equipped with a desk, TV & telephone. Some are fan-cooled & some have AC. $$

⌂ **Quinta Avenida** Avenida 5, No 8–32; ☎ 572 0086. Nice, bright, cheerful AC rooms come with private, modern bathrooms & a fridge. Rates include b/fast. There's also a swimming pool. $$

⌂ **Hotel Real Cúcuta** Most of the rooms at this reasonable dirt-cheap option are trpl bed but there are some sgls & dbls – all with fans or AC. $

WHERE TO EAT There are lots of fried-chicken joints, burger bars and pizza places in and around town as well as a good number of local restaurants, bakeries and cafés – some of them 24-hour. For fast food check out the **Presto** (☎ 577 5596) on Avenida Los Libertadores, **Kokoriko** (☎ 572 2822) on the corner of Avenida 0 and Calle 8 and **Los Carritos** (☎ 571 0097) on Avenida 0. For some good, uncomplicated local food head to **Punto Cero** (☎ 573 01533) on Avenida O where a menu offers traditional dishes in a homely atmosphere – even the most expensive big-plate meal costs no more than 10,000 COP. **La Mazorca**'s fine Creole set

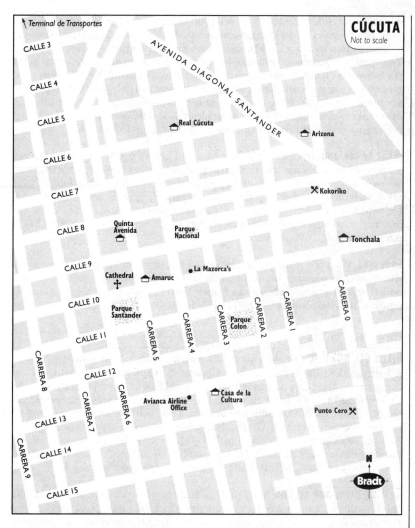

meals and decent wines are also great value at 4,000 COP. Find it on Avenida 4 and dine at a pleasant courtyard table.

OTHER PRACTICALITIES Staff at the Avianca airline office (✆ *571 5161*) can guide you through the complexities of the timetable from Cúcuta – find it downtown on Avenida 4. Numerous town-centre shops offer plenty of places to pick up essentials, with banks with ATMs on Avenidas 5 and 6 and a post office on Calle 8a. Travellers heading to Venezuela will need to visit the Departmento Administrativo de Seguridad (DAS) immigration post on the road to the border. The Venezuelan Consulate is located on Avenida Camilo Daza *en route* to the airport, 3km from the city centre.

Safety and crime Large numbers of travellers in Cúcuta have reported encountering the city's well-organised fraudsters who operate in and around the bus terminal and appear perfectly legit. Foreigners are targeted almost exclusively, usually by English-speakers, who either offer to help with bus tickets or offer to insure your cash against theft. Most carry official-looking documents and a triplicate pad of receipts but the tickets they tout are forgeries. The insurance is also a scam to part you from your cash. They push the benefits of insurance by telling an alarming story about recent hold-ups by bandits on buses and urge you to protect your cash against theft. However, the paperwork requires details of the cash you are carrying and once you have entered the amount, the con artists ask to count the money for clarification. At this point there is an almost invisible sleight of hand and suddenly, lo and behold, the amount is halved before your eyes. It's also important to watch your luggage like a hawk.

What to see and do Cúcuta isn't blessed with a host of sightseeing attractions but a reasonably sized **Casa de la Cultura** (*Calle 13;* ✎ *571 6689;* ⊕ *08.00–18.00 Mon–Fri, closed noon–14.00; admission free*) houses year-round exhibitions of local handicrafts and art. For slightly more excitement grab tickets for a Cúcuta Deportivo home match (see box, *Freed from football obscurity*) – or head to a local bar to watch the game on television when you hear cries of 'GOOOOOLLLLLL' echoing through Cúcuta's streets.

Shopping Cúcuta's many malls include a Unicentro on Avenida Libertadores, where an endless succession of shops include a Carrefour and a number of food outlets as well as a bingo hall and a casino. Ventura Plaza is the biggest shopping centre in the city, between Calle 10 and Calle 11.

AROUND CÚCUTA

VILLA DEL ROSARIO (*Telephone code:* 7) This town, located about 10km southeast of Cúcuta on the road to the Venezuelan border, is significant as the venue for the inauguration ceremony of Símon Bolívar as president and vice president of Gran Colombia in 1821. Today the Parque de la Gran Colombia signifies the spot where the New Granada of Colombia and Panama, Venezuela and Ecuador was unified to form the new nation of Greater Colombia. The town was founded by Don Asencio Rodriguez in 1750 on the Río Táchira and today forms part of the metropolitan area of Cúcuta. In 1813, Simón Bolívar liberated the city in the Battle of Cúcuta *en route* to Caracas, killing 20 Spanish fighters and injuring 14.

Getting there and around At about 20 minutes from the Venezuelan border, Villa del Rosario is easily reached by public transport and taxis from Cúcuta and Pamplona. It is also easily criss-crossed on foot and has several local taxi firms for those weighed down with luggage.

What to see and do Villa del Rosario's main claim to fame is its Símon Bolívar connections and the **Parque de la Gran Colombia** is the town's number one

COLOMBIA'S CONTRABAND CAPITAL

One of Colombia's contraband epicentres, Cúcuta is powered by numerous criminal syndicates that flex considerable muscle within local circles. Under the watchful eye of the city's kingpin players, Cúcuta's underworld has a tentacle-like control of trade and commerce, smuggling vast quantities of petrol over the border to sell at up to ten times the Venezuelan price. Contraband is big business in this frontier town and is a commerce that runs like clockwork – with battered old trucks carting goods over the border in back-to-back trips.

tourism attraction. It's been built on the remains of the Templo del Congresso where congressional talks and Bolívar's inauguration took place. Pretty red-tile pathways are flanked by large numbers of trees. Although the church was almost wiped out in the earthquake of 1875 it has since been restored, albeit not sympathetically. In the newer section of the church there's a marble statue of Bolívar and a few other related mementos. The park is also the site of the **Casa Natal de Santander** (☏ *570 0741;* ⊕ *09.00–17.30 Mon–Fri, closed 11.30–14.00; admission 1,600 COP*), former residence of Francisco de Paula Santander and today it houses a small exhibition relating to his life, including some photographs and letters.

.... thou who knoweth of the bounties which have been granted thy people, let me recall the blessings of the divine Coca which thy privileged subjects are permitted to enjoy through thy progenitors, the sun, the moon, the earth, and the boundless hills.

Ancient sacred ceremonial recital to the coca (Colombian Andes)

Although Spanish priests once denounced it as an evil *delusio del demonio*, this divine plant of the Latin American Indians remains Mother Nature's most effective remedy for altitude sickness. Chewing coca leaves is how the indigenous peoples have relieved symptoms of dizziness and nausea for centuries. Today thousands of trekkers in high regions of Latin America are following suit, although many prefer to ingest it in tea form than eat it raw. After a cup or two, most find that their headaches, nausea, vomiting, fatigue, shortness of breath and sleep disturbances are significantly eased. When a bunch of high altitude trekkers on Mount Everest were tested it worked a treat, significantly reducing the effects of altitude (palpitations, dyspnoea, anxiety and insomnia) compared with the placebo test.

Altitude sickness is the name given to human body's physiological and symptomatic reaction to low oxygen pressure ('thinner' air) at high altitude. About 20% of people experience mild symptoms at altitudes between 2,200 and 2,500m above sea level. These vary significantly from one individual to another and it is directly related to the rate of ascent. It is also related to how long a person stays at that height. At 3,000 to 4,000m the risk of altitude sickness is very real. More than 50% of travellers above 3,500m are likely to feel the effects of altitude with almost 100% suffering at 5,000m should they ascend without acclimatization. The altitude-related death rate is about 4% for trips above 7,000m. A person's level of fitness does not affect altitude sickness with even the most experienced athletes likely to suffer.

To lessen the effects of altitude take a graded ascent. If you feel ill at a particular height, come down to lower level. Drink plenty of liquids, avoiding alcohol. Stay warm. Signs of altitude sickness are usually evident in the first 36 hours. Those with heart and lung problems, pregnant women, children and people with severe diabetes and high blood pressure need to be especially careful at altitude.

Coca is honoured in sacred ceremonies in the Andes where Indians first chewed its leaves as a hunger pacifier before discovering its medicinal qualities. Homeopathic coca isn't available in the US due to FDA restrictions, but may be obtained from Indian, European, or Latin American pharmacies.

5

Los Llanos

Telephone code: 8

> Ah my Llanura! Green enchantment, where the blue of the sky gets confused with the soil of your vast expanse. In the dawn, the sun kisses you from the lake to the moriche. The air is full of herons and the palms whisper for liberty!
>
> Armulfo Briceño, *Ay mi Llanura* (album: Tributo Al Llano, 1999)

Los Llanos – 'the flat plains' – is a vast grassland savanna that sprawls to the east of the Andes in north-west Colombia and Venezuela. These cattle-clad seasonally flooded lowlands cover over 50% of the country's total landmass, comprising rolling grassy knolls, scrubby pasture and prairies dotted with ranches. The region's main river is the Orinoco with gentle slopes that lead away from higher elevations that barely rise above 200m. Herdsmen in Los Llanos raise mammoth droves of cattle over many thousands of acres with stud farms, horses and cow fields the lifeblood of Colombia's 'Cowboy Country'. Corralling, roping, ranging and lassoing are all-important skills in this rural hinterland where the nasal dialect of the Llaneros (plainspeople) remains peppered with phrases unchanged from the idioms of the first Spaniard settlers. The Llaneros are proud of their hard lives and are dedicated cowboys from the cradle to grave, spending long days enduring extreme heat and high winds in the saddle. Having learned how to 'break' horses while young, these gaucho-like ranchers enjoy a provincial culture rich in folklore, legends and stories. It is hard to image a Colombian song more poignant than those of Los Llanos' heartfelt lilting lyrics to the melodic strum of the *cuatro* guitar or harp. A true Llanero is a legendary figure on the ranches of Colombia and these accomplished horsemen often wear the distinctive traditional working clothes of a poncho, straw hat and *cotizas* (rope-soled sandals).

HISTORY

Niklás Federman, a German conquistador, approached the altiplano of Bogotá from the savannas of Venezuela navigating an inhospitable area created by the waters of the Orinoco Basin. Los Llanos, as the hinterland region was referred to, remained neglected by settlers for more than 300 years in favour of coastal territory. Few ventured east for fear of its problematic geographical obstacles and oppressive heat. However, in the 1840s, a small group of farming folk moved from villages in eastern Bogotá to establish the settlement of Gramalote, which officially became the parish of Villavicencio in 1855. Inhabitants of the plains became known as the Llaneros and these formidable horsemen first fought for the Spanish royalists and then for the Venezuelan and Colombian rebels during the war of independence. It is said they crossed the Andes with Bolívar to take the Spaniards by surprise on Tunja's plateau where they cleared the way for the taking of Santa Fé de Bogotá in August 1819. Villavicencio began to grow as the availability of medicine made this rural outpost more hospitable. Land was offered free to relocating farmers – the

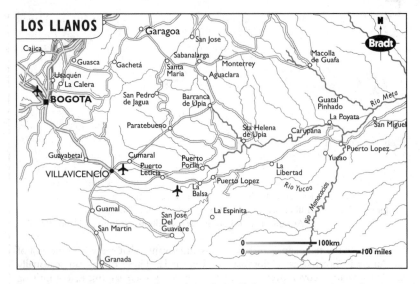

construction of a simple mule track made it all the easier to navigate. Soon new colonisers were building roads which improved access to the extremes of Los Llanos, enabling farming communities to better ship their produce and cattle to the markets of Bogotá.

THE ECOSYSTEM OF LOS LLANOS

South America's savanna ecosystem covers a total of 269 million hectares. Most of it (76%) belongs to the Cerrados of Brazil but about 11% forms the Venezuelan Llanos and 6% (16–17 million hectares) the Los Llanos Colombia. The plains of Venezuela and Colombia form a single eco-region, an area of extensive grasslands covered mainly by savanna vegetation. Geographically relatively young, at less than 10,000 years old, the region has experienced a major subsidence. The result is a striking landscape of dramatic alluvial plains and highlands.

The Llanos are some of the world's richest tropical grasslands, a diverse landscape of dry forests, grasslands, and seasonally flooded plains that teem with wildlife. It eventually disperses into a river delta of swamp forests and coastal mangroves as it approaches the Atlantic and harbours more than 100 mammal species and over 700 species of birds – around the same number of birds found in the entire United States. Boasting the largest river flow on earth, the mighty Orinoco cuts through the heart of the Llanos landscape.

WILDLIFE AND BIRDS One of the most critically endangered reptiles on the planet can be found in Los Llanos, the endemic Orinoco crocodile. The species can reach a length of 7m in maturity but scientific reports suggest that fewer than 1,800 of these magnificent individuals remain in the wild. The Orinoco turtle, giant river otter, ocelot, giant armadillo, black-and-chestnut eagle and several species of catfish are also in need of conservation. The capybara, the word's largest rodent at around a half-metre high, resides in wet, flooded savannas as does the anaconda, the largest existing boa, at over 7m long. The jaguar, the largest American felidae has been severely hunted in the Llanos, for both sport and to protect cattle. The tapir was once prevalent in the region but is now drastically reduced.

In contrast, no bird species are at serious risk of extinction in Los Llanos, although some are vulnerable. These include the sharp-tailed ibis, only found in Los Llanos and Colombia's most scarce ibis species. Colombia has the richest avifauna of any country in the world at more than 1,700 bird species although less than 40% is found in the region. At least 62 of the bird species in the Orinoco region are neo-tropical migrants, accounting for nearly 40% of the migratory species found in Colombia and Venezuela. Indeed, the wetlands of Los Llanos are among the most important areas for neo-tropical migratory birds, such as shorebirds like sandpipers and yellowlegs. Seasonal visitors to the region include the broad-winged hawk and swallow-tailed kite. There are renewed concerns for the future of the scarlet macaw as these are often captured and kept as pets.

Although relatively unaffected by negative human influences until recent times, the natural resources of Los Llanos have increasingly become important to the economies of both Colombia and Venezuela. Fire is used regularly to increase the quality of native grasses, while slash-and-burn tactics are used to increase pasture lands and natural plains are being replaced by introduced pastures. More than 1.3 million hectares of the Colombia Llanos are being used as introduced pastures with 15 million head of cattle in the region. This large-scale cattle production and commercial agriculture has seen the draining of sizeable expanses of wetlands. Rice and oil production have also damaged natural ecosystems. Dredging for ditches, dykes and ponds has also destroyed habitat, with the widespread use of agro-toxins in pest control also a concern.

In 2006, the Nature Conservancy in Colombia (*Carrera 7, No 80–49 Oficina 204 Bogotá, Colombia;* ↘ *571 321 4051;* e *colombia@tnc.org; www.nature.org/*) joined with the Colombian National Natural Parks Agency (Parques Nacionales) and WWF Colombia to lobby for a new 63,000 acre protected area of flooded grasslands covered by gallery forests. The proposed conservation area would be the first officially protected flooded plains in Colombia.

THE ROAD FROM BOGOTÁ

A modern road has shortened the driving time from Bogotá to 1½ hours, travelling east through Avenida Boyacá and passing the mist-shrouded peaks of Paramount Crux Verde. It cuts through Bogotá's notorious Sud Bolívar slum district, a distressing collection of shanty towns set back beyond the highway. Although dangerous, this stretch of 'no-go area' poses no danger to daytime drivers. Illegally constructed thrown-up shacks have no foundations, power or sanitation. Unsurprisingly, the nearby Río Tunjuelito is one of the most polluted stretches of water in South America. In the distance, the magnificent slopes of the mountains of Sumapaz National Park form a sharp contrast to the squalor in the foreground. Stretching 200km, the park's folds have effectively halted the continued growth of Bogotá's southern slums. Chickens peck at rotting garbage on the roadside by lotto-selling curb-side vendors while wealthy slick-haired urban cyclists on gleaming 100-million peso bikes head out to do battle with the peaks.

A Mobil-branded petrol station on the left at the end of a tatty cluster of houses signifies the end of the city – and the beginning of the route into Colombia's southeast. The first of three tunnels along the route is the Argelino Durán and it is around this point that the town of Caqueza can be sighted on the right, although the actual entry point is 28km further along. On the roadside there's a *lácteos la delicia* (dairy vendor) selling smoked cheeses, creams and yoghurt drinks. The route starts to wind through lush green grassy verges with wood-and-wire fencing. A shabby sign hails the Tienda la Piacita on the left, a stopping-off point for snacks and cold drinks.

It's not a banana – it is way too small. Sometimes green not yellow, or almost curved like a ball. What a treat that must have been to be the first to try one – must've created a din. It's a flexible delight, who has a mate with black beans and rice.

Doug Heyman (*The Plantain poem*)

Portuguese Franciscan monks are said to have introduced plantains to the Americas, although it was the Spanish who gave it the name *plátano* after spotting its similarity to the Spanish plane tree. Plantain and bananas belong to the Musaceae, known simply as the banana family. They can be eaten at different stages of ripeness, and their taste differs depending on how ripe they are. As the peel changes to brown or black, the flesh has a sweeter flavour. At this stage it smells more like a banana but still keeps its firm shape when cooked. The interior colour of the fruit remains creamy, yellowish or lightly pink, regardless of the stage of ripeness. Plantains are grown as a staple food in 52 countries worldwide on about 12.8 million acres. Today, Colombia produces roughly 2% of the world's bananas and 9% of the world's plantains. A typical 100g fruit comprises 66% water, 134 calories, 1.2% protein, 0.4% fat, 31% carbohydrates and 2.6% fibre. Plantains are eaten all over modern-day Colombia and are typically boiled, baked or fried. Patacones – a twice-fried flattened plantain patty – is one of the most delicious ways to enjoy this staple.

Soon, the second town of Chipague is just about in view as the road sweeps around to take in its shape. A small string of bars and shops has the rustic Restaurante PPC in its midst – a simple food joint where a plate of plantain, rice and grilled meat costs less than 6,000 COP. Giant orange rocks and a mustard-coloured mud bank are to the right-hand side of the road. To the left, a truly vast, breathtaking drop forms a stunning valley clad with green palms. In this region of Colombia there is no shortage of roadside eateries, mostly the omnipresent *asaderos* – the nation's much-loved wood-fired local grill. Both the La Vara and the Estadero la Fonda typify this rustic gastronomic favourite, serving big slabs of beef at tables set just yards away from grazing cattle herds.

Next up is the pit-stop town of Abasticos, little more than a row of snack stalls on the left of the road. The Restaurante Donde Mireya may not look much from the outside but it is always packed with truckers and passers-by. Rumour has it the *chorizo* is worth stopping for even if time is tight.

Running alongside the left-hand side of the road beyond Abasticos is the Quebrada Blanco. Look out for Hollywood-style white lettering in the hillside above – although not as glamorous as its Californian inspiration, the sign for 'Drogas Casa Ortiz' (a family-run drugstore) made from white pebbles is worth a peak nonetheless. Next up is the La Vara Sasados on the right of the road, a big local diner serving fried fish, *arepa* and grilled meat. Opposite, the Restaurante Cafetería sits next to a petrol station. Further up the road, a stretch of tiny snack shops and kiosks (*tienditos*) sell bits and bobs, sodas and sweets.

At this point the rocky banks become more densely covered in the so-called spoon tree. Rope-tethered soot-coloured bulls graze on spongy verges by the Quebrada La Honda. Nearby are a couple of tiny grill joints and a handful of small white single-storey fincas.

Then, hurrah! It's the long-awaited La Petite Source (2) Restaurant – the first in this family-run duo of fine diners that are loved by tourists and locals alike. Look out for a pretty stone-built building with lots of wrought-iron detail, flying a patriotic flag with great aplomb. Inside, the place is spotlessly clean with tiled floors and square wooden tables. A decent menu has plenty of seafood, chicken and meat dishes served in typical style with rice or *patacones*. A well-stocked Panadería Típica sells packed goods to take away with numerous sugary treats perfect for a road trip. A wide range of beers, liquor, wine and fresh juices sits on rows of wooden shelves along with jars of preserved fruits.

Half a kilometre on the right, the Parador Punta offers snacks with stunning views. Then it's La Petite Source (1) – the original restaurant and a similar concept to its sister, although much smaller and less popular with large families and groups as a result. Don't miss the waterfalls to the left – they are spectacular but often hidden by foliage.

Next it's the tunnel de Quebrada Blanca and onto the scrappy truck-stop town of Guayabetal where there's a small hotel, bakery, a handful of arepa stalls, some cell-phone minute vendors and a couple of local restaurants. The Rancho Grand is near to a drug store, Comcel phone shop and tiny kiosk while the Restaurante Don Pacho nestles between a couple of rickety beer shacks. On a backdrop of Andean forest of red, black and green hues there is lots of water gushing down from the mountains – it's crystal clear and deliciously drinkable, according to the locals. At exactly 70km from Bogotá by a bright yellow bridge it's possible to spot the remnants of the old road – an impossibly narrow crumbling strip under magnificent cascades of tumbling water and emerald creepers. There's another spectacular water feature around 5km further along the road, but more by accident than planning or Mother Nature. A thin stainless steel water pipe suspended across two high peaks hasn't been patched up in years and today spouts spray from at least half a dozen holes to create a ghostly apparition in the mist.

About 8km from Villavicencio, a handful of attractive plum-coloured fincas catch the eye just as an overpowering smell of chickens catches the breath. A steady climb leads to Alto de Buena Vista where, as the name suggests, the views are truly amazing. Pull in by the smallholding at the top on a clear day to look out across to Río Meta over a lush green valley – a true photographic opportunity. Nearby, there are a few shops for basics and snacks but not much more.

VILLAVICENCIO *Telephone code: 8*

A sign on the edge of town proudly announces your arrival in Villavicencio – the 'La Puerta al Llano' (The Gate to the Plains) it states, confirming its location. Sitting on the historical path from the Colombian interior to the vast savannas of the Colombian–Venezuelan plains between the Andes and the Amazon, Villavicencio is both a city and municipality and the capital of the Meta department. In a period of just over 40 years, this frontier outpost has been transformed from a hamlet of 30 people into a metropolis of more than 350,000. Dubbed 'Villavo' by its inhabitants, it lies on the banks of the Río Guatiquía in the footholds of the Andes range to the east.

Founded in 1840, it was named after Antonio Villavicencio, who was an early advocate of the struggle for independence from Spain. Today, Villavicencio serves as an important manufacturing and commercial centre for the plains and rainforests of eastern Colombia. Although its industries include a distillery, brewery, rice mills and saddleries, Villavo is primarily a cattle-raising centre. Today, a modern highway links the city to Bogotá 90km northwest making Villavicencio a commercial hub for roads from the northeastern and southern parts of the Meta department.

Although early and evening breezes from the mountains attempt to cool the city, Villavo is typically hot and muggy. Heat rises in a haze along a muddle of sun-

The Huitoto ('wuh-toe-toe'), also spelt Witoto, are recent arrivals in Los Llanos, a region without any surviving indigenous tribes. One of Colombia's largest indigenous groups, the Huitoto hail from a principal territory in the La Chorrera of the Amazon jungle and have only had a presence in the region for a few years. Artistically talented, the Huitoto make masks, rattles and blowguns as well as a range of jewellery made from bark cloth, seed and nuts coloured with vegetable dye. Bark cloth is made from a palm tree beaten until it is paper-thin. Traditional clothing for both sexes consists of a short skirt. Women used to be bare-breasted but now often wear traditional dress for ceremonial occasions only.

The Huitoto believe they emerged from the earth with tails thanks to their god, Jitoma. A bee removed their tails with its sting – and the Huitoto tribe were born. The Huitoto proceeded to a lake to wash where they came across an anaconda. Hungry, the Indians killed the snake, cutting it into four. This signified the birth of the tribe's four dialects.

However, over the years the Huitoto became increasingly marginalised until in 1990 the discrimination became intolerable for some. After first having contact with white rubber producers in 1980, the Indians suffered slavery. Then white missionaries attempted to convert them to Christianity, while the Colombian government made forceful inroads into eradicating Huitoto culture, language and beliefs. In 1999, the Huitoto denounced their oppressors, which by this time included drug-traffickers and guerrillas. Santiago Kuetgaje (✆ 578 664 8350; f 578 664 8105; www.etniasvivas.org) found his voice on Chorrera FM 104.9. However, his outspokenness prompted death threats and Kuetgaje judged these sufficiently serious to flee the Amazon in 2004, under cover of darkness. He eventually settled in Los Llanos where the rest of his 16 family members joined him, earning money as guides at the local zoo and making handicrafts to sell. Realising that the success of their new-established community lacked an economic foundation, Kuetgaje travelled to speak to tribal leaders in Peru. He learned about indigenous tourism and the dynamics of this emerging sector in Colombia, winning first prize in a Corporación Andina de Fomento (CAF, Andean Development Corporation) initiative for indigenous talent. Kuetgaje's award was US$22,000, a sum he used to establish the Los Llanos project. The objectives are to maintain the Huitoto culture, ethos, traditions and language whilst giving visitors an insight into how they live and think.

Key traditions the Huitoto are keen to explain include a woven stick (robaindias) they use to catch a partner. There is also the 'human–nature' connection they call 'el Mambeo' – a ritual that involves ingesting ground coca leaf to link with god. Eaten with a spoon, the coca powder is a stimulant that the Huitoto view as the 'female' energy of their version of ying and yang. The tribe also ingest tobacco in a thick, black jelly format. It is eaten from a small earthenware pot with a small toothpick. This is the male energy to counterbalance the coca leaf.

In the past, the women were allocated to a potential partner at birth, wrapped in a palm parchment. Today, a man and woman can have a relationship after the girl reaches puberty. The Huitoto are a patriarchal society with the Cacíque (chief) the most important male. Part of their belief system is shape-shifting into animal form. After el Mambeo the chief can better 'see' where his people should hunt in the jungle and his men shape-shift to become one with the animals to improve their hunting chances.

The Huitoto settlement is less than half an hour from Villavicencio but visitors should not turn up on spec to experience the dance, rituals, food, drink and handicrafts of this fascinating community. Villavicencio's Huitoto are 100% reliant on tourism for their income. After such a turbulent recent history they have many tales to tell.

parched streets that enjoy disorder born out of 40 years of crazed development. Unfortunately this expansion has been largely uncontrolled and poorly planned. Modern-day Villavicencio is not a pretty city. In 2007, many areas still lack clean water and decent sanitary systems. Many of its poorer neighbourhoods lack even the most basic amenity with an electrical grid that fails to keep pace with demand. This absence of town planning has left Villavo with a chaotic maze-like character. Concentrated clusters of colourful single-storey houses crowd highways, alleyways and plazas with makeshift markets and retail zones slammed up against swish residential streets. This manic development has encroached on the very outskirts of Villavicencio – a large roundabout with an Esso service station on the left denotes where the central urban spread begins in earnest. However, what it lacks in beauty it retains in importance and in the midst of a sprawling agricultural wilderness Villavicencio is a crucial commercial hub.

GETTING THERE AND AROUND Villavicencio's La Vanguardia Airport is served by Satena and Aires airlines with frequent 30-minute flights to and from Bogotá. The 98km overland route is around a three-hour drive from Bogotá – a far cry from a decade ago when the road was so bad it was a ten-hour haul. Several minibuses run from Bogotá including Bolívariano (✆ 1 424 9090; www.bolivariano.com.co), Macarena (✆ 1 425 4900; www.flotalamacarena.com), Velotax (✆ 1 429 6984; www.velotax.com.co) and Auto Llanos (✆ 1 263 0799). Costs range from 18,000–25,000 COP and some of the companies operate round the clock, departing every 15 minutes. Taxis are in plentiful supply throughout the city – and are the best way to get from A to B. Expect a cross-town journey to cost around 4,000 COP.

TOURIST INFORMATION
Oficina De Turismo ✆ 656 2728/672 5981; e enturismo_villavicencio@hotmail.com;

⊕ 08.00–18.00 Mon–Fri, closed noon–14.00, 09.00–13.00 Sat.

WHERE TO STAY Although there are plenty of shoestring places to find a bed for the night, the three nicest (and safest) hotels in the city are the most popular with foreign visitors. Those willing to chance a dirt-cheap joint will find umpteen throughout El Centro. The following offer a combined room-count of over 200 rooms but are often packed out so pre-booking is crucial.

🏠 **Hotel Del Llano** (110 rooms) Carerra 30, No 49–77; ✆ 671 7000; e hotellan@etell.net.co; www.colomguia.com/losllanos. Another bright, modern place that lacks a bit of soul but is perfectly adequate, catering for a mix of family vacationers, travelling merchants & overseas tourists. $$$
🏠 **Hotel Don Lolo** (57 rooms) Carerra 39, No 20–22; ✆ 663 1825; e donlolo@etell.net.co. This modern hotel has rooms that vary in size, ranging from some rather pokey sgls at 136,000 COP to trpls for 202,000

COP. As one of Villavicencio's most popular resting places the Don Lolo is packed to capacity during summer & public holidays, so be prepared to be disappointed if you turn up on spec. $$$
🏠 **Hotel María Gloria** (60 rooms) Carerra 38, No 20–26; ✆ 672 0197. This popular hotel has a wide range of rooms to choose from, so be sure to check out a few to compare. A spacious trpl or family room costs from 215,000 COP. $$$

Those keen to give large modern hotels a wide berth will find plenty of little-known alternatives on the outskirts of town. A growing number of fincas are offering home-stay programmes and bed and breakfast accommodation in pretty rural settings; many are located on working farms. Few advertise and as they tend to be set way back from the road they are often difficult to find without help. Independent tour operator Raman Vergel (✆ 311 281 9328) is a good person to call regarding agro-tourism.

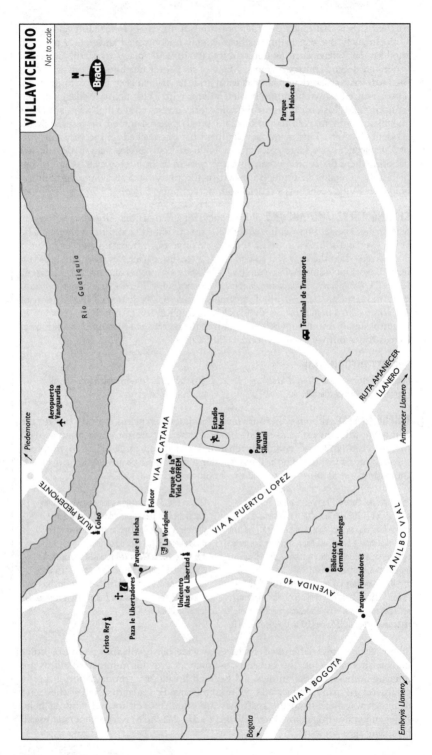

VILLAVICENCIO
Not to scale

Rio Guatiquia

Piedemonte

Aeropuerto Vanguardia

RUTA PIEDEMONTE

Coleo

Parque el Hacha

La Vorágine

Folcor

VIA A CATAMA

Cristo Rey

Paza le Libertadores

Parque el Hacha

Unicentro Alas de Libertad

Parque de la Vida COFREM

Estadio Macal

Parque Sikuani

VIA A PUERTO LOPEZ

Terminal de Transporte

Parque Las Malocas

RUTA AMANECER LLANERO

Amanecer Llanero

Biblioteca Germán Arciniegas

ANILBO VIAL

AVENIDA 40

Parque Fundadores

VIA A BOGOTA

Bogota

Embryis Llanero

CROONING COWBOYS

Heartfelt lyrics typify *música llanera* with proclamations of love and declarations of pride at top-of-the-lung-volume pride singing. The cattle-herding Llaneros are loyal to their homeland and proud working people that yearn for romance. Harp-led melodies in traditional *joropo* style blend machismo desires with big-hearted passion in this folkloric musical tradition. Beautiful words and poetic prose capture the essence of these vast cattle-and-horse-raising flatlands. Joyous, rhythmic, string-and-percussion-based songs are crafted on a *cuatro* (small, four-stringed guitar) and harp. Other instruments include a *bandola* (a pear-shaped guitar), bass and maracas and the songs of Llos Llanos are usually florid at a syncopated pace. Verbal contests called *contrapunteo* are often part of this musical tradition. Some of the famous musica llanera artists include such greats as Alma Llanera, Cimarron, Luis Ariel Rey, Carlos Rojas, Sabor Llanero, Arnulfo Briceño and Orlando Valdemarra. Visitors will hear this toe-tapping, infectious musical style everywhere in Los Llanos. It forms a constant soundtrack to a journey through the savannas, a melodic backdrop redolent of rural cattle-farming life.

✘ WHERE TO EAT Diners are spoilt for choice in the upscale areas of Villavicencio, such as El Barsal and El Caudal, as well as the city's two Zona Rosas. Expect to find numerous juice joints, bistros and grills on Carerra 32 as well as some of the city's best after-dark hangouts.

Travellers on the move will find plenty of cheap, rustic food places on the edge of town. Some of the best include Restaurante El Perico and Restaurante Judith (on the right as you come into town from Bogotá) and the Pescados Restaurante on the left. In the heart of the city (as well as the outer edges) there are umpteen budget fast-food joints. Clusters of reasonably priced local restaurants can also be found around the Plaza le Libertadores and around Carerra 39.

ENTERTAINMENT AND NIGHTLIFE Villavicencio's two Zona Rosas (Pink Zones) are awash with bars, clubs and restaurants. Find them in the southwest and the north of the city – but don't count on having an early night.

☆ **Los Capachos** Cra 48, No 17–87 Villavicencio; ✆ 578 662 2079; e info@loscapachos.com; www.loscapachos.com. Colombians travel miles across country to get to this frenzied party venue – a booming, pumping & neon-lit bar-cum-nightspot that even Bogotános consider oh-so cool. Expect big sounds & big drinking at Los Capachos, with non-stop dusk 'til dawn fun-fests every w/end that promise the ultimate in hedonistic merriment. Since it opened in 2002, Capachos has earned a formidable reputation for fun with a capital F. It's named after a set of rattle-style maracas used in Los Llanos created from hollowed gourd or totumo fruit & filled with achirilla or curcuma seeds – & after midnight in Los Capachos there are plenty of people shaking their maracas at this heaving wild night out.

SHOPPING At the time of writing, Villavicencio is undergoing sizeable redevelopment in its retail sectors. A large mall is slated for completion at the beginning of 2008 with dozens of smaller outlets due to open before 2009.

The city has all the usual large supermarkets, such as Exito as well as numerous boutiques and small shops in El Centro. In the middle-class district of El Barsal there are umpteen cosmetic surgeries, salons and beauty parlours, many funded by dubious means.

Carerra 39 is Villavicencio's makeshift market area, a mile-long stretch of counterfeit goods, cheap electronics, discount clothes, sunglasses, CDs and designer knock-offs. Endless street vendors and stalls attract big crowds of people in a street renowned for its low prices and redlight low life.

5

OTHER PRACTICALITIES As you'd expect from a large trading outpost, Villavicencio has numerous banks and ATMs. It is also a great place to stock up on hardware items, get tents and equipment repaired, and replace worn-out boots and T-shirts.

WHAT TO SEE On the large Unicentro roundabout on Avenida 40 stands a rather handsome monument in honour of the region's kidnapped persons 'Alas de Libertad'. Close by on the Avenida del Llano Vía Restrepo, there is also a statue commemorating Villavicencio's bullfighting tradition, 'Monumento Al Coleo'. On the Vía Marginal de la Selva a roundabout boasts a magnificent water feature with illuminated cascades designed to emulate harp strings accompanied by piped música típica.

About 15km from the centre of town is Villavicencio Zoo, complete with restaurants, souvenir stalls, vendors and taxis.

SAFETY COUNTS In the city's central Acacias district the Parque de Fundadores is a pleasant collection of seating under shady palms. However, in the area's central tree-lined boulevard the ambience is less tranquil. Muggings have increasingly become a problem in this most unlikely spot. Travellers are advised to be vigilant when in Acacias – and to avoid carrying excess belongings, valuables or sums of cash.

AROUND VILLAVICENCIO

CUMARAL This small town 10km from Villavicencio is named after the important palm 'cumares' – from which extracted fibre is used to make rope, hammocks and baskets. A wide main drag comprises a string of bars and restaurants serving excellent wood-fired grilled meats. A handful of essential shops include a small drugstore and a hardware vendor. One of the finest local eateries in Cumaral is the centrally located **Asadero los Camares**, an on-the-street food joint with inside and outside tables. Expect the patron to rush out with a plate of meat to sample before you make a decision to eat – it's standard practice and allows a little 'try before you buy'. If you like what you taste, grab a seat. A handful of waiting staff dressed in matching bright blue T-shirts attend to a dozen or so wooden tables, serving up hearty plates of chunks of grilled beef, salted potatoes with boiled yucca washed down with a ice-cold beer.

THE ROAD TO FINCA POTREOCHICO The road east towards Finca Potreochico near Paratebueno cuts through 65km of lush green fields, passing more local restaurants and cattle-breeding territories, vets, feed stores and farmers outlets. Fruit stalls dot grass verges scattered with maroon-coloured fincas with roadside vegetation dotted with the *morishes* palm – a clear sign that water is close by.

A DEVIL OF A PLACE

Ancient legend has it that the local children once swam in the river when the devil came to visit in human form. Over several weeks, he played with the youngsters and began to plot their demise, before being rumbled by the local priest. He exorcised the devil who was furious at the intervention and in an enraged state he decided to flood the river to wipe out the entire village. However, he'd been weakened by the exorcism and could only manage to create a crater – not the huge tidal wave he'd intended. This left Medina and its inhabitants unharmed 5km away. Today El Cañon del Diablo (Devil's Canyon) serves as a reminder of the villagers good fortune and the triumph of good over evil.

Devilish little rebel pebble, furious, fuzzy and vigorous.
Rumba rattle made of hollow gourd, with pebbles or lead shot inside.'
Ramon Guiraro, *The Maracas* (poem)

Maracas are one of the most recognisable percussion instruments on the planet and these rattles made from gourds are essential to Latin and South American music. Usually oval or egg-shaped, the maracas are filled with beads, beans or small stones, with a handle used for shaking. Traditional maracas are only made from natural materials including gourds or other plant pods, wood and leather. The word *maraca* is believed to have come from the Araucanian people of Chile and players of maracas in South America favour different varieties. In Colombia, traditional-style maracas are preferred above newer models with small *gapachos* popular in the Andes region filled with seeds from the gapacho plant. In Los Llanos, *clavellinas* similar to gapachos are played – and both these styles of maracas are heard in many forms of Latin music. This characteristic percussive sound is essential to traditional Colombian rhythms. Worldwide, maracas are often played at parties, celebrations and special events. Even rock and pop musicians have adopted the maraca, including Bo Diddley, Mick Jagger, and Bez from the Happy Mondays. The music of Los Llanos, 'música llanera', has maracas at its heart, accompanied by a harp and *cuatro* (a sort of four-string guitar).

Between Villavicencio and Pompeya, look out for landmark pineapple stall 'Papa Quiero Piña' – meaning 'Daddy, I want a pineapple' – a place dedicated to stocking the finest pineapple around. That the owner stole the name from a fellow trader in Cordoba in western Colombia doesn't seem to matter – if you've time, be sure to pull in to taste the sweetest, juiciest *piña* in town.

Pompeya (*Telephone code: 08*) This small town 25km from Villavicencio hugs a 2km stretch of main road with a couple of simple hospedajes, a small supermarket, a petrol station, burger bar and handful of drink kiosks as well as the inevitable half-dozen places selling 'minuto cellular'. A favourite stop-off with heavyweight trucks journeying back and forth across the Venezuelan border, at the end of town soaring gas exploration towers and a radiating glow of an aerated diffusion flame can clearly be sighted.

Alcaravan (*Telephone code: 08*) There are more power plants, drilling sites and energy companies at this tiny town 2km from Pompeya – a prime site of major US oil giant Harken Energy Corp. Harken Energy holds the largest net exploration acreage position in Colombia and is a driving force behind many of its so-called mega-projects. Beyond a thick-forested area lies one of the region's most important industrial shipping hubs, Puerta Porfía – a prime transit point for oil and industrial plant that is almost completely obscured from view. Harken Energy boasts the distinction of having US President George W Bush as a director – a relationship not without scandal. During a high-profile crackdown on corporate fraud, the President's own financial dealings came under scrutiny. This centred on Bush's decision to sell 212,140 shares for US$848,000 just before the company announced a 23.2m loss, causing the share price to drop to US$2.375 from US$3. The next day, Harken returned to US$3, but fell to US$1 at the end of 1990. A flagrant breach of disclosure laws was cited as grounds for prosecution by many of Bush's harshest critics. Bush supporters say that he did fully disclose the transaction, and that 'half of corporate America was filing forms late at that time'. An irritated Bush himself

5

said 'There was an honest difference of opinion as to how to account for a complicated transaction. Sometimes the rules aren't as specific as one would expect, and therefore the accountants and the auditors make a decision.'

Finca Potreochico The town of Paratebueno is actually 18 minutes from the Finca Potreochico (✆ *310 325 0060;* f *313 386 8059;* e *cauchoparr@yahoo.es*), travelling northwest from Villavicencio. A frequent bus service connects Villavicencio with Potreochico where it is possible to get a taxi to the Finca; just tell the driver you're staying with Rodrigo Escheverri. The Finca sits at the end of a long unmade off-road track that leads to the owner's sprawling 260km farmland where Echeverri has lived since childhood after his father left Bogotá for an alternative to city life. Today, his vast farm encompasses pasture, crops, cattle herds and jungle and enjoys a beautifully remote location in the heart of the countryside. Witty, charming and erudite, Echeverri is an engaging host who is enthusiastic about nature and adventure sports – especially cycling. His extraordinary stamina, skill and agility would put most men half his age to shame and Rodrigo Echeverri is a valuable source of local of knowledge, tips and advice. His tours are highly popular with adventurous types, mainly Europeans. Echeverri prefers individuals and small groups and is basically up for anything, from madcap downhill mountain bike rides to rappelling, rafting, caving and hiking. He likes nothing more than multi-day trips involving a bike, a boat and a tent, and advises guests to pack plenty of stamina – especially if they agree to do the eight-day 1,000km trip to the Río Orinoco. He operates under the name Wuajari Adventure Tours – and with Rodrigo Echeverri 'adventure' is just what you get.

On the farm itself, guests can horseride, cycle and hike across rubber plantations and through forests full of monkeys and grasslands with excellent birdwatching, fishing and numerous thermal springs. Echeverri embraces a management practice that involves educating locals in sustainable farming. He raises cows purely for organic fertilisers for the rubber plants and palm oil crops. He also promotes farming with great ecological focus over profit. White-water rafting is another of his passions on the Río Humea, Río Gasanta and Río Gasamumu.

Overnight accommodation is convivial with open-air lounges overlooking flower-filled trees and a lovely swimming pool – although guests should prepare themselves for plenty of wildlife. Frogs the size of sugar sacks hop around your feet. Farm rats scuttle along the rafters. Howls, shrieks, cries and yowls dominate the night air. Rooms are pretty basic but there's an outdoor shower in a space pod – yes a space pod. Let's just say this bubblegum-coloured finca is truly unique.

An overnight stay at Finca Potreochico costs 120,000 COP per person including breakfast, lunch and dinner – and the food is truly sublime ($$$).

MEDINA This small town 95km from Villavicencio was located elsewhere 50 years ago. After yellow fever almost wiped the whole population out the remaining half-dozen inhabitants relocated 10km to the north. Today, the 'new Medina' is a pleasant farming town of dusty muralled whitewashed walls and a good stock of shops for essentials, including a few small supermarkets, a hardware stall, a drugstore, bakery and grocers.

If you find yourself parched in Medina, be sure to pop into Los Centaurus, a pocket-sized beer and soda joint in the centre of town. It boasts the distinction of selling broom handles, root vegetables, bits of hardware and breakfast cereals at a makeshift counter. Choose from one of five plastic red chairs by a fully stocked candy rack and expect lots of loud *música típica*. At dusk this place is frequented by cigar-smoking moustached campesinos in ponchos that drink quietly, with purpose, until they drop.

They always put social experiments in the easiest, most fertile places. We wanted the hardest place. We figured if we could do it here, we could do it anywhere.

Gaviotas founder Paolo Lugari

Although it is rumoured to be totally impossible to find, Gaviotas (e *gaviotas@lists.greenbuilder.com; www.friendsofgaviotas.org*) – a small village of around 200 people – is one of the most unique communities on the planet. Set in the Vichado province in eastern Los Llanos, the settlement has redefined sustainability, developing revolutionary designs for power-collecting windmills and creating ground-breaking solar heating systems. Even their hospital has been hailed as 'One of the most important buildings on earth' by the *Japanese Architectural Journal*. This is no ordinary village – far from it.

In the late 1960s, Paolo Lugari encouraged a group of like-minded environmental engineers, scientists and researchers to join him in realising a vision of Colombian self-sustaining community. Yet although this may sound like a hippy plotline from a bad flower-power novel, Lugari and his colleagues were serious intellectuals who had little time for talk of cults. They arrived in Gaviotas and immediately began work, creating a reliable water supply in the inhospitable climate of Los Llanos, eventually designing a unique deep-soil water pump attached to a children's see-saw. The Gaviotan team also produced a sunflower-shaped windmill so effective that it is now found all over Colombia, thanks to their policy of not patenting their designs in order to ensure they are free to the world at large. The community's 16-bed hospital building is an elevated maze of glass skylights, steel columns and solar panels with an air-conditioning system that blends ancient wind ventilation techniques with modern technology. Although the hospital was closed by a shift in government policy, the building now provides a sterile environment for a new water and tropical fruit juice bottling operation. This fresh drinking water has reduced gastro-intestinal ailments and R&D staff have also designed a unique water bottle that children can assemble like Lego blocks. If the Gaviotan team have their way, an adjacent greenhouse looks set to contain one of the finest medicinal plant laboratories in the tropics. Even so-called failures have spawned ideas for future successes

Other noteworthy achievements include the reforestation of the Orientales Llanos – a replenishment project that began in 1984 with the planting of hardy Caribbean pines in an area that had been barren for centuries. At the last count, Gaviotas has planted 8,000ha of Caribbean pines, creating a 10% rise in the area's precipitation. The resin produced has been harvested for conversion to colofonia, which in turn has been sold for use in a range of products, such as cosmetics and household paints. More than 325ha of palm trees have also been planted for oil to make bio diesel, enabling Gaviotas to be entirely fossil fuel-free since 2004. Methane from cow dung provides fuel for kitchen appliances with solar pressure cookers used for most of the cooking. They farm organically and every family in the community enjoys free housing, community meals and schooling. Unlike most Colombian towns Gaviotas has no weapons, no police force and no jail – there isn't even a mayor.

Gunter Pauli, head of Zero Emissions Research and Initiatives (ZERI) has cited Las Gaviotas as the world's premier example of sustainable development. The United Nations named the village a model of sustainable development. Gabriel García Márquez has called Paolo Lugari the 'inventor of the world'.

See also Alan Weisman's *Gaviotas: A Village to Reinvent the World* (1998)

Los Llanos **AROUND VILLAVICENCIO**

5

The Llaneros are renowned throughout Colombia for their myths, legends and folkloric beliefs. Many remain intertwined with modern life in the plains and a powerful force within the local community, governing many unspoken social rules.

BOLA DE FUEGA (BALL OF FIRE) Many Llaneros report seeing balls of fire in the summer sun. Some, reportedly, have been of such ferocity that the balls have chased them into their homes. The locals believe that many balls of fire are successful in catching their victims and burning them and their homes to the ground. Llaneros view a small fireball as being close to them – and therefore presenting greatest danger. A fireball that looks large is far away and less of a threat. So what should you do if the fireball gets too close to you? Swear, apparently. Spilling your bad words and verbal poison will stop the fireball from burning you – but if the ball is tiny, you'd better be quick!

GENTE SIN CABEZA (HEADLESS HORSEBACK RIDER) According to local legend, the headless horseback rider only appears when the Llaneros gather together at night. Wearing black clothing and wielding a razor sharp machete, the horseman tries to attack the locals. The Llaneros believe that if they get caught they will be decapitated in an act of revenge. This belief stems from Colombia's bloody La Violencia era in the 1950s when enemies would kill each other in their sleep with machetes – the ultimate cowardly act.

LEYENDA DE DIABLO (DEVIL'S LEGEND) Llaneros believe that a man walking through the trees at night is exposed to the wrath of the devil. He appears, peering down from the leaves in the form of a witch. What does he want? The victim's soul in return for untold riches and all the women in the world. He can be highly persuasive, especially if the man has partaken of aguardiente.

A rough unmade track leads out of the centre of town up to a place the locals call El Cañón del Diablo (Devil's Canyon) on account of an old local legend. Don't be tempted to do this drive in anything other than a 4x4 as this crateous route is appalling. However at 5km another option is to tackle it on foot. Pass some big hibiscus shrubs past some remnants of the old drystone walls favoured by the villagers centuries ago. At the top of a steady, sloping climb, the track turns to grass running between two fenced-off paddocks. Carry on until the end and walk 200m to a gap in a barbed-wire fence (don't worry, this is an 'official' cut through). Walk about 100m northeast towards an obvious drop – you can't miss it, it's vast.

PACHAQUARO This 6km pit-stop stretch of rustic restaurants and small supermarkets is edged by expansive rice paddies. Pass by at dawn or dusk to spot feeding waterbirds in the low-lying sodden fields beyond. Pachaquaro is blessed by a good paved single carriageway free from billboards. A spare scattering of trees enables great views across open fields over fragile wood-and-wire fencing.

LA BALSA One good reason to stop at this small horse-farm town is its excellent smoked meat. Set your milometer for 70km from Villavicencio and look out for private residential homes with fresh cuts hanging from the porch. Other than that, La Balsa has a few basic shops selling essentials and a couple of cold-drink vendors. On a nice day, the views out to stud farms and cattle fields makes this a pleasant place to get out of the car and stretch your legs, with slender white ponies and herds of chocolate brown cows.

PUERTO LOPEZ Best described as a medium-sized small town, this modest port-side settlement on the Río Meta is around 99km east of Villavicencio. Crossing the wide, sluggish coffee-coloured Río Meta allows colourful views of rusting cargo boats, tethered horses, cattle carriers and hulking oil tankers with agriculture and cattle ranching the town's prime industries. Travellers passing through will find Puerto Lopez's restaurants well worth trying. Head for the roundabout in the centre of town to discover **Restaurante Tamanaco** (✆ 6450 630) – a first-class grill renowned for generous portions of good food. Other good options include the diner at the **Hotel la Prima** and the **Restaurante Mi Caseta** as well as the more basic **Asadero de la Mancheo**. Passers-by in a rush will also find plenty of places to eat on the hoof, including numerous fried-chicken joints, fish-and-rice street

---

A COWBOY'S TALE

Llanero cowboy Luis Abetardo Nieve is a former *El Coleo* (cow roping) champion. He was just a small boy when he first started working with horses and cattle. Today, in his late 30s, cattle and horses are his life:

'I started to help out with shoeing horses at the age of seven and soon learned the daily rhythm of work on the ranch. Today, I work full-time with cows and horses wearing the customary jeans, boots and a sombrero llanero (palm-woven cowboy hat) with a serrated knife in a holster on my hip (*cuchillo*). Horses mean a lot to me – they represent me as a Llanero. I am a man of The Plains so horses are my identity as well as my life. Today, I get up each day at 05.00 to milk the cows – a herd of cebú and criollo species. Another good Los Llanos working breed is pardo suito. Once this is done it is time to dedicate some time to the horses, so I get them ready to take out to graze on the grasslands after I have mucked out the stables.

After a quick lunch at home at 11.00 I train the new horses. I work with criollo as this breed is intelligent and good for speed. Other species in Los Llanos are more about brawn, not brains. First I use a rope and lasso to dominate the animal so that it eventually submits to being saddled. I use a stick-and-robe tool called a *muñeco* (meaning doll) and keep the horse still using rope ties. After about three days the horse loses its fear and accepts the saddle – and at that point it is ridden for the first time. Tied to the doll, I get the horse circling first anti-clockwise and then clockwise. At this point I start training a second horse as it is important to keep the momentum going. After another three days the horse is comfortable with being ridden and is six days into its training. Next, I teach the horse *quebrada* – how to move right and left. Also how to move at different speeds, from a trot and a gallop to a stop. Once the horse is happy with this instruction I attach the reins (*rienda*). Initially this is a double rein for strength but as the horse relaxes I remove the spare.

Once my work with the horses is finished, I return to the cows. I leave many of them out grazing overnight – after all the more grass they eat the better the milk. However, I do bring the calves in by rounding them up on horseback and herding them back to the stalls. After the cows are settled I wash down the horses. At about 17.00 my day is done and I can think about going home. To relax, I practise el coleo, or cow tailing – a horseback cattle-roping challenge when my skills are pitched against a strong wild herd. Every week there's a bull-roping festival somewhere in Los Llanos with an annual international fair in Villavicencio each year. This annual event attracts dozens of competitors from ten countries and is an incredible event that truly sets my blood pumping.'

stalls and snack kiosks. A few kilometres further along the road is Colombia's geographical heart – a mustard-coloured 100ft totem pole-like structure on a paved ledge of high land, the **Alto de Menegua.** A semi-permanent small market comprises vendors of woven bags, baskets, jewellery and carvings as well as some basic snack and drink options. Nearby, one of the nicest resorts in Los Llanos makes an excellent base from which to explore the region – the Lagos de Menegua Hotel & Resort not only benefits from breathtaking natural surroundings but is also spotlessly clean and an easy place to be based, especially off-peak. A programme of road improvement works has transformed the journey from Puerto Lopez for 33km east. More than 150km of paved road are expected to be completed by the end of 2008.

Where to stay

🏠 **Lagos de Menegua Hotel & Resort** (24 rooms)
🛎 315 326 6070/645 0013/645 0193;
e informacion@menegua.com;
www.lagosdemenegua.com. This hotel was newly refurbished in 2007 and many of its crisp, clean rooms boast a bright white 'Zen-like' décor. Although the place has plenty of modern resort trappings these play second fiddle to the setting, an incredible 100ha spectacular of lakes, peaks, hills & rivers. Don't be fooled by the subdued plains immediately around the resort; greater magic lies beyond. Rounded hillocks form a rippling landscape of numerous shades of green that roll down to scrubby grasslands that millions of years ago once lay under water. Coralline rocks & fossils can still be spotted amongst the scrub. Modest plateaus are dotted with dense, small wooded thickets close to forests of skinny palms. Expect to see lone hawks soaring above the savannas & to hear a cacophony of crickets at dawn & dusk. Lagos de Mengua is renowned for its truly awesome sunsets & sunrises, when the sky moves from tangerine to powder pink then baby blue & violet to inky midnight blue.

Tours at the resort range from gentle walks to full-on adventure hikes with birding, kayaking & horseriding. A loop of hiking trails overlooks large resplendent lakes & although camping isn't strictly on the menu, it can sometimes be accommodated in individual circumstances (although you'll need to demonstrate a responsible eco ethos). Standard accommodation can house 2–8 people & comprises white walls, white ceilings, white stone, terracotta floors, wooden beams, white linen, white drapes & white bedding. Rooms are equipped with towels, TV, minibar/fridge & AC. Showers are cold water but are big, clean & efficient. Communal amenities include an outdoors swimming pool, covered pagoda-style dining area, pool bar, ice-cream parlour, games room & large patio terrace. Guests can also use the internet although there are no telephones in the rooms. $$

RÍO MANÁCACIAS This pleasant waterfront setting is a favourite with fishermen but is largely undiscovered by tourists at a two-hour trip (108km) from Puerto Lopez. Yet those prepared to explore the river will find plenty of boatmen ready to make it happen. Expect to pay about 10,000 COP for a half-hour journey to the point where the Río Manácacias joins the Río Meta and Río Yucao. Pink river (boto) dolphins can be easily sighted here with plenty of places to picnic and chill out along the way.

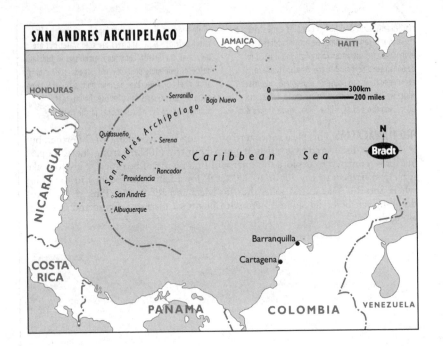

6

San Andrés Archipelago

San Andrés how beautiful you are. San Andrés how beautiful – it is a privileged place where God put his hand; a privileged place.

Francisco Zumaque, *San Andrés*

Colombia's only oceanic department – the West Indies Department – is one of the most isolated island regions in the Americas, located 800km northeast of the Colombian mainland, just 150km from the Nicaraguan coast. Laid-back locals pride themselves on being barefoot champions of leisure in a calypso culture that is a world away from fast-paced Bogotá. Warm Caribbean waters are home to a cluster of palm-scattered atolls, islets and cays in an archipelago where 300,000km² forms the main constituent of a UNESCO Seaflower Biosphere Reserve (Reserva de la Biosfera Seaflower). Fertile waters, grass beds and mangrove-clad lagoons host a magnificent array of bird species with isolated soft-sand beaches and undisturbed coral reefs rich in underwater flora and fauna. Three inhabited islands form the archipelago's geographical and spiritual heart as immortalised in the lyrics of Colombian musician Francisco Zumaque's catchy chart-topper 'San Andrés'. Around them lie five uninhabited atolls to the north and two to the south with a liberal scattering of sandbanks and cays in between, including the submerged islet of Alicia Shoal.

HISTORY

For a petite cluster of islands, the San Andrés Archipelago has a colourful history, steeped in tales of pirate plunder and glory-seeking conquistadors. Although claimed by English Puritans in 1627, it was first discovered by Dutch colonisers at least three decades earlier. They were also often visited by Mosquito Indians from the coast of Central America to trap sea turtles and collect bird eggs and guano. Unsubstantiated claims that Christopher Columbus unearthed the islands during his fourth voyage in 1502 add another theory to the pot. After quickly establishing San Andrés Island the English chose Providencía as a preferred settlement due to its advantageous lofty position and fresh water supplies. Slaves were shipped from Barbados and Jamaica to cultivate cotton and tobacco in 1633. Before long, Providencía became a pivotal centre for slave trading and a strategic hiding place for seafaring rogues touting contraband and pirates seeking shelter. The Spanish, furious at the prosperity of the English, launched an unsuccessful invasion of the island in 1635.

From 1670 to 1689, legendary buccaneer Henry Morgan arrived in Providencía, establishing a base from where he raided both Panama and Santa Marta. He is also reputed to have sacked Spanish galleons laden with gold, angering Spain and prompting another unsuccessful attack. According to local legend Morgan buried his treasure on the island during such an invasion where it remains undiscovered to this day.

The battle for control of the islands continued for over a century with England and Spain equally determined to conquer. In 1793 the signing of the Versailles Treaty recognised Spain's sovereignty over the archipelago, yet the Spanish had already begun to lose interest in the islands. Groups of former slaves soon established communities in the archipelago, fusing cultural influences of their English masters with the traditions of their African homelands. After independence from Spain in 1810, Colombia laid claim to the islands, a move fiercely contested by Nicaragua just 150km away. Colombia occupied the islands in 1822, although the United Province of Central America (a federation that comprised the states of Guatemala, El Salvador, Honduras, Nicaragua and Costa Rica) did not recognise this as legal and claimed ownership for itself. In turn, Colombia disputed the UPCA's occupation of the eastern coast of modern-day Nicaragua. After a civil war dissolved the federation, the resulting state of Nicaragua continued the dispute along with the Republic of New Granada (modern Colombia and Panama) that emerged from the collapse of Gran Colombia. In 1928, the signing of the Esguerra-Bárcenas treaty between both governments resolved the dispute temporarily in favour of Colombia. However, when the Sandinista government assumed power in Nicaragua in 1980 the treaty was renounced – and the archipelago's ownership has been contested ever since.

Nicaraguans claim that the treaty was signed under pressure from the US, while Colombia argues that it is valid. In 1999, Honduras and Colombia ratified the 'Lopez-Ramírez' Maritime Treaty that recognises the archipelago as Colombian territory, to a great Nicaraguan outcry. In 2001, the International Court of Justice received a claim from Nicaragua over a disputed maritime boundary of some 50,000km^2, including the islands of San Andrés and Providencía. Colombia reacted angrily, contesting the ICJ's jurisdiction over the matter. It also increased its military presence in and around the islands. As a basis for the Court's jurisdiction, Nicaragua invokes Article XXXI of the American Treaty on Pacific Settlement (officially known as the 'Pact of Bogotá'), signed on 30 April 1948, to which both Nicaragua and Colombia are parties. Nicaragua also refers to the declarations under Article 36 of the Statute of the Court, by which Nicaragua and Colombia accepted the compulsory jurisdiction of the Court, in 1929 and 1937 respectively. Nicaragua further indicates that it 'reserves the right to claim compensation for elements of unjust enrichment consequent upon Colombian possession of the Islands of San Andrés and Providencía as well as the keys and maritime spaces up to the 82 meridian, in the absence of lawful title'. According to Nicaragua, the treaty fixes its border with Honduras at the 15th parallel instead of the 17th, leaving 30,000km^2 in question. In addition, the accords give Colombia sovereignty over territory east of the 82nd meridian, which Nicaragua says deprives it of 100,000 km^2 of continental shelf.

Until 1953, the archipelago was virtually ignored by the rest of the world. However, once the Colombian government designated San Andrés and Providencía as a Free Trade Zone, flights to the island brought an appetite for commercialism to the archipelago. It also encouraged immigration from other parts of Colombia to the underdeveloped region, boosting economic activity through tourism and transforming the archipelago into a net contributor, rather than a drain to the government purse. However, this population explosion has done much to dilute traditional Riazal lifestyle, culture and language (see box, *Roots people*, page 201), something that island-wide community initiatives are striving to correct. In 1993, the Christian University of San Andrés was founded by a coalition of Baptist congregations from the archipelago to spearhead the economic, cultural, political and environmental future of the islands from a community standpoint. The United Nations Development Program (UNDP) is also involving

Although the combined landmass of the islands of the San Andrés Archipelago totals less than 60km² the marine area accounts for almost 10% of the Caribbean Sea. Declared a protected marine conservation area as part of the Man and the Biosphere (MAB) programme in November 2000, the reserve is recognised by the UN for its extraordinary coastal ecosystems. With UN help, local projects are attempting to reconcile the conservation of the biodiversity of the San Andrés islands with its sustainable use. Trademark pristine sparkling waters and pastel-coloured underwater gardens have survived threats of pollution and over-fishing, thanks to the widespread efforts of conservationists. Sedimentation and litter once saw the health of the coral reef spiral into decline as the marine resources of the archipelago suffered at the hands of industrial fishing vessels and poachers from the Colombian mainland, Central America and many Caribbean nations. A ramshackle collection of shanty towns became a prime source of coastal pollution due to inadequate sanitation, while rising levels of tourism threw the islands into a waste management crisis.

Today, the picture-postcard islands of San Andrés, Providencía and Santa Catalina; Bolívar Albuquerque, Cotton Haynes islets; Alicia and Bajo Nuevo sandbanks; and Grunt Johnny Rose, Easy Cay, Roncador, Serena, Serranilla, Quitasueño, Brothers, Rocky, Crab and Santander cays, are reaping the rewards of a decade-long forceful ecological drive that has worked hard to promote the crucial linkages between the biological systems of the islands – terrestrial, coastal and marine – with a healthy social system. In support, the Colombian government created a new officially sanctioned and funded agency, CORALINA (Vía San Luis; ↘ 512 0080; www.coralina.gov.co). Before CORALINA, native islanders played no part in the decision-making process in environment matters relating to the archipelago. CORALINA is charged with a number of ecological responsibilities, including the preservation of the archipelago's fragile coastal and marine ecosystems. Article 37 of the 1993 Law 99 defines the responsibilities of CORALINA as including the safeguarding of the islands' resources in a way that 'promotes economic growth and improvements in the quality of life and social well being, without depleting reserves of sustaining natural resources or damaging the environment, and preserving the right of the future generations to use and enjoy these resources'. Municipal tax revenues continue to fund a number of CORALINA environmental and community projects, striking a delicate balance between socio-economic pressures and the preservation of native trees, mangrove forests and other natural habitats. Achieving this equilibrium remains a challenge to the archipelago where flower-filled marshlands and salty coralline outcrops attract large numbers of migrant birds. Improved sanitation and refuge systems have ensured the translucent waters around these remote oceanic castaway islands remain home to some of the western hemisphere's most highly productive coral reefs.

However, human activities remain poorly managed and a key cause for concern. Sand stolen from beaches on the South Island in the 1950s left it seriously depleted – a resplendent strip called Baby Beach now a tiny reminder of how idyllic it once looked. More than 100 tonnes of refuse is produced on San Andrés Island each day with an unmet escalating demand for water. Despite an annual average rainfall of 1,800mm the islanders suffer from severe drought. Studies by CORALINA have revealed that 70% of groundwater is polluted. Saline intrusion from over-extraction and rising sea levels also pose a serious threat with rainwater collection on the island well below its potential. CORALINA's presence has undoubtedly furthered the archipelago's environmental goals. It has also brought this remote territory closer to the government administration in Bogotá where the ecological needs of a group of islands many thousands of miles away are all too easily overlooked.

racial, social and religious projects with the island Riazal population. Politics in this small archipelago remain a hot topic.

PEOPLE

The culture of the San Andrés Archipelago is intimately linked to its people, who have diverse ethnic origins. Islanders form three main groups: the Raizal people of African and British origin who speak Creole and English; the Continentals who preserve the Colombian culture and speak Spanish as their mother tongue; and foreign immigrants (mainly from Israel and Lebanon). The English/Creole speakers refer to themselves as 'natives' or 'islanders' in clear distinction from residents who migrated from mainland Colombia. In the new Colombian constitution, the native islanders are referred to as 'Raizal' (singular) or 'Raizales' (plural). Today, the modern-day inhabitants of the San Andrés Archipelago reflect its turbulent history and the diverse mix of races and cultures that have settled on the islands over the centuries. Strong English influences abound with English still the primary language on Providencía and names such as Mr Green, Mr Smith and Mr Brown commonplace throughout island communities. Many are devout Baptists, attending church in their Sunday best each weekend. Parlour games, afternoon tea and dancing the foxtrot are other telltale legacies of the archipelago's ties to a bygone England. Very, very different from the rest of Colombian society in every sense, the islanders remain linguistically, socially and culturally unique – a distinction that is heightened by the remote isolation of the Archipelago's geographic location.

LANGUAGE

The Colombian Constitution acknowledges English as the mother tongue of the native islanders. It also grants the archipelago two official languages – English and Spanish. The Raizal people speak a Creole-English patois quite unlike any other Caribbean islanders. This mesolectal, middle-class linguistic hybrid – called Bendé or Wendé – is a wholly unique English Lexifer, distinctly different from that spoken on the Caribbean and Pacific coasts of Colombia. It is also completely unintelligible to other patois or Creole speakers, despite its use of a language syntax derived in parts from African languages and similarity to Miskito Coastal Creole. Spanish-speakers are also utterly baffled by the languages of the San Andrés Archipelago, a place that feels very 'foreign' to visiting Colombian mainlanders, even though it is home soil. Confusingly, variants exist along with the choice of language. Creole tends to be spoken in the home and during social interaction in public places, while Spanish is often used for business and government matters. English is the language used in the many Protestant churches with Spanish spoken in the archipelago's Catholic places of worship. On San Andrés there is a greater use of Creole-English in the south while in the north social chatter is usually conducted in Spanish – even by native islanders. On Providencía, Creole-English is spoken as a primary language pretty much everywhere.

UNDERSTANDING THE NATIVE ISLANDERS

greetins to aal da peepl av di worl	greetings to all the people of the world
wi lov unu	with love to you
chaka chaka	messy, disorderly, untidy
no badda mi	don't bother me
bampa	grandfather
bama or bam-bam	grandmother

When the Colombian government prompted a large influx of migrants to head to the San Andrés Archipelago from the mainland it had just one goal; to create a self-financing region without costly reliance on the capital. It paid little heed to the cultural concerns of a small, native population and failed to anticipate the dramatic effects of the marginalisation of the Raizal people. Following General Rojas Pinilla's declaration in 1953 that made the archipelago a free port, changes to the region's make-up were marked. The population began to swell, the new Duty Free Zone prospered and the island became linked to the mainland via frequent flights. However, by the 1970s, native islanders began to complain of a lost identity. They also protested against discrimination and grew fearful over their increasingly marginalised status. Insularity, they argued, may have had its economic problems but it was a crucial tool in preserving their ethnicity, grounded in food, architecture, literature, oral traditions, music, religion, art and language.

By the 1980s the cultural and linguistic characteristics of native islanders were seriously under threat from Spanish-speaking dominance. In 1995, the government of Colombia began to take steps to preserve, restore and protect the rights and way of life of the Raizal people and other indigenous peoples living on the continent. In 1952 there were just 5,675 inhabitants in San Andrés – a number that 12 years later in 1964 had more than trebled to 16,731. In 1973 their population totalled 22,989. By 1988 it had almost doubled to 42,315. Today, the archipelago's indigenous population remains a minority at 25,000 people compared with 75,000 mainlanders, a significant demographic adjustment that has eroded many traditional ways of island life. Since the late 1990s new human rights legislation has been enacted and institutional support for indigenous communities encouraged. The region has also been designated as an official department within the Colombian administration with a governor appointed from the Raizal population. Each of these measures has helped foster a better understanding of the importance of Raizal identity to the community's social web. However, despite strict government measures to limit migration to the islands the issue regarding the diminished influence of Raizal culture remains one of contention. In November 2004 the Raizal people marched the streets of San Andrés Island in a peaceful Prayer-Walk in support of their human rights led by Pastor Raymond Howard. From Mount Zion Baptist Church in Perry Hill the Raizal crossed the island, singing hymns of praise along the way. Howard carried a large Moses-style walking stick as he led a crowd of men, women children with many elders over 80 years of age. This peaceful protest by the Raizal community passed without incident, unlike a 2002 rally when heavy-handed Colombian troops fired tear gas into the crowd.

pa	father
ma	mother
taanti	aunt
con	cousin
eda	brother
ta or *tita*	sister

FAUNA AND FLORA

MARINE LIFE The warm, fertile Caribbean waters that surround the islands are rich in marine life, including plentiful supplies of queen conch, spiny lobster, black crab, long-spined sea urchins, sea turtles and large numbers of fish. Fish and lobster larvae from the archipelago's vibrant reef systems are believed to travel as far as the Florida Keys, fulfilling a critical role in restoring depleted stocks there. Some 57 species of coral (including brain, fire, lace, black star and stony) have been identified in the archipelago, including at least 24 species of sponge and octacoral. The 273 recorded fish species include spotted drum, snapper, grouper (including the endangered goliath), indigo hamlet, bluehead, parrotfish, surgeonfish, snow bass, striped cardinal fish, tuna, yellow-cheeked basslet, bar jack, puffer, balloonfish, white hamlet, white spotted filefish, spotted scorpionfish and the winged flying gunard. Eels, octopus, dolphin, nurse shark and spotted eagle ray are also spotted frequently. Whales are not common to the San Andrés Archipelago although migrant species are occasionally sighted.

REPTILES, AMPHIBIANS AND MAMMALS A wide variety of resident and endemic reptiles, insects and other invertebrates can be found on the islands, including iguana, lizards, caiman, snake (boa), gecko, salamander and frog. One of the archipelago's two endemic swamp turtles (known locally as a *swanka*) is an endangered species. Bats are the only reported terrestrial mammal species. Four species of turtles nest in the archipelago, loggerhead, hawksbill, green and leatherback. Beaches on the northern banks and southern atolls are especially important nesting habitats. Sporadic nesting also still occurs on the island of San Andrés along with regular nesting at several spots in Old Providence, most notably Old John and Mona Bays on the northern coast of Ketlina.

Loggerhead turtles are the archipelago's most common nesters, favouring Seranilla Bank in June and July. Hawksbills also nest frequently on Serrana and Roncador banks during August. Sand mining remains a potential disruption to nesting and threatens the quality and size of some beaches in the archipelago.

TREES AND PLANTS Almost 400 plant species have been identified in the San Andrés Archipelago, 70% of them native and 25% identified as non-endemic. Indigenous beach vegetation includes sea grape, coconut palm, seaside mahoe and West Indian almond with shrubs such as bay cedar, beach bean, wild plantain, marigold and sea lavender. Although sizeable areas of woodlands have been cleared as grazing land for cattle, native trees can still be found in inland areas, mainly cotton tree, birch and cedar. Breadfruit, guava and citrus are also in good supply with numerous species of mangrove and large sea grass beds, including saltgrass and shoregrass species. This vegetation constitutes an important breeding group for many invertebrates and provides an important habitat for turtles. More than 18 resident and 76 migrant bird species also rely on the mangrove forests, including two endangered species and several endangered subspecies found only in the archipelago. Rainbird (or 'old man bird') is an endemic subspecies of the cuckoo and the subject of local legend. It inhabits swamplands and is in danger of extinction.

PRACTICALITIES

CLIMATE Expect high humidity, plenty of sunshine and average temperatures of 26–30°C. Light tropical showers aren't uncommon year-round. May and June are the driest months with rains heaviest September to December.

PEAK SEASON Flights and accommodation are in short supply during the peak tourist season. Pre-booking is essential late December to late January and throughout the Easter week. Crowds also swell from mid-June to mid-July with rooms like gold dust at Carnival time (Feb/March).

SAFETY Tourists in the San Andrés Archipelago benefit from one of the lowest regional crime rates in Colombia, with just a few hundred reported crimes each year. However, don't be fooled by the laid-back atmosphere; petty theft does happen. Most visitors come a cropper on the beach when they let their guard down

BIRDING IN SAN ANDRÉS

For a group of small coral outcrops, the San Andrés Archipelago is home to a lot of birds, attracting large numbers of migratory species from its location in the westernmost Caribbean Sea. This natural stopover point on the Western Flyway ensures the archipelago welcomes species en route further south from North and Central America. Many of Colombia's 150-plus hummingbird species can be found in the San Andrés Archipelago along with large numbers of neo-tropical migrants such as gadwalls, willows, alders and flycatchers. Birders can also expect to spot yellow-throated vireos and Nashville, Tennessee and Canada warblers. Green-breasted mangos and ruby-throats are also found on the island along with the bananaquit (a popular sight around the islands and called a 'wish-wish' by the locals), black-faced grassquit and an endemic species of black-whiskered vireo. Many species of hummers such as the colourful puffleg and dusky starfrontlet can be found flocked around a pink-flowered species of unnamed leguminous vine. The San Andrés vireo (Vireo caribaeus) is the archipelago's beloved endemic but endangered species. It serves as a poster-child for ongoing conservation efforts and is now restricted to an area of $17km^2$, where it is threatened by encroaching urbanisation, agriculture and coconut cultivation. Colombia's ornithological action-group, ProAves, a non-profit organisation, is highly active within the archipelago. The San Andrés vireo favour inland mangrove swamps as habitat and feed on arthropods and caterpillars in shrubby vegetation. Another endemic species under threat is the rainbird or 'old man bird', a bird steeped in local legend. A subspecies of the cuckoo, it also inhabits swamplands. Due to the erosion of mangrove forests the species has now become limited to a few localities on the southern half of San Andrés Island and is currently facing extinction.

and leave belongings unattended. This is also the place where drug dealers often tout for trade, selling 'weed' in 50,000 COP bags. Isolated muggings have been reported on the west side of the island between Morgan's Cave and the Blow Hole (Hoyo Soplador) when lone tourists were targeted for expensive watches and jewellery. Female travellers should avoid walking alone late at night, especially in remote and unlit areas.

WHAT TO PACK Cut-off jeans, flip flops and T-shirts are de rigueur in this oh-so-casual archipelago. Pack beach and swimming gear, snorkel and mask, water socks/shoes (some sea-bed areas are sharp), an underwater camera and plenty of sunscreen. Mosquito repellent is also essential as are sea-sickness pills for those that don't travel on water well.

ISLA SAN ANDRÉS *Telephone code: 8*

Seahorse-shaped San Andrés is the archipelago's principal island, an ancient volcanic landscape buffered with layers of coralline built up over many millennia. A small mountain range rises to 55m, criss-crossing the island from north to south covered in lush coconut palms. Sharp ravines, limestone deposits, white clay and coral sand meet dark red topsoil on a terrain characterised by farmland and rocky outcrops. Surrounding coral beds, particularly along the eastern shore, afford the water a beautiful array of oceanic hues described by the locals as 'The Sea of Seven Colours'.

Flanked by sandy beaches, San Andrés is the archipelago's largest island and prime tourism centre. Visitors arrive and depart from the airport and jetties, flying out to Providencía and the mainland and journeying to the surrounding cays. A congested town centre (El Centro) sits at the northwestern tip of the island's urbanisation to form the archipelago's commercial hub. A higgledy-piggledy jumble of duty-free shops, hotel blocks and restaurants occupy an austere collection of concrete buildings that are a vicious assault on the eyes. Vendors tout sunglasses, rice cookers, televisions, sports gear and perfume. Streets packed with tooting taxis, scooters and golf buggies spill down to the northern waterfront where the lion's share of boat launches and dive shops can be found.

In contrast, the brightly painted single-storey wooden houses of the local population sit amongst palms in the centre of the island. Rocking-chair porches overlook leafy, bloom-filled gardens in these fine examples of English-Caribbean architecture. A picturesque 30km paved road loops the entire island and is the main tourist trail for sightseeing and attractions. A tiny lagoon sits in the centre of San Andrés and is home to heron, pigeon and caiman with German Point (Punta Norte) the island's palm-fringed northern tip. A handful of quiet, inland roads weave across the undulating terrain of the interior, connecting the sleepy towns of La Loma and San Luis with the rest of the island. Although the nicest beaches are located on the island's eastern flank the first-class diving of San Andrés can be enjoyed all along the coast.

GETTING THERE Gustavo Rojas Pinilla Airport (also known as Sesquicentenario International) is a ten-minute walk northwest of the town centre (taxi 10,000 COP). International departures from San Andrés incur the same tax as elsewhere in Colombia (see *Chapter 2*, page 62). Cargo boats carry a limited number of paying passengers to and from Cartagena but there is no fixed schedule. Entry to the archipelago incurs a 20,000 COP tourist tax, usually paid at the airport of departure. Pack plenty of patience for navigating the slow-paced bureaucracy of San Andrés' airport arrivals process, as the sixth-busiest airport in Colombia in terms of passengers

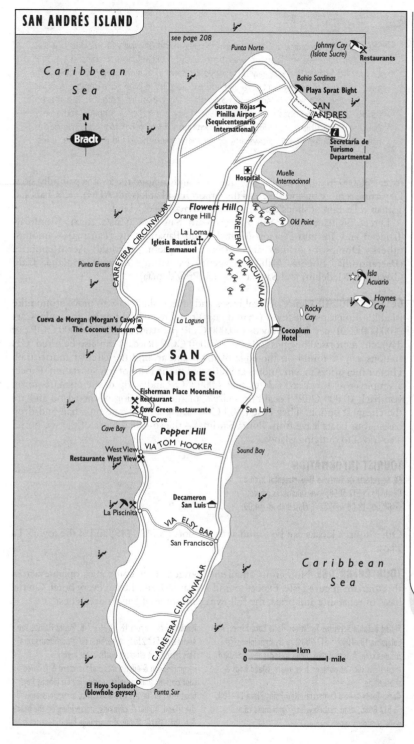

SAN ANDRÉS ISLAND

see page 208

Caribbean
Sea

N

Bradt

Punta Norte

Johnny Cay
(Islote Sucre)

Restaurants

Bahia Sardinas
Playa Sprat Bight

SAN
ANDRES

Gustavo Rojas
Pinilla Airpor
(Sequicentenario
International)

Secretaría de
Turismo
Departmental

Hospital

Muelle
Internacional

Flowers Hill

Orange Hill

Old Point

La Loma
Iglesia Bautista
Emmanuel

CARRETERA CIRCUNVALAR

CARRETERA CIRCUNVALAR

Punta Evans

Isla
Acuario

Haynes
Cay

Cueva de Morgan (Morgan's Cave)
The Coconut Museum

La Laguna

Rocky
Cay

Cocoplum
Hotel

SAN
ANDRES

Fisherman Place Moonshine
Restaurant
Cove Green Restaurante
El Cove

San Luis

Cove Bay

Pepper Hill
VIA TOM HOOKER

Sound Bay

West View
Restaurante West View

Decameron
San Luis

La Piscinita

VIA ELSY BAR

San Francisco

Caribbean
Sea

CARRETERA CIRCUNVALAR

0   1 km
0   1 mile

El Hoyo Soplador
(blowhole geyser)   Punta Sur

(over 830,000 in 2006) has lengthy queues – and baggage retrieval is painfully slow. Departing is more businesslike and the airport has a bank (with ATM), cafés, bars and a small collection of shops that make flight delays less of a bind.

Direct flights connect San Andrés with San José (Costa Rica), Montreal-Trudeau and Toronto-Pearson (Canada) and Panama City (Panama) – amongst others. Domestic airlines also offer a frequent schedule: AeroRepublica (Barranquilla, Bogotá, Cali, Cartagena, Medellín), Avianca (Bogotá, Cali, Cartagena, Medellín) and Satena (Bogotá, Providencía).

GETTING AROUND Plenty of local buses and taxis make it easy to move around the island. Numerous colectivos (shared taxis) trawl the island touting for trade. Cars (100,000 COP per day), mopeds (40,000 COP per day), bicycles (10,000 COP per day) and motorised buggies (60,000–200,000 COP per day) can also be hired. Gas stations can be found on the edge of town and around the circular tourist trail. Higher fuel prices in San Andrés are reflected in the price of transportation. Expect a simple cross-town taxi ride to cost 4,000 COP and a trip to the outskirts to set you back 10,000 COP. Local buses circle a large proportion of the island and are the cheapest option. They cost 1,000 COP a trip and operate on a hail-and-drop basis. Tour boats leave from Punta Sardinas – the so-called 'nose of the sea-horse' – to travel to outlying islands.

TOURIST INFORMATION

Secretaría de Turismo Departmental Avenida Newball; 512 5058; www.sanandres.gov.co; 08.00–18.00 weekdays, closed noon–14.00.

Other tourist kiosks can be found at the airport (512 1149) and at the town's La Playa.

TOUR OPERATORS Numerous small independent tour companies operate across this tourism-focused isle. Expect to find a tour desk attached to every hotel. On the basis of reliability and price, the following are some of San Andrés's best.

Flying Dolphin Servicios Turísticos Hotel Lord Pierre, Av Colombia IB–106; 512 9004; e flyingdolphins@tutopia.com. A decent tour menu includes the standard excursions such as pontoon boat tours, island hops & snorkelling.

Gema Tours Centro Comercial, New Point Plaza LI–108; 512 8666; e maclaudiavelez@gemtours.com; www.gemtours.com

Norbi Tours Carrera IB I-121 L-2-B, Punta Hansa, San Andrés; 512 2203; e norbitours@norbitours.com. This friendly & efficient outfit come highly recommended & offer a menu of standard & tailored tour options that includes snorkelling on Johnny Cay, boat trips to Haynes Cay & Acuario, excursions around the island, hiking & kayaking, horseriding on the beach & scuba safaris. It can also arrange full itineraries &

flights to Providencía – from day trips to a comprehensive 3-night/4-day jaunt that includes guides, lunches, transport, accommodation & activities, such as snorkelling in the Parque Nacional Macbean Lagoon, Caribbean cookery classes & dancing to reggae. **San Andrés Caribbean Tour Ltd** Sunrise Beach Hotel; ✆ 512 3977 ext 1303; e sacatur530@yahoo.es. An affable woman called Gladys organises all manner of tours & services, including bicycle rental, boat tours around the islands, car hire & horseriding.
Semisubmarino Manatí Av La Playa; ✆ 512 3349; e info@semisubmarinomanati.com;

www.semisubmarinomanati.com. This 1½-hr underwater tour provides a decent alternative to snorkelling or scuba diving. Large windows allow good views of the reefs around the island. Tickets (at 30,000 COP per person) can be purchased from several outlets on the town's beach.
Tren Blanco Regretfully, the island's tourist train is actually a tractor-pulled vehicle in disguise but its 3-hour circuit around San Andrés's key attractions is excellent value at 6,500 COP per person. Climb aboard from the bus stop on the cnr of avs Colombia & 20 de Julio – it departs every morning at about 09.30.

WHERE TO STAY Accommodation in San Andrés tends to be pricier than the rest of Colombia. However, as new places open the competition gets fiercer – a great basis on which to haggle. In simple terms, hotels fall into three main categories: large-scale resorts, beach hotels and mid-town options by the shops. All-inclusive packages are popular in Colombia and no more so than in San Andrés. Visitors keen to interact with the locals should also check out the island's excellent home-stay programme, Las Posadas Nativas.

Hotel Aquarium Decameron ✆ 512 9030; www.decameron.com. Out of all of the five Decameron Hotels on the island, this gets the best reports. Nicely located partially offshore, it sticks to the standard Decameron all-inclusive format. But despite this manages to offer pretty cabañas in a very nice spot for diving enthusiasts. Rates inc b/fast, lunch, dinner & all snacks, cigarettes & domestic drinks. Rooms come as twin or dbl & inc cable TV, fridge, safe & AC. $$$
Hotel Casablanca Av Colombia; ✆ 512 4115; f 512 6127; e vacaciones@hotelcasablanca.net; www.hotelcasablanca.net. This orderly 4-star hotel was one of the first to open up on the island & prides itself on being a 'big small hotel'. Guest accommodation comprises 11 modern fully equipped bungalows along with 39 large, comfortable rooms. Both the Casablanca Restaurant and SeaWatch Café have a fine menu, with red snapper au gratin at 20,000 COP & seafood spaghetti at 15,000 COP both particularly tasty. Rates start at 200,000 COP for B&B. $$$
Hotel Decameron Isleño (42 rooms) ✆ 512 3990; www.decameron.com. Located 3 mins from San Andrés Airport & just a few blocks away from shops of the town centre, this hotel offers terrace & balconies with ocean view along with 7 family cabañas. Amenities at this all-inclusive resort inc 3 restaurants, 2 bars & a swimming pool. $$$
Hotel Decameron Marazul (128 rooms) ✆ 513 2678; www.decameron.com. This all inclusive hotel lies between the sea & the jungle in the Orange Hill district & is popular with a Canadian package-tour crowd. Gym, 3 bars (Bar el Duende open 24-hrs), 3

restaurants, swimming pool, watersports, tennis, disco & volleyball are just some of the onsite amenities offered. $$$
Hotel Decameron Mary Land (65 rooms) ✆ 513 1818; www.decameron.com. Another Decameron chain hotel, this time located on the North End close to the boat launch at Punta Sardina, not far from the airport at the very edge of the hotel zone. Rooms are twin-beds & dbls, with a restaurant, 3 bars, swimming pool & the usual all-inclusive deal. $$$
Hotel Las Américas Av Las Américas; ✆ 512 3949; f 512 3870; e hotel-lasamericas@yahoo.com. Choose from dbl, trpl & suites in this 2-storey wooden hotel, centred on a garden terrace with pool. Rates inc b/fast, with rooms equipped with AC, minibar & cable TV. Onsite amenities include a perfectly reasonable buffet restaurant (with 24-hr room service) & laundry. $$$
Hotel Sol Caribe (225 rooms) Av Colón, No 2–77; e reservas.scsa@solarhoteles.com; www.solarhoteles.com. This modern, white-&-glass hotel in the heart of downtown is well positioned for shopping within easy walking distance of the beach & a 5-min drive of the airport. Four onsite restaurants offer seafood, themed buffets, grilled Caribbean food & an international menu. There are also 2 bars, a large swimming pool, gym, business centre, childcare services, solarium & a popular night club. Dbl, trpl, qdpl rooms & family suites come with cable TV, AC, fridge & phone. $$$
Nobelhouse Hotel (15 rooms) ✆ 512 8264; e info@sanandresnoblehouse.com; www.sanandresnoblehouse.com. This professional outfit

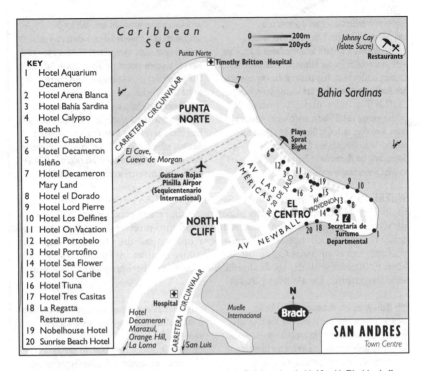

KEY

1	Hotel Aquarium Decameron
2	Hotel Arena Blanca
3	Hotel Bahía Sardina
4	Hotel Calypso Beach
5	Hotel Casablanca
6	Hotel Decameron Isleño
7	Hotel Decameron Mary Land
8	Hotel el Dorado
9	Hotel Lord Pierre
10	Hotel Los Delfines
11	Hotel On Vacation
12	Hotel Portobelo
13	Hotel Portofino
14	Hotel Sea Flower
15	Hotel Sol Caribe
16	Hotel Tiuna
17	Hotel Tres Casitas
18	La Regatta Restaurante
19	Nobelhouse Hotel
20	Sunrise Beach Hotel

SAN ANDRES
Town Centre

takes hospitality seriously, a legacy of its European ownership & fully trained staff. All rooms have a private bathroom, AC, minibar, satellite TV, safe & telephone in a central location. Services include tours, 24-hr room service, rental car & motorcycle hire with b/fast & internet use included in the room rate. Credit cards are accepted. Italian, French, Spanish & English spoken. $$$

🏠 **Sunrise Beach Hotel** (170 rooms) Av Newball, No 4–169; ☎ 512 3977; f 512 3825; e Hotel.sunrise@ghlhoteles.com; www.sunrisehotel.com. This landmark hotel is San Andrés's largest with spacious ocean-front rooms & FB packages. Facilities include a really nice pool bar on a large terrace that juts out over the water. There's also a private beach, 2 restaurants, 2 lounge bars, gym, spa, sauna, tennis, boat launch, kayaking, scuba instruction, water aerobics, live music & a disco. Rooms come with cable TV, telephone, minibar & AC. An expansive buffet dinner in the hotel's Henriette Restaurant is popular with families. An array of Pasta (Mon), Mexican (Tue), Caribbean (Wed), Oriental (Thu), Spanish (Fri) and barbecued meats (Sat) are served, 52 weeks of the year. $$$

🏠 **Hotel Arena Blanca** (72 rooms) Calle 2 1–51; ☎ 513 1199; f 513 1198; e arenabla@sol.net.co. The rooms include 6 large suites – all with balconies & sea views. Each is equipped with AC, cable TV, with a buffet restaurant, disco & swimming pool just some of the onsite amenities. Discounts available for longer stays. $$

🏠 **Hotel Bahia Sardina** (42 rooms) Av Colombia 5A–29; ☎ 512 3587; f 512 4363; e hbsardina@yahoo.com; www.geocities.com/bahiasardina. Most of the quaint little rooms in this yellow-and-blue ocean-front hotel boast views over the water. Each comes with AC. $$

🏠 **Hotel Calypso Beach** (100+ rooms) Av Duarte Blum; ☎ 512 3558; f 512 3852; e calypso@ sol.net.co. This modern, blue building sits on the ocean & has rooms equipped with AC, minibar, cable TV, rooftop pool & restaurant with sea views. $$

🏠 **Hotel Dallas Confort** (30 rooms) Av Costa Rica; ☎ 512 0883; fax 512 0883; e hdallasconfort@ yahoo.com. It's unlikely to win any awards for style, but this dingy little place is worth considering for budget travellers. The rooms vary in size but each comes with AC, minibar & telephone. $$

🏠 **Hotel el Dorado** Av Colombia 1A–25; ☎ 512 4155/512 4157 512 4056; f 512 7039; e dorado@ coll.telecome.com.co. A pleasant pool terrace is a nice feature of this mid-range hotel. Rooms have cable TV & AC – some with better views than others. An onsite restaurant serves a mix of international & local fare. $$

🏠 **Hotel Hermando Henry** Av Las Américas, No 40–48; ☎ 512 3416. The rooms may be old & tired, but they still represent good value for money. Each one has a TV, fridge, private bathroom, AC & balcony — and is spotlessly clean. $$

🏠 **Hotel Lord Pierre** (60 rooms) Av Colombia 1B–106; ☎ 512 7541; f 512 5666; e lordpierre@sol.net.co; www.lordpierre.com. This central hotel has dbl & trpl rooms plus 12 self-contained suites. Each has AC, tiled floors & colour TV. Amenities include a very nice outside pool terrace & safe sea bathing area with sunloungers & seating & a pool bar with stunning views. Expect perfectly reasonable fish, chicken & steak dishes at the onsite restaurant, Don Anibal. $$

🏠 **Hotel Los Delfines** (26 rooms) Av Colombia 1B–86; ☎ 512 4083; f 512 4013; e defines@sol.net.co. This sweet little motel-style place sits right on the beach so some of its rooms have uninterrupted views out to sea. Minibars, AC & cable TV all come as standard. There's also a palm-edged central swimming pool from which to enjoy the vistas. $$

🏠 **Hotel Mary May Inn** (8rooms) Av 20 de Julio; ☎ 512 5669; e ketlenan@yahoo.com. Budget travellers rave about this cosy little place opposite a cheap fried-chicken joint. It's nothing special, but the ambience is relaxed & friendly. Each room has a bathroom & colour TV. A neighbouring café serves a hearty b/fast at a bargain price. $$

🏠 **Hotel On Vacation** Av Colón; ☎ 512 3013; f 512 6057; www.tvg.com.co. This clean, comfortable mid-budget hotel sits in the midst of thrift shops & souvenir stalls. Rooms are well-appointed, all with AC, but lack style. However, with their all inclusive low rates who's complaining? $$

🏠 **Hotel Portobelo** Av La Playa; ☎ 512 5150; e reserves@portobelohotel.com; www.portobelohotel.com. It may not look much from the outside, but this little town-centre hotel has a beach, & rooms that overlook the sea. Each has AC, cable TV & minibar. Not a bad choice & a reasonable price. $$

Home-stay options

🏠 **Carson Hudgson Martínez** 'Mistic's Place' (La Loma) ☎ 513 0352

🏠 **Cleotilde Henry De Montes** 'Cli's Place' (El Centro) ☎ 512 6957

🏠 **Emerson Williams** 'William's Place' (La Loma) ☎ 513 0395

🏠 **Ethel Corpus Jay** 'Ethel's Place' (El Centro) ☎ 512 4502

🏠 **Fitarda Henry Valbuena** 'Henry's Place' (El Centro) ☎ 512 6150

🏠 **Hotel Portofino** Av Providencía No 1–115; ☎ 512 4212; f 512 2326; e reservasportofino@hotmai.com; www.hotelportofinosanandres.com. Rooms are small, but pleasant in this decent mid-budget hotel. All have AC & TV & rates inc b/fast & dinner. $$

🏠 **Hotel Sea Flower** (45 rooms) A Las América 1B–36; ☎ 512 0323; f 512 0322; e hotelsa@epm.net.co. All 45 rooms in this high-rise balconied hotel have AC & are a decent size. An onsite internet café & laundry are a boon although the restaurant has mixed reviews. $$

🏠 **Hotel Tone Beach** (144 rooms) Av Colombia 5A–25; ☎ 512 4251; f 512 4256. It's not hard to establish why this large, modern hotel is so popular with beach-going guests. Most of its rooms have balconies overlooking sand out to sea. Each comes with AC, colour TV & a safe. The hotel has a swimming pool, gym & very nice restaurant. $$

🏠 **Hotel Verde Mar** (44 rooms) Av 20 de Julio 2A–13; ☎ 512 5525; f 512 5494; e verdemar@sol.net.co. This functional resting place couldn't be closer to the shops. The rooms are basic but clean & equipped with AC, colour TV & telephone. A restaurant serves a respectable menu round the clock. $$

🏠 **Tres Casitas** Av Colombia, No 1–60; ☎ 512 6944; f 512 5880; e 3casitas@sol.net.co. This charming little blue-and-yellow wooden motel-style complex is popular with families as it faces the sea & has a safe, secure centrally located swimming pool. Each room has a colour TV, video, telephone, minibar, fridge, kitchen, water cooler & balconies. Rates inc b/fast & dinner. $$

🏠 **Posada Doña Rosa** (8 rooms) Av Las Américas; ☎ 512 3649. Lone shoestring travellers will enjoy the price of these dirt-cheap rooms. All fan-cooled rooms have private bathrooms. $

🏠 **Hotel Tiuna** (165 rooms) Av Colombia; ☎ 512 3235; f 512 3478; e reserves@tiuna.com; www.tiuna.com. This sprawling beachfront option has a bar, nightclub, restaurant, internet café, pool & cinema onsite with decent-sized rooms overlooking the sea. It's not plush, but it's comfortable — & good value.

🏠 **Gladys Bolaños** 'Gladys's Place' (El Centro) ☎ 512 1229

🏠 **Inéz De Macariz** 'Macariz Place' (El Centro) ☎ 512 6356

🏠 **Justina Pérez** 'Justina's Place' (La Loma) ☎ 513 3174

🏠 **Maximiliano Hooker** 'Maxi's Place' (El Centro) ☎ 512 5441

🏠 **Reolicia Duke Santana** 'Licy's Place' (La Loma) ☎ 512 9679

✕ WHERE TO EAT

✕ **El Rincón de la Langosta** Carretera Circunvalar; ✆ 513 2933; e langosta@sol.net.co www.rincondelalangosta.com. Charming patron Francisco Guzman has one of the most popular restaurants on the island, a waterfront seafood haven of great repute & a San Andrés tradition since 1994. Located in between the museum & Morgan's Cave on the northeast side of the island. Diners can eat in one of 4 different seated areas, including several indoor options & a breezy tropical outside dock-style terrace. Langoustine specials are order of the day here along with a long list of fresh island fish. Choose from garlic octopus, stuffed crab, prawn thermidor with coconut & buttered lobster tail. However the gastronomic crème de la crème at the Rincón de la Langosta is the lobster – it comes served grilled, steamed or roasted with a choice of 21 mouth-watering sauces. **$$$**

✕ **Gourmet Shop Restaurant** Av Atlántico; ✆ 512 9843; e service@gourmetshop.com.co; www.gourmetshop.com.co. Dine in style on wooden tables or reclaimed barrels, surrounded by an impressive cellar of vintages from all over the world. Walls racked with shelves are full of herbs, spices & bottled provisions in this sophisticated eatery. Expect beautiful glassware & good service in this true escape from Caribbean chaos. A menu of fine cheeses, smoked meats & foreign breads has a distinctly European feel. **$$$**

✕ **La Regatta Restaurante** Club Náutico, Av Newball; ✆ 512 3022; e info@clubnautico.org.co; www.clubnautico.org.co. The lobster, shrimp & crab dishes at the yacht club's lively on-the-water eatery are served under moody lighting amidst bobbing yachts & fish-filled waters. Arrive hungry to make the most of an excellent seafood platter – a plate piled high with grilled shrimp, langoustine, snails, calamari, crab claws & fried fish. Curried lobster tails, conch in coconut sauce & seafood stew are also recommended. Dishes come with warm bread & a choice of salads, potatoes & rice. **$$$**

✕ **Cove Green Restaurante** El Cove, Carretera Circunvalar. Ceviche & fried conch are just some of the Cove Green's specialities. Enjoy a plate piled high washed down with an ice-cold beer. **$$**

✕ **Fisherman Place Moonshine Restaurant** El Cove, Carretera Circunvalar. Daily specials depend on what the boats bring back to shore, but fried fish with garlic & langoustine in coconut are staples at this rustic food joint. **$$**

✕ **Niko's Restaurante y Bar** Av Colombia, No1–93; ✆ 512 7535. This wooden sgl-storey diner has a strong nautical theme with walls adorned with nets & ropes & a seafood menu at least a mile long. Eat casually outside under umbrellas or in a more formal indoor setting. Highlights include a delicious crab soup, roasted crab & lobster in crab sauce. The squid in garlic is also sublime. **$$**

✕ **Restaurante West View** Carretera Circunvalar. Expect loud reggae music & a tourist crowd at this on-the-water diner next to La Piscinita. It serves seafood dishes & acts as an unofficial changing room for swimmers & divers who, in turn, buy bags of bread to feed the fish. **$$**

✕ **Comida Típica Isleña** Carretera Circunvalar. This charming local eatery is nothing fancy but it serves generous helpings of fish, rice & plantains. Find it opposite some magnificent island mansions just down the road from Sharky's Dive Shop. **$**

ENTERTAINMENT AND NIGHTLIFE San Andrés has a reputation as a lively party town – even the local cemetery is next to a sign that says 'Caribe dreams … enjoy yourself!'. Venues have a relaxed, easy-going feel. Most can be found on Avenida Colombia and Avenida Newball with plenty of bars, restaurants, salsa clubs and live music also found in many larger hotels. The **Discoteca Blue Deep** can be found at the Hotel Sunrise (✆ *512 39*77) with **Discoteca Extasis** at the Hotel Sol Caribe Centro (✆ *512 3043*) and the **Discoteca Confetis** at the Hotel Mar Azul (✆ *513 2678*). Decent alternatives include **Willy's Disco Bar** and **Sweet Mama's Music Bar** downtown. Rustic rum shacks and thatched-roof seafood diners provide a real flavour of island life. These are a good fall-back off-season when the more sophisticated venues have yet to reach full swing. San Andrés also has a lengthy cockfighting tradition. Breeding and fighting is a serious business on the island where night fights take place in cockpits in Black Dog and North Cliff (see box, *Saturday night's alright for cock fighting*, opposite).

☆ **Café Bar Jet Set** Centro Comerical New Point, Av Providencia. This small outdoor plaza bar has a decent daily happy hour between 17.00–19.00. Its little-known generous measures & great 2-for-1 deals may just be the best-kept secret island-wide.

☆ **Casa de la Cultura** Av Newball; ✆ 512 3405. Frequent Caribbean-themed food, music & dance nights attract a lively crowd each Fri. Expect polished renditions of numerous Bob Marley classics washed down with rum punch & bowls of crab stew.

☆ **La Bodega** Av Colombia. This fantastic off-the-street salsa joint is next to Niko's. Video screens show MTV while a powerful sound system emits Colombian classics at deafening volume. A small dance floor is packed after 23.00, but it's cool to arrive early to grab a table & a bottle of aguardiente while the place fills up.

☆ **Mundo Marino** Centro Commercial New Point Plaza; ✆ 512 1749; e Munmarino@hotmail.co.uk. Join a mixed crowd of singles, couples & tour groups aboard this popular evening 'Morgan' party cruise. Live music has a reggae theme with accompanying dancers. Tickets cost 27,000 COP pp, departing Tue, Thu & Sat at 20.30.

☆ **Sailors Bar** Club Náutico, Av Newball; ✆ 512 3022; f 512 1666; e info@clubnautico.org.co; www.clubnautico.org.co. One of the best drinks menus in San Andrés can be found at the yacht club's watering hole, where punters can enjoy happy hour between 17.00–19.00 on a rustic dinghy dock overlooking the sea.

☆ **Wet** Av Colombia; ✆ 512 3287. This glitzy place looks a little out of place in laid-back San Andrés. Expect a menu of OTT cocktails at Manhattan prices. A dance floor has a sound system that is permanently cranked up to the max.

SHOPPING 'Retail therapy' is a San Andrés tradition and the island's duty-free shops are awash with mainlanders making their COP stretch. **La Riviera** has several stores of different sizes dotted around the town. This duty-free specialist stocks a large range of designer perfumes and big name brand cosmetics. Numerous other outlets offer sunglasses, electronic items, cameras and jewellery, including **Madiera** (✆ 512 5619) and **President Fashion** (✆ 512 6579), both on Avenida Providencía. Here, you'll find Lacoste, Polo, Ralph Lauren and Dior at 30% cheaper than in Europe. Sports goods such as Billabong, Speedo, Fred Perry and O'Neill are also dirt cheap.

At the time of writing, the town is in the midst of a major overhaul that is adding new malls and plazas. Local wine made from noni fruit and honey can be purchased from **César Palacío Santos** (✆ 513 2057) in La Loma. For an extraordinary array of exquisite goods and produce head to the **Gourmet Shop** (✆ 512 9843; f 512 6836; www.gourmetshop.com.co) on Avenida Atlántico where congenial patron Humberto Mejia truly knows his stuff. For hair-braiding look out for street hawkers outside the main hotels downtown. For a chance to buy leftover portions of dinner or extra baking look out for what the islanders call 'fair tables' by the side of the road.

OTHER PRACTICALITIES

Medical services The Timothy Britton Hospital (✆ 512 7392/512 3443) on the island of San Andrés is equipped with a hyperbaric chamber and is staffed by high standard, bilingual medical professionals. Emergency medical attention can be sought here at an outpatient clinic. However, the archipelago's diving community prides itself on an excellent dive safety record. Injuries are rare with sunburn and heat stroke the most common medical complaints from tourists. Find the hospital in the island's North End area in Sarie Bay next to the Hotel Decameron Mary Land. At last half a dozen pharmacies have premises in downtown San Andrés while the locals swear by bush rum as cure for toothache.

Money As you'd expect in a Duty Free Zone, the island of San Andrés is well served by financial institutions and few establishments will turn a credit card away. A decent handful of banks (with ATMs) and money changers can be found in El Centro and at the airport. Outside of town the options are much more limited. Travellers planning to journey further afield should therefore be sure to top up their wallet prior to departure. Given its remote location, the San Andrés Archipelago is more expensive than the Colombian mainland, as many goods are imported. To be safe, budget for at least 10–15% more than you would elsewhere. Transport and tours can also be pricey although food is generally good and cheap.

Internet and communications Many of San Andrés's larger hotels offer internet services – at a price. However, local-rate internet connections can be found at a handful of places in the town centre. The **Creative Shop** (↘ *512 3416*) on Calle 4 and the **Café Internet Sol** (↘ *512 2250*) on Avenida Duarte Blum are two of the best. At the time of writing a new speedy internet is slated to open at the New Point Plaza. The only post office in San Andrés is on Avenida Colón (↘ *512 9405*).

WHAT TO SEE AND DO

Playa Sprat Bight Also known as the 'town beach' or simply referred to as 'la playa' this sandy stretch in Bahía Sardinas is the island's main beach. Proximity to the town centre means this 450m white-sand stretch can get crowded. Despite this, those in the mood to let off steam will find it a fun place to hang out. Expect hair-braiding, volleyball, Frisbee-throwing and picnicking families. Those looking for sand to relax on in tranquillity should head to the island's eastern shore.

Cueva de Morgan (Morgan's Cave) This water-filled rocky cavern is steeped in legend and is where the locals believe Captain Henry Morgan buried his treasure. Every island tour and bus will make a stop here, although the grotto itself is secondary to the souvenir stalls and vendors that surround it. As the cave is waterlogged, entry is impossible. However, guides will take you through a historic narrative as you peer into the depths.

Coconut Museum For a chance to browse a collection of old artefacts and tools from the days of the coconut boom head to this bumper house of coconuts where plenty of coconut-related souvenirs range from carved shells to bizarre painted fronds – find it next to Morgan's Cave.

Johnny Cay This tiny coral islet is no larger than a football field 1.5km north of the coast of San Andrés. Sometimes called Islote Sucre, it's covered in coconut palms and edged by a beautiful white-sand beach. Most people visit to hang out and picnic on the sand – as a popular day trip Johnny Cay can often be deluged with tourists far beyond its capacity during peak season. However, in its quieter guise, the island is a fun place to spend the day. In the 1960s, Marlon Brando was spotted sunbathing on Johnny Cay's beach during a break from filming the movie *Burn* in Colombia. This gritty tale of slave revolt on an early 19th-century Caribbean island is arguably Brando's finest performance. The film won acclaim for using a cast of amateurs other than Brando and Rento Salvatori – along with 20,000 extras.

Saturday is horseracing day in San Andrés, a time of great excitement. Small crowds gather on the sand, their pockets stuffed with COP. Although the prize is officially honorific, bets are placed in hurried secret exchanges. Expectations are high. But first the beach must be blessed according to *obeah*, a type of voodoo witchcraft prevalent throughout the archipelago (see box, *Spirited and spellbound*, page 223). Spells are cast to give a horse extra power or weaken the competition. The ground is also checked for signs of evil or trickery, such as a buried dead dog or voodoo doll. Often just two horses race for the Saturday purse. Riders mount bareback, but such is the pace of this rousing exuberance, the race is over almost before it begins.

General Prada was played with wit and aplomb by a Colombian lawyer, while a British Petroleum employee starred as Mr Shelton. Johnny Cay was Brando's choice as a place for R&R away from the intensity of the film set. However, Brando got bored with Colombia and parts of the film ended up being shot in Morocco, Rome, St Malo, and the Virgin Islands. Johnny Cay has a handful of restaurants selling fish and rice dishes, beer and cocktails.

Isla Acuario Tours to Aquarium Island are often packaged with a trip to Johnny Cay. Littered with tourist huts, it sits in chest-high water next to Haynes Cay, off the east coast of San Andrés. Snorkelling gear can be hired from a dive shack. Other facilities are pretty rudimentary, but include toilets and a collection of small lockers for rental by the hour. Glass-bottom boats offer tours and jet skis are also available for hire. As a popular spot with holidaying families, Aquarium Island is packed to capacity at weekends and can all too easily become a hellish mix of screaming, sunburned kids and shrieking teens. Every fish is scared off by the racket and all the shade is taken, while lockers become like gold dust in the heat. Holiday weekends tend to be particularly unbearable, so stick to midweek if a more chilled-out vibe is your thing.

Haynes Cay This pretty, palm-covered isle is often part of a standard boat tour around San Andrés – usually as a half-hour stop-off for a spot of snorkelling in its shallow waters. Dense thickets of coconut trees provide plenty of shade not far from Acuario. Sharp exposed coral make water shoes essential for swimmers and divers.

La Piscinita Located west of West View just a little further along the coast from El Cover, La Piscinita is described by the locals as a sea-bath due to its calm warmth. Waist-high translucent waters are home to a rainbow of fish. A nearby restaurant serves as a changing room and snorkel-rental joint. It also serves a small but decent menu of seafood and rice dishes.

El Hoyo Soplador Every self-respecting holiday isle should have its own funny little natural phenomenon and this blowhole geyser is San Andrés's. A spurting jet of seawater blasts out of the coral rock in the southern tip of the island when the winds and tides collude – reaching heights of up to 15–20m and drenching onlookers in spray. Several enterprising locals have set up souvenir stalls and a restaurant to cater for the many tourists that visit. However, other less desirable instances of free enterprise have been reported at Hoyo Soplador. Belongings have been stolen from tour buses and hire cars and so-called free drinks haven't been quite as free as they seemed.

La Loma Most visitors head to the town of La Loma to visit its pretty Baptist church – the first to be built on San Andrés, in 1847. This red-roofed whitewashed building wouldn't look out of place in a sleepy English village and the Iglesia Bautista Emmanuel is very much at the centre of La Loma's daily life. The spire once served as a landmark for sailors – a kind of unofficial 'lighthouse' that guided ships into San Andrés. Islanders wear their best outfits on Sunday to attend church services. Despite being partially rebuilt in 1896 the building still provides a fine example of the traditional architecture of the island.

FESTIVALS San Andrés plays host to a Coconut Carnival in November each year to celebrate the birthday of the island and its coconut culture. Festivities abound during this three-day event – a loud, pulsating affair that requires earplugs and stamina. Christmas, Easter and Carnival are also big parties on the island. The 20 July celebration (Colombian Independence Day) sees processions of schoolchildren, military personnel, officials, brass bands and dancers take to the streets dressed in special costumes. A Pentecostal choir festival celebrates the island's choral history in musical merriment at the end of September each year. In May San Andrés hosts an International Triathlon on Johnny Cay. Other key festivals are the Battle of Boyacá celebrations in San Luis on 7 August and Columbus Day on 12 October in La Loma.

SAN LUIS

Visitors seeking a quieter alternative to the tourist-focused capital of San Andrés will enjoy San Luis. Located on the east coast, the so-called town is really just a hamlet – a simple string of houses. This former coconut-shipment port is notable for its traditional wooden island architecture. San Luis has a nice, relaxed feel and also some fine white-sand beaches and superb snorkelling. Despite having no real town centre, San Luis has a scattering of shops, restaurants, dive shops and hotels. Keen prices and fewer tourists are increasingly appealing to shoestring travellers and holidaymakers keen to interact with the locals. Frequent buses connect San Luis with San Andrés via a 15-minute journey.

WHERE TO STAY AND EAT As San Luis slowly establishes itself as a tourism centre, a growing number of enterprising locals are opening bed and breakfasts and simple food joints. On occasions it is also possible to rent a small house or apartment through word of mouth. **Karibik Diver** opposite the Cocoplum Hotel has a nice place that sleeps four people – ask at the office for rates as these vary throughout the year.

Decameron San Luis (323 rooms) ℡ 513 2144/0295. As one of 4 vast Decameron all-inclusive beach resorts on the island, this is pretty much true to form, although the use of authentic island-style architecture gives it a nicer feel. Rooms are set amidst palm trees & native trees with b/fast & lunch buffets & á la carte dinners & all snacks, cigarettes & domestic drinks inc in the price. A show wows the punters at 20.00 each night. Onsite amenities include tennis, volleyball, windsurfing, kayaking, snorkelling, 3 restaurants (including Japanese), 4 bars, 3 swimming pools, laundry & a disco. Rooms come as twin or dbl & inc cable TV, fridge, safe & AC – but no phone. However, several female guests at this resort have expressed concerns regarding personal safety. Beach vendors can also be a nuisance, singling out women & flogging coconuts for cash. $$$

Cocoplum Hotel (42 rooms) ℡ 513 2121/2421/2646/2087; www.cocoplumhotel.com. This comfy beach hotel has its own stretch of sand shaded by palm trees & offers good access to the snorkelling in nearby Rocky Cay. At the hotel itself, watersports inc snorkelling, diving, sailing, kayak & jet skiing. Typical island architecture is painted in vibrant dayglow aqua & lime with 24 dbl rooms & 18 family suites, bar service, swimming pool, beach chairs, hammocks, massage & a nice terrace. A decent restaurant can accommodate 80 people & serves casual fish-and-rice meals all day long. $$

⌂ **Ocean Beach Resort** ☏ 513 2866. This all-inclusive deal enjoys a magnificent palm-clad beachfront spot. Shoestring travellers shouldn't be put off by the advertised rack rates – in off-peak low season it is possible to forgo meals for a discounted price. $$.

⌂ **Villa Verde** ☏ 513 0155; m 315 7700 0785; e temporada@sol.net.com. This splendid green-roofed traditional wooden home enjoys a peaceful

location in a leafy palm-filled garden, just 5 mins from the beach & is one of the nicest places to stay in San Luis. It can be hired in full, or part & sleeps 8 people. A large lounge has a tiled floor & gorgeous wooden furniture. Three bedrooms, 2 bathrooms & a kitchen come with large wooden balconies & porched terraces overlooking lush vegetation. The house has partial AC, cable TV, swimming pool, maid service & optional car. Rates vary depending on the length of stay. Haggling is expected for durations of 1 night–3 months. $$

Home-stay options

⌂ **Caselita Forbes** 'Monica's Place' ☏ 513 2209   ⌂ **Vicenta Livingston** 'Centa's Place' ☏ 513 0183

DIVING IN THE ARCHIPELAGO

As the home to one of the largest barrier reefs in the Americas, the San Andrés Archipelago is a true diver's paradise. Dozens of operators offer scuba and snorkelling in a destination still relatively unknown in diving circles, despite being accessible. Underwater visibility is remarkable at an average of 30m year-round and as much as 60m in some spots. Conditions are calm with minimal currents and water temperatures of around 27°C.

Most boat dives are within a half-hour travel time with several only five minutes away. Steep walls, fine coral, sponges and sand shelves are often visible at about 70m. A spectacular 33km long reef is the third-largest on the planet. Volcanic crags and sunken shipwrecks add further excitement. The reefs on both Providencía and San Andrés are famous for their abundant array of varicoloured sponges. Giant purple sea fans gently wave in time with the ebb and flow of the sea. Brains, fingers, pencils and pillars are clouded by a rainbow of small fish. Feather bush hydroids sway like windswept grassy meadows amidst dense coral growths. Divers are also likely to spot turtles, lobsters, rays, barracudas, groupers and red snappers.

Most dive-specialist operators are based on San Andrés and offer two single tank dives each morning, departing at around 09.00 and returning at lunchtime. Many then run a single tank dive in the afternoon subject to demand. Night dives are popular and organised to order, departing half an hour before sunset. However, as with all things in San Andrés, dive times are more a general concept rather than a fixed constant. Most operators will also offer tailored dive tours for individuals and groups. Costs vary, so it pays to shop around. Budget for 18,000 COP for 1½ hours' snorkelling, including equipment hire. Scuba hire runs at about 55,000 COP for a morning's dive, including equipment. PADI courses start at 205,000 COP and rise to 900,000 COP for the full Dive Master certificate. A night dive with equipment will set you back at least 65,000 COP (about 40,000 without equipment) with a set of mask, fins and snorkel 9,000 COP per day and 10,000 COP for a wet suit. Sea urchins in the vicinity make water shoes a good idea.

Expect year-round water temperature of around 27°C with visibility of 23–33m. Only a few sites carry currents that make them only out of bounds for non-advanced divers. Although winds are stronger during the dry season, January–June, these tend to be from the east. The position of the barrier reef makes it possible to dive the western wall and the internal patch during these windier months, with no tidal problems. The archipelago's most popular sites have been buoyed by CORALINA in association with UNESCO and the Colombian government and include the following.

DIVE SITES

Anita Small coral caves surround this dilapidated wreck site, located on the outside of the reef opposite Crab Cay (Cayo Congrejo) at 10.5m. Although the site lacks maturity (the boat sunk in 2001) there are large numbers of tarpon resident to the area along big pillars of stony coral.

Bajo San Félipe Just 1km offshore, this sand-bottomed dive site reaches 13.5m in parts along a vast coral patch, in a spot famed for its abundance of colourful sponges and coral formations. Excellent visibility makes this a popular night-dive site.

Blue Diamond According to lore of San Andrés, the *Blue Diamond* sunk in 1995 after being impounded by the Colombian government for running drugs. Today it is one of the most popular dive attractions in the archipelago – a fascinating wreck full of little nooks and crannies that beg exploration. Resting not far off the eastern shore of San Andrés in about 35ft of water, this medium-sized freighter split as it sunk ensuring some decent gaps for adventuresome divers to swim through without running much risk of getting stuck or caught. A massive propeller is half-buried in sand while an open hatch in the bow leads to a passable hole in the side of the hull. Fans, corals and sponges cover the wreck – look for barracuda and other fish darting in and out of the cracks.

Cantil de Santa Catalina Initially sand, this scenic dive reaches maximum depths of 24m along a 12m wall. Large coral mounds include a plentiful supply of healthy star species as well as visiting chubs, queen conchs, lobsters and green morays.
Canal The abundant nooks, crannies, holes and ledges of this twin-site contain plenty of underwater creatures and fish species, located either side of the navigation channel into Catalina harbour. On the outer edge, a sand bottom at 21m at the wall's base rises to plateaus. Expect a wonderful mix of dramatic pillar corals and a variety of hard and soft species.

Confusion Divers can expect to encounter large numbers of blue runner jacks, yellow tail snappers and horse eye jacks as well as the Creole wrasse that hide along the wall. It starts out at 12m and is over a wall that plummets to the depths.

Connoly This enjoyable wall dive starts at 12m and has a site to the right where two walls of coral sit 9m apart. On the right, find three caves with two small caverns at 24m and a larger, swimmable cave at 27m that is home to nurse sharks.

Convento The edge of this coral edged sand basin starts at 15m with a wall offering diving to any depth to the recreational limit.

Cromis As the name suggests, this popular dive site is renowned for large numbers of blue cromis. It is usually dived in conjunction with the magnificent wall, Félipe's Place (see below).

Crystal A broken-down shipwreck sits on the edge of the reef in 11.5m of water, providing a good site for corals, sponges and a wide variety of fish. Expect to spot snapper and barracuda along with the occasional visiting nurse shark and a large number of chubs.

Dos Puntas Two Points consists of a duo of underwater ridges and starts at 18m sloping to 26m depths. Leading to the outside southern tip of the coral reef, the site offers super vistas of healthy stony coral.

El Jardín Not always an easy dive due to moderate currents, The Garden is so named for its bountiful healthy coral, sand carpets, grass and large sponges. Starting at 23m, the dive takes in some big mounds of coral that are home to fish and moray eels with good visibility throughout.

Espiral This sizeable cavern opens at 42m and features a spiral-like staircase – hence the name. Exit the cave at 30m to spot dog snapper and grouper before following the wall to a height of 21m.

Félipe's Place One of the region's finest wall dives, the site starts at a depth of 10m on a coral ledge. A sand spur leads to 24m over a steep wall with a small canyon to the right that is jam-packed with colourful fish.

Hippies' Place This super little horseshoed site used to attract an outdoorsy flower-power crowd, hence the name. Small, but perfectly formed, it is located on the east side of the island on the inside of the reef. Unusual coral formations on the deeper edge are home to large numbers of fish in a site that reaches maximum depths of 13.5m, 2m on top of the coral in parts.

Manta City Rather confusingly, despite the name, this site isn't home to manta rays but is a haven for southern stingrays – many of them with spans over 1.5m. It starts out over sand and hits a maximum depth of 13.5m around large patches of coral the size of a double-decker bus. Divers pass between coral mounds and sand over gardens of ghost feather dusters that are home to brown garden eels, a wide variety of fish, moray and lobster.

Nick's Place Numerous coral outcroppings are prominent features of this nice wall dive that starts at 15.2m where visiting marine life includes turtles and reef sharks.

Nitrogen Excess (NX) Advanced divers adore 'NX' as it starts deep and becomes deeper to 60m or more. Although short, the dive is worth it for the truly spectacular views alone, but requires immersion to the recreational limit.

Paulino's Place Located close to Manta City on the island's south tip, this pleasant sand-bottomed dive site features boat anchors and vast coral patches to a maximum depth of 13m. Southern stingrays are a common sight here with occasional reports of juvenile hawksbill turtles spotted.

Planchon A sunken barge forms a dramatic 90m-long feature of this dive, set in 22.5m of water on a flat terrain. Inhabited by numerous species of fish, corals and reef creatures, the wreck contains deteriorating oil drums and so cannot be entered, but is a fascinating experience nonetheless.

Snapper Shoal As the name suggests, this is an excellent site in which to see snappers and is also renowned for sleeping nurse sharks. Large jacks and spotted snake eels are also sighted in a site that has a maximum depth of 21m.

South Bank This submerged bank off the south end of the island is located outside the reef and starts at 24m – often in strong currents. Popular with drift-drivers, a key attraction of this site is its vast number of very large snapper and grouper. An enjoyable, if unpredictable dive, that experienced divers will find rewarding.

6

Stairway to Heaven At 24m, this deep dive starts in a sand shoot that leads to a striking gorge from which small plateaus form steps – hence the name. A vertical wall provides plenty of colours, with stunning views on a clear day.

Table Rock Popular with snorkellers and scuba divers alike, this shallow site has a depth of 8m blessed with large areas where the light play can be magnificent.

Tete's Place Located less than 1km offshore, this site has a maximum depth of 13m and very little current. Initially sand, it starts at 9m, forming a short 3m wall. Over a sloping coral bed blessed with a wide variety of fish species in large numbers, it is possible to spot mid-sized goat fish, squirrel fish, grunts and school masters in a dive that is described as 'like swimming an aquarium' by those in the know.

The Andy This broken-down wreck sits in 10.5m of water on the outskirts of the reef and boasts dozens of nooks and crannies. Reef and nurse sharks can be spotted on a sizeable coral and sand platform with good visibility.

The Bight Starting on a sand plateau at 18m, this wall dive is located on the point of the reef with a sand step at 45m. Dive at any depth up to the recreational limit to experience beautiful corals and multi-coloured sponges on the wall.

The Cave Plentiful colourful sponges are the appeal of this pleasant dive site characterised by a small cave at a depth of 33m and an array of resplendent orange, red, yellow, green and gold hues are not to be missed.

Timkam Channel At 10m this shallow dive leads through a cut in the reef in front of Manzanillo Beach, offering perfect visibility when conditions are right.

Tres Casitas Initially at 13.5m on the edge of the wall, a drop to 30m leads to flat sand bottom where a large gap in the coral allows plenty of opportunity to spot big groupers, Jewfish and hog fish.

Turtle Rock Frequently dived, this unique site has a strange structure that features a large rock on a short ledge separated from a wall. A rounded top and broad base give the rock the look of a turtle. Start at 18m approximately 45m from the wall to discover the top of Turtle Rock at 21m and its base at 36m. Follow the wall to rise to a small illuminated canyon with stunning views.

DIVE OPERATORS

⚓ **Banda Dive Shop** Hotel Lord Pierre L–102, San Andrés; ☎ 513 1080/2507; f 513 1060; e dive@bandadiveshop.com; www.bandadiveshop.com. Luis Miguel & Gloria are a friendly husband-&-wife team with a dive centre that boasts a sterling reputation. International certification in all levels of PADI, BIS & NAUI is offered, along with courses that range from a 3-day session to 20 days of dive master certification, using a modern 31ft boat with 2 115HP motors, a Ford truck, GPS navigation equipment & a MAKO 18.7cf compressor. A well-stocked shop offers a wide range of equipment & clothing for hire & sale, including TUSA & Oceanic accessories, Body Glove wetsuits and T-shirts. Visa & MasterCard accepted.

⚓ **Buzos del Caribe** Av Colombia 1–212, San Andrés; ☎ 512 8931; www.buzosdelcaribe.com
⚓ **Caribe Azul Dive Center** Pepper Hill Rd, San AndrEes; ☎ 513 0079; e ecoturismocaribeazul@gmail.com; www.caribeazulhotel.com. Bilingual instructors offer a wide variety of adults' & children's packages at this popular dive outfit owned by Hugo Arboleda, who videos dives for posterity.
⚓ **Karibik Diver** Av Newball 1–248, Edificio Galéon, San Andrés; ☎ 512 0101
⚓ **San Andrés Divers** Av Cincurvalar, San Andrés; ☎ 513 0347; f 513 0719; e info@sanandresdivers.com; www.sanandresdivers.com. This specialist dive operator has a 4-acre building complex in an idyllic

LOOK, BUT DON'T TOUCH!

Responsible divers understand that experiencing the magic of the underwater world is a privilege granted by Mother Nature. As coral reefs around the world come under extreme threat it is vital to ensure that future generations are able to enjoy the same honour. To help preserve the ecology, health and beauty of the planet's coral reefs the following responsible diving tips should be considered:

- Anchors cause serious damage to reefs. Only dive with an operator prepared to ensure the reefs will not be damaged via a responsible tourism and diving policy. Visit www.responsibletravel.com for further advice on choosing an ethical tour operator.
- Check that the point of entry into the water is away from fragile corals. Practise your buoyancy over sand before moving towards corals and reefs and vulnerable organisms.
- Resist the temptation to feed fish and discourage others from doing so. Feeding marine life upsets the normal pattern of behaviours. It can also encourage aggression.
- Contamination from poorly treated waste and water systems causes damage to corals. Choose a hotel that manages grey water responsibly.
- Keep time spent in underwater caves to a minimum to reduce the likelihood of leaving air bubbles behind as these can threaten organisms.
- Refuse to buy souvenirs made from corals, shells or earthwoods. Report any traders to Earth Dive via an online science log: www.earthdive.com.
- Be sure to take all litter – collect any that you see, not just your own.
- Finally, look but don't touch! Never step on live marine organisms and be mindful that even the gentlest of touches can destroy robust-looking corals, sponges and polyps.

palm-tree setting, bathrooms & lockers, new 80ft³ tanks using yoke valve systems, a BAUER compressor, NITROX fill station, & full rental gear availability as well as dive accessories such as lights, cameras etc & a tabled dive briefing area, training pool & AC classroom.
⚓ **Sharky's Dive Shop** Carretera Circunvalar; ☎ 513 0433/0420; e buceo@sharkydiveshp.com; www.sharkydiveshop.com. Since establishing ten years of experience this outfit has grown in size & stature &

now has a 31ft boat with 2 outboard 4-stroke motors of 115HP to whizz divers out to sites at speed. Other equipment includes a Ford 150 pickup truck; two Bauer compressors to fill 100 air tanks; 30 nitrox enriched air tanks; 25 BCDs & 25 Aqualung scuba regulators. Sharkey's specialities include day & night dives & underwater photography tours.
⚓ **Sirius Dive Center** Providencia; ☎ 514 8213; f 514 8808; e info@siriusdivecenter.com; www.siriusdivecenter.com

ISLA PROVIDENCIA Telephone code: 8

> In de Caribbean de very best, is de beautiful island of Prov-ee-dence.
>
> Willy B, Providencian musician

Idyllic can often be an over-used word, but in Providencía the beaches live up to the hype. Empty stretches of powder-fine palm-scattered white sand are lapped by languid waves. The water is warm, azure-green and like the proverbial mill pond – and often occupied by a sole bobbing wooden boat and a couple of wild horses frolicking in the lazy afternoon sun. In fact pretty much everything seems to move in slow motion in sleepy Providencía – an island with a laid-back energy. A handful of old American Chevrolets pass by at walking pace, fulfilling the role of taxi, an

San Andrés Archipelago ISLA PROVIDENCIA

6

absence of paintwork and door handles a testament to their advancing years. Calypso-shrouded open-sided restaurants care little for world-class service. Food comes served with a generous helping of good humour. Life unfolds at a leisurely pace. Friendly smiles lead to unhurried conversations. Time is an unimportant detail in this true get-away-from-it-all location – a place where it is impossible not to chill out and kick back.

Providencía's beaches are small, beautiful and often deserted. Bahía Manzanillo is the most popular with other fine ribbons of sand at Bahía Aguadulce and Bahía Suroeste. Numerous other tiny white-sand bays and idyllic stretches can easily be found dotted around the shoreline.

HISTORY Providencía's colourful history is intertwined with that of neighbouring San Andrés (see *Isla San Andrés,* page 220) attracting the first human settlers at the beginning of the 17th century. Traditionally known as Old Providence, the island is now commonly known under its Spanish guise. It is the second-largest in the archipelago at 17km² and lies 90km north of San Andrés. Unlike its younger, coralline neighbour, Providence is a mountainous island of volcanic origin. Occupied and besieged by pirates throughout its history including Dutch buccaneer Edward Mansvelt, Englishman William Dampier, Welsh privateer Henry Morgan and Frenchman Louis Michele Aury, the island is steeped in myth and legend. Like San Andrés, Providencía is rumoured to have been a final resting place for Morgan's buried treasure. Aury captured the island on 4 July 1818, establishing a settlement with a thriving economy based on plundered Spanish cargo. He unsuccessfully tried to rebuild good relations with Bolívar before being thrown from a horse and killed in August 1821. However, his death gave rise to a number of conspiracy theories that prompted some sources to claim he was alive and living in Havana in 1845. Aury dredged a channel between Providencía and Santa Catalina. Today, the two islands are united by a 100m floating bridge called 'Lovers Lane' or 'Bridge of the Enamoured'.

GETTING THERE There are no direct flights into Providencía's El Embrujo Airport other than those that connect it to San Andrés. Tickets for the 20-minute jaunt cost around 300,000 COP through a single airline, Satena Airways. Strict weight restrictions apply on these tiny little planes. Just 10kg is allowed for luggage before charges of 1,000 COP per extra kilo apply. Seats can be scarce during high season but most passengers turn up on spec so pre-booking online (*www.satena.com*) should be OK. Be warned, it is imperative to reconfirm a return flight to avoid your seat being given away.

Few tourists are even aware there are boats to Providencía as these cargo carriers lack facilities and comfort. If this option appeals head down to the Maritime El Cover del Muelle on Avenida Newball and ask for a boat called the *Doña Olga.* At the time of writing an unreliable schedule favoured a Wednesday and Friday. Pack a mattress, water and food and expect to pay 40,000 COP apiece.

GETTING AROUND It's easy to rent a car and drive around the island's 20km circuit of roads. Ask for car rental at the airport on arrival or head to the hamlet of Aguadulce on the west coast – the centre of the island's tourist industry, a 15-minute taxi ride away. Colectivo transport (shared minibuses) can also be found at the airport. Cycle hire is a good option for visitors keen to explore off the beaten track. The *chiva* is an easy way to circumnavigate the island's tourist trail. Tours by lancha (small boat) depart from Aguadulce. The chief settlement is Isabel Village in the north of the island, close southeast of Santa Catalina Island. Other villages are San Félipe on the west coast and La Paz in the southeast.

PROVIDENCIA & SANTA CATALINA

Map labels:
Santa Catalina
Lovers Lane floating bridge
SANTA ISABEL
see inset
Fundo de Promocion Turística Providencia y Santa Catalina
Old Providence Hotel
Banks
Hotel Flaming Trees
Crab Cay
Caribbean Sea
Bahía Catalina (Catalina Bay)
N
Bradt
Parque Nacional McBean Lagoon
Three Brothers Cay
Lazy Hill
El Reserva Natural El Pico
Iron Wood Hill
El Embrujo Airport
Bahía Agua Dulce (Fresh Water Bay)
Posada del Mar
Restaurante Rosa del Viento
Hotel El Pirata Morgan
Bahía Aguadulce
Cabañas Miss Elma
PROVIDENCIA
0 —— 1 km
0 —— 1 miles
Bahía Suroeste (South West Bay)
South West Cabañas
Café Studio
Cabañas Miss Mary
Bahía Agua Mansa (Smooth Water Bay)
Roland Roots Bar
Lighthouse
Bahía Manzanillo

Inset:
Inset
Cayos Catalina
Liza Bay
Bucaneer Point
Caribbean Sea
SANTA CATALINA
Posada Villa de Santa Catalina
Morgans Head Cannons
Lovers Lane floating bridge
Mona Bay
Providencia

Muitas Rent a Car Av Newball Edificio Galéon; ☎ 512 4590. Expect friendly & efficient service from Jorge García & Carlos Alberto García at this family-run firm.

A small fleet of buggy-style open-sided jeeps are clean & well maintained. Costs range from 160,000 COP in low season to 200,000 COP in high season.

TOURIST INFORMATION AND TOUR OPERATORS

ℹ️ **Fundo de Promocion Turistica Providencia y Santa Catalina** Santa Isabel; ☎ 514 8054; e providencia2004@yahoo.com; www.oldprovidence.com.co

Body Contact Bahía Aguadulce; ☎ 514 8283. This small, independent tour specialist offers a wide range of services, from kayak trips (25,000 COP) & horseback rides (25,000 COP) to hikes to El Pico (20,000 COP) &

boat excursions (20,000 COP pp). It also rents out bicycles (20,000 COP per day) & snorkel gear (12,000 COP per day) & handles flight reservations & currency exchange.

Rodolfo Bahía Suroeste; ☎ 514 8626. Superb tours on horseback are this tour company's forte. Most last a couple of hours (15,000 COP pp) & follow a mix of beach & mountain trails.

🏠 **WHERE TO STAY & EAT** As a tiny island, Providencía isn't blessed with umpteen hotel choices and accommodation tends to be more expensive than San Andrés as a result. A couple of upmarket options offer some luxurious touches but most

221

hotels are mid range or simple, rustic affairs. Like San Andrés, Providencía offers visitors home-stay accommodation as part of the archipelago's highly recommended Posadas Nativas project.

🏠 **Hotel El Pirata Morgan** Bahía Aguadulce; ☎ 514 8067; www.hotelpiratamorgan.com. Undoubtedly one of the best mid-budget hotels on the island & has the added benefit of being atop a decent supermarket. $$$

🏠 **Sol Caribe Providencia** Bahía Aguadulce; ☎ 514 8036; www.solarhoteles.com. This charming hotel rightly claims to be Providencía's finest – the bright & breezy blue-& orange-painted 2-storey building is a real delight. Built in traditional architectural style, the exterior wooden terraces are adorned with palm-filled pots & wind-chimes. Shuttered windows boast stunning views across leafy gardens. All-inclusive deals include cheerful rooms with AC, colour TV, fridge & phone. $$$

🏠 **Cabañas Miss Elma** Bahía Augadulce; ☎ 514 8229. A handful of fan-cooled rooms & suites with AC are comfortably furnished & right on the beach. A restaurant is a little pricey, but good nonetheless. Opt for the lobster if you feel like a splurge. $$

🏠 **Cabañas Miss Mary** (7 rooms) Bahía Suroeste; ☎ 514 8454. Highly recommended on the basis that it sits on a jaw-dropping palm-scattered beach, Miss Mary also has a fine seafood-&-rice restaurant as well as basic rooms with AC, right on the sand. $$

🏠 **Hotel Flaming Trees** (9 rooms) Santa Isabel; ☎ 514 8049. The spacious rooms are well appointed in this comfortable family-run hotel. Each has a private bathroom, fridge & TV & plenty of plug points for camera battery/mobile phone recharging. $$

🏠 **Old Providence Hotel** Santa Isabel; ☎ 514 8691. Dull, uninspiring rooms sit atop the Erika supermarket in the town centre. A good location, & despite a lack of charm, the rooms are faultlessly clean. $$

🏠 **Posada del Mar** ☎ 514 8168; e inforeservas@ posadadelmarprovidencia.com. Rooms in this beach-facing hostel have pleasant balconies slung with hammocks. It's clean, comfortable & a good budget option. $$

🏠 **South West Cabañas** Bahía Suroeste; ☎ 514 8221. Although it's not bang, smack right on the beach, this place is only 500m away. Sixteen large self-contained suites are ideal for longer stays on the island. Expect to pay 35,000 COP pp with discounted packages for 1 week plus. $$

🍸 **Roland Roots Bar** Bahía Manzanillo; ☎ 514 8417. This atmospheric open-air hangout is shaded by coconut palms & drenched in the sound of reggae rhythms from noon until dawn. Roland & his late-night revelry are legendary in Providencía. Before the serious drinking starts the bar also serves a decent menu. They serve some tasty fried fish & seafood dishes. Roland also has a room for rent – but earplugs are a must. $

✕ **Restaurante Rosa del Viento** Bahía Aguadulce; ☎ 514 8067; ⊕for b/fast at 07.00, this pleasant eatery serves food until early evening. Find it behind the Hotel El Pirata Morgan & expect a decent plate of fried fish, coconut rice, salad & patacones. $

Café Studio Bahía Suroeste; ⬛ 514 99076; 🕐 11.00–21.00 Mon–Sat. This coffee & cake joint is owned by a Canadian expat & almost everyone sipping espressos is a traveller far from home. However, the menu is exceptionally good with unsurpassed traditional favourites that include seafood & rice, pesto spaghetti & roasted crab. $$

Home-stay options

Victoria Bernard 'Miss Vicky's' (South West Bay); ⬛ 514 9152
June Marie Mow Robinson 'Miss June's Place' (Lazy Hill); ⬛ 514 8953
Josefina Huffington 'Miss Elma's' (Bahía Aguadulce); ⬛ 514 8953

Christine Huffington 'Christine Huffington's Place' (Bahía Aguadulce); ⬛ 514 8361
Joyce Hooker 'Joy's Place' (Bahía Agua Mansa)
Rosa María Fortune Archbold 'Posada Fortune' (Bahía Agua Mansa)

ENTERTAINMENT AND NIGHTLIFE Night owls will discover that Providencía is a simple place after dark. A dozen or so bars and a few open-air night clubs are frequented by a mix of islanders and tourists while groups of local musicians often perform on the beach. Those lucky enough to arrive on a full moon can join in the celebrations at Manchineel Bay or Southwest Bay. A bonfire is lit to the pulsating sounds of loud reggae music. Rum flows like water until the party ends at dawn.

Wherever you are in Providencía, you are sure to hear the loud slap of dominoes. Islanders play with great gusto on rickety wooden tables in the street, under the glare of a street lamp.

The music and dance customs and traditions of the island reflect the heritage of its inhabitants' mix of European, indigenous and Afro-Caribbean roots. European influences can be clearly found in schottische, polka and mazurka dances. Indigenous music known as 'string' is played using a washtub bass, fiddle, mandolin, maracas and jawbone of an ass. A mento comes from the Antilles and reggae from Jamaica. The island's calypso tradition stems from Trinidad with guitar pasillos from Spain. An entertainment known as 'rhyme' uses

SPIRITED AND SPELLBOUND

Ha I'm the Obeah woman, above pain, I can eat thunder and drink the rain
I kiss the moon and hug the sun. And call the spirits and make 'em run.
Niña Simone, 'Obeah Woman', *It is Finished* (2004)

Obeah is a style of Afro-Caribbean shamanism that uses ancient occult powers handed down orally over the centuries through the generations. Today, this aged spell-craft is practised throughout Africa and the Caribbean. In the San Andrés Archipelago it is prevalent, albeit in a watered-down form. Purveyors of present-day Obeah use traditional witchcraft, sorcery, shamanism, voodoo, palo, santeria, rootwork, hoodoo and tribal magic– yet it remains shrouded in secrecy. Islanders believe that Obeah is a potent force – a deadly and dangerous power in the wrong hands. Grown men believe they can be weakened by the spells of Obeahman. Those committing ill deeds render themselves powerless to the strength of Obeah. Nothing is free – there is always a pay-off somewhere at the hands of the spirits, they say. Spells relate to both black and white magic using charms, talisman, luck and mysticism. Obeah also came to mean any physical object, such as a talisman or charm that was used for evil magical purposes. However, despite its fearsome reputation, Obeah is also used to good purpose. Like many other forms of folk magic it contains traditions for healing and bringing about luck in love and money.

OUR FRIEND THE CRAB

We should praise the Lord for that we can be making so much crabs soup. All because of He bountiful goodness. We rich. He give us plenty crabs.

Mr Williams, Providencía resident

Islanders have a strong connection with the black land crab (*Gecarcinus ruricola*), an important symbol of native cultural identity and valued source of protein. Generations of islanders have celebrated the link between crab and human through story, folklore and song. An annual crab festival also honours the island's unusual relationship with this magnificent species of crustacean. Yet it is in April–May each year that the black land crab really makes its mark, journeying from the cool inland forests to the sea to spawn in a vast moving carpet. After two perilous weeks in the ocean, the young make the return trip, crossing treacherous paths and roads back to the relative safety of the woodlands. This extraordinary mass migration lasts a good two weeks and brings traffic to a halt in Aguadulce and Suroeste. Roads are covered so densely with crabs on the move that it is impossible to cross from side to side without decimating their ranks.

extemporaneous rhyming to poke fun at those present, an African tradition. North American country music can also be found in Providencía along with Colombian salsa, merengue and vallenato. **Roland Roots Bar** (↳ *514 8417; see above*) in Bahía Manzanillo is a popular place to hang out listening to reggae into the wee small hours.

Storytelling remains an important part of Providencía's lengthy oral tradition and some of the best historic tales of the island's former days come from Virginia Archbold. A former mayor of Providencía, Archbold's family were one of the first on the island. She often conducts historical tours and is happy to chat to visitors. To seek out this fountain of knowledge, just ask around.

SHOPPING Souvenir stalls and street vendors sell a diverse range of artwork and tourist tat, but some of the nicer handicrafts are the bright Caribbean paintings and woven baskets. A browse around Bahía Aguadulce's excellent Arts and Crafts is worth it for meeting the French owner alone. 'El Frenchie' is a great source of local information for travellers and whips up a mean fresh- fruit smoothie to boot. Local homemade fruit wine (tamarind and plum) can also be purchased. On Sundays, look out for stalls of freshly baked pies at the roadsides island-wide. These melt-in-the-mouth local delicacies (*tortas*) are truly delicious. Choose from coco, lemon, mango, pumpkin and papaya – at 2,000 COP each.

OTHER PRACTICALITIES

Money and banks Visitors are strongly advised to sort out cash and currency ahead of arrival as Providencía isn't blessed with facilities. Two banks in Santa Isabel are open from 08.00 until 13.30 Monday to Thursday. They extend the hours by 30 minutes on Friday and have an ATM. Other unofficial money changers operate on the island but most will only trade dollars – and rates are dire. Credit cards are not widely accepted.

Internet and communications Net Crawler (↳ *514 8956*) in Santa Isabel is open 08.00 until 21.00 (closed noon–14.30) each day. Although this is Providencía's only dedicated internet facility, **Body Contact** (see *Tour operators*, page 221), offers chargeable internet access in times of need. Be warned, connections on the island can be frustratingly slow.

Medical Dr William Burbano offers a clinic to visitors weekdays between 14.00–17.00 in Aguadulce (🔌 *514 8912*).

WHAT TO SEE AND DO

Hiking Providencía's craggy rise-and-fall volcanic terrain makes it a pleasant place to explore on foot. Several guides operate out of Casabaja and Aguadulce and will usually offer a hike to the top of El Pico (see *El Reserva Natural El Pico*, page 226) or along the mangrove coastal path to the west for 20,000–30,000 COP. The highest hills on Providencía are remnants of a carapace of felsic lava flows and domes. Trails lead through lush vegetation containing flocks of varicoloured birds. Stunning views and lots of small animals offer plenty of points of interest. An absence of poisonous snakes makes a walk in the wild non-hazardous although hikers should remain vigilant of mosquito swarms and biting ants.

Snorkelling Apart from the sites around the offshore belt near the islets of Cayo Tres Hermanos and Cayo Cangrejo, most of Providencía's finest dive spots are located on the island's western flank. Here, the coral reefs are even more remarkable than those around San Andrés with brightly coloured sponges and pristine fingers and brains. Snorkelling and scuba tour companies primarily operate out of Aguadulce, with most offering boat dives and instruction with a choice of half- and full-day tours. Crystal-clear waters make underwater photography popular – and even novices should pack a disposable waterproof camera to capture Providencía's stunning seabed views.

Fishing Islanders are practised masters of fishing and never come to shore empty-handed, even from the most difficult of waters. Little wooden boats bob close to shore in the early morning with larger vessels departing for deeper water at dusk. Many local fishermen offer one-to-one or small group tours, using nets and hooks and free diving in search of lobster, sea snail, bream, grouper, turtle, crab and other reef species. Ask around at Aguadulce – the guys at tour operator Body Contact usually come up trumps.

Parque Nacional McBean Lagoon (*Admission 20,000 COP*) On a volcanic terrain shaped by ancient streams, this 2,450-acre conservation zone at the northeastern end of the island was declared a national park in 1995. Underwater gardens account for more than 2,200 acres with a terra firma segment that encompasses a 500ft volcanic peak, Iron Wood Hill, and flat expanses of mangrove swamps. These

---

COOK WITH AN ISLAND GIRL

Flamboyant islander Lucy Trigigia Chow Robinson (🔌 *513 2233*; m *311 808 9039*; e *lucytrigidia@yahoo.com*; see box, *We Love Lucy*, page 206) is also an accomplished cook in the traditional style of San Andrés. She adores food and her enthusiasm for all things culinary is evident in the cookery schools she hosts. Packed with fun and gastronomic insight, Lucy takes students shopping for ingredients at the local fish and fruit markets. She introduces them to indigenous herbs and ancient cooking styles – and then they get to eat the results. Lucy's workshops cost from 20,000 COP (excluding ingredients). She can accommodate a maximum of five would-be chefs at a time.

complex marshland forests contain a predominance of red, yellow and white mangrove – an important breeding site for several species of turtles, fish, molluscs and birds. Shallow lagoon waters contain Crab Cay and Three Brothers Cay protected by sand bars and coral reef.

The vegetation on Iron Wood Hill is dry forest with cockspur the dominant species and a natural habitat for an aggressive biting ant. Pactá palms and several species of cactus and scrub can also be found on the slopes of the hill. In Crab Key (Cayo Cangrejo) vegetation is mainly coconut palm while in Three Brothers Cay (Cayo Tres Hermanos) the picus tree provides an important nesting place for frigate. Several extensive areas of sea grass surround the lagoon including a large prairie of marine phanerogams with coral outcrops on a rocky coastal strip home to several algae species. Sizeable numbers of multi-coloured lizard and bird species can be easily spotted throughout all areas of the park environments, including 56 migrant bird species from the western Caribbean. Birders will enjoy a slow meander along the 800m-long eco-path that winds through the mangrove systems.

El Reserva Natural El Pico Don't forgo a chance to tackle the 1½-hour ascent to the top of El Pico, the highest point of Providencía at 360m above sea level. It not only offers spectacular panoramic views across a stunning seascape but also provides a chance to enjoy some beautiful leafy bird-filled trails. Most people begin the steady climb in Casabaja although several paths criss-cross upwards. It's no hard slog, more a leisurely hike. However, tourists are recommended to use a guide to avoid getting lost. Most charge around 20,000–30,000 COP and can be booked through a tour operator or the tourism office. Making an early start is worth the effort to avoid the heat of the day. Take plenty of water for the trip as there are no shops or facilities along the way.

Festivals Providencía has a lengthy horseracing tradition with regular meetings on the beach. Cat-boat racing and domino tournaments are also staged year-round by the islanders – look out for the posters and ask around the bars for details of the venues or follow the crowds. The locals of Providencía are renowned for their love of tombola, carnivals and national and religious holidays. A potent local brew makes each festival or celebration a lively affair, but those not prepared for a mega hangover should pass on this fiery moonshine – officially called bush rum but known locally as 'bushy'.

Providencía's main annual event is a week-long Cultural Festival in June. Dancing, live music and parades culminate in an iguana beauty contest – well what else?

THE FOOD OF THE ISLANDERS

Native cuisine represents an important part of the island's culture and Providencía dishes have a strong Afro-Caribbean flavour. Islanders adore *rondón* (meaning rundown), a stew of conch, yucca, plantain and dumpling cooked in coconut milk. The island's sweet-fleshed crab is prepared in numerous ways, from a delicious soup served in deep terrines with sweet bread rolls and fried crab patty to simply cooked with butter in its shell. Fresh fish fried in coconut oil comes served with coconut rice and plantains with lots of conch and lobster dishes and fish meatballs. Another firm favourite is baked *po* (roasted pork). Islanders also have a very sweet tooth and so baked cookies, cakes and sweets are in good supply, including mango pies, Johnny cake and coconut bread. Meals are often accompanied by the home-distilled rum known as 'bushy'.

Now put your shirt on. You look much too naked for a decent English gentleman.
Captain Sir Henry Morgan – *The Black Swan* (1942)

Much has been written about Henry Morgan's seafaring exploits and maritime battles with the Spanish. In 1666 Morgan commanded a ship to seize the islands of Old Providence and Santa Catalina. He then took the well-garrisoned town of Portobelo using captured Jesuits as human shields to take the fortress. After escapades in Jamaica and Cuba, Henry Morgan recaptured the island of Santa Catalina in 1670, from where he planned the sacking of Panama's capital city. It was a bloody raid that saw Morgan leave with riches beyond his wildest dreams. As he departed, he burnt the city to the ground, massacring thousands. Morgan returned to the San Andrés Archipelago with his plunder and settled on Santa Catalina where islanders are convinced he buried gold and treasure. So are the locals on Providencía, who swear his booty lies in Cueva de Morgan.

However, this sacking of Panama violated a peace treaty between England and Spain. Morgan was arrested and returned forcibly to England in 1672 where he was able to prove he had no knowledge of the treaty. He was knighted in 1674 before taking up the post of lieutenant governor until his rowdy behaviour and drunkenness caused him to be replaced. Morgan's health steadily declined until his death in 1688.

Today he is immortalised in many diverse ways. Morgan appears in an array of films and fiction including John Steinbeck's 1926 novel *Cup of Gold* and Bob Marley and the Wailers' song 'You Can't Blame The Youth'. In 1942, cinema-goers watched Anthony Quinn in *The Black Swan*, a film that drew on the life of Sir Henry Morgan. Each year in early summer, Colombia's boating scene honours Wales's own menace of the seas. Mariners, boaters and cruisers complete a 400-mile race to Providencía in a good-natured battle that attracts a motley potpourri of sailing crafts. Morgan's Run (La Ruta de Morgan) takes place over several days, making landfall at Bajo Nuevo in the northernmost corner of Colombia before heading to Serrana and Low Cay. Providencía comes out in force to welcome the flotilla to the island before hosting a madcap rum-soaked award ceremony befitting of a man who liked his drink. On Providencía, several bars bear the name of Morgan. Santa Catalina has a Hotel El Pirata Morgan while a volcanic rock battered by the sea is said to resemble his face. Morgan is also the figurehead for Captain Morgan's Spiced Rum – an ironic legacy for a man whose alcoholism brought about his death from liver failure.

ISLA SANTA CATALINA *Telephone code: 8*

A brightly coloured 100m 'floating' bridge links the islet to neighbouring Providencía and exploring Santa Catalina on foot starts with a crossing. Green hills and rocky cliffs typify the landscape. Hidden caverns lie tucked away in volcanic outcrops edged by tiny soft-sand beaches. Santa Catalina has no roads. Some steep steps to the west of the bridge lead to a picture-pretty rocky beach, a decent spot from which to snorkel to spot octopus, lobsters and sea crabs.

On the southern flank of the island a small settlement contains a handful of fish-and-rice restaurants. From here, a short walk leads to Morgan's Head and the ruins of Fort Warwick – complete with cannons. History has ensured that Santa Catalina remains inextricably linked with Henry Morgan and several sites on the island are attributed to the Welsh buccaneer. Morgan's Head is a volcanic boulder carved by the breeze and now said to resemble the privateer's face. Under the rock, a natural pool is home to large barracudas; many thrill-seeking travellers jump from the rock straight into the depths. Santa Catalina's wild vegetation and rugged nooks and crannies are home to boa constrictors, iguana and numerous black crabs.

 ## WHERE TO STAY AND EAT

Posada Villa de Santa Catalina n/a. This pretty, private home is owned by Francia de Armas, a member of the Posadas Nativas home-stay programme. Leafy gardens surround this statuesque cream-painted wooden house with breezy terraces overlooking palms & lush shrubs. Snra de Armas opens her family home to tourists keen to learn about native island traditions and has a pleasant ochre-coloured dbl room for overnight guests. Typical dishes are served at mealtimes & cultural rituals observed. Rates vary, depending on the season. There's no phone at the Posada; just ask around town.

7

Amazonia

'Our land is special, a spiritual place. It's the lungs of the world, a rich botanical store-cupboard. I believe that the Earth gave us life. Our magnificent territory is sacred. Blessed by Mother Nature.'

Ticuna Indian elder (2007)

Few places in the world are as untamed and wild as the Amazon Basin, an isolated region swathed in vast, impenetrable jungle covering almost one-third of the Colombian territory. Exhilarating, humbling and awe-inspiring, the watershed is roughly the size of Germany, spanning 643,000km² and covering some 40% of South America as the largest lowland in Latin America. The river starts as a tiny trickle atop the snow-capped Andes Mountains and flows across the South American continent until it enters the Atlantic Ocean at Belém, Brazil. Reaching 40km in width at the height of the rainy season the mighty River Sea (as it is often referred to) can flood up to 350,000km² of land. Stretches of the Río Amazon are deep enough to accommodate ocean liners. Sections are fast-flowing and debris-scattered fed by over 1,100 tributaries, 17 of which are more than 1,000 miles long. This mammoth watershed contains over two-thirds of earth's fresh water in its rivers, streams and tributaries. From the headwaters of Peru's Ucayali-Apurímac river system the river flows for 6,400km to Brazil via Colombia, a distance slightly shorter than the Nile River but roughly the equivalent of a journey from New York City to Rome. Tiny wood-and-thatch Indian villages hug emerald vine-tangled riverbanks to the cacophony of squawking crimson parrots, chattering monkeys and whining insects in the treetops overhead. Piranha, crocodiles and dugout canoes navigate the waters of the mighty Amazon River and its many tributaries. Indian tribes hostile to strangers hide themselves away in the rainforest, living much as they did before European arrival, hunting, fishing, and eating a diet of berries, plants and fruit. Giant blue butterflies and water lilies the size of serving trays are just a couple of the highlights in this magical, surreal land. Hot, sticky conditions complete with vast swarms of hungry mosquitoes and reddish glue-like mud prevail along this brooding river stretch of inky green.

As a region, the Amazon is home to at least 7,500 species of butterfly, 1,800 birds, 800 insect species and almost 2,000 species of reptile and amphibian. It contains 3,200 species of fish and is home to a staggering 10% of all species found on the planet. Botanists have recorded 51,220 species of plant, but doubt they will ever be able to catalogue everything in the lifetime of the world. In a single acre of forest, as many as 100 arboreal species have been counted. Up to 121 million litres of water per second are generated by the Río Amazon with an average of 3 million tonnes of sediment deposited each day near its mouth. The annual outflow from the river accounts for 20% of all the fresh water draining into the entire world's oceans.

While the Colombian Amazon is, in reality, a small sector of the whole basin region, it is nonetheless complex and varied. Quite, quite different to the rest of

the region, it plummets from the Andes to low, forested plains. Extensive lowlands flank the river and its many tributaries (*várzeas*). Rapids and cascading waterfalls make Colombia's Amazonian waterways tricky to navigate but they are worth the effort nonetheless. Annual flooding is significant so soil is richer than the savannas with areas dotted with coarse igneous rock. Local tour operators generally include bits of Peruvian and Brazilian territories into their itineraries. Although this throws a mobile phone signal into confusion it does allow a greater chance to observe the astounding wonder of this unique environment. In some small way it also helps to capture the essence of scale in the Amazon's vast wilderness.

Today, despite the concerted efforts of humankind to dominate the natural resources of the Amazon region, this vast drainage basin remains intact. Carbon dioxide is absorbed at a phenomenal rate by this enormous, resplendent biomass – just one of the many environmental reasons that the Amazon is an important ecological component of the planet. Unlike the crude destruction of the forest in Brazil, the watershed remains a remote and undisturbed landscape in Colombia, primarily because it is inaccessible and foreboding. Razor-sharp machetes often struggle to slice a trail for even the most modest of treks through the Amazon's dense, multi-layered forest. These small clearings re-establish themselves relatively quickly. Unlike the commercial logging in Brazil, Colombia's indigenous communities rarely use an axe for large-scale deforestation, only felling the forest for their own small-scale needs.

HISTORY

Formed in the Palaeozoic period, somewhere between 500 million and 200 million years ago, the Amazon region boasts untold riches in geologic terms. Once, the

Amazon River flowed westward, possibly as part of a proto-Congo (Zaire) river system from the interior of present-day Africa when the continents were joined as part of Gondwana. When the South American and Nazca plates collided 50 million years ago, the Andes were formed, blocking the river and causing it to create a vast inland sea. Over time, the water became marshland and freshwater lakes prompting the evolution of marine life to adapt to this new saline-free environment. Some ten million years ago, the Amazon experienced its next geological milestone as the water forced its sandstone borders to begin the flow eastward prompting the birth of its forested areas. Mammals migrated, plants flourished and species spawned subspecies to create an incredible array of flora and fauna. During the Ice Age the levels of the great Amazon Lake dropped to become a river.

Isolated, inhospitable and riddled with disease-carrying biting insects, it is hardly surprising the Amazon was largely ignored by the civilised world until its discovery by Vicente Yáñez Pinzón in 1502. However, early European explorers were daunted by the tangle of dense vegetation through which they were forging and soon realised that it offered little in the way of fresh supplies of food. Pinzón ascended to a point about 50m from the sea, naming it the 'Río Santa María de la Mar Dulce'. He fast became known throughout the world as the first explorer to discover an estuary of the Amazon River. Yet it is Francisco de Orellana who is credited with giving the Amazon River its name. Born in 1511 in the town of Trujillo in the Spanish Esremadur province, Orellana was the son of a prominent family. The conquistador was hardly more than a boy when he first went to sea. He cut his teeth fighting Manca Inca but was tempted to venture further into South America in 1541 by tales of a land rich in gold – El Dorado. He had heard that the ruler of these lands dusted himself with gold each day and Orellana was keen to meet this fabled Golden Man. Orellana joined an expedition to a remote region east of Ecuador, trekking across rain-drenched mountains and hacking through native rainforest for seven months in desperate conditions. Eventually, the men arrived to the banks of a wide river, but not before some 4,000 of Orellana's comrades had died with many too sick or hungry to continue. The expedition set about building a boat to ferry the sick and dying upstream and soon the *San Pedro* was ready to sail. The men soon realised that the land ahead was vast and uninhabited, offering little in the way of food to help them survive. Orellano suggested that he take the boat and some 60 men down river in search of supplies as an alternative, agreeing to return within 12 days. However, the current was so strong that Orellano had no choice but to sail down river, with no hope of return.

During his terrifying journey Orellano's party survived several attacks by Indians, encountering a fierce tribe of warriors he swore were female. So strong and fearless were this tribe, Orellano compared them to Amazon women from Greek mythology, so when his crew made it alive despite near-starvation Orellano is said to have given the river its name. Historians now argue that the women were more likely long-haired male native fighters, although few alternative theories exist on how the river got its name. However, Orellano faced mixed fortunes on his return to Spain. Instead of being hailed a hero, he was widely viewed as a turncoat for deserting the rest of the expedition. Indeed he became known as the infamous 'One- Eyed Traitor' in certain circles, having lost an eye early in his career during one of many hand-to-hand battles. Francisco de Orellano returned to the Amazon region in 1549 where he died. Today he is credited with the distinction of having been the first man to have navigated the entire length of the Río Amazon, thus bringing recognition of its immensity to the world. He is honoured in Leticia by a park bearing his name.

The drum will be my home, the cradle my canoe
The river my road, the jungle my science
The land my base, the sun my reach
The air my lungs, the blood my sap.'

Francelina Muchavisoy, Inga Indian song, the Amazon (2006)

Even conservative estimates suggest that rainforest deforestation will destroy almost half of the world's 10 million species of plants, animals and micro-organisms or see them severely under threat within the next 25 years. Some 137 plant and animal species are lost every single day – a staggering 50,000 species a year. Serious conservation concerns exist in relation to the Amazon's role as one of the planet's most complex chemical storehouses. For although rainforests across the globe today provide sources for 25% of all modern medicines, a massive amount of untapped potential remains. Scientists are confident that some 70% of rainforest plants have some anti-cancer properties. However, at the current rate of deforestation, many of these plants will be extinct before studies can be carried out. The National Institute for Space Research (INPE) shows more than 25,000km^2 of forest were cleared in one year – with vast swathes of land logged to grow crops. Moderate figures suggest that in the last 15 years, more than 243,000 km^2 of the earth's forests have been destroyed. Just 100ha of Amazon rainforest can contain up to 1,500 different plant species, as many as in the whole of the UK.

A broader fear among ecologists is that deforestation and slash-and-burn has seen greenhouse gases increase. Other concerns include the impact of deforestation by the coca cultivation trade on the Amazon's ecosystem. In some of Colombia's key biodiversity hotspots vast quantities of glyphosate have been sprayed as part of a government initiative. Although figures suggest drug production has been slowed, it is far from eradicated. However, serious concerns surrounding the effects of the sprays continue to fuel protests from the local indigenous peoples, who claim surfactant chemicals and herbicides have penetrated the foliage of plants vital to their traditional medicines and diet. According to a survey by the Food and Agriculture Organization of the United Nations (FAO), deforestation in the Amazon rainforest suffered the largest net loss of forests between 2000 and 2005. However, in 2006 a WWF report suggested that deforestation rates in the Amazon were in decline, but warned that ranching, logging and agricultural activities were continuing to degrade the jungle, especially in the Brazilian Amazon where 17% of the natural vegetation has already been lost.

In a bid to protect their land, some indigenous tribes are using Google Earth, Global Positioning System (GPS) mapping and other technologies to combine traditional rainforest knowledge with Western technology to better conserve the Amazon's forests. The initiative, is designed to help the Indian communities preserve their ecosystem and medicinal plants through an enhanced understanding of their location and its threats. It is led by the **Amazon Conservation Team (ACT)** (✆ *703 522 4684;* f *703 522 4464;* e *info@amazonteam.org; www.amazonteam.org*), a US-based non-profit organisation working with a number of indigenous communities to help nurture a better understanding of conservation in the Amazon whilst protecting its biodiversity and rainforest culture. ACT was founded by Mark Plotkin, an accomplished author and renowned ethno botanist, who has spent much of the past 20 years with some of the most isolated indigenous groups in the world.

PEOPLE

Six comisariás (provinces) make up the Colombian Amazon region, Putumayo, Caquetá, Amazonas, Vaupés, Guainía and the Guaviare. The local Indian population is large and extremely diverse, though representing a thin spread (0.33 inhabitants per 1.6km²) across a territory that is still remarkably unexplored. Many of Colombia's ethnic and linguistic groups have their home in the world's largest rainforest, accounting for several hundred tribes and more than 100 languages and dialects.

The Tukanos, Gwananos, Taiwanos, Kubeos, Karapanás, Dsanos, Barasanas, Makunas, Sionas and Koreguajes all use the Tukanoan family of languages, while Witotan is spoken by the Boras, Witotos, Muinanes, Andokes and Mirañas. Many indigenous groups speak languages belonging to the Arawakan family, including the Yukunas, Tamimukas, Matapies, Kuripakos and Baniwas. A tiny population of Karibs speak a Karib derivative while numerous groups of nomadic Makús use a language that remains unclassified. Few large congregations of people exist outside of the administrative capital of Leticia. Unsurprisingly, this isolation has appealed to Colombia's narco-traffickers and leftist rebels who continue to seek sanctuary in the Amazon's secluded leafy depths.

Further information can be obtained from

Fundación Gaia-Amazonas Cra 4, No 26B–31, Bogotá; www.gaiaamazonas.org. NGO set up to strengthen indigenous conservation in the Colombian Amazon.

Indians of the Amazon e info@amazon-indians.org; www.amazon-indians.org. US-based educational resource for photos & videos of native indigenous people of the Amazon rainforest.

LETICIA *Telephone code: 8*

Providing a gateway to the Colombian Amazon, Leticia (*www.leticia-amazonas.gov.com*) sits on a narrow strip of land stretching south of the Putumayo River, at the point where the borders of Colombia, Brazil, and Peru meet (*tres fronteras*). Hot, steamy and often oppressively humid, Leticia retains the air of an isolated outpost despite good flight connections with Bogotá. Arrive on a small, low-flying plane to enjoy hours atop the rainforest canopy with no sign of human settlement. For a frontier town engulfed in wild, inaccessible jungle Leticia is actually remarkably pretty – and a welcome sight for new arrivals after several hours skimming across the Amazon's broccoli-like jungle. More than 500 miles from the nearest Colombian highway, it boasts a kaleidoscopic mix of restaurants, cafés and painted houses, set on grid-system streets that are parched in the dry season and boggy in the wet. Leticia and Tabatinga (Brazil) remain joined as a single city in many ways, with easy pedestrian and vehicular access and no clear border or patrol.

Leticia has grown considerably in the last decade to support increased levels of tourism. As the capital of the department of Amazonas, Leticia is home to the only major port on the river, although at first glance this seems a rather grand title for a muddy stretch of riverbank in Colombia's southernmost town. But while the port is nothing special, the atmosphere certainly is, amidst dozens of vendors and market stalls selling all manner of fruits beside a brightly coloured children's playground. Expect to find a mishmash of travellers sat patiently on their haunches by gently bobbing boats, from fresh-faced Scandinavian backpackers, American biologists and lone birdwatchers to an army of local Indians loading up giant sacks of maze, bananas and fish onto needle-thin dugout canoes.

Founded in 1867, this remote settlement of 37,000 people was originally christened San Antonio. Until 1932, it was part of Peru (see box, *Rumble in the jungle*, page 234) and because of this heritage and tri-border location, Leticia boasts

Amazonia LETICIA

7

Colombia's history of domestic warfare equipped it well to deal with its conflict with Peru. A powerful riverine fleet proved crucial in defending Colombian borders when the two nations went head-to-head over the control over the harbour town of Leticia in 1932. It wasn't the first time this Colombian Amazon settlement had been at the centre of a battle as Leticia had been up to its neck in boundary wrangles since the colonial era. An 1829 bilateral treaty was drawn up using the principle of *uti possidetis* (possession at end of war) but this failed to specify with true geographic accuracy the precise co-ordinates of the colonial boundary. A second agreement in 1930 was dismissed by Peru as biased to Colombian interests with four subsequent treaties in 1906, 1909, 1911 and 1922. However despite arbitration the opposing sides failed to agree on the nitty-gritty. Troops from both countries moved into the region and in 1911 things turned ugly. After Peruvian soldiers attacked the tiny Colombian garrison town of Puerto Córdoba both countries agreed a treaty limiting the number of troops in the area. In 1922, a subsequent treaty officially recognised the legitimacy of Colombia's boundary. However, Peru refused to ratify this agreement for six years. In 1928, the pact was finally signed and sealed with both parties confirming the lengthy border wrangle was resolved. In 1930, Colombia took formal possession of its territory although Peru took until 1932 to fully withdraw its troops.

Then, lo and behold, trouble flared up again when over 300 armed Peruvian civilians seized the town of Leticia in a bloody show of strength that saw arm-to-arm combat in the streets. Infuriated, Colombia immediately mobilised 1,500 soldiers to repel the invaders, prompting the Peruvian government to switch tact. Within a flash, it stopped openly criticising the actions of its unruly citizens and began speaking out in support of their protest. In early 1933, a Colombian river fleet was sent up the Amazon to Leticia to reclaim the town from the invaders. Months of diplomatic spite followed before both parties agreed on how to end the dispute. Brokered by the League of Nations, a provisional peace treaty was signed in May 1933, followed by yet another bilateral agreement in June 1934 when Leticia was formally returned to Colombian control. Peru issued an apology for the 1932 invasion, while Colombia pledged a non-aggressive future relationship based on mutual goodwill and bilateral co-operation. The agreement was ratified in September 1935 with relationships between the two cordial ever since.

plenty of linguistic, cultural and gastronomic influences born out of its past – and present. Leticia's melting pot of migrants includes umpteen ethnic fusions made up of Colombians from Cali, Medellín and Bogotá; Indians from at least several dozen jungle tribes across the Amazon; Peruvians; Brazilians; and those of a racial mix. However, few language barriers exist with a style of local 'Amazonian Spanish' generally spoken, littered with linguistic influences from Peru, Brazil and many indigenous cultures. Typical food also often fuses a myriad of culinary traditions, combining the hearty *sancocho* (soup) of Colombia with some fine Brazilian *churrasco* (barbecued meat) washed down with a glass of ice-cold Peruvian Cristal beer (see box, *Beer today, gone tomorrow*, page 236). However, around the town little has changed in generations. Indian tribesmen hunt and gather along the river while children swim and women wash in the shallows by the banks.

Today, like much of Colombia, Leticia is enjoying much improved safety. In the 1970s, the narco trade had an economic grip on the fortunes of the city. Trafficking became a new, fast way to make money in the region, along with shady contraband deals. Drugs were reportedly bought and sold in broad daylight with entire communities involved in the shipment of narcotics to some degree. For a time, Leticia basked in unprecedented prosperity as rich drugs cartels established themselves in the town. Vast sums of money were ploughed into big houses and river transportation. Bombarded with wealth, villagers chose to watch their brand-new televisions instead of gathering rubber plants. Prostitutes from Cali, Bogotá and Medellín worked two-week shifts in Leticia's three brothels making enough money in a six-month period to return home and live a life of luxury. Drugs were ferried along the Putumayo River to avoid the scrutiny of air carriers. Work also started on an ambitious 70km highway from Leticia to the Peruvian town of Tarapacá before the arrest of cartel members halted construction at the 12km mark. In a bid to eradicate the drug trade, a zero-tolerance police presence was installed in Leticia in the 1980s, followed by a significant investment in military strength. Today, this gateway to the Amazon is calm, safe and growing in confidence as a tourism destination. At sunset and dawn the town's Parque Santander becomes a cacophony of sound and colour as several thousand screeching *pericos* (small parrots) fill the skies in a magnificent, almost choreographed, display. Although the results of President Uribe's 2003 pledge to bolster the region's tourist potential have so far been a little disappointing, his visit to listen to the concerns of Leticia's townspeople in 2006 has given renewed hope. The sad fact is that Leticia is an all-too-easily overlooked jungle community. OK, it may be a metropolis by local standards, but it's a world away from the government bigwigs in Bogotá, and easily forgotten as a result.

YAGE: THE AMAZON'S LSD

This potent jungle brew is known by at least 42 indigenous names in the Amazon and is used by more than 70 of the region's several hundred indigenous tribes. Though widely separated by distance, language, culture and societal values, these very different communities each have this hallucinogenic tipple in common, be they in the jungle settlements of the Peruvian Amazon or the fishing villages of Ecuador, Colombia, Bolivia and Brazil. Called yage (or yaje) in Colombia, ayahuasca in Ecuador and Peru and caapi in Brazil, the drink is made from vines boiled with leaves from plants that include *Psychotria viridis* or *Diplopterys cabrerana* – to name just a couple. The result is a brew that is powerfully hallucinogenic thanks to alkaloids harmaline, harmine, d-tetrahydroharmine, and often N,N-dimethyltryptamine. Indigenous groups throughout the Amazon use yage as a medicine to enter the sacred supernatural world, to heal, divine and worship. Psychic effects vary depending on the amount imbibed but typically include brilliant visions in bright colours, macropsia (objects appearing larger than real life), seeing multiple people or animals, such as anacondas and jaguars. Nauseatingly bitter, yage is frequently drunk during dance ceremonies and generally causes vomiting and diarrhoea to the uninitiated. In recent years, the Western world has become increasingly curious about yage, prompting a growing number of Indian tour guides to tout it to pseudo-New Age/spiritual tourists. Some have reported extreme out-of-body-type experiences and an intense altered state of consciousness (ASC). Others report a sense of spiritual awakening or a strong (non-visual) acoustic 'psychedelic' trip.

The Unión de Médicos Indígenas Yageceros de la Amazonia Colombiana (Union of Yagé Healers of the Colombian Amazon, UMIYAC) (*www.amazonalliance.org*) was established in 1999, as a result of a gathering of 40 of the Colombian Amazon's most prominent shamans in Yurayaco, Caquetá. Seven tribes were represented in a meeting designed to share ideas relating to the future conservation of their forest, their medicine and their people.

An ice-cold beer is never far from the lips of most travellers in the Amazon. Sweat, mosquitoes, dust and dirt are the rasping tastes of the jungle. Searing heat and high humidity ensure dry, parched throats. Lips crack, tongues dry and the roof starts to burn. Suddenly saliva is in short supply. Mercifully, the Amazon's *tres fronteras* status means a decent cerveza isn't hard to find. Those prepared to devote a day to thirst quenching can savour the libation of three fine beer-drinking nations. For only in the Amazon can you sink a Skol, Brahma and Antarctica in Brazil in the morning, Cusqueña and Cristal in Peru ahead of an Aguila and a Póker at tea time back on Colombian soil.

In 2001, a national strike by brewery workers caused a widespread shortage that saw many Colombians wanting to cry in their beer. Annual total beer production of almost 80 million barrels makes Brazil the fourth-largest beer producer in the world. During the annual Carnaval period there is an explosion in beer consumption across South America. In these four days more beer is consumed in Colombia, Peru and Brazil than the total for the rest of the year. At any one time, more than 50% of the Colombian population has had a beer within the last seven days. According to the Latin American Association of Beer Manufacturers, Brazilians knock back an average of 47 litres of beer per year. Peruvians swear that Cusqueña is brewed with such purity it can be drunk without fear of a hangover. The average Colombian consumes 36.8 litres per annum. Between 1998 and 2005 the Peruvian beer market experienced a growth of 20%. Colombia's domestic beer market experienced a 30% decline in consumption between 1997 and 2002.

GETTING THERE

By air Catching a flight with AeroRepública (✆ 592 7666; *www.aerorepublica.com*) to Leticia's tiny Vásquez Cobo Airport remains your only option from Bogotá, although at the time of writing Leticia's tourist industry is campaigning heavily for increased competition in the market. Some seasonal fluctuations affect the frequency of the service, but expect three to four flights a week with high demand for seats during the peak months of January, August and December. From Brazil, a number of airlines connect Tabatina with Manaus, including Rico Linhas Aereas (✆ 92 4009 8333; *www.voerico.com.br.*). It has a main base at Eduardo Gomes International in Manaus (MAO). Both Leticia and Tabtatinga airports are served by a flurry of colectivos (communal taxis) that meet every flight and run back and forth all day. At the time of writing a twice-weekly service provided by small Peruvian airline Transportes Aereos Nacionales de la Selva (TANS) (*www.tansperu.com.pe*). from Santa Rosa to Iquitos looks under threat.

By boat As the only significant community for several hundred kilometres, Leticia may not be accessible by road but it does boast regular river connections with Iquitos (Peru), Manaus (Brazil), Florencia (Caquetá department) and other jungle towns.

To Manaus the super-fast express boat leaves from Tabatinga every day except Monday. The journey takes around ten hours and costs upwards of 100,000 COP. For a more leisurely pace opt for the three-day, four-night trip departing Tabatinga Wednesday, Friday and Saturday. Expect a 14.00 departure (but like most things on the Río Amazon this can be wide of the mark) and costs of around 95,000 – this is a real adventure if time isn't an issue. Additional boats sometimes run, so be sure to check this if a Tuesday, Thursday, Monday or Sunday departure is more preferable – you never know. Boats are likely to be packed out so be sure to board early in order to find a spot to hang your hammock (for sale everywhere in Leticia and Tabatinga at around US$8). Although food is included in the ticket price, bring plenty of bottled water and snacks for the journey as well as some toilet roll, a good lock for your luggage (theft on board can be a problem) and plenty of mosquito spray. Expect to pay around US$65 if you are bringing a hammock, or US$240 for a double cabin. The upstream trip from Manaus to Tabatinga takes a day or so longer and costs about US$110 (hammock) or US$330 for a double berth.

To Iquitos, the best way to travel from Tabatinga is on a high-speed passenger boat, departing in the early hours on a Sunday, Friday and Wednesday morning. The ten-hour trip costs about US$60 in either direction and includes breakfast and lunch in the price. Obtaining an exit stamp at Leticia's airport a day prior to departure is crucial. Another consideration is onward transport from Iquitos into Peru as there are no roads just riverboats (these take a week to reach Pucallpa). Another option is connecting flights.

GETTING AROUND The Colombian Amazon's difficult topography and isolation can make travel expensive, as it is practically impossible to navigate the region without a guide and a boatman. Many of the most reputable local independent tour operators are part of Fondo de Promoción Ecoturística del Amazonas (see *Tourist information*, page 238). Hiring a member of this organisation brings with it some guarantees in regards to quality and safety. It also avoids being ripped off on the basis of price and 'unforeseen' added costs and demands, a very good reason to resist the temptation to engage the services of a man on the street. Most visitors arrive by plane from Bogotá and feel an urgency to start exploring immediately. However, it's worth holding back from striding around Leticia as soon as you arrive in this quirky rainforest town – in the Amazon region there is no substitute for proper planning. Settle in slowly and see what's what at a nice, lazy pace. As with all jungle-based exploration, weather conditions play a major part in what is possible. Expect heavy rains from February to April when water levels can rise as much as 15m. Navigation is often easier in the dry months of July and August. The river peaks May to June and is at its lowest levels August to October.

All foreign arrivals are liable for an entry tax of 17,000 COP. Communal taxis (colectivos) nip backwards and forwards between the towns of Tabatinga and Leticia. Many visitors also travel between the two on foot or by local bus. Opposite

THE AMAZON'S NUMBER ONE GUIDE

Antonio Cruz is a rarity in Leticia, a worldly traveller who once lived in California but was born to a traditional Amazonian family. Twenty years of guiding have equipped him with considerable knowledge. This combined with a great enthusiasm for his homeland makes spending time with Cruz difficult to beat. His approach to guiding is simple: he gives visitors the experience that they want, rather than foisting on them what's simple. With flawless English and impeccable manners Cruz is also a plain-talking, easy-listening guy. Ask about the Amazon and its problems and he'll provide a wealth of intelligent insight into the challenges it faces. Antonio Cruz can organise anything in the Amazon Basin, from an exhilarating four-day wildlife trek or ecotour to a sedate cruise along the river. He owns Amazon Jungle Trips (see *Tour operators*, page 238) and is a founder member of the Fondo de Promoción Ecoturística del Amazonas (see *Tourist information*, page 238). He also speaks Italian and Portuguese. Cruz prefers working with groups smaller than half a dozen people and relishes trips that take him to the small nature reserves along the Río Yavarí.

lies the small Peruvian island of Santa Rosa. Frequent boats provide a shuttle service throughout the day. Several bike-hire shops and scooter rental yards are open seven days a week in Leticia. Expect to pay 30,000 COP a day for a scooter (plus petrol) and around 25,000 COP for a bike.

IMMIGRATION Moving between Leticia and Tabatinga is free from immigration formalities with no visa requirement or passport control. However, those planning to travel further into each country will need to meet normal immigration criteria, such as clearing passport control, getting an entry stamp and undergoing standard checks. This can be done at Leticia's airport or at the Policía Federal in Tabatinga on Avenida da Amizade 650 (closed noon–14.00). In Leticia, the Brazilian Consulate is open 08.00–16.00 (closed noon–13.00). Travellers should be sure to check visa requirements for entering Brazil from Colombia, especially those from Canada, the US and Australia who will need an ID photo and yellow fever vaccination certificate and will almost certainly be charged a fat fee. Crossing into Colombia from Brazil tends to be less bureaucratic. Visit the Colombian consulate on the Avenida Da Amizade Manaos in Tabatinga to check if in any doubt. Those travelling to or from Inquitos should pass through the Policía Internacional Peruviano (PIP) office on Santa Rosa to obtain an exit or entry stamp. Leticia's Peruvian Consulate is open Monday to Friday, but only from 09.00–14.000. Moving around the Amazon provides an excellent opportunity to add extra stamps in a passport, even for those on a flying visit.

TOURIST INFORMATION

Departamento Administrativo de Fomento Ecoturístico Calle 8, No 9–75; (8) 597 569; e turismoamazonas@hotmail.com

Fondo de Promoción Ecoturística del Amazonas Av Internacional, No 6–25; 310 229 9456. This self-regulating tourism association was established to raise standards across the local tourist industry. More than half of all businesses involved in tourism are now members. All work to a mandate of truthful service, customer focus & a spirit of co-operation.

Secretaria de Turismo y Fronteras Calle 8, No 9–75; 592 7569

TOUR OPERATORS Every hotel and backpacker joint will have umpteen tour guides they are happy to recommend. Taxi drivers at the airport will also try their best to introduce visitors to a cousin or friend. Tourist information offices will also be able to point you in the right direction. Due to recent reports of unscrupulous behaviour by guides touting for business, using a member of the Fondo de Promoción Ecoturística del Amazonas (see *Tourist information*, above) is highly recommended over a hustler on the street. Proper, registered Colombian tourist guides need a licence to operate legally. Cheap options are invariably a waste of money and unlike a registered, licensed outfit there is no recompense via a formal complaint. Engaging a guide who knows about red tape is also totally invaluable in the Amazon, given the complexities of negotiating a tri-country bureaucratic system that has more twists, turns and dead ends than the river itself.

Amazon Jungle Trips Av Internacional, No 6–25; 592 7377; e amazonjungletrips@yahoo.com. Visitors are spoilt for choice by an array of Leticia-based jungle tour companies, but this is undoubtedly one of the best. Punctual, reliable & multi-lingual (English, Italian, Spanish & Portuguese) this bunch are well organised. Opt for a standard 1-day tour or a more complex 3–4-day option. Good, knowledgeable guides – and nice people that care about what they do.

Paraíso Ecológico Carrera 11, No 6–106; 592 5111; e Paraísoecologico@hotmail.com. This small, independent tour company is run by the highly efficient Diva Mariá Santana Smith, a founder member of Leticia's Fondo de Promoción Ecoturística del Amazonas. Diva María organises tour programmes for groups or individuals & comes highly recommended. Although she speaks very little English herself she can engage bilingual guides on request.

I felt like urinating. I stood up. It was then it attacked me. It went deeper and deeper inside.

Silvio Barbossa, candirú victim (2006).

Forget the Amazon's predatory packs of carnivorous piranhas, prowling jaguars or giant anacondas, there are few more treacherous pastimes in the jungle than taking a pee in the river. Just uttering the word 'candirú' (*Vandellia cirrhosa*) can make a grown man wince. No, this isn't some mighty fearsome mammal with teeth the size of pitchforks, but rather a tiny vertebrate the size of a toothpick – sometimes known as the 'willy fish' in the Western world thanks to its loathsome reputation born out of its fondness for entering the human body via the urethra, the tube inside the penis. Once in, the barbs of the candirú jam it firmly into place. Squirm. Removal of this bloodsucker is a tricky procedure, that's if the patient survives the excruciating pain. Thankfully, only a handful of people have suffered a candirú invasion, but these isolated tales serve as a cautionary reminder to those caught short in the bush. Leg-crossing stories about the candirú have been horrifying men in the Amazon for generations, earning it the local name of 'vampire fish'.

One Amazonian fisherman reported being attacked as he waded naked in shallow water. The candirú swam towards him and forced its way at speed inside his penis. The man had tried to grab the fish but it was too slippery and fast.

Local shamen advise treating a patient with the xagua plant and the buitach apple. This does the trick, apparently, via insertion into the affected area (if space is tight, use an extract). Once the candirú is killed and dissolved it can be removed. There is no evidence the fish can survive once inside a human body.

Yurupary Amazonas Tours Calle 8, No 7–26; ☏ 592 4743; f 592 7983; e yuruparytours@hotmail.com. Reports are mixed about the standard of tours from this agency, based in the Yurupary Hotel. Programmes include Indian villages, dolphin spotting & trips out to the Jardín Zoológico Departmental.

AMAZON TOUR ITINERARIES Don't be fobbed off by a 'one-size-fits-all' tour package if it really doesn't appeal. The following itineraries are all pretty much standard, but can be easily tailored to a specific theme, such as birding or trekking.

Four days

Day 1 Leticia – Lake Yahuarcaca – Isla Santa Rosa (Peru) – Tabatinga (Brazil) – Leticia
Day 2 Isla de los Micos – Yagua and Ticuna Indian villages – Leticia
Day 3 Benjamin Constant (Brazil) – Leticia
Day 4 Leticia and Tabatinga city tour

or

Day 1 Leticia – Tarapacá
Day 2 Isla de los Micos – Yagua and Ticuna Indian villages – Reserva Natural Parana
Day 3 Full day at Reserva Natural Parana (kayaking, birding, hiking) – night safari
Day 4 Leticia and Tabatinga city tour

Amazonia LETICIA

7

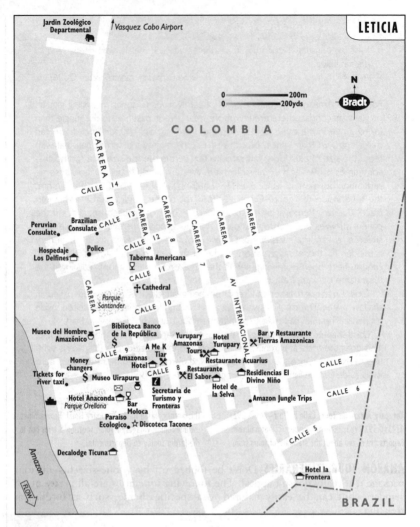

Five days

Day 1 Leticia – Reserva Natural del Zacambú (kayaking, birding, wildlife) – night safari

Day 2 Marajá Lagoon – Jungle wildlife tour – Zacambú Lodge

Day 3 Full jungle tour – night safari (optional jungle camping)

Day 4 Indigenous villages (Río Chítá) – Zacambú Lodge (hiking and wildlife spotting)

Day 5 Leticia and Tabatinga city tour

or

Day 1 Leticia – Tarapacá

Day 2 Isla se los Micos – Yagua and Ticuna Indian villages – Puerto Nariño

Day 3 Lake Tarapoto – Insituto OMACHA – Reserva Natural del Zacambú – night safari

Day 4 Marajá Lagoon – Jungle wildlife tour in Parque Nacion al Amacayacú – Zacambú Lodge
Day 5 Benjamin Constant (Brazil) – Leticia

Seven days
Day 1 Leticia – Tarapacá
Day 2 Benjamin Constant – Reserva del Zacambú – night safari (optional jungle camping)
Day 3 Full day in the jungle (kayaking, birding, hiking and wildlife spotting)
Day 4 Islas de los Micos – Yagua and Ticuna Indian villages – Puerto Nariño
Day 5 Full day in Parque Nacional Amacayacú (kayaking, birding, hiking and wildlife spotting)
Day 6 Full day in Parque Nacional Amacayacú (kayaking, birding, hiking and wildlife spotting)
Day 7 Return to Leticia (via Lake Tarapoto and Lake Yahuarcaca)

WHERE TO STAY Leticia has dozens of small hotels that offer good value for money. Most are clustered in the centre of town, by the park or near to the border. Unless you are an especially hardy soul, don't scrimp on a room without air conditioning or a particularly efficient fan.

Decalodge Ticuna Carrera 11, No 6–11; ☎ 592 6948; www.decameron.com. Visitors keen to enjoy the finest accommodation the Colombian Amazon has to offer should check out this luxury option. Top-notch thatched-roof cabins offer space, style & elegance overlooking a palm-edged terrace & pool area. Cocktails are served in a huge open-air bar by an army of smart-suited staff while a restaurant menu offers gourmet dining Amazonian style. $$$

Amazonas Hotel Calle 8, No 10–32; ☎ 592 8026/9859 28027. This rather bland green-painted building with yellow signage is located next to the very reasonably priced Restaurant Viejo Tolima, opposite the Panadería y Pastelería la Sevillana, one of Leticia's

BEWARE THE PIRANHA

They are undoubtedly among the most ugly fish on the earth today with powerful dentition famous for a lethal bite. Piranha have a sizeable presence in the waters of the Amazon, forming carnivorous congregations that have been known to attack livestock and even humans. Hatching from microscopic eggs, piranhas come into the world armed and dangerous, feeding on small crustaceans, seeds, fruits and aquatic plants. Their physical characteristics vary with location, population and age. Generally piranhas are reddish-orange ventrally and silver-grey-green dorsally with a black dorsal fin, black anal fin, and reddish-orange pectoral fins. Short, powerful jaws have a triangular, interlocking row of teeth that are not dissimilar to razor blades. Once they grow in size, piranha hunt in packs, using a wide array of hunting strategies to kill and devour their prey. Piranhas eat other fish and also practise cannibalism and infanticide. They also prefer to feed on their victims while still alive. Feeding frenzies can churn up the waters of the Amazon as in an effervescent blood-red bubble and when the piranha attack with true ferocity they can strip flesh from the bone within seconds. More than two dozen species of piranha have been catalogued in the Amazon so far. However, despite a fearsome, aggressive reputation, only a handful pose any threat to human life, such as the red-bellied piranha, *Pygocentrus nattereri*. However, many experts believe the ferocious reputation of the piranha is totally unwarranted. Yet, uncorroborated reports claim 300 people lost their lives to these toothy fiends when a boat capsized in the Amazon in the 1980s.

finest bakeries. Rooms have AC, TV, phone & private bathroom. There's also a bar, laundry, restaurant & a small swimming pool. $$

🏠 **Hotel Anaconda** Carrera 11, No 7–34; ☎ 592 7119; fax 592 7005; e Leticia@hotelanaconda.com.co; www.hotelanaconda.com.co. Past guests include Michael Palin and a host of Hollywood stars and the bright AC rooms in this well-located hotel are difficult to beat. Each has a large private bathroom & is clean, spacious & equipped with a minibar, phone & TV. Electrical plug sockets are also in good supply. Expansion in 2006 maximised the outside pool area to include a larger bar & restaurant. Ask for a room at the front of the building for balcony views across the Francisco de Orellana Park & out to the river (room 301 has 3 sgls & a huge bathroom) — perfect for those keen to be right in the thick of it during fiesta season. $$

🏠 **Hotel la Frontera** (16 rooms) Av Internacional, No 1–04; ☎ 592 5600; e fronterahotel@hotmail.com. Drive too fast across the Tabatinga–Leticia border & you'll miss this nice little hotel. The AC rooms include a good mix of dbls, trpls & family-sized accommodation & are meticulously clean. Views of both Brazil & Colombia can be enjoyed from a breezy rooftop terrace bar & restaurant. Look out for the huge painted mural-style advert for this place as you wait patiently in the heat by the luggage carousel at Leticia's Aeropuerto Internacional Vásquez Cobo Airport. $$

🏠 **Hotel Yurupary** Calle 8, No 7–26; ☎ 592 7983; e hotelyurupary@hotmail.com; www.hotelyurupary.co.nu. This good-value option is well located 50m from a dirt-cheap 24-hr diner & has

large, clean brightly furnished rooms set around a picturesque, leafy courtyard. The hotel's substantial buffet b/fast costs just 6,000 COP with lunch & dinner options from 12,000 COP & a well-stocked bar. Look out for the red & yellow sign set back from the road. $$

🏠 **Hospedaje Los Delfines** (9 rooms) Carrera 11, No 12–81; ☎ 592 7388; e losdelfinesleticia@hotmail.com. This friendly family-run small hotel has simple courtyard rooms that come with a fan & private bathroom. No frills, but good value. $

🏠 **Hotel de la Selva** Calle 7, No 7–28; ☎ 592 7616; e hoteldelaselvaleticia@hotmail.com. Dbls, trpls & quadruple accommodation may be small & sparsely furnished but each room has AC, private bathroom, TV, phone & minibar. An onsite restaurant & laundry are also a real boon for those on the go. A reliable & popular option with a loyal clientele — look for the painted green entrance. $

🏠 **Hotel Fernando** Real Calle 9; ☎ 592 7362. Simple fan-cooled rooms are without frills but OK nonetheless. Located a few doors down from the Tropical Casino opposite the A Me R Tiar Restaurant. $

🏠 **Residiencias El Divino Niño** Av Internacional, No 7–23; ☎ 592 5598. Shoestring travellers rave about this tatty-looking little border hotel because its dirt-cheap room rates are great for stretching a budget. Twenty fan-cooled rooms with a private bathroom are clean & well cared for by kindly housekeeper Betty. Owners Karen & Edgar are renowned for their hospitality & this warmth makes the El Divino Niño a very pleasant place to stay. $

✗ **WHERE TO EAT** Leticia is blessed with dozens of good cafes, bars and restaurants with decent food served as the norm. In the centre of town a number of no-fuss local eateries serve Amazonian fare from early til late at shoestring prices. Some of the best include the Amazon Sazón Restaurante, Restaurante Viejo Tolima, Restaurante Los Paisano and Restaurante Marina where a daily menu of fresh fish (usually gamitana or pirarucú), rice and plantains comes in at under 6,000 COP. Other good options as follows.

✗ **Bar y Restaurante Tierras Amazónicas** Calle 8, No 7–50; ☎ 592 4748; ⊕11.30–late. Don't be put off by the fact that this quirky food haunt is aimed squarely at the tourist — the menu is as terrific as the Amazonian clutter hanging from the rafters. Jungle bric-à-brac & Indian artefacts adorn every inch of wall space in this wooden-clad diner. Huge tropical ceiling fans whir slowly over bench-style tables with mezzanine & street-side seating when the restaurant gets full. A wooden menu has soups, juices, grilled meats, fish, chicken dishes a mile long as well as numerous cocktail options — beware the potent Caipirina Limón as it really packs a punch. $$

✗ **A Me K Tiar** Carrera 9, No 8–15; ☎ 592 6094; ⊕noon–midnight. This popular grilled-meat joint attracts a mixed crowd of locals & tourists with low prices & a good menu ensuring the place is always packed out. $

✗ **Restaurante El Sabor** Calle 8, No 9–25; ☎ 592 4774; ⊕everyday. The 24-hr cheap, tasty food makes this a popular backpacker hangout. Hearty chicken-&-rice meals come in well under 6,000 COP & include an unlimited refill of fruit juice. Other menu items include salads, vegetarian burgers & fruit pancakes. $

✕ **Restaurante Acuarius** Carrera 7, No 8–121; ✆ 592 5025; ◷ 07.00–21.00. Serving some of the best fish in the city, the Acuarius is celebrated for its pan-fried pirarucú & gamitana & is a nice place to grab a bite in the open air.

ENTERTAINMENT AND NIGHTLIFE Some of Leticia's most innocuous buildings transform themselves into lively salsa bars and drinking dens after dark. Many are clustered along Calle 8 with some in Calles 11 and 10. During peak tourist months the Bar y Restaurante Tierras Amazónicas (see *Where to Eat* above) is the place to party when the staff crank up the volume on the CD player and the salsa doesn't stop until dawn. Numerous impromptu fiestas take place in the Parque de Orellana while many of Leticia's larger hotels host live music during the busiest months. Leticia's only legal gambling joint is the garish-looking **Tropical Casino** on Calle 9, a hotbed of local gossip and scandal and an *en vogue* place to be seen.

♗ **Bar Moloca** Carrera 11, No 7–34; ✆ 592 7119; ✆ 592 7005. For a sundowner away from the hubbub of Leticia's street noise, head to the open-sided poolside bar at the Hotel Anaconda. Cocktails, beer & wine (by the glass, half-bottle or bottle) are served to salsa classics on an aged jukebox while flocks of pericos screech overhead.
☆ **Discoteca Tacones** Carrera 11, No 6–14; ✆ 592 7719. This rather uninspiring nightspot is the place in Leticia to let your hair down. A decent dance floor is heaving in peak season when a sea of sweaty bodies strut their stuff to raunchy Latino beats.
♗ **Taberna Americana** Carrera 10, No 11–108. Few places in Leticia can boast as much aguardiente consumption as the Taberna Americana. Swaying glassy-eyed men burst into song to the distorted sounds of salsa emitting from the speakers. For a night of drink-soaked camaraderie this rustic booze-joint has a certain charm.

SHOPPING Leticia has a reasonable range of shops geared to tourists passing through, but is far from being a retail paradise. T-shirts, souvenirs and trinkets are sold from stalls along the street with some interesting artefacts and rustic art for sale in some scruffy-looking makeshift galleries opposite the Parque de Orellano. Those stocking up on food supplies ahead of a day in the jungle should be sure to pay a visit to one of Leticia's many excellent bakeries. La Casa Pan on Calle 11 is highly recommended as is Panadería Las Delicias on Calle 9 and the first-class Panadería y Pasteleria la Sevillana on Calle 8. Leticia's biggest souvenir and handicraft shop is the Uirapuru Galería Artesanal, an open-fronted place on Calle 8 (✆ *592 7056*). Expect to find all manner of indigenous knick-knacks, some more authentic than others, including handwoven hammocks, spears, tablemats, pottery and jewellery made from seeds and nuts.

OTHER PRACTICALITIES
Banks and money As you'd expect in a commercial triple-border town, Leticia is blessed with dozens of places to change money. Most are around Calle 8, Carrera 11 and the market where it is easy to obtain US dollars, Colombian COP, Peruvian soles and Brazilian reais. Rates vary dramatically so be prepared to shop around if clinching the best deal in town is important to your pocket. Leticia's three banks are located on the corner of Calle 10 and Calle 7. All have ATM facilities but are loath to change dollars and have unpredictable policies regarding travellers' cheques. Both reais and COP are generally widely accepted in Tabatinga and Leticia, especially by larger businesses and hotels.

Emergency numbers
Police ✆ 112 or 592 5066

Internet Internet cafés continue to spring up across town. Expect to pay about 2,000 COP per hour, possibly as much as 3,000 COP in the newer, swanky places.

You can't scream if you can't breathe.

Anaconda, 1997

Hunting its prey with considerable stealth before crushing it into a breathless state, the mighty green anaconda (*Eunectus marinus*) is revered by Amazon Indians and Hollywood film-makers alike. Reaching 10m long and around 130kg in weight, the world's largest snake lives both in water and on land, hunting in the rainforests and river systems of the Amazon amongst swamps and sluggish streams. Olive green in colour with black blotches down the length of its body, the green anaconda has a narrow head with distinctive orange-and-yellow stripes on both sides and high-set eyes. It can survive for around three months on a sizeable kill, using its vast, powerful muscular body to coil and constrict birds, reptiles and mammals. Although large anacondas may occasionally consume large prey such as deer, caiman, tapir and capybara, such large meals are rare.

Exaggerated tales of anaconda attacks on humans frequently do the rounds in the Amazon, but can rarely be proven. Strikes are rare and are generally attributed to self defence. However, this hasn't prevented the green anaconda from becoming one of the most exaggerated animals on earth in regards to tales of its size. Unconfirmed reports abound about sightings of beasts up to 40m, with the Brazil–Colombia Boundary Commission claiming an anaconda of some 27.5m in 1933. In 1948, a 30.5m-long anaconda was reportedly killed in Fort Tabatinga on the Río Oiapoc, giving rise to the sorts of fearsome jungle myths of which films are made. In the 1997 blockbuster film *Anaconda* some of the terror that this vast reptile can create unnerved cinema-goers across the globe. Yet despite starring Jennifer Lopez and rapper Ice Cube the movie failed to impress the world's herpetologists due to the script's many fundamental errors. Not only did the film portray the anaconda's speed, reproductive habits and feeding rituals incorrectly, in one scene the animatronic anaconda shorted out and can clearly be seen out of control in the final cut. An ill-conceived storyline of an ill-fated *National Geographic* expedition also took a bit of swallowing, as did the

However, one thing is certain: wherever you choose to log on in Leticia – the connection is sure to be painfully slow. Some of the better options include Indio.net at the Centro Commercial AcuaRíos on the corner of Carerra 7 and Calle 8 and AMI on Carrera 10. Both offer printing, photocopying and other sundry services and sell a limited stock of consumables.

Laundry, supplies and repairs Leticia's good handful of drug stores and pharmacies are mostly centred on Calle 8 with almost every hotel offering laundry services at competitive rates. At the Hotel Anaconda, one of Leticia's most expensive hotels, a whole set of clothes can be laundered for about 6,000 COP – that's a shirt, a pair of shorts, socks, underwear and a pair of jeans. Laundry at the Hotel Amazonas is slightly cheaper with the cost of laundering the entire contents of a suitcase unlikely to exceed 55,000 COP. At the Lavandería Aseo Total on Calle (↘ 592 6051) a kilo of washing costs US$1.50. Travellers in need of twine, tent pegs, tarpaulins, mallets and machetes will find at least three hardware vendors in the centre of town. There's also a camera repair shop and a couple of places that will mend boots and shoes.

SAFETY Leticia is a calm and safe town posing few problems for travellers. On the river, all prime points of interest can be visited without concern. However, long treks deep into the jungle require careful planning, as forested areas can be egg-hatching scene – anacondas don't lay eggs, they give birth to live snakes. Unsurprisingly, this modest box office hit was critically panned, garnering six nominations in the 1997 Golden Raspberry awards. Many critics sniped that the CGI (computer generated graphic) snake had also upstaged other members. The green anaconda is not officially registered as threatened, but it is protected by the **Convention on International Trade in Endangered Species** (CITES) (✆ +41 (0) 22 917 81; f +41(0) 22 797 34 17; e info@cites.org; www.cites.org).

Further information from **Come Back Alive** (✆ 1 800 504 0640; www.comebackalive.com), author and adventure traveller Robert Young Pelton's live-dangerously stay-safe site, and the **Adopt an Anaconda Programme** (e jesus@anacondas.org), an independent funding initiative for anaconda conservation worldwide.

FACED WITH AN ANGRY ANACONDA? The US government Peace Corps Manual suggests that its volunteers in the Amazon jungle do the following to survive an anaconda attack:

- Do not run. The snake is faster than you are.
- Lie flat on the ground, put your arms tight against your sides and your legs tight against each other.
- Tuck your chin in.
- The snake will begin to nudge and climb over your body.
- Do not panic.
- The snake will begin to swallow your feet first.
- You must lie perfectly still. This will take a long time.
- When the snake has reached your knees, reach down, take your knife, slide it into the side of the snake's mouth between the edge of its mouth and your leg.
- Quickly rip upward, severing the snake's head.
- Be sure you have your knife.
- Be sure your knife is sharp.

inaccessible and also unsafe. Advice from the British Foreign Office at the time of writing is not to visit Putumayo or Caquetá. Putumayo, close to the Ecuador border, has become a prime focus of the government's coca-plant crop-spraying programme in accordance with the US$44 billion US-sponsored anti-drug effort, informally known as Plan Colombia II (see page 12). It also has a history of leftist FARC guerrilla activity, right-wing paramilitary units and regular Colombian military force. Caquetá is also a drug-trafficking centre where left-wing insurgents remain strong.

WHAT TO SEE AND DO

Jardín Zoológico Departmental (*Avenida Vásquez Cobo;* ⊕*08.00–17.00 daily, closed noon–14.00; admission 2,000 COP*) Located near the airport, the place has a rundown, ramshackle air – and although it has just a measly entrance fee it isn't an attraction for those who truly love wildlife. A reasonable collection of Amazonian animals look forlorn and listless. However, those prepared to overlook this can witness huge anacondas on an up-close-and-personal basis. A zookeeper asks visitors who'd like a photo taken with a snake, before plopping a massive anaconda around their neck with great aplomb. Other species include tapir, ocelot, owl, eagle, macaw and some little monkeys. Every animal is named, so if you like your caiman called Paulisto or your manatee called Polo, this is the zoo for you.

'Neither whisper, sweetest, soft from the peaceful springs that slip away across the
meadow fair;

nor the howl a forest downpour brings,

those through the thickness to the ear supplied;

nor starlight splendours vivid flair,

beacons hanging up on high when sparkling, beauteous, in midair, amidst the mists of dark
night's sky,

have not ever terrible deep marks produced,

those unnameable impressions in me loosed like when I gaze upon your course's pitch
and roll Oh! I feel you, sacred river! in my soul.'

Fabriciano Hernàndez, Amazonian poet (*Hymn to the Amazon*, 1868)

Although many of the native tongues of the Amazon are without a written form, the
region has produced many generations of poetry, song and verse. Most have their
roots in the myth, history, geography and cultures of the Amazon. Many centre on the
power of the river as a crucial life force. Indeed, the Amazonian vast water system
unifies much of the work of these wordsmiths through the rich colours of the poetry,
stories and verses of the Amazon's traditional indigenous groups. Many themes explore
the dismay felt at the threat to their survival or look at the complex relationship
betweens humans and nature. Some describe colonial and neo-colonial exploitation of
the land and its inhabitants by bards who frequently assumed the role of spokesperson
for social justice. One story born out of the myth of the magical *boto* (pink river
dolphin) tells of its metamorphosis into human form. Another recounts the origins of
the Amazon River through the inconsolable and torrential weeping of a beautiful love-
struck girl. Jungle life has provided the Amazon tribesfolk with an extraordinary number

Museo del Hombre Amazónico (*Carerra 11, No 9–43;* ☎ *592 7729;* ⏰*09.00–14.30
Mon–Fri, 09.00–13.00 Sat; free admission*) This small collection of artefacts contains
some household items and implements gathered from a small number of
indigenous communities in the region.

Museo Uirapuru (*Calle 8, No 10–35;* ☎ *592 7056*) This backroom collection is at
the rear of Leticia's biggest handicraft and souvenir shop, the Uirapuru Galería
Artesanal. If, like me, you like your wildlife to be alive this depressing range of
dusty stuffed animals, snakeskins, turtle shells and pickled birds will fail to
impress.

Biblioteca Banco de la República (*Carrera 11 No 9–43; open 9.00–15.00
Tues–Sat; free admission*) Housed in this modern orange-coloured building is a
fine (if small) collection of artefacts including masques, instruments and pots
gathered from the Ticuna and Huitoto Indian tribes. It is funded by the Banco
de la República as a lobby showpiece. A guide is obligatory, but only speaks
Spanish.

Birding around Leticia Birdwatchers in the Amazon have reported sighting a wide
range of birdlife in the forested areas immediately surrounding the town centre.
These include the white-vented euphonia, purple-throated fruitcrow, grey antbird,
spot-winged antbird, ochre-bellied flycatcher, black-spotted barbet, cinereous
antshrike, reddish hermit, black-throated hermit, violaceous trogon, ocellated
woodcreeper and brownish twistwing.

above **Open-air thermal baths at Santa Rosa**
(DITUR) page 326

left **The quiet country lanes of Barichara, Santander**
(DITUR) page 162

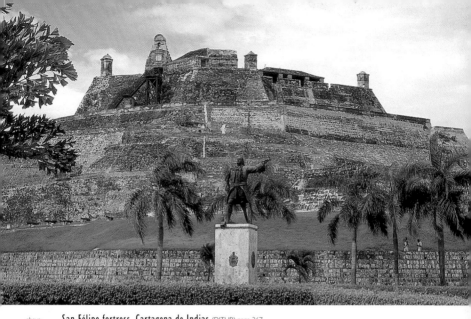

above   San Félipe fortress, Cartagena de Indias (DITUR) page 367

below right   Stone carving in Parque Arqueológico — one of Colombia's World Heritage sites — in San Agustin. (DITUR) page 278

below left   The coast at La Guajira (DITUR) page 395

above **The looming rock face of El Peñol, Medellín** (DITUR) page 307

below left **One of the five permanently white-tipped volcanoes in Los Nevados National Park** (DITUR) page 318

below right **Salto de Tequendamita — 132m high** (DITUR) page 308

above **Lush forests of Manizales ecological park** (SW) page 311

below **The salt flats at Manaure** (DITUR) page 400

above   **Anaconda**
(*Eunectes murinus*)
(AH) page 421

left   **Blunt-headed tree snake**
(*Imantodes cenchoa*)
(AA) page 421

below left   **Red-eye tree frog**
(*Agalychnis callidryas*)
(AA) page 422

below right   **Helen's morpho butterfly**
(*Morpho helenor*)
(AA) page 422

above left **Green violet-ear hummingbird**
(Colibri thalassinus)
(AA) page 419

above right **Capybara**
(Hydrochaeris hydrochaeris)
(AH) page 419

right **Giant anteater**
(Myrmecophaga tridactyla)
(KS) page 418

below left **Keel-billed toucan**
(Ramphastos sulfuratus)
(BRM/TIPS) page 419

below right **Pink-toe tarantula**
(Avicularia metallica)
(FT/TIPS) page 423

top **Brazilian tapir**
(Tapirus terrestris)
(AH) page 418

above **Three-toed sloth**
(Bradypus variegates)
(AA) page 418

left **Ocelot kitten**
(Felis pardalis)
(PO) page 417

of folk legends evoking numerous magnificent legacies that honour one of the world's most important river cultures.

In the 1970s Russian poet Yevgeny Aleksandrovich Yevtushenko added his unique style of poetry to the Amazon's lengthy literary heritage. This spokesman for the post-Stalin generation of Russian poets travelled through the Amazon, spending some time in the town of Leticia, from where he spotted a large fire burning on the south side of the river. Alarmed, he suggested to his Colombian hosts that they all cross the river to help extinguish the flames, but they were dismissive. 'No importa; es del lado peruano' ('Who cares; it's on the Peruvian side'), they shrugged. Yevtushenko was appalled, putting pen to paper to create a poem in Spanish to encourage better Amazonian unity:

No hay lado colombiano (There is no Colombian side)
No hay lado peruano (There is no Peruvian side)
Solo hay lado humano (There is only the human side)

Yevgeny Aleksandrovich Yevtushenko

Some of the Amazon's most acclaimed modern-day poets, essayists and authors include Thiago de Mello, Paes Loureiro, Raúl Otero Reiche, Pedro Shimose, Nicomedes Suárez Araúz and Julio de la Vega, among others. In *Folklore de la Foresta*, a range of Amazon-inspired children's tales, such as *Ranito*, is based on actual events around Leticia. In *Yumo* a young boy watches the tribal elder cross the Amazon River and dreams of being able to walk on the bottom like the chief.

Further information can be obtained from the Centre for Amazonian Literature and Culture (CALC) (e *nsuarez@sophia.smith.edu; www.smith.edu/calc*) and Poets and Writers Against the Destruction of Amazonia (PWADA) (*www.smith.edu/calc/pwada*)

AROUND LETICIA

LAGO YAHUARCACA This picturesque lake island is edged by multi-coloured heliconias and palms dotted with parrots, but it is for its giant lilies (*Victorias regias*) that most people visit. Easily reached via a short jaunt from Leticia, this natural collection of the world's largest water lily (named after Queen Victoria) is a favourite with local tour guides, many of whom will explain its 93-day lifecycle and the co-existence role it supposedly plays with piranha. Try to pluck the lily from the water and you're likely to sustain a scratch from a thorn, attracting piranha from far and wide with the smell of blood.

PARQUE NACIONAL AMACAYACU This 293ha expanse of rainforest is located about 75km upriver from Leticia, occupying a large part of the Amazon trapezoid. Jointly run by the municipalities of Leticia and Puerto Nariño this stunning protected stretch of wilderness is accessed by an exhilarating boat ride up the Río Amazon to the Quebrada Matamata at the edge of the park. The name *Amacayacú* means 'Hammock River' in Quechua, the widest-spoken Indian language in the world today. In 1542, the Spanish conquistador Francisco de Orellana discovered Kahuapanas, Jeberos, Boras, Kotuenes, Jiduas, Muinanes, Mirañas, Andokes, Huitotos, Omaguas, Yaguas, Cocamas, Otucunas and Ticunas in this part of the Amazon Basin. Today only the Tikunas remain in their ancestral land. Amacayacú's terrain has two very different landscapes, the rolling and relatively dry scrubland that supports vegetation and the swampy marshes of the floodlands. A spectacular array of trees can reach up to 100–130ft high on drier terrain. Mammoth ceiba trees

7

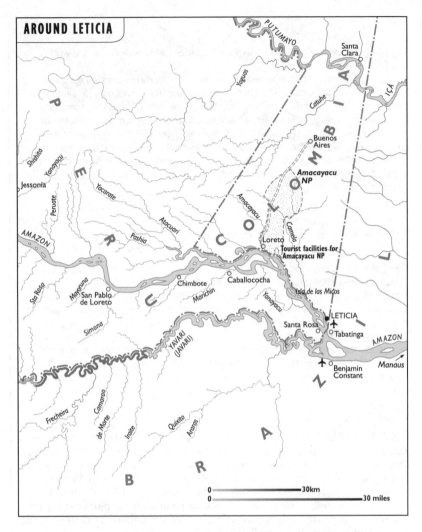

(map labels)

PUTUMAYO

Santa Clara

Yaguas

ICA

Catuhe

P E R U

COLOMBIA

Buenos Aires

Amacayacu NP

Shishita

Yanayacu

Yacarate

Jessonia

Peruate

Amacayacu

Camela

Atacuari

Pashia

Loreto

AMAZON

Tourist facilities for Amacayacu NP

Sta Rosa

Chimbote

Caballococha

Isla de los Micos

Mengruna

San Pablo de Loreto

Marichín

Yanoyacu

LETICIA

Santa Rosa

Tabatinga

AMAZON

Simona

YAVARI (JAVARI)

Benjamin Constant

Manaus

B R A Z I L

Frecheira

Camaraco

de Morte

Iraite

Quixito

Araras

0 ——————— 30km

0 ——————— 30 miles

need up to 30 people to fully encircle their girth. Other species include red and white cedar, mahogany, rubber, balsam, caoba and uvo. In the boggy wetlands the spectacular Victoria lily, Capiron and Munguaba trees are typically found along with 150 mammals and dozens of reptiles and snakes, Species range from caiman, boa snake, anaconda, danta, jaguar, otter, pink dolphin (boto), black alligator, coral snakes, and monkey (including the small but resplendent golden lion tamarin) to the jabuti, the world's largest freshwater tortoise. More than 500 species of birds include flocks of brightly coloured parrots. Short-tailed swift, thrush-like wren, screaming piha, yellow-browed antbird, yellow-browed tody-flycatcher, rufous-bellied euphonia blue-throated piping-guan, red-throated caracara, scarlet macaw, chestnut-fronted macaw, black-spotted barbet, lettered aracari, cuvier's toucan, fasciated antshrike, striped woodcreeper, Amazonian umbrellabird, chestnut woodpecker, scarlet-crowned barbet, black-fronted nunbird and dusky-chested flycatcher have also been sighted here, while parcucú and piranha are among the park's rich abundance of fish. With the aid of a guide, the Río Yavarí is the perfect arterial for a four–seven-day trip. Look for anaconda with a torch at night or learn the art of basketry from an Indian craftsman. Sling a hammock to escape the ferocity of the afternoon heat after dining on palm-wrapped fish, rice and plantain.

Excursions into the wilds of Amacayacú begin at the confluence of the Quebrada Matamata and this is where every birder, hiker and kayak launch departs. Every visitor is assigned a local guide for a range of tours that include night safaris, camping, fishing and visits to Indian villages. Prices vary but entry for non-nationals starts at 20,000 COP per person with group rates and discounts that alter depending on the season. Most people allow a good couple of days to do Amacayacú justice. Book at the Aviatur office on Calle 7 near Carrera 11 (*www.grupoaviatur.com*).

Further information may be had from **Territorial Amazonía–Orinoquía** (*Calle 14, No 8–79 Piso 2; Bogotá;* \ *2431940;* e *amazonia@parquesnacionales.gov.co; www.parquesnacionales.gov.co*).

Getting there and away The best way to reach the park is to catch the daily passenger boat from Leticia to Puerto Nariño. It passes by the Amacayacú Park Visitor Centre so simply ask to be dropped off on the way. To be sure of a seat, don't leave things to chance. Book in advance at 20,000 COP for a journey that will take about two hours. For the return trip, a certain amount of patience is required, unless you have found a way to secure a seat. Try enlisting help from staff at the visitor centre as they are usually prepared to flag a boat down at around about noon and 16.00 each day.

Where to stay

Amacayacú Resort \ 284 90 12; www.decameron.com. This collection of thatched-roofed cabins is run by hotel chain Decameron with 3 twin cabañas named after the Yacaruna, Huito and Tangarana indigenous tribes of the Amazon while a family-sized cabin bears the name of the region's giant lily, *Victoria amazonica*. Although Decameron is usually associated with mid-range to luxury accommodation, the Amacayacú is a simple, rustic affair. However, each cabin does have a private hot-water bathroom. It also offers a cheaper standard of accommodation with an overnight stay in a hammock or bunk available. These are in large dormitory-style cabins that are pretty well protected from bugs & insects. Camping is not permitted within the park. Onsite facilities include a decent restaurant where meals start at 10,500 COP. There are also communal showers & toilets with bedding provided. Bring plenty of mosquito repellent (enough to give clothes, skin & hair a major dousing), a torch & some waterproof gear. Accommodation can be booked at the Aviatur office on Calle 7 near Carrera 11 (*www.grupoaviatur.com*) or direct with the resort.

PUERTO NARIÑO (*www.puertonarino-amazonas.gov.co*) This tiny pedestrianised jungle town has a population of fewer than 5,000 with quiet sleepy streets that make even Leticia feel like New York's urban sprawl in comparison, albeit just 75km away. At the heart of the community is a dual-use basketball and football court, flanked by the might of the river one side and a raised wooden boardwalk on the other. Young boys clad in Brazil football shirts hone their keepy-uppy skills while women braid hair and sew in the shade. Billiard games, dominoes and idle gossip centre on this hub of town in weathered open-fronted buildings. After dark every resident of Puerto Nariño young or old seems to descend on the wooden bench seats overlooking the courts, from giggling toddlers and love-struck teens to groups of wrinkled elders.

Neat, paved footpaths divide Puerto Nariño, characterising the town as improbably tidy. Cars are banned, apart from a battered VW van that collects the trash. Puerto Nariño is also the only place in Colombia to embrace recycling as a citizen-led initiative, an idea that on the face of it seems more likely in an urban centre than a small jungle outpost. Yet the residents of Puerto Nariño are surprisingly well versed in environmental matters, possibly as a result of the many biologists, ecologists and conservationists that pass through (see box, *An Eden for ecologists*, opposite). A piece of rogue litter would likely be seized upon within minutes, if not seconds. Rubbish bins are in plentiful supply, gardens are well maintained and neighbourhoods seem to positively burst with community pride. This neatness is challenged a little when the rainy season arrives and its children's playground resembles a paddling pool; even more so when the population swells to accommodate entire communities seeking sanctuary from rising tides. Kids attempt to play five-a-side in murky knee-deep water while men wade through thick mud with giant crates of yam and yucca. Yet most fresh arrivals will be greeted by Puerto Nariño's pseudo-suburban scene of a green public park on a backdrop of turquoise-painted single-storey wooden houses edged by lush garden palms. It has freshly swept pavements and an electricity supply that ceases with an abrupt clank at 22.00.

Tourist information
🖳 **Puerto Nariño Informacion Turistica** `313 2688 901`

Getting there The easiest way to reach Puerto Nariño from Leticia is by booking a seat with one of the handful of boat companies that run a daily weekday schedule of passenger services there. This is easily organised via all Leticia-based hotels and hostels or can be booked direct with the boat operators in offices on Calle 8 near the riverfront. Departures are at around 09.30 and 13.30 but are often affected by the water levels of the river and weather conditions. Pre-booking a ticket (about 25,000 COP) is a wise precaution as these boats are often full. Try Expreso Tres Fronteras, Transporte Amazónico or Expreso Líneas Amazonas. Another alternative is to book one of the umpteen tour companies that include Puerto Nariño as a final port of call on its full-day itinerary. Chartering a vessel can be an expensive option at 120,000 COP unless there are others in a similar predicament prepared to chip in and share the cost.

Getting around As a tiny, pedestrian town Puerto Nariño is easily navigable on foot. To visit local points of interest along the river simply head down to the riverfront. You'll find several local boatmen waiting to ply their trade as well as other travellers keen to share the cost.

🏠 Where to stay
🏠 **Casa Selva** (12 rooms) `310 221 4379`; e casaselvahotel@yahoo.es. The comfortable rooms in this fine wooden 2-storey building are without a doubt Puerto Nariño's most luxurious option. Each has a private bathroom & fan or AC with shuttered windows & a small balcony. Simple, wooden furniture, white linen & white towels give the place a monastic elegance. A decent restaurant seats 40 people at yellow-clothed tables & offers excellent value for money. Expect a hearty b/fast to cost less than 6,000 COP with a 3-course lunch & dinner menu at 10,000 COP apiece. A bar serves beer, water & soda. Guests can lounge around in the hotel's communal hammock lounge or grab a seat in a pleasant leafy courtyard. To find it, take the road that leads up from the riverbank & look for the bright blue COMCEL sign that signifies a left turn to the hotel. Pre-book & a member of staff will meet you off the boat to save you lugging your gear 2 blocks uphill. $$

🏠 **Brisas del Amazonas** `311 281 2473`. This former grand family home on the waterfront needs a decent lick of paint & a spring clean, but is still a good dirt-cheap option. Some rooms are better than others, so be sure to have a look at a few & check for damp. $

🏠 **Hotel Paiyu** `313 237 0840`. Budget travellers highly recommend this small family-run hotel. Simple rooms are small but clean & equipped with a fan. Look out for a sgl-storey wooden building with a red tin roof opposite the Casa Selva. $

As you might expect, the Colombian Amazon attracts dozens of ecologists and conservationists, keen to observe the region's extraordinary biodiversity and unique habitat. Some establish study bases in the jungle or along the river. Others operate on a more nomadic basis throughout the region as a whole. Many choose to centre themselves in the town of Puerto Nariño, because it enjoys a location close to Lake Tarapoto (Lago Tarapoto) and Parque Nacional Amacayacú. One such organisation is the OMACHA Foundation (📞 57 1 236 26 86; e info@omacha.org; www.omacha.org), a non-government and non-profit organisation created to study, research and protect the Colombian Amazon's fauna and aquatic ecosystems. Since 1987, OMACHA has worked closely with local communities in the Putumayo, Caquetá and Apaporis rivers and tributaries to devise programmes for the sustainable development of aquatic resources. The biological station and laboratory opened in 1993 to focus on two species of river dolphins that inhabit the Amazon region: the boto (Inia geoffrensis) and tucuxi (Sotalia fluviatilis), both of which face possible threat. Other studies have concentrated on the fish population, especially the largest fish species in the Amazon, the cucha (Pterygoplychthes multiradiatus) and the pirarucú (Arapaima gigas).

In recent years, OMACHA scientists have begun studying river wolves (Pteronura brasiliensis) and otters (Lontra longicaudis) in Puerto Nariño. It also rehabilitated an Amazonian manatee calf (Trichechus inunguis) following the capture and death of its mother at the hands of local fishermen. Whilst raising and observing the behaviour of the calf (named Airuwe, meaning 'manatee' in the Ticuna language), OMACHA began a series of studies on the Amazonian manatee in conjunction with native Ticunas, Yukunas, Tanimucas and Macues along with the mixed-race fishermen from Puerto Nariño and the Caquetá and Apaporis rivers areas. The Florida-based Sirenia Project fitted the manatee with a belt and radio to enable researchers to monitor it via telemetry techniques. The Amazonian manatee is the smallest of the living sirenians and the only manatee species to live entirely in fresh water. An educational project was launched within local communities where manatees are hunted as a food source. National and international film-makers followed the project, making documentaries about the pioneering nature of the manatee conservation efforts. In 2002, the OMACHA Foundation and the Puerto Nariño community returned Airuwe to the wild at three years eight months old, in Lake Tarapoto, a fertile manatee feeding area. OMACHA's manatee project captured the hearts and minds of many people Colombia-wide and has since furthered the Amazon's conservation profile to a large degree.

Visitors will find the Fundación Omacha centre right on the riverfront. It is open to the public and has a small exhibition space. Pop in to learn about the projects and Adopt a Dolphin programme or to lend much needed volunteer support.

✗ Where to eat and drink As you'd expect from a small jungle town, Puerto Nariño doesn't have many gastronomic hangouts, but a couple of places a block from the riverfront serve decent fish-and-rice meals. Both **Las Margaritas** and **Doña Francisca** are open for lunch and dinner with a set soup-and-main-course option costing under 9,000 COP. Domino-playing men mainly populate a handful of drinking holes with the **Granero Bodega** and **Alvear** two of the best. Both overlook the basketball courts and have a few plastic chairs on the boardwalk, a perfect spot from which to people-watch at dusk with an ice-cold cerveza con limon.

Many of the pinprick-sized riverbank Indian communities in the low-lying Colombian Amazon are used to abandoning their homes during the wet season. A cyclical climate makes this necessary as close to 3m of rain can pound the land each year. Yet this dousing isn't viewed as a flooding disaster zone, but rather simply the Amazon's way. Rising river levels can see the water increase by up to 15m. Entire wood-and-thatch villages are engulfed, with huge tracts of jungle immersed and only the highest ceiba trees able to peak out above the surface of the water. Once the rains subside and water levels fall, villagers return to reclaim their homes for the dry season. Much of the Amazon lowlands is richer and more fertile after this prolonged soaking thanks to plant matter decomposition and nutrients from the river. Fish feed on berries and seeds from the forest ahead of reproduction.

Generally speaking, river swelling occurs between the end of December and the end of June, with levels reaching their highest level in March–the beginning of June. During this rainy season the volume of the Amazon River increases, flooding the forest. Large lagoons and swamps are formed to provide ideal areas for observing birds, caiman and *Victorias regias* (water lilies) and fishing for piranha. Ebb tides begin in mid-July and last until the beginning of December, reaching their lowest levels in July–November. During this time, sandbanks are formed at the river borders. Turtles nest and lay their eggs, Indian people plant rice on exposed beaches and fishing is at its most popular.

What to see and do

Mirador Nai Pata (*admission 5,000 COP*) The charge is a small price to pay for the breathtaking views this lookout affords from the west of the town. Gaze out over the river, lakes and Puerto Nariño from this wooden purpose-built tower set atop the town's highest point, built in 2004.

San Martín A number of walking trails lead in and out of this Ticuna village, where tourists are welcome to learn about traditional medicine, indigenous plants, local customs and the history of the community. All hotels offer tours out to the village (or can point you in the right direction). Walk out of the town along a leafy path bathed in sunlight. Artisans in San Martín offer visitors plenty of opportunity to buy Ticuna crafts on arrival. A Catholic church stages mass on a Sunday when it is visited by a famous Amazonian *fraile* called José Rivera. This community-spirited monk opens his home to travellers and is renowned for his genuine hospitality. If you bump into him expect a fund of stories. He is also a great source of tips and information on how best to interact to get the most from local life.

Ask anyone in Puerto Nariño for directions to the 'Frailes place' and you'll be guided by scribbled maps and wild hand signals from a host of helpful passers-by. **Fraile José Rivera's cabañas** are a welcome sight after a sweaty hour-long hike from the town centre, high above a flooded forest by the river bank amidst palms and coloured blooms. As you'd expect from a monk, the fraile is a rather unique host in the wilds of the Amazon. However, this remarkable fountain of knowledge is a superb source of information for travellers as he was posted to the region many years ago. He left once, at the Church's suggestion, but returned to build a home after missing the jungle so much. Today, the fraile works with local communities, taking in travellers that take the time to pass by. Simple, wooden cabañas are without any home comforts but up to 12 guests are welcome to a jungle retreat that has a dining area and a rustic cold shower. Verandas are slung with hammocks where the only distraction is birdsong and jungle chit-chatter. A viewing tower affords truly magnificent views and is a big hit with birders that make it this far. The fraile is respectful of traveller independence but is happy to arrange boat trips and local guides for those that need them. He also has a couple of wooden kayaks for guests keen to explore the river.

San Francisco For a chance to explore some wildlife-rich trails close to Río Loretoyacu ask a guide in Puerto Nariño to take you on a stomp around San Francisco. Eminent traditional herbalists reside in this pretty indigenous Ticuna village and may also accompany visitors on a tour around the trails' vast array of curative plants.

Birding around Puerto Nariño Visiting birdwatchers prepared to explore in and around Puerto Nariño and San Martín are likely to spot numerous species in the many walks that loop the town. Recent sightings include the black-tailed tityra tui parakeet, white-bearded hermit, rufous-breasted hermit, rusty-fronted tody-flycatcher, spotted tody-flycatcher, yellow-bellied dacnis, glittering-throated emerald, scarlet-crowned barbet, bare-necked fruitcrow, campo oriole, dark-breasted spinetail, plain-breasted piculet, maroon-tailed parakeet, hooded tanager, lesser yellow-headed vulture, sapphire-rumped parrotlet and white-eared jacamar.

Lago Tarapoto This large, magical expanse of water is edged by ficus trees and is a famous location in which to spot pretty rose-coloured dolphins (boto) and admire the vast *Victoria amazonica* (giant lily). Located about 9km west of Puerto Nariño and 80km from Leticia, the lake is only accessible by boat via the river with trips costing about US$25 (for 4 people) for a half-day. Canoes can also be hired from the local Indian settlements that dot the lake for about US$8 per day. Most full-day tours from Puerto Nariño will take in Lago Tarapoto with a host of local boatmen prepared to depart from the riverbank every day. In 2002, Lago Tarapoto was the site chosen by the OMACHA Foundation and the Puerto Nariño community (see box, *An Eden for ecologists*, page 251) for the return to the wild of a three-year-old Amazonian manatee. The lake is a well-established manatee feeding area and a sacred place for many local people, many of whom believe it has special powers. Myths are important to the Indian communities of the Amazon and centre on integration with nature. At Tarapoto, legends relate to a strange green light that illuminates the night sky, an eerie glow that has prompted many fishermen to return home after setting their nets. Rumours say that those who choose to fish

---

BE PREPARED

Unfortunately, many of even the Amazon's most seasoned guides are hopelessly poorly equipped. Many carry torches with low-watt bulbs, even if they plan to hike the jungle overnight. Few have binoculars, waterproof matches or a basic first-aid kit. Others don't have any firm ideas of what they'd do in an SOS. Don't be afraid to request a full briefing ahead of even the most straightforward itinerary to check that you pack what you need. As a rule of thumb, always wear boots – even in the dry season. Light baggage is the way to go as you'll probably have to lug it on and off boats and along unmade roads. Choose lightweight clothing that includes swimming gear, long trousers, long-sleeved shirts and waterproofs. Be sure to pack a hat, sunglasses and sun block as protection against the harsh equatorial sun. Candles and matches are also advisable as most lodges only have electricity between 18.00–21.00 each night. Be sure not to forget your camera (fast film is recommended) and binoculars. Carry water and *lots* of mosquito repellent and keep a mobile phone (a quad band works best) close at hand.

By Peter Hutchison, co-author of Amazon: the Bradt Travel Guide *(third edition, August 2007) with Roger Harris.*

The most important requirements for a successful trip are to have a purpose and a plan. Your expedition must have a definite goal otherwise you will just drift from place to place. Ask yourself why you want to mount your own expedition. If it's so that you are free to go where you want when you want, to stay away as long as you wish and to be in total control of your own destiny; then to achieve that much freedom you will need to finance it yourself. If you are sponsored, commissioned or under contract to carry out some sort of research you won't have complete choice in where you go and what you do.

Most expeditions use local guides, porters and boatmen. For a first-time independent jungle trip, travelling, camping and daily chores will take up most of your time and all your energy; you would need experience to be able to carry out project work as well. If you plan to write a book when you return home or make a film while you're there, then you will have to compromise your freedom. The main things you need to concentrate on are:

GETTING TO KNOW YOUR DESTINATION The more information you can gather about your destination the better equipped you will be to handle any unforeseen circumstances that arise – and arise they will. Buy the best maps and plan your route, then start doing the detective work. Contact embassies, ministries, tourist boards, but keep your enquiries brief and concise.

GAINING PERMISSION Whether or not you need a visa to enter the country itself, make thorough enquiries about requirements to enter the area you will visit. Some officials are sensitive if there is logging or mining activity. To travel in a national park, a protected area, or the home of indigenous tribal people may take six months or longer to gain

overnight under the light have been found dead and headless in the lake in the morning. Some say pirates ascend from the water's depths killing unsuspecting fishermen as the light shines. Others say the body parts are harvested for research purposes by scientists from the United States.

EXPLORING THE RÍO YAVARÍ

This mighty, winding tributary reaches into large unbroken stretches of rainforest, meandering into some of the most magnificent areas in which to observe Amazonian wildlife first hand. An increasing number of small private reserves have sprung up along the Río Yavarí to offer adventure activities with the services of a guide, such as night safaris, alligator spotting, birding, jungle hikes along old Indian trails and jaguar trekking. Simple accommodation tends to be basic at best, usually in the style of mud-and-thatch cabins with rudimentary, communal washrooms. Food is generally included in the cost of your stay with tours and transfers extra. Those travelling in a group will find there are plenty of discounts up for grabs on accommodation and tours. The Río Yavarí stretches from the border between Brazil and Peru's Loreto department, flowing northeast for 870km. It joins the Amazon River near the Brazilian outpost of Benjamin Constant, so enquiries regarding visa requirements for each territory should be made prior to travel.

Journeying the Río Yavarí allows plenty of opportunity to spot the Amazon's pretty pink river dolphins (*boto*) as well as the silver-coloured tucuxis (*Sotalia fluviatili*) – start scanning the water from the moment you leave downtown Leticia. In the permission. Be patient, polite and persistent and remember that some of the most interesting places cannot be visited on a whim.

WHEN TO GO In the dry season the rivers will be low, sometimes so low that the riverbed is exposed, making river travel arduous. But in the dry season you will see lots more wildlife and camping is more pleasant because it's not raining all the time. In the rainy season it rains nearly every day and river levels are high. Rivers will be flowing fast and the jungle may flood. Clothes that get wet take ages to dry, while mould grows on camera equipment and film. But the rainy season does have its compensations, particularly if you are visiting a waterfall.

CHOOSING YOUR BOAT Dugout canoes are the most common means of travel on Amazonian rivers. They are strong, and respond well under power, but they are heavy and sit low in the water. Sometimes the sides are built up with planks, which makes them more stable but even heavier. Fibreglass, plastic and aluminium canoes are light, fast and responsive under power. But they are not so readily available and are much more fragile than dugout canoes. Take this into consideration if your river is a rocky one. If you choose this type of boat you will probably have to take one from your home country. Inflatable boats are excellent, particularly for the novice. They rarely capsize even when punctured or full of water; they bounce off rocks, carry enormous weights and are repairable and comfortable to sit on day after day. But on fast water they slide, they spin, they are slow and almost impossible to paddle. However, for a first trip my choice would be an inflatable powered by an outboard engine light enough for one person to carry.

WHAT TO TAKE It may be possible to buy most of the things you will need in larger towns, but if an item is essential take it with you.

virgin rainforest swatches within the reach of the river, expect to find common squirrel monkey, black-mantle tamarin, black agouti, Amazon dwarf squirrel, pygmy marmoset, night monkey, brush-tailed rats and white-fronted capuchin. Also red howler, titi monkey, woolly monkey, monk saki, short-eared dog, collared peccary, tapir, oncilla, giant armadillo, sloth, jaguar, ocelot and giant otter. Foliage along the riverbank runs an entire spectrum of green, from garish paintbox-green ferns and black-green mangroves to olive-green reeds, yellow-green palms and a tangle of lush emerald-green creepers. The colour of the river also alters dramatically from a creamy swirl of thick vanilla to a deep brick red. Ichthyologically speaking, the Amazon and its tributaries are some of the most exciting on the planet. Even on a slow day, fishermen can expect to find cardinal tetras, discus, angel cichlids and armoured pleco catfish with thin-nosed tube-snout knifefish, freshwater dogfish, motoro, tooth-lip knifefish, tiger stingray, faulkner's stingray, Harald Schultz's cory, arowana, American lungfish, hatchetfish, giant peacock bass, tambaqui and goliath pirarucú. Piranhas are omnipresent as are electric eels and river stingrays. Since 1960, more than 50 species of fish have been discovered, named and catalogued in the Amazon per annum. The number of identified fish species currently stands at 3,200 but experts agree the true figure is likely to exceed 4,000 – at least.

 WHERE TO STAY
Río Yavarí

🏠 **Reserva Natural Palmari** Contact the multi-lingual owner Axel Antoine-Feill at his Bogotá HQ; ☎ 1 482

7148/0081/7593/0769; 📠 1 6170 280; www.palmari.org. Dolphin views abound from this sprawling wooden

Many of the eco-lodges in the Amazon region prefer their guests not to use the hard stuff. Citing health concerns relating to high chemical content as well as the damage it is said to cause the environment, there is also a joke in the Amazon that Western sprays seem to attract more mosquitoes than they repel. An increasing number of herbal insect repellents can be found on the market. Many are 100% natural, contain no chemicals, are organic and fully biodegradable. Some are safe enough to use even in pregnancy and suitable for people of all ages, including children and babies.

Many eco-conscious travellers swear by citrus essential oils in the Amazon, liberally applied to clothes, hair and skin. Citrosa geranium has up to 40% of the repellent power of DEET, great when added to crushed lemon thyme (*Thymus citriodora*), which itself has over 60% of DEET's repellence.

In the Amazon, many Indian tribes have developed their own ecological repellent for the use of whey-skinned bug-bitten tourists. Each has been designed for multiple use in generous drenching quantities to cope with the prevalence of mosquitoes in the region. The following recipe comes highly recommended:

Mix alcohol with menticol in equal measures in a jug. Add a chopped bar of nopikex soap and six camphor tablets. Pour into a blender to make a paste. Add three tablespoons of 10% eurax (for every 300ml of alcohol) with 30cc of citronella essence and four tablespoon of Johnson's Baby Oil. Mix well before pouring the liquid into a bottle, preferably with a pump spray attachment. Use the lotion to spray clothing ahead of travel to the Amazon, repeating this process for a good three or four days. Before direct exposure, apply liberally to the skin (taking care to cover the head, hairline, ear lobes and other 'forgotten' areas). Douse the outer edges of bedding, sleeping bags, hammocks and mosquito netting. The mixture is also effective in reducing pain and inflammation from existing bites.

lodge with a viewing tower that ensures prime vistas from a lofty vantage point. Rooms have private bathrooms while a circular communal building is hung with dozens of hammocks. A decent restaurant serves hearty meals & the lodge has a number of guides. Prices start at 30,000 COP for food & board (hammock) rising to around 45,000 COP for a bed, with tour packages at around 80,000–100,000 COP per day. Tours include hiking, birding, kayaking, night safaris, camping & trips to Indian villages. The reserve is a full-fledged research facility so the focus is ecological. Guests can also swim in natural springs, fish in the surrounding waters, dolphin watch, have a temporary pigment tattoo applied by local Indian tribesfolk, learn about neo-tropical flora in the lodge's purpose-built library on a complimentary basis. More than 541 species of bird have been recorded in & around the environs of the reserve. These are from 62 different bird families with seven species unclassified as unknown. Note: guests are forbidden to bring any manufactured insect repellents to the lodge. Ecological recipes are allowed (see box, *A Green way to keep the mozzies at bay*, above).

🏠 **Reserva Natural Zacambú** (30 rooms) Book accommodation and tours through Amazon Jungle Trips; Av Internacional, No 6–25, Leticia; ✆ 592 7377; e amazonjungletrips@yahoo.com. Overlooking Lake Zacambú, this mangrove-flanked lodge offers simple, earthy rooms with mosquito nets & hammocks but without private bathrooms. An all-in price includes meals of fish & yucca in a setting where you can actually hear dolphins frolicking in the water. Canoeing in the lake is easy from a boardwalk dock from where caimans can be spotted up to a few metres in length. Machete-wielding patron Jorge is fond of after-dark caiman hunting using a powerful flashlight strapped to his head. He utters strange guttural sounds to emulate the call, sweeping a beam of light along the shore. Walking trails are limited around the reserve with almost every excursion by boat. However the chirping of frogs, humming insects & local anteaters has a certain charm. Birders are sure to sight egrets, kingfishers and parrots on the shores of the lakes with piranha fishing as easy as throwing a piece of string into the water.

🏠 **Reserva Natural Heliconia** Book at the Reserva Natural Heliconia office; Calle 13, No 11–74, Leticia;

🤙 601 8709 or 311 5085 666, 310 300 6025; ⓔ info@amazonheliconia.com; www.amazonheliconia.com. Located on the Yavarí River amidst palms & trees that exceed 100m in height, the wood-&-thatch cabins of the Reserva Natural Heliconia sit on 15ha of beautiful, preserved jungle. Only environmentally friendly materials are used in the running of the lodge. The reserve's philosophy also extends to a number of conservation projects in the Amazon in conjunction with non-profit groups, including a protection programme for the native cultures that inhabit the surroundings of the lodge. A wide range of boat & hiking tours include dolphin watching, kayaking, fishing & canopy exploration. Birding tours have become something of a speciality of the lodge with observation towers & onsite guides. Rates vary depending on the tours chosen & the season but it is well worth taking advantage of a transfer from Leticia Airport & the assistance Heliconia staff offer in regards to immigration arrangements with Colombian & Brazilian authorities, DAS & Federal Police.

Río Amazonas

🏠 **Reserva Natural Marasha** Book through Amazon Jungle Trips; Av Internacional, No 6–25, Leticia; 🤙 592 7377; ⓔ amazonjungletrips@yahoo.com. The boat drops arrivals on a muddy riverbank ahead of a good hour-long trek through the jungle, but the Marasha Reserve is worth the effort – even in the rainy season. For a start, the people that work there are a breath of fresh air – dedicated, friendly & prepared to go the extra mile. Secondly, the setting makes a great base for some deeper exploration into the wilds. Set on a sparkling lake & surrounded by peaceful waterways, the reserve is blessed with wildlife-rich trails full of monkey, sloth, toucan, eagle, owl & butterflies. Stay overnight in simple, slung hammocks along with a resident pair of parrots, a couple of titi monkeys & a curious coati that thinks he's a cat. Overhanging branches are festooned with creepers & bromeliads with the Marasha's oldest giant ceiba tree, over 400 years old. A wide range of day & night jungle excursions range in price depending on the number of people but it is worth budgeting at around 85,000 COP for a full-on full-day trip (inc lunch).

BENJAMIN CONSTANT

This small Brazilian river town is named after Benjamin Constant Botelho de Magalhães (1836–91), a military man and political thinker. Like many Amazon settlements it isn't blessed with endless attractions but the town's compact Magüta Museum has some interesting artefacts relating to the region's endemic tribes, including books in Ticuna language. All in all, Benjamin Constant could probably be walked from end to end within 30 minutes. Dominated by a cathedral and a timber mill, the town is a popular refuelling point with boats travelling to and from Manaus. A handful of decent restaurants and bars also make it a good place to stop off for lunch. Benjamin Constant is one of the oldest agricultural frontier areas in eastern Brazil with a population of small-scale farmers practising subsistence agriculture. Relying on the existence of secondary forests, the local communities use 135 plant species to survive, producing food, tubes, latex, oils, fibres, resins, gums, balsams, condiments, candles and cellulose from their natural environment. In 1988, the town gained international notoriety following the mass slaughter of Ticuna Indians at the hands of logger Oscar Castelo Branco. Some 14 Ticuna were shot to death with 23 wounded, in a brutal attempt to prevent them from reclaiming their traditional forestlands. The Ticuna are one of Brazil's most populous indigenous groups, with some 95 villages mainly scattered along the banks of the Upper Solimões River and its tributaries. Despite being home to more than 50% of the world's Ticunas (Colombia and Peru also have Ticuna peoples), Brazil has only recently started to invest in native language education. Brazilian Ticunas now have written literature and an education provided by the Brazilian National Foundation for the Indian (FUNAI) and the Ministry of Education. Ticuna is a tonal language similar to Chinese with the meaning of a word varying greatly simply by changing the tone.

PARQUE NACIONAL CAHUANARI

This 575,000ha expanse of lowland tropical rainforest lies in the western region of the Amazon Basin where Río Cahuanari and Río Bernardo meet, with the Río Caquetá River forming its northern border. Characterised by a high degree of both terrestrial and aquatic biodiversity, the park also overlaps two of Colombia's legally declared indigenous territories: the Predio Putumayo and Miriti Parana. Brackish rivers, sparkling creeks and alluvial plains provide a wide variety of ecosystems with a mix of lowland forest and flooded forest covering about 90% of the land. Soaring trees reach 40m entwined with vines and epiphytes. However, a history of intensive fishing and hunting of black caiman, otters and various primates has seriously depleted wildlife numbers. Rare and endangered animals found in Cahuanari include jaguar and the magnificent giant river otter, for which the lower Río Caquetá is a last remaining habitat. Another species under severe threat is the endemic Charapa river turtle. Other inhabitants include the white-lipped peccary and tapir with very little research conducted into bird species, which include the nocturnal curassow, grey-winged trumpeter and blue-and-yellow macaw.

Accessing the park is problematic with the area subject to safety concerns due to its remoteness, but many of those that have made it there have been mightily impressed. Cahuanari is certainly a landmark in the conservation of Colombia's indigenous patrimony. Traditional cultures have been preserved and the lessons of conservation offer considerable potential to other communities in educational terms. One of the most well-preserved forests in the Colombian Amazon, the park is of great importance to the 1,500 indigenous people who live within its boundaries. Rubber exploitation was threatening to devastate the land and people. Today, the park protects the indigenous groups that survived and the amazing tropical rainforests in which they live.

Before visiting the Parque Nacional Cahuanari be sure to check on the latest safety advice on the ground. At the time of writing, accommodation seems to be limited to a couple of basic cabins and an undeveloped camping area. Visitors must pre-book ahead of arrival at a Parques Nacionales office (*call the Bogotá EcoTourism office for details on* \ *243 1634*). Entry is prohibited to anyone who hasn't engaged the services of a recognised guide with permits awarded on a discretionary basis only if the park isn't in use for community projects.

Further information can be obtained from **Territorial Amazonía – Orinoquía** (*Calle 14, No 8–79 piso 2; Bogotá* \ *2431940;* e *amazonia@ parquesnacionales.gov.co; www.parquesnacionales.gov.co*)

TABATINGA

Leticia's Brazilian twin-town lacks the charm of its Colombian neighbour but it does serve as an alternative base for those keen to swap salsa for samba. Hotel accommodation tends to be much pricier than in Leticia but Tabatinga has a good range of decent restaurants and some lively bars. Travellers planning to board an early-morning launch to Iquitos may find staying overnight in Tabatinga makes good logistical sense. Locals often refer to crossing over 'Checkpoint Charlie' when describing the Leticia–Tabatinga border. However there is no distinguishable boundary, no guards or passport check and no immigration red tape.

WHERE TO STAY Much like Leticia, Tabatinga is blessed with umpteen hotels and budget hostels but is rather light on luxury options. Most of the dirt-cheap options are clustered around the border area. Others can be found a stone's throw from the port.

When Slovenian Martín Strel (*www.martinstrel.com*) announced plans to swim the entire length of the Amazon River in 2007, the world thought he was mad. For not only did Strel's route stretch a gruelling 5,800km, the river is also a proverbial soup of piranha, crocodiles and other predatory water-borne beasts. The Slovenian also chose to conduct his mammoth swim during the rainy season. Rising water is at its most hazardous at this time of year with the river scattered with fast-moving debris from the flood-ridden jungle. Strel's goal was to average 85km per day, departing Atalaya Peru on 1 February 2007. He entered Colombian waters after 26 days in the water and on 11 April a huge party welcomed Strel to the riverbanks of Belém where he finally limped ashore. During his arduous trip, the Slovenian swimmer became a legend throughout the Amazon with every small village dispatching a flotilla of dugout canoes packed to the gills with awestruck Indians as he passed their way. After suffering chronic sunburn on the stretch of river approaching Colombian territory, Strel donned a mask fashioned out of an old bedsheet and wore a floppy sun hat. Proceeds from the charity fund-raising marathon swim have helped numerous indigenous communities along the Amazon River, improving sanitation and basic living conditions (*www.amazonswim.com*). Guinness Book record-holder Strel is no stranger to challenge. He swam the Danube in 2000, the Mississippi in 2002, the Paraná in 2003 and the Yangtze in 2004. A documentary about the Amazon swim (*Big River Man*) was broadcast in Latin America in 2007 to much acclaim. Strel's slogan for his repeated feats of endurance is 'Swimming for Peace, Friendship and Clean Waters'.

🏠 **Hotel Takana** Rua Oswaldo Cruz 970; 📞 3412 3557. Although this hotel is on the outskirts of town, those looking for something swish will find that it is Tabatinga's most upscale option. Spruce, AC rooms boast a pleasing décor surrounded by mature leafy courtyard garden with a restaurant & swimming pool. $$$

🏠 **Hotel Bela Vista** Rua Marechal Rondón 1806; 📞 3412 3846. Just a few steps from the port, this cheap & cheerful resting place is a popular option with shoestring travellers. It's nothing much to look at, but the location is unbeatable & the rooms have AC. $$

🏠 **Pousada do Sol** (7 rooms) Rua General Sampaio 50; 📞 3412 3987; 📠 3412 5122. The decent-sized rooms have AC, a fridge & private bathroom & are within easy walking distance of the launches for Iquitos & Manaus. It's close to a handful of good local restaurants & also has a courtyard garden & a small swimming pool. $$

✕ **WHERE TO EAT** Tabatinga has numerous places to eat from sizzling food stalls and fried-chicken joints to funky curbside cafés and seafood diners. Typical Brazilian fare is easy to find, such as feijoada (black beans) and coquetel de camarao (shrimp cocktail) and, of course, Brazil's delicious Skol beer.

✕ **Blue Moon Restaurantes** 📞 3412 2227. Located right on the side of the port, this cream-coloured single-storey restaurant may not look much, but there are few better places to dine while waiting patiently for a boat. Brightly coloured hanging baskets give the place a cheery feel but it is the prices that truly put a smile on your face at less than US$5 for a big plate of chicken and rice. $

✕ **Churrascaria Tia Helena** Rua Marechal Mallet 12; 📞 3412 2165. The décor may be functional but the food is cheap & hearty – & with an all-you-can-eat option that's a budget traveller's delight! Melt-in-the-mouth meat is brought to the table on skewers from the grill on demand. It's then carved in true flamboyant Brazilian style with flashing blades, with much aplomb. $

✕ **Restaurante Tres Fronterias do Amazonas** Rua Rui Barbosa; 📞 3412 2341. Dine in style in this pleasant thatch-roofed open-sided restaurant where a simple menu of grilled chicken, fish & meat dishes rarely disappoints. $

Amazonia TABATINGA

7

259

GETTING AROUND Exploring Tabatinga on foot is easy enough with taxis in good supply. Hail one on the street or head to the port where you'll find a number waiting for trade, including a fleet of Faz Freet taxis (☎ *915 10393*). Citywide, the streets are a swarm of motorbikes and scooters with plenty of places to hire by the day or hour. Down by the river, dozens of boats and wooden dugouts vie for position under the pale, stone-terraced steps of the portside. Goods and chattels form ugly piles in ready-to-board preparedness while backpackers catch 40 winks on rolled-up hammocks by sacks of bananas. All boats leave Tabatinga from this launch point, be they hulking great grey cargo ships or leisurely dolphin cruises.

OTHER PRACTICALITIES Very much a town designed for travellers passing through, Tabatinga has everything for people on the move. Supermarkets, mini-markets and kiosks can be found in abundance with the excellent Mini Mercado Baratinho a popular fallback for backpackers dashing to board the boat. A large permanent market is a great place to pick up spare T-shirts, flip-flops, hammocks, boots, hats, sunglasses and replacement luggage. Public toilets can be found on the portside just a short walk from a row of shops that includes a drugstore, mobile phone shop and internet café.

ISLA SANTA ROSA

A big blue sign welcomes arrivals to Santa Rosa with 'Bienvenidos al Perú' on arrival, but most visitors are simply passing through. Dozens and dozens of boats zoom in and out hurriedly for a visa stamp. Passengers that do disembark are usually party-goers from Leticia, arriving in Peru to make the most of its dirt-cheap beer and chicha bars. Larger boats that berth are crammed with pigs, chickens, lumber and electrical goods and, of course, backpacking tourists. Santa Rosa's local population is a mix of Peruvian government administration, immigration officers and local farming folk.

A cluster of decent bars and restaurants hug the shoreline and Letician townsfolk eagerly cross the river on the basis of Santa Rosa's excellent ceviche and ice-cold Cristel. Music is teeth-rattlingly loud at the Bar El Delfin Enamorado while the wild parties at El Paisa are rumoured to rage until dawn. However, during daylight hours Santa Rosa is a much more sedate place to be. Expect to see border controllers washing their clothes at the water's edge while their colleagues snooze on benches in the shadows. Sleepy dogs roam the dusty streets with the action the frenzied refuelling of passing boatmen on the move.

8

The Southwest Interior

Colombia's inner southwest region is home to some of the country's most diverse topography amidst a dizzying array of altitudes and contrasting terrain. Impenetrable folds of jungle stretch to snowy mountain peaks with patches of arid desert leading to dusty country towns. Dramatic green valleys give way to rugged highlands and magnificent rolling hills. Delve into the countryside to discover the southwest's host of pretty *pueblitos* and fine colonial cities along with some of the most important pre-Columbian sites in the Americas. The region is also home to the nation's third-largest city, Cali, Colombia's ultra-modern urban hub. Renowned as the 'Salsa Capital of Colombia' Cali boasts a lengthy dance tradition and this hot, rhythmic musical pulse has made the city famous worldwide. Expect hundreds of sweaty, sexy salsa joints and sassy movers in a city devoted to partying hard – a sharp contrast to the region's genteel religious centres and pilgrim prayer sites.

VALLE DEL CAUCA

That an entire department is named after a single valley reflects the importance of the Valle del Cauca to the region where fertile soils produce bountiful crops of sugarcane, tobacco, maize and cotton. Wedged between the Cordillera Occidental and Cordillera Central, the Valle del Cauca's 22,140km² terrain is riddled with nourishing rivers. Emptying into the mighty Río Cauca, these mountain waters have nurtured the region's prosperous agriculture-based economy in which sugarcane remains the fiscal bedrock. Cotton, tobacco, soy and coffee are also grown, alongside bagasse-based (sugarcane fibre) pulp and paper mills and a growing number of cement works. Good access to Buenaventura port on the Pacific coast enables the efficient import and export of goods to the rest of Colombia – and beyond. Despite Valle del Cauca comprising large swathes of countryside, more than 80% of the population live in cities or towns. The coverage of public services is among the highest in the country.

PRACTICALITIES Personal safety in some areas of the Valle del Cauca Department is a major priority, especially in the rural areas near the cities of Pradera and Florida. Once the stronghold of FARC rebels, safety is much improved in many areas, although pockets of guerrilla and military remain. In June 2007 the kidnapping in 2002 of 12 local politicians grabbed the world's headlines. After being held for five years by FARC to pressure a prisoner exchange with the Colombian government, guerrilla leaders suddenly announced that 11 had been killed, despite recently releasing so-called live video footage of the hostages. FARC claimed that the deaths occurred after the group became caught up in crossfire during an attack by an 'unidentified military group'. The only hostage survivor was Sigifredo López, who for security reasons was travelling in another group of FARC operatives. In September 2007, the Red Cross was allowed to recover the bodies and return them

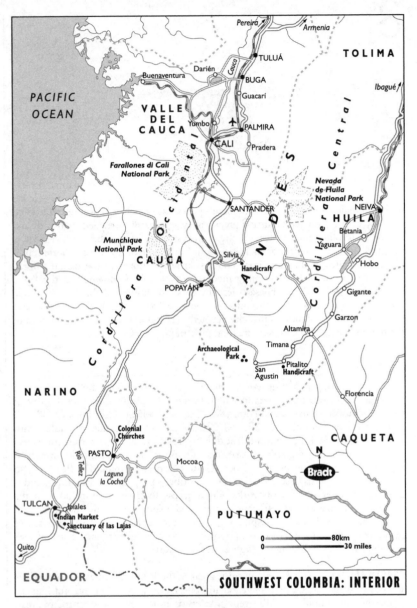

PACIFIC OCEAN

TOLIMA

Pereira

Armenia

TULUÁ

Darién

Cauca

BUGA

Buenaventura

Guacarí

Ibagué

VALLE DEL CAUCA

Yumbo

PALMIRA

CALI

Pradera

Farallones di Cali National Park

A N D E S

Nevada de Huila National Park

NEIVA

HUILA

Cordillera Occidental

SANTANDER

Betania

Munchique National Park

Silvia

Yaguara

Hobo

CAUCA

Handicraft

Gigante

POPAYÁN

Cordillera Central

Garzon

Altamira

Timana

Archaeological Park

Pitalito

San Agustin

Handicraft

NARIÑO

Florencia

CAQUETA

Colonial Churches

PASTO

N

Río Tellez

Mocoa

Laguna la Cocha

Bradt

TULCAN

Ipiales

Indian Market

Sanctuary of las Lajas

PUTUMAYO

Quito

0 ————— 80km
0 ————— 30 miles

EQUADOR

SOUTHWEST COLOMBIA: INTERIOR

by helicopter to their families. In the same year Diego Montoya who ranked alongside Osama Bin Laden on the FBI's Ten Most-Wanted Fugitives list was arrested at a small farm in the Valle del Cauca, following a nine-year manhunt. As one of Colombia's most powerful and dangerous drug baron, Montoya is thought to have been responsible for 80% of the cocaine in the United States and Europe. Even conservative estimates value his exports since 1993 at 500 tonnes of cocaine worth more than US$10 billion. The FBI had offered US$5 million for information leading to the arrest of Montoya and his capture has been hailed as the biggest victory in the drug war since Medellín cartel leader Pablo Escobar was killed in a 1993 shootout. Known as 'Don Diego', Montoya is alleged to have infiltrated Colombia's military and boasted a well-organised gang of several hundred bodyguards known as the 'macho men'.

Although the security situation in the Valle del Cauca makes these types of incidents rare – that they happen at all is a stark reminder of the region's struggles. A legacy of violence, drug trafficking and kidnapping in Valle del Cauca place these small, isolated rural pockets off-limits to those keen to travel off the beaten track. Never travel alone, use a trusted guide who is native and knows the region well. Stay on main highways, especially at night. The city of Cali itself is no stranger to FARC activity, although it has been much reduced. On 9 April, 2007, a 45kg car bomb gutted Cali's five-storey police HQ before dawn, killing a taxi driver and injuring over 30 people. Authorities blamed FARC and three days later tens of thousands of Caleños marched through the city's streets in protest carrying giant banners reading 'I reject terrorism' and 'Death to fear'.

CALI *Telephone code: 2*

In Cali, look, they know how to enjoy. By day it's burning sun, make my Cali hot…
Let the band tune up, because this year we're going to explode!
    lyrics from *Oiga, mira ve* by Qrquesta Guayacán, 1992

Caleños consider their passion for music and their beautiful women a source of great pride. Cali appears to be permeated by an irrepressible rhythmic pulse as Colombia's undisputed 'salsa city'. Every arterial in this modern urban sprawl seems to throb with a percussive Latin beat as Cali's party people come out to play. Having imported salsa and other Latin American musical genres from Cuba and Puerto Rico, Caleños are rapturous about staccato *merengue* rhythms, samba and rumba classics and syncopated ta-tum-ta-tum bossa nova beats. Even on a weekday, hip-swaying *salseros* can be found sashaying and snaking through downtown *arepa* stalls bound for downtown *salsotecas* (salsa bars). High-heeled women in skin-tight garb click their heels to the sound of drumming timbales and claves while car stereos emit the powerful boom of *tumbao, cuica* and *cavaquinho*. A row of neon-lit basement dancehàlls emit a cocktail of pan-Latino

CITY OF SALSA CHAMPIONS

We have received from our ancestors the passion for Salsa Dancing. We live it with all intensity and we transmitted this passion outside Colombia. All the energy and speed we have in our hearts and run through our blood.

    Viviane Vargas,
    Cali resident and Word Salsa Federation Champion 2005 and 2007

Cali is home to a number of world-champion salsa aficionados, including the dance troupe Swing Latino (winners of the Team Division 2006), John Vazquez and Judy Aguilar (winners of the Cabaret Division 2006) and Viviane Vargas and Ricardo Murillo (World Salsa Federation Champions 2005 and 2007).

The latter couple also performed at the Festival Encounter Latino in London in July 2006, the Carnaval Del Pueblo, Europe's largest free Latin American fiesta, and Birmingham's Latin American Festival in 2007.

Further information: World Salsa Championships (www.worldsalsachampionships.com), World Salsa Federation (www.worldsalsafederation.com), Carnival Del Pueblo (www.carnavaldelpueblo.co.uk), Latin American Festival (www.abslatin.co.uk).

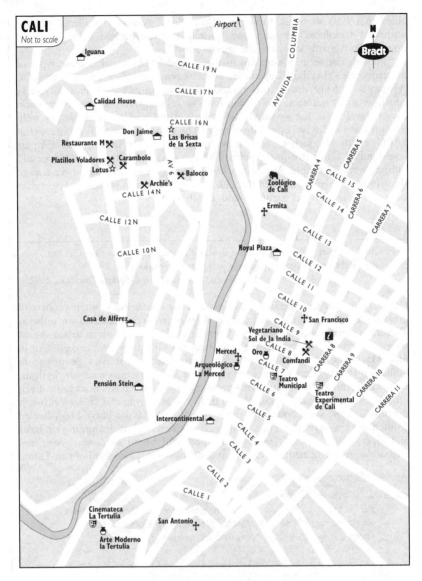

CALI
Not to scale

Airport

COLUMBIA

N

Bradt

Iguana

CALLE 19 N

CALLE 17 N

Calidad House

AVENIDA

CALLE 16 N

Don Jaime

Las Brisas
de la Sexta

Restaurante M

Platillos Voladores
Lotus

Carambolo

Balocco

AV 6

Archie's

CALLE 14 N

Zoológico
de Cali

CARRERA 4

CARRERA 5

CALLE 15

CARRERA 6

CALLE 14

CARRERA 7

CALLE 12 N

Ermita

CALLE 13

CALLE 10 N

Royal Plaza

CALLE 12

CALLE 11

CALLE 10

Casa de Alférez

San Francisco

CALLE 9

Vegetariano
Sol de la India

CARRERA 8

Merced

Oro

CALLE 8

Comfandi

CARRERA 9

Arqueológico
La Merced

CALLE 7

Pensión Stein

Teatro
Municipal

CALLE 6

Teatro
Experimental
de Cali

CARRERA 10

CARRERA 11

Intercontinental

CALLE 5

CALLE 4

CALLE 3

CALLE 2

CALLE I

Cinemateca
La Tertulia

San Antonio

Arte Moderno
la Tertulia

melodies so sweet it can almost be imbibed. More than 130 salsa orchestras, 5,000 salsa students, dozens of music stores and instrument makers, over a hundred *salsotecas* and numerous conga, bongo and maracas players give Cali its character – along with an energetic nightlife that requires plenty of stamina. Cali is also home to a week-long salsa festival – the largest salsa festival on the planet that celebrated its 50th anniversary in 2007. This colourful kaleidoscope of music and dance is not for the faint-hearted. Indeed, it's as hot, claim the Caleños, as the women of the city (see box, *Chicas calientes*, page 270) and its year-round sultry heat.

In Glynis Anthony's travel narrative *Colombia: Land of Tomorrow* a tale is told of a Cali taxi-driver who is transporting a newly arrived French businessman across the city. Cali born and bred, he is boasting of the city's progressive stance and developments and asks his passenger if it was really true that Parisians still lived in houses that were over 400 years old. The Frenchman, rather mystified by the question, confirmed that this was true. Aghast, the taxi driver proudly asserts that Cali, whilst not as famous as Paris, doesn't have a building dating any further back than 1990 – all the older structures having been torn down. This is a slight exaggeration, but isn't *that* wide of the mark, with Cali's architectural make-up largely modern. Some interesting colonial buildings can be found hidden amongst the skyscrapers, flyovers and shopping malls with some nice, leafy pathways along the Río Cali.

HISTORY Before the arrival of the Spanish, the land on which Cali now sits was inhabited by a number of indigenous tribes, including the cannibalistic Morrones and large Calima communities. Fiercely protective of their fertile valley, the Indians offered stiff resistance when Sebastían de Benalcázar and his men arrived fresh from founding Quito and Popayán and conquering the Incas. However, he was able to establish a settlement in 1536 – dubbed Santiago de Cali – and shipped in thousands of African slaves to work the sugarcane plantations. In 1540, Santiago de Cali fell under the jurisdiction of Popayán's political and economic administration after Benalcázar decided a cooler climate would aid governance. The settlement continued to grow and by 1793, Cali had a population of over 6,500 of which more than 1,100 were slaves. Strategically positioned for trade among the mining regions of Antioquía, Chicó and Popayán, Cali soon spawned a trail for mules and horses to the coast at Buenaventura. However, it was the arrival of the railway in the early 20th century that brought true prosperity to Cali as it enabled the fast and efficient movement of goods to world markets. By the 1940s, the city had witnessed explosive growth to become a dynamic, industrial centre. Today it is Colombia's third-largest urban settlement after Bogotá and Medellín and is the prime trade and commercial hub in the nation's southwest. With a population of around 2.6 million, Cali is home to more than half the people of the Valle del Cauca. It continues to grow in size and girth on a grid-based layout, neatly divided by the Río Cali. The locals describe the city as 'La Sucursal del Cielo' – meaning 'The Branch Office of Heaven'.

GETTING THERE Cali is served by the Alfonso Bonilla Aragon International Airport (CLO) – also known as Palmate International Airport. An important national and international hub, it is Colombia's second-largest airport in terms of passengers (transporting 2,171,551 in 2006) that serves much of Colombia's southwest region. Located 16km northwest of the city it has daily international flights to and from the US, Spain, Ecuador and Panama – amongst many others. Minibuses between the airport and the bus terminal run every ten minutes (2,000 COP, 30 mins) until mid-evening. Avianca operate frequent flights direct throughout the day to Bogotá as well as a number of other Colombian cities, including Cartagena, Medellín, Pasto and San Andrés. American Airlines and Continental Airlines have flights to the US.

Long-distance buses arrive at and depart from the city's bus terminal, a 25-minute walk northeast of the city centre – or a ten-minute taxi ride. Frequent buses run regularly to Bogotá (55,000 COP, 12 hrs), Medellín (40,000 COP, 9 hrs) and Pasto (30,000 COP, 9 hrs). The Pasto bus also serves Popayán (13,000 COP, 3 hrs) as do minibuses (15,000 COP, 2½hrs).

GETTING AROUND At the time of writing, Cali is awaiting the launch of its brand-new mass transportation system, the Masivo Integrado de Occidente (MIO), modelled on Bogotá's pioneering TransMilenio network. It will replace the aged and disorganised buses and independent transport providers and has been dubbed 'El Mio' – and has already come in at a whopping 350% over budget at a cost of US$345 million.

TOURIST INFORMATION

Z Secretaria de Cultura y Turismo Carrera 7 (between Calle 9 & Calle 10); Edificio Palacío de San Francisco; 886 0000; ⏱08.00–14.00 (closed 12.30–14.00) **Department website** www.valledelcauca.gov.co

Local government website www.gobernaciondelvalle.gov.co
City website www.cali.gov.co

TOUR OPERATORS Numerous tour operators offer tours around the city and outlying areas with day trips to Popayán a popular option – the tourist office has a good range of leaflets and maps. A great little after-dark *chiva* bus tour runs at the weekend at 35,000 COP per person, subject to demand: **Viajes Oganesoff** (892 2840; *www.viajesoganesoff.com*).

WHERE TO STAY

Cali Penthouse 954 557 8250; e jamesr24@comcast.net; www.calipenthouse.com. This luxury penthouse apartment has a state-of-the-art home theatre, jacuzzi, sauna & steam room – a decadent option for visitors planning a longer stay. A 7-day min applies as does a US$500 security deposit, payable by PayPal. $$$

Casa de Alférez Avenida 9N, No 9–24; 661 8111; www.sofitel.com. An elegant lobby sets the scene at this luxury property where the rooms are superbly appointed with stylish décor. $$$

Hotel Intercontinental 882 3225; www.interconti.com. Expect top-notch amenities at this high-end option, including a swimming pool, tennis courts, restaurants, bar & gym. $$$

Hotel Don Jaime Avenida 6N, No 15N; 667 2828; www.hoteldonjaime.com. Choose from a range of comfortable AC rooms in an ultra-central location in this perfectly OK mid-range hotel, popular with visiting blue-collar workers. $$

Hotel Pensión Stein 661 4999; www.hotelstein.com.co. Another Swiss-owned option,

the Stein is a rather fine small hotel, offering top-notch accommodation in a grand stone building. Expect simple, clean rooms that are high in demand with good-value rates that include b/fast. $$

Hotel Royal Plaza Carrera 4, No 11–69; 883 9243. Although the rooms could do with some TLC, views from the upper storeys across the Plaza Cayecedo are rather nice. $$

Calidad House (4 rooms) Calle 17N, No 9AN–39; 661 2338. Dorm-style rooms with shared bathroom are the only option in this basic backpacker favourite. There is also a communal kitchen, luggage storage, a traveller's notice board & laundry. $

Guest House Iguana Calle 21N, No 9N–22; 661 3522; e iguana_Cali@yahoo.com. This great little Swiss-run budget traveller's lodge is excellent value with large, clean rooms, a shared kitchen, laundry & internet access in a quiet backstreet close to the thick of it. Staff are friendly & helpful & will organise guides, tours & salsa lessons – that the owner speaks fluent English, Spanish & German is the icing on the cake. $

WHERE TO EAT
Dining out in Cali is rewarding and well priced with numerous restaurants, cafés and diners offering every possible cuisine. Visitors looking for cheap eats will not be disappointed as Cali's rustic local food joints offer simple meat-and-rice dishes for well under 5,000 COP.

Archie's Avenida 9N, No 14N–22; 653 5383; ⏱noon–22.00. One of Cali's *en vogue* salad & pizza cafés, Archie's attracts a well-heeled crowd with a relaxed ambience & gourmet menu. $$$

Platillos Voladores Calle 14N, No 9N–32; 668 7588; www.platilloslosvoladores.com; ⏱lunch & dinner. Expect an experimental fusion-style menu at this oh-so fashionable eatery with oriental, European

and Colombian influences mixed to glorious effect using the freshest local produce. $$$

Restaurante Carambolo Calle 14N, No 9N–18; 667 5656; ⏱lunch & dinner. Expect tables of power suits & media types at the slick dining establishment where an ultra-funky ambience & neat eats are as stylish as the punters. $$$

Like all Colombian cities, Cali has its own distinctive dialect and local vernacular with numerous homespun jargon not found elsewhere.

como fue que?	what's up? what's going on?
malandro	bad person or criminal
chino/chinaso/parcero/pana	friend
flacha veloz	fast arrow (meaning slow-witted)
cabeza de motor	big head
no me coja de destrabe	don't mess me around
pa las que sea!	I'm up for anything!
prendido	tipsy
bolqueta	drunk
bochinchero	somebody that fabricates stories
que destrabe	having a good time
ruñidera or ruñiendo	a two-faced backstabber
sisas	yes
todo bien	all good

✗ **Restaurante M** Avenida 9N, No 15N–39; ✆ 660 1785; ⏱noon–21.00. For a splurge book a table at this opulent upscale eatery set in a grand mansion house where a rather fine menu of Asian-fusion food has wowed the critics. $$$

✗ **Restaurante Balocco** Avenida 6N, No 14N–04; ⏱lunch–early evening. Choose from a tiny menu of simple hearty local fare at this super little family-run restaurant $

✗ **Restaurante Comfandi** Carrera 6, No 8–22; ⏱weekdays only. This is a great place for budget travellers to fill their boots at lunchtime with inexpensive self-service dishes of meat, chicken, rice, plantain, sweet potatoes & pasta. $

✗ **Restaurante Vegetariano Sol de la India** Carrera 6, No 8–48; ⏱weekdays lunch only. A menu of mild curried vegetable-&-rice dishes make this a good cheap vegetarian option – the breads & deep-fried pakoras are particularly good. $

ENTERTAINMENT AND NIGHTLIFE With so much going on throughout the city it is worth swotting up on Cali's 'what's on' listing in *El Pais* newspaper. There's also a decent entertainment section online at www.terra.com. It's hard to go wrong when heading for a night on the town in Cali as *caleños* could turn a visit to the dentist into *la rumba* (partying) on a grand scale. After an early-evening beer in the city's Zonas Rosas on Avenida Sexta and Calle 5, the pace begins to fasten as cocktails are downed and punters begin to move to a host of Latino beats. At around midnight (but not before) the crowds head to the Juanchito district 12km to the east of the centre (20 minutes by taxi at a cost of around 5,000 COP). A slim selection of what's on offer is listed below but the best way to discover Cali's excellent salsa-infused nightlife is to just throw yourself in – feet first.

♀ **Fanaticos Sports Bar** Palmetto Plaza Shopping Center; ✆ 300 600 2637. This lively sports bar is open 7 days a week & is popular with college students & young professionals. Expect dead-cheap beer, loud music & 4 flat-screen TVs.

♀ **Kukaramakara** Calle 28N, Bis–97; ✆ 653 5389. Famous throughout the city for the beautiful women it seems to attract, this simple watering hole often has live

music & is located in the north of the city. To get a table, order a bottle of liquor or a half-bottle to sit at the bar. That there isn't a dance floor doesn't seem to matter as everyone climbs on the table tops after about 23.00.

☆ **Las Brisas de la Sexta** Avenida 6N, No 15N–94; ✆ 661 2996. This popular hangout is one of the largest bar-cum-discos in Cali. The cocktails are strong & the music deafening in this hot & steamy salsotecas.

♀ **Lotus** Calle 15, No 9N–27; ↘ 681 5906. Chill-out music & moody, glowing walls attract Cali's style-setters in this decent early-evening option. ⊕from 19.00 for first-rate cocktails Thu–Sun.

♀ **Tin Tin Deo** Calle 5, No 38–71; ↘ 514 1537. Expect ear-splitting Música del Pacífico (African-Colombian music from the Pacific Coast) at this crowded bar, which attracts an easy-going mixed-age crowd.

Juanchito The Juanchito district south of Cali's city centre contains at least 30 salsa bars and salsotecas with new places opening up – and closing down. Two of the best-known salsa nightspots are both located on Juanchito's legendary Vía Cavasa.

Changó (↘ 662 9701) is a classic Juanchito nightclub that heaves with crowds of gorgeous, sexy movers in a smoke-filled atmosphere that positively sizzles with body heat. Not as swish, but still highly charged is neighbouring **Agapito** – a popular dance hall that plays the salsa fast and loud until 06.00.

Theatre

🎭 **Teatro Experimental de Cali (TEC)** Calle 7, No 8–61; ↘ 884 3821. Cali-born Enrique Buenaventura, one of Colombia's most successful dramatists, poets & theatre directors, founded this innovative company. It has since won considerable national & international acclaim for its ground-breaking drama & adaptations.

🎭 **Teatro Municipal** Carrera 5, No 6–64; ↘ 684 3578; www.teatromunicipal.net. Cali's oldest existing theatre dates back to 1918. It offers a year-round calendar of varied performances from classical concerts to opera & ballet.

Cinema As with Colombia's other two major cities, Cali has a number of multiplex commercial cinemas. One of the most popular is the **Multiplex Chipichape** (*Centro Comercial Chipichape, Av 6N, No 39N–25;* ↘ *644 2463; www.chipichape.com*), a large facility screening Hollywood offerings. The **Cinemateca La Tertulia** (*Museo de Arte Moderno La Tertulia, Av Colombia No 5, Oeste–105;* ↘ *893 2939*) is Cali's best art-house option. It's located in a fine facility established in 1536.

SHOPPING Cali has at least half a dozen shopping malls of which the Comercial Chipichape on Avenida NN, No 39N–25. is one of the best. Expect plenty of fashion brands, electronic shops, CD stores, perfumeries, handbags, and shoe shops. For a full listing visit www.chipichape.com.

OTHER PRACTICALITIES Cali has everything a traveller could need, from numerous banks with ATMs and dozens of great shopping malls to internet cafés, pharmacies, large supermarkets, hardware stores, camping shops, drug stores, camera shops, international payphones and gas stations. The biggest concentration of internet cafés can be found along Avenida Sexta where most charge around 2,300 COP per hour. The Bancolombia on the corner of Calle 15N and Avenida 8N is a favourite with foreign visitors as it changes travellers' cheques, offers cash advances on credit cards and changes currency. Medical centres are in good supply with a 24-hour city ambulance service (*dial 123*). Good hospitals include Clíníca Fundación Calle de Lili (↘ *331-9090*) and Clíníca de Occidente (↘ *660 3000/608 3200*) – both are open round the clock.

WHAT TO SEE AND DO

Zoológico de Cali (*Cnr Carrera 2A Oeste & Calle 14 Oeste; www.zoologicodecali.com.co;* ⊕*09.00–17.00; admission 7,000 COP*) With an excellent collection of species native to Colombia and a magnificent host of lush, green gardens, Cali's zoo is easily the nation's finest. Spread across 10ha around lakes and mature shrubs, the zoo is home to about 1,200 animals, representing some 180 species – from armadillos and condors to bears and butterflies. A key centre for research and conservation studies, the zoo's flower-filled picnic areas along the picturesque Río Cali make this an extremely pleasant place to spend the day.

Museo Arqueológico La Merced (*Carrera 4, No 6–59;* e *museolamerced@telesat.com.co; www.musarq.org.co/fpc/museo_merced.htm;* ⏰*09.00–13.00 & 14.00–18.00 Mon–Sat*) Cali's oldest existing building dates back to around 1538–40 and was formerly La Mercad Convent but today houses an archaeological museum containing a fine collection of pre-Columbian pottery. All of central and southern Colombia's ancient cultures are well represented, including Calima, Tierradentro, San Agustín, Quimbaya, Tolima, Nariño and Tumaco.

Iglesia de la Merced (*Cnr Carrera 4 & Calle 7;* ⏰*06.30–10.00 & 16.00–19.00; admission by donation*) The first foundation for Cali's oldest church was laid in 1545, just nine years after the founding of the city, and it was built in the best Spanish colonial tradition. A beautifully whitewashed exterior masks a rather simple interior of wood and stucco containing a long, narrow nave and a gilded, Baroque high altar.

Iglesia de San Antonio (*Colina de San Antonio;* ⏰*07.00–16.00; admission by donation*) The nuns at this pretty little hilltop church keep it in tip-top condition. Built in 1757, it contains some highly valuable *tallas quiteñas* from the 17th century – a rather fine set of Quito carved-wood statues of saints. It's an easy ten-minute walk westward from the old town centre. There's also a little stall selling religious art.

Museo del Oro (*Calle 7, No 4–69;* ⏰*10.00–17.00 Mon–Sat; free admission*) This small collection of Colombian gold is rather modest. There is also some pre-Columbian pottery made by the ancient tribes of Calima Indians.

Iglesia de la Ermita (*Cnr Av Colombia & Calle 13;* ⏰*mornings; free admission*) This early 20th-century construction contains an 18th-century painting *El Señor de la Caña* (Lord of the Sugarcane) that is said to have produced many miracles.

Museo de Arte Moderno la Tertulia (*Av Colombia 5 Oeste–105;* ✆ *893 2942;* ⏰*10.00–18.00; admission 2,000 COP*) Home to the city's best art-house cinema and a range of fine temporary exhibitions of contemporary paintings and photographic design, this fine collection is located just outside the centre of the city.

Iglesia de San Francisco (*Cnr Carrera 6 & Calle 10; free admission*) This 18th-century neo-classical church is next to the Convento de San Francisco and Capilla del la Immaculada and stands opposite a fine example of Mudejar art, the Torre Mudéjar bell tower.

Hacienda el Paraiso (✆ *256 2378;* ⏰*09.00–17.00 Tue–Sun; admission 3,500 COP*) A number of old sugarcane plantations outside Cali are now open to the public. One of the best is the Hacienda el Paraíso about 40km north of the city. Numerous tour operators run half-day trips & it is a fascinating way to see how the 19th-century Colombian elite lived. Today, this lovingly restored mansion is a well-stocked museum containing beautiful furnishings, paintings & books from a bygone Cauca era. The manor house also boasts literary connections as the setting of Jorge Isaacs's romantic period novel *María*.

Football The first Colombian city to host the Pan American Games in the 1970s, Cali is home to two of the nation's most successful soccer clubs, **Deportivo Cali** (*www.deporcali.com*) and **América de Cali** (*www.america.com.co*). Two vast stadiums

– Estadio Deportivo Cali (built in 2007, capacity 58,000) and Estadio Olímpico Pascual Guerrero (built in 1937, capacity 45,625) – cater to Cali's enthusiastic soccer nuts. Deportivo Cali is the older club, founded in 1912 with América de Cali established 15 years later. Fierce rivalry exists between the two, which are divided by clear class distinctions. Deportivo Cali is mainly supported by the affluent upper class with fans of América de Cali primarily working class from poorer outskirts of the city. Bad vibes have existed since the early 1930s when after a local derby América de Cali's players accused the referee and Deportivo Cali of fixing the match. In 1982, 24 people were killed and 250 injured during another bad-tempered clash after a stampede at the Pascual Guerrero stadium. At the time of writing, Deportivo Cali has the edge, having won 19 of the 39 league derby matches played in the last decade. The team plays in a green-and-white strip with the América de Cali team kit all red.

FESTIVALS AND EVENTS

My mother used to tell me that when I wasn't even one year old I would grab the bars of my baby bed and dance to the rhythm of Noel Petro's song Cabeza De Hacha.

Carlos Molina, Cali musician and owner of the Museo de la Música

Feria de Cali (*Dec; www.feriadecali.com*) Cali is famous throughout Latin America for its long-established Feria de Cali, Colombia's biggest festival. It runs from Christmas to New Year and pulls crowds from all across the region, filling up every bar, venue, park and salsa hall citywide. Expect lots of music, dancing and aguardiente-drinking in party-loving Cali plus a host of events that range from beauty pageants and *cabalgata* (parade of horseback riders) to bullfights, processions and salsa competitions.

Fiesta de Salsa (*Jul*) This week-long free summer salsa festival includes concerts by the world's great salsa musicians and dancers. Expect flamboyant costumes and 'melomano' competitions in which salsa connoisseurs try to outdo each other by digging deep to discover long-lost salsa classics.

DAPA (*Telephone code: 2*) Located 13km outside of the city, this little mountain settlement sits amidst cool mountain trails and cloud-shrouded peaks. Once too dangerous to visit, due to guerrilla and military activity, Dapa is now becoming a popular place for urbanites visiting at the weekend. A paved road winds up a mountain from the city passing little food kiosks on the way. Stream-fed natural bathing pools attract Caleños keen to escape the heat of the metropolis – they dip to cool off while eating arepa and chorizo on a Sunday. Crisp breezes fan the mountains with temperatures dropping dramatically the higher you climb. Fields and fields of coffee plants lead to vast stretches of forest and meadow. A popular area for kite-flying and horseriding, the area around Dapa is also popular with people keen to slide down the side of the mountain on a piece of cardboard – an exhilarating pursuit that draws the crowds. Peaceful walking trails delve deep into the heart of the mountains past creeks, wild poinsettias, rivers, ice-cold lagoons and hanging vines (*bejucos*) that are strong enough to swing on Tarzan-style. The town itself has a handful of friendly, local restaurants selling beer and simple meat-and-rice dishes. More and more makeshift roadside signs are also advertising cabañas and places to camp. Several local guides offer treks out across the rocks to Dapa's Cueva del Indio (Indian Cave).

Where to stay

El Parque Racaman Dapa \ 258 0185/880 1818. At the time of writing, this upmarket vacation accommodation 7km from Dapa is slated to open. Stylish tiled rooms boast en-suite bathrooms with a jacuzzi, swimming pool & a large mountain-front terrace. $$$

El Rincón de Dapa \ 664 9598/256 0256/312 721 2101. This charming casa de campo is owned by the patrons of the Juan de Farra (see *Entertainment and nightlife*, below), a young Colombian couple called Juan & Adriana. A comprehensive set-up offers guests every conceivable option, from a simple overnight camping stay to a full set of outdoor pursuits that includes horseriding, rappelling, fishing, hiking, buggy tours & hotel accommodation. Juan is an energetic, enthusiastic guide who enjoys nothing more than heading out into

the mountains to set up camp by the river & cook freshly caught fish over a fire. At the time of writing, 4 brand-new cabins offering luxury accommodation are set to open. Options range from 10,000 COP to camp to 250,000 COP for a cabaña that sleeps 4. $$

Hostel Mochileros \ 315 4200 315; e hostelmochileros@gmail.com; hostelmochileros.googlepages.com. Run by extreme-sport nut Fernando Urzuz, this dirt-cheap option is fine for those used to roughing it, offering empty rooms for backpackers equipped with a sleeping bag. A simple, clean wooden house designed around a large feature window affords magnificent views across the mountains. Urzuz runs rock-climbing tours, hikes, camping trips & horseriding. A local bus connects the hostel with the centre of Cali at 1,400 COP pp. $

Tour guide Affable **Juan Jaime Benítez** (*Juana de Farra;* \ 550 8049 or 312 288 9934) offers a range of guided trips around the Dapa area, from genteel river walks and camping to full-on extreme sports and mountain buggy drives.

Entertainment and nightlife

Juná de Farra \ 300 774 3592/613 0289; e juanadefarra@hotmail.com. This ultra-stylish open-sided bar sits right in the upper side of a mountain, wedged in amongst some stunning countryside & offering truly memorable views. Even on a dreary day, Juana de Farra's outlook is totally captivating – but in

clear, dry, sunny weather it'll draw an involuntary intake of breath. A huge drinks menu offers numerous cocktails, liquors & beers with a wooden bar & seating illuminated by candle lanterns. Expect atmospheric ambient music & a relaxed star-gazing crowd. Find it 7km from Cali on the Dapa road – look out for the sign.

Shopping

You'll find numerous small handicraft stalls and vendors along the Cali–Dapa road selling an array of bags, jewellery, woven crafts, scarves and knick-knacks. In Dapa itself, there is a small market of baskets, beaded bracelets and carved woods.

YUMBO (*Telephone code: 2*) Heavily industrialised with large paper-pulp factories, metal works and one of Colombia's largest breweries (a US$55 million Bavaria plant), Yumbo offers very little to tourists, apart from the usual practicalities for those passing through. Numerous gas stations, car repair shops, restaurants and hardware stores can be found on the town's outskirts as well as several small supermarkets and snack kiosks. Those keen to stop overnight will find a number of billboards for *hospedajes* and hotels on the approach road.

Tourist information
Local government website www.yumbo.gov.co
Yumbo city website www.yumbovalle.com

THE ROAD TO BUGA From Yumbo the road north towards Buga offers some extraordinary views from a winding mountain road that climbs and plummets in rolling waves. Startling green meadows lie permanently cloaked in haze with stud farms, haciendas and sugarcane fields as far as the eye can see. The occasional *poker* (beer) kiosk and rustic diner sits by the side of the road until at about 7.5km from Yumbo the Area de Servicio – complete with restaurant, toilets and showers – appears on the right. At about 18km from Buga on the left amidst cattle fields and horse farms you'll see the Restaurante Taypa, a fine-looking wooden building set high above the road that can't be missed. Further along, a string of juice vendors, snack stalls, watermelon sellers and a small kiosk sit opposite the Restaurante Fogonaza as you enter an area dubbed 'Little Switzerland' on account of its pine-clad slopes, flower-filled gardens and chalet-style houses.

BUGA *Telephone code: 2*

Founded in 1650, the agricultural town of Buga (*www.buga.gov.co*) sits on the Pan-American Highway and on a main route between Bogotá and Buenaventura. An important hub for trading cattle, rice, tobacco and sugarcane, the town has a population of 145,000. Despite pleasing temperatures that average 23°C year-round it is Buga's famous El Señor de los Milagros (Miraculous Christ of Buga) that prompts three million people to visit the town per annum. This vast basilica totally dominates the plaza and attracts numerous pilgrimages throughout the year. At the time of writing, Buga is undergoing a sympathetic beautification project to smarten up its streets and give the main square some TLC. Until just a few years ago, the town was considered off-limits due to guerrilla and paramilitary activity. In 2001, the United Self Defence Forces of Colombia (AUC) executed 24 people in Buga at point-blank range. Cancer victim Andrés Félipe Perez (aged 12) also earned the town worldwide media attention when he repeatedly appeared on Colombian television news. Perez was calling on rebels of the Revolutionary Armed Forces of Colombia (FARC) to free his kidnapped father, policeman Norberto – but died after his appeals were ignored. Today, Buga is making more cheery headlines and is enjoying vastly improved safety. The town stages a highly popular Agricultural Fair (*www.feriadebuga.com*) each July and celebrates Festibuga (*www.festibuga.com*) in August.

Although it has limited tourism facilities, Buga hopes that a new planned development 3km away will help bolster its profile. Vertigo Park at Club Estancia (*www.vertigothemeparks.com*) will span more than 2.5 million square metres and offer an outdoor eco-equestrian sports complex, 3,000 luxury timeshare units and

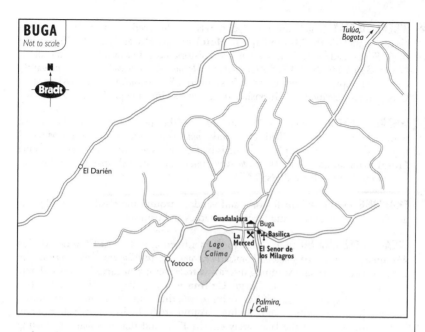

a shopping centre that will house outlet bargain stores, restaurants, a cinema, arcades and a theme park.

GETTING THERE AND AROUND Guadalajara de Buga can be reached by a 40-minute minibus journey from Cali's main bus terminal. Buga-based bus, coach and *buseta* companies include Trans Calima (✆ *227 7853*), Coop Ciudad Señora (✆ *237 0522*) and Montebello (✆ *228 3111*). It may also be possible to cadge a lift from the steady stream of Bugueños who travel back and forth, usually for around 10,000 COP. Taxi's are easy to find with Cootaxbuga (✆ *227 9495 / 237 4949*) and Unitax (✆ *227 7931*) two of the most reliable firms. Cross-region buses include Expreso Palmira (✆ *227 6586*) and Expreso Trejos (✆ *227 1171*). From Cali, the Tren Turistico Café y Azuca steam train connects with Buga via a seasonal schedule. Pick up a time-table from Cali's Central Station or contact the reservations office (*Avenida Vásquez Cobo No. 23N – 47, Piso 2;* ✆ *666 6899* & *620 2324;* e *trenturistico@ert.com.co; www.trenturisticocafeyazucar.com*).

By bus Buses run from Cali to Buga early 'til late seven days a week, every 20 minutes or so. Expect to pay around 9,000 COP for a one-way journey in a comfortable mini van. Services run 05.00–20.00 from Buga and 04.30–21.00 from Cali. Buses to Darién from Buga depart every 90 minutes, costing around 8,000 COP.

By taxi A cab across Buga will cost around 3,000 COP rising to 6,000–8,000 COP for trips to the outskirts. Expect to pay around 85,000 COP from Buga to the airport in Cali where frequent flights connect to Bogotá and Medlelin.

TOUR GUIDE John Howard (✆ *315 526 2053;* e *howie1006@hotmail.com*) speaks better English than many Britons, having studied it for many years. He teaches English at Buga's university and works as both translator and guide. Howard is also a thoroughly nice bloke with a staggering vocabulary – and is highly recommended to visitors to Buga.

WHERE TO STAY Buga's small, budget hotels are clustered on or around the main plaza and include the **Meson España Hotel** and the **Hotel Casa Del Peregrino** ($$). For considerably more style, head to historic **Hotel Guadalajara** on Calle 1, No 13–33 (❱ *236 2611;* f *228 2468; www.hotelguadalajara.com.co*) where 67 elegantly appointed rooms (including 18 suites) overlook a stunning courtyard garden. Onsite amenities include a Turkish bath, jacuzzi, swimming pool and sauna ($$$).

WHERE TO EAT A string of local restaurants edge the right-hand side of the basilica with almost all serving grilled meats and *rapido comida*, including the **La Merced** ($). However, the nicest place to dine is by far the restaurant at the grand colonial **Hotel Guadalajara** (see *Where to stay*) where delicate fish-in-sauce dishes are served by tuxedo-clad waiters ($$$).

SHOPPING Dozens of small stores and vendors around the Basilica sell religious artefacts, from necklaces and charms to statues and paintings.

WHAT TO SEE AND DO Buga's only tourism attraction is the vast **El Señor de los Milagros** basilica (e *info@milagrosodebuga.com; www.milagrosodebuga.com*)on the main square. It boasts a stunning interior with lavish use of carved wood and gilt.

Outside of the town, the **Largo Calima** is a popular out-of-town day-trip excursion. Expect windsurfing, fishing, boating, kite surfing, paragliding, waterskiing, jet skiing and diving around this hydro-electrical reserve. Temperatures around the lake rarely exceed 17°C and that national kite surfing championships are staged here is indicative of how windy it is. Depending on the season, it is also possible to camp here overnight – look out for the roadsigns by the side of the road for *cabañas* and *zona de camping*. The road out to the lake climbs up to a magnificent lookout, known locally as **El Panorama** – a great spot for a photo.

Reserva Natural de Yotoco This important state-managed 559ha woodland reserve is central to numerous conservation projects and studies and contains many of the region's 3,000 orchid species. It is also home to over 1,000 howler monkeys. Several high-profile behavioural studies by eminent international scientists have centred on the community of monkeys and their feeding, breeding and social characteristics. Other research projects include how the health of butterflies and insects in the reserve has been affected by changing weather patterns from the Pacific Ocean. Unfortunately, at the time of writing, a plan to enlarge a stretch of road looks as if it may impact the reserve to detrimental effect. Two trails – Sendero the Corbón (1 hour) and Sendero the Cedar (1 hour) wind through mosses, pine, cedar and bamboo. Visitors to the reserve need to seek permission ahead of arrival (❱ *228 1922; www.cvc.gov.co*). It is also possible to camp overnight and meet resident biologist, Pablo Emilio Florez Brand (e *pablo-emilio.florez@cvc.gov.co*).

AROUND BUGA

DARIEN (*Telephone code: 2*) This pleasant little town was founded in 1912 and is a nice place to explore on foot with neat streets and a pretty little plaza – and plenty of useful shops. Dozens of tiny restaurants, bars, kiosks and a bakery flank the main square, where the locals park their cars in haphazard style. There's also a pizza joint, laundry, doctor's surgery, dentists and a hardware store. There are a handful of small budget hotels just off the plaza, including the **Hotel Casa Blanca**, **Hotel Leyenda Calima** and **Hotel Calima Plaza**. For good local food try the **Café Monalva** and the **Restaurante Porvenir**. Darién's major tourist attraction is the **Museo Arqueológico** on the edge of town (◐*08.00–17.00 Tue–Fri, closed*

13.00–14.00, 10.00–17.00 Sat/Sun; admission 2,500 COP). It contains an impressive collection of pottery from the Calima culture.

HUILA AND CAUCA

For many years these two adjoining departments were too dangerous to visit due to a strong rebel presence that ruled all travel out. Today, the region is once again 'open for business' allowing a growing number of tourists to discover for themselves the treasures of the triangular route connecting the colonial gems of Popayán, San Agustín and Tierradentro's pre-Columbian marvels – each real 'must sees'. However, travellers should be aware that the British Foreign Office advice remains unchanged from years ago, stating: 'We advise against all but essential travel to the rural areas of Cauca and Huila, including to San Agustín and the Parque Arqueológico San Agustín'.

NEIVA *Telephone code: 8*

Although its full name is Nuestra Señora de la Limpia Concepción del Valle de Neiva, most people just call it Neiva, the capital of Huila with a population of

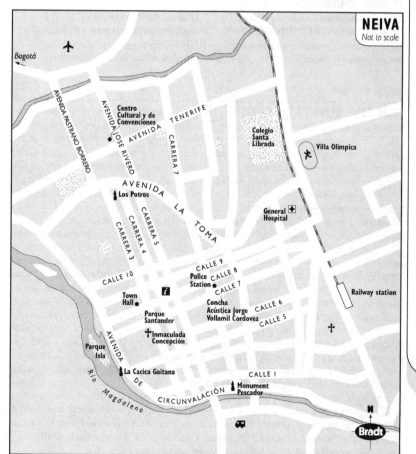

around 400,000 people. Close to the Equator and at a low altitude, Neiva is hot and dusty year-round with average daytime temperatures of 30°C. Most visitors arrive by plane flying low above the soupy Río Magdalena, a creamy-butterscotch expanse flanked by spongy grass. Home to several notable universities but just a meagre scattering of historic monuments, Neiva may not be on the radar of most international tourists but is important nonetheless. Providing a gateway to Bogotá and the world for the region's oil, coffee and vegetable farmers, the city provides an economic lifeline to the region. Mainly *mestizo* (mixed race) in ethnic make-up, Neiva has a strong folkloric tradition and stages three colourful annual fiestas, the Festival Folcórico, Reinado Nacional del Bambuco and Muestra Internacional del Folclor. However, most tourist arrivals in Neiva don't plan to stay, as they are hot-footing it to Popayán, San Agustín and Tierradentro

GETTING THERE AND AROUND Avianca flies thrice-daily from Bogotá to Neiva's Benito Salas Vargas Airport with regular direct connections to half a dozen other Colombian cities. A colectivo departs every 30 minutes or so from Bogotá's main bus terminal (18,000 COP, 9 hours). Driving from Bogotá to Neiva takes about six hours.

TOURIST INFORMATION

Z **Secretaría De Turismo Y Cultura Departamental** Cnr Carrera 4 & Calle 8; ↘ (8) 875 3042/ 2995; f (8) 8671300; e benjamin.vinasco@gobhuila.gov.co; www.gobernacionhuila.gov.co

Z **Oficinas Municipales De Turismo** Calle 16, No 7–45 Antigua Estación del Ferrocarril; ↘ (8) 871 2439/7621; f (8) 8714135; www.gobernacionhuila.gov.co **Neiva town website** www.alcaldianeiva.gov.co

AROUND NEIVA

ROAD FROM NEIVA TO SAN AGUSTÍN This five-hour drive makes for a superb road trip through dry, dusty farming towns hemmed by rice paddies and vegetable fields. First, pass through the rice-growing village of **Campoalgre**, a gritty working town with a few simple food joints serving breakfast for 1,500 COP, before hitting **La Vega Da Oriente**, a place famous for its *alfarería* pottery. At the humble carrot-farming town of **El Hobo** there are numerous sizzling food stalls around a small plaza as well as a handful of local restaurants and a fried-chicken joint. A string of roadside banana stalls and ceiba trees hail the approach road to **Gigante**, a busy little chocolate-making town. A couple of restaurants and a hotel sit on the left tucked amongst the trees with a small tourist information office by the main square – look out for green signs. Around the plaza you'll find a bakery and half a dozen restaurants with beer shack 'El Gaucho' on the right on the road exiting the town. A kilometre on, on the **Quebrada la Honda** (Honda Creek) there's a nice open-sided wood-and-thatch grilled-meat place. Then it's past some particularly charming rose-coloured fincas by the **Río Oro**. The town of **Garzon** is notable as the first Catholic settlement in Huila and has become an important religious centre, attracting pilgrims in their droves. It's also a town of considerable hubbub with numerous shops, banks, drug stores, restaurants and cafés – and also boasts a 1km stretch of cheap-food stalls. Leaving the town behind to pass tethered mules and scrawny chickens by the roadside, the road snakes into cattle-grazing country dotted with smallholdings to **La Juaga**. This handicraft centre is famous for its bags, mats and jewellery boxes made from *figue* (palm fibre). The town is also reputed to be the home of Las Brujas (witches), slow-speaking long-haired women with mystical powers that are said to curse. At **Altamira**, 75km from San Agustín, the Amnesia Latin Club makes a decent place to stop for a drink – it's open dawn until dusk; look out for a bright orange building.

A terrifying hairpin bend heralds breathtaking views of the **Río Magdalena** at a point used as a suicide spot by ancient Indians in the village of **Pericongo**. Vast cliffs overlook the fast-flowing river, a reminder that Huila means 'Mountain with life' in the language of indigenous tribes. In the horse-and-trap town of **Timaná** you'll pass cute little single-storey houses in pastel hues. The main square has a rather fine pinky-red brick cathedral with a handful of basic amenities nearby. Huila's second city **Pitalito** is famous for its coffee, a rich, full-bodied and distinguished coffee with citrus acidity and a tart undertone. Cows nibble on the verges that edge the city's outskirts alongside a necklace of stalls selling milk, cheese and vegetables. Farmers ferry their crops across town in the *zorras* (horse-pulled carts), careering around a busy main plaza edged by cycle shops, hardware stores, bakeries, drug stores and local restaurants. Founded in 1818, Pitalito has around 100,000 inhabitants and is 188km from Neiva. The city averages daily temperatures of around 19°C and is served by Contador Airport, located 6km outside of town on the road to San Agustín. The road out of Pitalito is edged with brightly coloured gardens selling plants, shrubs and flowers. Sombrero-wearing campesinos walk their prize bulls to market past fields of sunflowers and vegetables and hedges of violet bougainvillea. Soon wooded slopes and gushing streams soften dramatic views of the mountains. Lush, green thickets of vegetation mean that San Agustín is nearing – fast.

SAN AGUSTÍN (*Telephone code: 8*) Tourism has more than doubled since the safety situation began to improve dramatically and today San Agustín is fast becoming one of Colombia's most talked about attractions. City-dwellers from Bogotá visit at weekends and during *puentes* (extended breaks). Although the town itself is nice enough, it is San Agustén's fascinating archaeological zone that people come to see, 2.5km to the west.

Getting there and around Regular minibuses run from Neiva (11,000 COP, 5 hours) with buses from Bogotá (35,000 COP, 12 hours) and Popayán (13,000 COP, 8 hours). Battered taxis nip back and forth around San Agustín's tree-lined streets but most attractions can be reached on foot.

Tourist information
🅩 **Tourism Office** Cnr Calle 3 & Carrera 12; ✆ 837 3062; 🕔08.00–17.00 Mon–Fri, closed noon–14.00

San Agustin town website www.sanagustin.com.co

Tour guides **Fabio Burbano** clearly relishes every aspect of San Agustín's mysterious history and as the owner of **World Heritage Travel** (✆ 837 3940; e *viajespatrimoniomundial@yahoo.es*) offers a range of archaeological tours to the area's 18 sites. Prices vary with itineraries arranged to suit individual needs.

🏠 **Where to stay** At the time of writing a number of new hotels are in the planning, but only one is near completion as detailed below. Unfortunately accommodation in San Agustín falls well below the Colombian average so be prepared to shop around and check out different rooms. Half a dozen signs had also sprung up on the roadside by the Hotel Yalconia advertising cabins and camping. All accommodation tends to suffer from damp and mustiness due to the local climate.

🏠 **San Agustin International Hotel** e imturcol@gmail.com. More likely to appeal to domestic tourists than international visitors, this global-themed collection of 6 individual houses seems a little out of place. Each has been built to a unique design & reflects American (à la New England), Mediterranean, Arabic, oriental, Scandinavian & traditional Colombian architecture. Houses can be shared or hired & can accommodate between 8–12 people. It's located just slightly outside of town. $$$

🏠 **Hotel Yalconia Vía al Parque Arqueológico** \ 837 3001; e hyalonica@hotmail.com. Probably the best

option at the time of writing, with OK rooms & an OK restaurant about 1km from the centre of town. $$

🏠 **Casa de Nelly** \ 837 3221. This simple boarding house is located just on the edge of town to the west & rooms overlook a garden. $

✗ **Where to eat** There are numerous eateries around town, including lots of small, inexpensive local places. In the centre there's everything from burgers and pizza to Chinese. However, **Donde Richard** (*Vía al Parque Aqueológico;* \ *311 809 3180*) is the best value and the most consistent restaurant in San Agustín. It serves up big plates of grilled meat, fish, pork, sausages and chicken from a pleasant open kitchen with wooden tables and chairs on a tiled floor.

Entertainment and nightlife San Agustín is not renowned for its party scene, but there are a handful of bars and a couple of clubs in the centre of town, including the **Santelmo Disco Bar** and the **Casa de Tarzan**.

Other practicalities There are a number of banks but none reliably offers anything other than cash withdrawal – and even then there is only a single ATM at the **Banco Ultrahuilca** (*Calle 3, No 12–73*). There's a reasonable internet café opposite the tourist office: the **Internet Galería Café** (⊕*08.00–22.00*).

What to see and do Declared a UNESCO World Cultural Heritage Site in 1995, the site of the **Parque Arqueológico** (⊕*08.00–16.00 year-round; admission 6,000 COP*) is shrouded in mystery as almost nothing is known about its exact origins or purpose. An incredible array of carved monumental stones of varying shapes, styles and sizes are believed to have been erected to honour the dead. That they have remained so perfectly untroubled and intact is almost impossible to rationalise, given the history of unrest in the region. However, it is easy to fathom why an ancient civilisation would choose this stunning setting as consecrated ground – it is a beautiful and other-worldly spot. Yet without a written language to go on, experts have applied scientific guesswork to unravel the history of the site – but why or how the entire culture was wiped out nobody knows. Set amidst 78ha of massifs and canyons, the ceremonial stones symbolise continuity, birth and evolution and are thought to date from the second century BC to the tenth AD. Megalithic tombs, small temples, sculptures and anthropomorphic figures span a wide range of themes, both human and beast. The monuments were first discovered by Juan de Santa Gertrudis in 1758. He wrote a book, *Natures Wonders*, prompting a thorough investigation by German Koonrand Theodor Preuss.

A particularly interesting cluster of 34 stones is located by a riverbank, thought to be a foot-washing area, **Fuente de Lavapatas**. Carvings include a birthing chair, snakes, frogs, birds, human faces and eagles. A path winds up to the **Alto de Lavapatas** where the oldest archaeological site is located. As well as some magnificent statue-guarded crypts there are astounding views. At the entrance of the park the **Museo Arqueólogical** contains some of the artefacts discovered on the site.

Other fine archaeological attractions can be found at the **Alto de Los Idolos**, located 4km southwest of San José de Isnos on the other side of the Río Magdalena. It is notable for the largest ceremonial stone in the San Agustín area, and many visitors choose to access the park via a very pleasant three-hour walk across the Magdalena Gorge. **Alto de las Piedras** is 7km north of Isnos and contains a distinctive collection of stones dyed black, red and yellow. **El Tablón**, **La Pelota**, **El Purital** and **La Chaquira** are often visited in a single trip as they are situated quite close together, a five-hour hike or four-hour horseback trek. Other lesser-known archaeological sites include **Naranjos**, **El Jabón** and **La Parada**. Appointing a specialist guide is highly recommended (see *Tour guides*, pagte 277).

TIERRADENTRO (*Telephone code: 2*) This remote little town is notable for its remarkable catacombs – a collection of tombs complete with pillars that boast an elaborate décor. Hundreds have been recovered so far, but archaeologists expect to unearth more in the future as they are often set as deep as 9m underground. Some are painted with geometric patterns in black and red with carved figures hewn out of the chamber walls. Some of the tombs measure up to 7m in diameter and have been expertly scooped out of rocky volcanic terrain. Amidst verdant, mist-cloaked hills, the site is thought to date between the 7th and 9th centuries AD, but very little is actually known about the civilisation that created the tombs. Spread across five separate sites, Tierradentro consists of four underground and one above-ground tomb. Tierradentro was declared a World Heritage Site by UNESCO in 1995.

Getting there and around At least three buses pass El Cruce de San Andrés, a 15-minute walk from the museums, on their way to Popayán (13,000 COP, 6 hours). Two direct buses connect with Bogotá and San Agustín with a more frequent service from Pitalito a 45-minute colectivo journey away.

Where to stay and eat Accommodation is scarce and simple in and around Tierradentro – but the good news is it's cheap. Close to the museums, the **Hotel El Refugio** (↘ *824 0220;* $$), is the most comfortable option and has a swimming pool, sauna and restaurant in lovely gardens. The best shoestring hotel is the nearby **Hospedaje Pisimbalá** ($).

Other practicalities Most hotels are happy to arrange guides, horses and maps in the absence of a dedicated tourist office. Temperatures average 18°C and it can be damp at times. When visiting the tombs, pack a torch – but don't bother with a camera as photography is forbidden.

What to see Most people head to museums first as most attractions lead off from this part of town. A combined ticket offers admission to both museums over two consecutive days and also includes entrance to all archaeological sites. Decorated pottery forms the centrepiece of the collection at the **Museo Arquelológico** while the **Museo Etnográfico** houses an exhibition of Páez Indian artefacts. Both are open 08.00–16.30 daily.

To explore burial sites and tombs, walk for 15 minutes north uphill to **Segovía** where there are 28 catacombs and some of the best preserved. From Segovía, walk another 15 minutes uphill to the four tombs of **El Duende** before heading to the five tombs of **Alto de San Andrés**, two of which are perfectly intact. Close by, **El Tablón** comprises ten elaborate stone monuments, like those found at San Agustín. The 30-plus tombs at El Aguacate are a two-hour walk from the museum high on an isolated mountain ridge. All have been raided so are something of a disappointment, although the walk itself offers magnificent views.

LAGUNA BETANIA Approached by a giant causeway 9km from Hobo, this vast water reserve has become a sport-fishing and fish-farming centre. Developed as a hydro-electrical resource by the Colombian government in 1997, 80% of the energy generated is sold to Ecuador. The reserve is now Chilean owned. However, fish stocks at the Laguna Betania were severely affected by a drought in April 2007 after an estimated three million died after a four-month drought. Water levels fell so drastically – 25m in just a few months – that there was insufficient oxygen in the lake to sustain its dozens of hatcheries. More than 1,320 tonnes of tilapia floated to the surface during soaring temperatures. The local fish industry, which exports the tilapia as fillets to the United States and Europe, lost more than US$2 million after burying and incinerating the dead fish. To protect consumers from the threat of contaminated fish, Colombia's government placed a temporary ban on the sale of fish produced in Betania's hatcheries. It pledged US$700,000 in federal subsidies to help fishing stocks recover and asked Spanish power company Endesa SA to help restore the reservoir's water levels by scaling back production of electricity at the dam. Views around this 541-megawatt hydro-electric facility are well worth enjoying. A number of tourist facilities have begun to spring up around the shores of the dam, including kayaking and fishing boats. There are also usually a handful of taxis and local colectivos hanging around.

YAGUARÁ (*Telephone code: 8*) A sculpture of a bull and *campesino* in the ultra-neat Parque Angel María Paredes forms the centrepiece of this small farming town. Founded in 1623 as a cattle-breeding centre, 49km southwest of Neiva, Yaguará was largely neglected until 2005 after being effectively cut off by rebel violence. Today mass investment by Mayor Luis Ernesto García has put the town and its 9,200 population back on the map. At the time of writing, a swanky tree-lined waterfront promenade is about to open, replacing a stretch of wasteland – a US$30 million, 1.2km regeneration project that has revitalised Yaguará. A gleaming tourist information booth reflects the townsfolk's optimistic outlook for the future. Also on the boardwalk are a stone-built open-air auditorium and paths for rollerblading, cycling and jogging – all with superb views over the lake. In the fullness of time a further 2.8km will be added to the main drag to include a conservation area complete with ecological trails. There are also plans to construct a bridge from the promenade to the other side of the lake. Largely pedestrianised, with taxis and bicycles the only vehicles allowed, Yaguará's promenade already has a couple of very nice restaurants and is poised to attract many more. It is also the launch point for cruise boats and water taxis out to lake-based attractions on a picturesque body of water created by the Betania Dam.

Getting there and around Frequent buses and colectivos connect with Neiva and the surrounding area with Yaguará's many taxis huddled around the square.

Tourist information

🛈 **Yaguará Secretaría De Turismo** Calle 4, No 3–91 Alcaldía Municipal; ☎ 838 3066; 📠 838 3069; 🖂 yaguara@coll.telecom.com.co ; www.municipioyaguara.gov.co

🛈 **Department website** www.yaguara-huila.gov.co

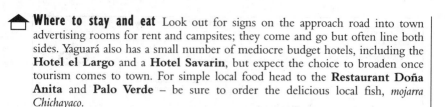

Where to stay and eat Look out for signs on the approach road into town advertising rooms for rent and campsites; they come and go but often line both sides. Yaguará also has a small number of mediocre budget hotels, including the **Hotel el Largo** and a **Hotel Savarin**, but expect the choice to broaden once tourism comes to town. For simple local food head to the **Restaurant Doña Anita** and **Palo Verde** – be sure to order the delicious local fish, *mojarra Chichayaco*.

What to see No visit to Yaguará is complete without taking to the waters of **Largo Yaguará** – an extraordinarily beautiful expanse set amidst lush, green rolling hills. Ferries depart at the weekends at 15.00 for four-hour trips around the lake's most scenic spots. Costs vary, but expect to pay around 10,000 COP with food and drink extra from the café on board. Another option is to hire a boat for around 120,000 COP – they typically seat about six passengers and come with two drivers. Highlights include the **Bahía de Chichayaco** where the water reaches a depth of 15m and the **Quebrada de Chichayaco** (Chichayaco Creek) which runs into the lake. This is where Yaguará's plentiful stocks of freshwater *mojarra Chichayaco* are found and on the surrounding hills a growing number of deluxe mansions owned by Colombia's affluent business reflect the growing popularity of the area with second-homers. One such area is the **Costa Brava,** a stretch that overlooks rice fields, and offers outstanding lakeside views. At the beautifully contoured **Punta Catalina**, thick folds of vegetation form a patchwork of different shades of green. **Santa Helena** used to be a simple farm, but is now a Mecca for watersports enthusiasts with boats, jet skis and kayaks for hire amidst former chocolate fields. Two particularly undulating mounds, known as **Las Tortugas** (The Turtles), denote another prime spot to fish. An Italian construction team working on the dam named the **Cuevas del Amor** (Caves of Love) in 1988. These Tolkein-esque labyrinths hewn from towering pink rock became a favourite spot for the workers to engage in a bit of romantic activity – and it remains popular with courting couples today.

There are some rather fine houses in the street beyond the promenade where the buildings were once home to families and their livestock. Vast wooden doors are a common characteristic of these aged properties as the entrance needed to be big enough to accommodate both man and beast. Now beautifully restored, this fine-looking street – dubbed **la calle de puertas** (the street of doors) – makes for a pleasant stroll as is Yaguará's most historic quarter. It begins at the church on the plaza and heads right down to the water.

POPAYÁN *Telephone code: 2*

Renowned throughout Colombia as 'La Ciudad Blanca', Popayán is an architectural treasure, which joins Villa de Leyva and Cartagena as the nation's most handsome colonial cities. Surrounded by the undulating Valle de Cauca, Popayán (at an altitude of 1,737m) was once a strategic stop-off between Quito and the Caribbean coast – a transfer point for riches bound for Spain. It was founded in 1537 by conquistador Sebastián de Benalcázar but takes its name from the indigenous *po* (meaning two), *pa* (meaning straw) and *yan* (meaning village) – a reflection of a time when Popayán was just a couple of straw-roofed villages. Although very little is known about the pre-Hispanic history of the town, Popayán has an ancient Indian pyramid known as El Morror de Tulcán. The structure was already abandoned when the Spanish first arrived to the city but is thought to have been a burial site. Local legend has it that the inner structure holds treasure and gold.

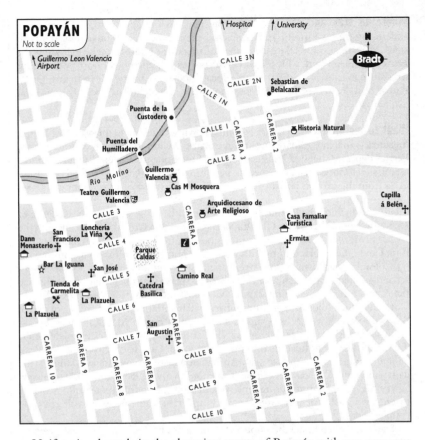

POPAYÁN
Not to scale

Hospital | University

Guillermo Leon Valencia Airport

CALLE 3N

CALLE 2N

Sebastian de Belalcazar

CALLE IN

Puenta de la Custodero

CALLE I

Puenta del Humilladero

CALLE 2

CARRERA 3

CARRERA 2

Historia Natural

Rio Molino

Guillermo Valencia

Teatro Guillermo Valencia

Cas M Mosquera

Arquidiocesano de Arte Religioso

CARRERA 4

CALLE 3

Lonchería La Viña

San Francisco

CALLE 4

Parque Caldas

CARRERA 5

Casa Famaliar Turistica

Ermita

Capilla á Belén

Dann Monasterio

Bar La Iguana

San José

CALLE 5

Camino Real

Tienda de Carmelita

La Plazuela

CALLE 6

Catedral Basilica

La Plazuela

San Augustin

CALLE 7

CARRERA 6

CALLE 8

CARRERA 10

CARRERA 9

CARRERA 8

CARRERA 7

CALLE 9

CARRERA 4

CARRERA 3

CARRERA 2

CALLE 10

Bradt

Uniformity abounds in the charming streets of Popayán with one gorgeous whitewashed street connecting to another. Numerous churches reflect the town's religious importance and Popayán's many monuments, cobbled paths and pretty plazas are a true delight. On 31 March 1983 a violent earthquake caused massive devastation moments before the city's much-celebrated Maundy Thursday procession was set to depart. It was a highly destructive 18 seconds, causing widespread damage to much of Popayán's historic core. The quake measured 5.4 on the Richter scale, killing about 250 people and injuring 1,500. More than 2,400 homes were completely destroyed with another 6,900 suffering major structural damage. Also destroyed were streets, schools, health facilities, shops, commercial and office buildings, rural infrastructure and bridges. The damage made it difficult for the government to function as public utilities needed major repair. The loss of electric power greatly complicated initial disaster relief efforts, such as providing emergency shelter. The resulting restoration took more than two decades to complete but the results are stunning with very little signs of any destruction evident today. Historically, Popayán has suffered major earthquakes at intervals of around 80 years – a cyclical pattern that will no doubt worry residents in 2063.

Popayán is famous throughout Colombia for its cultural and political life. It was once the nation's capital and boasts the distinction of producing more Colombian presidents than any other city – 17 to be precise. Popayán has also played an important role in the arts as the home of poets, painters, playwrights and composers and is synonymous with enlightened, progressive thinkers keen to lead and effect change. Today the city's sizeable student population enjoys some of the oldest academic establishments in the country, bringing 2.4 million COP to Poyayán's economy. The city's traditional colonial-era layout of neat linear narrow streets has a quirky peculiarity: two curved roads – the Calle de Banano and the Calle del Caiho – named after a banana and a horn.

GETTING THERE AND AROUND At the time of writing, flights to Popayán are shared by Aires and Satena – but with just two a day seats need to be pre-booked. At the time of writing, the airport is situated 15 minutes' walk north of the city next to the bus terminal. However, a brand-new airport is under construction and is scheduled to open in 2009.

Ten different buses provide an excellent range of overland options, including departures to Cali every 15 minutes (18,000 COP). At the time of writing a new road to the Pacific coast is slated to open in 2010, enabling a 2½-hour drive to Guapi with connections to Isla Gorgona.

Numerous taxis operate throughout the city, charging 3,000 COP for a ride across town.

TOURIST INFORMATION
🛈 **Oficina de Turismo de Popayán** Carrera 5, No 4–68; 📞 824 2251; 🕓 08.00–18.00 Mon–Fri (closed noon–14.00), 09.00–noon Sat

WHERE TO STAY
🏠 **Hotel Camino Real** Carrera 5, No 5–59; 📞 824 3595; www.hotelcaminoreal.com. Another of Popayán's finer hotels, the Camino Real is a resplendent colonial building that offers stylish rooms on a grand scale. $$$

🏠 **Hotel Dann Monasterio** Carrera 4, No 10–14; 📞 824 2191; www.hotelsdann.com. This former Franciscan monastery is Popayán's landmark hotel with plush rooms set around a vast courtyard & a host of top-notch onsite amenities, inc a swimming pool. $$$

🏠 **Hotel La Plazuela** Calle 5, No 8–13; 📞 824 1084; e laplazuela@hotmail.com. This ultra-handsome whitewashed colonial mansion is packed with character, from its lovely arcaded courtyard garden & hulking wooden doors to its tiled lobby & antiques. A restaurant serves particularly good food, inc delicious home-baked rolls. Family run, spotlessly clean & well located. $$

🏠 **Casa Familiar Turística** Carrera 5, No 2–07; 📞 824 4853. This shoestring option doesn't look much but it is clean, practical & convenient – & is a gathering point for international backpackers. Expect simple rooms & a shared kitchen. $

WHERE TO EAT
Restaurants are easy to find in and around the historical centre and are well supplemented by street vendors selling tamales, juice and the local specialities, *empanadas de pipián* (a delicious empanada recipe using peanuts and potatoes), and a refreshing drink made from rice and *lulo* fruit, *champús*.

✗ **Lonchería la Viña** Calle 4 No 7–79; 📞 824 0602. This family-run diner is rather schizophrenic in character with a restaurant section featuring a collection of nicely laid tables & suited waiters accompanied by a blaring TV, vending machine & take-away service. However, it is open when everything else is shut & serves decent food. $$

✗ **Los Kingos de Belén** Calle 4, No 0–55. It's just a simple little local food joint but the Kingos de Belén serves up generous portions of regional fare with a choice of set meals & snacks. $

✗ **Tienda de Carmelita** Calle 5, No 9–45; 📞 824 4862. This scruffy little snack shack serves cheap & delicious empanadas de pipián & cold drinks, but is – rather annoyingly – closed at lunchtime.

ENTERTAINMENT AND NIGHTLIFE For a student town, Popayán has a distinct lack of nightlife. Try **Bar La Iguana** on Calle 4, No 9–67, for pumping salsa and cheap beer. For a night of retro tango head to **El Sotareño** – an outmoded Popayán institution renowned for its passé style, elderly vinyl records and faded décor.

SHOPPING At the time of writing, the town's old airport is scheduled for conversion into a shopping plaza. It is located 15 minutes' walk north of the town and is scheduled to open in 2009.

OTHER PRACTICALITIES Popayán has a decent handful of banks, all with ATMs. As with most student towns, it also has numerous internet cafés, including the **El Universitario** on Carrera 6, No 3–47, and **C@feto** on Carrera 9, No 5–42. Both charge 2,000 COP per hour. Lone travellers seeking to hook up with others should head to **Tienda de Faby** on Calle 5 to check out its well-used notice board.

WHAT TO SEE Popayán's historic centre is home to all of the city's main sites of interest with narrow streets set within ten blocks that are easily navigable on foot. Almost all of the churches are open daily at around 08.30 and 17.00 for mass. Wear comfy shoes and prepare to put in some leg work to see the lot within a single day. A stop-off at the leafy **Parque Francisco José de Caldos** makes a pleasant spot for respite amidst shoe-shiners and domino-playing elders. A statuesque **clock tower** bears a clock face donated by the British Embassy in 1983 after the earthquake.

Popayán's largest colonial church is the **Iglesia de San Francisco** (corner Carrera 9 & Calle 4), a very handsome building with a stunning high altar. The **Iglesia de San Agustín** (corner Carrera 7 & Carrera 6) and the **Iglesia de San José** (corner Calle 5 & Carrera 8) are other fine churches to visit. As the oldest church in the city, the **Iglesia la Ermita** (corner of Calle 5 and Carrera 2) dates back to 1546. On Parque Caldos, the neo-classical **Catedral** is Popayán's newest religious building, built between 1859 and 1906 after an earthquake destroyed the previous church.

Museo Arquidiocesano de Arte Religioso (*Calle 4, No 4–56;* ✆ *824 2759;* ⊕ *09.00–17.00 Mon–Fri , closed 12.30–14.00, 09.00–14.00 Sat; admission 2,000 COP*) Housed in an attractive colonial building set around a courtyard, this large collection of religious art re-opened in 1989 and includes some magnificent silver items. Artefacts have been gathered from churches all over the region and include jewel-encrusted altarpieces, communion vessels, paintings and statues, many from the 17th century but some dating to 1580. Only a small proportion of the entire collection is on display at any one time – the rest of the time it's housed in eight vast vaults that are protected by an automatic locking system that only opens twice a year. The building itself dates back to 1763 and today it also plays host to a number of important religious congresses.

Museo de Historia Natural (*Carrera 2, No 1A–25;* ✆ *820 1952;* ⊕ *08.00–17.00 daily, closed noon–14.00; admission 3,500 COP*) This sizeable collection contains a much-acclaimed array of insects, stuffed birds and butterflies.

Casa Museo Mosquera (*Calle 3, No 5–38;* ✆ *824 0683;* ⊕ *08.00–17.00 daily, closed noon–14.00; admission 3,500 COP*) Once home to General Tomás Cipriano de Mosquera, Colombian president between 1845 and 1867, this colonial mansion contains an interesting collection of personal artefacts relating to his life. After suffering face wounds during a battle in 1824, Mosquera was forced to wear a metal prosthesis. This earned him the nicknamed 'Mascachochas' by his critics.

Museo Guillermo Valencia (*Carrera 6, No 2–65*; ☏ *824 2081;* ⊕ *10.00–17.00 Tue–Sun, closed noon–14.00; admission 2,000 COP*) This sizeable collection of period furniture, paintings, documents and old paintings relates to the Popayán poet who lived in this gorgeous 18th-century building. Guillermo Valencia's son, Guillermo León Valencia, was Colombian president 1962–66.

To the north of the historic centre on the Río Molino, two bridges can be seen. The **Puente de la Custodia** is the smaller of the two and was built in 1713 as a crossing point for priests to enable them to administer to the city's poorer outlying areas. The larger bridge, **Puenta del Humilladero**, was constructed 160 years later alongside it to provide a more robust crossing – and this rock-solid 178m structure is still used today. It is overlooked by the majestic slopes of the **Cerro del Morro**. Close by in the **Archivo Central del Cauca**, over four million ancient documents contain the history of the city dating back to 1541 in rows and rows of dusty tomes stored in vast oak cabinets.

Don't pass up an opportunity to poke your head into the doorway of the **Teatro Municipal Guillermo Valencia** – the 900-seat auditorium was restored in 1987 but retains a retro style. Opposite, spot the fabulous wrought-iron gates of the **Colegio Mayor del Cauca** English school.

The tiny hillside chapel of **Capilla e Belén** offers magnificent city views just east of the centre. Thought to be an old Indian burial site, **El Morro de Tulcán** also affords stunning vistas and is home to a statue of the town's founder, **Sebastián de Benalcázar**. Sadly, in sharp contrast to the pristine historic centre, this is graffiti-adorned and littered with rubbish.

FESTIVALS Crowds of some 20,000 people descend on Popayán for the city's famous **Semana Santa** (Holy Week) when stunning night-time processions snake through the streets. In 2006, the event celebrated its 450th anniversary, having taken place every year since 1556. Each year's procession is so complex it takes 12 months of planning and follows a route of 54 stopping points across the city over the five-day event. Vast religious wooden figures of elaborate design are carried by townsfolk as part of the procession. Each weighs over 500kg and requires eight bearers who will then have to take the strain for over four hours across 20 blocks, from 20.00 to midnight. Every icon is assigned a *sindico* between each year's event who are required to maintain and restore it.

A **Gastronomic Festival** in early August is another major tourist draw with food stalls, markets and cook-offs throughout the city.

AROUND POPAYÁN

NACIONAL PARQUE PURACÉ This 83,000ha reserve 45km south east of Popayán contains some heavenly hiking trails amidst a geothermal wonderland of hot springs, waterfalls and grasslands – as well as an inactive volcano from which it derives its name. Created in 1961, the reserve sits at an altitude of between 2,500–4,750m above sea level, so offers plenty of geological biodiversity, rising from boggy, humid jungle to the snowy chill of rugged peaks. More than 50 lakes and a dozen creeks are home to many species of frogs, birds, butterflies and insects. The black-and-chestnut eagle, rainbow-bearded thornbill and yellow-bellied chat tyrant are all resident in the park. The volcano itself is a pleasant four-hour trek along a leafy trail that climbs up from the visitors' centre. The park's Cascada del Bedón (waterfall) and major lake (Laguna de San Rafael), is an 8km hike from the road from the nearby village of Pilimbalá. Less than 2km from the falls you'll find the hot springs of the Termales de San Juan, in what is a scenic 15km round-trip.

Other trails lead to caves (Cueva de los Guácharos) and smaller lakes, including the Laguna de la Magdalena. A striking characteristic of the landscape is its defined patches of colour. Visitors can stay overnight in three rustic cabañas; each sleeps six and there is also camping in four tents that accommodate five apiece. Entrance is 18,000 COP with a dorm bed 13,000 COP per night plus 10,000 COP for three square meals. Visitors need a permit to enter the park from the Parques Nacionales Naturales de Colombia and should prepare for sharp temperature variations as these can range from 12–20°C. A very helpful ranger has maps and route plans for most of the trails – find him in the visitors' centre.

NARIÑO

Colombia's most southwesterly department boasts a checkerboard terrain from blankets of thick jungle to towering Andean peaks. An array of indigenous cultures and strong Ecuadorian influences ensure the cultural make-up of Nariño is quite unlike any other part of the country. Some of Colombia's finest ceramics and textiles are produced in the region where a strong artistic tradition prevails. Pasto's Carnaval de Negros y Blancos is one of the nation's most riotous while the region's hybrid ethnicity ensures the food is a wholly unique fusion of flavours.

However, the Nariño has become synonymous with many of Colombia's ills as a centre for coca production and cross-border conflict in recent years. The jungle geography and the rivers along the Colombia–Ecuador border make it perhaps one of the continent's most complex regions to patrol. It remains a hotbed of guerrilla activity with petroleum plants, including the San Miguel de Orito pipeline, relentlessly targeted by FARC. In times of upheaval, the region has also experienced massive flows of displaced people. Drug traffickers frequent the Colombian–Ecuadorian border, which is notorious for a steady flow of contraband. Goods are ferried in and out in vast quantities by any means possible, from human couriers and trucks to mules, buses and bicycles. Some of the most toxic and dangerous agrochemicals in the world are also shipped for use in cocaine production. In 2005, the authorities seized over 1,093 tonnes of solid supplies and 182,000 gallons of liquid substances used for the purpose. Corruption is said to have permeated all levels of the military and government on both sides of the border.

As Colombia's largest drug producer, Nariño is prolific: conservative estimates put the number of hectares planted with coca plants at 13,875 – but the reality is that it is almost certainly much, much more. Figures closer to 70,000ha are often quoted by the local population. Official figures reckon that 44 tonnes of cocaine is produced in Nariño each year – much of it bound for the US via Ecuador. Amidst this scenario, Colombia's Washington-supported aerial spraying of coca crops has caused considerable cross-border tension. Although coca has been grown in Nariño for more than 25 years the amount of crops has increased markedly since the late 1990s. Official reports suggest that 103,343ha of illicit crops were sprayed in the first seven months of 2005 alone. A highly toxic herbicide containing glysophate is used in Colombia's anti-narcotics aerial spraying programme and this has sparked fierce complaints from farmers on both sides of the border who claim it has seriously affected human health and poisoned livestock and vegetables. Demands by the Ecuadorian government for a 10km no-spray zone have failed to impress the Colombian authorities who remain committed to their programme. So far, it has failed to meet its goal of eliminating 50% of illicit crops in the country, despite an investment of nearly US$1.2 billion. More than four times the initial area of coca has been sprayed.

In 2005, both the United Nations and the US government reported an increase in the area covered by illicit coca crops. A BBC investigation in the same year revealed that just eightweeks' production in a single Nariño coca production plant can amount to £800 million worth of cocaine in UK street prices, enough to buy Manchester United football club. At the time of writing the security situation in Nariño is best described as 'patchily turbulent'. Mixed reports from travellers crossing the border from either side suggest the situation is potentially volatile with months of calm suddenly becoming 24 hours of turmoil overnight. The British Foreign Office advises against all travel to Nariño with the exception of the border town of Pasto. Visitors should only travel during daylight hours and never cross the city after dark.

PASTO *Telephone code: 2*

Most visitors to Pasto are simply travelling through: hopping on or off a bus to Ipiales to cross the border to Ecuador or boarding a plane to Bogotá – or beyond. Like most transportation hubs Pasto lacks any real beauty, despite having several rather fine colonial buildings. An earthquake in 1834 destroyed many of its oldest buildings, leaving Pasto without a great deal of character. As Nariño's administrative and political capital the city has a busy commercial centre. Despite its reputation for shady dealings, Pasto is a friendly place to be during daylight hours. It was founded in 1537 by Lorenzo de Alana and sits at the eastern base of the volcano La Galera at an altitude of 2,530m. Pasto is famous throughout Colombia for its barniz de Pasto, a glossy vegetable resin used to decorate wooden artefacts, and numerous examples of these colourfully decorated bowls, mats and boxes can be seen throughout the city.

GETTING THERE AND AROUND Colectivos nip back and forth to the airport 33km to the north of the city every 45 minutes (6,000 COP) from Calle 18 at Carrera 25. Get your hotel to pre-book this for you and the driver will pick you up. Both Avianca and Satena run flights to Cali and Bogotá with connections to other cities.

Frequent buses, minibuses and colectivos connect with Ipiales (8,000 COP, 2 hours), Cali (30,000 COP, 9 hours), Popayán (25,000 COP, 6 hours) and Bogotá (75,000 COP, 22 hours). The bus terminal is 2km south of the city, a 4,000 COP taxi ride away.

TOURIST INFORMATION

Oficina Department de Turismo de Nariño Calle 18, No 25–25; 🕾 723 4962; ◴08.00–18.00, closed noon–14.00

City website www.gobernar.gov.co

 Where to stay There are plenty of hotels in the city but choose one with a restaurant to avoid having to cross the city after dark.

Hotel Agualongo Carrera 25, No 17–83; 🕾 723 5216; f 723 0604. Pasto's most luxurious central hotel contains 12 storeys of large modern rooms & top-notch private bathrooms overlooking the Plaza de Nariño. $$

Hotel Concorde Calle 19, No 29A–09; 🕾 731 0658. Located close to the Plaza de Nariño, this basic mid-range option isn't big on style but represents good value near to all central amenities. $

Hotel Rey del Sur Carrera 9, No 15A–10; 🕾 720 7909. This inexpensive hotel near the city's bus terminal 2km outside of the centre is modern & clean. Expect simple rooms with private bathrooms & cable TV. $

Koala Inn Calle 18, No 22–37; 🕾 722 1101. This backpacker haunt comes highly recommended & is a popular choice with travellers crossing to & from Ecuador. It has all the usual budget travel amenities, from a book exchange & noticeboard to a laundry & shoestring restaurant. Choose from a collection of spacious rooms set around a courtyard, some with a private bathroom. $

WHERE TO EAT

Caffetto Calle 19, No 25–62; ✆ 729 2720; ⏰ noon–late. One of the city's upmarket options with an international menu of salads, soups, sandwiches, juices & milkshakes. $$

Picantería Ipiales Calle 19, No 23–37; ⏰ 09.00–21.00 Mon–Sat, 10.00–18.00 Sat. Choose from a simple menu of delicious home-cooked meals, including fish-&-rice and grilled chicken, as well as plenty of fast food & snacks.

Restaurante Tierra Colombiana Chipichape Calle 18, No 27–19; ✆ 772 8992; ⏰ 07.00–21.00 Mon–Fri, 07.00–15.00 Sat. This cheerful diner serves simple local chicken-&-rice dishes & decent b/fasts. $

Salón Guadalquivir Plaza de Nariño; ✆ 723 9604; ⏰ 08.00–19.30 (closed 12.00–14.30) Mon–Sat. Expect plenty of Colombian staples at dirt-cheap prices in this bustling little place, such as meat-filled empanadas & crispy tamales.

OTHER PRACTICALITIES Almost every bank, internet café, *casa de cambio* and international payphone is centred on the Plaza de Nariño. Those crossing to Ecuador should change their money here rather than rely solely on Ipiales.

WHAT TO SEE

Museo Taminango de Artes y Tradiciones (*Calle 13, No 27–67;* ✆ *723 5539;* ⏰ *08.00–18.00, closed noon–14.00; admission 1,000 COP*) Dating back to 1623, this is one of the city's oldest houses, a large restored mansion that houses an eclectic mishmash of antiques and books.

Museo del Oro (*Calle 19, No 21–27;* ✆ *721 9108;* ⏰ *08.30–18.00, closed noon–14.00; admission free*) This small collection of pre-Columbian gold and pottery from the indigenous cultures of Nariño is actually pretty impressive.

Iglesia de San Juan (*Plaza de Nariño*) Check out the largely restored city church's lavish gold interior décor and ornate colonial Baroque detail. The building itself dates back to the 16th century but had lots of 18th-century attention.

FESTIVALS AND EVENTS

Carnaval de Negros y Blancos (*Jan*) Be prepared for lots of uptempo processions and music during this two-day festival, celebrated since the time of Spanish rule. The city fills with the rhythmic sounds of beating drums and dancers in colourful garb and painted faces. It's a mad-cap high-energy event that goes back to the days of slavery and culminates in a messy merriment of black and white paint, flour and talc.

AROUND PASTO

VOLCÁN GALERAS The hiking trail from Pasto to the summit of this vast brooding volcano takes about 4½ hours and climbs up to 4,276m along some beautiful scenic paths past farms and meadows. Although it was active as recently as 2006, several guides offer treks along the 9km trail – including those employed by the tourist board. Views from the top take in a spectacular panorama across the city and beyond. An eruption in November of 2005 threw smoke and ash across Pasto and surrounding villages, prompting 8,000 to evacuate their homes.

LAGUNA DE LA COCHA Everybody raves about the beauty of this beautiful lake and cloudforest – and it more than lives up to the hype. Located 30 minutes east of Pasto, the Laguna de la Cocha is a peaceful and resplendent place in which to fish for trout. An offshore island reserve (La Corota) offers magnificent views across the water and can be reached by boat. At 75m in depth and 20km long by 5km wide the lake is one of the largest in Colombia and is an important scientific research centre under the auspices of the University of Nariño. Colectivos from Pasto serve the lake from the front of the church on Pasto's main square. The 20km trip will cost around 4,000 COP.

IPIALES (*Telephone code: 2*) Located 5km from the Ecuadorian border, Ipiales is every inch the ugly frontier town: grimy, seedy and functional with very little soul. Everyone is on the move to somewhere more inspiring. That there is nothing to see or do makes it all the more dreary – a town that people visit as a necessity, not for joy. Set on the banks of the Río Guáitara at 2,897m above sea level it was founded in 1585 by Spanish missionaries. Apart from its border role, Ipiales is famous for its Indian markets and the manufacture of woollen and cotton textiles. The city has a population of around 75,000 and is often visited by pilgrims heading to the sanctuary of the Virgin of Las Lajas, reputed to be a site of miracles.

Getting there and around Avianca flies to Bogotá with connections to other cities but there are no flights from Ipiales to Ecuador. Ipiales Airport is 7km northwest of the city, a 13,000 COP taxi ride. Ipiales bus terminal is new and efficient 1km northeast of the centre. Frequent buses connect to Bogotá (75,000 COP, 25 hours), Cali (30,000 COP, 10 hours), Popayán (25,000 COP, 8 hours) and Pasto (4,000 COP, 2 hours). Numerous colectivos, taxis and minibuses serve the border at Rumichaca (1,000 COP) – cross on foot before jumping in a taxi for the 6km trip to Tulcán, where there is a small airport.

Where to stay The city has a number of hotels as befitting a busy frontier post; some are better than others but most represent decent value. For a good choice of restaurants head to the Plaza de la Indepencia. You'll find everything from burger bars and French fries to fish-and-rice and *empanadas*.

Hotel Metropól Calle 14, No 7–30; ☎ 773 3851. Conveniently located opposite the bus terminal, this modern hotel has simple, but comfortable rooms, each with private bathroom. $$

Hotel Belmonte Carrera 4, No 12–111; ☎ 773 2771. This little cheapie favoured by backpackers has cold-water bathrooms but is friendly, clean & family run with decent-sized rooms. $

Hotel Los Andrés Carrera 5, No 14–44; ☎ 773 4388; f 773 3255. For smart rooms, excellent amenities & swish décor don't look anywhere else – this super hotel is top value & has a gym & sauna. It is also home to the finest restaurant in the city, the Restaurante Las Colinas.

Other practicalities Ipiales's Puente Internacional de Rumichaca border closes 22.00–06.00 so allow enough time for border-crossing formalities. The city's internet cafés are notoriously slow; head to Internet (*Calle 16, No 6–51*) for the speediest connection. Several banks are clustered around the Plaza la Pola, some with ATMs. None change travellers' cheques or offer currency exchange but there are a handful of money changers nearby.

What to see Ipiales is renowned for being the home of **Sanctuario de las Lajas**, but this pilgrim site is actually located 7km south of the city. An enormous vertical rock is believed to have great religious significance and has attracted those in need of a miracle since the mid 18th century when an image of the Virgin Mary is believed to have emerged from the stone. Set 45km above the river, the rock is surrounded by plaques of prayer and edged by a church built between 1926 and 1944. Grab a colectivo from Ipiales (1,000 COP, 15 minutes), from Carrera 6 at Calle 4 or hire a cab for the return trip for around 10,000 COP.

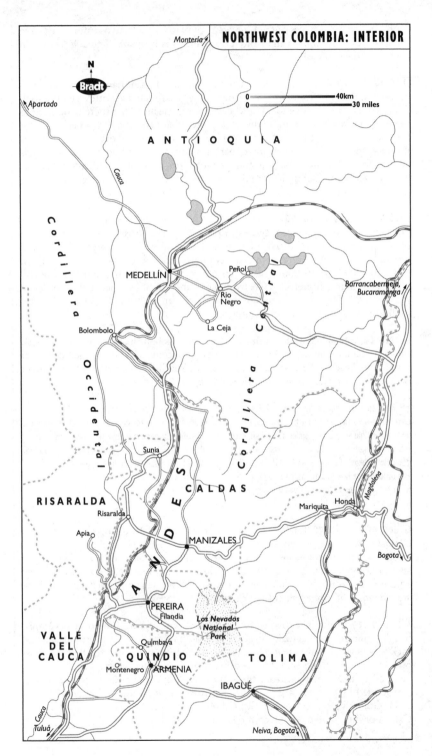

Monteria

N

Bradt

0   40km
0   30 miles

Apartado

A N T I O Q U I A

Cauca

MEDELLÍN

Peñol

Rio Negro

Barrancabermeja, Bucaramanga

Bolombolo

La Ceja

Cordillera Occidental

Cordillera Central

Sunia

A N D E S

C A L D A S

RISARALDA

Risaralda

Mariquita

Honda

Magdalena

Apia

MANIZALES

Bogota

PEREIRA

Filandia

Los Nevados National Park

VALLE DEL CAUCA

Quimbaya

Q U I N D I O

Montenegro

ARMENIA

T O L I M A

IBAGUÉ

Cauca

Tuluá

Neiva, Bogotá

9

The Northwest Interior

Our home, our mountains, our family for those we toil. Our hearts, our God, our pride for those we sweat. País Paisa for ever.... our homeland.

Anon, *'País Paisa'*

Colombia's northwest interior region is a landscape of two distinct characters, deftly defined by the majestic peaks of the Andes range. Sharply rising terrain soars up from steamy flatlands to cooler, verdant highlands and snow-capped mountaintops. Fertile valleys clad with thick, lush vegetation are home to folds of coffee, plantain and banana crops set in nutrient-rich soils. Pretty wooden haciendas sit enveloped by rolling meadow overlooked by fog-cloaked forests atop scrub-covered hills. Horseriding *campesinos* cart sacks of coffee beans to market while oxen plough the fields. The region's aged colourwashed colonial settlements are some of Colombia's most inviting with cobbled streets, flower-filled baskets and sleepy plazas seemingly lost in time. Tangled clumps of sky-high ferns form uniformed lines on plump waterlogged terraces. Winding lanes are shaded by palm leaves the size of bathtowels aside rocky rivers.

ANTIOQUÍA

Spanning 63,612km², the department of Antioquía occupies the central northwestern part of Colombia with a narrow strip that borders the Caribbean Sea. Comprising some of South America's most mountainous terrain with deep lush valleys and fast-flowing rivers, Antioquía's population of almost six million are true country folk. These so-called 'Texans of Colombia' have a strong cultural identity linked to the geography of the region, a territory isolated from the rest of Colombia from the 17th until the mid 19th century when the Antioquía expansion began. Many Antioqueños are known as Paisas (a shortened version of the Spanish 'Paisano' meaning countryman) although strictly speaking Paisa Country (País Paisa) is a larger region made up of Caldas, Risaralda, Quindío, the north of Valle

FAMOUS PAISAS

- Alvaro Uribe: President of Colombia 2002–10
- Pablo Escobar: leader of the Medellín drug Cartel
- Juanes: pop star, song writer and anti-landmine campaigner
- Fernando Botero: artist who donated works worth US$120-million to Colombia
- André Escobar: footballer murdered after scoring own goal in 1994 World Cup
- Santiago Botero: professional cyclist and World Time Trial Champion 2002

del Cauca and the northwest Tolima and just 80% of Antioquía. Paisas are true country folk who relish their strong cultural identity linked to the mountainous geography of the region. Isolated from the rest of Colombia until the mid-19th-century expansion, Antioquía's remoteness plays a crucial role in the make-up of the Paisa psyche – proud, resolute and self-sufficient. Alternately the butt of jokes and the object of envy for many Colombians, what makes Paisas stand out is their rugged individualism and nose-to-the-grindstone hard-work ethic. This reputation stems from the mid 19th century when Antioqeños seized the government's carrot of free land and cleared their hinterland for agriculture. Huge progress ensued, earning them a certain status throughout Colombia. Soon, they became synonymous with industriousness, thriftiness and skill at turning a profit. Today that reputation persists with the term Paisa meaning anything related to, or originating from, the region – with perhaps the biggest Paisa contribution to Colombia being its coffee. At the very heart of Paisa Country is the mushrooming metropolis of Medellín – Colombia's former murder capital – a city now transformed into one of the nation's most progressive. Lush, rolling coffee fields lie scattered with pretty fincas and Paisa homesteads, encircling the cities of Manizales, Armenia and Pereira in the Zona Cafetera de Colombia. Unknown even to native Colombians until the mid 2000s, the 'Coffee Zone' is the country's fastest upcoming tourist attraction – a place where visitors can harvest coffee beans, learn about crop yields, discover the history of coffee growing and sample an array of rich, dark aromatic Colombian varieties. It is also an excellent base from which to explore one of Colombia's most exceptional national parks, the **Parque Nacional Natural Los Nevados**.

HISTORY By the 18th century, almost all of the Antioquía's indigenous Indians had been wiped out by disease or Spanish settlers. They belonged to the Caribe ethnic group, which in its turn was divided into three tribes and families: the ferocious Catíos (who inhabited Urabá and Chocó), the fearsome Nutabes (located between the Cauca and Porce rivers) and the peaceful Tahamíes (who lived between the Porce and the Magdalena rivers). Fighting the Spanish with bows and arrows, often laced with poison, the Indians slowly lost their territory, eventually surrendering to slavery and ultimately to death.

The first Basque families from northern Spain began arriving in the 16th century, establishing small homesteads in what is now eastern Antioquía. The terrain, similar to that of the mountainous northern Spain region, soon had numerous settlements of family units. That these were not just communities of single men made a big impact to the local culture. Close-knit and hard-working, these early Basque pioneers began to shape the identity of the Antioquía. To this day, Paisas speak using a distinct Castilian sounding 's' with Basque less commonplace. They also tend to be more conservative than other Colombians with a clear devotion to family life. But above all, *Antioqueños* have a formidable settler's drive – and a strong and determined will.

MEDELLÍN

The city of Medellín used to be synonymous with Colombia's deadliest drug wars and was also a critical hub for guerrilla activity. However, the city's security situation has undergone a dramatic improvement in recent years. Many of Colombia's largest drug cartels – once a powerful fixture in Medellín – have now been dismantled, with the city's left-wing warring factions significantly reduced in size and clout. The Colombian president Alvaro Uribe is a home-grown *Antioqueño* (see box, *Famous Paisas*, page 291) and has been widely praised for cracking down on crime via a zero-tolerance stance. As a consequence Medellín has blossomed into a fine city of considerable elegance with high-end restaurants, swanky bars, chi-chi boutiques, iconic street art and plush galleries in abundance. Today, it is hard to believe that stylish, cosmopolitan Medellín was once under the violent control of drug lord Pablo Escobar, Colombia's most deadly cocaine baron who ruled his empire by savage means. In the 1980s Escobar's leadership saw Medellín become one of the most murderous cities on the planet. After his death at the hands of the police in 1993 Medellín entered a new era. It now ranks amongst the safest metropolises in Latin America – although some hidden dark forces remain. In June 2007, 49-year-old Regulo Leal (aka Arley Leal) was arrested in Medellín on homicide and kidnapping charges. He is reported to be the commander of the 32nd Front of FARC (Revolutionary Armed Forces of Colombia), the nation's most dominant guerrilla militia group. Leal is thought to have overseen a 1996 attack on a military base in which 28 soldiers were killed and 60 others kidnapped. His capture served as a shock reminder of a chilling era of evil to the people of Medellín – a breed renowned for their friendly, sunny disposition.

HISTORY As the former capital of the world's cocaine trade, Medellín's history is sufficiently colourful to warrant several chapters in its own right. From the 1980s until the late 1990s, the city was the base of the world's most powerful international drug-trafficking organisations. It was also a city bloodied by the very worst of Colombia's violent conflict. Social unrest and street gangs made Medellín one of the most violent cities on earth with 6,349 homicides recorded in 1991 alone – 11 times that of Chicago. Today, much has changed and Medellín has done much to shake off the notoriety of its past. The image of the city has undergone a massive transformation, with tangible results. In 2005 the homicide rate was 35 per 100,000 people, the lowest in over 20 years, and one of the best improvements of any city on the planet.

In 2007, huge infrastructure projects continue to redefine Medellín's skyline, with new public libraries, congressional centres, expansive plazas, schools and strong community programmes in the pipeline. The city's 2.4 million inhabitants are fiercely proud of their new, improved metropolis – and justifiably so. As the second most populated city in Colombia after Bogotá, Medellín is a leading industrial centre as well as a cultural hub of international repute. Heavy urban development is evident throughout the city with Medellín's construction of new skyscrapers outpacing all other major Colombian cities. As of August 2007, there were over 120 high rises under construction in Medellín with 60 more proposed, more than in the cities of New York City, Los Angeles and Philadelphia combined, according to government statistics. Medellín is also home to over 30 universities, including some of Colombia's most important public and private establishments such as the Universidad de Antioquía, Universidad EAFIT and Universidad de Medellín.

The 100th most populous urban area in the world, Medellín was founded in 1616 by Francisco Herrera y Campuzano but was first discovered by Spanish explorer Jeronimo Luis Tejelo in 1541. It was originally named San Lorenzo de Aburra but this was changed in 1675 to Villa de Nuestra Señora de la Candelaria de Medellín but has also been known as San Lorenzo de Aná, Valle de San Bartolomé, Aburrá de los Yamesíes, San Lorenzo de Aburrá, Villa de la Candelaria de Medellín and Medellín over the years. In the 1960s, Medellín's now infamous drug cartels turned the city into a violent battleground and the world's cocaine capital. Bloodthirsty gangs roamed the streets, extortionists preyed on residents who feared for the lives of their families and narcotics traffickers attacked the police. It was a bleak era for Medellín with seemingly little hope of change. However, change did come thanks to a city blessed with true Paisa grit and determination. A large-scale clean-up transformed huge areas of Medellín in an urban regeneration project unprecedented in Colombia. Decaying hovels used by drug dealers, hookers and hit-men have been turned into swish new office complexes stylishly renovated in upscale mews. Large international conglomerates and more than 70 foreign organisations now have their Colombian HQ in Medellín, among them Phillip Morris, Levi's, Renault, Toyota, Kimberly Clark and Mitsubishi. Educational parks have been built all over the city. In 2005, a 30,000ft^2 convention centre opened to much acclaim and now hosts a dozen international congresses each year, an enterprise that alone generates over US\$100 million in investment and business deals. Medellín's fashion industry is second only to São Paulo's in Latin America; its medical sector a leader in organ transplants, AIDS and cancer research. The city has over 30 universities and attracts 130,000 students each ear. Pleasant open-air settings are adorned by the sculptures of Medellín-born artist Fernando Botero (see page 37), replacing a seedy red-light district and tatty open-air street market.

That the city is now a living renaissance of peace and hope is due in no small part to the vision of the Mayor of Medellín, Sergio Fajardo – a man considered instrumental in the rebirth of Medellín. His evangelical enthusiasm for spearheading what he calls 'From Fear to Hope' has captured the hearts and minds of Colombia. Since taking office, he has pushed ahead with a programme of rehabilitating the homeless and has continued to eradicate street crime. Fajardo has also effectively closed down Medellín's most notorious no-go areas. Turning blight into beauty, leafy parks and statues have replaced dimly lit scrubby wastelands and rubbish-strewn alleyways – a regeneration symbolised by the city's iconic central mural 'Horizontes' in which two Paisas are depicted looking forward and beyond.

CLIMATE Medellín's location, 1,500m above sea level, equips it with pleasantly warm year-round weather with an average annual temperature of 22°C and minimal variations. This agreeable 52-week spring-like climate has earned Medellín the nickname of 'La Ciudad de la Eterna Primavera' (City of the Eternal Spring), with weather that is more characteristic of a humid sub-tropical zone than that of a tropical region.

GETTING THERE International flights arrive and depart via Medellín's José Mariá Córdova International Airport (MDE) (*www.aerocivil.gov.co/Aeropuertos/Rionegro*) in the Rionegro suburb, 35km from the city with daily flights to and from Miami, New York, Caracas, Quito, Panama City, Porlamar, Aruba and many other cities worldwide. Medellín's domestic hub is Olaya Herrera International Airport (EOH) (*www.aeropuertoolayaherrera.gov.co*), serving mainly regional flights, commuter, charter and light aircraft. It was once the city's only airport and ceased handling international flights once José Mariá Córdova was built. Aerolineas de Antioquía (ADA) (❧ 255 99 99) operate flights to Armenia, Bahía Solano, Bucaramanga, Cali, Capurgana, Carepa, Cartagena, Caucasia, Condoto, Corozal, El Bagre, Manizales, Monteria, Necocli, Nuqui, Pereira, Puerto Truinfo, Quibdo, Remedios, San Pedro and Turbo. Aires Colombia (❧ 361 13 31) fly to Apartado, Barranquilla, Bucaramanga, Carepa, Cartagena, Cúcuta, Ibagué, Manizales, Monteria, Pereira and Quibdo, while Satena (❧ 361 40 56) offer frequent flights to Apartado, Bahía Solano, Barranquilla, Bogotá, Bucaramanga, Cali, Carepa, Corozal, Nuqui, Pereira, Quibdo and Villavicencio.

GETTING AROUND Medellín is divided into six metropolitan zones and these are subdivided into 16 communes that are in turn split into barrios and urbanisations. The city contains more than 230 barrios (districts) and five corregimientos

Dining on the gut-busting Antioquian traditional dish is an enormous undertaking that is best avoided by those watching their waist. Created to provide sustenance for hard-working country folk, Bandeja Paisa is not for the faint-hearted. It is often served on plates the size of a tea tray and is an incredibly filling man-sized meal. Is it healthy? No – it's high in calories, carbohydrates and saturated fats, but this didn't stop attempts by the Colombian government to make it the national dish. The idea was rubbished by everyone outside of Paisa Country, most of whom favoured sancocho (soup). Nonetheless, many commercial organisations choose to use the image of Bandeja Paisa when promoting Colombia. In this respect it is almost certainly the nation's most recognisable dish.

INGREDIENTS

4 cups kidney beans	1 chorizo sausage
1 tablespoon salt	2 cups of white rice
2 tablespoons tomato paste	2 tablespoons oil
2 diced green plantains	Sliced plantains
Grated carrot	4 oz pork crackling
1 roasted pork trotter	1 arepa (or soft corn tortilla)
1 x 8 oz steak	1 large egg

Rinse the beans before cooking, then place them in a pressure cooker half filled with water and add 1 tablespoon of salt. Cook the beans for approximately 30 minutes. Then add the tomato paste, diced green plantains and grated carrot before cooking for another 20 minutes. Add the trotter.

Grill the beefsteak and chorizo for 5 minutes each side and steam the white rice for 20 minutes. Fry the sweet plantains until golden brown. Roast the pork crackling until crispy (1 hour). Warm the tortilla and fry the egg, placing it onto the portion of rice in the middle of the plate. Add the beans to the left and position the remaining items to the right … then loosen your belt.

(subdivisions) and is divided north to south by the **Río Medellín** (Medellín River). Medellín's six zones are defined as the Northwestern Zone (Castilla, Doce de Octubre and Robledo); Northeastern Zone (Aranjuez, Manrique, Popular and Santa Cruz); Southeastern Zone (El Poblado); Southwestern Zone (Guayabal and Belén); West Central Zone (Laureles, La América and San Javier); and East Central Zone (La Candelaria, Villa Hermosa and Buenos Aires). Streets are laid out according to the Cartesian grid system with calles running from east to west and vice versa with numbers increasing south to north (except in upmarket El Poblado where numbers increase north to south). However, most locals refer to streets by colloquial names, not numbers – and this can be confusing. That aside, Medellín's compact city centre is easy to navigate around the Parque de Bolívar with almost all of its first-class nightlife and restaurants found along Calle 10.

Medellín is rightly proud of its public transportation system, a pioneering joined-up network of diesel buses, cable cars and an urban train referred to as the Metro de Medellín that connects the city with outlying areas. Line A departs from Itagüí to Niquía, while Line B goes from San Antonio to San Javíer. Line K comprises a cable car, locally known as Metrocable, and serves a sprawling, ramshackle neighbourhood on a mountainside that was once geographically remote. Line K begins on Acevedo station on Metro Line A, and continues uphill ending in Santo Domingo Savio. At the time of writing, Line J is earmarked to open any day and will connect San Javíer with La Aurora. The Metro de Medellín operates from 05.00–23.00 Monday to Friday and from 07.00–22.00 Sunday and public holidays with a train every three minutes during peak hours (see box, *Worth every penny*, opposite) at a cost of less than 1,000 COP. Using public transport is highly preferable to attempting to navigate the roads of Medellín. Traffic is chaotic as the number of vehicles continues to exceed the capacity of local highways. Impassable gridlocks are common and even short journeys are arduous. Those mad enough to try it will find hire car agencies throughout the city and within each airport.

Medellín has two bus terminals, conveniently named Terminal del Norte and Terminal del Sur. The northern terminal serves all destinations to the north, east and southeast and is located 3km from the city centre (a 4,000 COP taxi ride or five-minute metro journey). The southern depot is 4km southwest of the city centre (4,000 COP by taxi) and handles all traffic to the south and west of Medellín. Frequent services connect to most major cities, including Barranquilla (65,000 COP, 15 hours), Santa Marta (70,000 COP, 16½ hours), Popayán (22,000 COP, 5 hours). Bogotá (45,000 COP, 9 hours), Cali (40,000 COP, 9 hours) and Santa Fé de Antioquía (8,500 COP, 3 hours). Shuttle buses run back and forth from José María Córdova Airport to the city centre every 30 minutes or so – the journey takes about an hour and costs 5,000 COP. Taxis are also in plentiful supply Medellín-wide – a cross-town trip will set you back about 10,000 COP with an airport run around 35,000 COP. Taxis are metered and clearly show the exact fare, unlike Bogotá. Small *busetas* operate throughout most of the metropolitan area until around 23.00 and are clearly marked. At the time of writing, a brand-new Metroplus network is scheduled to open. This bus service will have an exclusive road route to allow faster transit and will operate much like Bogotá's TransMileno system. Most of the city will be served by the network, which should help alleviate the city's traffic congestion problems. All buses will run on natural gas in an effort to limit air pollution.

TOURIST INFORMATION

⏹ **Fomento y Turismo** Palacío de Exposiciones, Aveninda Alfonso López; ☎ 232 4022; ⊕ 08.30–17.30 Mon–Fri, closed 12.30–13.30. This well-stocked tourist office is located about 1km southwest of the city and has maps, flyers & a hotel-booking service.

TOUR OPERATORS Dozens of local companies offer day trips around the city, from self-guided open-top buses to tailored itineraries for singles or groups. Canadian-educated **Natalia Mejia Jiménez** (e *nataliamejiajimenez@gmail.com*) speaks excellent English and offers guided tours to fit in around her medical studies. Medellín born and bred, Natalia is passionate about her home town and is extremely well versed in its social and modern history. Medellín's excellent **Turibus** service (☎ 285 1978) journeys from sight to sight across the city. It picks up and drops off at numerous points from its main departure point on Parque de Bolívar for a single-priced ticket (9,000 COP) Tuesday to Saturday 09.00–17.00. The 2006 'Meet Your City' has also made this highly popular with local sightseers. A more turnkey tour solution is provided by **Las Buseticas** (☎ 262 7444; *www.lasbuseticas.com*) – a professional outfit that offer a range of flexible itineraries to suit individual needs from 50,000 COP, including a guide and lunch. To enjoy Medellín's spectacular views from a bird's-eye vantage point contact the city's premier paragliding school. **Boomerang** (☎ 254 5943; e *piloto_x@hotmail.com*) – exhilarating tandem flights across the skyline require no previous experience and cost 60,000 COP. The city's government-sponsored army of **tour guides** is largely made up of tourism students. Look out for a uniform of bright blue T-shirt and baseball cap but don't expect much more than directions and a map.

It may have cost the city over US$1.6 billion, but in societal terms the debt of the Metro de Medellín (*www.metrodemedellín.org.co*) is worth its weight in gold. Sure, it will take at least 60 years to pay off, but it's a small price for a ground-breaking feat of modern engineering that has revolutionised the social fabric of a city. Before the Metro de Medellín and its cable cars, vast swathes of the city's outlying neighbourhoods were only accessible via an arduous trek across the mountains on foot. Today, these once isolated ramshackle suburbs may still cling desperately to the slopes but they are just a few minutes from Medellín's commercial centre – not a gruelling day-long hike. Not only has this improved employment prospects and fostered better social interaction it has opened up economic participation – just a few lasting benefits of Medellín's revolutionary mass transportation system that remains the envy of many cities in the world.

Medellín's complex urban transport system has transformed Medellín from a provincial town to a world-class commercial centre, crossing the metropolitan area from north to south and from centre to west. An important social and cultural tool that has redefined the city, the Metro of Medellín has created a metropolis in which workers of every class can travel from A to B with ease. After the inaugural journey at 11.00 on 30 November 1995 the Metro of Medellín soon became a symbol of the city, heralding the unification of its remote, poorer and marginalised neighbourhoods with affluent areas. An absence of graffiti, chewing gum and litter in its pristine carriages is testament to how much the system is adored by the locals. That it is clean, efficient, safe and respected is a real source of Paisa pride. Genteel, patient, orderly queues are very much the norm.

At the time of its launch, the Metro had 25 stations – today it has more than 30, with over 90 cable cars shifting 14,000 people per day at a rate of ten per cart along four separate lines. Trains run mainly at ground level apart from a stretch along a viaduct. The cable car route climbs up a steep hillside and offers magnificent views frighteningly close to the rooftops. These communities are now fully employed – once an impossible dream due to their ostracised locations.

In every way, the Metro of Medellín continues to redefine the city, spawning dozens of important public areas along its routes. Plazas, galleries, restaurants, libraries, parks and recreational zones are still being added, awarding new vision and fresh cultural dimensions to the communities in Colombia's burgeoning second city.

WHERE TO STAY Medellín has many places to stay and offers reasonably priced accommodation, from the shoestring hostels in El Centro to El Poblado's grand five-star hotels.

Hotel Dann Carlton Carrera 43A, No 7–50; 444151; www.hotelesdann.com. Without a doubt one of the most upmarket hotels in the city, the Hotel Dann Carlton offers every 5-star amenity you'd expect in a privileged location in El Poblado. Large, luxurious rooms are equipped with safety deposit boxes, TV with cable, phone, internet, iron, minibar & AC with onsite restaurants, bars, pool, spa, business centre & a gym just some of the many top-notch guest amenities. $$$

Hotel InterContinental Calle 16 No 28–51; 319 4450; f 315 4404; www.intercontinental.com. Located about 30 minutes' drive from the international airport, the InterContinental Hotel Medellín enjoys stunning views across the city & valley beyond & offers a range of sumptuous rooms & suites. Facilities include a business centre, tennis courts, 9-hole mini golf course, heated swimming pool, health club, restaurants, pastry shop, bar, nightclub & laundry. The hotel is also connected to a commercial arcade with drug store, travel agency, hair salon. Rooms come with a safe, TV (cable), en-suite bathroom and 24-hr room service. $$$

Hotel Nutibara Calle 52A, No 50–46; 511 511; www.hotelnutibara.com. Rumour has it that this was

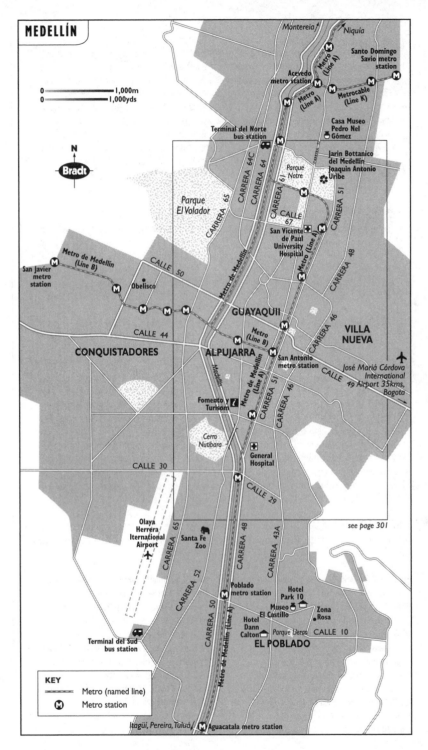

MEDELLÍN

0 ————————— 1,000m
0 ————————— 1,000yds

N

Bradt

Montereia

Niquía

Santo Domingo
Savio metro
station

Metro
(Line A)

Acevedo
metro station

Metro
(Line A)

Metrocable
(Line K)

Terminal del Norte
bus station

Casa Museo
Pedro Nel
Gómez

CARRERA 64C

CARRERA 64

CARRERA 61

Parque
Notre

Jarin Bottanico
del Medellín
Joaquin Antonio
Uribe

CARRERA 65

Parque
El Volador

CALLE
67

CARRERA 51

San Javier
metro
station

Metro de Medellín
(Line B)

CALLE 50

San Vicente
de Paul
University
Hospital

Metro (Line A)

CARRERA 48

Obelisco

GUAYAQUII

Metro de Medellín

CARRERA 46

VILLA
NUEVA

CALLE 44

CONQUISTADORES

ALPUJARRA

Metro
(Line B)

San Antonio
metro station

José Mariá Córdova
International
Airport 35kms,
Bogota

CALLE 19

Medellín

Metro de Medellín
(Line A)

CARRERA 51

CARRERA 46

Fomento y
Turisom

Cerro
Nutibara

CALLE 30

General
Hospital

CALLE 29

see page 301

Olaya
Herrera
International
Airport

Santa Fe
Zoo

CARRERA 65

CARRERA 48

CARRERA 43A

CARRERA 52

CARRERA 50

Metro de Medellín (Line A)

Poblado
metro station

Hotel
Park 10

Museo
El Castillo

Zona
Rosa

Hotel
Dann
Calton

Parque Lleras

CALLE 10

Terminal del Sud
bus station

EL POBLADO

KEY

━━━━━━ Metro (named line)

Ⓜ Metro station

Itagüí, Pereira, Tuluá, Ⓜ Aguacatala metro station

where the Colombian president used to stay before the more luxurious Hotel Intercontinental was built. It's still got plenty of charm & character, albeit a little faded in places, with lots of original 1940s Art Deco. Large AC rooms offer super views & there is also an outdoor swimming pool & gym for guests. Rates include an ample buffet b/fast. $$$

🏠 **Hotel Park 10** Carrera 36B, No 11–12; ↘ 266 8811; e gerencia@hotelpark10.com.co; www.hotelpark10.com.co. This rather showy & fancy 5-star place is geared up for midweek business executives – with prices to match. Travellers on a budget will find weekend discounts make this a more affordable option – otherwise prices are steep. That aside, the location of this postmodern hotel is nigh-on perfect with the Parque Lleras just a stone's throw away with its art galleries, restaurants, pubs & boutiques. $$$

🏠 **Hotel Capitolio** Carrera 49, No 57–21; ↘ 512 0012; f 11 5631. For no-nonsense good value, this mid-range option is worth a try as it wins points for clean simplicity. Expect basic rooms with little or no added extras. However, a little open-air bar next to the swimming pool sets this apart from the rest. $$

🏠 **Black Sheep Hostel** Transversal 5A, No 45–133; ↘ 311 15 89/1379; www.blacksheepmedellín.com. Well located in a quiet El Poblado neighbourhood, this New Zealand-owned hostel has won rave reviews since opening in 2005. Spacious rooms & communal areas offer plenty of places to hang out, with a garden, kitchen, BBQ, TV room (with cable), hammocks & internet for guest use. With El Poblado's nightlife just a 15-minute walk this is a good option for anyone keen to make the most of Medellín's excellent bars & restaurants. A Metro

station is also just 8mins down the road. Everyone speaks English here so it's also a boon for those with iffy Spanish. A choice of dorm rooms contains 4, 6 or 8 beds with 3 dbl rooms available & a sgl. En-suite bathrooms are equipped with hot power showers & extra-long European-style beds (great for those over 5ft 8in). On Sundays the owners throw an all-you-can-eat BBQ party with sausages, steak, chicken, salad & potatoes. $

🏠 **Hostal Odéon** Calle 54, No 49–38; ↘ 513 1404. Budget travellers unconcerned with cheerful décor will find this a good, cheap option. Rooms come with private bathrooms & offer plenty of space. Located just up from Parque de Bolívar. $

🏠 **Hotel Cristal** Carrera 49, No 57–12; ↘ 511 5631. What this place lacks in frills & fuss it makes up for in cleanliness with a decent collection of small, simple rooms close to Parque de Bolívar. Ask to see a choice of rooms if you can as some are nicer than others. All have private bathrooms but not all have windows. $

🏠 **Palm Tree Hostal** Carrera 67, No 48D–63; ↘ 260 2805; e palmtreemedellín@yahoo.com; www.palmtreemedellín.com. A highly popular backpacker option located in a residential area northwest of metro Estadio, the Palm Tree is just three blocks from the Metro that connects to any part of the city. Painted bright orange, the building is just a few metres from a large Exito supermarket, & offers a collection of private rooms & dorm beds. Communal facilities include hot showers, laundry service, bar, book exchange, BBQ, TV room (cable), DVD movies, internet & free all-day coffee. There is also a fully equipped kitchen for guest use & a chill-out lounge with hammocks. Discounts are available for long-term stays. $

✖ **WHERE TO EAT** Medellín has at least 200 places to eat with new food joints springing up across the city. Standards are high and prices low with plenty of dirt-cheap Paisa dishes found in the city centre. For more upmarket dining options head to El Pablado where you'll find every type of international cuisine, from sushi and soul food to tapas and maize. Most of Medellín's fast-food outlets are clustered around the streets that make up El Hueco. Expect to find snack bars, fried-chicken joints, diners, burger vendors and pizza places in abundance. Like most of Colombia, vegetarians aren't particularly well catered for.

PUEST IS BEST

Listen to the Medellínenses in conversation and you'll notice a very strange characteristic, the almost habitual, liberal use of the regional uttering 'puest' – a word with no literal meaning. Expect to hear it at the beginning, end and middle of every sentence – at the very least.

Central Medellín

✘ **Café Colombo** Carrera 45, No 53–24; ☎ 513 444; www.colomboworld.com. Be prepared to be distracted by the stunning views from this stylish 10th-floor restaurant located in the cultural institution, Centro Colombo Americano. Overlook the city & mountains in elegant contemporary-modern surroundings where the meals are as light & tasty as the décor. $$$

✘ **La Estancia** Parque Bolívar. This cavernous diner packs in the locals with a simple lunch at shoestring prices. Don't expect anything fancy but La Estancia remains unrivalled on the basis of cost – & is a good place to sit & watch city life unfold. $$

✘ **Restaurant Hatovejo** Carrera 47, No 52–17; ☎ 251 2196. For great local meat dishes & traditional favourites this place is difficult to beat. Expect a menu of big-portion beef & pork dishes typically served with beans & corn tortilla, including the gut-busting Antioquian speciality Bandeja Paisa (see box, *Man-sized meal*, page 295). $$

✘ **Salón Versalles** Pasaje Junín, No 53–39; ☎ 251 7416. Ask anyone about Salón Versalles & they'll

mention the delicious Argentine empanadas they serve, as they are famous citywide. Tables are in demand at lunchtime when local office workers descend in their droves. Priced a little high for meals but better value for snacks. $$

✘ **Mango Maduro** Calle 54, No 47–5; ☎ 512 3671. Travellers wax lyrical about this wonderful little place that must be one of Medellín's best-kept gastronomic secrets. Funky, bohemian-style décor welcomes diners to 9 small tables at lunchtimes only for a single set menu. Expect excellent food that offers Colombian classics with a twist at incredibly low prices. Be prepared to scour the streets for this place as it's an inconspicuous above-street diner delightfully tucked away. Arrive early to grab a seat along with the academics, poets & artists who favour this great find. $

✘ **Restaurante Govinda's** Calle 51, No 52–17; ☎ 512 9481; ⊕ Mon–Sat for lunch only. This cheery little upstairs restaurant is run by Medellín's friendly Hare Krishnas who serve excellent vegetarian fare. First-rate prices & great service. $

El Poblado

The best way to discover the many excellent eating places in El Poblado is to stroll around the Zona Rosa perusing menus and sussing them out. Numerous restaurants offer all manner of dining options, from Brazilian steak houses and Japanese noodles to Tex-Mex and fish and chips, almost all with outside seating.

✘ **Tramezzini** Calle 9A, No 37–56; ☎ 311 5617; ⊕ lunchtime until late Mon–Sat. This unassuming Italian bistro is continually highly acclaimed by Medellín's food press. Expect all the usual Italian classics served in simple style in this upmarket restaurant. A great place to spot the local glitterati dressed up to the nines. $$$

✘ **Resturante y Bar Nuqui** Carrera 42, No 10–49; ☎/f 312 3749. Located a block from Parque Poblado,

this fine seafood restaurant is renowned for its top-quality menu of lobster, shrimp & squid dishes. The grilled mero & langoustine soup is also particularly tasty. Expect turquoise walls, red paintwork & a nautical theme. $$

✘ **Thaico** Calle 9A, No 37–40; ☎ 311 5639. This funky Thai restaurant attracts a hip pre-party crowd who nibble on great noodle dishes & battered chilli prawns on an atmospheric outside terrace. $$

NIGHTLIFE Cocktail lovers and bar-hoppers are spoilt for choice in Medellín's El Poblado district where practically every place is alive with Martini shakers, slammers and flaming sambuca. Start at the Parque Lleras and follow the crowds from beer joints and vodka bars to neon-lit champagne lounges – there is no shortage of options with over 50 different watering holes to choose from in this up tempo Zona Rosa. The El Rojo and Basilica are popular restaurants with people-watchers as they are positioned in a superb corner plot where big-screen televisions show important football matches to cheering crowds. Other good hangouts include Niagra (the oldest bar in the city), El Forno, La Grappa, New Orleans and the Restaurant la Plaza – there's even a British pub (The Liverpool) and a Scottish pub (Pub Escocia).

Parque Lleras is busy every night of the week, although Thursday, Friday and Saturday are when it's standing room only. Bars close at around 03.00 but party-goers with stamina congregate around the Parque until dawn to drink, smoke and

MEDELLÍN
City Centre

Terminal del Norte bus station

'Metocable' Line K, Niquía, Montereja

Casa Museo Pedro Nel Gómez

CARRERA 65

CARRERA 64C

CARRERA 64

CARRERA 61

CARRERA 52

CARRERA 48

CARRERA 51

Parque Notre

Parque El Volador

Jarin Bottanico del Medellin Joaquin Antonio Uribe

Antioqui University

Parque de los Deseos

San Vicente de Paul University Hospital

CALLE 67

National University

CARRERA 55

CARRERA 52

Metro de Medellin (Line A)

Obelisco

Museo de Arte Moderno

CALLE 50

Metro de Medellin

CALLE 58

CARRERA 48

CARRERA 57

Minorista José María Villa Market

CALLE 53

Museo de Antioquia

Ermita da la Veracruz

CARRERA 51

Metropolitana Cathedral

Parque Bolívar

Mercado de San Alejo

Hotel Nutibara

NOTE
MANY MINOR ROADS ARE OMITTED

CARRERA 65

CARRERA 64

CARRERA 61

Centro Commercial Palacio Nacional

Parque Berrio

CARRERA 16

CALLE 44

Metro de Medellin (Line B)

Basílica de la Candelaria

San Antonio metro station

Hotel Inter Continental

Pablo Tobón Uribe Theatre

Parque San Antonio

CALLE 49

CALLE 44

Parque de los Pies Descalzos

CARRERA 55

Medellin

CARRERA 51

José Mariá Córdova International Airport 35kms, Bogota

Metropolitano Theatre
Palacio de Exposiciones

Metro de Medellin (Line A)

N

Bradt

Fomento Turisom

CARRERA 16

Pueblito Paisa

Parque de las Esculturas

Cerro Nutibara

KEY

Metro (named line)

Metro station

General Hospital

CALLE 30

Olaya Herrera International Airport

CARRERA 52

CARRERA 50

CARRERA 48

CALLE 29

0 ———— 500m
0 ———— 500yds

CARRERA 65

CARRERA 43A

Terminal del Sud bus station

Poblado, Itagüí, Pereira, Tuluá

El Poblado, Zona Rosa

chat the night away. Cigarettes, alcohol and street food can be bought from an army of vendors until the last person heads home. Bars open up and close down with alarming frequency but it is still almost impossible to choose a dud. A couple of venues particularly worthy of note include the well-established **Ave María Bar & Restaurant** which serves perfect cocktails and has a first-rate menu of international fare to the sound of jazz and salsa music. Moody chill-out tracks attract a chic crowd at the **Melodie Lounge** on Carrera 37, a trendy bar with glowing walls and kaleidoscopic cocktails. Medellín's finest nightclubs are located out of town in the south of the city. Each offers ravers unsurpassed partying on a truly grand scale. Eccentric, quirky **Vinacure** (*www.vinacure.com*) is in the Caldas district and is a circus-cum-disco-cum-bar that is also part-gallery. Images, statues and mannequins hang from the ceiling and rooms are adorned with all manner of pseudo-religious Hollywood kitsch. Weird photo galleries lead to an Amsterdamesque erotic-themed room and packed-to-the-gills dance floor in an old former house that is roughly a 20,000 COP taxi ride from El Poblado. Another venue for a top night is **Mango's** in the Itagüí district where wild live shows feature choreographed cowgirl dancers on stages with a Wild West theme. Mango's is rated as one of the best nightclubs in South America by E! Entertainment television and is next door to Medellín's hottest new nightclub, **Palmahía**. Arguably the best dance club in the city, Palmahía is certainly the largest – with a capacity for 3,000 punters and a central all-female boxing ring. Vinacure, Mango's and Palmahía are each about a 25,000 COP taxi ride from the centre of Medellín – it's a bit of a haul but well worth the trek.

ENTERTAINMENT Medellín plays host to numerous cultural shows, exhibitions, concerts, events and film festivals throughout the year in venues citywide. For a full list of what's on pick up a Thursday edition of the daily *El Colombiano* newspaper (*www.elcolombiano.com*) – it includes a special weekend entertainment supplement and is Medellín's definitive listing. Monthly local entertainment magazine *Opción Hoy* varies in the quality of its content but is still worth a flick through – it's sold in newsagents throughout the city at 2,000 COP.

Medellín's vibrant arts scene offers everything from black comedy and drama to experimental art-house cinema. A dozen or more theatres stage regular performances including alternative theatre at the Teatro Matacandelas (✆ *215 1010; wwwmatacandalas.com*), midstream plays at the Teatro Pablo Tobón Uribe (✆ *239 7500*) and musicals at the Teatro Metropolitano (✆ *232 4597*), home to Medellín's fine Philharmonic Orchestra. More than 20 commercial cinemas are mainly multiplexes although a handful of *cimematecas* offer more than just the usual blockbuster fare. These include the Museo de Arte Moderno de Medellín (✆ *230 2622*), the Museo de Antioquía (✆ *251 3636; www.museodeantioquia.org*) and the Centro Colombo Americano – all of which screen foreign-language films and shy away from the Hollywood norm.

SHOPPING Medellín is one of Colombia's finest retail hubs with dozens of gleaming shopping plazas, malls and markets selling all manner of items, from coffee and bric-a-brac to designer brands. Traditional flower markets throw their doors open at dawn while vendors start to ply their wares on the city's street corners well before 06.00. Medellín is also the nation's prime textile production centre and host of numerous fashion and clothing exhibitions, including the world-renowned **ColombiaModa** (*www.colombiamoda.com*) – a glittering three-day showcase event that features catwalk shows, retail booths and 450 exhibitors and is the most important annual fashion fixture in South America. It also has a dedicated fashion district, an impressive succession of colourful boutiques, dressmakers, designers and unique clothing stores (see box, *First for fashion*, page 304).

Medellín's prime shopping centres include the **Centro Commercial Palacío Nacional** (☎ *381 8144*) on the corner of Carrera 52 and Calle 48 in a pedestrianised bargain retail district nicknamed El Hueco (The Hole) by the locals. Here over 200 shops sell goods at shoestring prices in a grand building dating back to 1925 surrounded by a succession of 'todo a 100 pesos' (everything 100 COP) outlets. At the **Mercado de San Alejo** on the Parque de Bolívar a collection of handicraft stalls sell plenty of cut-price bags, paintings and jewellery on the first Sunday of the month. The vast covered daily market at the **Mercado Minorista José María Villa** on Carrera 57 and Calle 55 isn't for the faint-hearted with more than 2,500 vendors selling food, knick-knacks and clothing. Medellín is also the birthplace of one of Colombia's biggest supermarket chains, **Exito** (*www.exito.com*) – a retail institution with 15 outlets in the city alone. Once a small independent thrift store, the past 30 years have seen Exito transformed into the symbol of Medellín's penchant for shopping. Look out for the bland brick and yellow buildings across the city with a rather garish sign.

OTHER PRACTICALITIES Medellín is a well-equipped big city that offers every conceivable convenience. Expect to find dozens of internet cafés in the streets that lead from the Parque de Bolívar (2,000 COP per hour) as well as numerous pharmacies, banks (with ATMs), money changers, shoe-repair shops, payphones and luggage retailers. The city's largest internet facility is Café Internet Doble-Clik (☎ *511 4183*) on Calle 50, No 43–135. It not only opens seven days a week but is also ultra-speedy with new machines and a decent stock of consumables. In 'El Centro' – the main artery at the heart of Medellín – there are dozens of clinics and drug stores. José María Córdova International Airport is well equipped with ATMs, cafés and international payphones and also has a newsagent that stocks a limited range of English-language magazines. For medical attention contact the city's ambulance service (☎ *123 or* ☎ *235 3001*) or head to the Clinica las Américas (☎ *342 2262/1010/7070*) and Clinica Soma (☎ *576 8480/8400/6415/8555*) – both are open 24 hours.

SAFETY Transformed from murder capital to corporate boom town, Medellín has been hailed as a rare urban success story for neo-conservatism in South America. However, although the city is a much, much safer city than it was a decade ago, visitors should still exercise caution when walking after dark. Although the police have a presence in every neighbourhood, don't be tempted to venture into Medellín's poorer neighbourhoods. Care should also be taken in the crowded confines of the city's smaller backstreet parks. The lively, popular districts of Poblado and Laureles are both safe and well patrolled, day and night. Use an ATM in a safe part of town and apply common sense – never flaunt cash and keep wallets out of sight. Single men should also be aware that Medellín has a large number of so-called prepagos (meaning pre-paids), generally stunningly beautiful middle-class girls who are often university students or professional models. Prepagos work secretly as prostitutes to fund their lavish 'IT Girl' lifestyles and commonly target foreigners in a blatant gringo-hunt – much to the annoyance of their regular punters, many of whom are of dubious, but powerful, pedigree.

WHAT TO SEE It is impossible to list everything worth seeing in Medellín. The city is fast evolving, thanks to multi-million-dollar investment, and rapid change continues at a staggering pace. Medellín has more than 20 parks, dozens of museums and many, many fine monuments to discover. Visitors with limited time will find the city easy to navigate with much of Medellín's attractions centred on the middle of town.

As the home of Colombia's fashion industry Medellín is blessed with lots of home-grown creative talent, much of it nurtured in the city's prestigious Colegiatura Colombiana de Diseño. Wholesale clothing distributors, dress designers and bespoke fashion boutiques all have their base here in a sector that prides itself on being cheap and good quality with manufacturing 100% sweatshop-free. ColombiaModa, Medellín's international fashion show, forms the heart of Fashion Week in the city in a dazzling star-studded display of glitz and glamour. Clothing buyers, style journalists, film crews and catwalk queens descend on Medellín from all over the planet to witness Colombia's latest fashion collections – a creative pool that is arguably South America's finest.

Designer Johanna Logreira is a bright example of Medellín's gifted fashion leaders, an independent designer who has been instrumental in showcasing individual talent. In 2005, she joined forces with others involved in fashion and textiles, forming a collective that soon had the backing of Medellín's mayor and ColombiaModa. They established a fashion district on Vía Primavera (www.primavera.com), rejuvenating the streets with street lights, flowers and seating areas. Today, the collective has over 30 members, from boutique owners and couture specialists to fashion cafés and jewellery designers in a trendy, stylish urban space that attracts a growing number of style tourists. The group remains committed to being 100% Colombian owned, using local materials and employing local people. It has also dispensed with the usual envy-based mistrust of the fashion industry in order to promote a true sharing of talent, skills, ideas and resources. Each business within the collective is involved in local education initiatives and is, in turn, mentored by an elder from Colombia's godfather – Bella, a major fashion house.

Another focus of the Vía Primavera fashion district is making sophisticated clothing styles available to the masses. In Medellín, women are extremely fashion conscious but tend to stick to a uniform look, favouring tight jeans, bare midriff, high heels and a clingy top – regardless of age, shape or social group. By producing a broader range of clothing without astronomical price tags, Vía Primavera (*www.primavera.com*) has widened Medellín's fashion scope at street level. Consumers have greater choice and are proud to buy a 100% Colombian item from a community-led business that is dedicated to giving something back.

Central Medellín City planners have prohibited new construction in central Medellín that doesn't include public art within its blueprint and the result is a glorious outdoor gallery. At the very core of Medellín's centre are the much-photographed giant, rounded sculptures of Medellín's very own Fernando Botero, a prolific artist whose work is synonymous with the regeneration of the city. More than 90 sculptures have been donated to his home town, the most famous of which can be seen (and are also frequently touched and fumbled, see box, *Touchy feely*, page 307) at the **Plazoleta de las Esculturas**. More of Botero's work is displayed at the **Museo de Antioquía** in the resplendent **Palacío Municipal** (*Carrera 52;* ✆ *251 3636; www.museodeantioquia.org;* ⊕*09.30–17.00 Mon–Sat, 10.00–16.00 Sun; admission 7,000 COP*). Alongside Botero's fine donations are some magnificent pre-Columbian, colonial and contemporary works. His massive bronze of woman's torso, **La Gorda**, is sited outside the Banco de Berrío while in the Parque San Antonio three further pieces include the **Bird of Peace** (Pájaro de Paz) – today, somewhat ironically, this symbolic piece is terribly scarred by a guerrilla bomb.

More fine monuments represent the work of Rodrigo Arenas Betancur, who wowed Colombia with numerous architectural triumphs until his death in 1995.

In 1974, he unveiled the ultra-impressive **Monumento a la Vida** (Monument to Life) – a 14m-high twisted, semi-spiral structure in Centro Suramericana. His dramatic **Monumento a la Raza** (Monument to the Race) depicts the evolution of Antioquía at the Centro Aministravo la Alpujarra in a powerful, robust sculpture that represents the forces of good and evil.

Much of the **Parque Berrío** is dominated by the **Basílica de la Candelaria**, a structure that dates back to the early 1770s and was Medellín's cathedral from 1868 to 1931. The most important of the city's religious buildings, the basílica contains some beautiful, vivid interior decoration including an ornate ceiling with stunning recessed panels. Widely regarded as Medellín's oldest church, the **Ermita de la Veracruz** dates back to 1682 when the first brick was laid. Handsome and stone-built, it is located on the corner of Calle 51 and Carrera 52 and has a simple whitewashed interior adorned with wooden carvings and splashes of gold. However, it is the **Catedral Metropolitana** overlooking the Parque de Bolívar that can claim to be Medellín's largest place of worship, having been constructed using more than 1.2 million bricks – as the locals are very keen to point out. A cavernous interior is adorned with paintings by Gregorio Vásquez de Arce y Ceballos while huge stained-glass windows glow in a myriad of vibrant hues. A number of architects played a part in creating this fine cathedral and this is reflected in an interesting hybrid of influences that contribute to a rather pleasing neo-Romanesque design.

Another not-to-be-missed is the ultra-modern **Parque de las Luces** (Park of Lights), a vast rectangular concrete plaza dotted pin-cushion-style with 300 needle-thin pillars that resembles a giant birthday cake when illuminated with white lights at night. At the nearby Zen-themed **Parque de los Pies Descalzos** (Barefoot Park) visitors are encouraged to kick off their shoes to walk through a bamboo forest before dipping their toes in cascading water fountains and freshwater pools.

Southern Medellín Almost every visitor to the city feels compelled to visit **Pueblito Paisa**, a rather well-constructed mock-up of a typical traditional Antioquian settlement in miniature form. Despite being aimed squarely at the tourist dollar, it is worth a trip out as there is something rather charming about the little faux church, town plaza and mayoral residence atop Cerro Nutibara. At Christmas the whole place is illuminated by fairy lights and lanterns – a truly beautiful sight. Views from the summit of the 80m-tall hill are also magnificent. Pueblito Paisa is 2km southwest of the city centre and can be easily reached by taxi for 4,000 COP – get the driver to drop you at the bottom of the slope to enjoy a short walk up a paved path to the top where a couple of nice bars and a restaurant serve good, hearty Paisa meals.

For some particularly fine abstract sculpture head to the **Parque de las Esculturas** (Sculpture Park) – it is also on the slopes of Cerro Nutibara and contains works by a host of South American artists, including Carlos Cruz Díez and Edgar Negret.

The grandiose **Museo El Castillo** (℡ 266 0900; ◷09.00–17.00 Mon–Fri, closed 11.00–14.00, 09.00–11.30 Sat; admission 4,500 COP) was once the home of a landowning family who spared no expense in creating a mock-Gothic castle fit for a king. Today this 1930s building remains a monument to that era and is open for guided tours and exhibitions. Each room is laid out with original furniture and furnishings and contains the family's belongings and personal effects. The museum is located in El Poblado on Carrera 9 about 5km south of the city centre – a taxi will cost around 6,000 COP.

Northern Medellín A visit to the city's truly gorgeous **Jardín Botánico del Medellín Joaquin Antonio Uribe** (*Carrera 52; www.jbmed.org;* ◷09.00–17.00

daily; admission 2,500 COP) is highly recommended. Since opening in 1978, the garden has grown in size and stature and is now a wonderfully mature green space in which many urbanites choose to while away the hours. Botanists have collected more than 600 tree and plant species – including numerous orchids – and the gardens boast a thoughtful, contemporary layout that uses colour and textures to dramatic effect. At the weekends, choral and orchestral concerts are often staged in a small open-air auditorium to appreciative crowds sipping espressos on wrought-iron tables and chairs. Other attractions include a lovely lake, a herbarium and Orquideorama that houses a sizeable orchid display in March and April.

Opposite the botanical gardens is the uber-trendy **Parque de los Deseos** (Dream Park), a concrete complex constructed along minimalist lines that is a popular place for many of Medellín's 130,000 students to hang out. Sleek cafés/diners open out onto modern leafy garden areas designed to inspire hopes and dreams. There is also a planetarium, library, internet café and science building.

Housed in the former home of Medellín's beloved Pedro Nel Gómez (1899–1984), the **Casa Museo Pedro Nel Gómez** (↘ *233 2633; ⊕09.00–17.00 Mon–Fri, closed noon–14.00, 09.00–noon Sat; admission 4,500 COP*) on Carrera 51B is wholly dedicated to the life and works of this most prolific artist. The highlight of the museum is a 2,000-piece collection of his murals, drawings, watercolours and sculptures. Find it 3km north of the city centre (4,000 COP by taxi).

FESTIVALS AND EVENTS Paisas love to party and enjoy nothing more than dressing up to the nines to make merry all night long. Joining in this revelry is a rewarding way to get to Medellín's heart – there are numerous festivals to choose from, from a Fiesta of Humour to an Artisan Fair. Some of the most important events include the following.

La Feria de las Flores (*early Aug*) The Festival of the Flowers is a key event in the Antioquian calendar, filling Medellín's streets with brightly coloured blooms and horse-drawn floral displays. The celebration has taken place every year since 1957 and culminates in a spectacular 400-strong procession of flower-bearing campesinos from the mountains in the Desfile de Silleteros (flower carriers' parade).

Festival de Poesia de Medellin (*Jun; www.festivaldepoesiadeMedellín.org*) This headline-grabbing poetry festival is fast gaining global repute and was the recipient of the 2006 Right Livelihood Award. In 2007, Medellín's Poetry Festival attracted 72 poets from 52 countries from all continents during the ten-day event. The event is sponsored by the Municipality of Medellín and it has financial support from Hivos, Doen Foundation, Cordaid, Embassy of Switzerland in Colombia, Agence Internationale de la Francophonie, Prince Claus Fund, Fundación Heinrich Böll and Caja Cooperativa Confiar and is dedicated to the pursuit of peace.

Parade of Myths and Legends (*Dec*) This exceptional fairy-lit event occurs every year on 7 December and features a pre-Christmas parade on deeply rooted traditional themes, such as the 'Patasola', the 'Madremonte', the 'Sombreron', the 'Ruanón' and the 'Judío Errante'.

Feria Tuarina de la Macarena (*Jan/Feb*) This event sees the bullring packed to capacity with 15,000 cheering fans as the Plaza de Toros La Macarena plays host to one of the most important bullfighting fairs in Colombia. A retractable rooftop ensures a rainproof event in this Moorish-style building on Autopista Sue on the corner of Calle 44. Expect large crowds, ticket touts and a riotous carnival atmosphere.

AROUND MEDELLÍN

The lush, mountainous areas to the southeast of Medellín seem to have been untouched by the modern world. Sleepy Paisa villages edge winding lanes that climb the slopes in the Circuito de Oriente where the rain-nourished Cordillera Central is rich with vegetation and sparkling streams. Most visitors embarking on a day trip to the region opt for a standard one-day itinerary that is offered by numerous local tour companies. Costs average 80,000 COP per person – an excellent price for the opportunity to witness some truly memorable Antioquian scenery and towns. Those keen to go it alone can journey by bus from Medellín to connect to the following key day-trip attractions.

MARINILLA (*Telephone code: 4; www.marinilla.gov.co*) This beautifully preserved city boasts some stunning Antioquian architecture, much of it dating back to the early 18th century. One of the oldest towns in the region, Marinilla is 45km from the centre of Medellín – a one-hour journey by bus. Expect pretty whitewashed churches, leafy plazas and a little weekday market. A decent collection of local restaurants and budget hotels are clustered around the main square.

EL PEÑOL Meaning literally 'the stone' this 200m moss-covered granite monolith rises from the banks of an artificial lake, soaring 649 steps from the Embalse de Peñol. Those with plenty of stamina will find the climb rewards the effort with incredible views over the lake and beyond. A handful of grilled-meat restaurants and roadside cabins cater for tourists. Buses run to and from Medellín every hour or so, taking two hours. El Peñol Lake is fast becoming a fishing Mecca with weekending anglers from the city.

RIONEGRO (*Telephone code: 4; www.rionegro.gov.co*) This aged city has plenty of gorgeous buildings to wander around on a rural backdrop of rolling farmland and tree-lined meadows. Founded in 1663, Rionegro lies around 50km southeast of Medellín, and has a number of interesting museums and monuments, including the Monumento a José María Cordoba, a fine statue commemorating the War of Independence. Numerous Paisa-style buildings can be found just off the main plaza where the vast 200-year-old Catedral de San Nicolás casts its shadows. The backstreets are home to a handful of small hotels and restaurants. Frequent buses nip back and forth to Medellín, taking around 1½ hours.

CARMEN DE VIBORAL (*Telephone code: 4*) Most people come to this small Paisa town to visit its many ceramic stalls, pottery factories and workshops. Carmen de Viboral is renowned throughout Colombia for its fine ceramic industry with most of its production still managed by hand. Buses connect to Rionegro 9km away every hour, taking 20 minutes. Half a dozen budget hotels are located around the plaza.

LA CEJA (*Telephone code: 4; www.laceja.gov.co*) This charming town centres on a handsome main plaza where balconied Paisa buildings adorned with brightly coloured flowers boast traditional Antioquian décor. Two gorgeous churches offer plenty of stunning religious art. A number of small handicraft stalls can also be found in the streets beyond the square. La Ceja has a handful of basic mid-range hotels and is served by an hourly bus to Medellín (1½ hours). Surrounding attractions include the **Hacienda Fizebald**, a lovely old mansion house dating back to 1825 that houses a collection of 150 species of orchids. Also the **Salto de Tequendamita**, a stunning waterfall with a very nice restaurant at its base.

RETIRO (*Telephone code: 4*) Prepare to be charmed by this pretty little cattle-ranching town, founded in 1800. Surrounded by emerald hills dotted with colourful haciendas, Retiro is one of the region's most scenic towns, with a beautiful main plaza edged by Paisa-style buildings. For a small town, Retiro also boasts a good stock of restaurants and hostels and makes an excellent stopoff for lunch. Buses to Medellín 41km away run every 35 minutes, taking an hour.

SANTA FÉ DE ANTIOQUÍA Telephone code: 4

A visit to this sleepy agricultural town allows a step back in time through handsome streets that have remained unchanged since the early 18th century. As the oldest settlement in the region, Santa Fé de Antioquía is also the most beautifully preserved, set in a low-lying steamy valley watered by the Río Cauca and Río Tonusco. Founded in 1541 by Jorge Robledo as Villa de Santafé on the western bank of the Río Cauca, the town received its shield of arms and the title of City of Antioquía from King Phillip II of Spain in 1545 and was elevated to parish status in 1547 by the Bishop of Popayán. In 1584 it became the capital of Antioquía, a role it served until the government relocated to Medellín in 1826, 80km to the southwest. Since then, Santa Fé de Antioquía has remained totally overshadowed by its neighbour – more than a little aggrieved by its diminished status. However, in rivalry terms, the town has little competition when it comes to its architectural core with stunning single-storey pastel-coloured colonial houses along narrow streets and gorgeous courtyards and plazas. Elaborate carvings decorate each vast wooden doorway beside patios planted to capacity with a rainbow of flowers. Balconies and windows are also adorned with blooms in what must be one of Colombia's prettiest streetscapes. In 1960, Santa Fé de Antioquía and its charming maze of cobbled paths was declared a national monument. The very recent completion of the Tunnel of the West in 2006 has cut travelling time from Medellín to a lazy hour-long drive. This has stimulated a surge of renewed interest in Santa Fé de Antioquía as a weekend destination and today tourism is fast becoming an economic bedrock of the town, along with maize, coffee and beans.

GETTING THERE AND AROUND The town is well served by a good, frequent bus service to and from Medellín (8,000 COP, 2 hours) with another half-dozen minibuses (11,000 COP) and an on-demand collective service.

TOURIST INFORMATION

🛈 **Oficina de Fomento y Turismo** Plaza Mayor; ✆ 853 2314; www.santafedeantioquia.gov.co; ⏱08.00–18.00 Mon–Fri, closed noon–14.00

WHERE TO STAY AND EAT Rates at many of Santa Fé de Antioquía's decent handful of hotels can double when there are festivities in town – so it is well worth booking in advance. The town is often deserted until the weekending urbanites arrive on Friday night, so it pays to haggle midweek. Almost every hotel has a restaurant with simple meat-and-rice dishes the norm. Santa Fé is also reputed to be home to finca nudista, a hotel catering wholly for those who prefer to B&B in the buff.

🏠 **Hotel Mariscal Robledo** Carrera 12, No 9–70; ✆ 853 1111/1563. This beautiful hotel is the place to stay if you want the best in town. Expect stunning décor, a big courtyard swimming pool with great views, pretty rooms & understated elegance throughout. Rates may be Santa Fé's highest but it's a real bargain when you consider they include 3 meals & free drinks from 15.00–19.00. $$$

🏠 **Hostal Guaracu** Calle 10, No 8– 36; ✆ 250 50 07. Look out for the orange sign for this mid-range tourist hotel, located just off the main plaza. Each room has AC & a TV & is clean if a little soulless. $$

🏠 **Hospedaje Franco** Carrera 10, No 8A–14; ✆ 853 1654. Located just a block from the main plaza, this super hotel has simple fan-cooled rooms centred on a leafy patio. Each is small & comes with a clean private bathroom. Rooms are like gold dust here in January. $

🏠 **Hotel Caserón Plaza** Plaza Mayor; ✆ 853 2040; e Halcaraz@edatel.net.co. Well located, right on the main plaza, this former private residence has an aristocratic past. Courtyard rooms are clean, cheerful & nicely appointed with a swimming pool, restaurant & pleasant garden. $$

🏠 **Hostal Plaza Mayor** Parque Principal; ✆ 853 34 48/316 281 6799. This great little place is set right on the main square & is renowned for its friendly staff. Rooms are small but clean & have a private bathroom. A rather nice patio area & a tiny swimming pool offer plenty of spots in which to relax. $

🏠 **Hotel Espana Colonial** Calle 10, No 7– 60; ✆ 311 641 42 63. This nice little budget option is located a couple of blocks from the main square and has basic, clean rooms with private bathroom that are popular with the festival crowd. $

✕ **Restaurante y Hospedaje El Méson de la Abuela** Carrera 11, No 9–31; ✆ 853 1053; ⏱early–late. This decent local restaurant serves robust meals in an outdoor dining room. Expect generous b/fasts at a dirt-cheap price, tasty lunches & dinners of fish, chicken & meat. Rooms are basic but come with fans & a private bathroom around a plant-filled courtyard. $

SHOPPING Be sure to try the local *pulpa de tamarindo*, a mega-sweet candy with a touch of sour made from tamarind grown in the surrounding valley. Numerous vendors on Plaza Mayor sell it throughout the day from battered wooden stalls opposite the church.

WHAT TO SEE AND DO In reality, the biggest attraction in Santa Fé de Antioquía is the town itself – a stroll through the narrow streets is an absolute delight. Most people head for the impressive **Iglesia de Santa Bárbara** on the corner of Calle 11 and Carrera 8 and the **Catedral Madre** on Plaza Mayor before heading to the 17th-century **Iglesia de Chiquinquirá** on the corner of Carrera 13 and Calle 10 and **Iglesia de Jesús Nazareno** on the corner of Carrera 5 and Calle 10. All open for evening mass and boast a fascinating array of religious artefacts. There are more sacred objets d'art at the **Museo de Arte Religioso** (✆ *853 2345*) on Calle 11, No 8–12, including paintings by Gregorio Vásquez de Arce y Ceballos. It opens at weekends and on public holidays and costs 2,500 COP admission, next to Santa Bárbara church.

Out-of-town attractions centre on the **Puente de Occidente**, one of the first suspension bridges in the world. This metal-and-wood single-lane construction was built by the famous Colombian architect – and renowned big drinker – José María Villa (1850–1913). Villa trained in Hoboken, New Jersey, and helped build New York's Brooklyn Bridge. On his return to Colombia he built four bridges on the Cauca River. The Bridge of the West boasts a distinctive design with twin turrets on either end and took eight years to complete between 1887 and 1895 at a cost of 171,300 COP. Most of the materials used were shipped from England to create this 291m feat of engineering. It carried traffic until 1978 when it was declared a National Monument and is now used only by light vehicles. Buses connect to the bridge from Santa Fé or you can walk it in about an hour on the road to Sopetrán.

FESTIVALS

Semana Santa (Holy Week) Crowds swell and room rates soar during this highly popular week-long festival. Expect numerous colourful processions steeped in traditional pageantry and half a dozen religious ceremonies and services.

Antioquia Film Festival (*early Dec; www.festicineantioquia.com*) This popular event attracts film-lovers from all across the country with a broad range of cinematic treats from Colombian studios and film-makers from all across Latin America.

Fiesta de los Diablitos (*end of Dec*) Dating back to the colonial period, this festival has been celebrated with gusto since 1653. In the past Spanish fiestero Don Manuel de Benavides laid on bullfights, dancing and parties. Today, things are much the same – but faster-paced and more crowded. Expect lots of food, handicrafts and a beauty pageant.

ZONA CAFETERA (EJE CAFETERO)

Colombia's rugged and green Zona Cafetera is the nation's principal coffee-growing area, providing half of the country's 66-million-tonne coffee production in a region that represents just 1% of the country's landmass and 2.8 million people. Rolling plantations and quilted terraced slopes are hemmed by banana plants, shaggy coffee bushes, bamboo groves and vibrant heliconia thickets. Lush tufted grassy knolls and verdant valleys richly nourished by frequent rainfall are dotted with phosphorus hot springs and bubbling pools of mud. Expansive meadows are home to wooden white fincas with red and green window frames, shutters and broad shady balconies. Narrow, winding lanes scattered with podgy chickens lead to the snow-capped peaks of the Andes and aged volcanic crags. Here, between the magical altitudes of 800m and 1,800m, about 10% of the world's coffee supply is grown. However, since the plummeting prices of the 1990s, Colombia's coffee growers have woken up to smell a new crop – tourism. Today, coffee *finca* tourism is a growing business, offering a taste of plantation life to visitors, whilst supplementing the income of the region's 300,000 growers. Centred on three coffee-growing regions in the west of the country – Quindío, Caldas and Risaralda – more than 1,000 farmers have opened up their homes. There is even a highly popular Disney-style coffee theme park, complete with a Broadway-esque Show del Café cabaret show that honours Colombians' beloved beans.

HISTORY The Spanish didn't settle in the area that makes up the Coffee Zone until the mid 19th century, but once Antioquía began its phase of post-colonisation growth the region became ripe for development. By 1905 it was sufficiently large and populated to become a department in its own right and Caldas was born. However, widespread economic differences prompted the department to divide into three smaller areas, namely Quindío, Risaralda and Caldas. Today, the Zona Cafetera is dominated by the cities of Manizales, Pereira and Armenia, each departmental capitals and not terribly inspiring places. Sombre architecture and gnomish buildings reflect the region's fear of recurring earthquakes. Both Pereira and Armenia – along with 33 smaller towns – were badly damaged during a devastating burst of seismic activity in 1999. Some 2,000 people were killed or badly injured and entire streets razed to the ground after a quake that measured 6.2 on the Richter scale. It left more than 200,000 people homeless and was the third earthquake in 20 years. Ninety aftershocks wreaked havoc across the region for almost 24 hours with poor construction codes and ageing buildings contributing to the carnage. Since then, international aid has helped rebuild and expand the city. Numerous new government buildings and highways have been constructed with the subsequent rebuilding project costing more than US$500-million. The Coffee Zone's seismic vulnerability is due to the triple junction that occurs at the northwest corner of the South American plate where the Nazca, Cocos, and Pacific plates converge. The 1999 earthquake had a sizeable impact on coffee production in the region, adding to the woes of growers facing falling prices worldwide.

PRACTICALITIES At the time of writing, there aren't any specialist tour operators outside of Colombia offering coffee finca tours, as the Coffee Zone is relatively new to international tourism. Most people visit independently under their own steam, or organise a tour to the region once in the country. A good first step is to pick up a copy of *Haciendas del Café*, the region's finca directory. It lists dozens of coffee farms that offer accommodation to tourists. Some have pools and all are traditional buildings with balconies, spacious rooms, gardens and coffee fields. Prices start at about 55,000 COP per person per night, including breakfast. Another good source of reference is *Turismo Rural*. It also lists a good dozen or so *fincas agrotouísticas*; contact TurisCafé for a copy (✆ *310 538 1590*).

There's also some useful information and links at the following websites:

www.turiscolombia.andes.com/coffee_region.htm
General guide to the area with some accommodation options

www.ColombiaFarmVacations.com Specialist portal under development at the time of writing, but which promises fincas countrywide

MANIZALES *Telephone code: 6*

A crucial part of the Colombian coffee-growing axis and the capital of the Caldas department, Manizales has long been an important commercial hub. Due to a succession of devastating earthquakes and a terrible fire in 1925, the city has very little remaining historical character. Where grand period buildings would have once flanked the plaza there are now bland, concrete monstrosities: a dismal, grey reminder of Manizales past despairs. Modern high-rise towers fail to add glamour – and finding charm requires considerable patience – yet the climbing streets that lead from the centre have a certain appeal. In the oldest part of the city, a vast cathedral is famous for its elaborate gold canopy and beautiful, large stained-glass windows – and is a rare structure of beauty. A large student population lends Manizales a European feel in part. Academics and scholars are omnipresent walking to classes or sitting in the many cosy little cafés along Avenida Santander or sharing notes in the Plaza Bolívar. Enter Manizales from Pereira to pass the city's vast white bullring on the right: venue of the Feria de Manizales.

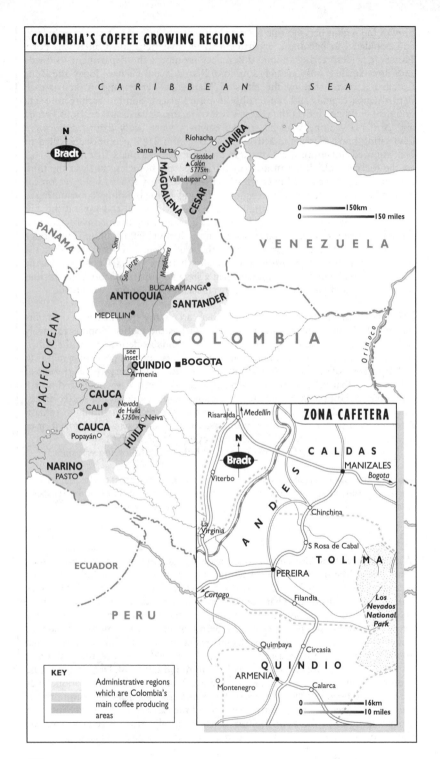

COLOMBIA'S COFFEE GROWING REGIONS

N
Bradt

CARIBBEAN SEA

PANAMA

PACIFIC OCEAN

Ríohacha
Santa Marta
GUAJIRA
Cristóbal
Colón
5775m
Valledupar
MAGDALENA
CESAR

VENEZUELA

0   150km
0   150 miles

Sinú
San Jorge
Magdalena

BUCARAMANGA
ANTIOQUIA
SANTANDER
MEDELLÍN

COLOMBIA

Orinoco

see
inset
QUINDIO ■BOGOTA
Armenia

CAUCA
CALI   Nevada
de Huila
5750m Neiva
CAUCA
Popayán   HUILA

NARINO
PASTO

ECUADOR

PERU

ZONA CAFETERA

Risaralda Medellín

N
Bradt

CALDAS
MANIZALES
Bogota

Viterbo

Chinchina

ANDES

La
Virginia

S Rosa de Cabal
TOLIMA

PEREIRA

Cartago
Filandia
Los
Nevados
National
Park

Quimbaya Circasia

QUINDIO

ARMENIA
Montenegro   Calarca

0   16km
0   10 miles

KEY

Administrative regions
which are Colombia's
main coffee producing
areas

HISTORY Founded in 1849, Manizales was born out of a desire by a group of Antioquian colonists to escape the ravages of civil war. At a height of about 2,153m, the land on which it is built offered relative sanctuary from the warring Liberal and Conservative factions. The original settlement is said to have comprised just 20 families, including that of Manuel Grisales, after whom the new city was named. Manizales remained an isolated, fair-skinned settlement until other ethnic groups arrived in the early 20th century, once the universities were established and diluted the pure Spanish influences. The city's early development was seriously hampered by two devastating earthquakes in 1875 and 1878. Prosperity came late to Manizales, once it became the capital of the newly created Caldas department and a pivotal part of the coffee trade.

GETTING THERE AND AROUND At the time of writing, Avianca is the only airline flying to Manizales with several daily flights. The city's La Nuba Airport is located about 8km southeast of the centre, just off the road to Bogotá (10,000 COP by taxi). Buses from the main terminal on Avenida 19 northeast of Plaza Bolívar depart frequently to Bogotá (35,000 COP, 8 hours), Cali (25,000 COP, 5 hours), Medellín (22,000 COP, 5 hours). Shorter hops are served by minibuses, including Pereira (7,000 COP, 1½ hours), Armenia (11,000 COP, 2½ hours) and Salamina (9,000 COP, 2½ hours).

TOURIST INFORMATION

Tour guides One of the most knowledgeable local guides is a specialist on the Parques Nacional Los Nevados ecosystem – and a man who loves to spend time in the mountains. Those who want true adventure in the wild with someone who knows their stuff should contact Giovany Coñon Pochin (☎ *300 394 6425; e giovanyguia@hotmail.com*) – he has some rusty English that he's keen to practise and will arrange itineraries, supplies, maps and accommodation.

Tour operators Most of the city's main tour operators offer day trips out to the Nevado del Ruiz, the highest volcano in the Parque Nacional Los Nevados, as well as longer stays in the park itself. Some of the most established include Bioturismo Arte y Café (☎ *884 4037*) in the Centro Comercial Parque Caldas, Tesoro Tours Manizales (☎ *883 7040*) in the Hotel Escorial on Calle 21, No 21–11, and Ecoturismo (☎ *880 8300; www.aventurascolombia.com*) on Calle 11, No 63–05. Expect to pay around 80,000 COP per person for a standard full-day package, including lunch.

WHERE TO STAY

Hotel Estelar Las Colinas Carrera 22, No 20–20; ☎ 884 2009; e ventas@hotelesestelar.com; www.hotellascolinas.com. Comfortable rooms come in a choice of dbls or large sgls & are equipped with a desk, satellite TV, minibar & private hot-water bathrooms. Other amenities onsite inc internet access & room service. $$$$

Hotel Fundadores Carrera 23, No 29–54; ☎ 884 6490; www.hotelfundadores.com. This faux-Paisa building offers reasonable-sized rooms with decent beds & attractive, roomy décor. Rates include a good b/fast. $$$

California Hotel Calle 19, No 16–37; ☎ 884 7720; f 880 0906. Despite being opposite the bus terminal, this hotel isn't bad. Modern rooms are small, but clean with pleasing prices that make it a good-value option. $$

Unlike beans from other origins, Colombian coffee is 'washed' in style and it is this that gives it a distinctive rich taste and aroma. There are approximately 60 types of coffee trees in the world, but only ten are mass cultivated. The most widespread are Coffea arabica, Coffea canephora and Coffea liberica. Of these Coffea arabica is the most cultivated on the planet, representing 90% of the world's coffee production and the most valued of the species. Colombian coffee plants are grown in a nursery from selected beans that are sown close together. After about eight weeks, the seeds germinate and roots develop, and the healthiest plants are selected for nurturing. When the seedlings have grown to about 2ft in height, they are transplanted to the plantation where they are carefully cultivated. An average coffee tree will take about four years to grow to full size and to blossom. The first fruit appears about six months later. Coffee trees bear ripened fruits and flower at the same time with each tree producing around 455g of coffee per year. Coffee beans are ready for harvesting when they are a rich, red colour. They are picked individually, bagged up and loaded on mules for transportation to the only mechanical part of the farming process – the de-pulping.

A machine removes the pulp from two seeds in the centre of each berry, leaving the beans, encased in a tough parchment husk. These are put into concrete tanks where they are soaked in cold mountain water for 24 hours before being carefully washed. Twigs, debris and poor-quality beans are discarded at this stage before the good beans are placed in straw baskets. They are then spread out on open-air terraces to be dried in the sun before being sold at market. The beans are tested for aroma, colour, size, moisture and texture with only the best crops sold and distributed for export. Many Colombian growers sell their crops to the National Federation of Coffee Growers, an organisation founded in 1927. Beans are brought to the mill and fed into machines that remove the tough parchment husk and silvery skin. Different screening processes free the beans from impurities and sort them by size, weight and shape. After a final critical inspection to assess aroma, acidity and uniformity, they are packed into bags and sealed for export.

The Colombian Coffee Federation (FNC) is entirely owned and controlled by Colombia's coffee farmers (cafeteros), of whom there are over 500,000. Most growers only have around 2ha of land but by joining together they can benefit from the clout of a large organisation. All profits from the FNC are channelled back to the cafeteros with the organisation providing a buffer against the volatile and unpredictable international coffee market. When the market took a dramatic dive in the early 1990s, this system served to compensate the farmers' US$1.5 billion shortfall. Colombia's farmers are under no obligation to sell to the FNC as no commercial monopoly exists. Over 50 private

---

🏠 **Hotel Carretero** Calle 36, No 22–22; ☎ 884 0255/1498; 📠 884 0821; www.hotelcarretero.com. This nice mid-range option attracts business travellers on a budget with decent rooms, an excellent b/fast & clean comfortable rooms. $$

✕ WHERE TO EAT

🍴 **Cafetería Alejandrío** Plaza de Bolívar; 🕐 07.00–21.00. Situated right on the plaza, this family-run little café serves dirt-cheap tasty snacks in lacklustre surroundings. Expect to pay 250 COP for *pan mariquiteño*, 600 COP for empandas & 300 for coconut bread amidst a glum-looking crowd of diners. There is a payphone here & the tinto is good at 400 COP a cup.

✕ **Mall de Comida** Cable Plaza, Carrera 23, No 61–11; www.cableplaza.com.co; 🕐 10.00–22.00 every day.

On the upper floors of the Cable Plaza you'll find a high-quality food court, containing Sandwich Cubano (Cuban snacks), Patacón Pizzao (pizza), Frisby (fried chicken), Brunos Huerta al Carbon (grilled meats), Jennies (pizza), Taco's & BBQ & a coffee house all under one roof.

✕ **Punto Rojo** Carrera 23, No 21–39. The city's best 24-hr diner is conveniently centrally located – and dirt cheap. $

shippers and 40 co-operatives operate independently within the Colombian coffee trade.

Colombians swear that the basic rule for making the perfect cup of coffee is to start with fresh cold water. Using two level tablespoons of 100% Colombian coffee, add six ounces of boiling water – the perfect quantities and ingredients for a truly splendid cup of a coffee.

- There are 566,000 coffee growers (cafeteros) in Colombia.
- A cup of coffee from a street vendor will cost around 200 COP.
- Coffee is the most popular drink worldwide with around two billion cups consumed every day.
- 90% of Colombians drink coffee daily.
- Globally, the coffee industry is worth over US$60 billion per annum.
- It takes 42 coffee beans to make an espresso. However, an espresso has one-third of the caffeine of a regular cup of coffee.
- Colombian coffee is grown across seven geographic areas and in 86 microclimates.
- Coffee is the second most traded product in the world after petroleum. Worldwide coffee production tips the scales at about six million tonnes.
- Central and South America produce approximately two-thirds of the world's coffee supply. Colombia is second only to Brazil in terms of production.
- A Belgian living in Guatemala invented the first instant coffee in 1906 and later emigrated to the United States. His name, ironically enough, was George Washington.
- Coffee plants were first grown in Colombia around 1830.
- Caffeine is on the International Olympic Committee list of prohibited substances. Athletes who test positive for more than 12 micrograms of caffeine per millilitre of urine may be banned from the Olympic Games. This level may be reached after drinking about five cups of coffee.
- Vietnam is now the third-largest producer of coffee with Japan the third-largest consumer. Americans drink over 400 millions cups of coffee per day.
- Some 25 million families worldwide are totally dependent on the coffee crop as their only source of income.

The official site of the Colombian Federación Nacional de Cafeteros (www.cafedecolombia.com) offers coffee industry news, yields, prices and statistics for the nation's various coffee-growing regions.

✖ **Restaurante El Pylon** Calle 21, No 21–21 ☎ 883 2021; ⏰12.00–19.00. Expect good service & robust local dishes at this simple diner where set meals won't set you back more than 10,000 COP. $$

✖ **Restaurante Zaguán Caldense** Carerra 23, No 30–64; ☎ 883 6360; ⏰lunch & dinner. This bamboo-clad local eatery suffers from off & on days but is worth a risk. Choose from a host of local Paisa classics, such as crispy pork, tripe & beans. $

ENTERTAINMENT AND NIGHTLIFE The city has a **municipal auditorium** that stages a wide range of concerts, operas and classical music and boasts some decent nightlife along **Avenida Santander**. Here you will find many of the best discos and restaurants in Manizales, many of them aimed squarely at the city's vibrant student population. For three nights, Thursday to Saturday, the area is packed to the gills around the fast-food restaurants and pizza bars in the area. Dozens of clubs and discos serve up a powerful repertoire of R&B, house, trance, rock, salsa and tango music. The smaller residential neighbourhoods of Batallon and Milan in the

MANIZALES
(not to scale)

CARRERA 16
CARRERA 17
CARRERA 18
CARRERA 19
CARRERA 20
CARRERA 21
CARRERA 22
CARRERA 23
CARRERA 24

Food market

N

Bradt

California Hotel

CALLE 21

CALLE 19
CALLE 20
CALLE 22
CALLE 23
CALLE 24
CALLE 25
CALLE 26
CALLE 27
CALLE 28
CALLE 29
CALLE 30
CALLE 31

Tourist Information ℹ
Palacio del Gobierno El Libertador
Tamanaco
Hotel Escorial, Tesoro Tours Manizales
Plaza de Bolívar Cafetería Alejandrio
Restaurante El Pylon
Centro Comercial Parque Caldad, Bioturismo Arte y Café
Iglesia de la Immaculada Concepción ✝
Fundadores 🏛
Hotel Estelar Las Colinas
Punto Rojo
Catedral de Manizales
Museo el Oro
Hotel Fundadores
Restaurante Zaguán Caldense
Cable Plaza

south of the city are home to a collection of rather fine dining options and upmarket bars. **Cable Plaza** (*www.cableplaza.com.co*) on Carrera 23, No 61–11, is the hottest new entertainment hangout in Manizales. It houses a five-floor state of the art, shopping and entertainment centre that includes a cinema, luxury supermarket, fast-food restaurants and bars. For theatrical shows and art-house films head to **Teatro Los Fundadores** on the corner of Carrera 22 and Calle 33 (✆ *884 5633*).

SHOPPING For some fabulous local colour, throw yourself into Manizales's food market – it's open everyday from dawn until the vendors shut up shop at about 16.00. The squeamish should close their eyes as they pass the cow eyes, pig heads, chicken feet and horse jaws in the meat section. The fruit and vegetable section is a little less taxing as is the herbs and spices market across the road. Prepare for a noisy, crowded shopping experience where haggling is expected. Look out for a big oval-shaped building in the middle of the intersection of Calle 23 and Carrera 16.

OTHER PRACTICALITIES First-time visitors can be caught out by Manizales's cool year-round temperatures, which can feel like the Arctic for those fresh in from the Caribbean coast. Pack waterproofs, a thick fleece and dispense with the beach gear – especially during the rather bleak rainy months, March to May and September to November. Those planning to hike, trek or camp will need thermal clothing and cold-weather sleeping bags.

Thankfully, the city's large student population has caused numerous internet cafés to spring up citywide. Most charge around 2,500 COP per hour. Some of the most central include the **Internet Café Tamanaco** (✆ *888 6290*) on the corner Calle 23 and Carrera 21 and **Café Internet Fundadores** (✆ *884 2538*) on the Carrera 23, No 30–59.

Almost all of the **banks** in Manizales have ATMs and are located in and around Calle 21 and Carrera 22, including the Bancolombia, Cambios Country and the Banco Unión Colombiano.

WHAT TO SEE At the heart of Manizales is the **Plaza de Bolívar** where, even on a dull, wet day, there are always plenty of shoeshine stands and vendors braving the relentless drizzle. In the middle, stands an unusual statue by Rodrigo Arenas Betacur. It's dubbed Bolívar-Cóndor and depicts **El Libertador** as a bird. The plaza is flanked to the north by the **Palacío del Gobierno** (Governor's Palace), a nice-looking neo-classical building dating back to 1927. On the south, the Gothic **Catedral de Manizales** dominates the view and is the third church to occupy the site following earthquakes and fire. Two colourful murals decorate the wall under the cathedral steps and are as strange as the oddball assortment of decorative styles inside the church. The east and west of the plaza are edged by an eclectic array of nondescript shops and restaurants. East, the 20th-century **Iglesia de la Immaculada Concepción** has some fine woodcarvings to admire. A block south you'll find the **Museo el Oro** (884 3851; ⊕08.00–18.00 Mon–Fri, closed 11.30–14.00; free admission) on Carrera 23, No 23–6, where a small collection of Indian gold and ceramics help tell the history of the Quimbaya people.

FESTIVALS AND EVENTS

Feria de Manizales (Jan) One of Colombia's biggest events after the Barranquilla carnival, this annual party features parades, concerts, dancing and bullfighting – plus a beauty pageant to crown the Coffee Queen.

Festival Latinoamericano de Teatro (Sep) For over 40 years, this week-long festival has showcased some of Colombia's finest film-makers as well as the most cutting-edge cinematic talent in Latin America. Today it is arguably the nation's second most important film event, after the festival in Bogotá. Free concerts attract film fans from all over Colombia – and beyond.

AROUND MANIZALES

There's a fabulous lookout point offering astounding views about 18km from the city, on the Manizales–Pereira road. **El Mirador** also has a rather nice restaurant which, as the name suggests, also boasts to-die-for vistas. Swirling mists create ghostly shapes over emerald hills. Vultures sit poised on twisted palms ready to swoop into the valley below. Creeper-clad trees sprout up from tufted grass, shrubs and mile-high ferns.

The 70ha humid rainforest-cum-ecological theme park **Ecoparque De Selva Humeda Tropical Yarumos** (875 5598; admission 2,000 COP) lies to the west of Manizales and is divided into two zones: education and adventure. Funded by public funds, the park contains 60 plant species, numerous migratory and endemic birds, dozens of butterflies, monkeys, frogs, snakes, iguanas and at least 13 species of tree. Two separate manmade trails wind 1.5km and 2km along waterfalls and are used by scientists from the Alexandra von Humboldt Institute for bird research. In the sector devoted to adventure, there is a covered ice-rink (the second biggest in Colombia), a kids' playhouse, rappelling and a forest canopy ride – the highlight of the park. In the gardens, 200 peacocks strut around a museum of stuffed animals and pickled exhibits. A very ethereal chill-out zone has been built on the roof of the museum building, featuring a vast stone-paved Zen-inspired plaza in which relaxing music is piped day-long. The park attracts 152,000 visitors each year. It has a sister attraction ten minutes away to the north. Founded in 2002, **El Bosque de Popular** (875 5511; ⊕08.00–18.00 daily; free admission, small charge for vehicles) is a conservation and public space. One million visitors per annum use this picturesque 56ha parkland, a scenic spot with wooded and recreation zones. Close by, the National Coffee Federation-run **El Recinto del Pemsamiento** (*www.recintodelpemsamiento.com*) has some nice gardens to visit that are home to over 300 orchid species and a lake. A 1.5km trail skirts a museum devoted to Colombian rum past a butterfly house and out along a pretty, leafy path. The 179ha site also contains cable cars and a coffee-tasting pavilion. Admission is 5,000 COP to simply walk around or 10,000 COP all-in, including a guide.

PARQUE NACIONAL LOS NEVADOS (*www.parquesnacionales.gov.co*) Travellers keen to

hike through some of Colombia's most striking terrain will find this 583km² stretch of the Andes fits the bill. Not only does this snow-caked range of volcanic peaks — topped by the 5,325m-tall Nevado del Ruiz – offer truly incredible views from trails that climb through cloudforest but it is also relatively easy to access and, most importantly, safe. However, it is very cold and the altitude can pose problems health-wise. On this basis, anyone not feeling 100% fit should give Los Nevados a miss.

A hike to the summit of the still-active Nevado del Ruiz takes about three hours. Varying altitudes ensure a collection of well-maintained paths wind through considerable diverse terrains, from humid thickets and cool highland scrubland to crisp, white snow and ice. Popular with skiers and budding volcanologists, the range comprises El Tolima (5,215m) at the southern end followed by El Quindío (4,750m), Santa Isabel (4,950m), El Cisne (4750m), and then El Ruiz in the north. The park attracts mountaineers from all over the world, many of whom traverse all four peaks. This takes about seven days to complete and is a highly popular challenge.

But it is not just the climbing that has made these mountains famous. On 13 November 1985 at precisely 21.08 Nevado del Ruiz erupted – with catastrophic results. Within four hours vast lava flows had travelled over 100km, leaving total devastation in their wake. More than 23,000 people were killed and more than 5,000 injured. The town of Armero (population 27,500) at the mouth of the Río Lagunillas canyon was hardest hit, disappearing entirely under the mud. Thousands of villagers along the Chinchiná, Gualí and Lagunillas rivers fled in fear as their homes surrendered to the lahars.

Earlier eruptions of Nevado del Ruiz occurred in 1595 and 1845 spewing melted snow and ice and forcing mudflows out into the surrounding valleys. However, when El Ruiz began showing clear signs of unrest in 1984 scientists feared the worst. A series of pyroclastic flows from the summit crater and phreatic (steam) explosions were an early warning system but weren't enough to enable a firm prediction of when an eruption would occur. El Ruiz had been observed closely for a whole 12 months when, suddenly, pumice and ash began to fall in heavy rain. Within minutes, hot rock fragments melted about 10% of the volcano's ice cover, gauging channels 100m wide and up to 4m deep. A vast sluice of water, ice, pumice and rocks began to flow into the six major river valleys draining the volcano. In one river, the Azufrado, scientists found a 2m piece of ice over 3km from the crater. It is estimated that lahars reached speeds of 60km per hour along the Río Guali and were up to 50m thick, quadrupling in size as they eroded soil, loose rock debris and stripped vegetation from the riverbanks. The eruption of Nevado del Ruiz remains the second mostly deadly in the 20th century (Mount Pelee in Martinique was first, killing 29,000 people in its 1902 eruption.)

The volcano actually has three craters: Arenas, Olleta and Piraña. Arenas – the main one and the crater responsible for the 1985 disaster – is reached by a relatively easy trek on snow. Olleta has a soil-covered summit that is usually snow-free. It is also extinct, so after the climb to 4,850m many visitors opt to descend into the crater for an alternative view. For a superb meander through beautiful scenery

The trio of towns that make up the Zona Cafetera are fierce rivals in every way. Each thinks that it's commercially savviest. They also think their football teams (Deportivo Pereira, Once Caldas Manizales, Athletico Quindío) are better, their women more pretty, and their countryside more beautiful. In fact, the populations of all three are actually pretty closely linked; strong family ties exist throughout the region, with inter-marriage and shared forefathers common.

follow the 40km path to El Cisne and Santa Isabel, where the sparkling waters of the Laguna del Otún at 3,950m are a spectacular sight – and a great place for a spot of trout fishing.

Since 1985, the volcanoes have been relatively quiet apart from the occasional puff of smoke, although global warming continues to cause some ongoing shrinkage to the volcanoes due to decreasing levels of annual snowfall. According to a report entitled 'The Thawing of the Peaks' by the director of the Colombian Institute of Hydrology, Meteorology and Environmental Studies, this will have a devastating impact on the local population, severely affecting fresh water supplies within the next 100 years.

Spectacled bear (Andean bear), tapir, moose, deer, rabbit, puma, mountain lion, armadillo and squirrel are all found in the park along with sparrow hawk and eagle. It is also notable for its various species of bromeliads, fern and moss.

Practicalities It is only possible to explore the park with a registered guide. Most visitors enter the park via the northern access road, a gateway frequently used by those day tripping from Manizales. It's a long day, so be sure to allow at least ten hours in which to reach around 5,100m and enjoy some truly magnificent views. Vehicles can only gain access via the northern access road so if your route involves the southern entrance you'll need to do it on foot. The northern road begins as La Esperanza just off the Manizales–Bogotá road and climbs up to 4,800m to the base of El Ruiz. Visitors pay their admission fee (8,000 COP) at the actual entrance to the park in Las Brisas at 4,050m. It takes around three hours to ascend to the Arenas crater of El Ruiz at 535m and about 1½ hours to reach Olleta at 4,850m. Two trails offer access to the southern section of the park. One begins in Cocora and climbs up to the highlands and to del Quindío. The other links the Parque Ucumarí to the Laguna del Otún via a 15km uphill path. All visitors should pack boots (or trainers), gloves, thick clothing and waterproof clothing and should be sure to stay close to their guide. As it is usual to stop off for a dip in the hot springs at the Hotel Termales be sure to have a bathing suit with you too. Those staying overnight should be properly equipped with basic essentials, including cold-weather sleeping bags and a torch. Guides should have a satellite phone, emergency flares and a detailed map.

When to go The park is open all year round with paths that are passable most days. However, it is more rewarding to avoid days shrouded with mist, fog and heavy cloud as they totally void the views, so plan your trip according to the local weather.

Getting there and around The park isn't served by public transport but most visitors will find that a transfer by jeep or van is included in the cost of a guide – but be sure to double check. A milk truck offers rides out to the park bright and early each day for 4,000 COP – every hotel in town knows the driver, so just ask around.

The Northwest Interior AROUND MANIZALES

9

🏠 **Where to stay** If a ten-hour day trip seems a tad too strenuous, staying overnight in the park may offer a more leisurely pace. Options are limited to a couple of basic campsites and a couple of cabins but they are well located. All accommodation should be pre-booked through the Parques Nacionales Naturales de Colombia in Bogotá. Expect to pay around 12,000 COP for a dorm bed and 4,000 COP per night per person to pitch a tent and be prepared to bring food, drink and provisions.

A handful of hotels located close to the park entrance supplement the ranger's accommodation, including he following.

🏠 **Hotel Termales del Ruiz** ☎ 851 7069/870 0944; e hoteltermalesruizgo@terra.com; hoteltermalesruizgo.es.tripod.com. This comfortable hotel is a firm favourite with most of the tour guides & operators in Manizales – with good reason. At 3,500m, it boasts the distinction of being Colombia's highest & is conveniently located just outside the northern perimeter of the park. Expect simple rooms & friendly staff along with a decent restaurant & thermal pools. $$$

🏠 **Hotel Cisne** Another simple but comfortable option on the outer edges of the park. At the time of writing it isn't connected by phone but can be contacted via the Parques Nacionales Naturales de Colombia in Bogotá. Rooms are good value at around 70,000 COP with camping in the grounds at 5,000 COP pp per night.

🏠 **Hotel Las Brisas** Located directly outside the entrance of the park at 4,050m, this nice little basic option has guides for day-long trips – & longer. It is also possible to camp here at 5,000 COP pp per night.

🏠 **Chalet Arenales** Comprising solely dirt-cheap dorm room beds at 4,150m this rustic hostel is a popular backpacker choice at around 11,000 COP per night.

✗ **Where to eat** Apart from the hotel restaurants the only other place to buy food is **El Refugio**, a simple shack selling drinks and snacks. As it opens and shuts at whim it is wise not to rely solely on this option – to be on the safe side pack a picnic and bring plenty of water.

SALAMINA (*Telephone code: 6*) This popular day-trip destination from Manizales attracts coach-loads of devotees of the colonial era who visit Salamina to simply stroll through the town's genteel streets and breathe in the ambience of yesteryear. Streets of pretty buildings are dominated by a particularly fine cathedral, built in 1865 by an English architect. One of the oldest settlements in the Zona Cafetera, Salamina was founded in 1825 and has retained much of its original charm. A typical pueblo Paisa with a population of around 20,000, its houses boast lots of traditional architectural characteristics, such as ornately carved wooden doors and windows. A small handful of local restaurants and budget hotels can be found in and around the main plaza. Salamina was declared a National Monument in 1982. A frequent bus service connects it with Manizales (9,000 COP, 2½ hours) with supplementary colectivos that nip back and forth throughout the day (11,000 COP, 2 hours) – both pass through the town of Neria, another pretty colonial settlement.

PEREIRA *Telephone code: 6*

With a population of almost totally 590,000, Pereira is Colombia's sixth-biggest city and the largest in the Zona Cafetera – and as the capital of the department of Risaralda, Pereira has coffee coursing through its veins. Founded in 1863 by priest Remigio Antonio Cañarte, the city was named after Francisco Pereira Martínez, the former owner of the land on which it stands. Dubbed 'the Pearl of the River Otún' Pereira sits within a fertile valley at the very epicentre of the Coffee Zone and is equidistant from Cali and Medellín at around 230 km. A succession of destructive earthquakes has dramatically reshaped the city over time. Today, much of Pereira is modern in construction with just a few telltale historic buildings in the city centre – but this hotchpotch of mismatched patched-up architecture is undoubtedly part of its charm. Pereira is not a tourism destination but a gritty commercial hub. As such, it has little to offer in the way of attractions per se. However, it makes an excellent base from which to explore the region. The city is also renowned for its partying stamina and love of soccer, so expect plenty of passion and gusto (along with generous measures of aguardiente) when Deportivo Pereira kick off on home soil. Pereira is twinned with Miami and enjoys close links with the Floridian city. Although no firm statistics exist, a large number of Pereirans reside overseas. Anecdotal evidence suggests that more than 50% of homes in Pereira have a family member living abroad, mainly in Spain and the US.

HISTORY Before European colonisation, what became Pereira was the domain of Quimbaya, a particularly fierce-fighting tribe of Indians. Although the Spanish established a small settlement in the area around 1540 the city itself wasn't founded until August 1863. On his death, landowner Francisco Pereira Martinez bequeathed the ground to the priest Remigio Antonio Cañarte for the specific purpose of building a city. Six days later, Pereira was inaugurated on what today is the Plaza de Bolívar. The settlement soon began to attract migrant farmers from Antioquía, ready to exploit Pereira's economically strategic location, fertile soil and good weather. In vast swathes of the mineral-rich volcanic soil of the Andes, they planted coffee crops, heralding the start of an era of prosperity. Over 140 years later, coffee still remains the bedrock of the city and the dynamo that powers its economy.

GETTING THERE AND AROUND At the time of writing, there are plans to relocate Pereira's Matecaña Airport to the nearby town of Cartago, although this is unlikely to happen until 2010. At present, the airport is located 5km west of the centre of the city. Avianca operates eight flights a day to Bogotá where connections can be made to other Colombian cities and international destinations. It also runs five direct flights to Miami per week.

Pereira's bus terminal is on Calle 17, No 23–157, about 2km from the city centre. Numerous buses pass by and from El Centro; it's an easy 12-minute trip. Here frequent departures serve Bogotá (35,000 COP, 9 hours), Medellín (25,000 COP, 5 hours) and Cali (20,000 COP, 4 hours). Minibuses to Armenia (6,000 COP, 1 hour), Marsella (4,000 COP, 1 hour) and Manizales (7,000 COP, 1½ hours) leave every 15 minutes.

The city's US$36 million mass transport system opened to much acclaim in 2006. The Megabus (*www.megabus.gov.co*) is modelled on Bogotá's hugely successful TransMilenio system and is a public–private partnership. Although the entire scheme hasn't been fully rolled out, a frequent all-day service is already in place. This is designed to replace the city's 1,000-plus privately owned colectivos with an integrated system of dedicated transit lanes and high-quality stations. Megabus comprises articulated buses and is scheduled to expand to serve the surrounding areas of Cartago and Santa Rosa de Cabal. Megabus is showing impressive results, achieving about a 2% shift from private cars to public transportation across the city as a whole.

TOURIST INFORMATION
Dirección de Fomento al Turismo Palacío Municipal, Carrera 7, No 18–55; 324 8030: ⏱08.00–16.00 Mon–Fri, closed 11.30–14.00

Local government website www.pereira.gov.co
Local tourism website contratacion.pereira.gov.co

⌂ WHERE TO STAY

⌂ **Gran Hotel** Calle 19, No 9–19; www.granhotelpereira.com. Despite its faded façade & tired décor, this massive Art Deco building retains a certain charm. Expect large rooms with grand architectural flourishes. A rather slow restoration project has yet to gather pace – but here's hoping. $$$

⌂ **Hotel Abadia Plaza** Carrera 8, No 21–67; ☎ 335 8398; e hotelabadiaplaza.etp.net.co. This is fast becoming a firm favourite with discerning domestic tourists from Bogotá due to its plush décor, upmarket funkiness & gorgeous bathrooms. Rooms are also fitted with soundproofed glass so there is minimal disruption from the noise of the city below. $$$

⌂ **Hotel de Pereira** Carrera 13, No 15–73; ☎ 335 0770; www.hoteldelpereira.com. By rights, this large, rather swish, modern hotel should be snooty & unwelcoming, but instead it has all the friendliness of a small family-run concern. A large, circular foyer boasts a sunken lounge with daily newspapers & a business centre. Large rooms are well equipped with modern private bathrooms with bath & shower, TV (cable), minibar, desk, phone, safe & room service. Onsite amenities include a pool, restaurant & bar. Highly recommended, if a little out of town. $$$

⌂ **Hotel Cataluña** Calle 19, No 8–61; ☎ 335 4527; f 333 0791. This great-value option is located close to the Plaza de Bolívar & has clean, cheerful rooms, some of which have balconies overlooking the street. $$

⌂ **Hotel Dann Soratama** Carrera 7, No 19–20; ☎ 335 8650. Centrally located, this large hotel offers some of the most convenient & comfortable rooms in the heart of the city. It's not big on style, but it's pretty big on value. $$

⌂ **Hotel Tequendama** Carrera 7, No 22–34; ☎ 335 7986; f 334 3079. Unlike the Hotel de Pereira, the Tequendama is right in the thick of it, a factor that makes earplugs a must for every guest. Located next to a busy casino that keeps late hours, the hotel is a hive of activity. For those that sleep through anything, this hotel is a bargain with good rates, nice staff & decent rooms. $$

✗ WHERE TO EAT
There are dozens of funky upmarket international-style restaurants in and around the Zona Rosa's Avenida Circunvalar and the Turín-La Popa district, from pizza joints and Chinese diners to French bistros and Mexican cantinas. In the centre, restaurants largely serve typical Colombian dishes and Paisa specialities. Perhaps the biggest dining thrill would be to try the unnamed restaurant in Calle 12 that looks just like an ordinary house from the street. The locals advise that callers knock three times on the last door in the street. There's no sign, but apparently the patron serves meat priced according to weight in a wide variety of styles – Pereira's best-kept secret.

✗ **El Balcón de los Arrieros** Carrera 8, No 24–65; ☎ 335 3633; ◷ noon–21.00'ish. This rustic local eatery is a popular Paisa fixture. Choose from a menu of man-sized meat-based dishes, from grilled oxen to spicy chorizo. $

✗ **G&G Restaurante** Plaza de Bolívar. This 24-hr diner serves pastries, pizza, drinks & snacks overlooking the cell-phone minute vendors & shoeshine stands. $

✗ **Grajales Autoservicios** Carrera 8, No 21–60. This 24-hr food joint is permanently full of people, largely because it is dirt cheap. An onsite bakery is consistently good, but the quality of meals is patchy. Self-service style. $

✗ **La Carreta** Bolívar Plaza Mall. Fans of the largest chain of Cuban fast food will enjoy this upper-floor diner, overlooking the main square in the centrally located mall. $

✗ **Restaurante El Túnel** Carrera 7, No 23–41; ☎ 335 0226; ◷ 07.00–22.00. Serves up plates of hearty Colombian staple dishes, from tripe & sancocho to suckling pig & goat. $

ENTERTAINMENT AND NIGHTLIFE
The locals describe the city as '*Querendona, transnochadora y morena*' – meaning sleepless, loveable and dark – as everyone in Pereira loves to party, from the city's twenty-something student population to the aged grandparents. You'll find an ever-changing club scene that offers rumba, tango, salsa, rock and techno music along with numerous bars. Most of them are located on Avenida Circunvalar and the Turín-La Popa district, home to more than 50 discos, bars and nightclubs. Failing that, take a walk through the centre of the city and see what's happening – there's bound to be music playing somewhere; just follow your ears.

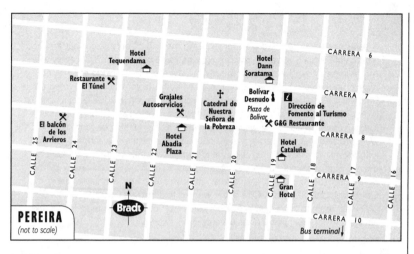

Map labels:
Hotel Tequendama
Restaurante El Túnel
Grajales Autoservicios
Hotel Dann Soratama
Catedral de Nuestra Señora de la Pobreza
Bolívar Desnudo
Plaza de Bolívar
Dirección de Fomento al Turismo
G&G Restaurante
El balcón de los Arrieros
Hotel Abadia Plaza
Hotel Cataluña
Gran Hotel
Bus terminal
CARRERA 6
CARRERA 7
CARRERA 8
CARRERA 9
CARRERA 10
CALLE 25, CALLE 24, CALLE 23, CALLE 22, CALLE 21, CALLE 20, CALLE 19, CALLE 18, CALLE 17, CALLE 16
Bradt

SHOPPING Pereira's Bolívar Plaza Mall is conveniently located in the centre and is the most accessible of the city's seven shopping malls. As well as a cinema and paintball centre it includes dozens of shops and a food court – and is a good place for sporting goods, mobile phone consumables and clothing. Throughout Pereira you'll see makeshift markets and vendors selling goods laid out on blankets on the sidewalk. Much of it is knock-off, especially the sunglasses, watches and leather belts. On the outskirts of town on Avenida de Río there is a vast Carrefour superstore – you can't miss it.

OTHER PRACTICALITIES Pereira is home to dozens of internet cafés, many of which are centred on or around the main plaza. Most cost about 2,500 COP per hour with **Cybernet** on the square (℡ *335 0554*) open seven days a week. Similarly, all of the city's banks are clustered together. Most have ATMs, including the **Banco Unión Colombiano** and the **Bancolombia** on Calle 8. For laundries, head to Carrera 12.

WHAT TO SEE Much like Manizales, Pereira has a rather unusual monument to Simón Bolívar in the form of Arenas Betancur's **Bolívar Desnudo**. This 11-tonne 8.5m-high bronze sculpture of El Libertador naked on horseback was created in 1963. 'It was left the man naked, so a Christ to horse', Betancur, a teacher, wrote at the time. 'Naked the horse, naked the fire – as in the hands of Prometheus – naked the flags. Nothing else, nothing less than Prometheus: the man flying with the fire on the beast and mountains in where the men sleep and generate. Blind that looks for the light. Slaves who look for the freedom. Bolívar – Prometheus. Bolívar – storm. Bolívar – fire. So it is my statue. Another thing a yearning of freedom to know was not the independence wars …, to live, to create.'

Pereira's once fine **Catedral de Nuestra Señora de la Pobreza** is a shadow of its former self, having been remodelled, rebuilt and repaired several times since the first foundation was laid in 1874. Apparently it has skeletons in the walls.

Centro Recreativo y Vacacional Comfamiliar (℡ *335 2033; f 333 5562*) This sprawling 47ha leisure resort about 10km from Pereira is open for day trippers and vacationers and is a Mecca for urbanites seeking some country fresh air. Hemmed by a shallow forest, the park-style complex is centred on a wide range of sports and leisure attractions, including six swimming pools, half a dozen football pitches, tennis courts, hiking trails, fishing lakes, boating, basketball courts and cycle paths. It's all

A sex strike may seem like a rather extreme method of persuasion, but for the women of Pereira it was a last-ditch effort in the name of peace. In 2006, every wife and girlfriend of gang members in the city called a sex ban in a bid to get their men to give up the gun. Hundreds took part in what the Colombian media called the 'strike of crossed legs', a protest backed by Pereira's mayor. In 2005, a total of 480 killings were reported in the city (90% of the victims were aged 14–25), prompting a disarmament scheme. However, many wives and girlfriends of gang members were worried that their partners were not handing over their weapons. They met with the mayor and came up with the idea of a sex strike as a clear message to disarm. Studies found that local gang members were drawn to criminality by the desire for status, power and sexual attractiveness, not economic necessity, Colombian radio reported. One of the women told Britain's Guardian newspaper: 'We want them to know that violence is not sexy.' The sex ban lasted ten days and attracted widespread global press coverage.

a bit formula-driven and borders on tacky in places – but visitors at weekends top 3,000 a day with up to 40,000 people visiting each month. Accommodation options range from camping zones and cabins to hotels, with five hotels reflecting different regional styles of Colombian cuisine. Entrance is 54,000 COP with cabañas from 90,000 COP per person per night and camping (200 pitches) from 32,000 COP.

AROUND PEREIRA

CERRITOS You'll find the rural area of Cerritos just 5km outside the urban sprawl of Pereira city centre, past hammock stalls and springy grass verges. The Pereira–Cartago road has numbered milestones – look out for 'Entrance 4' on the left-hand side as it leads to a number of fincas open to tourists. This collection of large, old farmhouses has been tastefully converted into stylish hotels, bars and restaurants – all of them to great effect. Travellers seeking superb boutique accommodation away from the city should certainly consider the following option.

 Where to stay

Finca Sazagua 337 9895; f 313 2291; e info@sazagua.com; reserves@sazagua.com. A sumptuous high-end former farmhouse that looks like something out of Architectural Digest. Elegant furnishings adorn every one of the 10 stylish rooms in a property where no compromise has been made on the quality of décor. Fittings, fixtures & drapes ooze good taste in rooms that overlook handsome gardens & a delightful outdoor pool. The finca is also home to a highly acclaimed restaurant & outdoor bar. $$$

Hacienda Malabar 337 9206; e malabar@une.net.co. A neighbouring property 7km from Pereira. Offering a range of dbls & family suites with beautiful tiled floors & blood-red colourwashed walls, this aged finca has wooden shutters & chunky wooden furniture & ornate balconies overlooking flower-filled gardens. Huge baskets piled high with bananas flank the hallway as do vast vases of birds of paradise. A rather good restaurant boasts a lime-green décor with exposed stone. Rooms start at 138,000 COP for a dbl, but don't include b/fast. $$$

SANTUARIO OTÚN QUIMBAYA In the early 1990s, this 5km² of Andean forest was under threat. Today, its staggering biodiversity is beautifully preserved. Located 15km southeast of Pereira, and sitting at altitudes of between 1,800m and 2,400m, the Santuario contains several pleasant ecological trails, a basic lodge for overnight stays and a small restaurant. Since 1996 it has been part of the Colombian government's national conservation programme. Rare plant species and vulnerable wildlife have been protected and the integrity of the natural environment restored. Today the area is used purely for ecological studies and ecotourism with five different well-maintained paths that climb through mountain forests where the average temperature is 16°C. Those wishing to combine a visit with a trip to the Parque Ucumarí can do so on foot in about four hours. Butterflies and birdlife are particularly rich along this wooded route.

Getting there and away Catch a chiva from Pereira towards El Cedral and jump off at La Suiza at the entrance of the park.

Where to stay and eat The reserve's only option, **La Suiza**, has beds in a dorm room for around 25,000 COP a night and serves simple chicken-and-rice meals for around 5,000 COP. Accommodation should be pre-booked with the Parques Nacionales Naturales de Colombia in Bogotá (*www.parquesnacionales.gov.co*).

MARSELLA (*Telephone code: 6*) Located 30km northwest of Pereira, this homely small town is home to around 8,500 people and is totally surrounded by emerald carpets of coffee fields. Founded in 1860 by Antioquian farmers, Marsella is every inch the typical Paisa town. Most people visit to mooch around the tiny streets and the **Jesús María Estrada cemetery** before heading out for a stroll around the **Jardín Bontánico Alejandro Humboldt** (368 5233; 08.00–18.00 daily; admission 4,000 COP), where an hour-long trail along a cobblestone path winds through orchids, ferns and bamboo. Created in 1979 as an education and research facility, the gardens offer plenty of insight into the ecosystem of the Zona Cafetera. It contains a museum dedicated to promoting the protection of local bird species. The **Museo de la Cauchera** (Slingshot Museum) has actively sought to discourage local children killing birds with catapults – once a much-practised pastime. Today it offers free entrance to the park in return for discarded caucheras.

Getting there Minibuses run to and from Pereira each day until around 19.00, every 15 minutes (4,000 COP, 1 hour).

SANTA ROSA DE CABAL (*Telephone code: 6*) Tourism has become a focus of the town of Santa Rosa de Cabal, once a delightful one-horse pit-stop that welcomed travellers *en route* to the surrounding thermal pools. Today, it has a handful of basic budget hotels, including the **Hotel Turistica** at 15,000 COP per night and is pushing itself forward as a destination to be reckoned with – it has even, rather successfully, renamed the thermal springs to include its name. Those that stay in the town can hop aboard a chiva that heads to the thermals three times a day for 2,900 COP each way. Times vary but are 09.00, noon and 15.00 at the time of writing. The hotel can also help you hire a driver and a jeep for around 35,000 COP return trip.

The **Termales de Santa Rosa** (*once known as the Termales Arbeláez*) (⊕*08.00–midnight; day-guest admission 13,000 COP*) are located 8km east of the town on the Pereira–Manizales road. A resort aimed squarely at tourists is totally engulfed by its natural surroundings in a truly stunning location that prompts audible involuntary intakes of breath. A 170m waterfall provides a formidable backdrop to the complex where hot springs reach temperatures of 70°C but cool to around 40°C in the pool. Other amenities include a restaurant, bar and a hotel. Many choose to stay overnight at the very nice Hotel Termales (✆ *364 5500/1322*) where a wide range of accommodation offers something for every guest. Opt for the Casa Veja where rooms can comfortably accommodate up to seven people at 90,000 COP per person or stay in the newer La Montaña cabins (five to seven people) at 110,000 COP per person – it's not cheap, but it is worth the splurge and rates include full board.

ECOTERMALES SAN VINCENTE (*Telephone code: 6*) Another popular thermal bath close to the Termales de Santa Rosa, this newer resort-style set-up is located 18km east of Santa Rosa de Cabal at the end of an unmade road. Leafy trails lead out to waterfalls and bloom-filled thickets on a complex that comprises a hotel, campsite, cabins and several thermal pools. There is also a place to take a mud bath and enjoy a massage. Packages range from a day-long visit (10,000 COP) to a full-week stay.

Getting there and away The trip to the Termales de Santa Rosa takes just over an hour from Pereira. Transportation departs daily from the Ecotermales San Vincente office at around 08.00 with the return leg at 17.00. Cost 10,000 COP.

Where to stay and eat Accommodation ranges from a double room with or without a bathroom and a cabaña that sleeps six (45,000 COP pp) to camping (25,000 COP per tent). Rates include breakfast and use of the pools. A restaurant serves lunch and dinner at around 10,000 COP a head.

Other practicalities All visits to the Ecotermales San Vincente must be pre-booked with the office on the corner of Calle 16 and Carrera 13 in Pereira (✆ *333 6157; www.sanvicente.com.co*). The most cost-effective option is a full-day package as it includes return transportation, lunch and a couple of guided walks at 35,000 COP. Accommodation also needs to be booked in advance. It's possible to hire tents for a 5,000 COP premium. You'll need to pack towels and bathing costumes.

PARQUE UCUMARÍ A trail links this 43km² natural reserve with the Parque Nacional Los Nevados, winding along the Río Otún and through a magnificent gorge. Located about 30km east of Pereira, Parque Ucumarí was established in 1984. It offers a range of decent bird-filled hiking paths that rise up through forest-clad hillsides past waterfalls onto cloud-shrouded summits – some more gruelling than others. More than 185 bird species have been recorded here in a single day and the park is also home to a rich abundance of wildlife, including the spectacled bear. Rugged boulders and ice-cold streams pepper a rugged terrain covered in vibrant-green lush vegetation. Mules and horses can be rented from the reserve's Refugio – a worthwhile expense for those with camping gear, especially on the eight-hour trek to the Laguna del Otún.

Getting there and around From Pereira, local chivas will take you up the El Cedral, about 25km from the centre of town. It's a rough road but the scenery makes it a pleasant hour-long drive. From El Cedral (at 1,950m) the 5km uphill trek along the Río Otún to La Pastora will take around two hours. An enterprising local lad sometimes tethers his horse to the start of the trail to attract custom from those lacking stamina. Expect to pay around 20,000 COP for a one-way trip.

Where to stay and eat The reserve's **Refugio La Pastora** sits at 2,400m and can accommodate 28 guests in rooms that sleep four to eight. However, there is almost unlimited capacity for those prepared to sleep on mattresses around the camp fire and there is also plenty of space for those prepared to pitch a tent. A decent breakfast (3,500 COP), lunch (6,000 COP) and dinner (7,000 COP) are served from a rudimentary kitchen. The Refugio hires out guides at 45,000 COP per day. It costs 13,500 COP per person to stay overnight.

Other practicalities Visitors need a permit to visit the reserve and will also need to pre-book and pre-pay for any accommodation. Both can be done via the Grupos Ecológicos de Risaralda (GER) office in the Centro Comercial Fiducentro Local A 119 in Pereira (↙ *325 4781;* e *grupos_ecologicos@yahoo.com*) – they can also help with transport, maps and guides.

ARMENIA *Telephone code: 6*

Bearing the battle scars of earthquakes past, Armenia is not a city renowned for its beauty, with streets that have a rather makeshift, make-do feel. What hasn't been patched up seems to have been rebuilt in functional style. Construction born out of urgent necessity rarely wins awards for elegance and Armenia makes little pretence of that. However, the city does sit on some of the most beautiful countryside in the Zona Cafetera between a luxuriant valley and the peaks of the Cordillera Central. Almost a third of Armenia's historic centre was razed by the region's 1999 earthquake. That it re-established itself with both speed and determination is testament to the gritty fortitude of the Armenian population, many of whom played an active role in, literally, piecing the city back together. Today Armenia is very much back in business and dubbed 'Ciudad Milagro' (Miracle City), a bustling trade centre with coffee, bananas and plantains at its heart. This busy transportation hub seems permanently jam-packed with tooting cars, street markets, horse and carts, buses, taxis and shoeshine stands with cargo-laden highways that lead into the chaotic mix.

HISTORY Armenia was founded in October 1889 by hunter Jesús María Ocampo, a man whose success at trapping jaguars earned him the nickname Tigrero (meaning 'tiger killer'). He bought the land for 100 pesos in gold coins and set about building a trade centre to serve the settlements that were beginning to spring up in the region. Within six months of its founding, Armenia's population had soared to 100 people, gaining it legal recognition by the government. Initially called Villa Holguin after the then president of Colombia, the name was changed to Armenia to honour the Armenian people murdered in the Hamidian massacres of 1894–97.

Armenia's rapid growth and expanding economy were hampered by poor transportation with mule trains used to traverse the mountainous terrain. The construction of an asphalt road in 1927 gave the city's prosperity further impetus and Armenia soon became a thriving distribution centre. In 1966 it became capital of the newly created Quindío department. In 1999, disaster struck in the form of an earthquake. It measured 6.2 on the Richter scale and reduced large areas of the city to rubble. The devastation was immense and destroyed 70% of the homes in Armenia. More than 1,180 people were killed and 5,000 injured. Over 28,000 people were still living in 'alojamientos' (multi-family spaces) in transitory camps two years after the disaster, placing enormous pressure on the provision of basic sanitary services, water supplies and food. A ten-strong team of search and rescue experts from Scotland helped recover survivors. Volunteers from the International Rescue Corps (IRC) had previously been called on after earthquakes in Afghanistan, Iran and Japan.

GETTING THERE AND AROUND El Edén Airport is well outside of the city, 20km southwest on the road to Cali. Avianca offer about half a dozen flights a day to Bogotá where domestic and international connections can be made. The city's bus terminal is located on the corner of Carrera 19 and Calle 35 1.5km southwest of the centre. It is served by the many, frequent buses that run along Carrera 19 and is a 4,000 COP taxi ride from the centre of town. There's a good service to both Bogotá (33,000 COP, 8 hours) and Cali (18,000 COP, 4 hours) with minibuses serving Pereira (6,000 COP, 1 hour), Manizales (11,000 COP, 2½ hours), Filandia (4,000 COP, 1 hour), Salento (4,000 COP, 50 minutes) and the Parque Nacional del Café (2,500 COP, 30 minutes) every 15 minutes.

TOURIST INFORMATION
🛈 **Secretaría de Turismo** Plaza de Bolívar; ☏ 741 2991; ⊕ 08.00–18.00, closed noon–14.00

TOUR GUIDES Fernando Vargus (☏ 316 554 5708) can often be found distributing tourist maps by the side of the La Tebaida–Armenia road. Look out for the billboard advertising the Las Camelias Hotel on the right-hand side – and Vargus is generally sitting opposite. He not only guides on a tips-only basis but guarantees to find accommodation for an average of 30,000 COP per night.

WHERE TO STAY There are numerous makeshift signs for many of Armenia's small bed and breakfasts, cabins and hostels located along the road from La Tebaida. Those in a hurry can also call on the services of Fernando Vargus (see above).

In the city centre, there are a number of large hotels. Rates are competitive although very few look very much from the outside.

🏠 **Hotel Bolivar Plaza** Calle 21, No 14–17; ☏ 741 0083; e hotelbolivaplaza@telsat.com.co. As the city's most lavish accommodation, this hotel's major selling point is its stunning mountain views as its rooms are actually quite small. However, many look out onto the Cordillera Central – & some have balconies. Each has a private bathroom, cable TV & a minibar with onsite facilities that include a laundry, café/bar & a very nice upper-floor restaurant, again with rather fine views. $$$

🏠 **Hotel Centenario** (50 rooms) Calle 21, No 18–20, ☏ 744 3143; www.hotelcentenario.com. Don't be put off by the rather synthetic façade of this central hotel as the interior is very nice. The rooms are clean & comfortable with cable TV, minibar & room service available in configurations that include 2 large family rooms & 48 dbls. The hotel's top-floor restaurant, Los Cristales, is widely praised & can accommodate 60 diners, offering a varied menu of delicious comida típica & international dishes until 22.00 each day. There is also an onsite gym & sauna. $$

🏠 **Hotel El Quijote** Carrera 15, No 25–8; ☏ 744 0663. Offering some of the quietest rooms in the city, the El Quijote is set beyond the worst of the traffic & mayhem. It's nothing special, but rooms are modern &

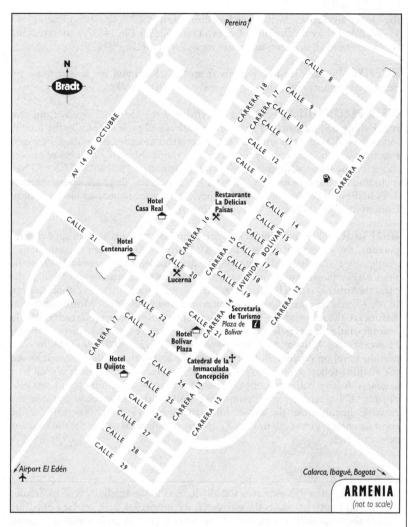

Pereira

N
Bradt

CALLE 8

CALLE 9

CARRERA 18
CARRERA 17
CALLE 10

CALLE 11

AV 14 DE OCTUBRE

CALLE 12

CALLE 13

CARRERA 13

Hotel
Casa Real

Restaurante
La Delicias
Paisas

CALLE 21

CALLE 14

CARRERA 16

CARRERA 15 CALLE 15 (BOLIVAR)

Hotel
Centenario

CALLE 16

CALLE 20
Lucerna

CALLE 17

CALLE 18 (AVENIDA

CALLE 19

CARRERA 14

Secretaría
de Turismo

CARRERA 12

CALLE 22

CARRERA 21

Plaza de
Bolívar

CARRERA 17
CALLE 23

Hotel
Bolívar
Plaza

Catedral de la
Immaculada
Concepción

Hotel
El Quijote

CALLE 24

CARRERA 13

CALLE 25

CARRERA 12

CALLE 26

CALLE 27

CALLE 28

CALLE 29

Airport El Edén

Calarca, Ibagué, Bogota

ARMENIA
(not to scale)

clean in this relatively new hotel. All rooms are dbls &
come with private bathroom. $$
🏠 **Hotel Casa Real** Carrera 18, No 18–36; ☎ 741
4550. This decent budget option has small, pokey

rooms with private bathrooms & is spotlessly clean &
well equipped. Choose from sgl or dbl – each has
cable TV. $

✗ **WHERE TO EAT** On the main drag into town from the airport on the city's outer
edge you'll find a number of dirt-cheap places serving good local food. Aimed
squarely at the locals, none of them are particularly fancy. The **Tierra Mia
Restaurante** (chicken-and-rice), **Rincón Asada Llanero** (grilled meats) and the
Ructica Café all come recommended as is **Don Frijoles**, a big, modern wooden-
fronted open diner with a first-class menu near to a row of jugo de naranja (orange
juice) stalls.

More centrally, check out the many 24-hour diners and budget restaurants that
serve set meals for under 5,000 COP. Try the **Restaurante La Delicias Paisas**
(☎ 745 5365), an above-the-street fuss-free sandwich shop. It offers great round-

the-clock Paisa snacks, including a lunchtime deal at 4,000 COP on Calle 17, No 15–22. Another local favourite is **Lucerna** on Calle 20, No 14–37, a convivial café that is crowded all day long and offers meals for around 5,000 COP.

SHOPPING On the road into the city from La Tebaida and the airport there are numerous vendors selling handicrafts and woven hammocks.

OTHER PRACTICALITIES You'll find everything you need in Armenia, from tyre repair shops and car batteries to camping outlets and cycle shops. On the heavily industrialised main strip into the city there are numerous gas stations, garages, supermarkets and hardware stores. In the city centre there are a number of camera shops, phone shops, computer retailers and pharmacies. The banks all have ATMs, including the Bancolombia on Calle 20, No 15–26, and there are several internet cafés in the centre. Most of the best money changers are housed within the Centro Comercial IBG building on Carrera 14, No 18–56.

WHAT TO SEE There isn't much to sightsee amidst Armenia's urban sprawl with, perhaps, the exception of the **Plaza de Bolívar**. An elevated location atop a gentle slope affords good views of the mountains, where would-be Tour de France champions can often be seen training. As in Manizales and Pereira, the plaza in Armenia is also home to a rather eccentric monument to Simón Bolívar, in this instance the Rodrigo Arenas Betancur-designed **Monumento al Esfuerzo** (Monument to Effort). The rather grim-looking **Catedral de la Immaculada Concepción** is also on the main square but is no object of beauty. However, the **Museo de Quimbaya** (\ *749 8433;* ⊕*10.00–18.00 Tue–Sat; admission free*) on Avenida Bolívar is definitely worth closer inspection. It closed for a while, following the 1999 earthquake, but has reopened with several new artefacts. A large collection of pre-Columbian artefacts includes about 400 gold objects, 104 pieces of anthropomorphic pottery and 22 stone sculptures and carvings mainly from the pre-Columbian Quimbaya civilisation. One of the most important pieces is a fine gold poporos, a traditional gadget for the chewing of coca leaves.

AROUND ARMENIA

LA TEBAIDA Armenia's airport is actually located in the small town of La Tebaida and as you journey towards the city you'll see numerous stalls on the right-hand side of the road, selling milk, netted bags of oranges and great hands of bananas. There are also a couple of handicraft vendors, including the **Artisanas de Tebaida** and numerous snack kiosks and food stalls as well as the **Restaurante Paisa**, a rustic local eatery selling set meals for 6,000 COP. Just before you enter Armenia there are another couple of decent food joints, including the **Estación Paraíso** – a restaurant and coffee bar with outside seating and a children's playground.

PARQUE NACIONAL DEL CAFÉ (\ *753 6095; www.parqunacionaldelcafe.com;* ⊕*depending on the season; admission fees reflect the number of rides you may want to go on, starting at 16,000 COP and rising to 43,000 COP for the works*) On the face of it, a coffee-themed fun park may seem like an odd concept, but the National Coffee Park is one of the most visited tourist draws in Colombia. Building work on the park began in 1991 and since the Colombian Federation of Coffee Growers first threw open its gates in 1995 it has continued to attract crowds in their droves – 6,000 a day at its peak. Originally a 12ha site, it has since grown by over 48ha, with every single square metre dedicated to Colombia's beloved bean. Disney it isn't, but that doesn't prevent the daily hordes from reaching fever-pitch excitement, especially during one of the highly popular 'How del Café' musical extravaganzas. Five performances a day take place in a packed auditorium where the atmosphere is as highly charged as a boy-band concert. Clapping, whooping and hollering accompany a series of songs and dances that tell the story of how the coffee crop became the bedrock of the Colombian economy. It's a slick, well-choreographed visual production with beautiful costumes and catchy bambuco and pasillo music. Lyrics centre on the happy life of a Paisa campesinso coffee picker with lots of machete-throwing dark-haired hombres in neckerchiefs. It's a real crowd-pleaser – and well worth the queue. Other attractions at the park include cable cars, buggy rides, go karts, fun-fair rides, roller coasters, shops, dozens of restaurants and a number of ecological trails through coffee fields. Expansive gardens, lakes and pools lead to plazas and fountains. There is also a museum and, of course, places to buy and drink Colombian coffee. A food court offers Paisa dishes, pizza, fried chicken, Tex-Mex and sandwiches. For 12,500 COP, the Cazuela de Frijoles at the Babor de mi Terra is highly recommended – but only for those with a big appetite.

Getting there The Parque Nacional Del Café is located in Montenegro about 15km west of Armenia and is well served by minibuses from the city.

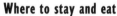
Where to stay and eat

⌂ **El Delirio Quinio** ☎ 745 0405/310 438 9005, e casadelirio@hotmail.com. Ignore the fact the gates are locked at this beautiful, old finca on the Montenegro road to the Café – simply toot your car horn or hang around expectantly & someone will turn up to let you in. Set in stunning, mature gardens, the property is a handsome farmhouse in the truest sense & a fine example of the Coffee Zone's rustic chic. Enjoy fine views across immaculate grounds in stylish surroundings. A handful of rooms can accommodate up to 18 people for 70,000–90,000 COP pp FB – exceptional value.

⌂ **Finca Villa Nora** (6 rooms & cabin) ☎ 752 1121/741 5472/310 422 6335. Conveniently located within 2.5km of the Parque del Café and 16km from Armenia, the Finca Villa Nora seems from a bygone era. Set off the road to Quimbaya on the outskirts of a small village, this traditional red & white painted wooden plantation home is truly magnificent offering lofty views across coffee & banana fields amidst a cacophony of birdsong. Although the present house was built 85 years ago, the farm has been in the same family since 1892 & owners Nohora Londoño & Roberto Echeverry are a mine of information on local history & culture. Generous, attentive & friendly, the couple genuinely enjoy inviting foreign guests into their beautiful home. Acts of extraordinary kindness appear to be very much the norm here, be it a delicious menu of your personal favourite Colombian delicacies or the loan of a car for the night. Nohora & Roberto turned to agricultural tourism in the early 1990s when coffee prices fell to an all-time low. They still farm 15ha of guayaba, bananas, macadamia nuts and cattle but have worked hard building up a sterling reputation at their finca. Six traditional wooden-floored rooms with solid oak furniture, rugs & throws each have private bathrooms. A cabin in the grounds can accommodate small groups. Three very good meals are included in the room rate of 100,000 COP per person.

PARQUE NACIONAL DE LA CULTURA AGROPECUARIA
(☎ 758 2830; e panaca@panaca.com.co; www.panaca.com.co; ⊕ 09.00–18.00 daily; admission 36,000 COP) This agricultural attraction is part fun, part education, a complex with a strong ecological ethos set up to showcase the importance of farming to Colombia. 'Without the country, there is no city', says the literature – and in the rural communities of the Coffee Zone the locals are vehement that this is true. The park opened in December 1999 and is privately funded by donations. A high proportion of visitors to PANACA are wide-eyed urbanites with little idea of what agriculture involves. Thematic displays explain just exactly what is involved in getting milk to

9

Bogotá in time for the city to eat its cereal. They also detail the sheer hard work required to rear livestock, grow crops and harvest. Visitors are transported by an old jalopy to eight different farming zones that span 103ha to vast self-contained farms that centre on individual species, such as poultry, cows, pigs, dogs and horses. PANACA produces its own eggs, milk, meat and fruit for the half-dozen restaurants onsite. The milk is sold throughout Colombia under the brand name 'Colanta'. Everything on the farm is organic and recycled with almost all of its fuel derived from manure. Visitors are encouraged to feed, touch, taste and smell everything in interactive exhibitions and live demonstrations. There are numerous picnic areas, lookout points, a medicinal plant zone and a composting plant. A silk farm is one of PANACA's newest ventures and there are already plans to make and sell sarongs, scarves and neckerchiefs.

The land in which the farms are set is extremely beautiful with rolling fields that rise and fall in soft curves. Large thickets of needle-thin guadua (bamboo) provide the raw materials for many of the buildings in the park – there is a plentiful supply as this rampant species grows at a rate of 6cm per day. There are also numerous birds, cacti and flower-filled hedgerows along well-maintained paths. Activities include canopy rides, horseriding, ecological hikes, bull-roping, equestrian shows, camping and sheep shearing.

Getting there The park is located just outside of the town of Quimbaya on the Filandia road. The park isn't served by public transport but can be reached by colectivo from Quimbaya or Filandia.

Where to stay and eat

Hotel Panaca \ 758 2111; f 758 3389; e hotel@panaca.com.co; www.panaca.com.co. This gorgeous C-shaped ochre-coloured finca overlooks a charming courtyard full of vibrant blooms, birds & antique farm equipment. Located on the outer edges of the park, the hotel offers a range of lovely dbl & sgl rooms with tiled floors, en-suite bathroom & TV. Rates inc b/fast & a crack-of-dawn tour to watch the cows being milked. Expect cockerels, goats & sheep to be wandering around your feet in the open-air lobby overlooking horse paddocks. A restaurant onsite serves a nice, varied menu of Paisa staples. $$$

Malocas Panaca \ 310 404 2238; e resevashotel@panaca.com.co; www.panaca.com.co. Large groups of between 10 & 130 people are well catered for in a more rudimentary lodge in the park. The rate inc all food, use of the pool & local transportation at 36,000–70,000 COP.

EL BOSQUE DEL SAMAN (\ 336 55590; e reserves@fincahotelbosque.com; www.elbosquedelsaman.com) This private reserve is located 15km north of PANACA park and is renowned for its forest canopy tours – especially those run at night. At 2,000m, the views are incredible over surrounding village rooftops and open country. It also offers a range of tailored guided tours including rappelling, rope-bridging, hiking, horseriding and ecological walks. Overnight accommodation is offered in two separate buildings. An older typical Antiochian finca has 11 cheerful rooms complete with private bathroom and television, and there's also a new construction with 20 larger rooms equipped with en-suite bathroom, television and balcony with hammock. Communal facilities include a lounge, restaurant, outdoor terrace and swimming pool. Seasonal rates and special discounts apply. $$

FILANDIA (*Telephone code: 6*) This small, well-preserved pueblo paisa has just a handful of modern buildings to blot its landscape and is legendary as the setting of popular RCN telenovela (soap opera), *Café Con Aroma de Mujer* (Coffee With the Scent of a Woman) – a Fernando Gaitán Salom series of Ugly Betty fame. As a result, Filandia attracts a smattering of tourists, most of whom spend half a day strolling the streets.

Juan Valdez (*www.juanvaldez.com*) is Colombia's most famous name in coffee, an iconic brand and fictional character more instantly recognisable to Colombian citizens than McDonald's. Wearing his poncho and sombrero, Juan Valdez stands alongside his faithful mule, Conchita. He has Colombia's rugged mountains in the background – a moustached hero who has embodied Colombian coffee since 1981. The brand was developed to reflect old-time Colombian cafeteros, the coffee-bean pickers of the nation's Zona Cafetero. The image was created to strengthen consumer loyalty to 100% Colombian coffee that has been inspected and approved by the National Federation of Coffee Growers of Colombia. It served to highlight that Colombian coffee isn't a mix of different beans and qualities. The face of Juan Valdez guarantees that the coffee is wholly and only Colombian. Consumers now look for the label so they can be assured they're drinking the real McCoy.

The National Federation of Coffee Growers of Colombia appointed the Doyle Dane Bernback advertising agency to develop the brand. It chose the name 'Juan Valdez' because of its generic popularity on the basis that Latin America would readily identify with such common Hispanic names. Yet Juan Valdez isn't purely a logo, he is also a real live person – or three people to be more precise. Juan Valdez was initially portrayed by José F Duval in both print advertisements and on television until 1969. José Duval died in 1993 at the age of 72. In 1969, Juan Carlos Sánchez took over the role (although he was voiced by Norman Rose). In 2006, Sánchez announced his retirement after taking Juan Valdez to unprecedented heights across the globe. He was replaced by Carlos Castañeda, a grower from Antioquía, after open auditions nationwide.

Getting there Minibuses from Armenia nip back and forth throughout the day (3,500 COP, 1 hour).

SALENTO (*Telephone code: 6*) Salento is fast-becoming one of Colombia's laid-back backpacker haunts; a charming small-town in the midst of rural coffee country that is easily overlooked but shouldn't be missed. After trawling some of the Coffee Zone's large, uninspiring settlements, Salento is a breath of fresh air wrapped in mountains and rich in character and culture. Don't expect to pass through on a day-trip as the chances are you'll end up getting hypnotised by Salento's jaw-dropping sunsets – they have a rather pleasant stupefying, brainwashing effect. Almost as surreal are the region's enormous wax palms (Palms de Cera), an almost other-worldly plant that ranks amongst the tallest in the world at up to 60m. They add to Salento's fairytale fantasy feel and dippy-trippy character and provide a backdrop to the settlement's brightly-painted little houses, cutesy plazas, hummingbirds and eclectic artisan shops. A single road leads in and out of Salento to connect to the Armenia/Pereira highway. It a series of hairpin bends, it crosses the scenic Quindío valley offering joyous views of the rolling, lush green hills and tufted coffee bushes. They have a saying in Salento that describes the town as '*el pueblo calles cortas y recuerdoes largos*', meaning the town of short street and long memories – and as the oldest settlement in Quindío (founded in 1850), this just about sums it up. Yet, for a small town, Salento has some much-needed traveller amenities from a decent supermarket (*Super Cocora*), an ATM (in the *Banco Agrario* on the main square, Visa cash advances only) and internet cafes (between Calle 3 & 4) to a weekly market of fruit, meat and vegetables stalls plus some great little restaurants serving delicious local trout. Behind the main plaza a cluster of tourist shops sell all sorts of local handicrafts, from palm-woven sun hats to leather sandals, bangles and beads. If you're passing, stick your head around the door of the fire station – a fine collection of lovingly polished elderly engines are a real blast from the past.

Getting there and away Salento is served by minibuses that run to and fro every 15 minutes or so from Armenia (2,800 COP, 50 minutes).

Where to stay and eat A growing number of Salento's handsome old Paisa buildings are being turned into bed and breakfasts and restaurants with most concentrated around Calle Real. During high season, Fiesta de Salento (first week in January) and Easter Week, prices can inflate in Salento and reservations are imperative.

El Portal de Coroca ✆ 759 3075; e anaisabel@telesat.com. This out-of-town option is located on the Cocora road, about 500m from the centre. A rather nice restaurant offers super meals on a garden terrace. Two cabañas have cooking facilities & stunning views across the Valle de Corora. $$

La Posada del Café ✆ 759 3012; e malenacafe@yahoo.com. Central, clean & spacious, this delightful old building boasts plenty of character & has a gorgeous courtyard garden. $$

Hostería Calle Real Carrera 6, No 2–20; ✆ 759 3272. This traditional Paisa home offers small, basic rooms but is clean & conveniently located – & run by a very friendly family. B/fast is optional at 3,500 COP. $

The Plantation House Alto del Coronel, Calle 7, 1-04; ✆ 759 3403/759 3147/315 4097039 (Spanish), 316 2852603 (English); e theplantationhousesalento@ yahoo.co.uk; www.theplantationhousesalento.com. Travellers rave about this spacious backpacker haunt for all sorts of reasons, from its laid-back atmosphere & first-rate tours to its sunset views & über-fine book exchange. Owned by Briton Tim Harbour & his Colombian wife Cristina, the Plantation House has 5 private rooms & 10 dormitory beds split across the main hostel building & 2 cabañas. Expect to pay 15,000–16,000 COP per person for a dorm room with private dbls 32,000–35,000 COP (with shared bathroom) or 45,000 with private en suite. Sgl occupancy runs from 27,000 to 40,000 COP with onsite amenities that include internet access, garden hammocks, terraces, self-catering kitchen & dining area, b/fast (3,000 COP) & free coffee on tap all day. $

Hospedaje La Casona Carrera 6a No. 2-15, Calle Real; ✆ 759 3008, 317 250 2745; e antoniomfl1@ yahoo.es. This no-frills hostel opened in Dec 2007 in a newly renovated colonial-style building just 5mins walk from the main plaza close to shops, bars & restaurants. Owner José Antonio also runs Salento's restaurant El Rincón Campestre, a prize winner for its *Trucha criolla en salsa de café* (creole trout in coffee sauce). 5 rooms can accommodate 30-plus people in a variety of configurations, from sgls & dbls to interconnected family suites – all with shared bathrooms. Expect to pay upwards of 15,000 COP per person per night – or from 5,000 COP if camping. $

What to see Hiking the local countryside is the prime activity in scenic Salento, where several tour operators offer guides and jeeps to take travellers out of town. A path leads from the end of Calle Real out to the Alto de la Cruz and is well worth the climb for stunning views across the valley. Alternatively, catch a jeep to the small neighbouring town of Cocora (3,000 COP, 35 minutes) – or do the 11km on foot for a pleasant 2-hour stomp. From here it is possible to hire a horse to explore the Valle de Cocora in-depth. East of Cocora is especially magnificent, follow the bridge over the Río Quindío and follow the path uphill. Other popular tours include trips out to nearby villages and fishing in trout-rich rivers along with full-on excursions to *Los Nevados* for camping and cloud forest mega-hikes. Trucha y Montaña (✆ 096 744 3912) in Calle Real arrange a variety of day tours.

10

The Pacific Coast

'Magic days, golden nights, and the summer is forever.
It's the endless summer . . . And I'm all about Pacific Ocean Blue.'

                    lyrics from album *A* (Hollywood Records, 2002)

The region known simply as El Pacifico is one of the wettest on earth, stretching for 1,300km along Colombia's western flank and lavished by an annual rainfall of up to 10m. Curved bays sit aside a jungle of extraordinary biodiversity with cliffs and beaches lined with mangrove forests criss-crossed by rivers of great girth. Outlying islands are renowned for their resplendent flora and fauna with fertile waters home to migratory whales *en route* from the Antarctic. Vast volcanic crags explode upwards from the sea amidst coral outcrops teeming with marine life. El Pacifico is an important component of an eco-region known as the Chocó Biogeografico, a key part of the Tumbes-Chocó-Magdalena ecological hotspot. This magnificent expanse of rainforest terrain runs from the Río Atrato near Panama to the Mataje River bordering northwestern Ecuador along the entire Pacific coast of Colombia and is bordered by Mesoamerica to the north and the tropical Andes to the east – a landmass larger than Costa Rica. Until recently the region's dense forest, abrupt mountains, deep gorges, marine flats and fast-flowing rivers stood in the way of so-called progress, dividing Colombia's key commercial centres from the western shore. However, this unique, moist ecosystem is now recognised as one of the richest lowland regions on the planet – a swathe of land blessed by isolation and inaccessibility and large volumes of freshwater run-off. Fertile coastal sediments have helped ensure an abundance of biologically distinct endemic plant, bird, amphibian and butterfly species. Today, despite multiple threats by commercial developers, much of El Pacifico is protected by conservation status. It remains a culturally rich region with numerous indigenous reserves (*resguardos*) and settlements as well as a burgeoning ecotourism and birding destination.

More than 85% of the population along the Pacific coastal stretch are Afro-Colombian – almost 60% are jobless and poor. Indigenous Emberá Indians account for 5% of the local people, living in reserves and communities by the Río Valle and Río Juná. The remaining 10% are *mestizo* (mixed race). Most inhabitants of the Pacific coast earn a living from subsistence farming, hunting, fishing, forestry and mining in terrain rich in mineral and natural resources. Since the early 19th century, large amounts of platinum and gold have been excavated in the region and sizeable deposits of zinc, nickel, tungsten, bauxite, manganese, tin, copper and chromium remain. It's little wonder former president of Colombia Carlos Lleras Restrepo called this resource-rich beautiful area 'our country's piggy bank'. Yet, vast swathes of the Pacific coastal region remain untroubled by industry, commerce or modern technology. Cars are rare, electricity scarce and mobile phone signals poor. Daily life continues much as it did in generations past with freshly harvested

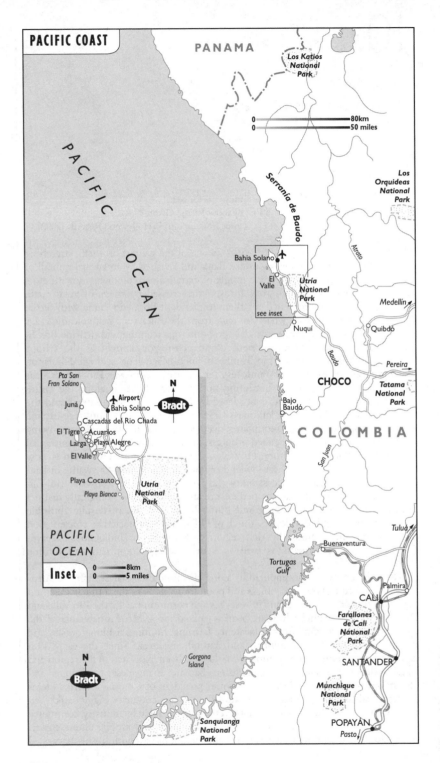

rice drying on hessian sacking while men fish silently in wooden dugout canoes. Children play in shallow rivers while their mothers wash big bundles of clothes on rocks by the bank. Entire communities live in *tambos* (stilt mud-and-thatch huts) that teeter along the shoreline while stray dogs and chickens pounce on scuttling crabs on the sand.

FLORA AND FAUNA

The Pacific coast is home to eight species of mangrove in a region where expanses of forest over 20m in height extend up to 30km inland. Almost 3,000km^2 of mangrove thickets account for about 7.5% of Colombia's total Pacific exploitable forest, forming a complex drainage system in the region's hot, steamy lowlands. More than 70% of Colombia's mangroves are located along the Pacific coast and these evergreens play a vital role in the health of the seaboard's ecosystem, providing a component in the transition between land and sea. Mangrove habitat provides a breeding ground for 60% of the world's fish species with red mangroves, white mangroves, black mangroves and button mangroves found throughout El Pacifico.

Heavy rainfall and numerous rivers feed an abundance of lush vegetation with a rich network of tributaries running to the ocean. Conservationists estimate the number of plant species in the Tumbes-Chocó-Magdalena region at around 11,000 of which around 25% are endemic. More than 5,000 of these are found in the wet or pluvial forests of Chocó where more than 300 trees per hectare have been recorded, including the nispero (loquat) whose seeds are scattered by the Pacific's tidal currents. Although conservation status has protected large areas of forest in the Colombian and Panamanian portion of the Pacific coastline the degradation in Ecuador continues – and is severe.

MARINE LIFE Coral reefs on the Pacific coast are small and scattered but provide important shelter for a wide range of marine fauna. Prime reef areas include Gorgona Island and Malpelo Island, both of which are protected national parks. Over 20 coral species have been recorded in Pacific waters. Dramatic volcanic extrusions rise from the ocean, seemingly undisturbed by sea spray, strong winds or tides. El Pacifico is home to an abundance of fish species and marine mammal populations. Regional fish production represents almost 50% of Colombia's national total – a figure that state officials believe is as little as 15% of its estimated potential. Whales breed in the warm Pacific waters during June–November each year. The Bay of Málaga, located about 50km northwest of Buenaventura boasts one of the highest whale-calf birth rates in the world. It welcomes between 470 and 1,200 humpback whales annually – more than 25% of the total estimated whale population for the southeast Pacific region. A popular local song contains the lyrics 'they take care of their children and drive their husbands away' – a reference to the mating ritual of the whales that visit. It forms part of a chorus sung by the local women (*cantaoras*) after they have danced a *currulao* of African origin. Humpback whales are just one of at least a dozen species of marine mammals observed in the region.

GETTING THERE AND AROUND

Due to its relative inaccessibility and absence of infrastructure, the Pacific coast is only reachable by boat and air. Only a single overland route links Colombia's interior to the commercial hubs of Buenaventura and Tumaco. Buses serve this 200km route but tend to do the journey overnight. Flights connect via Medellín to

Ardent birders will be amazed by what the Pacific coast has to offer as one of the richest areas of avian endemism in the entire neo-tropics. According to ProAves, the forests of the Tumbes-Chocó-Magdalena region contain around 900 bird species of which 14 are endemic and at least 110 can't be found anywhere else in the world. As Colombia's undisputed 'No 2 Birding Hotspot', the Pacific coast is only second in avian diversity to the Atlantic coast's Santa Marta and contains Endemic Bird Areas (EBAs) as defined by BirdLife International. The shoreline is a critical feeding, wintering and stopover site for millions of migratory shorebirds. The Chocó EBA has a total of 51 confirmed bird species – a total second only to the Atlantic Forest Lowlands EBA. In 1991, a new species was discovered in the Colombian Chocó and was named in 1996 as the Chocó vireo (*Vireo master*) through an auction of its scientific title. Dr Bernard Master won the bid, paying 70,000 COP to a fund for the conservation of threatened rainforest habitat along the Pacific coast. Rare, endangered or vulnerable birds found in the region include the esmeraldas woodstar, little woodstar, sapphire-bellied hummingbird, lava gull, ochre-bellied dove, banded ground-cuckoo, grey-backed hawk, plumbeous forest-falcon, blue-billed curassow, rufous-headed chachalaca, white-winged guan, bearded guan, tacarcuna wood-quail, brown wood-rail, long-wattled umbrellabird, slaty becard, Peruvian plantcutter, mangrove finch, medium tree-finch, tumaco seedeater, saffron siskin, hood mockingbird, cerulean warbler, tawny-chested flycatcher, great green macaw, grey-cheeked parakeet and Colombian tinamou. In 2007, more than 100 different bird species were spotted by birders on the Pacific coast in just 72 hours, including the fabled harpy eagle – the largest eagle in the Americas.

the tiny airports of Bahía Solano and Nuquí but often incur delays due to rainy conditions. Because of a scarcity of roads, navigating El Pacifico relies almost entirely on journeying by boat. What transport exists is very rudimentary: expect a decrepit old van without tyre tread, windows, shock absorbers or clutch to ferry you from the airport along craterous unmade roads to the nearest town.

PRACTICALITIES

It rains a lot on the steamy Pacific coast where humidity frequently tops 90%. Be sure to pack waterproofs and plenty of lightweight clothes as the mud and rainfall will mean frequent changes. You'll also need a torch as few places have electricity and all paths are unlit. Don't forget to pack a decent pair of binoculars if visiting during whale-watching season, June–November. Arrive with enough cash (in low denominations) as few places accept credit cards and ATMs are scarce. At the time of writing, there is a high incidence of malaria in Colombia's lowland tropical areas with a marked increase in the number of reported cases of dengue across the region. Travellers should take proper precautions (see *Health* in *Chapter 2*, page 65) to minimise exposure to mosquito bites – with repellent and suitable clothing essential.

BAHÍA SOLANO *Telephone code: 4*

This steamy little jungle town has a population of about 7,000 people, most of them of African descent. Outlying indigenous Emberá communities are mainly located upstream along the river and comprise a handful of basic mud-and-thatch huts teetering on the banks. Local people eke a living from fishing and a small amount of tourism with boat owners adamant they can offer the best deep-sea fishing in the world. However, Bahía Solano is largely devoid of foreign tourists, so expect to be the only gringo in town. At the time of writing, a road is being built to link the town with El Valle – but it's been hard going and workmen are only progressing at a rate of 15m per day, so this 16km project could take some time.

GETTING THERE AND AROUND Satena and ADA fly daily direct to Bahía Solano's Aeropuerto José Celestino Mutis from Medellín. Another option is to travel overland to Buenaventura to catch a fast boat – it runs Monday and Thursday (COP 120,000, 6 hours). There's also the slower cargo boat but it doesn't appear to adhere to any firm schedule (although it tends to leave on a Thursday or Friday at around 80,000 COP) – turn up at the port and ask around if you fancy chancing your luck for a 30-hour slog. At the time of writing, the bus from Medellín and Pereira to Quibdo (Chocó's capital) isn't recommended on the basis of safety. Buses leave for Nuquí every Tuesday, Thursday and Saturday (50,000 COP, 2 hours). The boat for Buenaventura advertises a Saturday departure at 16.00, but this is a very fluid schedule (see *Safety*, page 345). A ticket costs 80,000 COP and includes simple meals and a bed.

TOURIST INFORMATION AND TOUR OPERATORS

[i] **Oficinas Municipales De Turismo** \ (4) 682 7049
– 682 7418; f (4) 682 7049;
e alcaldiabahiasolano@hotmail.com

Mr Jerry's Eco Tours \ 513 1200; e mrjerryBahía
solano@telesat.com.co; www.mrjerryBahía
solano.com

WHERE TO STAY The town and surrounding area has around 30 hotels and lodgings that offer approximately 400 beds with additional 'unofficial home-stays' prepared to top-up during whale-watching season.

⌂ **Eco-Hotel Kipara** \ 682 7909;
e hotel_kipara@hotmail.com. Choose from nine
pastel-coloured cabins with terraces that overlook the

jungle in a small complex that offers numerous
activities & tours, including whale watching & birding.
A large swimming pool is edged by palm trees near a

STAYING SAFE ON THE PACIFIC COAST

Guerrilla forces and paramilitary groups were once highly active in the region, targeting civilian communities that collaborated with the security services and occasionally kidnapping tourists for ransom. However, today 4,000 marine troops patrol the Pacific coastline with a police force of 60 officers in Bahía Solano alone. Serious incidents impacting safety are increasingly rare and the Pacific coast is doing its utmost to consign the troubles of its past to history. Tourism is slowly rebuilding and visitor figures are increasing year on year and although some isolated pockets remain off-limits to tourists between Pasto and Tumaco, the coastline north of Buenaventura is considered safe. Towns like Bahía Solano are strategic points for the Colombian army with a sizeable presence based there year-round. Travellers considering journeying on the Cali–Buenaventura road should check on the current safety situation. Buses serving the Medellín–Quibdó and Medellín–Turbo routes are not safe at present. At the time of writing, the US Bureau of Consular Affairs warns against using any inter- or intra-city bus transportation. The British Foreign Office also advises against all travel to the port of Buenaventura. A spate of bombings in the city in June 2007 saw temporary curfews imposed throughout the city. However, tour operators remain satisfied that using the city's dock as a launch point to Isla Gorgona carries little risk to tourists.

Bahía Solano's tiny airport is named after José Celestino Mutis (1732–1808) a Spanish-Colombian naturalist, physician and mathematician who assembled one of the richest botanical collections in the world of his time. He was born in Cadiz in Spain on 6 April 1732 but spent the last 48 years of his life in Bogotá after studying medicine and philosophy at the University of Seville. Using scientific subsidies from the Spanish government, Mutis visited Stockholm, where he worked alongside the great Swedish botanist Carolus Linnaeus. He then accompanied Viceroy Pedro Mesia de la Cerda to Bogotá in 1760 where he actively furthered botanical research for almost half a century. He was the first to explain Newton's theories in that part of America and gained membership of the Academy of Science of Paris and of Stockholm. His observational diary encapsulated discoveries in natural sciences from 1760 to 1790 and he was especially acclaimed for his studies of quinine. Mutis created the Botanical Mission in 1783 as a research centre for Colombia's flora and fauna and employed artists to prepare thousands of coloured drawings of the nation's many species. Mutis's magnificent collection of 24,000 specimens represents some 5,000 distinct species and the book he created remains indispensable to this day. In his later life, Mutis was ordained a priest. He died in his adoptive homeland of Colombia on 11 September 1808 and is buried in Bogotá. Today, the spectacular Jardín Botánico Botanico José Celestino Mutis (www.jbb.gov.co) on Carrera 66 con Calle 56 in Bogotá remains one of the city's premier attractions.

small snack kiosk & bar. Each cabin can accommodate 4–5 people with all-inc packages from around 550,000 COP for a 3-night stay. $$$

Hotel Los Delfines Choose this as a last resort if everything else is full. Rooms have a private bathroom for 20,000 COP but only a few have a window – and those that don't are cramped, oppressive & stuffy. $$$

Mr Jerry's Eco Hotel ℡ 513 12 00; e mrjerryBahía solano@telesat.com.co; www.mrjerryBahía solano.com. Although this rambling wooden hotel does take room-only guests off-season it is primarily set up as an all-inclusive place with rooms on a package basis. Three-night 4-day basic deals start at 290,000 COP inc meals, drinks & some tours with extra nights at 90,000 COP. More comprehensive, specialised packages cost around 70,000 COP for an 8-day 7-night stay with absolutely everything all-in. $$$

Cabo Marzo This highly recommended B&B option is owned by a very friendly Colombian–American couple, Enrique & Nancy. Fishing fans should note than owner Enrique is a knowledgeable deep-sea fishing & diving enthusiast who offers a wide range of tours.

Expect to pay 25,000 COP for a pleasant room & a decent b/fast. $$

Hotel Balboa Plaza (23 rooms) ℡ 682 7075; f 682 7401; e hotelbalboaplaza@hotmail.com. This rather nice central hotel has clean, spacious rooms with TV, minibar, private bathroom & AC with a garden pool, restaurant, bar & solarium. Staff can arrange fishing & boating trips & a wide range of jungle treks. $$

Mapara Crab Eco Lodge (4 cabins) ℡ 315 488 7670; e hotel@maparacrab.com. Feedback has been mixed in regards to the pros & cons of this place. The cabins sleep up to 21. Offers transfers & fishing tours. $$.

Marlin Azul Lodge ℡ 682 7779; www.marlinazul.com.co. This very pleasant family-run lodge can accommodate up to 17 guests in a variety of room configurations. Rates start at 578,000 COP for a 2-night 3-day all-inclusive package with additional nights from 90,000 COP – meals, drinks, transfers (20 mins from Bahía Solano) & some tours are part of the deal. $$

Hotel Bahía Expect to pay 15,000 COP for a simple sgl room with a private bathroom & a fan. Some of the nicest also have a TV for a 5,000 COP premium. $

✖ **WHERE TO EAT** There are a couple of open-fronted rustic local food joints near to the airport serving simple fish-and-rice dishes and cold beers. At the other end of town several local residents offer tourists seafood meals from their kitchens and there are numerous kiosks selling sodas, snacks and beers.

WHAT TO SEE There isn't a great deal to see in Bahía Solano itself. Most people use it as a base to explore outlying areas. A pretty, if muddy pot-holed road leads out of Bahía Solano, hugging the coastline on one side with a steep jungle bank on the other. Hidden beyond the palms are several beautiful waterfalls – you'll need to keep your eyes peeled as these are well camouflaged by thick jungle. Close by, a rustic coastal bar sells ice-cold beer – it's a popular watering hole with the military and a good place to let off steam. Migratory humpback whales arrive in numbers between July and October and local boatmen offer tours to the Nacional Parque Ensenada de Utría for around 50,000 COP. There are also plenty of local guys keen to rent out their boats for fishing trips for around 30,000 COP for a morning on the bay.

FESTIVALS
Festival De La Bahía (*Aug*) Decorated boats, folkloric shows, processions, beauty pageants and dancing celebrate Bahía Solano's local culture on and around the bay.

PLAYA ALEGRE *Telephone code: 4*

This silver-grey stretch of sand has its back to a jungle canvas and looks out to open sea. A handful of hotels have created a decent mini-resort area aimed at ecotourists with gorgeous beach walks, gushing creeks and plentiful birdlife. The beach is quite, quite beautiful and offers lots of crab-ridden trails from the sand out to waterfalls in the rainforest. Playa Alegre makes a very nice base from which to explore the surrounding area. It's quiet, sleepy and very pretty – and some of the beachfront hotels are undoubtedly some of El Pacifico's finest. Stroll along the sand to discover vast volcanic boulders – some with wooden houses built precariously on top. Towering ferns and palms edge the sea-grass-scattered beach with creeks that empty into the sea. Surfers can expect 3m waves when the season hits full pelt in September and October and February to March.

GETTING THERE AND AWAY Although Playa Alegre is only 16km or so from the centre of Bahía Solano the hard-going one-hour drive can take twice as long in the rain. A deeply pot-holed unmade road winds, dips and climbs and is only the width of a single car. Thick jungle flanks both sides in a track that has literally been carved from the forest. Cloying pinky-brown mud and unpredictable boulders make a 4x4 the vehicle of choice. Grab one of the colectivos or haggle with a driver at the airport – the journey should cost no more than 8,000–10,000 COP. El Valle is just 1.5km away. Boats out to Utría National Park and other attractions leave from La Bocana, a small riverbank dock a 20-minute stroll south along the sand.

TOUR OPERATORS Staff at the **El Almejal Eco Lodge** offer a wide range of different local tour options, including kayaking (2 hours, 35,000 COP or a half-day

---

ONE HELL OF A QUAKE

On 26 September 1970, three giant earthquakes wreaked havoc along the entire Pacific coast. More than 300 aftershocks followed in what was a first for Colombia – no other old fault had ever shown clear signs of new life in the country's seismic history. Tsunamis followed in the wake, although no-one was killed and only two people were hurt. However, some 40% of Bahía Solano's buildings were razed to the ground with land suffering subsidence of 20–30cm. Tremors were felt by residents in Colombia's central and north-western provinces hundreds of kilometres away.

10

45,000 COP), surfing (1 hour @ 15,000 COP or 2 hours 25,000 COP), body surfing (10,000–18,000 COP with board hire or 5,000–8,000 with own board) and fishing (full day for 20,000 COP). It also runs a trip out to the Emberá village of Posa Manga, 2½ hours away, for 50,000 COP to witness traditional dance and handicrafts as well as a range of night safari treks in the jungle, all of which are priced to order.

🏠 WHERE TO STAY AND EAT

🏠 **Almejal Eco Lodge** (12 cabins + upper cabaña) ➤ 230 6060 (Medellín); e almejal@une.net.co; www.almejal.com.co. Set in gorgeous tropical landscaping overlooking the ocean, the Almejal Eco Lodge opened in 1982. A fine collection of luxury cabañas have been built to an exceptional standard to combine rustic style with elegant touches. Each has a separate lounge & bedroom with a terrace looking out onto the beach. Private bathrooms are well appointed with owner César Isaza demonstrating a keen eye for detail where it counts. Expect wooden furniture & flower-filled vases with each cabin named after a local species of bird. Señor Isaza is a fanatical birder & an enthusiastic conservationist & paintings on the wall throughout the lodge depict flora & fauna from El Pacifico. The food at the Almejal Eco Lodge is truly sublime – in fact a visiting 'celebrity chef' from Bogotá was astounded to learn that the cook was a self-taught mother of three not an academy-trained culinary virtuoso. After trying every possible form of bribery to acquire the recipe for a particularly good soup he had enjoyed, he finally accepted defeat – &

promptly ordered another bowl. Twelve wooden cabins are complemented by a large open-sided restaurant & an upper cabaña with a dbl bed & bunk beds in the jungle high above the sea. Set on a terraced ledge, the cabin has a freezer & dining table & a deck with amazing sunset views. However, steep steps make this an unsuitable option for anyone unsteady on their feet. Rates range from 645,000 COP pp for a 3-night 4-day stay (all inc) to 1,035, 000 COP for a fantastic 5-night 6-day stay with boat transport, airport transfers, meals & an expert guide part of the price. $$

🏠 **Hotel Playa Alegre** ➤ 511 229; e playalegre@une.net.co; www.playaalegre.com. This battered-looking sea-worn wooden hotel neighbours El Almejal but lacks any of its charm. However, it may suit travellers keen to secure dirt-cheap alternatives – although the leaking roof & rotting untreated timber structure may be enough to put you off. Rates centre on multi-day packages, from 3–7 nights. Expect to pay from 531,000 COP for all inc 3-day 4-night stay with tours, meals, drinks & a guide. $$

WHAT TO SEE AND DO If you can, visit the **Reserva el Almejal** behind the Almejal Eco Lodge – a magnificent 47,000km² private reserve established by César Isaza, patron of the hotel. A scenic trail contains fossilised ferns and winds through thick rainforest, *bosque húmedo tropical*, along a rocky creek. A 24m jungle canopy is due for completion by the end of 2008 and will offer views at 55m above the sea. There's also a short trail from the hotel along the beach to a small waterfall – turn right out of the entrance and look right after about 200m. The Almejal also runs a **turtle conservation project** in a bid to better protect the nesting habitat of the olive ridley sea turtle (*Lepidochelys olivacea*) that lay their eggs on Playa Alegre each year. Operational now for 15 years, the project has since helped approximately 60,000 of these most magnificent marine creatures. The World Tourism Organisation identified the Almejal as one of Colombia's most important ecotourism models in 2006 and its educational programmes have achieved considerable success. One of the region's most prolific turtle hunters is now a project leader. Guests at the lodge can play their role during nesting season (July–November) and hatching (August–early January) by giving the volunteer workforce a hand.

Beaches Sandy beaches account for almost 25% of the 1,300km Pacific coast and some of the nicest can be reached from Playa Alegre. **Playa Larga** lies about 4km north and is accessible by boat or by a two-hour medium–difficult hike through the jungle. A pretty 1.5km dark-sand beach has a waterfall close by. **Playa el Tigre**

is a 15-minute boat trip from Playa Alegre and this charming 200m soft-sand stretch has falls that cascade into the sea. Stretching 2km between waterfalls, **Playa Chado** lies north via a tricky half-day hike that takes you past lagoons and sparkling pools along some beautiful leafy tracks – those not feeling quite so fit can get there by a 20-minute boat journey. **Playa Juná** is the last in a succession of four beaches and offers golden sands and clear waters with magnificent views. A single family live on Playa Juná – they are often prepared to cook a fish-and-rice lunch for beach-goers at 8,000-10,000 COP per person.

PARQUE NACIONAL ENSENADA DE UTRÍA

This 777,750ha national park reopened to the public in October 2006 and contains 18,850ha of marine fauna and waterways, including inlets, estuaries and creeks. Bordered by Corregimiento Valle to the north, Jurubira Nuquí to the south, the mist-shrouded Alto Baudo (at 1,200m) to the east and the Pacific Ocean to the west, the Parque Nacional Ensenada de Utría comprises three distinct ecosystems – rainforest jungle, mangroves (eight species) and coral reefs (hard and soft species). Sandy stretches provide important nesting sites for turtles while forested areas contain over 1,000 species of trees. Many of the park's 300-plus bird species are easy to spot along ten well-defined trails. Sendero Utría is the longest trail at 11km – it takes around three hours to hike and is medium-level difficulty traversing forest and mangroves to a pretty beach called Playa Cocalito. A community of Emberá Indians can be visited along a two-hour trail. The Resguardo Boroboro is home to 21 families and this population of a little over 100 has plenty of handicrafts for sale. Another 1km track takes about an hour to complete during low tide or can be tackled in a canoe. It passes through seven species of mangrove and leads to a magnificent creek (Quebrada Estero Grande y Chocólate) where there are many, many birds. An abandoned scientific research station once staffed by conservationists from Natura Fundación lies derelict – a memento of a past era of troubles that saw 26 kidnaps in the park in a single day in 2002. Today, security is good in the area and that the park has once again opened for business is a clear indication of safer times.

Many of the waterways are navigable by kayak, although at the time of writing visitors will need to bring their own equipment to the park. Marine fauna in the park is diverse and plentiful and includes 105 species of crustaceans and several species of whales, including the region's famous humpback. Other wildlife species include sting rays, turtles, fruit bats, insect bats, toucans and poison frogs. An education centre contains a small exhibition and there are also whale and dolphin skeletons at the entrance on the riverbank. On the park's southern limit, an area known as Morro Mico has water depths of 40m and is popular with free divers. There's also a protected coral garden that ranks as South America's largest. A liberal scattering of van-sized black volcanic extrusions reach up from the seabed on the outskirts of the park – a treacherous obstacle course for canoeing Indian fishermen in the dark.

GETTING THERE The park is about an hour by boat from Nuquí and Bahía Solano and is offered by almost every tour operator in both towns.

WHERE TO STAY AND EAT Stay overnight in cabañas for 16,000 COP (low season) and 23,000 COP (high season). An onsite restaurant serves three meals a day.

OTHER PRACTICALITIES Permission should be gained from Dirección Territorial Noroccidente (✆ *422 0833; www.parquesnacionales.gov.co*) in Medellín prior to visiting the park – your tour operator will organise this as part of the package price. Entrance is 24,000 COP. Plastic bags, aerosol sprays, chemical products and litter are all prohibited in the park environs.

EL VALLE *Telephone code: 4*

Just 3,000 residents make up El Valle's fishing and farming community. A rather nice shoreline contains a several-kilometre-long volcanic beach. Several big lava shoots sit amidst a magnificent stretch of jungle dotted with colourful flowers and huge blue morpho butterflies. On the Río Valle, a large partial-suspension bridge spans a slow-moving cloudy expanse. Tethered horses nibble from grain sacks on the riverbanks by a ramshackle collection of rustic wooden homes. Children giggle in huddles by lines of drying washing flapping in a warm, damp breeze.

GETTING THERE AND AWAY A regular chiva (open bus) connects Bahía Solano with El Valle and takes about 1½ hours to do the bone-shaking trip.

WHERE TO STAY

⌂ **Hotel Valle** (10 rooms) ✆ 682 7907. Although this place is run by a rather haughty Chocónita, don't let this put you off as this family-run posada is clean, comfy & efficiently run. Dbl rooms have a shared bathroom (or pay 55,000 COP for 1 of the 5 that has a private en suite). The price includes 3 decent meals. $$

⌂ **Hotel Coty** (10 rooms) ✆ 682 7948 690. This character-packed family home is decorated in simple style with colourful bedspreads and blue painted walls. All rooms have a shared bathroom. Owner Doris Agadia also cooks up a storm in her backroom kitchen. $

⌂ **Hotel Dasma** (16 rooms). Patron Domingu Gonzalez offers 25 beds for 45,000 COP apiece,

including 3 good meals a day. Seven rooms have a private bathroom – choose room 4 or room 1 at the back of the property for sea views & a balcony.
Posada Villa Maga ✆ 682 27900; e magapacifico@yahoo.com; www.villamaga.net. This lovely reasonably priced out-of-town option is run by Pepe Murillo & Carmen Lucía Gómez & is close to the beach. The centre of El Valle is a 10-min walk along the sand. Each bamboo-&-thatch cabaña is nestled in jungle gardens with a small balcony & a sunken shower. It's conveniently located near Playa Respingue, close to La Bocana where all boats depart out to surrounding areas. $

WHERE TO EAT Almost all of the hotels and posadas in El Valle offer meals as part of their package. Subsequently the town is not blessed with other dining options. For light meals and snacks pop into **Julevi** close to the school.

SHOPPING A rather anonymous-looking little shop sells rucksacks, shorts, sunglasses and T-shirts next to the Hotel Dasma in the town centre. For delicious jars of freshly made local fruit jams head to **Las Ballenas** – a small factory that produces wonderful preserves using guava, pineapple and mango. For water and other essentials head to the Granero Kevia grocery store while a small supermarket by the church (La Iglesia del Valle) sells beer and other items. There's also a drug store and a COMCEL telephone office close to the Discoteca el Trasmallo.

WHAT TO SEE Numerous boatmen in El Valle offer trips along the slow-moving creamy-green length of the **Río el Valle**. Bromeliad-clad trees and shrubs shade the water and are home to kingfishers, hawks, morpho butterflies and a myriad of purple, red and yellow flowers. Expect to haggle with rates about 30,000 COP.

BUENAVENTURA Telephone code: 2

As the Pacific coast's prime seaport, Buenaventura is a typical commercial hub – an ugly and grimy centre of freight and cargo that creeps along the shoreline. Roughly the size of Los Angeles's metropolitan area with a population of over 300,000, Buenaventura is a crucial distribution point for raw materials and goods for Colombia – and one of the Pacific coast's few metropolitan conurbations. Sadly, while many of the nation's larger cities have calmed, Buenaventura has bucked the trend and today the city has a reputation as a breeding ground for drug trafficking and violence. An underpowered police force struggles to cope with a frightening number of homicides each year – the murder rate doubled in two years to top 300 in 2006 (24 times that of New York City and double the national average). Lying some 345km southwest of Bogotá, Buenaventura is also a key through-point for the cocaine industry – more than 20 tonnes were seized in and around the city in 2006 alone. According to government figures, some 80% of Buenaventura's population survives on less than US$3 a day while an unemployment rate of almost 30% means that many residents have little option other than crime. In a bid to quell the violence, special marine forces control the worst areas of the city where poverty and violence are rife. Although it's not a place that most visitors would choose to spend large amounts of time, Buenaventura does offer a transit point for travellers keen to head out to Bahía Málaga and Isla Gorgona. There are also some fine beaches a short boat ride out of the city centre while the Río San Juan is a great place to spot humpback whales and dolphins.

SAFETY In June 2007, Buenaventura witnessed a flare-up in violence. Several bombs and grenades exploded at a police station and commercial centres, injuring 23 people. Rebels detonated explosives near a vehicle used to transport beach-goers to Juanchaco outside the city. Police and army patrols stepped up the military presence and the mayor imposed a night-time curfew. Travellers are advised to check the situation on the ground ahead before planning a visit. This recent wave of bombings was triggered by the killing of Milton 'J.J.' Sierra, a top FARC commander who authorities say was in charge of Pacific drug operations.

GETTING THERE Frequent buses and colectivos run from Cali's bus terminal – the 100km journey takes about three hours and costs 10,000 COP but before travelling overland be sure to check out the safety situation as the route is prone to security problems. Another consideration is that the road is often affected by landslides in the rains, resulting in a serious gridlock of traffic.

WHERE TO STAY AND EAT Buenaventura has numerous hotels throughout the city although anyone who values their personal safety should be sure to choose wisely. Don't be tempted to entertain any establishments that don't have soldiers in combat fatigues guarding the foyer. Proper security measures are paramount in Buenaventura so for a safe hassle-free overnight stay there is little sense in scrimping. On this basis, avoid the many dirt-cheap hotels near the bus station. As the city isn't safe after dark it is advisable to eat in your hotel. The following are recommended.

Hotel Estación (70-plus rooms) Calle 2, No 1A–08; 243 4070; f 243 4118; e reservas@ hotelesestelar.com; www.hotelesestelar.com. This fine neo-classical building was built in 1928 and has rooms that range from sgls & twins to dbls, trpls & suites. An elegant restaurant Las Gaviotas has plenty of ornate stucco & grandeur & serves a pan-Colombian seafood menu with plenty of international style. There's also a decent bar for cocktails, lunches & snacks. Rooms have central AC, cable TV, telephone, minibar & a safety deposit box as standard & start at 150,000 COP. A competent tour desk also offers diving & waterfall trips with a guide as well as a three-day whale-watching package inclusive of accommodation & meals for 600,000 COP. $$$

Hotel Los Manglares Carrera 4, No 2–18; 242 4344. This large city hotel is aimed squarely at the business executive, with services & amenities that reflect this market. Choose from a wide range of rooms that vary in size & price but include b/fast. $$

FESTIVALS
Festival Folclórico del Litoral Pacifico (Pacific Coast Folkloric Festival) (*Aug*)
Musical concerts, dancing, street processions, religious services, beauty pageants and art exhibitions celebrate Buenaventura's colourful mix of cultures across a wide range of venues in the city.

ISLA GORGONA

This former penal colony was once Colombia's Alcatraz, an impenetrable place of confinement for the nation's most notorious criminals. Located about 50km offshore, the 10km-long and 2.5km-wide island was declared a national park in 1985. Colombia's worst-of-the-worst law-breakers were shipped to the mainland in 1983 allowing 'Devil's Island' to become a popular tourism destination. It is surrounded by numerous smaller atolls and is separated from the continent by a 270m deep underwater depression. Today, a portion of the prison buildings have been converted as a research centre, lodgings and restaurant and this stunning volcanic isle is covered by dense, tropical rainforest. It contains a breathtaking array of colourful flora and fauna and although famous for its poisonous snakes, Isla Gorgona is home to numerous other endemic species, including lizards, monkeys, bats, turtles and caiman. The island has at least 25 permanent freshwater streams. Sheltered lagoons and creeks are home to pelicans, blue-footed boobies and frigate birds and more while the surrounding waters contain sea turtles, dolphins, sharks and lots of fish. In fact, some of the beaches on the island are important turtle-nesting sites. Prime stretches of sand include Playa Blanca, Playa Pizarro, La Azufrada, Playa Palmeras, Playa Yundigua and El Antiguo Muelle – and these are also fabulous spots from which to spot humpback whales from mid-June until

November each year. Males can clearly be seen breaching while females and their offspring come in close to the island to surface and breath. Exploring the island is only permitted with a guide – whose services are free. Tours include the former prison area and one jungle trail that leads to the other side of the island. A dive shop supports scuba and snorkelling on some magnificent dive sites that are teeming with sea turtles, moreens and whitefin sharks. It offers PADI open water or a PADI advance course and has equipment for hire. Prior to the arrival of the Spanish the island was inhabited by Indian tribes who left petroglyphs, artefacts, stone statues and a ceremonial site called El Templete. The island was discovered by Francisco Pizarro in 1527 and, along with the nearby small islet of Gorgonilla, became a pirate's lair. Amidst birds, boas and monkeys it is hard to imagine a nicer place to be incarcerated than this jungle mountain isle, where a stunning cloud-shrouded mountain overlooks deserted beaches and open seas. Some of the prisoners on the island penned beautiful poetry based on their experiences of Isla Gorgona.

GETTING THERE Traditionally, the departure point for boats to Isla Gorgona has been the port of Buenaventura. The boat from Buenaventura is a cargo vessel and the trip can take up to 12 hours overnight. Conditions can be rough and amenities are basic on a boat that is often packed to capacity. A ticket costs around 60,000 COP (✆ *244 6089*) from the Bodega Liscano close to the wharf. Faster options include the Embarcaciones de Turismo *Asturias* (✆ *242 4620*) for a four-hour trip at about 200,000 COP return while the *Pacifico Express* speedboat takes around five hours at 80,000 COP per person (✆ *241 6507*). All boats leave from Muelle el Piñal on the portside.

OTHER PRACTICALITIES All visits to the Isla Gorgona need to be pre-booked via tour operator Aviatur on behalf of the Parques Nacionales Naturales de Colombia – the earlier this can be the better as trips are often over-subscribed. Entrance to the park costs 21,000 COP and has to be paid in advance. There's a fee of 25,000 COP for an overnight stay in a room that sleeps four. Any Aviatur office can organise a permit – there's an office in Buenaventura as well as locations in Cali (✆ *664 5050*).

A rustic restaurant serves up three set meals a day, hot and cold snacks, juices and non-alcoholic drinks for 25,000 COP a day. Pack anything you need as there aren't any shops or services on the island, so make room in your daypack for waterproofs, swimming gear, snorkel and mask, a hat, sunglasses, sunscreen, a torch and mosquito repellent. In the rainy season you will need to wear rubber-soled boots. Travellers prone to seasickness should pack motion-sickness tablets or wristbands. Isla Gorgona is hot and wet year-round with temperatures that average 27°C and 90% humidity. September and October are wetter than others with February and March the driest months. Mobile phones rarely work on Isla Gorgona as the signal is so patchy.

BAHÍA MÁLAGA *Telephone code: 4*

This mixed community of black Afro-Caribbean and indigenous peoples is located around 20km northeast of Buenaventura amidst rocky outcrops and verdant jungle. The La Plata Archipelago sits in the middle of the bay and comprises more than 100 islands that form a maze of canals and boggy swamps. Hourly changes to this coastal area mark the tidal ebb and flow that covers islands and exposes beaches charting the rhythm of the Pacific Ocean. Two of the great regions of the Colombian Pacific coast meet at Bahía Málaga, making it a superb spot for biological conservation. The mountains of Baudó and Los Saltos dominate to the north of this jungle-covered coastline where an enormous diversity of flora and fauna include many species unique to the area. Bahía Málaga has 60 species of amphibians, 114 reptiles, 16 species of freshwater fish, 148 species of saltwater fish, 57 different marine birds and 360 terrestrial birds. Between July and October humpback whales arrive from the Antarctic to give birth to their young – the calves then grow up to 20cm per day.

The community of La Plata contains fewer than 70 wooden huts on stilts whose residents are keen to develop ecotourism to its full potential. WWF has been instrumental in furthering a strong environmental ethos in Bahía Málaga, helping to launch a Migrations Festival. Today the local community celebrate in October by playing traditional music on handcrafted wind and percussion instruments accompanied by lyrics that celebrate the beauty of the whales, birds and turtles and their natural habitat. In 2007, WWF Colombia and its partner in the Colombian Pacific coast – the Yubarta Foundation – celebrated the decision of the Colombian government to become a member of the International Whaling Commission (IWC). Along with Brazil, Argentina, Chile, Mexico, Panama and Belize, Colombia is now a part of the 'Latin American Front' of IWC – an important coalition of countries who oppose reopening commercial whaling.

During the migratory period (June–November) local communities in and around Bahía Málaga offer whale-watching tours to the 20,000 tourists that visit. Guides have been tutored by staff from the Yubarta Foundation – a conservation organisation that has been present in the area for over 15 years. Yubarta has not only developed environmental-awareness campaigns with local people but has also established guidelines for ecological whale watching in the bay. Other tours offered to visitors include boat trips around the mangrove swamps along the shoreline on a backdrop of low-lying jungle out to La Piscina, a natural pool at the mouth of a small river with a little waterfall and a leafy trail. Another highlight is La Sierpe, where two 50m waterfalls cascade into the bay. At the time of writing there are sizeable campaigns opposing a plan by the Colombian government to build a port in the Bahía Málaga. That this important breeding site and area of biodiversity has even been considered for such development has shocked local residents. The government insists that its decision is purely commercial as Bahía Málaga is large and deep and doesn't have rivers running into it – this saves on high dredging costs as the pristine waters are sediment free. The bay is also big enough to accommodate post-Panamax ships – vessels too large to dock at the Buenaventura port, which handles 53% of Colombia's foreign trade and 80% of its coffee exports. Should it go ahead, the first phase of the project will cost US$300 million, according to the Colombian Transport Ministry. A 204km pipeline will transport 40,000 barrels of fuel a day and there will also be an oil terminal capable of storing 700,000 barrels of gasoline and diesel fuel along with 40,000 barrels of liquefied gas.

GETTING THERE AND AROUND Check with your tour operator regarding the current state of the road to Bahía Málaga before travelling. The journey is less than 20km but it pays to take local advice before making the trip to gauge the current level of safety – and hiring a guide could be a worthy investment.

SAN CIPRIANO Telephone code: 2

San Cipriano is a teeny-weeny settlement situated at 200m above sea level, hidden deep in tropical rainforest of the brightest green. It's an important area that generates much of the drinking water for the nearby port town of Buenaventura where vast expanses of the river's watershed are protected in order to maintain water quality with the thick surrounding jungle largely unspoilt. Remote and almost inaccessible, San Cipriano has no roads and its fast-flowing river is too shallow to easily navigate. To overcome this problem, the locals have devised an ingenious transit system using a stretch of railway track. It runs past the village and consists of transportation known as 'Brujita' – there are various designs ranging from a wooden pallet with bearings as wheels and customised old mopeds, each powered by men the size of giants. These strange contraptions are pushed along with a pole in a style similar to punting with frightening speeds up to 50km per hour achieved on downhill stretches. This journey is *not* for the faint-hearted as the single track makes little allowance for anything travelling in the opposite direction. The route is also still occasionally used by a cargo train. An absence of any safety measures and numerous blind bends and having just a shoe for a brake make this an exciting (but ludicrous) way to arrive. A sign seemingly in the middle of nowhere declares 'Bienvenidos a San Cipriano' – and this is certainly a welcome sight after the 15-minute white-knuckle ride that propels you into town.

GETTING THERE AND AROUND San Cipriano is at least 10km from the nearest road but buses (6,000 COP, 2½ hours) from Cali to Buenaventura pass by the entrance of neighbouring Cordoba. Here you'll find the guys who run the Brujita to San Cipriano – just walk over the suspension bridge down the hill and head for the railtrack. Expect to pay 4,000 COP per person for the 15-minute ride into town, unless the Brujita operators relent and accept the local rate of 2,000 COP.

WHERE TO STAY AND EAT Numerous locals offer rooms for the night with **Casa David** one of a handful of the town's small hostels. Expect to pay around 10,000 COP per person for a clean, comfortable but basic room in a simple wooden house. The friendly owners also serve a cheap lunch, dinner and breakfast as well as soft drinks and beers. For a small town, San Cipriano has plenty of places to buy food and drinks.

OTHER PRACTICALITIES There's a very good reason why San Cipriano is so incredibly green – it is very wet. So pack a waterproof jacket, a change of clothing and a towel. Night falls in an instant and there are no street lights in town so a torch is essential. You'll also need swimming gear for tubing and messing about in the sparkling waters of one of the cleanest rivers on the planet. However, take heed of rising water levels – the river can swell alarmingly in seconds flat.

WHAT TO SEE Although the town itself is little more than two dirt roads lined with wooden huts, San Cipriano has a great atmosphere. A local population of about 500 is friendly and welcoming and there is something cathartic about being someone so isolated and removed from the outside world. Most visitors head out to hike into the jungle along a truly beautiful one-hour trail out of town. Swimming in the river is another delight and there are some beautiful cascades and crystal-clear pools at a place called *refugio del amor*. Ask the locals to show you the best spots – there are plenty of people prepared to guide for the day.

San Cipriano is also an excellent place for birders due to the unspoilt natural birding habitat in the area. Just follow the dirt track out of town to spot lesser swallow-tailed and grey-rumped swifts, white-thighed swallow, tawny-crested tanager, chocó toucans and dusky-faced tanagers, black-chested jay and spot-crowned barbet – it's also possible to hear plenty of golden-collared manakin. In a thick palm concentration there are purple-throated fruitcrow and chestnut oropendola with cinnamon and crimson-bellied woodpeckers in the trees nearby. Other species include the short-tailed pygmy-tyrant, half-collared gnatwren, blue-black grosbeak, white-ringed flycatcher, purple-crowned fairy, white-headed wren, masked tityra, buff-throated saltator, and rose-faced parrot. Look out for the bay-breasted warbler in the winter months.

NUQUÍ *Telephone code: 4*

Colombian vacationers heading to the Pacific coast have long favoured Nuquí, a rustic but charming fishing settlement on the beautiful Gulf of Tribuga 50km south of Bahía Solano. This traditional Chocóan village has beautiful beaches surrounded by vine-tangled tropical jungle. Cascading waterfalls, stream-fed pools and rambling forest trails make this popular with a wide range of visitors, from serious ornithologists, divers, fishermen and hikers to artists, poets, beach bums and anyone who enjoys nature. Much like Bahía Solano, Nuquí serves as a base for whale watching June–November and ecotours with numerous operators and eco-resorts offering a wide range of packages. July is a prime month for diving in Nuquí and is a great time to spot giant mantas and large numbers of dolphins. Nuquí's beaches and that of nearby Pijiba consistently rank amongst Colombia's finest in tourist polls. However, given their location the beaches are rarely crowded except at Christmas and New Year and during major surfing events when Nuquí's population of 7,500 can rise by at least 20% overnight.

GETTING THERE AND AROUND Nuquí's Reyes Murillo Airport is served much like Bahía Solano with frequent flights from Medellín (50 minutes on a small twin Otter plane carrying 20 passengers). Boats to and from Buenaventura depart to an unpredictable schedule at 80,000 COP per person. The ticket price includes three simple meals and a bed.

TOURIST INFORMATION
☑ **Oficina De Turismo** Carrera 2, No 2–10; ☏ 683 6006; f 683 6005; e alcaldiadenuqui@hotmail.com

WHERE TO STAY AND EAT
Many of Nuquí's nicest places to stay are out of town along the coast in the jungle where some particularly fine eco-resorts offer a wide range of adventure packages. Almost all offer an all-inclusive package, but if you do decide to eat elsewhere (or manage to negotiate a cheaper room-only rate off-season) try the Restaurant El Paisa and Pola's Place (ask around) – both serve good food for 5,000 COP.

⌂ **Ecolodge Nautilos** ☏ 310 896 8364; e info@nautiloslodge.com; www.nautiloslodge.com. This right-on-the-sand wood-&-thatch lodge has brightly painted balconies that offer superb views across open water. Popular with surfers & fishing nuts, the lodge also offers a range of guided jungle treks to waterfalls, hot springs & lesser-known beach areas – as well as whale-watching trips. Rates start at US$265 for a 3-night stay all-inc (meals, drinks, transfers, taxes & 2 tours) with surfboard hire (US$8) & jungle hikes (US$10) extra. $$$

⌂ **El Cantil Eco Lodge** ☏ 252 0707/352 0729; e elcantil@epm.net.co; www.elcantil.com. This innovative eco-resort hosts a wide range of themed 1-week activities, from surfing vacations & jungle survival schools to diving, climbing, dancing & well-being weeks. During June–October it offers highly popular humpback-whale tours as well as year-round dolphin spotting, birding & fishing trips – the waters are full of sailfish, marlin, tuna, mackerel, wahoo & snapper in May & June. Dive masters offer 15 years experience & a full equipment rental service. Established in 1998, El Cantil is located south of Nuquí near to Termales (a 35-min boat transfer that is inc in the price) & boasts a splendid spot right on the ocean with magnificent views. Seven comfortable rooms with private bathrooms can accommodate 6 people & have an ocean-view terrace. A communal area has a restaurant & sundeck & the resort is equipped with surfboards, kayaks & boogie boards. Prices vary but expect to pay around 150,000 COP per night for one of a wide range of 3–10-day packages. $$$

Although much of the Pacific coast's natural habitat remains largely intact and undeveloped there remains widespread concern regarding proposed large-scale development in the area. In the name of progress, a number of public and private investors have pushed for roads, inter-oceanic canals, railways and hydro-electric dams in El Pacifico with slash-and-burn agriculture, logging and mining an ever-present threat to the integrity of the region's forests. These state plans – known collectively as the Plan Pacifico – aim to tap into the local resources more systematically as part of a strategy for increased trade with the outside world.

Amphibian diversity offers more than 200 species in the Pacific coast region – 30 of them endemic. Scientists are struggling to keep up with the pace of new discoveries with shelves of specimens awaiting analysis at the National Herpetological Collection in Bogotá. However, several species remain under threat, with the Pacific horned frog, pink-sided treefrog, golden poison frog, green poison frog and Myers' Surinam toad endangered, critically endangered or vulnerable.

More than 285 mammal species have been recorded in the region – 11 of which are endemic. Species under threat include the bush dog, spectacled bear, smoky bat, equatorial dog-faced bat, Kalinowski's mastiff bat, fraternal fruit-eating bat, greater long-tailed bat, southern long-nosed bat, western nectar bat, long-snouted bat, Tacarcuna bat, Central American woolly opossum, Baird's tapir, silvery-brown bare-face tamarin, cotton-top tamarin, lemurine night monkey, red crested tree rat, Gorgas' rice rat and a giant anteater.

Scientists estimate that El Pacifico is home to more than 320 reptile species, of which nearly 100 are endemic. The American crocodile, marine iguana, Santa Fé land iguana, Dahl's toadhead turtle, green turtle, leatherback sea turtle and Dunn's mud turtle are currently listed as endangered, critically endangered or vulnerable species. Poaching remains a problem in the Pacific region – in 2007 Colombia's navy intercepted a boat containing nearly 80 dead sharks (approximately two tonnes of shark meat). Officials charged the crew with illegally fishing in a protected sanctuary. They were caught 25km southwest of the island of Malpelo, a World Heritage Site. Among the sharks trapped were several blacktip sharks, a species listed as threatened by the World Conservation Union. Colombian fishing boats have been reportedly poaching hammerhead and other shark species near Malpelo for some time, selling the fins to Asia for shark fin soup.

⌂ **Hotel Turqui Eco Hotel** www.hotelturqui.com. This lovely little eco-resort is located in the Cabo Corrientes (meaning end of the river current) a 45-min speedboat journey from the centre of Nuquí. Wood-&-thatch cabins sit inside the jungle overlooking the seashore & accommodate up to 60 people in a range of dbl & family-sized rooms or hammock dorms. Communal space has decks over the beach, a fresh seafood restaurant, bar, diving centre & 7km beach. Fishing trips use 25ft Yamaha twin-engine fibreglass boats with 25 sets of diving gear, instructors & international diving experts, Bauer compressor, GPS, sonar & dbl tanks. Packages range in price from US$382 for a 4-day 3-night stay to US$814,000 for 8 days 7 nights of fishing & inc all transport, transfers, meals, guides & tours. $$$

⌂ **Lodge Piedra Piedra** Calle 10B, No 35–03; ☏ 311 2358; e info@piedrapiedra.com; www.piedrapiedra.com. This jungle lodge is 15 km south of the centre of Nuquí between the tropical rainforest & the ocean. Rooms can accommodate a total of 17 people across 2 3-storey cabins close to beaches, rivers, waterfalls, thermal springs & jungle trails. It gets pretty full during whale-observation months (Jun–Nov) & is also a popular base camp for birders. Dolphins & a great variety of fish can be seen in the surrounding waters with kayaking, fishing, surfing & swimming from a lovely wooden deck. An onsite restaurant serves 3 meals a day & there's a bar, communal lounge & laundry. Rates start at 100,000 COP for a basic overnight stay although 3–7-day inclusive packages offer better value for those keen to whale watch, fish & hike. Transfers are included. $$

The Pacific Coast NUQUÍ

10

OTHER PRACTICALITIES Bring enough money (in low denominations) as there are no ATMs in Nuquí. Pack rubber boots, waterproof clothing and plenty of bug spray. It's also advisable to bring a candle and matches (or a torch) as paths are unlit.

WHAT TO SEE Surfers, windsurfers and kite-surfers head to Nuquí's **Playa Olympica** west of the airport where the water is calm close to shore. The big waves happen about 100m out where they break to a height of 2.4m. Pick up some supplies, fresh fish and tin foil from Nuquí before crossing the lagoon by canoe to set up a day camp on the beach. **Guachalito** is another popular tour and has some very nice sandy stretches an hour's boat ride south of Nuquí with whale watching, dolphins, sport fishing and diving all along the coast to the **Cabo Corrientes**. A rather nice **Birding Trail** that leads out of town along the river where a wide variety of species can be easily spotted. Expect to see purple-throated fruitcrow, chestnut-backed antbird, black-striped woodcreeper, southern nightingale-wren, mourning warbler, blue-grey tanager, golden-hooded tanager, great-billed crimson-crested woodpecker, rufous-tailed jacamar, white-tailed trogon, ringed kingfisher, Amazon kingfisher, orange-chinned parakeet, blue-headed parrot, streak-throated hermit, purple gallinule, long-tailed tyrant, black-crowned tityra, seed-finch, buff-throated saltator, baudo oropendola, scarlet-rumped cacique, Wilson's plover, southern lapwing, roadside hawk, red-breasted blackbird, olive-crowned yellowthroat, dusky-faced tanager and great-tailed grackle – to name quite a few.

11

The Atlantic Coast

Colombia's most accessible coastal stretch is also its most tourist-friendly with around 1,750km of palm-fringed coastline dotted with fine historic cities, Caribbean resorts and numerous attractions. Containing a vast range of ecosystems and six distinct sub-regions, the many contrasting facets of the Caribbean shoreline begs thorough exploration. From the Andean Mountain range a massif plain extends to the Sierra Nevada de Santa Marta and the Guajira Peninsula at Colombia's most northerly point. A criss-cross of rivers and the vast Ciénaga Grande de Santa Marta marshland lead to idyllic carpets of white sand on terrain bordered by Panama's impenetrable jungle swathe to the east and humble Venezuelan fishing villages to the west. From the windblown dry cacti-clad coastal desert in La Guajira and the steamy virgin rainforest of Parque Nacional Tayrona to the fine-looking colonial city of Cartagena and its exquisite UNESCO-listed architectural beauty, the Atlantic coast is steeped in history and legend. Myths continue to dominate modern culture with many versions of *La Llorona* (The Crying Woman) in existence. The region's nine-million laid-back *Costeños* are mainly of African descent, renowned for their slow-paced simplicity and pulsating reggaetón, porro and champeta Afro-Caribbean rhythms. The Atlantic coast is also synonymous with Colombia's wildest festivals with the eye-popping Carnaval de Barranquilla an especially raucous affair. Various dialects of Caribbean-Spanish exist within each sub-region, along with several indigenous languages including Wayúu. La Guajira is also home to one of Colombia's concentrations of Middle Eastern émigrés in the border town of Maicao.

HISTORY

The Caribbean coast boasts the distinction of being the first conquered by the Spanish and contains Colombia's two oldest surviving cities, Santa Marta (founded in 1525) and Cartagena (1533). However, various indigenous groups inhabited the region long before the conquistadors' arrival. Two communities evolved into highly developed civilisations with the Tayrona in the Sierra Nevada de Santa Marta and the Sinú in the region's southwest particularly industrially advanced. Both Santa and Cartagena were important strategic shipping posts for vast riches amassed by the Spanish plunder. Mules ferried gold from besieged Indian tribes in the interior regions to galleons bound for Spain. As a consequence Cartagena was subject to sustained attacks and vicious assault throughout its early years.

CLIMATE

Expect brutally hot, steamy conditions and temperatures that rarely drop below 28°C. Two rainy periods run from April to May and October to November with December to April and July to September typically dry. Cooling winds during December to January make this a pleasant time to visit.

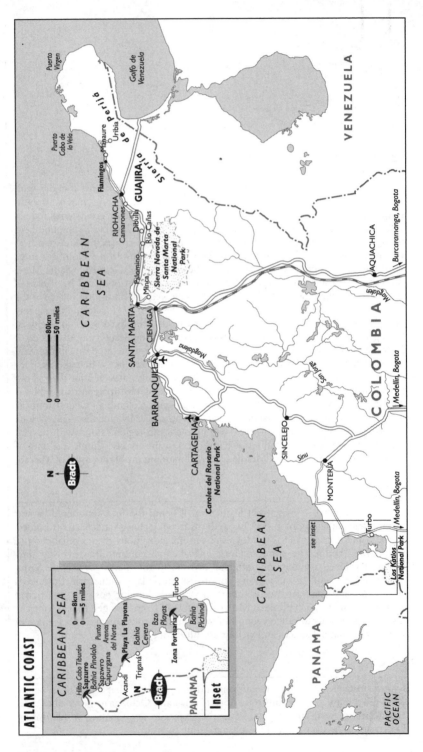

ATLANTIC COAST

CARIBBEAN SEA

VENEZUELA

Golfo de Venezuela

Puerto Virgen

Puerto Cabo de la Vela

Flamingos

Manaure

Uribia

Sierra de Perijá

RIOHACHA

Camarones

GUAJIRA

Dibulla

Río Cañas

Palomino

Minca

Sierra Nevada de Santa Marta National Park

SANTA MARTA

CIENAGA

BARRANQUILLA

Magdalena

CARTAGENA

Caroles del Rosario National Park

SINCELEJO

Sinú

MONTERIA

San Jorge

COLOMBIA

AQUACHICA

Barcaramanga, Bogota

Medellín, Bogota

Magdalena

Turbo

see inset

Medellín, Bogota

Los Katios National Park

PANAMA

PACIFIC OCEAN

CARIBBEAN SEA

N Bradt

0 80km
0 50 miles

Inset

CARIBBEAN SEA

0 8km
0 5 miles

Hilo Cabo Tiburón

Sapzurro

Bahía Pinololo

Punta Arenas del Norte

Sapzwro

Capurgana

Playa La Playona

Acandí

Trigana

Bahía Cevera

Bzo Playas

Zona Portitaria

Turbo

Bahía Pichindi

PANAMA

N Bradt

BOLÍVAR

One of the most visited regions of Colombia, Bolívar extends from the coast at Cartagena near the mouth of the Río Magdalena before sweeping south along the river to a border with Antioquía. Pretty offshore islands and the resplendent colonial buildings of the walled city of Cartagena make the department a major tourist draw. Much of its 25,978km² terrain consists of hot, humid, forested lowlands. Aside of tourism, Bolívar's economy relies on the production of livestock, sugarcane, tobacco, cotton, cereals, coffee and forest products. Cartagena's port has ensured the region is an important centre for commerce with strategic waterway connections via the Canal de Dique along the Río Magdalena.

CARTAGENA Telephone code: 5

Abandon all thoughts of ticking off sightseeing attractions in Cartagena; simply take to the city's picture-perfect streets and meander through one of the greatest cultural treasures in the Americas. Stroll along an enchanting puzzle of cobbled paths complete with horse-drawn carriages past bloom-covered archways and fine colonial buildings painted a dazzling array of bold hues. Pristine leafy plazas adorned with vibrant bougainvillea and handsome palms lead to ancient fortifications with stunning sea views. Outdoor cosmopolitan cafés bustle with cappuccino-sipping tourists amidst street theatre, basket weavers and flower sellers. Facing the Caribbean Sea to the west with Cartagena Bay to the south, Cartagena was declared a World Heritage Site by UNESCO in 1984 as the region's true jewel-box of Spanish colonial ostentation. Expect sweet, sticky heat in a city that seems to be in a permanent state of festival with plenty of unique historic character of which slavery, sainthood and swashbuckling buccaneers are all a part.

HISTORY Founded in 1533 by Pedro de Heredia on the site of the Carib Indian settlement of Calamarí, meaning crab, Cartagena formed a vital part in the Spanish defence strategy. A walled military fortress was constructed to protect the city against plundering pirates from England, Holland and France. Cartagena's first buildings were destroyed when fire ravaged the city in 1552. Since then, only stone, tile and brick have been allowed in construction. As the main northern gateway into South America, Cartagena soon grew into a busy port used by the Spanish to store and ship looted Indian gold. Despite its robust design, the city was subjected to numerous attacks, with five violent assaults in the 16th century alone. Sir Francis Drake sacked the port at dawn, forcing the inhabitants to take refuge in the neighbouring village of Turbaco. He destroyed the nave of the cathedral and demanded a staggering 107,000 ducats (10 million COP) in ransom in return for agreeing not to raze the town to the ground. In a bid to better protect Cartagena, the Spanish engaged some prominent European military engineers to undertake the construction of a series of fortresses. In March of 1741, English admiral Edward Vernon and his troops attacked Cartagena with an enormous fleet of 186 ships and 25,000 men. Blas de Lezo (1688–1741), a Spanish officer who had already lost an eye and a leg in earlier fighting, only had six ships and 3,600 men. After weeks of intense fighting, the siege was repelled by the Spanish commander. He lost his remaining leg and died shortly after but is honoured in a statue outside the San Félipe fortress as the saviour of Cartagena. Vernon had not expected defeat and, before he attacked, overconfident of victory, had ordered medals bearing: 'True British Héroes Took Cartagena, April 1741'. A statue of Vernon and a replica of this medal were erected as a permanent laughing stock. Never count your chickens, especially when fighting the Spanish and with incalculable amounts of treasure at stake.

In the early 17th century, Cartagena was granted a shared monopoly of the Caribbean slave trade with Vera Cruz in Mexico. The first slave ship arrived in 1564 to send thousands of slaves all over the continent. More than one million slaves were brought by ship to Cartagena during this era, providing cheap labour to ensure the sustained growth of the Spanish Empire and becoming the greatest slave market of the New World. After an exhausting sea crossing the African captives were offloaded from their ships and taken straight to auction at the *feria de negros* (slave market) at the entrance of the old city. The slaves brought their culture, traditions, songs and dances from Africa and these soon became mixed with Catholic ritual with animist and Islamic rhythms. Today, Colombia's beloved Cumbia Cienaguera songs remain heavily laced with the influences of Cartagena's slavery in music that retains African beats and plenty of *sabor* (flavour) and *ambiente* (atmosphere).

In 1650, the construction of the Canal del Digue strengthened Cartagena's gateway role for ships heading to ports along the river. It continued to be one of Spain's most important colonial strongholds, serving as a warehouse for the wealth of the country before it was loaded onto boats for the journey to Seville. However the self-rule movement began to gain momentum in Cartagena and in 1810 the city was one of the first to proclaim independence from Spain, signing a declaration on 11 November 1811. A four-month siege followed as the Spanish attempted to calm the revolt under the leadership of Pablo Morillo in 1815, during which time more than 6,000 inhabitants lost their lives. Although Simón Bolívar defeated the Spanish at Boyacá in August 1819, Cartagena wasn't liberated until 1820. Nationalist troops eventually freed the city by sea and it was honoured by Bolívar with the name 'La Héroica', the Heroic City. 'Si Caracas me dio la vida, vosotros me desteis gloria,' he declared –'Caracas may have given me birth, but you gave me glory.'

Today, Cartagena's population has soared beyond one million. It is Colombia's number one tourist draw and in 2006 hosted the Central American and Caribbean Games. In the same year Cartagena became the home of an overseas spin-off of the Hay Festival, bolstering its status as Latin America's essential detour for sun-seeking literati seeking also a new style of libertarian hedonism. This celebration of contemporary literature has a head start as the home of 'Gabo', Gabriel García Márquez, author of *A Hundred Years of Solitude* and Colombia's Nobel laureate. So far the bill has attracted guests such as Christopher Hitchens, Asne Seierstad, Manuel Rivas, Wole Soyinka, Junot Díaz and D B C Pierre. In 2007, Bob Geldof performed 'I Don't Like Mondays' in the city's main square to rapturous applause. During the event, Geldof was presented with a guitar made from a decommissioned guerrilla AK47.

CLIMATE Due to Cartagena's tropical location, the city's climate has little variation with an average high of 32°C and an average low of 25°C throughout the year. Humidity is generally around 90% so it is permanently hot and sticky. A rainy season runs typically in October to November with the driest months December to April, although tropical showers occur year-round.

ORIENTATION The locals divide Cartagena into five distinct zones: Historic, Tourist, North, South and Residential. The Historic Zone (known by its original name Calamarí by the locals and also Centro Histórico) is, as the name suggests, the old quarter in the west containing the Ciudad Amurallada (Walled City) and the aged neighbourhoods of San Diego, La Matuna, Getsemaní and Santo Domingo. The Tourist Zone of Bocagrande, Castillogrande and Laguito sits to the south of the old city in an odd-shaped peninsula that is home to the city's main beaches with Cartagena Bay to the east and the Caribbean Sea to the west. Flanked by a succession of modern, high-rise Miami-esque hotels, the Avenida San Martín forms the backbone of this vibrant area renowned for its nightlife, shops and restaurants. The Rafael Núñez International Airport is in the Northern Zone in the suburb of Crespo. Cartagena's poorest residential neighbourhoods are in the city's southeast.

GETTING THERE Cartagena's ultra-efficient Rafael Núñez International Airport (*www.sacsa.com.co*) is located in Crespo, 3km northeast of the old city and handles more passengers than any other airport in the region. ADA, AeroRepública and Aires Avianca offer frequent flights to the Colombian cities of Medellín, Bogotá, Cali, San Andrés, Barranquilla and Pereira. The US, Panama and Venezuela (Miami, Panama City and Caracas) are also well served with numerous seasonal operators serving Europe direct. The airport is serviced by frequent local buses with *colectivos* (shared taxis) departing to Crespo from Monumento a la India Catalina. Arrivals at the airport can catch a bus to the centre (it's marked El Centro) for about 500 COP.

It is also possible to travel by sailboat from Cartagena to Panama – it takes around five days. However, this is not a regular service so no schedules exist. Boats include the *Melody* (☏ *315 756 2818*, e *freshaircharters@yahoo.com*) and the *Golden Eagle* (☏ *311 419 0428*) – both offer one-way sailings for around 250,000 COP plus food, including a couple of days snorkelling at Kuna Yala (Panama's islands of San Blas). Passengers are dropped at the island Porvenir where a small airport connects to Panama City for around US$40. This is a preferable option to negotiating a place to hang a hammock on a passing cargo boat – safer, better equipped (with kitchen etc) and not involved in contraband or drug smuggling.

Cartagena's main bus terminal is on the eastern edge of the city and is served by Metrocar buses from the city every ten minutes or so. Half a dozen daily buses to Bogotá (90,000 COP, 20 hours) and Medellín (80,000 COP, 13 hours) with buses to Barranquilla (9,000 COP, 2 hours) running every 15 minutes.

GETTING AROUND Numerous yellow taxis serve the Cartagena area with a ride across town 4,000 COP, an airport run 12,000 COP and a trip to the outskirts 8,000 COP. To keep costs down ask the driver to drive to the Green Church at Crespo rather than the airport – it's a simple walk across the road to the airport and avoids incurring the expensive airport tariff. Taxis are not metered so fix the price beforehand – for a full tariff visit www.cartagenainfo.com/taxis.

The city's famous horse-drawn carriages operate around the historical centre and the tourist zones after 17.00 – ask for a general tour or give them a specific drop-off point for around 25,000 COP. A system of buses and *colectivos* serve all areas of the city and these are useful for getting to the beach at Bocagrande.

Cartagena's public transport has been invaded by 'mototaxis' – check out the many postings of harrowing footage on YouTube for a zillion good reasons why to give this cheap option a miss. At the time of writing a multi-million dollar mass transportation system was slated to open; for an update visit www.turismocartagena.com.

TOURIST INFORMATION

☑ Turismo Cartagena de Indias Av Blas de Lezo; ☏ 655 0211; www.turismocartagena.com;

⊕ 08.00–18.00 Mon–Fri, closed noon–14.00, 08.00–noon Sat

Tour guides

Nico Medes ☏ 315 710 8700/674 0336. Expect an abundance of great historical facts & background

from the oh-so likeable Nico, a quietly spoken charming man who has been guiding in the city for 20 years. He speaks English fluently & is a popular man around the city. To explore Cartagena on foot is a genuine delight such are his good-natured style & attention to detail. Nico has a regular tourism slot on Cartagena TV station C5.

Jorge Coneo 🤙 301 386 874; e georgeconeo@ hotmail.com. Jorge comes highly recommended by the backpacker crowd who rave about his insider knowledge when it comes to the best places to party. He lived in the US for a number of years & speaks fluent English.

Tour operators Hop aboard a *chiva* (colourful, open-side traditional Colombian bus) for Cartagena's four-hour city tour; they depart daily at 14.00 from Bocagrande. Another tour option is to take a horse-drawn carriage from Bocagrande for a trip around the walled city and along the waterfront. These operate from 17.00 each night and last about one hour. Numerous tour operators offer boat trips out to the islands, especially Islas del Rosario (see page 369). Cartagena also has lots of diving centres with the largest concentration in Bocagrande, including the Caribe Dive Shop (🤙 *665 3517; www.caribediveshop.com*) at the Hotel Caribe. To hire a captain and 52ft luxury yacht that can accommodate 15 people, complete with kitchen and bar, contact Relax 2 Yacht (🤙 *664 1117; www.cartagenarelax.com*). It costs 1.4 million COP for a full day on the ocean, with 48 hours notice required.

WHERE TO STAY Cartagena has a growing range of accommodation in every price bracket, but tends to be pricier than many Colombian cities. Getsemaní is the centre of backpacker hostels; the Tourist Zone (Bocagrande and El Laguito) is home to the majority of mid-to-high-end options while El Centro and San Diego are renowned for their upscale boutique hotels. At the time of writing, Getsemaní's red-light activity has made it risky for female travellers. On this basis, only hotels in the less sleazy parts of town are listed – but double checking on the ground is advised.

For a range of well-maintained apartments for rent contact **Colombia Rental** (*www.colombiarental.net*), an independent outfit run by an American guy called Michael. The company deals with short-term and long-term lets in all areas of the city.

Getsemaní

🏠 **Casa Relax B&B** (10 rooms) Calle de Pozo, No 20–105; 🤙 664 1117; www.cartagenarelax.com. Visitors rave about this French-run B&B housed in a beautifully restored colonial building. It has comfortable, AC rooms (8 dbl/2 twin) with a TV & nice, clean private bathrooms. There's also a communal kitchen, laundry, shared lounge, internet, bar, snack bar & a pool. Staff speak English & French as well as Spanish. Rates include a delicious French-style b/fast. $$$

🏠 **Casa Viena** Calle San Andrés, No 30–53; 🤙 664 6242; e hotel@casaviena.com; www.casaviena.com. This Cartagena budget travel institution started in 1992 & is a firm favourite with backpackers, offering simple rooms with shared facilities & a lot of practical help. Austrian owner Hans knows the backpacker trail well & is well versed in tours, boats to Panama, treks, etc. Communal amenities include laundry services, cooking facilities, book exchange & individual safety deposit boxes. $

🏠 **Hotel Behique** (38 rooms) Calle Tripita y Media, No 31–29; 🤙 664 3511. This comfortable hotel offers clean, simple rooms with either fans or AC. A little tired around the edges, but well equipped with onsite internet. $

🏠 **Hotel Holiday** Calle de la Media Luna, No 10–47; 🤙 664 0948. Another popular shoestring joint, the Hotel Holiday lacks the amenities & ambience of Casa Viena but on the basis of price is a worthy second choice. Choose from a handful of fan-cooled rooms with private bathroom set around a courtyard garden. $

🏠 **Hotel Marlin** Calle 30, No 10–35; 🤙 664 3507. Choose from a range of poky rooms with private bathroom in this cheap little backpacker option – ask to see a few as some don't have windows & are claustrophobic. $

🏠 **Hotel Villa Colonial** Calle de las Maravillas, No 30–60; 🤙 664 4996; e Daniela.akel@gmail.com. Choose from a collection of clean, if sparsely furnished, rooms in this simple family-run hotel in a colonial building – some have AC, others just a fan. $

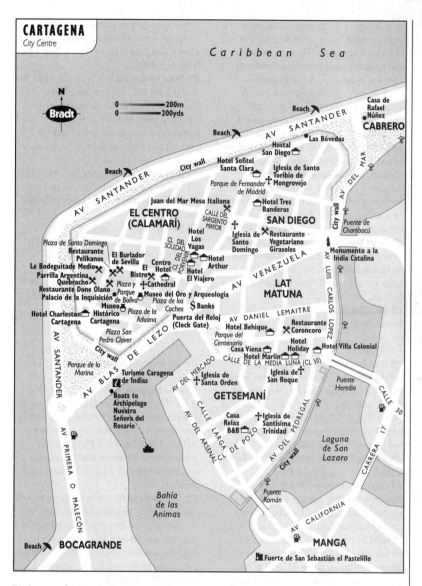

CARTAGENA
City Centre

Caribbean Sea

N

Bradt

0 ——— 200m
0 ——— 200yds

Beach

Casa de
Rafael
Núñez

CABRERO

Beach

Las Bóvedas

Hostal
San Diego

Hotel Sofitel
Santa Clara

AV SANTANDER

City wall

Beach

Iglesia de Santo
Toribio de
Mongrovejo

Parque de Fernandez
de Madrid

AV SANTANDER

Juan del Mar Mesa Italiana

EL CENTRO
(CALAMARÍ)

CALLE DEL
SARGENTO
MAYOR

Hotel
Los
Vagas

Hotel Tres
Banderas

SAN DIEGO

AV DEL MAR

City wall

Puente de
Chambacú

Iglesia de
Santo
Domingo

Restaurante
Vegetariano
Girasoles

Plaza de Santo Domingo
Restaurante
Pelikanos

Le Bodeguitade Medio
Parrilla Argentina
Quebracho
Restaurante Done Olano
Palacio de la Inquisición

Hotel Charleston
Cartagena

El Burlador
de Sevilla

CL DEL
SOLEDAD

CL DEL
PORVENIR

Centro
Hotel

El
Bistro

Hotel
Arthur

Hotel
El Viajero

AV VENEZUELA

Monumento a la
India Catalina

AV LUIS CARLOS LOPEZ

LAT
MATUNA

Plaza y
de Bolíva

Cathedral

Museo del Oro y Arqueología

Museo
Histórico
Cartagena

Plaza de la
Aduana

Plaza de los
Coches

Banks

Plaza San
Pedro Claver

City wall

AV DANIEL LEMAITRE

Puerta del Reloj
(Clock Gate)

Parque del
Centenario

Hotel Behique

Restaurante
Coroncoro

AV SANTANDER

DE LEZO

Parque de la
Marina

AV BLAS DE

Turismo Caragena
de Indias

Casa Viena
Hotel Marlin

Hotel
Holiday

Hotel Villa Colonial

CALLE DE LA MEDIA LUNA (CL 30)

AV DEL MERCADO

Iglesia de
Santa Orden

Iglesia de
San Roque

Puente
Heredia

CALLE 30

Boats to
Archipelago
Nuestra
Señora del
Rosario

GETSEMANÍ

CALLE LARGA

AV DEL ARSENAL

CL DE POZO

Casa
Relax
B&B

Iglesia de
Santísima
Trinidad

AV DEL PEDREGAL

City wall

CARRERA 17

Laguna
de San
Lazaro

AV PRIMERA
O MALECÓN

Bahía
de las
Animas

Puente
Román

AV CALIFORNIA

Beach BOCAGRANDE

MANGA

Fuerte de San Sebastián el Pastelillo

El Centro (Calamari) & San Diego

⌂ **El Marques Boutique Hotel** (8 rooms) Calle
Nuestra Señora Del Carmen, No 33–41; ☎ 664
4438/7800; f 664 7957; e
elmarqueshotelctg@gmail.com;
www.elmarqueshotelboutique.com. Expect classy
furnishings & chic styling at this newly opened boutique
hotel set within one of the nicest 17th-century colonial
buildings in this part of the old city. A lavish
restoration programme has equipped this fine historic
property with a host of high-tech amenities in what

was once the home of a famous New Yorker, Sam Green
– the boyfriend of Greta Garbo who regularly
entertained Yoko Ono & the Kennedy family. Six
luxurious rooms & 2 suites overlook an elegant
courtyard garden with LCD-screen controls, cable TV,
minibar & safety deposit boxes. El Marques also has a
swimming pool, sushi bar & spa. A pricey option but an
enjoyable extravagance nonetheless. $$$$
⌂ **Hotel Sofitel Santa Clara** (180 rooms) Calle del Torno;
☎ 664 6070; www.hotelsantaclara.com. Without a doubt

one of Cartagena's classiest accommodation options, this landmark colonial building used to be the Convento de Santa Clara & dates back to 1621. No-expense-spared luxurious touches attract a well-heeled clientele with rooms & suites decorated in sumptuous grandeur. Amenities include a gym, business centre, 2 upscale restaurants & a chic bar. The Santa Clara boasts its fair share of visiting Hollywood starlets, movie-makers & political leaders. Colombian Formula I star Juan Pablo Montoya had his wedding here & past lunch guests have included Bill Clinton. Worth a splurge. $$$$

🏠 **Hotel Charleston Cartagena** (113 rooms) Plaza Santa Teresa; ☎ 664 9494; www.hotels-charleston.com. Two idyllic arcaded courtyard rooms & suites of tasteful décor at this elegant hotel. Guest amenities include a rooftop pool, 3 good restaurants & a gym. $$$

🏠 **Centro Hotel** Calle del Arzobispado; ☎ 664 0461; www.centrohotelcartagena.com. Just a few metres from the Plaza de Bolívar, the Centro is a good mid-range option with nice, clean AC rooms set around an open courtyard. Rates include b/fast. $$

🏠 **Hostal San Diego** (27 rooms) Calle de las Bóvedas, No 39–120; ☎ 660 0986;

e hostalsandiego@enred.com. Choose from comfortable rooms set around a pleasant courtyard in a pretty, quiet street in the north of San Diego close to the thick of it. $$

🏠 **Hostal Tres Banderas** Calle Cochera del Hobbo, No 38–66; ☎ 660 0160; www.hotel3banderas.com. This beautifully decorated alcohol- & tobacco-free hotel is drenched in colour. Rooms are larger on the 2nd floor & have a balcony. A stylish courtyard has waterfalls & palms beyond a bloom-clad tangerine exterior adorned with a fine wrought-iron gate. $$

🏠 **Hotel Arthur** Calle San Agustín, No 6–44; ☎ 664 2633. A little tatty, but reasonable on the basis of price, the Arthur can be noisy so ask for a room at the back. $$

🏠 **Hotel Las Vegas** Calle San Agustín, No 6–08; ☎ 664 5619. Another noisy option with rooms on the street, Las Vegas has simple, clean rooms with TV – but light sleepers should pack a pair of earplugs. $$

🏠 **Hotel El Viajero** (14 rooms) Calle del Porvenir, No 35–68; ☎ 664 3289. This good-value budget hotel has clean & comfortable AC rooms, a courtyard & communal kitchen. $

Bocagrande

🏠 **Hotel Caribe** (380 rooms) Carrera 1A, No 2–87; ☎ 650 1160/665 0155; www.hotelcaribe.com. Grand, imposing & with a pink-washed stucco exterior, the palatial Caribe sits adorned with flags in lush, tropical gardens. Built in 1940, the hotel boasts ultra-posh rooms & self-contained suites. Expect top-notch service, with prices to match. $$$$

🏠 **Hotel Capilla del Mar** (200-plus rooms) Cnr Carrera 1 & Calle 1, No 8; ☎ 650 1500; f 665 5145; www.hotelcapilladelmar.com. This high-rise beachfront hotel's rooms were fully renovated in 2006 & are cheerfully decorated, spacious & well appointed with modern private bathrooms. Choose from a range of AC dbl rooms & suites with safety deposit boxes, telephone, minibar, cable TV & hairdryer. Three restaurants, a pool & business centre are just some of the Capilla del Mar's many amenities – it even has a slow-moving rotating

21st-floor bar offering panoramic views across the city. $$$

🏠 **Hotel Bocagrande** Avenida San Martín, No 7–159; ☎ 665 4435; e hotelbocagrande@hotelesdelmar.com; www.hotelesdelmar.com. Comfortable, simple rooms come with AC & balconies at this tourist hotel close to the beach & are equipped with minibar, cable TV, private bathroom & telephone. Amenities include a restaurant serving a mix of fast food & Colombian specialities. $$

🏠 **Hotel Estrella del Mar** Avenida San Martín, No 4–46; ☎ 655 1349/6144; e estrella@hotelesbarahona.com. Set a block or so from the seafront, the Estrella del Mar is a fuss-free lower mid-range option, popular with vacationing Colombians looking for a cheap place to stay a short walk from the beach. Basic AC rooms have a private bathroom & cable TV. $$

✘ **WHERE TO EAT** Good food is easy to find in Cartagena with an abundance of choice in the historic centre and in and around Bocagrande in the Tourist Zone. Local specialities include delicious small smoked meatballs (*butifarras*), deep-fried cheese sticks (*dedos de queso*) and egg-filled fried maze (*arepas de huevo*) – all are sold throughout the city by street vendors. There are way too many restaurants to list, but the following will provide a starting point.

✘ **Club de Pesca** Fuerte del Pastelillo; ☎ 660 4594/5863/7065; e restaurante@clubdepesca.com; ⏲ lunch & dinner. Cartagena's affluent gastronomes

like to eat at this great lunch spot where oh-so-chic tables are laid in grand style underneath a giant tree on a patio overlooking a posh marina. Expect a superb menu, fine wines & lots of designer garb in Cartagena's oldest fort. $$$

✗ **El Bistro** Calle de Ayos, No 4–42; ✆ 664 1799; ⏱all day. Expect casual fare & light meals at this pleasant German-owned backstreet café where the travel tips for backpackers are as good as man-sized sandwiches & pasta dishes. $$

✗ **El Burlador de Sevilla** Calle Santo Domingo, No 33–88; ✆ 660 0866; ⏱noon–midnight. Styled in traditional Spanish fashion with matador posters & wall-mounted bulls' heads, this is Cartagena's best place for tapas, paella & roasted suckling pig. $$

✗ **Juan del Mar Mesa Italiana** Plaza San Diego; ✆ 664 5108; e delmarsa@telecom.com.co; ⏱lunch & dinner. Choose from a menu of grilled fish with basil, homemade mozzarella pizza & pasta dishes at this charming place with indoor or outdoor seating. $$

✗ **La Bodeguita de Medio** Calle de la Mantilla, No 3–32; ✆ 660 1436; ⏱noon–midnight. Coloured walls displaying rebel-rousing posters supporting *la revolución* give it a studenty feel with lots of hardline political items relating to Castro & Guevara. A small menu offers Cuban bean-&-rice dishes & grilled meats. $$

✗ **Parrilla Argentina Quebracho** Calle de Baloco; ✆ 664 1300; ⏱lunch & dinner Mon–Thu, all day Fri/Sat. Meat-lovers will die & go to heaven at the sight of spit-roasted pig, huge slabs of steak & chorizo sausage – washed down with a big cellar of Argentine wine. $$

✗ **Restaurante Coroncoro** Calle Tripita y Medio, No 31–28; ⏱08.00–20.00. Expect simple, filling local food at this inexpensive family-run restaurant where most meals come in at under 4,000 COP. $

✗ **Restaurante Done Olano** Calle Santo Domingo, No 33–08; ✆ 664 7099; ⏱noon–23.00 Mon–Sat. A French-Creole menu offers some interesting dishes a little different from the norm, such as jambalaya & garlic fish. $$

✗ **Restaurante Pelikanos** Cnr Calle Santo Domingo & Calle Gastlebondo; ✆ 660 0086; ⏱11.00–late. Superb value is the order of the day at this chilled-out bohemian diner where a set 6-course meal comes with limitless wine & inc four mini-appetisers. $$

✗ **Restaurant Vegetariano Girasoles** Calle de los Puntales, No 37–01; ✆ 664 5239; ⏱noon–22.00. This San Diego meat-free joint offers tasty beans-&-rice dishes and soups at budget prices. $

✗ **The Santa Clara** Calle del Torno; ✆ 664 6070; www.hotelsantaclara.com; ⏱lunch & dinner. It's difficult not to gush about this truly gorgeous setting, amidst blood-red paintwashed walls, hand-thrown tiles & towering leafy palms. Rugged antiques, lavish drapes & fine furnishings offer unabashed luxury. Choose from a French menu at El Refectario (the former convent's dining area), snacks at El Corro (where the nuns intoned their ecclesiastical chants) and El Caustro Café (a relaxed outside brasserie-style lunch spot) for some of the most memorable dining in Cartagena's swishiest locales. $$$

Bocagrande As you'd expect from a seafront tourist zone, Bocagrande offers plenty of vacation food, from hamburgers and pizza joints to indulgent family diners. Most of the restaurants are along Avenida San Martín. Menus don't tend to offer the sophistication or choice of the historical centre – the following are just a handful of what's around at the time of writing.

Enjoy first-rate beef kebabs at **El Otoyal** on Avenida 4 diagonally opposite the Carulla supermarket. For some of the most mouth-watering coconut macaroons head to **Pan De Bono**, while **El Kiosko de Bony** in front of the Hotel El Caribe is renowned for its excellent fried fish. Another **rustic seafood joint** is found opposite the Capilla de Mar Hotel on Carrera 1A in a blue-roofed hut on the sand. It boasts a sterling reputation for simple Caribbean-style seafood; simply sit at one of just a handful of tables and ask what's just been reeled in. A few doors down from the hotel on Carrera 1A the **Ranchería Restaurante** (✆ 665 6163) has a good 13,000 COP menu of typical Colombia fare served at outside covered tables set back from the road. For great snacks head to the **Restaurante Crepes and Waffles** on Carrera 3, No 4–76. Other good dining options include the fabulous gaucho-style meat joint **Restaurante Dany El Churrasco Argentino** (✆ 665 4523) on Calle 5, No 2–104, and the pasta specialists **Restaurante Granditalia** on Carrera 2, No 8–19 (✆ 665 6326). Reviews of the lobster dishes at the **Nautilus Restaurante** on Carrera 2, No 9–145 (✆ 665 3964), are consistently good.

ENTERTAINMENT AND NIGHTLIFE In Cartagena music is everywhere, from the blaring radios of public transport and car stereos to the booming sound systems in

11

bars, restaurants and even offices. Latin music dominates the local music scene, from champeta and vallenato to Latin rock and reggaetón. The retro salsa of the 1970s and '80s with its heroes like Hector Lavoe, Celia Cruz, Willie Colón, Ruben Blades and local lad Joe Arroyo is much adored. Cartagena's touristy nightspots are clustered around El Centro and Bocagrande with the bars on Avenida del Arsenal in Getsemaní at the heart of the backpacker scene. For *real* local nightlife check out the salsa bars and watering holes near Castellano – an area the locals refer to as Avenida de la Rumba (Party Avenue). A taxi from El Centro will cost 4,000 COP, or catch a bus for 500 COP. Nightly chiva tours are popular with both Colombian and foreign tourists and include live music, unlimited rum and Coca-Cola, some snacks, a stop at Las Bóvedas, and free entry and a complimentary drink at the La Escollera disco in Bocagrande. At the time of writing Cartagena's best gay clubs are centred on Centro Calle del Porvenir and Centro Calle de la Soledad; visit www.guiagaycolombia.com/cartagena.

SHOPPING Cartagena has a sophisticated mix of small craft shops, antique stores and stylish boutiques. Elegant jewellery stores boast dazzling displays of emeralds while exclusive outlets offer Silvia Tcherassi creations that have graced the runways of Milan, Paris and New York. Las Bóvedas in the centre of the walled city stocks the biggest range of handicrafts and souvenirs, including Costeña dolls or Guajiran hammocks. Makeshift markets can be found all over Cartagena, especially in the Tourist Zone and the Plaza de Santo Domingo. A growing number of antique shops (many American-owned) have made Cartagena a popular place for collectibles. Try the Anticuario Cartagena de Indias (↘ *664 971*), Anticuario El Arcón (↘ *664 5304*), La Ruta de las Indias (↘ *664 9960*) and Anticuario de Lupita (↘ *660 1067*).

OTHER PRACTICALITIES

Costs According to government statistical agency DANE, Cartagena is the most expensive city in Colombia, followed by Manizales and Villavicencio. Accommodation, food and tours are all significantly higher in price than in other areas – a consideration for those travelling on a tight budget. However, low-cost and efficient public transportation renders car hire unnecessary. Avoid the most touristy areas where prices are heavily inflated and everyone has something to sell for cheaper eats and less expense.

Internet, post and telephone Many of Colombia's numerous **internet cafés** are open early til late seven days a week. Centro Uno contains half a dozen places

---

CARTAGENA'S CHAMPEDUROS

Dirty-dancing champeta is Cartagena's most popular street music: a gutsy, sleazy rhythm born out of African beats. Musicians would lay down tracks at a rudimentary studio in Bazurto market. It was a rudimentary set-up, with local artists paid 10,000 COP per song. Within hours the tapes had been passed round Cartagena's bus drivers. Copies were bootlegged. Lyrics were learned. And the latest hot champeta hit was on the lips of every working-class *champeduro* citywide. Once considered scandalous and outlawed by Church elders, champeta caused some disapproving parents to seek police intervention such was the lyric content. Today champeta is a more mainstream musical style but retains its earthy origins. In 2005, celebrated local champeta star John Gutiérrez Cassiani (aka 'El Johnky') was shot in gang violence. More than 8,000 dancing fans joined his funeral procession in a moving tribute that brought the streets of Cartagena to a standstill.

With its showbiz glamour, glitzy looks and big-screen presence it is little wonder Cartagena is a film star: a city that has many years of movie credits under its belt. OK, the Cartagena-based story of *Romancing the Stone* starring Michael Douglas was actually filmed in Veracruz, Mexico, but the film *La Quemada*, better known under the Brazilian title *Queimada* or the English translation *Burn*, put Cartagena on the cinematic map. Since then it has made several cameo appearances in films, documentaries and travelogues. However, when Gabriel García Márquez finally agreed to bring his Cartagena-set romantic novel *Love in the Time of Cholera* to Hollywood, Cartagena became an A-lister overnight. Producer Scott Steindorff brought screenplay writer Ronald Harwood (*The Pianist*), British director Mike Newell (*Four Weddings and a Funeral, Mona Lisa Smile, Harry Potter and the Goblet of Fire*) and Oscar-nominated actors Javier Bardem and Giovanna Mezzogiorno to film in the city – to the jubilation of Cartageneros. Past movie productions have seen Robert de Niro, Marlon Brando, Jean Seberg and Klaus Kinski work in Cartagena. During the filming of *Burn*, Italian actor Salvo Basile (*Once Upon a Time in the West* and *Chronicle of a Death Foretold*) liked Cartagena so much, he bought a house there and became a permanent resident.

alone, with a cluster opposite the Hotel Capilla del Mar in the Tourist Zone and lots in the streets around El Centro. Try the Café Internet (✆ *664 3003*) on Calle Roman No 32–03, Micronet (✆ *664 8409*) on Calle de la Estrella No 4–47 and Intranet (✆ *660 0005*) on Avenida Daniel Lemaitre. Visitors staying longer term can take advantage of Cartagena's pre-paid wireless service (*www.davilate.com*).

Numerous **payphones** can be found throughout the city and most internet cafés place international calls.

The city's **Adpost** (✆ *664 3173;* ⏲ *08.00–18.00, closed noon–14.00*) office is located on Avenida Concolón. If sending mail to a local address, pay a bit more and use a courier service to ensure its safe arrival. International post is fine.

Medical services Medical services are in good supply in Cartagena with two of the best healthcare centres found at the Hospital Bocagrande (✆ *665 5270/0873/5759*) and Hospital Naval de Cartagena (✆ *665 5360/61/62/63/64*).

Money Head to the historic centre for the largest concentration of *casas de cambio* in and around Plaza de los Coches and to Avenida Venezuela for Cartagena's numerous banks, including Davivienda, Bancolombia and Banco Colombiano – all have ATMs. Unlike other South American countries, there is no money-changing black market so do not be tempted to take up any 'great deals' offered on the street. This is almost certainly a scam involving fake bills or is a ploy to snatch your wallet. Some of Cartagena's larger businesses accept US dollars, but offer a poor rate of exchange.

Safety Cartagena has not been a violent city by tradition but it does have its seedy side – and with many locals earning around 5,000 COP a day the threat of petty theft is real. Over 60% of the population live below the poverty line with unemployment running at almost 20% – statistics that serve as a reminder to keep valuables out of the public glare. Muggings have been reported on the walls, Las Murallas, at night and the road from the Convento de la Popa to Cartagena should not be walked at any time of day or night – catch a cab.

In recent years, counterfeit Colombian currency has been a problem in Cartagena. Fakes tend to be passed off in taxis or dimly lit bars – check that yours

The Atlantic Coast CARTAGENA

11

has a watermark and a metallic thread running through. Coins are also counterfeited, especially the 1,000 COP. These lead fakes are checked by hurling them on the pavement – if they don't bounce you've got a nickel-plated dud.

Street hawkers and hustlers can be an annoyance in Cartagena but generally back off when proffered a firm *'No gracias'*. Propositions centre on all manner of products and services, from island tours and sunhats for sale to uncut cocaine (*perico*) and money-changing at so-called fantastic rates. Be wary of pushy vendors waving T-shirts in your face – this is often a distraction ploy to allow an accomplice to relieve you of a handbag or camera.

Like most Colombian cities, Cartagena has a criminal underbelly, although according to a report by the Centro de Observación Social y Seguimiento del Delito en el Distrito de Cartagena (COSED) this is largely contained. Its murder rate is lower than many Latin American cities with homicides concentrated in Cartagena's poorest suburbs. At the time of writing there have been no reported violent incidents involving foreign visitors, with just two drug-related arrests since 1996, both relating to Italian citizens.

WHAT TO SEE AND DO Cartagena's prime attraction is its beautiful *centro histórico*, comprising Calamarí, San Diego, La Matuna and Getsemaní. This large old city is packed with magnificent colonial architecture, beautiful churches, attractive plazas, mansion houses and cobblestone streets and forms one of the finest colonial cities in the Americas. Overhanging balconies draped in bougainvillea offer both colonial (wooden) and republican (stucco) styles. Vast leafy courtyards shaded by palm trees lie behind grand archways. Fetching monuments, resplendent towers and Baroque façades sit against ochre-coloured walls and houses of bubblegum pink. The following list details just some of the many gems to take in during a walk around town.

Las Murallas Construction of these thick stone walls began towards the end of the 16th century, after the city was subjected to a particularly costly attack by Francis Drake. Due to pirate battles and storm damage the project took two centuries to complete. The walls were finally finished in 1796, just 25 years before the Spanish were eventually overthrown. Today Las Murallas remain in remarkably good condition with walkways that offer some breathtaking views. Some of the oldest sections of the walls date back to 1616 and contain cannons from a later date.

Puerta del Reloj (Clock Gate) This fine butterscotch-coloured tower is much photographed and signifies the entrance to the inner part of the walled city, Calamarí. Comprising three arched doorways, the central entrance once had a drawbridge that connected to Getsemaní. The outer doors were used as an armoury and a small chapel. Today the entrance houses a small booth selling maps for walking routes around the city. There is also an eclectic collection of stalls selling antique books and bric-a-brac. A four-sided clock and republican-style tower were added in 1888. The Puerta del Reloj was originally known as the Boca del Puente.

Plaza de los Coches Cartagena's infamous slave market was once known as the Plaza de la Yerba, but today this triangular-shaped courtyard has a statue of the city's founder, Pedro de Heredia at its core. An L-shaped collection of shops, restaurants and bars are housed in some handsome balconied houses as well as El Portal de los Dulces, a string of candy stalls.

Plaza de la Aduana A painstaking restoration has brought the old Royal Customs House back to its former glory and it now serves as Cartagena's City Hall. As the largest and oldest of the Old Town's plazas it was used for ceremonial events and as a military parade ground. A statue of Christopher Columbus takes pride of place in the centre surrounded by a plethora of banks with ATMs.

Plaza de San Pedro Claver This small rose-coloured tree-scattered tiled square is home to the **Museum of Modern Art** (📞 *664 5815*; 🕐 *09.00–19.00 Mon–Fri, closed noon–15.00, 10.00–13.00 Sat; admission 1,000 COP*), a prestigious gallery with three sections containing the works of many avant-garde Colombian artists, including Cartagena-born Alejandro Obregón. An array of interesting wrought-iron sculptures outside the museum depicts traditional local trades. They were created by Eduardo Carmona and form a permanent display. Another dominant attraction is the **Convento de San Pedro Claver** (📞 *664 4991*; 🕐 *08.00–17.00 Mon–Sat, 08.00–16.00 Sun; admission 4,000 COP*), formerly San Ignacio de Loyola, a Jesuit convent that dates back to the early 17th century and was renamed in honour of Spanish monk Pedro Claver (1590–1654). He took his vows aged 22, writing that he wished to 'do God's service, as if I were a slave'. He was ordained by Cartagena's bishop in 1616 at the age of 35 and worked with Father Sandoval, author of the book *Salvation and Catechizing the Negroes*. Together they ministered to the slaves at the slave markets where Claver was appalled by the treatment they received. On 3 April 1622 he wrote in his diary: 'Pedro Claver, slave of the slaves forever. He worked ceaselessly to care for the many unkempt, starved, diseased and frightened men, women and children that arrived by ship each day.' Over 40 years Claver baptised 300,000 slaves ignoring all pleas to slow down. In his latter years he suffered from a degenerative disease that slowly rendered him bedridden. After his death, he was beatified in 1850, and canonised a saint by Pope Leo XII in 1888. Today the convent's padre is an excellent source of information on the life of Pedro Claver. Contact Father Tulio Aristizabal (✉ *tari39@hotmail.com*).

Part of the cloisters is open to visitors in this monumental three-storey building where a collection of graphic paintings tell the story of Claver's work with the slaves. In an adjoining courtyard a sundial commemorating the Centenary of Independence can be seen topped by a small 12ft cannon. In 2001, a 2m statue of San Pedro helping an Angolan slave created by Colombian sculptor Enrique Grau was unveiled in front of the cloister. It has been set at ground level to enable it to be accessible to people on the street, just as San Pedro was in real life.

Next door, the **Iglesia de San Pedro Claver** (📞 *664 7256*; 🕐 *06.45–07.15 Mon–Sat, 10.00–19.00 Sun*) was completed in the early 18th century and boasts some magnificent stained-glass windows. The remains of the body of Cartagena's 'Slave of the Slaves' and 'Apostle of the Blacks', Pedro Claver, are housed in a glass coffin under the altar.

On Calle San Juan de Dio, the **Museo Naval del Caribe** (📞 *664 7381*; 🕐 *09.00–19.00 daily; admission 3,000 COP*) opened in 1992 to commemorate the 500th anniversary of Columbus's discovery of the New World. A collection of models depicts ancient ships and maritime Cartagena with numerous historic artefacts relating to the Colombian navy.

Some of the city's finest colonial buildings flank the pretty **Plaza de Bolívar** with a statue of Simón Bolívar at its midst. Formerly known as the Plaza de Inquisición, the Plaza de Mayor and the Plaza de Catedral, it is a popular gathering point as numerous lively restaurants, street musicians, jugglers and mime artists are found in the surrounding streets. The park is also frequented by groups of locals playing draughts, dominoes and cards amidst shoeshiners, scattered pigeons and swaying palms.

Opposite the park, a statuesque white-washed building with a grand stone entrance houses the **Museo Histórico Cartagena** (🕐 *08.00–16.00 daily, closed* *noon–14.00; admission 3,000 COP).* Dating back to 1738 it boasts some particularly attractive balconies and contains an interesting array of historical documents and archaeological finds.

Witness fiercely fought board-game battles at Cartagena's **Liga de Ajedres** (Chess League) housed in an open-sided building on the corner of Plaza Bolívar. A dozen or so tables and chairs have been set up in a beautiful colonial building with a large stone arch – just pop in.

One of Cartagena's most beautiful buildings, the **Palacío de la Inquisición** (✆ 664 4113; ✆09.00–19.00 daily; admission 3,500 COP) is worth a visit for its magnificent entrance hall alone. Once a Punishment Tribunal of the Holy Office, it primarily dealt with crimes relating to blasphemy and black magic. Culprits were anyone the Church viewed as heretic and the death sentence was issued on guilt with a resulting *auto-da-fé*. Around 800 people were condemned to death and executed between 1776 and 1821 and today a museum contains numerous instruments of torture. A small, barred window is the place where sentences handed down by the tribunal were announced to the public outside.

Cartagena's gold museum the **Museo del Oro y Arqueología** (✆ 660 0778/0808; ✆10.00–18.00 (closed 13.00–14.00) Tue–Fri, 10.00–17.00 (closed 13.00–14.00) Sat; free admission) contains a fine selection of riches from the Sinú tribes of the region. There is also a replica of a traditional Indian dwelling complete with household tools and utensils.

Although the construction of the plaza's **Catedral** began in 1575 the building work was partially destroyed in 1586 when the site was hit by cannons fired by Francis Drake. Work resumed in 1598 but was not finally completed until 1612 with further alterations made between 1912 and 1923 when it was given a terracotta-coloured stucco overhaul. A simple interior contains an 18th-century altar-ledge worked in gold leaf.

On the Calle de Santo Domingo the late 16th-century **Iglesia de Santo Domingo** is little changed from colonial days and is the oldest church in the city. Architecturally, it has some quirky characteristics born out of construction imperfections. The bell tower is decidedly skewed but local legend has it this was the work of the devil, who knocked it in a fit of pique.

Facing the small Parque de Fernandez de Madrid, the **Iglesia de Santo Toribio de Mongrovejo** on Calle del Sargento Mayor is relatively small. The church was built between 1666 and 1732 and boasts some fine Mudejar panelling and a pretty wooden altar covered with gold ornamentation. Although the building was hit by a cannonball during Vernon's assault on the city there were no casualties – despite it smashing through a window during a packed service. Today the ball is displayed in a glass container on the wall.

The 23 dungeons of the city walls, **Las Bóvedas**, were built between 1792 and 1796 in stone 15m thick. During the republican era they were used as a prison. Today they form a colourful succession of bunting-adorned handicraft stores, boutiques and tourist shops.

Just outside of Las Bóvedas in the Cabrero district, the historic green-and-white **Casa de Rafael Núñez** (✆ 664 5305; ✆08.00–18.00 daily, closed noon–14.00; admission 3,500 COP) was the former home of the Colombian president, lawyer and poet. Cartagena-born Rafael Núñez was also the celebrated composer of Colombia's national anthem, creator of the Banco Nacional and mastermind of its constitution – and the only president of Colombia to be elected four times. Núñez was born in 1825, and was an elected congressman by 1853. He spent some time in Europe as a consul in Liverpool and Le Havre before returning to Colombia in 1875. This grand, old two-storey wooden mansion in Antillean Caribbean style built in 1858 was home to Núñez for 17 years. He died in Cartagena on the 18

September 1894 and is buried alongside his wife Soledad in the Ermita de Cabrero, a small red-and-white church opposite his home. Today the property houses a museum commemorating his life, poetry and his political thoughts. It contains photos, documents relating to the Delegates Council of 1886 (the basis of the Colombian Constitution), his will and testament and a memorial poem by his contemporary Rúben Dario, entitled 'Qué Se Je?' (Who Am I?). His famous motto is now painted above the doorway of the museum: 'Regeneration or Catastrophe' could not have been more apt, even with the benefit of hindsight.

Sculptor Eladio Gil's **Monumento a la India Catalina** was erected in 1974 to commemorate its pre-colonial past. It's located at the entrance to the Old Town in tribute to the Carib Indians, the indigenous group that inhabited the region before the arrival of the Spanish. This lovely bronze statue depicts the beautiful Indian translator who worked with Pedro de Heredia, a courageous warrior called Catalina. It stands by Puente de Chambacu in the middle of the traffic island. Smaller versions of this statue are coveted as distinguished awards presented during the annual Cartagena International Film and TV Festival held in March.

In the Getsemaní district in the northeast of the Old Quarter, the **Iglesia de Santísima Trinidad** (Church of the Holy Trinity) was built in the second half of the 17th century but retains very little original character having been modified without preserving its architectural style. A church-built school to the rear of the building was established to educate the poor and is still in use today.

To the east of the Holy Trinity, the **Iglesia de la Santa Orden** has an interesting wooden ceiling with ornate carved cross-pieces in the central vault. Legend has it that heroic Don Blas de Lezo is interred here.

North of Santa Orden Church is the leafy **Parque del Centenario** (*http://www.cartagenainfo.net/image/fotos/parquecentenario.jpg*) which was built to celebrate independence in 1912 and received an impressive makeover in 2006. However, despite being popular with families with its grassy areas, fountains, statutes and ponds, it's also a hangout for bums, hookers and crack-heads – so be vigilant. It's just a few minutes walk northwest of the Clock Gate.

To the west of Parque del Centenario, the **Iglesia de San Roque** was created in 1674 to celebrate the life of a saint who cared for plague victims. Legend has it Saint Roque was struck by the disease himself and so retreated to the wilderness to die. There he was befriended by a dog that brought him scraps of food and was able to drink water that rose up from the soil. He recovered after the appearance of an angel and was able to continue his work.

No visit to Cartagena is complete without a visit to **Castillo de San Félipe de Barajas** (℡ *656 0590/666 4790;* ⏰*08.00–18.00 daily; admission 6,000 COP*) on Avenida Arévalo, Colombia's largest and most impregnable colonial fort tower. Set on a 40m hill, east of the historic centre, it is the strongest fortress ever built by the Spanish in the colonies. The original, smaller fort was built between 1639 and 1657, but in 1762 extensive rebuilding work led by engineer Antonio de Arévalo

HORN OF PLENTY

Visitors to Castillo de San Félipe de Barajas should look out for an entrepreneurial trumpet player at the entrance of the fort. As tourists pass he guesses their nationality and heralds them in with a rousing rendition of their very own national anthem – the reward is a 1,000 COP tip. Of course, he occasionally gets it wrong but has become highly skilled at distinguishing Costa Ricans and Peruvians from Panamanians and Nicaraguans – but scratches his head when a gringo comes to town.

11

enlarged it considerably to cover the entire hilltop. A matrix of complex underground tunnels enabled an efficient distribution of supplies. They were built to maximise even the smallest sound to allow approaching troops in the distance to be clearly heard in the fort. Today, a guided walk through these claustrophobic conduits is the highlight of a visit – and does much to explain why despite many attempts this powerful bastion was never taken by pirates. Cannons and an old military hospital also form part of this vast site.

Los Zapatos Viejos (Old Shoes Monument) was built in honour of Luis Carlos Lopez (1883–1950), a famous satirical Cartagena-born poet and writer nicknamed 'One-eyed Lopez'. Declaring that he loved Cartagena 'as much as he loves his own shoes' in a poem, Lopez was honoured after his death by his friends and literary contemporaries with Los Zapatos Viejos, located at the back of the San Félipe Fort.

As one of Cartagena's first battle defences, the **Fuerte de San Sebastián el Pastelillo** is located at the western end of Isla Manga. Small and built in the 16th century, today there isn't much to look at. It is the home of the Club de Pesca marina and is just a short walk from Getsemaní.

Perched on a 150m hill known as La Popa (the Stern), it is thought to resemble the back end of a ship. The 400-year-old **Convento de la Popa** (\ *666 2331; ☉09.00–17.00, admission 5,000 COP*) lies about 1.5km from Castillo de San Félipe de Barajas. Officially named Nuestra Señora de la Candelaría, the convent was founded in 1607 by the Augustine order. It contains a beautiful image of La Virgen de la Candelaría, Cartagena's patroness, in the chapel. Superb views abound from this pleasant spot, but don't be tempted to walk here from the city as the road is dangerous – take a taxi (4,000 COP).

The **Fuerte de San Fernando** and the **Batería de San José** guard the entrance to the Bahía de Cartagena through the Bocachica Strait. The Spanish strung a heavy chain between them to further strengthen defences. There used to be a second gateway to the bay, Bocagrande. After Vernon's attack is was blocked to ensure it was impassable – and it remains so today. Built between 1753 and 1760, the fortress is only accessible by boat, but much of the original structure can still be seen. Tours cost 19,000 COP including lunch and admission. Boats leave daily from the Muelle Turístico at around 09.00 and return in the afternoon.

FESTIVALS AND EVENTS

Feria Taurina *(Jan; www.cartagenataurina.com)* The first week of the year hails the start of the bullfighting season with a crowd-packed calendar of local and international matadors at the bullring on Aveninda Pedro de Heredia.

Festival Internacional de Música *(Jan; www.cartagenamusicfestival.com)* Cartagena's long-standing celebration of classical music attracts musicians from all over the world with a host of performances and gala concerts citywide.

The Hay Festival *(Jan; \ (UK): 01497 822 620; f (UK): 01497 821 066; www.hayfestival.com)* Colombia's Hay Festival has captured the hearts and minds of Cartagena, attracting a high pedigree of Latin American literary greats and some high-profile international artists, including Gabriel García Márquez and Hanif Kureishi.

Festival Internacional de Cine *(Mar; www.festicinecartagena.org)* The oldest film festival of the continent and the biggest cinematic event in Colombia, this glittering showcase of around 60 feature films include movies competing for the India Catalina Awards.

Carnaval de Cartagena (*Nov; www.carnavalcartagena.com*) This high-tempo week-long fiesta celebrates Cartagena's Independence Day (11 November) with an array of street processions, parties, parades and marching bands. The Reinado Nacional de Belleza – Colombia's national beauty pageant – paralyses the city. Although tickets to the judging and testimonial dinners sell out months in advance, the locals head to bars to watch it live on television.

AROUND CARTAGENA

ARCHIPELAGO NUESTRA SEÑORA DEL ROSARIO Cartagena's surrounding islands, the Archipelago Nuestra Señora del Rosario, sit amongst coral reefs and warm turquoise waters that make up the Parque Nacional Natural Corales del Rosario y San Bernardo 35km southwest of the city. Extending over 100ha, the islands were once inhabited by Caribe Indians who were slowly driven to the mainland after sustained attacks from pirates *en route* to test Cartagena's defences. The region contains important marine grasses, 113 plankton species, hundreds of crustaceans, 215 species of fish, 5 mangrove species, dozens of migrating seabirds, many seaweeds, 197 mollusc species and wildlife. Despite widespread erosion, many of the region's 52 coral species have been successfully spawned in an ongoing recovery effort. Some 30 coralline islands range in size with the largest containing coastal lagoons, tourist facilities and dry tropical forests. As the name suggests, Isla Grande is the archipelago's biggest island at around 200ha. A forested walking trail leads to a lagoon and sandy beach. Isla del Rosario is also popular with day trippers with the nearby Isla de San Martín de Pajarales home to a small aquarium containing sharks, turtles, rays and dolphins. Isla de Barú, which forms a part of the archipelago, is in fact a jutting spit of mainland 20km from the city. It offers one of the finest beaches around Cartagena with coral reefs close to the shore – so be sure to pack snorkel gear. Most tour boats take in three or four islands. Since the 1970s, many of the smaller atolls have been snapped up for private ownership. Even Colombia's most infamous drug lord, Pablo Escobar, got into the act, ploughing his ill-gotten gains into real estate in this most scenic spot. Today this is home to some of Colombia's more exclusive second homes with many islets home to a single luxury pad.

Getting there and around Tour boats depart year-round from Cartagena's Muelle Turístico at around 08.00 and return late afternoon. Choose from large, slow-moving cruisers that accommodate up to 150 passengers or smaller speedboats that seat fewer than a dozen – there are pros and cons for each. However, most boats follow a similar route past the old Spanish forts and out to Isla Grande, Isla del Rosario, Isla de San Martín de Pajarales and Isla de Barú. Expect to pay between 35,000–40,000 COP including lunch but allow an additional 20,000 for extras, such as drinks and snacks, entrance to the national park (3,800 COP), tickets for the aquarium (10,000 COP) and admission to the fort (4,000 COP). A Sunday morning bus departs early from Cartagena to the beach on the tip of Isla de Barú.

Where to stay and eat Staying overnight on the archipelago is becoming increasingly popular with a growing number of accommodation options springing up. These range from dirt-cheap hammocks on the beach and rustic camping to renting a house or booking a room in a plush boutique hotel. Many places are run by Europeans who offer boat tours, snorkelling trips and transfers from the mainland.

⌂ **Hotel Agua** (6 cabañas) Isla Barú; ☎ 664 9479; f 664 9431; e info@hotelagua.com.co; www.hotelagua.com.co. This striking boutique hotel opened in 2006 and offers the most upscale accommodation on the islands, with trendy open lounges in contemporary style. A gorgeous bar area has

11

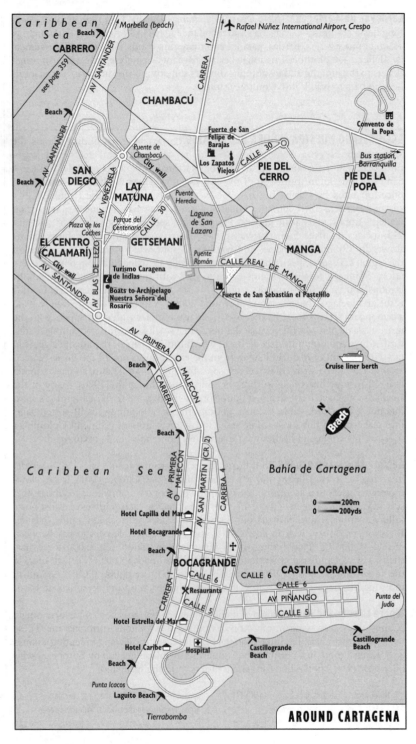

Caribbean
Sea

CABRERO

Beach

Marbella (beach)

Rafael Núñez International Airport, Crespo

CARRERA 17

AV SANTANDER

see page 359

CHAMBACÚ

Beach

Convento de
la Popa

Fuerte de San
Felipe de
Barajas

CALLE 30

Bus station,
Barranquilla

AV SANTANDER

SAN
DIEGO

Puente de
Chambacú

City wall

Los Zapatos
Viejos

PIE DEL
CERRO

PIE DE LA
POPA

Beach

AV VENEZUELA

CALLE 30

LAT
MATUNA

Puente
Heredia

Laguna
de San
Lazaro

MANGA

Plaza de los
Coches

Parque del
Centenario

AV BLAS DE LEZO

EL CENTRO
(CALAMARÍ)

GETSEMANÍ

Puente
Román

CALLE REAL DE MANGA

City wall

AV SANTANDER

Turismo Caragena
de Indias

Boats to Archipelago
Nuestra Señora del
Rosario

Fuerte de San Sebastián el Pastelillo

AV PRIMERA O MALECÓN

Beach

CARRERA 1

Cruise liner berth

N
Bradt

Beach

Caribbean   Sea

AV PRIMERA O MALECÓN

AV SAN MARTIN (CR 2)

CARRERA 4

Bahía de Cartagena

0 ——— 200m
0 ——— 200yds

Hotel Capilla del Mar

Hotel Bocagrande

Beach

BOCAGRANDE

CASTILLOGRANDE

CALLE 6

CALLE 6

CALLE 6

CARRERA 1

Resaurants

CALLE 5

AV PIÑANGO

Punta del
Judio

CALLE 5

Hotel Estrella del Mar

Hotel Caribe

Hospital

Castillogrande
Beach

Castillogrande
Beach

Beach

Punta Icacos

Laguito Beach

Tierrabomba

AROUND CARTAGENA

inlaid-pebble flooring, rattan swinging chairs, coralline pillars & oversized cushions. Gentle ambient mood-music plays from an upper terrace where wooden loungers look out onto open sea & palms. Staff in crisp, white uniforms jump to attention under slowly whirring ceiling fans amidst chic décor. Accommodation at the Agua comprises 6 luxurious cabañas that sit in a staggered layout on a terraced slope and boast private pools. Room rates vary throughout the year but are not cheap – with an additional 180,000 COP on top for the transfers to and from Cartagena.

🏠 **Campamento Wittenberg** Isla de Barú; ✆ 311 615. Run by affable Frenchman Gilbert, this place is a backpacker favourite with hammocks under a simple thatched roof & mosquito nets. He picks up once a week from Casa Viena in Cartagena and charges 6,000 COP a night plus 12,000 COP for the transfer. Meals are extra. $

🏠 **La Sirena** Isla de Barú; ✆ 310 661 1964. At the time of writing the future of this long-established bed-for-the-night is unsure, amidst rumours of a government land-grab. It's run by Ángel González Camargo & his wife Carmen & offers rustic rooms & simple seafood meals. $

🏠 **Hotel Kokomo** Isla Grande; ✆ 673 4072; e hotelkokomo@hotmail.com. This Norwegian-run budget set-up offers cabañas and hammocks as well as food. It also rents out snorkel gear and sells drinks and snacks.

LA BOQUILLA For a charming fishing village and exquisite fresh seafood take time to visit La Boquilla, 7km north of Cartagena where fishermen work with *atarrayas* (round fishing nets) on the sand. Head to a collection of wood-and-thatch huts on the beach for ice-cold beers and delicious fish-and-rice dishes – this is also where locals sell handicrafts and wares. La Boquilla is a great place to hang out, enjoy a boat trip or take a canoe tour out through the mangroves amidst marine birds, and is best visited at weekends. The countryside around the village is a popular birding destination in the months of September to April when an influx of North American waders arrive. Look out for Wilson's plover; red knot, gull-billed and large-billed terns are regular. Also look for grey kingbird, lesser kiskadee, cattle tyrant, Wilson's phalarope, collared plover, least and semi-palmated sandpipers, solitary sandpiper and semi-palmated plover, black, least, brown-throated parakeet, Louisiana and little blue herons, reddish egret and ringed kingfisher.

Getting there and around Catch one of many frequent buses that run to La Boquilla from the monument of India Catalina in central Cartagena – they are clearly signed (800 COP, 30 minutes).

🏠 **Where to stay and eat**

✗ **Restaurante y Hospedaje Marlene** El Paraíso; ✆ 300 831 5704. For friendly, family-run kitchens & accommodation this charming little beachside restaurant is well worth a visit. A simple palm-thatched open-fronted diner is hung with all manner of fishing paraphernalia, from nets to ropes & buoys. A menu offers a wide range of shellfish & fish dishes, from *pargo rojo* (red snapper) & *langostinos al ajillo* (garlic shell-on prawns) to *arroz de marisco* (seafood rice) & the house speciality *bandeja marisco* – a man-sized plate of mixed seafood. Chairs, tents & hammocks are offered free of charge to anyone that orders a decent meal. The owners also provide guided tours out to the mangrove swamps, passing through the túnel del amor (tunnel of love) & the tunnel of happiness (túnel de la felicidad) to Punta Icaco – all areas used as a film set for movie-makers shooting the García Márquez film

VOLCÁN DE LODO EL TOTUMO The crater of this 15m-high volcano is full of warm mud as thick as cappuccino and offers a therapeutic dip to visitors prepared to yield to this nutrient-rich natural bath. Located about 52km northeast of Cartagena, Volcán de Lodo El Totumo is the subject of considerable myth and legend. The locals swear that it once spewed fire, lava and ash but that this was considered to be the work of the devil by a priest. He sprinkled it frequently with holy water and it slowly extinguished, drowning the devil in mud. A makeshift wooden banister leads the way to the top of the volcano. Visitors can bathe from dawn til dusk for 1,000 COP with a neighbouring lagoon the perfect place for a post-dip clean-up. Don't be surprised if local villagers turn up – a massage is often part of the deal.

Getting there and around A growing number of tour companies are including the Volcán de Lodo El Totumo in their packages, so ask around. To visit independently, catch the hourly bus from Cartagena's main terminal bound for Galerazamba but ask the driver to drop you off at Lomita Arena (3,000 COP, 1½ hours). The volcano is a 3.5km walk (45 minutes). Be sure to be back at Lomita Arena by 16.00 to catch the last bus back.

JARDÍN BONTÁNICO DE GUILLERMO PIÑERES This pleasant 8ha garden is planted with 250 coastal species of flora, including umpteen palms and grasses. Located 15km southwest of Cartagena on the outer edges of the city of Turbaco, it makes a nice half-day detour by bus – pick up the Turbaco service that passes the Castillo de San Félipe frequently (1,500 COP, 45 minutes) and ask the driver to drop you off; the turn-off is a 20-minute walk from the park entrance.

MOMPÓX *Telephone code: 5*

As they sailed down to the coast the river had grown more vast and solemn, like a swamp with no beginning or end, and the heat was so dense you could touch it with your hands.

The General and his Labyrinth (1990) Gabriel García Marquez

An isolated colonial country town that was the setting for Gabriel García Márquez's literary classic *Chronicle of a Death Foretold*, Mompóx (also spelt Mompós) is an old-time settlement bearing much beauty from the past. Located 249km southeast of Cartagena amidst swampy rivers and thick vegetation, the city has all the hallmarks of remoteness. Much of its colonial character (*arquitectura Mompóxina*) remains unchanged from times gone by with a notable absence of many of the modern trappings of the 'outside world'. Founded in 1537 by Don Alonso de Heredia on the eastern branch of the Río Magdalena, Mompóx hasn't always been a sleepy backwater relic. Up until the 20th century, it was the one of Colombia's most important commercial hubs as a port for the transportation of goods upriver into the country's interior. Mompóx even established a royal mint and became famous for its many goldsmiths. However, once the silt-laden Río Magdalena altered its course Mompóx was left high and dry: a city isolated and much decreased in importance. Today it relies on a fledgling tourism industry hampered by the perils of isolation along with fishing and some commerce generated by raising cattle. The name Mompóx comes from the last cacique (Indian chief) of the Kimbay tribe that populated the region before the arrival of the Spanish. In 1812, Simón Bolívar gathered over 400 recruits to form the basis of an army to liberate Caracas, earning it the title Ciudad Valerosa, or Courageous City. UNESCO declared the city a World Heritage Site in 1995 on account of its historic splendour. Mompóx is famous throughout Colombia as the home town of singer Sonia Bazanta Vides, better known as Totó la Mompóxina (see box, page 375). At the time of writing, the mayor is investing heavily in promoting tourism, with a bridge under construction at El Banco. This will place it within easy-ish reach of the Bogotá–Santa Marta road from 2009 – and is certain to herald the imminent arrival of hordes of tourists as Colombia's next big thing.

GETTING THERE AND AROUND A new road has also been earmarked and speculation abounds about new long-distance bus services to and from a host of Colombian

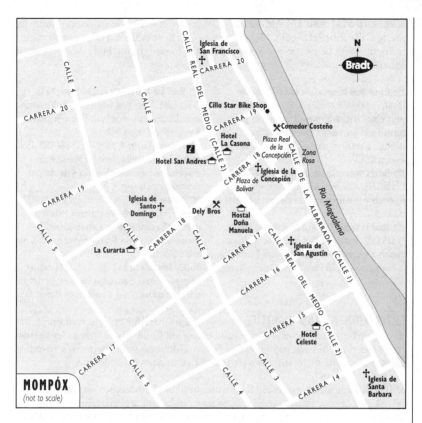

MOMPÓX
(not to scale)

cities. At present, most travellers arrive via an eight-hour bus ride from Cartagena
(30,000 COP) – it leaves at 07.30 with the return leg departing Mompóx at 06.30.
Other routes include Bogotá by bus to El Banco (80,000 COP, 17 hours) then
colectivo to Mompóx (20,000, 3 hours). For updates on Mompóx transportation
visit the tourist office (see *Tourist information* below). Apparently, it's also possible to
travel from Bogotá by bus to Magangue to catch a ferry to Bodegas to pick up a taxi
(7,000 pesos) to Mompóx (1 hour), but I have been unable to verify this.

Mompóx is easily navigable on foot and this is the best way to explore the town.
If the oppressive heat gets too much, bikes can be rented to ease the strain at
around 4,000 COP per hour – head to Cillo Star Bike Shop (✆ *684 0636*) on
Carrera 1A, No 18–81.

TOURIST INFORMATION
Ｉ Tourist office Plaza de la Libertad; ✆ 685 5738;
🕐 08.00–18.00 Mon–Fri, closed noon–14.00

Tour guides A number of local guides offer walking tours around the streets of the
colonial centre and along the riverfront. An hour's tour of Mompóx on a mototaxi
(10,000 COP) is a good way to get your bearings and learn some of the local
history. Don Ernesto, a former teacher and well-respected local, is well worth
seeking out – he resembles a living encyclopaedia and has lots of botanical
knowledge and their medicinal properties. He offers guiding and enjoys meeting
international visitors, so ask around town.

WHERE TO STAY AND EAT Almost all of the hotels in Mompóx are strung along the pretty Calle Real del Medio. Most represent excellent value and offer a good choice of rooms – but be sure to pre-book if you plan to visit during Holy Week (Semana Santa).

Hostal Doña Manuela Calle Real del Medio, No 17–41; 685 5621; e mabe642@hotmail.com. This upscale hotel is the priciest you'll find in town, but boasts a pool & restaurant. Choose from a fine collection of rooms set around 2 large plant-filled courtyards. $$
Hotel Celeste Calle Real del Medio, No 14–174; 685 5875. A charming & friendly family-run residencía with inexpensive spotlessly clean fan-cooled rooms. $$
Hotel La Casona Calle Real del Medio, No 18–58; 685 5307. Another excellent inexpensive option with comfortable, clean & well-appointed rooms & some nice communal areas – plus a fast, efficient laundry service. $$

Hotel San Andrés Calle Real del Medio, No 18–23; 685 5886. A very good budget choice with common areas, laundry & a nice courtyard filled with parakeets, & well-equipped rooms. $$
La Cuarta Carrera 4, No 18–57; 684 6127. This modern little shoestring option has both AC & fan-cooled rooms. Expect friendly service & the cheapest accommodation in town. $$
Comedor Costeño Calle de la Albarada, No 18–45; 685 5263; 05..30–late afternoon. Head to the riverfront for some of the cheapest restaurants in Mompóx with nice views & decent *bocachico* fish-&-rice meals. $$
Dely Bros Calle 18, No 2–37; 685 5644. Expect inexpensive chicken at this simple food joint with a choice of inside & outdoor seating & a good range of sodas. $$

ENTERTAINMENT AND NIGHTLIFE Mompóx has a handful of local watering holes that serve beer until dawn – and beyond. Most are found on the streets leading off from the plaza outside the Iglesia de Santo Domingo with the town's so-called Zona Rosa along the riverfront a pleasant place to enjoy a sundowner.

SHOPPING For locally produced fruit wines head to ViniMompóx on Carrera 3, No 20–34, and choose from a range of flavours from banana and guayaba to orange and tamarind. You'll find stunning filigree work at a number of silver workshops around Calle Real del Medio and Mompóx's famous wooden rocking chairs are also in good supply.

WHAT TO SEE By far the best way to discover the delights of Mompóx is to wander aimlessly through this sleepy town, passing wrought-iron grilles, clay-tiled roofs, whitewashed walls, elaborate fronts, flower-shrouded balconies and pretty patios – it's a genuine journey back in time.

Mompóx has half a dozen churches of which the **Iglesia de Santa Bárbara** is one of the finest, dating back to 1630 and situated on the Plaza de Santa Bárbara. Boasting a Mudejar balcony, ornate moulding and Baroque figures, the church has an octagonal bell tower that ends in a crown-shaped dome. Others include the **Iglesia de San Francisco**, one of the oldest in Mompóx .The **Iglesia de la Concepión** is the largest local church while the **Iglesia de San Agustín** houses much of the richly gilded religious items at the heart of the Semana Santa processions.

FESTIVALS AND EVENTS
Semana Santa Mompóx honours *Semana Santa* (Holy Week) with several extraordinarily elaborate processions that bring the entire population out onto the streets on Maundy Thursday and Good Friday nights. From midday on the Thursday, the penitents leave to make a pilgrimage to all the churches and sacred sites of the town, amidst the mournful sound of trumpets and the tolling of bells. On Good Friday there are morning church services, afternoon sermons and a six-

The drums make your body vibrate and make it react in an instinctive and spontaneous manner. That is when you come out of yourself and forget everything around you. Nothing matters anymore.

Mompóx-born Totó La Mompóxina

Totó La Mompóxina was born plain Sonia Bazanta Vides in Mompóx but today boasts international acclaim. She comes from a family of five generations of musicians and as a young girl travelled from village to village, learning the rhythms and dances in the art of the *cantandoras* (traditional village singers). In 1968 she formed her first group and began to tour Colombia before playing all over the continent and eventually heading to Europe. In 1982, she accompanied Gabriel García Márquez to Stockholm to play at his Nobel Prize ceremony. In 1991, Peter Gabriel's world music organisation WOMAD invited her to take part in a number of festivals throughout the world. She recorded 'La Candela Viva' for Real World in 1992. Her musical style draws on the musical and dance traditions of the Caribbean and its mix of cultural influences, bringing a fusion of African (slave), Spanish (colonist) and South American (indigenous Indian) rhythms to the masses using musicians playing traditional instruments. Her unique sound blends drums, gaitas (flutes), brass (trumpet and bombardino), tiple (12-stringed guitar), bass and percussion to create cumbia, bullerenge, chalupa, garabato and mapale.

hour evening procession from the church of San Agustín to the church of San Francisco. Saturday sees a serenade in the church of San Francisco with a dawn procession of the Resurrected Christ. On Sunday morning, the procession of Minerva takes to the streets of Mompóx – a solemn and stately affair.

ATLÁNTICO

Colombia's third-smallest department spans just 3,388km² but is home to a population of more than 2.2 million, making it one of the most crowded at over 670 inhabitants per square kilometre. Bordered by the Caribbean Sea to the north, the Río Magdalena to the east and the Magdalena department to the west, Atlántico sits on a coastal plain earning its capital city the nickname La Arenosa (meaning the Sandy City). Almost 75% of the population live in Barranquilla, one of Colombia's most active port cities and a major industrial centre. Large-scale cotton production, sesame crops, cattle rearing and fishing remain key areas of commerce as well as fluvial and maritime transportation. The department was established in 1905, boasts great economic diversity and is strategically positioned at the mouth of one of the continent's major rivers. Barranquilla is also known as Colombia's Golden Gate (La Puerta de Oro de Colombia).

BARRANQUILLA *Telephone code: 5*

A chaotic concrete muddle, Barranquilla is proud to be home to South America's first airport, the Ernesto Cortissoz International, built in 1919. The world's second-oldest commercial airline was also founded in the city – and SCADTA (Sociedad Colombo Alemana de Transporte Aéreo, now Avianca) is still in business today. SCADTA's first aerial transportation route pioneered civil aviation with the Río Magdalena easily landed by seaplanes at almost any point. On 19 September 1921 the first scheduled service flew from Barranquilla and Girardot

11

in what today is widely regarded as the most significant date in Latin American aviation history. After Bogotá, Medellín and Cali, Barranquilla is Colombia's fourth-largest city. It is famous throughout Latin America for its wild four-day carnival. In 2003, UNESCO honoured the Carnaval de Barranquilla as a Masterpiece of the Oral and Intangible Heritage of Humanity, the only one of Colombia's most riotous festivals to have been recognised in this way. Barranquilla people are often referred to as *curramberos* (literally meaning 'party people'), a telling insight into the gregarious temperament of the city's fun-loving population. Nobel Prize-winning writer Gabriel García Márquez lived in Barranquilla during his early years as journalist. Today his old bohemian literary hangout is an artsy-chic bar containing mementoes relating to the intellectuals and philosophers who made up the Barranquilla Group (see *Nightlife and entertainment*, page 379). Colombian-Lebanese pop sensation Shakira was born and bred in the city and has an apartment in the north. A massive six-tonne statue stands in her honour outside a school helped by the singer's Fundación Pies Descalzos (Bare Feet Foundation), founded in 2001. Another famous Barranquillo is Dr César Carriazo, a home-grown ophthalmic specialist who pioneered Lasik eye surgery worldwide.

HISTORY Although no official records exist regarding the foundation of Barranquilla, the city is known to have been settled in 1629. However, modern Barranquilla was inaugurated in 1813 and it is this birth date that is commemorated citywide with gusto on 7 April each year. Barranquilla grew slowly in its early years before the city's Puerto Colombia – the nation's first port – began to handle both fluvial and sea vessels in the late 19th century. Barranquilla also welcomed large numbers of immigrants from Europe during the two world wars and a sizeable population of Middle Eastern and Asian migrants give the city a cosmopolitan cultural fusion. This ethnic mix differentiates Barranquilla from other big Colombian cities, with over half of the population of foreign descent. Gastronomic influences from Italy, Germany, China and Lebanon have fused with Hispanic traditions and Colombian cultures and makes for an interesting multi-racial mix. Unlike Medellín, Cali and Bogotá the city also has large numbers of followers of non-Catholic faiths, including Protestants, Muslims and Jews. Barranquilla is home to the largest number of synagogues in Colombia with Jews representing 1.1% of the city's population as well as kosher delicatessens and Ashkenazi and Sephardic cemeteries. The main wave of immigration took place during the Holocaust in 1944. Regardless of origin, those that hail from Barranquilla are known as *barranquilleras* or *barranquilleros*.

CLIMATE Barranquilla is dusty, hot and very humid with daytime temperatures that typically sit at around 32°C. January–February and June–July are the coolest months at around 25°C. April–June and August–November are the wettest periods with Barranquilla prone to flooding, often resulting in the loss of life. These deep fast-flowing torrents (called 'arroyos') are the result of a lack of drainage in some sectors of the city – and render many streets out of bounds after heavy rains.

GETTING THERE Some 10km south of the city, the Ernesto Cortissoz International Airport (*www.baq.aero*) serves as both a domestic and international hub. Most of Colombia's domestic carriers serve Barranquilla, including Avianca (✆ *330 2255*), ADA (✆ *334 8253*), Satena (✆ *334 8019*) and AeroRepública (✆ *368 4040*). About 1km from the southern edge of the city is Barranquilla's main bus terminal (*www.ttbaq.com.co*). A dozen buses connect with Bogotá each day (75,000 COP, 18 hours) Bucaramanga (60,000 COP, 10 hours) and Medellín (65,000, 14 hours).

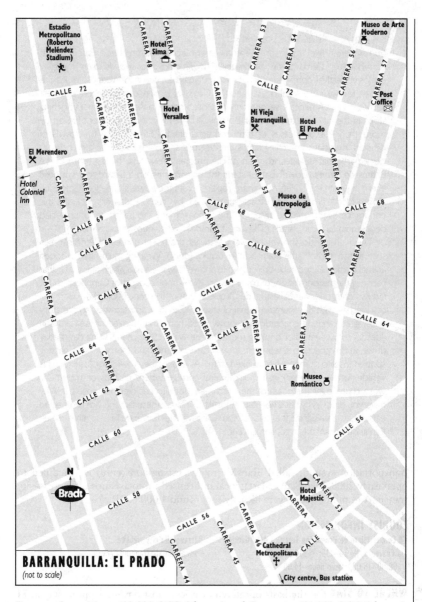

BARRANQUILLA: EL PRADO
(not to scale)

Estadio
Metropolitano
(Roberto
Meléndez
Stadium)

CARRERA 48
CARRERA 49
Hotel
Sima

CARRERA 53
CARRERA 54
CALLE 72

CARRERA 56
CARRERA 57

Museo de Arte
Moderno

Post
Coffice

CALLE 72

CARRERA 46
CARRERA 47

CARRERA 50

Hotel
Versalles

Mi Vieja
Barranquilla

Hotel
El Prado

El Merendero

CARRERA 48

CARRERA 53

Museo de
Antropología

CARRERA 56

Hotel
Colonial
Inn

CARRERA 44
CARRERA 45

CALLE 69

CALLE 68

CALLE
68

CALLE 68

CARRERA 49

CALLE 66

CARRERA 58

CARRERA 54

CARRERA 43

CALLE 66

CALLE 64

CALLE 64

CALLE 62

CARRERA 47

CALLE 62

CARRERA 50

CARRERA 53

CALLE 64

CALLE 64

CARRERA 46

CARRERA 45

CALLE 60

Museo
Romántico

CARRERA 44

CALLE 62

CALLE 60

CALLE 58

N

Bradt

CALLE 58

CARRERA 53
CARRERA 53

Hotel
Majestic

CARRERA 47

CALLE 56

CARRERA 46
CARRERA 45

CARRERA 46

CARRERA 44

CALLE 56

Cathedral
Metropolitana

CALLE 53

CARRERA 56

City centre, Bus station

Buses to Santa Marta (19,000 COP, 2 hours) and Cartagena (11,000 COP, 2 hours) leave every 15 minutes.

GETTING AROUND Barranquilla's layout is relatively simple. To the east the city is bordered by the Río Magdalena with the remaining sector looped by a bypass called Circunvalar. A grid system divides the city using calles (streets north to south) and carreras (avenues east to west) with Barranquilla's downtown area located near the river on the city's eastern limits. Most tourists spend time in the district of El Prado, one of the city's most pleasant areas about 3km to the northwest of the centre. At the time of writing Barranquilla's Bogotá-style mass

Curramberos like their pre-Lenten celebrations full-on hedonistic and at Barranquilla's Carnaval de Barranquilla (*www.carnavaldebarranquilla.org*) a truly explosive festival dominates the city for four days before Ash Wednesday. As the largest festival in Colombia, Barranquilla Carnaval is one of the biggest and best parties in Latin America – second only, the locals claim, to Río de Janeiro. Everything stops in the city to make way for Barranquilla's revelry, a riotous event fuelled by more than 100,000 cases of rum and aguardiente. Streets fill with crowds of dancers, musicians, marching bands, processions and masquerades in a round-the-clock party that deviates from an official programme amidst boozy high jinx. La Battala de Flores (Flower Battle) starts the celebrations on a Saturday, a symbolic event in which the bullets of war are replaced with the flowers of peace. Colourful, bloom-filled carriages and floats surrounded by cumbia dancers kick off this endurance event in grand style. On the Sunday, many thousands of costume-clad people join La Gran Parada (The Great Parade) as it sweeps through the city.

This high-tempo showpiece event features drumbeat dances of African origin such as the 'torito' (little bull) and the 'diablo' (devil). Wearing multi-hued wooden animal masks painted in black, red, white and yellow, it is a noisy high-spirit affair that narrates the historical story of black slavery. A 24-hour concert of Caribbean music follows on Monday at El Festival de Orquetas before the conclusion of the Carnaval on Tuesday with the figurative burial of Joselito Carnaval. Joselito was, so the story goes, a Barranquilla coach driver who worked hard and enjoyed himself only on Tuesday. However, after drinking more that he was accustomed to one day, he lay down in the coach to sleep it off. In was carnival time, and merry-makers passing spotted Joselito slumped in a drunken state. As a joke, they took poor Joselito in his vehicle to the cemetery in a mock funeral cortege where crowds of 'mourners' were crying over the death of the coachman. 'Joselito has died, oh! Joselito! Why have you died? Why have you left us, Joselito?' Today these laments are re-enacted each year and signify the end of the Carnaval de Barranquilla – a time when Barranquilla can at last get some sleep.

transportation system, called TransMetro (*www.transmetro.gov.co*) is scheduled to open early 2008. Like Santa Marta, local unlicensed mototaxismos offer cross-city transport to pillion passengers illegally for around 1,000 COP.

TOURIST INFORMATION

⛏ Comité Mixto de Promoción Turística del Atlántico
Vía Cuarenta, No 36–135; ✆ 330 3862;
🕑08.00–18.00, closed noon–14.00

Barranquilla city website
www.alcaldiabarranquilla.gov.co

🏠 **WHERE TO STAY** On the basis of safety not price, most travellers opt to stay in El Prado where pleasant streets can be walked without fear after dark. Those happy to stay holed up in the city's cheapest options will find numerous shoestring choices clustered on and around Paseo Bolívar (Calle 34).

🏠 **Hotel El Prado** Carrera 54, No 70–10; ✆ 369 7777; www.hotelprado.com. Housed in a beautiful old mansion house built in 1928, the hotel is set in palm-filled gardens bursting with colour. Boasting the swankiest rooms in Barranquilla it offers plenty of space & elegance with a pool, internet, AC & hefty prices. $$$

🏠 **Hotel Majestic** Carrera 53, No 54–41; ✆ 349 1010/2002; www.cotelco.org. Another top-notch option, this Moorish-style building is renowned as one of the city's nicest places to stay with its restaurant as celebrated as the stylish collection of AC rooms. $$$

Hotel Versalles (80 rooms) Carrera 48, No 78–188; ☏ 368 6970; www.hotelversallesinn.com. This modern well-appointed hotel offers a range of dbl rooms & suites in widely differing décor as well as a rather nice French-styled restaurant. Onsite amenities include a pool, spa, sauna, gym & business centre with internet. B/fast is inc in the room rate. $$$

Hotel Colonial Inn Calle 42, No 43–131; ☏ 379 0241. This city-centre mid-range option isn't big on fuss but it does offer simple, comfortable rooms with AC, TV & private bathroom. $$

Hotel Sima Carrera 49, No 72–19; ☏ 358 4600; e hotelsima@enred.com. One of El Prado's best-value options offers clean, comfortable rooms including b/fast. Interestingly, this place is popular with visiting dignitaries. $$

✗ WHERE TO EAT Barranquilla isn't short of cheap dining options with dozens of cafés, fast-food outlets and shoestring eateries along the Paseo Bolívar. For more upmarket cuisine head to El Prado where you'll also find a good range of food-court fare in the district's shopping malls. Local delicacies include *arroz con coco* and *sancocho de guandul* (a soup of peas or 'guandules' and meat), *bocachico frito* (fried fish from the Río Magdalena), *sancocho*, *arepas de huevo* (egg-filled fried maize) and empanadas.

✗ El Merendero Carrera 43, No 70–48; ☏ 345 095; ⏰ 11.00–midnight. A meat-lovers' paradise, with big plates of grilled steak in man-sized slabs & all the trimmings served under wood-&-thatch. $

✗ Mi Vieja Barranquilla Carrera 53, No 70–150; ⏰ 11.00–15.00 & 18.00–22.00 Mon–Thu, 11.00–15.00 & 18.00–03.00 Fri–Sat, 11.00–16.00 Sun. This open courtyard garden has been styled on a colonial plaza & is a popular place with local vallenato musicians. A good, simple menu draws the crowds as does the ice-cold Aguila beer. $$

✗ Restaurante La Cueva Corner of Calle 20 de Julio & Carrera 59; ☏ 379 2886/340 9813; e reservas@ fundacionlacueva.org; www.fundacionlacueva.org; ⏰ lunch–late. Apart from being a fine monument to the so-called Barranquilla Group literary community, La Cueva is an exquisite restaurant in which diners can choose from airy terrace tables or a dark-panelled dining room amidst a gallery of memorabilia. A large menu & numerous special dishes offer a good range of seafood, pasta, salads & grilled meats in Colombian-European fusion style in an ambient atmosphere. $$

ENTERTAINMENT AND NIGHTLIFE Barranquilla's nightclubs come and go so it is best to simply stroll around the city's Zona Rosa to see what catches your eye. At the time of writing, **Froggs Leggs** (☏ *359 0709*) on Calle 93, No 43–122, is considered one of the best. Clubs generally open from Thursday to Sunday. Also popular are the city's many *estancos* – rustic liquor stores with battered tables outside where the music often comes from a car audio system. Be sure to also try a *canelazo,* Barranquilla's local rum-laced cocktail that gives Brazil's potent *caipirinha* a run for its money.

♀ La Cueva Cnr Calle 20 de Julio & Carrera 59; ☏ 379 2886/340 9813; e reservas@fundacionlacueva.org; www.fundacionlacueva.org. A one-time drinking den where Colombia's finest writers, journalists, poets, playwrights and philosophers hung out in the wild, hedonistic 1950s, La Cueva is a handsome corner-plot building that today houses a rather nice restaurant, bar, cultural centre and video theatre. The outfit behind this project also offer bursaries to young creative talent and have painstakingly restored this important part of Barranquilla's 20th-century literary heritage. Original photographs of Gabriel García Márquez, Álvaro Cepeda Samundop, German Vargas and Alfonso Fuenmayor, members of one of the most productive literary communities of that era, adorn the walls. Gunshot damage to one of the paintings on the wall is testament to the consequences of urinating in someone's drink. In an attempt to persuade the owner to open one day, artist Alejandro Obregon rode an elephant to the door – look out for a footprint at the entrance. La Cueva hosts a wide range of artistic events, talks, workshops, performances, recitals and book launches. Check out the website for a rolling calendar of evening events.

SHOPPING For artesanal souvenirs head to the corner of Calle 72 and Avenida 46. This is where the largest collection of cheap handicraft kiosks are located as well as the more expensive Artesanías de Colombia store.

11

OTHER PRACTICALITIES As a vast heavily industrialised city, Barranquilla has plenty of basic essentials with drug stores, clinics, laundries, hardware stores and **internet cafés**. Some of the fastest connections can be found at Chat Net (❧ *369 2600*) on Carrera 54, No 71–111 and Prado Web Place (❧ *358 4577*) on Calle 70, No 53–33 – both at 1,800 COP per hour. The city's **Avianca Post Office** (❧ *330 2255*) is located on the corner of Calle 72 and Carrera 58. Numerous ATMs are clustered along 53, including **Bancolombia** at No 68–69. A number of **hospitals** offer 24-hour medical care, including the Clínica del Caribe (❧ *334 6143*) and Clínica del Caribe SA (❧ *378 6013/337 7226/356 4861*)

WHAT TO SEE Barranquilla doesn't pretend to be a tourist town and hasn't conspired to produce any so-called attractions for the sake of it. Apart from a few museums and a church or two there isn't much to see – but as most people visit for carnival or business this doesn't really matter.

Museo de Arte Moderno (*Carrera 56, No 74–22;* ❧ *360 9952;* ⊕ *15.00–19.00 Mon, 09.00–19.00 Tue–Sat, closed 13.00–15.00; free admission*) Ferdinand Botero is just one of the many fine home-grown artists featured in this collection where works range from contemporary sculpture to photography and film.

Museo de Antropología (*Calle 68, No 53–45;* ❧ *358 8488;* ⊕ *08.00–17.00 Mon–Fri, closed noon–14.30; free admission*) Located on the second floor of the Universidad del Atlántico offices, this small collection of pre-Columbian pottery has been gathered from all across Colombia from a variety of indigenous communities.

Museo Romántico (*Carrera 54, No 59–199;* ❧ *344 4591;* ⊕ *08.30–17.30 Mon–Fri, closed 11.30–14.00, 09.00–15.00 Sat; admission 5,000 COP*) Don't expect a homage to Casanova as this museum has a purely historical focus with exhibitions that tell the story of Barranquilla's founding and multi-cultural mix. It has a rather confusing name for what is a standard city collection, but it's a worthwhile browse nonetheless.

Catedral Metropolitana (*Cnr Calle 53 & Carrera 46*) The interior of this ugly modern church has some pleasant surprises, including some beautiful stained-glass window designs and two wall mosaics using coloured German glass. Highlights include an over-the-altar 16-tonne, 16m-high bronze sculpture by Rodrigo Arenas Betancur.

Iglesia de San Nicolás (*Cnr Paseo Bolívar & Carrera 43*) If the warden has left the doors open, take a peak inside this mock-Gothic building for its elegant altarpiece and handsome pulpit.

FESTIVALS AND SPORT Known as 'The Sharks', Barranquilla's beloved soccer team is Atlético Junior (*www.juniorbarranquilla.com*), also known as Corporación Deportiva Popular Junior. The pride of Colombia's Caribbean coast, the club enjoyed a golden age during the mid-1990s when Carlos 'El Pipe' Valderrama was instrumental in the championship wins of 1993 and 1995 (see *Santa Marta's mop-haired hero,* page 386). Atlético Junior play at the Estadio Metropolitano (also known as the Roberto Meléndez Stadium), home also to the Colombian national team. The stadium holds 58,000, making it the largest in Colombia. It was built for the failed Colombian World Cup bid in 1986.

See also box, *Colombia's wildest party,* page 378.

Overcome by your moving temple, overcome by this holiest of altars. So pure, so rare to witness such a lovely goddess. I bear witness to this place, this lair, so long forgotten. So pure, so rare…

lyrics from *Magdalena* by A Perfect Circle (album: Mer de Noms, 2000)

A relatively small department at approximately 23,188km², Magdalena (*www.gobmagdalena.gov.co*) is beautiful nonetheless, with a territory blessed by genuine contrasting landscapes that a wide variety of ecosystems bring. Powder-fine beaches and coastline in the north leads to the snow-covered peaks and swamplands in the west. Inland cloudforest and grasslands edge urban centres surrounded by farmlands and arid shrubby desert on a backdrop of valleys and rocky rivers. Four drainage basins are fed by dozens of lakes, lagoons, marshlands, creeks and waterways of which Río Magdalena is the most important. Bordered to the north by the Caribbean Sea; La Guajira to the northeast; the department of César to the east; and edging Atlántico in the northwest and Bolívar in the west and southwest, Magdalena is divided by Río Magdalena to the west. Thick jungle, fine national parks and peaks that soar 5,700m offer excellent hiking trails in a region that is undoubtedly one of Colombia's most picturesque.

SANTA MARTA *Telephone code: 5*

Hot, sticky and with its colonial grandeur now largely faded, the waterfront city of Santa Marta is steeped in history as the place where El Libertador Simón Bolívar died. As a popular domestic tourist destination, Santa Marta is a byword for relaxation. Most Colombians visit to enjoy plenty of beer, rum and sun along with the leisurely delights of the beach. As the capital of the Magdalena department, the city is an important maritime port although tourism is increasingly important to the local economy. In recent years Santa Marta has attracted large numbers of migrants displaced by conflict, drastically increasing the city's population. At the time of writing there are plans to restore many of Santa Marta's colonial streets. The city's mix of old architecture and modern beachfront complexes offers considerable past-and-future contrasts. Open-air reggae bars and palm-edged cafés make Santa Marta a pleasant place to spend time and from which to explore the local area. Exotic tropical fruit stalls adorn every street corner. Fruit can be bought whole or whipped up into a smoothie by vendors who hotwire electricity pylons into blenders all over town. Families huddle around disco-sized speakers listening to blasting *vallenato* at several million decibels as impromptu parties break out on the city's beach.

HISTORY The land on which Santa Marta was founded was populated by indigenous Indians before the arrival of Spanish explorers who inaugurated the city in July 1525. On naming it after Saint Marta, Spanish conqueror Rodrigo de Bastidas planted a flag accompanied by some 200 of his men. Spanish colonisation began in earnest as the surrounding lands were conquered. Bastidas had previously reconnoitred the area and using this intelligence was able to pinpoint where the region's gold-rich indigenous settlements were located. Santa Marta's strategic location at the base of the Sierra Nevada de Santa Marta served the Spanish well and allowed the efficient transportation of untold treasures to the Old World via the Caribbean Sea. Fierce resistance from the natives prompted sustained attack that saw the Tayrona Indians completely wiped out by the end of the 16th century. It was from Santa Marta that Jiménez de Quesada and his troops set off to march

11

the Magdalena Valley in 1536, an expedition that later led to the founding of Bogotá.

During the colonial era Santa Marta lost its importance to the nearby port city of Cartagena, a more dynamic commercial centre and better fortified. In 1871, the city became a university town when the University of Magdalena was founded, initially with law and medicine faculties. The export of coal and bananas gave Santa Marta's sluggish port trade a boost in the 20th century but was hit by industrial unrest in 1928. When the Colombian army was sent in to dispel workers campaigning for improved pay and conditions the situation turned ugly. Troops opened fire in what has become known as the Santa Marta Massacre. The official death toll was 47 but the reality was much worse. In 1961, the Atlantic Railway connected Bogotá with Santa Marta, and in 1968 the government decentralised the Port Authority, giving Santa Marta more autonomy. Today, Santa Marta is still a busy trading port although tourism is the economy's fastest-growing sector in this city of 600,000. The date of Simón Bolívar's death in Santa Marta on 7 December 1830 after liberating six Latin American countries is honoured nationwide.

CLIMATE Temperatures in Santa Marta range can top 30°C but fall dramatically during the climb up the surrounding peaks of the Sierra Nevada de Santa Marta. During the stormiest months, Santa Marta's streets can become rivers due to rainfall and flooding from the sea.

SAFETY Santa Marta and the surrounding areas are generally safe for tourists despite being home to some *paracos* (paramilitaries), a few FARC operatives, some *narcos* (narcotics traffickers) and a handful of drug labs. Incidents of tourists being caught up in this murky underworld are extremely rare, but do happen. In September 2007, at Donde Chucho, a famous fish restaurant in the centre of El Rodadero popular with tourists, armed men walked in and opened fire. Eight people were injured, none of them seriously. A known narcotics trafficker had just left the building. Two months earlier a 13-year-old girl was shot after she witnessed the murder of a taxi driver, allegedly at the hands of paramilitaries.

There remains considerable debate about the wisdom of journeying to Ciudad Perdida, the so-called Lost City built around 500 BC but only discovered in 1976. A six-day trek or an extortionate helicopter ride are the only ways to the ancient settlement. The trek is an arduous but rewarding affair along muddy trails across a seemingly endless succession of mountains. The British Foreign Office advises against all travel to that part of the region as does the US government. This follows the unprecedented kidnapping in September 2003 of eight travellers on the site by ELN guerrillas. The guerrillas tied up the guide and chose those foreigners most fit and equipped to walk for days in the jungle: four Israelis, a couple of British guys and a Spanish man along with a German girl. The hostages were treated well by their kidnappers and eventually released, the last after 102 days.

Since then the threat of kidnappings has been a recurring topic of discussion between hikers considering the trek. Some feel it was a one-off occurrence and others feel concerned that in such a remote spot the risk is just too great. The ELN said the purpose of the kidnapping was to draw attention to the problems faced by local communities in the Sierra Nevada. No kidnapping attempt has been reported since then. Today the local people of Santa Marta consider the trek to be safe for tourists. The Ciudad Perdida is cared for by the indigenous Indians that still live in the area. They have linked up with local guides Turcol, the only company they permit to bring tourists. The area around the Lost City remains under the control of the paramilitaries. Turcol is said to pay 20,000 COP per visitor to them as a safety tax – a measure that has, at the time of writing, been effective for over five years.

GETTING THERE The 98km stretch between Barranquilla and Santa Marta passes through numerous one-horse towns and pretty villages once it leaves the city's zillions of car repair shops in the industrial outskirts behind. A frenzied riddle of garages, workshops and tyre-fitting centres populated by tooting gridlocked traffic gives way to gas stations, roadside vendors, kiosks and grilled-meat joints. It then becomes much less frenetic as the road becomes much slower paced. Essentials are easy to find *en route* with water sellers plying for trade at junctions and windscreen washers at each toll. Mudflats and drier, dustier terrain turns to palm-fringed wetland expanses as the tropical resorts of Santa Marta's come into view.

Santa Marta's El Rodadero Airport is easily reached by well-marked city buses, 16km (45 minutes) south of the city on the Barranquilla–Bogotá road. Avianca (✆ *421 4018*), AeroRepública and Aires service Santa Marta, with direct flights to Bogotá and Medellín.

Frequent minibuses connect with the main bus terminal on the southeastern outskirts of the city. Buses run daily to Bogotá (95,000 COP, 16 hours), Bucaramanga (60,000 COP, 9 hours) and Barranquilla (9,000 COP, 1¾ hours) – some stop at Cartagena (22,000 COP, 4 hours). Daily buses from Santa Marta serve Maracaibo in Venezuela (65,000 COP, 7 hours) where passport formalities take place in the border town of Paraguachón.

GETTING AROUND Buses and colectivos run along the seafront on Carrera 1C (Av Rodrigo de Bastidas) with frequent minibuses serving Taganga (15 mins), El Rodadero (15 mins) and Mamatoca (20 mins).

Santa Marta is easy enough to navigate on foot with taxis widely available between carreras 1 and 5. Although illegal, motorbike taxiing is a highly popular form of local transport – and dirt cheap. It costs 1,000 COP to cross the city and is the fastest way to negotiate the traffic, albeit a little scary.

TOURIST INFORMATION AND TOUR OPERATORS

Z Etursa Calle 17, No 3–120 ✆ 421 1833; ⏰ 08.00–18.00 Mon–Fri, closed noon–14.00
Atlantic Divers Calle 10C, No 2–08; ✆ 421 4883. This decent little dive school offers a number of tour packages, from half days & full days to night dives.

Turcol Carrera 1C, No 20–15; ✆ 421 2256; e turcol24@hotmail.com. Every hotel in town offers tours out to Ciudad Perdida through this outfit, one of Santa Marta's longest-established specialists.

WHERE TO STAY Santa Marta's centrally located hotels tend to be budget or mid-range options with larger resorts and plusher accommodation found on the outskirts of town. Generally speaking, finding a rooms isn't difficult in the city unless it's during Carnaval, Christmas, New Year or Easter when it is imperative to book ahead. Signs at the entrance to town advertise camping and cabins.

Hotel Irotama Vía Ciénaga KM 14; ✆ 432 0600; e reserves@irotama.com; www.irotama.com. This super resort-style complex boasts ultra-friendly staff & top-notch facilities & boasts spectacular views from a 12th-floor rooftop bar & restaurant complete with jacuzzi. Located a 5-min drive from the airport & set across 23ha, the Irotama is surrounded by lush, tropical gardens & numerous exotic birds & edged by a 1km sandy beach. Spacious modern rooms in condo-style units have tiled floors, a lovely private bathroom, TV, minibar & balcony. The complex also has a collection of cabins, villas & suites. Onsite amenities include business centre with internet, swimming pool, gym, spa, restaurants & bar. Travellers that have roughed it for weeks will enjoy the splurge. Rates vary with a wide range of packages available with significant discounts for 7-day stays off-peak. $$$

Hotel Zuana Beach Resort Carrera 2, No 6–80; ✆ 432 0455; f 432 0672; www.zuana.com.co. This huge tropical-style resort complex has large, cheerful rooms with tiled floors, wicker furniture & brightly coloured décor. Amenities include pools, bars, snack bars & a buffet-style restaurant. $$$

11

Hotel Las Vegas Calle 11, No 2–08; ℡ 421 5094. Rooms lack style, but do have AC with street-side balconies & basic bathrooms. $$

Hotel Nueva Granada Calle 12, No 3–17; ℡ 421 1337; www.hotelnuevagranada.com. Expect good value for money from this mid-range option in the centre of town. Small rooms are simple but clean – but only some come with much-needed AC. There's also a flower-filled courtyard & small swimming pool. $$

Hotel Yuldama Carrera 1C, No 12–19; ℡ 421 0063; e hotelyuldama@reservashoteleras.com.co. For mid-range accommodation with AC & sea views this is a decent choice; rates inc b/fast. $$

Casa Familiar Calle 10C, No 2–14; ℡ 421 1697; www.hospederiacasafamaliliar.freeservers.com. Shoestring-priced rooms at this clean high-rise hotel

attract the backpacker crowd. Choose from a range of different sizes and configurations, some with private bathrooms. A nice rooftop terrace offers excellent views. $

Hotel Miramar Calle 10C, No 1C–59; ℡ 423 3276; e elmiramar_santamarta@yahoo.com. This backpacker favourite has become complacent in recent years & has let rooms & communal areas fall well under par. However, it is a great place to meet up with other travellers so those that can cope with its scruffy dilapidated state will enjoy the congenial atmosphere. A simple café serves dirt-cheap meals, beer, soft drinks & snacks. $

Hotel Republic Colonial Calle 17, No 2–43; ℡ 421 2942. Stuffy rooms are small & pokey in this functional mid-range hotel conveniently located a couple of blocks from the beach in the centre of town.

✖ **WHERE TO EAT** Santa Marta has a lot of little food joints serving inexpensive meals as well as fast-food bars and upmarket cafés. Meander along calles 11 and 12 or trawl the beachfront – and simply follow your nose. There is a sizzling 2km string of ramshackle food stalls along the PanAmerica, from meats grilled in makeshift oil-can barbecues to freshly fried empanadas and cauldrons of stew. Dozens of fruit vendors sell an excellent array of fresh produce citywide.

ENTERTAINMENT AND NIGHTLIFE There is plenty of nightlife on the streets of Santa Marta; just wander along the palm-lined beachfront strip to discover crowds spilling out of numerous bars and restaurants and music at ear-splitting volume. In peak months, roads are closed to accommodate the sheer traffic of people crawling through the streets. Expect the air to be full of a heady mix of rock, salsa, techno, reggae and calypso as the bars attempt to compete with each other. At weekends, most of Santa Marta stays open until daybreak. Follow the throng to the innocuous-looking hangout **La Puerta** on Calle 17, No 2–29 (⊕ *Tue–Sat*), for full-on salsa music or to the Flemish-owned **Barrio Samario** (℡ *310 710 9649*) on Calle 17, No 3–36, for a party atmosphere that doesn't end until dawn. Open-air dance bar **Peskaito** (℡ *310 729 4818*) on Calle 16, No 2–08, opens mid-afternoon and doesn't close until daybreak. Head to the silver sand of the city beach for regular live music – it's not uncommon for vallenato groups to simply turn up and play.

OTHER PRACTICALITIES Santa has a few **internet cafés**, but connections can be painfully slow. Try Mundo Digital (℡ *431 9418*) on Calle 15, No 28–19 – although it's pricey at 3,000 COP per hour. DialNet (℡ *431 5493*) on San Francisco Plaza is one of the best in town and is just 1,900 COP. The **post office** is located on Calle 3, No 17–26, and is open weekdays 08.00–18.00 (closed noon–14.00) and Saturday 08.00–13.00. A decent collection of **ATM**s supplement a couple of walk-in banks. **Bancolombia** (℡ *421 0185*) on Carrera 3, No 14–10, changes travellers' cheques with a number of **currency exchange** places along Calle 14 between Carreras 3 and 5. **Telecom** (℡ *421 1977*) on Calle 13, No 5–23, offers long-distance and international calls.

WHAT TO SEE Expect to find shoeshine vendors, ice-cream stalls, melon sellers and balloon stalls in the **Parque Simón Bolívar** along with elderly card-playing women and children playing the dice game *arranque*. There's a backdrop

SANTA MARTA
(not to scale)

of fine colonial buildings complete with vast wooden doors and ornate balconies.

Museo del Oro (*Calle 14, No 2–07;* ✆ *421 0953;* ⊕*08.00–11.45 & 14.00–17.45 Mon–Fri; free admission*) A decent collection of gold from the Sierra Nevada is housed in Santa Marta's Gold Museum in a fine colonial mansion known as the Casa de la Aduana (Customs House). It contains some rather fine Tayrona objects and some pottery from the Kogi and Arhuaco cultures in rooms set off a circular lobby.

Catedral de Santa Marta (*Cnr Carrera 4 & Calle 17*) Ignore claims that Santa Marta's hulking great whitewashed cathedral is Colombia's oldest church – construction didn't finish until 1766. The ashes of the town's founder, Rodrigo de Bastidas, are contained in a vault by the entrance. Simón Bolívar was also buried here in 1830 but his remains were returned to his birthplace in Caracas in 1842.

Monumento Carlos 'El Pibe' Alberto Valderrama Palacío (*Eduardo Santos Stadium*) This PERM-anent 7m bronze statue of Colombian football legend Carlos Valderrama captures the great man perfectly, right down to his wild, frizzy hair. It was created by Colombian artist Amilkar Ariza and attracts tourists from all over the country. Find it outside the stadium, a 23,000 capacity complex built in 1951 that is home to the Unión Magdalena squad.

Quinta de San Pedro Alejandrino (*4km east of the city, a 20-min bus journey from Santa Marta's beachfront strip or a 10,000 COP taxi ride;* ✆ *433 0589/2994;* ⊕*09.30–16.30* *daily; admission 10,000 COP*) Meaning the Quinta of Saint Peter Alexander this grand hacienda was built in the 17th century and was the estate where Simón Bolívar spent his final days. He died in 1830 as the guest of the Spanish owner, Joaquín de Mier, a loyal supporter of Bolívar's push for Colombian independence. The hacienda produced rum, sugarcane and honey and had its own mill. Now a shrine and museum honouring Bolívar, this magnificent homestead contains a number of fine monuments to the liberator. Works of art in the Altar de la Patria have been donated by artists from all of the countries in Latin America freed by Bolívar's campaigns. A vast white marble memorial built in 1930 contains a centrepiece statue that offers a trick of the eye. Look at it head on and Bolívar is standing proud with a swagger. Step to the right and he is a generation older, wizened and visibly weaker. Stand to the left and he is younger and looking forward to the distance, wearing a knowing smile. The house, the Museo Bolívariano and the monuments can each be visited and the grounds are well worth a stroll.

Mamancana Natural Reserve (*Not far from the Hotel Irotama just off the road to the airport out of Santa Marta;* \ *438 27 37/438 27 38/312 659 0658/312 659 0652;* e *ventas@mamancana.com; www.mamancana.com*) This eco-centre and adventure sports complex, Mecca for downhill cyclists, Mamancana played host to Colombia's national competition in 2006 and offers a host of canopy rides, hiking trails and mountain-bike routes as well as a climbing wall and extreme sports, including paragliding. Sailing, kayaking and fishing take place on a large lake with 4x4 off-road tracks and 600ha of thick forest. A lofty lookout point offers breathtaking views out to the coast amidst springs, cactus, palms, ravines, rocks and nesting birds. A large open-fronted wooden lodge has to be one of the funkiest in Colombia with a part-canvas sail-style roof and a tasteful restaurant that transforms into a bar at weekends, complete with DJ. Wildlife in the park includes monkey, foxes and wild cats. It is also home to numerous species of butterflies and migratory and indigenous birds. Guests can stay overnight in dorm beds (14) or double rooms and can handpick a range of activities. Rates include breakfast ($$).

FESTIVALS AND EVENTS

Las Fiestas del Mar (*mid-year*) Santa Marta's Festival of the Sea is celebrated during peak season and is a modern concept aimed squarely at tourists. Expect beauty pageants, parades and parties under the festival's slogan 'Santa Marta, la magica de tenerlo todo' (Santa Marta, the magic of having it all).

Festival de la Cumbia (*Jul*) An annual celebration of dance and song in tribute to the native tradition of Cumbia with colourful processions and non-stop merriment and lots of stalls.

AROUND SANTA MARTA

EL RODADERO (*Telephone code: 5*) Once a sleepy little seaside town, El Rodadero is now practically a beachside suburb of Santa Marta, with white sands surrounded by contoured scrub-clad slopes. Popular with volleyball players, and with calm waters for windsurfing, swimming and diving, El Rodadero is located 5km south of downtown Santa Marta. All the main resort amenities are clustered close to the beach with modern hotels, rental apartments, open-side restaurants, dive schools, campsites, supermarkets, discos, casinos, a post office and a couple of internet cafés easily accessible on foot. Sun-loungers and sunshades can be hired for the beach along with kayaks and paddle boats. Popular with Colombian holidaymakers, El Rodadero can get very crowded at weekends and during public holidays. It is also quite lively after dark when a host of beachfront bars fill with the sound of salsa, vallenato and cumbia.

Getting there and around All buses heading south of Santa Marta will drop off at El Rodadero. A taxi will cost around 4,000 COP. A local pilot called Donaldo (↘*311 427 3939*) offers scenic flights and air transfers across the region in his light aircraft. He charges 350,000 COP for the first hour then 300,000 for each additional hour.

Tourist information There's a small **tourism booth** on the beachfront. It offers maps, hotel reservations and books tours and is open daily 08.00–18.00.

Where to stay El Rodadero has dozens of hotels that offer similarly-styled vacation accommodation, many in high-rise blocks. Look out for signs around the beach and on the approach road advertising cabins and camping. Some of the larger family-run restaurants also rent out rooms in peak season.

Hotel Arhuaco S A (59 rooms) Carrera 2, No 6–49; ↘ 422 7166; f 100 0000; e reservas@solarhoteles.com; www.solarhoteles.com. One of the best hotels in the area, the Arhuaco is newly opened & boasts a gleaming ultra-swish lobby & spotless swimming pool. Rooms range from standard dbl to trpl, each containing TV & AC. There is also a laundry service, a couple of restaurants & indoor & outdoor bars. $$$

Hotel Arrecifes Caribeño Calle 19, No 6–54; ↘ 422 3028/3265. This archetypal El Rodadero hotel is modern & close to the beach with a range of different-sized rooms, some better than others. $$$

⌂ **Hotel El Rodadero** Calle 11, No 1–29; ✆ 422 8323; f 422 8295; www.hotelrodadero.com. A large beachfront hotel with pool, restaurant, café & games room & modern rooms with AC & private bathrooms. $$$

⌂ **Hotel La Sierra** Carrera 1, No 9–47; ✆ 422 7960; f 422 8198. Another much-of-a-muchness to look at but a popular option nonetheless, close to the action with good amenities & first-class views from a decent collection of AC rooms with balconies. $$$

⌂ **Aparta Hotel Tiskirama** Carrera 2, No 5–159; ✆ 422 7903. This perfectly acceptable budget option has functional suite-style rooms that can accommodate larger groups or families. $$

⌂ **Hotel Betoma** ✆ 422 7340; e hotelbetoma@etb.net.co. This homely little place offers some of the cheapest rooms in the area as well as distant views of the Sierra Nevada Mountains. Each clean, freshly spruced-up room has a fridge & hot water – good value all round. $

Numerous outfits offer cabañas sleeping four–ten in and around El Rodadero, including **Cabañas Costa Azul** (*Calle 18, No 2–48;* ✆ *422 9749;* $$) and **Cabañas Cooedumag** (*Calle 21A;* ✆ *422 5650;* $$).

A number of private individuals offer apartments for rental in and around the beach area of the town, including the following options. An American-owned **holiday condo** (✆ *(US): 305 219 0292*) at the Breezas del Lago resort is for rent on a monthly basis at around 1,200 COP, sleeping six–eight. An **oceanfront apartment** (✆ *(US): 786 252 9957;* e *jecaicedo@aol.com*) is available for rent on a weekly or monthly basis in a superb location offering magnificent views containing washer and dryer in well-appointed accommodation. It has televisions in every room, a DVD and VCR player along with air conditioning, ceiling fans, a communal pool and 24-hour security. Daily cleaning and cooking are also available. The apartment rental agency **Vista Mar Colombia** (✆ *422 3890/315 446 8028/312 757 2535;* e *reservas@vistamarcolombia.com; www.vistamarcolombia.com*) has a number of seafront units in and around El Rodadero.

✖ **Where to eat** As befitting a touristy seaside resort, El Rodadero has plenty of fast-food options and ice-cream parlours. Places come and go so take a stroll along the beachfront to see what takes your fancy.

✖ **Asadero Girón** Carrera 3, No 7–20; ✆ 422 0143; ◷ lunch–23.30 Mon–Sat. Expect big plates of delicious grilled meat & plantain at this decent family-run food joint. $

✖ **Asadero Rico Pollo** Carrera 4, No 19 A–09; ✆ 422 4727; ◷ all day. The speciality here is chicken – & it's cheap & good. A good choice for generous portions & lunchtime deals. $

✖ **El Encarrete Paisa** Calle 12, No 2–04; ✆ 422 2063; ◷ noon–23.00. A menu of traditional Colombian fare includes dishes from many regions, including some great Caribbean fish plates. $$

✖ **Emanuel Restaurante Y Comidas Rapidas** Calle 9, No 2–39; ✆ 422 7306; ◷ 11.00–15.00. This family-run fast-food place serves up lots of fried snacks at lunchtime for vacationers on the go. $

✖ **Holguer Pizza** Calle 8, No 2–57; ✆ 422 6861; ◷ 11.30–midnight. People rave about the pizza from this place. It can be ordered whole or by the slice with all manner of toppings. $

✖ **Restaurante Casa China** Carrera 3, No 6–43; ✆ 422 8069; ◷ lunch & dinner. El Rodadero's best Chinese diner has a reasonable choice of menus, from seafood noodles & sweet-and-sour shrimp & rice to spicy stir-fried octopus. $$

✖ **Restaurante El Pibe** Calle 6, No 1–26 L–101; ✆ 422 7973; ◷ noon–midnight. Named in honour of Santa Marta's home-grown footballing talent Carlos Valderrama, this restaurant has a good ambience & has posters of the midfield virtuoso on the wall. $$

Entertainment and nightlife After dark it gets lively in El Rodadero with two of the nicest options the upmarket club and restaurant **La Escollera** (✆ *422 9590;* ◷ *Wed–Sun*) with its fun open-air bar and the funky **Latino Café** (✆ *422 7089*).

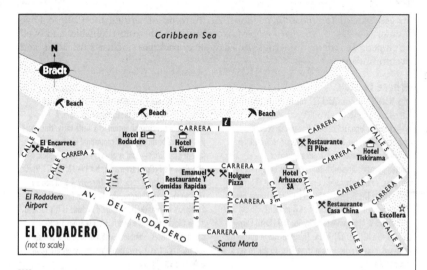

What to see

Acuario y Museo Del Mar (✆ *422 7222;* ⊕*09.00–16.00 every day; admission 2,500 COP*) Founded in 1966, this aquatic complex contains an aquarium which is home to sharks, dolphins, seals, turtles and other species of marine life. A dolphin show takes place when the audience is sufficiently large to warrant it. An adjoining museum houses an eclectic assortment of local artefacts. The aquarium can be reached by hopping on any bus heading northwest. Numerous small boats also depart from the beach at El Rodadero – a ticket will cost 6,000 COP return.

TAGANGA (*Telephone code: 5*) This tiny fishing village is much favoured by visiting backpackers and alongside nets and boats you'll find ramshackle stalls selling hippy paraphernalia. Set on a horseshoe-shaped bay, Taganga divides opinions. Some visitors describe it as paradisiacal and wax lyrical about its simplistic beauty. Others are horrified by Taganga's many flaws. Dabbling in some of Colombia's illicit crops is certainly a popular pastime here, so if this isn't your scene opt for the beach-life in Rodadero. Although some upscale boutique hotels have sprung up, Taganga remains very much the domain of body-pierced, hair-braided, guitar-strumming *ganga*-smoking gringo. Most drop by *en route* to Venezuela after trekking to the Lost City. Many get caught up in Taganga's simple vibe and end up spending several months there, idly swinging in hammocks and making the most of cheap beer. Unfortunately, a once-idyllic palm-scattered beach is now in dire need of a clean-up. Describing Taganga as 'rubbish-on-sea' (as one French visitor did in 2007) may be a little unkind, but the main drag is certainly unkempt. Trash-strewn sands edge paths blocked by piles of rubble with vast pot-holes in the road. For a more picturesque stretch of sand walk 20 minutes northwest of Taganga to the Playa Grande (or take a boat for 2,000 COP) where beachside restaurants are pleased to see you and serve plates of delicious fish-and-rice.

Getting there and around Taganga is easily reached from Santa Marta's beachfront with numerous minibuses nipping back and forth throughout the day (500 COP, 15 minutes).

Tour operators Taganga offers some of the best-value scuba diving in Colombia and a number of operators run PADI/NAUI courses. Standards vary enormously, so ask around for recommendations. At the time of writing the Calipso Dive Center (✆ 421 9146; www.calipsodivecenter.com) is the most reliable and well equipped. It offers numerous full-day dive packages inclusive of food and accommodation.

🏠 Where to stay

🏠 **Hotel La Ballena Azul** (27 rooms + 4 suites) Carrera 1CI, No 18; ✆ 421 9009; www.hotelballenaazul.com. A fine upmarket option on the main drag, the Blue Whale offers a mix of different styles of accommodation, from minimalist contemporary suites with sunken baths on ultra-chic terraces, to homely rooms that look in need of bringing up to date. The hotel's seafood restaurant comes highly recommended. There's also a bar & internet. $$$

🏠 **Hotel Y Apartamentos Mirador Del Mastil** Carrera 1B, No 18–107; ✆ 421 9206. This mid-range option has received mixed reviews from travellers, so ask to see a couple of rooms. $$

🏠 **Hotel Y Restaurante Bahía Taganga** Calle 4, No 1B–35; ✆ 421 9049. It's nothing special, but this family-run place is perfectly OK as a budget option with comfortable rooms & a restaurant that serves tasty seafood-&-rice dishes. $$

🏠 **Cabañas Techos Verdes** Calle 8, No 4–39; ✆ 421 9148. Expect inexpensive, simple, basic accommodation at 'Green Roofs' where cabins sleep 4–6 people. $

🏠 **Casa Blanca** (10 rooms) Carrera 1, No 18–61; ✆ 421 9232; e barbus85@latinmail.com. A reasonable beachfront option, if a little tatty, this hotel has private bathrooms & a communal kitchen with laundry facilities – and is always full, so pre-book. $

🏠 **Casa de Félipe** Carrera 5A, No 19–12; ✆ 421 9120; www.lacasadefelipe.com. Nice, friendly & well run by Frenchman Jean Philippe, this is a firm favourite with European backpackers, but the downside is it's located a few blocks from the beach. Choose from 3 self-contained suites, complete with kitchen, or 3 standard rooms. Each has a private bathroom. Rates are room-only or B&B. $

🏠 **Divanga Casa Francesa** Calle 12, No 4–07; ✆ 421 9092. Many shoestring travellers have recommended this family-run place on the basis of friendliness & affordability. $

🏠 **Hostal Pelikan** Carrera 2, No 17–04 Entrada Principal; ✆ 421 9057. Another inexpensive hangout for budget travellers, located reasonably close to the beach with clean, simple rooms. $

✗ Where to eat

✗ **Asados Al Carbon Y Comidas Rapidas Yiu Nu Sagu Taganga** Calle 13, No 2 A–86 ✆ 421 9137. A popular place to grab a lunchtime bite & take-away food, this grilled-meat café is excellent value but lacks service-with-a-smile. $

🍽 **Los Baguettes De Maria** Calle 18, No 3–47; ✆ 421 9328; ⊕ until late afternoon. Choose from a menu of sandwiches, juices, shakes & salads. $

✗ **Restaurante Las Velas** Carrera 1, No 18–95; ✆ 421 9072; ⊕ early–late. Las Velas serves tasty, inexpensive fish-&-rice dishes. $

Entertainment and nightlife Of the open-sided bars in Taganga, the liveliest is **El Garaje** (✆ 421 9003; ⊕ Wed–Sat), a popular gringo hangout that plays salsa and reggaetón until the early hours.

Other practicalities Although a couple of local shops stock a few tourist essentials, don't rely on this if you plan to stay. Bring everything you need with you, from suncream and cash reserves to over-the-counter medicines. Taganga also has a couple of internet cafés and a poorly stocked drug store.

PARQUE NACIONAL TAYRONA (*Admission 20,000 COP; horse 25,000 COP. Visitors travelling by road pay toll, 5,800 COP*) One of Colombia's easily accessible and most popular national parks, Tayrona offers some stunning beaches set within deeply contoured bays and hemmed by coconut trees. Bordered by the Bahía de Taganga in the west to the mouth of the Río Piedras 35km to the east, Tayrona was once home to the indigenous Tayrona community. Today all that is left of their ancient civilisation are ruins of the pre-Hispanic town of Chairama (or Pueblito in Spanish). It is thought that this was once the main settlement for the Tayrona people. Today, Tayrona's gorgeous sandy stretches are edged by large coral reefs in an expanse that can be explored on horseback or on foot. Rocky ravines edge gushing rivers amidst dense rainforest and cacti-clad arid slopes. Wildlife includes wild pigs, spider-monkeys, lizards, frogs and snakes with parrots, vultures and crows. Spider webs the size of tablecloths stretch from tree-to-tree above a crocodile of mules piled high with rice bound for the park's Indian villages. Surrounding fertile waters are home to grouper, red snapper, octopus, mackerel, shark, lobsters, squid and eels. A hand-shaped terrain has its fingers round the coves of Concha, Chengue, Gairaca, Neguange, Cinto, Guachaquita and Palmarito. More than 37,000 acres include 12,000 of mainland and 3,000 of coastal waters. Bathers should take precautions at beaches with strong currents, including Arrecifes (see box *The Gringo trail*, page 393) and Cañaveral. The safest waters are found at La Piscina.

Neguange can be reached by the road to Palangana, which also goes to Gayraca and Playa Coralina. Through Cañaveral you can walk to the beautiful beaches of Arrecifes and El Cabo, or go to Pueblito to see the old Tayrona settlement, Chairama. Naranjos can be accessed from Cañaveral along some leafy trails amidst dense vegetation, or from a path leading out from Bahía Concha. From Los Naranjos there are numerous tracks to the mouth of the Piedras al Mar River, Playa del Muerto, Playa Coralina, Bonito Gordo, Concha Bay, Chengue Cove, Gayraca Cove, Cinto, Guachaquita. From Arrecifes, a half-hour trail connects with La Piscina, a deep bay with waters that are calm enough to swim and snorkel. A 20-minute walk leads on to the stunning beaches of Cabo San Juan de la Guía where a one-hour trail climbs up to Chairama (Pueblito). Tayrona's park rangers can provide details and maps of these and other trails. El Zaíno heralds the entrance to the park 34km east of Santa Marta, where a 4km paved road connects to Cañaveral. At Cañaveral there's an administrative centre and a place to organise horses and a guide. Be sure to check about routes that are off-limits due to bad weather or high seas.

Where to stay and eat In Cañaveral, 11 park-run hillside thatch-roofed cabañas called **Ecohabs** enjoy magnificent views out to sea. Each can accommodate two to four people and have been designed to reflect Tayrona style with wooden floors and simple beds cooled by coastal breezes. A two-bed cabin costs 76,000 COP with a four-bed 112,900 COP. Book through the Parques Nacionales de Colombia (*www.parquesnacionales.gov.co*).

Below the staggered collection of Ecohab buildings there is a rather nice open-sided **restaurant** (**$$**) that serves excellent meals, such as seafood rice, lobster and grilled fish.

Cañaveral is also the venue for the park-run **campsite** (5,300 COP pp). You'll need a tent, a mattress, sleeping bag and torch along with food and cooking implements should you not want to eat in the restaurant. The place is very, very basic and only for hardened backpackers with little regard for comfort.. Book through the Parques Nacionales de Colombia (*www.parquesnacionales.gov.co*).

In Arrecifes, there are two accommodation options. **Finca El Paraíso** (\ *310 691 3626;* $) sits close to the beach and offers dead-cheap rustic cabins, covered hammocks and camping. **Rancho Lindo** ($) is on the approach trail to the beach and offers the same basic accommodation. Both have simple restaurants that serve freshly cooked inexpensive meals as well as snacks and drinks.

Further west a ten-minute walk along the beach is the rustic lodge **Bucarú** ($). Basic cabañas, hammocks and camping are also offered here; again it's pretty cheap. It's owned by the same people as Finca El Paraíso.

At the end of the trail in Cabo San Juan de la Guía you'll find a cheap little backpacker haunt with **hammocks** at 4,000 COP apiece.

11

Just before the park entrance, a string of small rustic restaurants offer local dishes, including grouper soup at 2,500 COP.

Getting there and away To get to Cañaveral take a minibus from Santa Marta to Palomino and get off at El Zaíno (6,000 COP, 1¼ hours) – they leave every half-hour from downtown. A jeep ferries passengers (every half-hour) between El Zaíno and Cañaveral (1,500 COP, 10 minutes) with the walk taking about 45 minutes.

Other practicalities There is rarely any mobile phone signal in the park, so don't rely on this. Two small kiosks – Refresqueria Anita and Refresqueria Abril – are located immediately outside the entrance. Both sell bottles of cold water, sodas and snacks. Pack plenty of bug spray and drinking water.

MINCA (*Telephone code: 5*) Located at 650m on the slopes of the Sierra Nevada de Santa Marta, the town of Minca may only have a population of 600 people but it is the centre of one of the most exciting birding regions in the world. Birdwatchers from all over the world visit Minca, a mountainous settlement that makes a great base to explore the surrounding birding paradise. Surrounding forests are also home to indigenous Kogi Indian tribes who fled higher into the mountains and have managed to remain isolated to this day as the only tribe unconquered by the Spanish. This reclusive group of about 12,000 people have a deep mistrust of cultures born out of the Spanish invasion (see *Safety* below). However, Kogi culture is evident throughout the town and is highly respected. Things are still done the old-fashioned way in flower-filled Minca, including the cultivation, harvesting and roasting of the local coffee. MinCafe is made entirely by hand from the planting under thick cloudforest to picking on the steep slopes. The town has three grades of MinCafe which is sold throughout the town along with aromatic herbs and shrubs.

Safety In the mid 1990s, Minca suffered at the hands of paramilitary activity. Peace was restored to the area in 2000 although the town remained under peaceful paramilitary control until March 2006. It was then that the forces demobilised in a deal with the Colombian government. Today Minca is becoming a favourite destination for many mountain bikers, bird enthusiasts and hikers.

Minca's surrounding Kogi Indian tribes are deeply suspicious of outsiders. It is not advisable to attempt to photograph a tribe member without asking permission – they may not have seen a camera before and believe it to be a weapon. Even Kogi that are familiar with photography may believe that taking an image is stealing their soul. Minca is surrounded by Kogi history and trails around the Río Minca contain shards of Indian pottery. In the event that any objects are spotted, it is not advisable to touch or remove them. This could be construed as an act of theft or grave robbing.

Tour guides Numerous locals offer guide services to birding spots and trails, just ask at the Sans Souci Restaurant (✆ 310 710 8563) in the centre of town.

Getting there and around Minca is reached by an hourly pick-up truck from Santa Marta (3,200 COP, 35 minutes) or a take a taxi for around 20,000 COP.

Where to stay and eat

Debajo los Mangos ✆ 421 9972. A small family-run affair with comfortable rooms for hire & a decent restaurant serving traditional dishes. $

Finca Sans Souci ✆ 310 710 853; e sanssouciminca@yahoo.com. Simple rooms & good food make this smallholding a decent base in Minca –

Long you live and high you fly,
But only if you ride the tide,
And balanced on the biggest wave,
You race towards an early grave.

Pink Floyd, 'Breathe', *Dark Side of The Moon* (1973)

When author Mark Mann wrote about Parque Nacional Tayrona in his travelogue *The Gringo Trail* (1990), he conjured up the atmosphere with considerable skill. He describes 'climbing up rocky slopes and dropping into dry creeks' when walking to Arrecifes where 'an arc of white sand curved away to two rocky headlands … a wild empty beach with waves pounding the shore and palm trees swaying behind'. Mann spent many months living within the park's confines, illegally. He was part of an oddball community of worldwide travellers who arrived and set up camp on the beach. They fished with harpoons, slept in hammocks and ate fresh coconut. Playing chess, reading books, playing cards, collecting driftwood and talking became the order of the day. They drank Colombian rum and made jewellery from seashells before building a camp fire. At night the moonlit air was thick with the sweet smell of cannabis and howling monkeys as crabs scuttled across the sand.

Yet life in Arrecifes wasn't perfect as the surrounding waters have a deceptively strong undertow. A dozen people had apparently drowned there in the 12 months prior to Mann's arrival. When tragedy struck for a 13th time it was his travelling companion who lost his life to the sea. 'Suddenly, a big churning wave crashed over him and, instead of coming in, he was dragged back out again,' he writes. 'He was gone. Dead. Drowned.'

Today only a handful of dreadlocked, skinny-dipping backpackers remain encamped at Arrecifes. A sign reading 'Dangerous water, don't dream of swimming' the only visible monument to a life lost to the sea.

there's even use of the kitchen for those that prefer to self-cater. The German owner is also a good source of local info & will organise mountain bikes, horseriding & local guides. It is also possible to pitch a tent here in the grounds. $

La Casona Hostería Ecológica ☎ 421 9958; e lacasona@colombiaexotic.com. A good restaurant, camping, rustic rooms & a guiding service make this a popular choice with outdoor types. $

Los Paisas Somos Así ☎ 421 9904. As well as specialising in inexpensive tamales & chorizos this place rents out cabañas. Rates vary but won't break the bank. $

Sierra Sound Resort ☎ 421 9987/310 277 1544/312 638 5353; e minca2505@yahoo.es. This sweet little *finca* offers nice, clean rooms with private bathrooms as well as a terrace restaurant that serves traditional Colombian & Italian cuisine. There is also a TV room & a very pretty garden containing lots of mature fruit trees. $

Piqueteadero Liliana ☎ 421 9911. Expect fried chicken, pork, empanadas & *arepas* at this little food joint along with a good selection of *jugos naturals* (fresh juices).

Restaurante Doña Ana ☎ 421 9977. Try a bowl of delicious *sancocho de gallina Criolla* (soup) at this town-centre restaurant to taste it at its very best. $

What to see

Birds The Sierra Nevada de Santa Marta has about the same number of bird varieties as can be found in the whole North American continent. More than 620 known bird species inhabit the region, including the yellow-billed toucanet, Santa Marta warbler, white-lored warbler, Santa Marta sabrewing, vermilion cardinal, Santa Marta woodstar, coppery emerald, white-tailed starfrontlet, rufous-browed conebill, streak-capped spinetail, blue-knobbed curassow, Santa Marta antpitta, slender-billed inezia, sapphire-bellied hummingbird, buffy hummingbird, tyrian

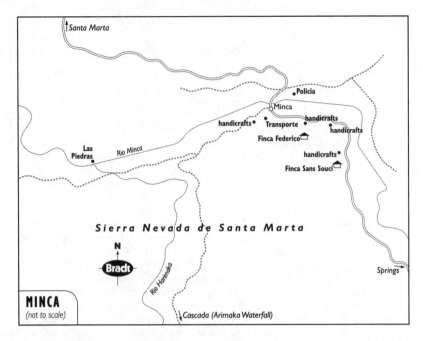

metaltail, bronze-brown cowbird, yellow-crowned whitestart, Santa Marta bush-tyrant, black-fronted wood-quail, chestnut-winged chachalaca, bearded helmetcrest, band-tailed guan, white-tipped quetzal, chestnut piculet, Santa Marta parakeet, black-backed thornbill, black-backed antshrike, brown-rumped tapaculo, Santa Marta tapaculo, white-whiskered spinetail, rusty-headed spinetail and Santa Marta wren – to name many. Over 70 migratory species from the United States and Canada journey to this Endemic Bird Area (EBA B08), including red-tailed hawk, broad-winged hawk, orange-billed nightingale-thrush, Swainson's thrush, chimney swift, common nighthawk, yellow-billed cuckoo, olive-sided flycatcher, eastern wood pewee, black-throated blue warbler, bay-breasted warbler, cerulean warbler and gray catbird.

Las Piedras A 15-minute walk from the centre of Minca leads up to this large rock formation where freshwater pools offer an inviting spot to take a dip. The warm waters of the Río Harimaka meet the colder Río Minca and create natural whirlpools. To reach this stunning spot take the road out past the church and follow the signs to the Buruake and Doña Ana restaurants. Continue for about 500m beyond Doña Ana to the confluence of the two rivers.

Arimaka Waterfall This beautiful 45-minute walk along a leafy trail from the centre of Minca leads to a hidden waterfall that was once a sacred location for the Kogi Indians. After the Kogi fled to higher ground they used other sites for ceremonial rituals and today the Arimaka Waterfall is used purely as a place to swim. Dark, craggy rocks and deep cool pools are surrounded by clay thought to have curative qualities.

CIUDAD PERDIDA (LOST CITY) One of the largest pre-Columbian archaeological sites discovered in the Americas, Ciudad Perdida lay undiscovered on the remote northern slopes of the Sierra Nevada de Santa Marta until 1972. A series of stone steps led treasure hunter (*guaquero*) Florentino Sepúvedaup and his two sons to the abandoned city believed to have been built between the 11th and 14th centuries but with origins dating to the 7th century. They named it 'Green Hell' due to the extraordinary effort it had required to reach it through thick mountain jungle. Officials revealed the site's existence in 1975 when its gold figurines and ceramic urns began to appear on the local black market. Fights broke out as people rushed to loot it, resulting in a military crackdown in 1976. Archaeologists were sent in to study and survey the entire city. It appears the site was once a major political and economic centre, housing between 2,000–4,000 people over 2km². Known as Teyuna by its indigenous inhabitants, Ciudad Perdida sits on the Río Buritaca at an altitude of between 950–1,330m. It consists of a series of 169 terraces carved into the mountainside with a network of tiled roads and small circular plazas. The entrance to the city is a climb of some 12,000 stone steps through dense jungle. Today the Lost City is partially overgrown but this seems to add to its character. It was apparently abandoned during the Spanish conquest and although local Arhuaco, Kogi and Assario tribes knew of its existence, they told no-one.

Getting there and around It is not possible to do the trip out to Ciudad Perdida alone, and with only a single tour company granted permission to visit the site (see *Safety*, page 392) choice is limited. Turcol in Santa Marta is the tour outfit with that status (see *Tour operators*, page 383). It charges around 350,000 COP per person for the all-inclusive six-day programme, including transport, food, accommodation (hammocks), guides and permits. Porters are part of the deal too but only carry the cooking gear, not backpacks. Travellers should be sure to pack waterproof clothing, a torch, insect repellent and a water bottle. They should also bring a medical kit. Although the Lost City is just 40km from Santa Marta as the crow flies, the journey has to make allowances for an absence of access roads to navigate thick, impenetrable jungle and impassable mountains. It is a hard slog across muddy terrain that begins with a three-day arduous trek uphill. Tour groups are usually between 4–12 people with departures every week or so.

LA GUAJIRA www.laguajira.gov.co

Colombia's most northerly department is populated mainly by Wayúu Indians and their descendents and is distinctly different from any other region – from the guttural language and dialects of the Guajiros and their walnut-coloured skin to the coloured robes adorned with pom-poms and face-blackening to protect the skin from the fierceness of the sun. Dry, arid deserts dominate the peninsula, bounded by the Caribbean Sea to the north and west and the Gulf of Venezuela to the southeast. Although much of this sparsely populated peninsula lies in Colombia, La Guajira extends into Venezuelan territory. Approximately 120,000 Guajiros have lived in the region since before the Spanish conquest. After their arrival, the Guajiros adopted horses and cattle from the Spanish and lived a pastoral lifestyle. They acquired weapons from the Spanish and built temporary wattle-and-daub huts in the inhospitable barren desert – but were far from isolated. Many became involved in trade and smuggling and lived a life of co-existence with pick-up trucks and wage labour on Venezuelan farms. In the late 1990s, large-scale mining began in La Guajira, severely disrupting the livelihoods of the Guajira people and placing their culture and lifestyle under threat. However, under the leadership of Governor José Luis Gonzalez – himself a Wayúu Indian – the department has positioned itself as Colombia's centre of cultural tourism. Considerable investment has gone towards the preservation of sacred sites and conservation of local cultures and traditions. La Guajira people also have a greater political voice and are intent on ensuring their rituals survive. As a result, visitors will find it easy to access some of

11

the seven Indian groups that inhabit the province, including the Wayúu and Kogi peoples. La Guajira is also an excellent place to buy high-quality woven crafts, including hammocks, basketry and shoulder bags (*mochilas*). A growing number of folkloric festivals also allow tourists to learn more about the region's unique ethnic roots, language, societal structures and proudly upheld traditions.

THE ROAD TO RÍOHACHA The 166km journey northeast to Ríohacha on the road from Santa Marta initially skirts the palm-flanked foothills of the magnificent **Sierra Nevada de Santa Marta** – a terrain of lush vegetation so rich and fertile the locals say a rusty nail could sprout green shoots. A successive string of flower-filled towns sit surrounded by carpets of emerald foliage with even a most humble dwelling blessed with a garden of healthy crops. Vast banana plantations tumble down to the sea from roads hemmed with vegetable stalls and fruit. Cattle, horses and tunic-clad Indian farm workers dot large, verdant fields. Sausages hang in every doorway of the little village of **Pericoaguardo**, a community with a strong livestock tradition. Then it's on to **Palomine**, a town that signifies the border between the departments of Magdalena and La Guajira, 42km from the coast. Stand by the **Río Palomine** on a clear day to enjoy fine views of the Sierra Nevada's highest peak Pico Cristóbal Colón (5,775m). It's a good spot to stop for breakfast at a little roadside joint, **La Saga** – a plate of arepas, grilled ham, juice, eggs, toast and steak washed down with sweet coffee costs less than 3,000 COP. A little further up the road just before **Río Ancho** there's another good-value stop-off, **Restaurante Glario,** close to a sign advertising cabañas for rent. After crossing the Río Caña into the bustling agricultural hub of Mingueo with its permanent food market and fresh-fish stalls you'll see a ramshackle wooden food joint that appears to be nearing collapse. Parada doesn't look much but it offers good rustic food at low prices amidst palms, pecking chickens and the sound of a crackling transistor radio. After a stretch of waterlogged pasture and grazing mules, enter the fruit-growing village of Dibula, 53km from Ríohacha – where the ground is suddenly drier and yellow rather than green. A brand-new paved road takes over at Pelucha as the surrounding forest gradually becomes less tropical and more scrub. At about 20km from Ríohacha take a left-hand turn down a mangrove-flanked road signed to the village of **Camarones** (meaning prawns). Cross a small bridge past saltpans and freshwater lakes that are home to flamingos and sea birds hunting for shrimp (see box, *Birds, birds, birds*, page 401). Every little kiosk and bohío-style restaurant in Camarones sells prawns in one guise or another – try the mural-covered **Restaurante Mira Mar** right down on the beach for good local dishes and incredible, uninterrupted sea views. After the detour rejoin the road to Ríohacha, a stretch that becomes uglier the closer you get and passes numerous stalls selling knock-off Venezuelan petrol in cola bottles.

RÍOHACHA *Telephone code: 5*

After decades of living in the past and letting the present die, Ríohacha is finally beginning to look more like a department capital. The city's once mournful central streets and grubby buildings have had a cheery facelift. Spotless pastel-coloured plazas have been built where filth and decay prevailed. Ríohacha still has its neglected, rundown areas but it can now, at least, hold its head up high. Founded by Nicolás Federman in 1535 as an important pearl-trading port, Ríohacha has another commercial focus today, namely contraband from Venezuela. The city's post-colonial fortunes have been mixed, but largely depressing: the result of Colombia's central governments distinct lack of interest. In the early 1900s Ríohacha had a fishing fleet of 150 but just 40 years later this had dwindled to fewer than half a dozen. Most of the inhabitants are 'in the trade' today as it is easier and more lucrative. The result, however, is that few people are prepared to work hard to develop local resources. In its darkest days, Ríohacha's dirty, rubbish-strewn streets were home to neighbourhoods of single-storey hovels – many containing Scandinavian fridges, Italian coffee-makers and piles of boxed electronic goods and designer brands unseen in Bogotá.

Ríohacha was inhabited by La Guajira's Wayúu Indians when the territory was sighted by Spanish sailor Alonso de Ojeda in 1498 from the sea. During its time as a major pearl-shipment centre it was the subject of many attacks including one led by Francis Drake in 1596. It became the capital of the newly created La Guajira department in 1964. A rather nice palm-scattered beach, some interesting historic buildings and a strong handicraft tradition form the backbone of Ríohacha's tourism ambitions.

GETTING THERE AND AROUND The city's Aeropuerto Almirante Padilla (↘ 727 3914) is located just west of the town and is well served by local taxis and colectivos. A daily Avianca (↘ 727 3624) flight to and from Bogotá is the only option at the time of writing. Bogotá departures are at 10.15 and Ríohacha flights leave at noon. Much of Ríohacha can be easily covered on foot with the town's cyclotaxi fleet a cheap and fun alternative. The city's motorised taxis are easy to spot along the main drag (↘ 728 5555) – expect to pay 2,500 for a cross-town trip and 6,000 COP to the airport.

TOURIST INFORMATION
◪ Riohacha Oficina de Turismo Calle I Antigua Terraza Marina; ↘ 728 3781/3782; f 7271015; ⊕ 08.00–18.00 Mon–Fri, closed noon–14.00, 09.00–13.00 Sat

Riohacha city website www.alcaldiaderiohacha.gov.co
Community portal www.miriohacha.com.co

Tour guide and operators Although a guide isn't necessary for Ríohacha itself, it is imperative to engage someone with a 4x4 and some local knowledge if travelling further north. Much of the journey is through inhospitable desert where an absence of defined tracks means getting easily lost is a genuine threat. On the basis of reliability, good humour and musical taste, **José Barros** (↘ 315 749 1431) at Tourismo Ecológico comes highly recommended. Not only does he navigate the ever-changing desert trails with ease and a smile but he also dances as he drives. Few people are as passionate about Vallenato, so just stick a CD of Los K Morales on and watch him groove.

A growing number of large and mid-sized tour companies operate out of Ríohacha, including Aviatur (↘ 728 7523), Guajira Magica (↘ 728 5758; e *guarijamagica@hotmail.com*), Guajira Tours (↘ 727 3385; f 727 5450), Guajira Viva (↘ 727 0607; e *guarijaviva@hotmail.com*) and Sol-Era Viajes y Turismo (↘ 727 2317; e *sol-eraviajes@yahoo.es*).

 WHERE TO STAY Ríohacha's hotels are located near the beach on Avenida la Playa or in the streets that lead off it, but the city isn't known for its fine accommodation, so be prepared to shop around.

🏠 **Hotel Almirante Padilla** Carrera 6, 3–29; ↘ 727 2328; e hotelalmirantepadilla@hotmail.com. Expect clean but bland rooms at this high-rise hotel, just a block or so from the beachfront main drag. It's got a restaurant, bar & rooms have AC & TV. $$

🏠 **Hotel Gimaura** (42 rooms) Av la Playa; ↘ 727 0019/2234; f 727 4546. This hotel sits on the banks of the Río Ranchería adjacent to the beach & over the Río Ranchería bridge. Expect the best service in town & comfortable AC rooms close to the pier, restaurants & tourist office. $$

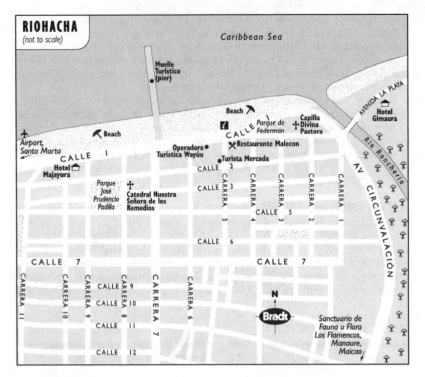

RIOHACHA
(not to scale)

Caribbean Sea

Muelle
Turístico
(pier)

Beach

Beach

Parque de
Federman

Capilla
Divina
Pastora

CALLE

Hotel
Gimaura

AVENIDA LA PLAYA

Río Ranchería

Airport,
Santa Marta

CALLE   I

Operadora
Turística Wayúu

Restaurante Malecon

Turista Mercada

Hotel
Majayura

CALLE   2

CALLE 3

AV

CIRCUNVALACIÓN

Parque
José
Prudencio
Padilla

Catedral Nuestra
Señora de los
Remedios

CARRERA 5

CARRERA 4

CARRERA 3

CARRERA 2

CARRERA 1

CALLE   5

CALLE   6

CALLE 7

CALLE 7

CARRERA 11

CARRERA 10

CARRERA 9

CALLE 9

CARRERA 7

CARRERA 6

CALLE 10

N

Bradt

Sanctuario de
Fauna u Flora
Los Flamencos,
Manaure,
Maicao

CALLE 11

CALLE 12

🏠 **Hotel Majayura** Carrera 10, 1–40; ☎ 727 5242.
This reasonable mid-range hotel is set back from the
beachfront strip at the opposite end of the pier, 100m
from the shoreline. Rooms are clean & have TV & AC but
the staff are indifferent. A restaurant serves decent food
but has a blaring TV – try the little bars & restaurants
opposite for a more enjoyable ambience. **$$**

🏠 **Hotel Miramar** Calle 1, 1–05; ☎ 728 0083. This
decent budget option is close to the thick of it, but
rooms at the front can be noisy. Expect simple
furnishings & a fuss-free service. **$$**

✗ **WHERE TO EAT** Typical dishes can be found in plentiful supply in the town's
numerous rustic local eateries, including rice-and-shrimp, grilled goat, goat stew
(*friche*) and a minced shrimp-and-onion meal (*salpion de camarones*). Opposite the
pier you'll find a string of fast-food, fried-chicken and pizza joints, including
Leonardo's Pizza. Try the nearby **Restaurante Malecón** opposite the park for
something a tad more refined (☎ 727 6762), the neighbouring upscale **Yotojoro**;
seafood joint **La Casa del Marisco** next door or fish specialist **La Tinaja**. The
consistently good **Pavillon Bay y Restaurante** (☎ 727 5555) is four blocks
north. Candy sellers on the beach boast an array of sticky-sweet treats typical of
the region – listen out for the sing-song cry from women that carry vast pots on
their heads.

ENTERTAINMENT AND NIGHTLIFE Rather surprisingly, the typically machismo
town of Ríohacha also has a highly evident community of transsexuals. They
don't don girly garb but wear typical Colombiano male attire – whilst sporting a
full face of make-up. For a more mainstream night, head to the **Sol y Luna Café
Bar** on the main drag opposite the beach – it serves up good, cheap cocktails and
light bites. For a lively full-on noisy fun-fest head to the Restaurante Malecón

after 23.00 – once the diners are finished this place rocks til daylight. Some funky little tequila bars and grilled-meat joints can be found along Calle 10 opposite the Hotel Majayura.

SHOPPING There is no shortage of vendors, stalls and hawkers selling cheap handicrafts around town, with bracelets, bags, hammocks and beaded jewellery the most popular crafts. The tourist office also has a small craft retail section but this tends to be pricey. One of the best-stocked independent stores specialising in Wayúu crafts is the Operadora Turística Wayúu on Calle 1, No 4–35 (✆ 728 7720; e *operadoraturisticawayuu@hotmail.com*). Another good option on the main drag is the Turista Mercada (✆ 728 3684; e *turismoyelisgomez@hotmail.com*), a small shop packed high with sombreros, Wayúu crafts and bags, run by helpful Yeliz Solano.

OTHER PRACTICALITIES Most of Ríohacha's banks are set back a block from the beach in a long succession of buildings with ATM booths outside. A couple of internet cafés are located on the main drag near to the tourist office.

WHAT TO SEE There's not a huge amount of sightseeing attractions as such in Ríohacha but a few points of interest are worthy of a closer look, including the **Catedral Nuestra Señora de los Remedios**, the city's principal church. Close by, the **Muelle Turístico** (Muelle de Santa Lucía) – Ríohacha's 1,200m, 70-year-old wooden pier – is a popular promenade with strolling, ice-cream eating families, hand-holding teens and snoozing elders. Thrill-seeking children jump into the water below amidst much shrieking and laughing. The pier fell into disrepair 50 years ago and began to rot into the sea. Today it has been restored to its former glory and is the tourist centrepiece of the main drag and a great place for a *paseo de la playa*. Nearby, the old **Capilla Divina Pastora** (chapel) sits in the **Parque de Federman**. A stretch of pavement adjacent is inlaid with symbols and flanked with six fine columns, adorned with mosaic designs and images relating to the Wayúu belief system connected to Mother Earth.

FESTIVALS AND EVENTS
Fiestas Nuestra Señora de los Remedios (*Feb*) Ríohacha's main festival brings crowds of locals out onto the streets in celebration of its patron saint – and sees hotel prices soar.

Feria Comercial Artesanal y Turística de la Guajira (*Jul*) This artisan extravaganza celebrated its seventh birthday in 2007 and showcases the region's rich handicraft tradition.

AROUND RÍOHACHA
SANCTUARIO DE FAUNA U FLORA LOS FLAMENCOS At Boca de Camarones 20 minutes south of Ríohacha, the **sanctuary** is a nesting ground for large numbers of small, salmon-pink flamingos. Large numbers of birds build mud nests in this oppressively hot 7,682ha mangrove forest around the areas of Manzanillo, Laguna Grande, Ciénaga del Navío Quebrado and Tocoromanes. Gondola-style canoes are hired for 10,000 COP (with a boatman) from the visitor centre for the 45-minute journey out to the nesting zone. Boarding the boat requires wading out across very slippery weed-covered sandbanks. The sun is also incredibly fierce out on the open waters, so pack plenty of water, sun block and a hat – and binoculars are a must. Shrimp farmers fish the lake with all surrounding communities 100% reliant on this economically. Eagle-eyed tourists have spotted

frogs and snakes in the mangroves, including large boa. Look out for flying fish in the Laguna Grande.

CENTRO DE EDUCACION E INVESTIGACION DE TORTUGAS (⊕*06.00–17.00 daily; free admission*) Attached to the flamingo sanctuary is a small turtle conservation centre complete with hatcheries, nurseries and clinic. Since 1977, it has collected approximately 40,000 turtle eggs from local beaches. Today it draws almost 5,000 visitors a year and regularly hosts conservation talks and workshops.

SALINAS DE MANAURE With its charming waterfront and stunning views, it's difficult to believe that the pretty little seaside town of Manaure is home to the most important and most extensive salt mines in Colombia. More than 700,000 tonnes of salt are mined here each year across 4,200ha and these vast silvery mounds are quite astounding and can be seen on the coastline beyond the beach. A pleasant plaza is just a 50m walk from the waterfront where children skip the lazy waves. Local boat owners sometimes ply for tourist trade by hammock-strung cabañas. Try the chicken a la plancha with frijoles, rice, plantain and salad at Restaurante y Panadería (10,000 COP) – it's in the centre of town.

RANCHERÍA EGNOTURISTICA WAYÚU IWOU>YAA (✆ *315 716 7197;* e *rancheriatour@ hotmail.com; www.geocities.com/tour-rancheria; admission 16,000 COP, must be pre-booked. Overnight stays are accommodated in rustic cabañas for 40,000 COP pp, inc all meals*) This small Wayúu community have opened up to tourism and offer talks, tours and demonstrations to provide an insight into the origins of their beliefs and culture. IWOU>YAA means 'Star of Spring' and the settlement is run along traditional lines. As a matriarchal society, the oldest woman has the greatest power and is highly respected. She has the final word and wears black pom-poms as a symbol of her status. When a girl is born there is much merriment. Once married, a woman is the controlling force with the husband joining her family. Domestic issues are also resolved within the community. If a wife fears infidelity on the part of her husband she seeks help from the *piache* (medicinal leader) who then concocts a potion using plants and herbs to win him back. Negative thoughts and insecurity are banished by the wearing of a stone in the waistband. Women are schooled in marriage from seven years old. During ceremonies and celebrations the Wayúu drink a potent liquor made from fermented trupillo fruit. Visitors are plied with the mega-strong *chirrinchi* during their tour and are also treated to dancing, singing and traditional food.

THE ROAD TO CABO DE LA VELA The road to Cabo de la Vela (Sail Cape) crosses the Ahuyama Desert and is not for the feeble or fragile. Unmade, unmarked, treacherous desert trenches are hard going for the toughest 4x4 on the last stretch to the cape (known as Jepira in the language of the Wayúu). It's relentlessly bumpy but exhilarating; just check the vehicle has decent shock absorption and air conditioning. Another essential is plenty of water.

Initially a wide stretch of paved road runs parallel with a stretch of train track, cutting through dark orange sand flanked by scrub. Birds of prey perch on a large billboard advertising Cabo de la Vela. At this point you are 17km from the cape – and just about to enter the undulating desert. This barren terrain of cactus-edged rugged sands is an alien land to the uninitiated – much like the most remote areas of the Australian Outback. As it is totally unlit and poorly drained, this sand expanse should not be attempted in bad weather or after dark.

CABO DE LA VELA (*Telephone code: 5*) In 1499, Spanish explorer Alonso de Ojeda named this rocky outcrop El Cabo de la Vela after spotting what he thought was a

The village of Camarones is rich in birdlife with rufous-vented chachalaca easily spotted in the early morning when they feed on the maize thrown down for the chickens. In the surrounding countryside, just beyond the village, Orinocan saltator, Caribbean hornero, bare-eyed pigeon, green-rumped parrotlet, scaled dove and brown-throated parakeet have been sighted. Thick, cactus-rich scrub is the preferred domain of the black-crested antshrike, vermilion cardinal, straight-billed woodcreeper, buffy hummingbird, red-billed emerald, pileated finch, chestnut piculet, white-fringed antwren, crested bobwhite and red-crowned woodpecker. Beyond the dry scrubland is a seasonally flooded flat plain favoured by terns, cormorants, herons, egrets and Ibis. It's also a good place to sight wood stork, roseate spoonbill and greater flamingo – white-rumped sandpiper has been recorded here.

white sail from his ship. Today this rustic little fishing village on the tip of the peninsula is home to a friendly Guajira community, thought to be the inspiration behind the tribe featured in Henri Charriere's *Papillon*. Women clad in brightly coloured flowing *yonnas* serve as a reminder that Cabo de la Vela is 99% Wayúu. Distinctive palm-thatched huts and battered fishing boats are the predominant feature in the beachfront settlement El Cabo, an idyllic spot with an 8km sandy stretch. Shallow waters form a theatrical contrast to the surrounding desolate tract and give it an oasis feel. Sparsely populated at just 800 people, it's an easy place to hang a hammock and simply shoot the breeze.

Getting around Several local boatmen offer their services to tourists, including Machorrito (312 630 637). Expect to pay 40,000 COP for a return trip to the lighthouse and 80,000 COP for salt mines at Pilón.

Where to stay and eat Most of Cabo de le Vela's dozen small, family-run hotels are little more than hammock-strung huts – and almost all are on the beach at El Cabo. However, one of the nicest places to stay is a few kilometres along the main drag. Beachfront **Refugio Pantu** is run by friendly owner Claudia and her two young daughters, Kelly and Katiara. Two rustic cabañas have small private bathrooms and open up right on the sand at 30,000 COP, including breakfast – just ask someone around town to point you in the right direction. Other options in central El Cabo include the **Ranchería Jarrena** (310 603 2517), **Ranchería Jeke'Tumana** (311 416 4004) and **Restaurante y Hospedaje Mahannain**. Many will also allow camping.

Many of the local restaurants also rent out rooms. Try **Restaurante y Hospedaje Jarrinapi** (311 683 4281), **Restaurante Utta** (310 644 4450/311 415 3933/300 825 0133), **Mar y Sol**, **Restaurante Mauicha**, **Restaurante Bonita**, **Restaurante Calamar**, **Restaurante Salaaima** and the **Restaurante Cabo Mar**. Local dishes tend to revolve around seafood, especially snapper, prawns and lobster – but goat is also on the menu. Food is generally served 07.00–21.00 each day with restaurants supplemented by vendors selling empanadas and sodas on the beach.

Shopping A couple of souvenir shops have opened up along the seafront. Most sell shells and local handicrafts, including *mochilas* (woven bags).

Other practicalities As a simple, rustic place without electricity or running water, visitors should expect accommodation and services to be basic. A bucket of water per person constitutes a bath with all generators switched off at 22.00. Pack a torch,

For many people, the closest they will ever get to a sea turtle is the creature gliding through a tank in their local aquarium. Adult sea turtles are elusive at best, and the majority of hatchlings crawl from their beaches and into the surf, disappearing from human radar. Adult sea turtles spend most of their lives in the water migrating, foraging or mating. Females will return to the beach in order to lay eggs, and males will occasionally leave the water to 'bask', raising their body temperature by sitting in the sun. With the use of radio-tracking devices and a multitude of international tagging projects, researchers have created a map of migration routes, and we now have a concept of a sea turtle's life at sea. Sea turtles are reptiles, and demonstrate reptilian characteristics, such as cold-blooded body temperatures, and laying their eggs on land.

Female sea turtles lay their nests in sand and never return, leaving their offspring to hatch, evacuate the nest, avoid predation and find the ocean all by themselves. Once the hatchlings emerge, they instinctively move into the water as quickly as possible. After the initial arduous journey ends, the turtles become very passive, drifting in the water instead of actively swimming. Juvenile hatchlings are a feast of the seas, as their carapaces (shells) are still quite soft, leaving them defenceless. Hatchlings become a snack for a variety of predators, including sharks, large fish and sea birds. This time of mystery, labelled by noted researcher Archie Carr as 'the lost year', can eventually be reconstructed – in a very general sense. The hatchlings are floating in deep water, and eventually reappear as much larger juvenile sea turtles in their juvenile foraging habitat. With an idea of the location of this habitat, a typical hatchling's path can be recreated by paying attention to ocean currents, gyres and other hydrographical features.

In their first nesting season, sexually mature sea turtles migrate into poorly defined courtship/mating areas, which are generally much closer to the nesting beaches. After insemination male turtles return to their foraging areas and females move into nesting sites in the same region as their birth. The belief that a turtle has an uncanny ability to return to the exact beach where it was born is an exaggeration. Sea turtles do in fact return to the region of their birth (impressive considering their foraging habitats could easily be 1,000km away) but not necessarily the beach where they hatched. Within her birthing region, a female turtle selects a nesting beach (utilising an unknown selection process) and returns to that very precise area for her successive nesting seasons approximately every three to five years.

Sea turtles nest at night, although there are specific exceptions to that rule, including but not limited to arribadas. However, it is still important to note that as cold-blooded reptiles, the majority of turtles nest during the cooler night-time hours, due to a decreased risk of overheating under the hot sun. A female crawls ashore, a laborious process during which she may change her mind and return to the sea for no apparent reason. She may also select a nesting site (habitat choice is varied by species – green turtles and leatherback turtles lay nests in open sandy areas, while hawksbills often lay under trees and shrub cover), often facing away or parallel to the water. After selecting a site, she clears a surprisingly deep body pit with long, sweeping movements of her front flippers. When the pit is cleared sufficiently, the turtle begins digging her nest hole. This amazing process

bring a book and maybe a card game – and bring snorkel gear etc. If you can, buy mineral water in Ríohacha as this is in short supply.

What to see Most visitors simply hang out on the beach eating fresh seafood before napping in a hammock and enjoying a swim in some of Colombia's bluest waters. However, those keen to do some sightseeing should take in the **Faro de la Vela** (lighthouse) – it's high up on an out-of-town headland that offers some truly begins by her first easing one rear flipper into the sand, scooping up a 'flipper-full', and tossing it to the side. Then, she immediately places the flipper on top of the loose sand, effectively keeping it from sliding back into the nest. This process is continued as she alternates flippers while digging. This is a lengthy procedure that eventually results in a flask-shaped nest. The turtle will keep digging until her flippers cannot reach any more sand and never turns around to check on the progress of her nest.

When the turtle is ready to lay her eggs she positions herself directly over the top of the nest chamber. It is at this point in her nesting process that most permitted researchers will tag, measure and gather data since the turtles become much more tolerant of noise, light and other distractions. Once all of her eggs are deposited, the turtle begins a methodical process of covering them. She scoops up sand with one rear flipper, places it on top of the eggs, and taps it down. This continues until the eggs are totally covered.

Although her eggs are covered, she is not yet ready to return to the sea. As she moves forward slowly, she will stop and use her front flippers to sling massive quantities of sand behind her before advancing. This returns the beach environment surrounding the nest to its original condition, and, as researchers late in marking their nests have found out, it also serves as an effective camouflage. She then slowly makes her way back to the sea. Females create nests, deposit their eggs, and return to sea multiple times in a single nesting season. Although it is extremely variable among and between species, this process is commonly completed as often as every two weeks but usually no more than four times in total.

Six to 13 weeks after laying, the hatchlings begin to emerge in a brief period of intense activity, termed 'a hatchling frenzy'. This consumes most of the resources provided by the egg yolk and their instinct is to immediately get to the water. Environmental cues, such as sand temperature, light reflection and the slope of the beach are significant tools that prompt ascending from the nest and aid in orienting their advancement towards the ocean.

Marine turtles can be traced back to the Jurassic era, over 150 million years ago, evolving and adapting to include modifications to the forelimbs, shell and rear limbs for swimming.

La Guajira is one of the biggest nesting grounds for Loggerhead turtles in Colombia. Turtles migrate thousands of miles through warm-water oceans and, according to experts, cry real tears. In La Guajira stories are told of when beaches were so full of turtles, men could not manoeuvre their boats out to sea. Today, all of Colombia's marine turtles face extinction and conservation groups now use volunteers to walk the beaches each night during the season in order to protect, tag and monitor those that arrive. Conservation groups throughout South America now collaborate on recorded data and research – a vital move as turtles vary nesting patterns over the years. Marine turtles are also threatened by fishing wire and nets, which cause many to drown, as like all reptiles they need to breathe air. Visitors can help stop the illegal poaching of turtles by refusing to buy eggs, meat or shell, if offered it. Sadly many tourists are still tempted by claims that the eggs act as an aphrodisiac. While locals are slowly responding to education concerning the threat to turtles, many believe that they will simply never die out.

magnificent views. The area also has a salt pile (**Pilón de Azúcar**) that is worth a peek. Both are covered by local tour guides.

SOUTHERN ATLANTIC COAST

The sprawling department of Chocó just manages to stretch to the Atlantic coastline and is the only Colombian province able to boast that it is also bordered by the Pacific Ocean. Set within the northeastern part of the Gulf of Urabá this tiny ribbon of land is home to some rather nice seaside towns on a backdrop of yucca plantations, maize crops and plantain trees. It is also perfectly placed for jungle treks, tours to Kuna Yala (San Blas islands) and hikes across the border into neighbouring Panama and is flanked to the west by the mighty Serranía de Darién.

CAPURGANA Telephone code: 4

This small coastal settlement of 2,800 inhabitants is carved out of the jungle on the northwestern Atlantic coast. Nudging the Darién Gap just a stone's throw from the Panamanian frontier, Capurgana overlooks the Gulf of Urabá where the waters of the Río Atrato run into the ocean. Two simple, but gorgeous beaches attract a fledgling tourist crowd that more than doubles the local population in high season from December to January. The northern beach is famed for its crystal-clear waters, so is a popular spot to watch the surf or snorkel in near-perfect visibility, especially during the rainy season when the water is calm. Although pebbly, the southern beach is an exciting place to spend time listening to the roar of the crashing waves against the shore. Island hopping, diving and kayaking are the prime occupations. It's also a great place to enjoy some superb seafood dishes at candle-lit tables looking out across the ocean. Traffic-free and largely Afro-Colombian, Capurgana has a funky laid-back beach town vibe.

GETTING THERE Three daily flights depart from Medellín during high season, arriving at the tiny Aeropuerto Narcisa Navas in about 75 minutes. Regional airline ADA (Aerolínea de Antioquía) operates a fleet of small 19-seater aircraft which fly to Capurgana. Departure times from Medellín are highly dependent on weather conditions so the timetable is best described as 'fluid' – it's worth preparing for possible delays. On arrival, passengers will discover a quirky taxi fleet primed for action. Coché's – Capurgana's makeshift pony and traps – transport luggage and passengers to hotels across town for 2,000 COP. Those arriving during the rains will find themselves serenaded by a zillion croaking frogs – they live in large numbers in the jungle behind the airport and hit high volume every time it showers.

GETTING AROUND Compact Capurgana is easily navigable on foot. Without roads or motorised vehicles (apart from a single motorbike) the only other option is the local horse-and-cart transport (coché) – plastic garden chairs with their legs removed have been roped to the hulk as seats and, other than a wheelbarrow, this eccentric taxi is the best way to get luggage to/from the airport at a cost of 2,000 COP.

TOUR GUIDE AND OPERATOR Amiable local guide **Walter Restrepo** (✆ *314 796 4455/314 643 5492*) specialises in horseriding tours, camping and jungle treks. One of his favourite stomping grounds is a large area of primary forest, Vereda el Brillante – home to a large number of wildlife species including boas, titi monkeys, armadillos, puma, eagles, toucans and parrots. Walter has 60 horses and tents for 20 people and overnight treks at 120,000 COP per person include cooking freshly caught fish and freshwater shrimp over an open fire. Other tours include two-hour treks up to La Cielo (12,000 COP) and half-day trips to Bahía Aguacarte (50,000 COP inc lunch) on foot or on horseback as well as tours to Los Rios (50,000 COP inc lunch) up from a rainforested valley dotted with rocky creeks and natural pools.

Small tour operator **Excursiones Ecologicas** (✆ *682 8789*) has an office opposite the park. It runs snorkelling trips and organises horseriding and jungle treks and will lend a hand with hotel bookings.

Visitors rave about the quality of fishing in and around Capurgana. Today, the town generates 90% of its revenue from tourism with just 10% from fishing, ensuring there are plenty of fish in the sea for enthusiastic amateurs. Large numbers of marlin, prawns, tuna, jacks, needle fish, angel fish, queen fish and red snapper can be found in the surrounding waters. Numerous boatmen offer fishing trips out around the bays and islands for around 20,000 COP per person.

WHERE TO STAY Capurgana's first hotel opened 30 years ago. Today, five large hotels and a good handful of smaller places offer rooms to rent – often with meals thrown in. Shoestring travellers will also find some camping options and a youth hostel – all within a ten-minute walk of the beach. However, those keen to stay near the park should pack a pair of earplugs unless they are immune to loud music and revelry 24 hours a day.

Casa Blanca (11 rooms) ☎ 682 8789. As the name suggests, this white building has white fittings & furnishings with AC rooms that sleep 37 people at 75,000 COP pp per night all inc. Owner Ariel Palacios Palacios is open to discounts for stays of more than a week & offers plenty of nice touches, such as welcome cocktails.
Centro Náutico Hotel (12 cabins + 3 suites) ☎ 362 2158; e alcazarcapurgana@une.net.co. This sister hotel of the Alcazar is also its immediate neighbour and can accommodate 70 people. Most guests have booked as part of a watersports holiday package but rooms are available on a per-night basis. Rates vary depending on the season (all-inc rates apply in the peak months).
Hostal Capurgana (8 rooms) ☎ 824 36111; www.hostalcapurgana.com. This charming *pensionado* is located opposite the Tiende y Restaurante Don Blas. Room rates of 45,000 pp inc b/fast & dinner – with lunch available for an extra 15,000 per night. Rooms are set around a leafy courtyard where wooden tables & chairs enjoy a cooling breeze amidst palms, trees & flowers. In low season the hotel offers rates of 20,000 COP pp room only & is open to negotiation regarding discounts for longer stays.
Hostal Marlin This big wooden building located at the end of the main drag overlooking the bay, has large balconies & is notable for its sizeable carved marlin over the porch. Prices pp per night start at 55,000 COP inc meals but rooms vary so be sure to ask to see a few.
Hotel Alcazar (29 rooms) ☎ 362 2158; e alcazarcapurgana@une.net.co. Although originally from Medellín, charismatic general manager Sergio Osorio Fernandez adores Capurgana so much he has declared it his spiritual home. Built in grand Moroccan style on a staggered beachside plot, the Alcazar is an architectural mix of domes, towers & archways. Influenced heavily by the 7 saints of Marrakech, each of

the rooms at the Alcazar has been inspired by Arabic mosques, palaces & riads using inlaid wood, painted glass, minarets, copulas & aged tiles. All-inc packages at the Alcazar represent excellent value per night with a choice of dbl & sgl rooms (in low season room-only rates apply) – choose room 402 for stunning views across the rooftops out to sea. The Alcazar's zany waiter-cum-barman-cum-guide-&-handyman Dairo Gonzales boasts the distinction of first discovering Capurgana's blowhole – he's also a good source of tourist information & local gossip. $$
Hotel Amar (49 rooms) ☎ 366 262; e almar@epm.net.co; www.almar.com.co. This beachfront hotel opened 24 years ago & is one of the most established & most popular all-inclusives in Capurgana. Onsite amenities include a jacuzzi, bar, spa & TV lounge. AC rooms aren't particularly plush but are reasonably comfy & the hotel does have a facelift in the offing. White wooden balconies overlook pretty hedged tropical gardens. Buffet-style meals inc seafood, meat, chicken & salads with beer, wine & cocktails & snacks all part of the all-inc package of 180,000–200,000 COP pp per night.
Hotel El Uvito ☎ 824 3002. It's been 25 years since El Uvito opened for business & some of the rooms in this small family hotel are definitely beginning to show the strain. However, overlook the slightly shabby décor & this hotel is perfectly adequate. Ask to see a couple of rooms as some are more comfortable than others.
Hotel Las Mañanitas ☎/f 824 3412; e hotelmananitascapurgana@hotmail.com; www.hotellasmananitas.com. This pretty single-storey all-inc hotel has views over open water & is the last building on a sandy coastal track. Just a 10-min walk from the airport, Las Mañanitas is built in Mediterranean style with ceramic tiling, paved terraces

11

& paintwashed terracotta-coloured walls. An open-sided restaurant has pretty tables covered in orange cloths & vases of yellow heliconia. Archways guarded by tubs trailing bougainvillea lead to a large pool edged by a ochre-coloured balustrade.

⌂ **Luiz de Oriente** ↘ 824 3719. Essentially a restaurant (see *Where to eat* below), the Luiz de Oriente is located right by the dock between the town & the beach. Pleasant fan-cooled rooms above the diner are 50,000 COP with rates fully inc of meals.

⌂ **Posada los Laureles** (4 rooms) ↘ 311 622 5937. This little pensionado above Almacén Accesorios Mannix sleeps 13 people in rooms with private bathrooms.

Rates are 20,000 COP pp room only or 55,000 COP for dinner, B&B.

⌂ **Tacarcuna Lodge** (35 rooms) ⅋f 412 2552; e info@hotelsdecostacosta.com; www.hotelesdecostacosta.com. This beautiful wooden orange & blue building oozes style with terracotta floors & inlaid rocks adorned with flower-filled tubs & planters. Hanging baskets brim with varicoloured blooms under a wood-&-thatch roof hung with shells, molas & wind chimes. Rooms offer sgl, dbl & trpl accommodation at 105,000 COP pp all inc — but don't stay here unless you have a high noise tolerance as this hotel is right, bang smack in Capurgana's local party zone.

✗ **WHERE TO EAT** The beachside **Restaurante y Marisqueria Josefina** (*Playa Caleta near Hotel Almar;* ⊕*daily for dinner; $$*) serves up arguably the finest seafood dishes in town. Choose from prawns in coconut, red mullet in garlic, fish soup, squid and langoustine.

On the edge of Playa Caleta, near the bridge that connects with the town, the **Luiz de Oriente** (↘ *824 3719; $$*) has a distinctive Asian décor. Red lanterns hang around the wooden frontage in a restaurant adorned with bamboo, lacquered fittings and teak. Yet, rather confusingly, the menu appears to be 100% Spanish-influenced with paella a speciality. This place also has rooms (see *Where to stay*, above) and a cocktail bar.

For a tiny kiosk, the **Cocteleria Emilyn** ($) drums up a lot of trade. Find it on the dock and don't expect anything more complicated than prawns and soda.

The **Tiende y Restaurante Don Blas** ($) serves up snacks, drinks and simple fish-and-rice meals for less than 8,000 COP to eat in or take away. Look out for this family-run eatery in the centre of town – it has dayglow green walls.

Nearby, the red-painted **Venta de Jugos Naturales** ($) whips up endless fresh tropical juices, such as papaya, mango, pineapple and orange.

For big plates of meat head to the **Restaurante Doña Fatima** ($) – a popular *carne a la plancha* joint located opposite the juice bar, where seasoned beef with plantain and a beer will set you back less than 9,000 COP.

The **Restaurante Mi Barcito** ($) has a menu of grilled meat and chicken, fried fish and sancocho soup. You'll find it near the artisan vendors at the dock end of town.

Doña Ofelia ($) serves traditional tropico chocóano food using regional recipes and is renowned for delicious *arepa con carne* (meat arepa), *frijole beans* and *maza morra* (maize soup) – a real treat and dirt cheap.

There are chips, chips and more chips at the aptly named **El Palcio del Frito** ($) (The 'Palace of Fries') located opposite the **Restaurante Café** where a basic fare is served at tables on a corner shingle plot. If it's fried chicken and fries you want head to **Chocó Pollo** on the park, a greasy spoon popular with Capurgana's drinking crowd on a Sunday afternoon.

ENTERTAINMENT AND NIGHTLIFE Capurgana's main park is little more than a square patch of grass that doubles as a town plaza-cum-soccer-field. It is also a popular grazing spot for horses and chickens. A small string of noisy local bars and a solitary disco pump out music until dawn each day, each playing competing tracks at deafening volume until the sound systems explode. The worst offenders are El Empate, Guayabo Loco, El Wasa and Sohido Nitido. Each has a set of mile-high distorted speakers and is located opposite the goalposts. At the nearby Estadero del Almendro old men stagger around a makeshift dance floor swigging from bottles of *aguardiente*. However, most gringos choose to give the local drinking dens a miss in favour of the beach bars and restaurants by the dock.

SHOPPING In the centre of town, along the Calle del Comercial, a string of handicraft shops and vendors sell jewellery, bags, trinkets, baskets and souvenirs. There's also a stall selling local crafts outside the Hotel Almar – the Arte el Machi sets up early in the morning and closes at dusk and proudly displays a sign guaranteeing '50% discount' year-round. By the park, Almacén Accesorios Mannix stocks a nice range of jewellery, jeans, beachwear and belts. There are also a couple of souvenir shops at the airport. María Canamo and Helados both stock Kuna molas, jewellery and other handicrafts.

OTHER PRACTICALITIES Capurgana's city chiefs have dissuaded traders from hawking their wares on the beach and it is very rare to be hassled on Playa Caleta – or anywhere in the town. Pack a torch as Capurgana has many unlit paths with an electric supply that runs until 02.00. Capurgana's COMCEL office in the centre of town offers a fax and airmail service with national and international calls and also sells mobile phone chargers. Next door, the town's small ADA airline office has a stock of timetables and a ticket desk (✆ *682 8817*).

WHAT TO SEE AND DO
Beaches The picturesque palm-edged sandy stretch of **Playa Caleta** fronts some of Capurgana's largest hotels but is gorgeous nonetheless. It's easily accessible and a popular place for a morning stroll or jog. Pristine sands are swept daily and there are plenty of shady spots under palms in which to escape the rays. Sweeping **Playa Soledad** (aka Playa Alta) is a popular stop-off with day trippers while **Playa Media** is an idyllic 100m strip of golden soft sand fanned by palms. This Robinson Crusoe beach is accessible by boat or a six-hour hike on foot and is a gorgeous picture-postcard stretch. **Playa la Mora** (Blackberry Beach) is named after the fruit-laden bushes that edge the sand. Other small beaches within reach of Capurgana include **Playa Los Locos**, **Playa Bélen** and **Playa Sucia**.

Bahía Aguacarte (Avocado Bay) Most people visit Bahía Aguacarte as part of an organised boat trip, arriving to snorkel in the middle of the morning before a lunch of fried fish overlooking the bay. With this in mind, those arriving under their own steam may be wise to give it a wide berth between 11.30 and 14.00 as the place is much less likely to be crowded once the lunchtime rush has died down. Bahía Aguacarte is a beautiful spot with an avocado-shaped bay edged by thick jungle slopes and crimson san juaquin blooms. Diners can enjoy views from the open-sided **Restaurante Doña Diana** (known locally as simply 'La Aguacarte') of bobbing fishing boats and open seas. The food is great and served at rustic wooden tables with plastic chairs set out under a thatched awning. Choose from the catch of the day with patacones and salad, grilled beef or seafood soup – all for less than 8,000 COP. Four-hour tours on horseback depart from Capurgana with boat trips daily from the dock at around 09.30. At the time of writing, plans for a hotel on Bahía Aguacarte are well under way. German owner Dairio Peñaloza expects the Hotel Puerto Ventura to open early 2008.

Isla de los Pajaros (aka Isla Sucre) Although renowned for its many species of nesting seabirds, this island has a dual persona as Sugar Island – a name born out of its sugar-like 'frosting' of crystallised salt. As a protected breeding site, the island is not accessible to humans. However, large numbers of birds can be easily sighted from the surrounding waters (especially at around 16.30). A trio of bottle-nosed dolphins can also often be spotted here.

El Hoyo Soplador (The Blow-hole) Madcap Dairo Gonzales (the Alcazar Hotel's medallion-wearing sexagenarian) claims to have first discovered Capurgana's blow-hole decades ago. Today, this spouting cavity forms part of the daily tour schedule – a natural phenomenon that lies at the inland end of a rocky outcrop washed by waves. Water is funnelled up towards a gap in the rocks to create some spectacular soaring jets of water, although the height of the gushes very much depends on the state of the weather. In the right conditions, air is either blown out or sucked into the hole at considerable pressure with resulting spouts that reach speeds of 20 miles per hour.

El Cielo (The Sky) A simple walking tour along this rocky rainforest trail costs around 10,000 COP with horseback a popular alternative option at 12,000 COP – the trek is a 10km round trip along a gradual slope upwards. Local guide Walter Restrepo (see *Tour guide and operator* above) keeps his horses fit, well trained and healthy and is highly recommended. On foot, the round trip will take around four hours. By horse, it is 45 minutes each way. Expect to spot titi monkeys high above waterfalls, sandy creeks and rocky rivers. A nice little rustic eatery – the Esmeralda Restaurante – serves fish-and-rice meals, sodas and beers at La Cielo. Thick jungle and creekside views make this a memorable pit-stop ahead of the trek back down. Another option is La María Restaurante towards the end of the journey or the Ultimo Recurso at the point the trail begins.

Piscina de Los Dioses (Pool of the Gods) Plunging into the sparkling waters of this deep, natural pool from the surrounding rocky ledges is a popular dare-devil pursuit. However, those less fearless will still enjoy swimming in the pristine depths of this beautiful spot – Mother Nature's own jacuzzi.

Kuna Yala (San Blas) Kuna Yala is an autonomous region of 400 islands and a 230km needle-thin strip of mainland coastline in Panama inhabited solely by indigenous Kuna people. Meaning 'Kuna-land' in Dulegaya, the unique language of its people, Kuna Yala has been self-ruled since 1930, when the Panamanian government granted the tribe the right to govern its own land. Many of these beautiful palm-fringed islands surpass every travel brochure 'paradise island' cliché. Most have white-sand beaches, some have thatch-and-mud villages, but all are blessed with uncluttered ocean views. Only 40 are inhabited with communities that range in size from five to 5,000. The people of Kuna Yala are believed to be descendants of people from the land known today as Colombia, whose tribes migrated to Darién to escape disease in the Colombian jungle in the 1600s. Since settling on the archipelago the Kuna have struggled as outsiders in Panama, isolated by culture and location. The last 130 years have been a period of immense change for people that have fought to retain their traditions against a background of economic, discriminatory and political challenge. Declining fish stocks in recent years have caused the Kuna Yala to look elsewhere for revenue, and its modern-day economy is becoming increasingly reliant on the exploitation of its culture. Tourism is a contentious issue that is endorsed by some but not all Kuna. Traditionally a barter economy, the sale of mola to tourists is bringing greater cash orientation to the islands, a cause of some social tension. Yet in many respects there are few discernable differences between the people of Kuna Yala and those olden settlements in northern Colombia. Men hunt, fish and gather wild tapir, agouti, monkey, deer, bird, peccary and iguana using blowguns, spears, bow and arrow and a variety of traps and pits. Women cook on open fires in one-room bamboo-and-thatch huts while children play in the rivers and on the shoreline with coconut husks and palm fronds. All are practised oarsmen whose only method of transport is dugout canoe (*ulu*). To the

Kuna the world is a dual civilisation containing the 'world of spirit' and the 'world of subsistence'. The world of spirit surrounds and resides inside every material thing, underpinning the world of subsistence and giving it power. Spirits respect those who reinforce tradition and so the Kuna respect 'spirit sanctuaries' where these spirits dwell. These sanctuaries are usually on what would be quality agricultural land but because of the Kuna belief, it remains forested and intact. Violation of these sanctuaries would cause the spirits to rise up in rage and harm the community, a principle based on the earth as the body of the Great Mother who in union with the Great Father gave birth to all plant, animal and human life.

The distinctive dress of the Kuna women comprises a mola (blouse), gold nose rings, a long skirt, a red and yellow headdress, gold breastplates and colourful long strands of beaded leg wraps (uini). A long black line is painted on the face from the tip of the nose to the forehead and women adopt this dress after puberty rites when they are properly named. Until this point they are known only by a nickname but after menstruation a woman's position is reinforced in matrilineal Kuna society by a name. This strong female status is further strengthened by the income generated by mola sales, a practice that began in 1945 after a missionary purchased one as a souvenir. Today making molas for tourist revenue represents an important part of the region's economy, and one that is wholly reliant on its women. Many Kuna are keen to connect with foreigners and are curious, candid and engaging. However, they often do not understand the blatant disrespect they receive from visiting tourists. Many feel their cultural sensibilities are ignored by 'guests' who should know better. That tourists can disregard Kuna values has horrified entire communities in the archipelago, resulting in a further tightening of the grip on tourism. Skimpy clothes may be de rigueur in Acapulco but they are alien attire in Kuna Yala. Nudity is strictly prohibited and men are asked not to go shirtless. The offence it causes and the image it creates present the Kuna with an unfavourable picture of the 'outsiders' and often breed cynicism in those once keen to show their homeland to the world.

Each of the 400 islands is privately owned by the communities of Kuna Yala. At the time of writing none of the nine communities on the mainland is geared up for visits by 'wagas' (the Kuna word for foreigner) and the archipelago is the focus of visitor activities. Every visitor that steps onto any island in Kuna Yala needs to pay a fee to its people. The rate varies from island to island but is about US$35. This is generally included in the cost of a tour and is paid to the village elders. Visitors should be sure to carry plenty of US$1 bills, as a dollar fee is payable to the subject of each photograph that you take. The photogenic Kuna and their colourful clothes make striking subjects, but visitors should never take a photo without first gaining permission. The issue of photography is a sensitive one in Kuna Yala and can lead to some misunderstanding. However the rule is simple ('no fee no photo') and is rarely wavered. Kuna elders enforced this law after learning that photographs of Kuna Yala were being used for commercial gain without any financial benefit to its people. Today the value of its culture in terms of 'bankability' has been a valuable lesson learned, especially by the many Kuna with a photogenic smile. The two-hour trip to Kuna Yala is offered by almost every hotel tour desk and operator. Prices include a guide and lunch at around 110,000 COP for adults (80,000 COP for children) with 24-hour permission to visit granted by the Kuna elders. Trips generally depart at 08.00 and return to Capurgana at 17.00.

AROUND CAPURGANA

SAPZURRO It is difficult not to take this tiny seaside community to your heart, such is its charm, beauty and laid-back seafront feel. Just 150 inhabitants live in this 120-year-old settlement, located right, bang smack on the Panamanian border – Colombia's so-called 'Last Town of The North-West'. A yellow-and-black-striped wooden jetty leads to Sapzurro's main drag – a colourful 100m waterfront stretch. A couple of bars and restaurants overlook bobbing boats and rainforest-clad slopes along the bay. Sandy paths wriggle with burrowing crabs in flower-filled neighbourhoods of candy-coloured wooden houses. Fruit trees bearing mango, avocado, lemon, lime, kumquat and tamarind edge a thick emerald-green jungle mass tumbling down to bright blue waters.

Safety Colombia's military forces have successfully pushed the FARC guerrillas that once controlled the region back deep into the jungle and FARC operatives are now based in Panamanian territory in the Darién. Here, FARC's Frente 57 continues to engage mainly in logistical planning. In 2007, it is hard to imagine that in June 1999 guerrillas briefly took over Sapzurro and had ultimate control. Today, local residents boast that Sapzurro is the 'safest place in Colombia' as it has a four-to-one ratio of lawmen (local police, army, coastguard and federal police) for every citizen. The entire border region is heavily guarded by both the Colombian and Panamanian armies with posts every half-mile. It feels exceedingly safe with all traces of guerrilla presence gone.

Getting there Timetabled tour boats leave from Capurgana throughout the day, but for a more direct route find a boatman prepared to do the short trip. However, don't be rushed to board a vessel clearly not fit for the purpose, especially in rain or high seas. Over the past couple of years at least one elderly boat has broken in half during the trip from Capurgana. The motor immediately sunk and although everyone aboard was eventually rescued (or was able to swim the miles to shore) an absence of insurance, life vests and radio in choppy seas wasn't a recipe for a carefree journey.

Getting around Sightseeing on foot is your only option in pedestrianised Sapzurro, but that's just fine as the pretty paths are a pleasure to walk and the jungle treks totally stunning.

Tour guides Martha Rubio (♦ 314 622 3149) is an excellent independent tour guide. She offers a wide range of trips from jungle treks and visits to Kuna tribes to birding, fishing and 'meet the people' tours. Martha speaks a little English and is also involved in conservation projects in Sapzurro. She can arrange tailor-made camping and snorkelling trips and trips to local farms. Martha is a member of the Colombian Ornithological Society and a practised birding guide.

Andrés Buendia (\ *313 624 1329*) knows his way around the islands, bays and jungle tracks (from short stomps to full-day hikes and three-day camping trips). He can also organise a boat and guides across the border into Panama.

Where to stay and eat For a teeny-weeny town, Sapzurro sure has a lot of places to stay. A collection of cabins, home-stays and campsites offer well over 150 beds a night – an incredible achievement that should make many of Colombia's larger resorts take note.

Restaurant & Hotel Doña Triny (22 rooms) \ 312 751 8626. Patron Triny is proud of her hotel and restaurant – & it shows. This spotlessly clean yellow-&-lime waterfront building is immaculately maintained with pretty rooms at 60,000 pp, inc b/fast & lunch (or dinner). Seafood & chicken dishes in the restaurant are priced at around 9,000 COP for red snapper with delicious soups & snacks from 3,000 COP.

Hotel Uvalí (4 rooms). This simple family-run hotel has fan-cooled rooms at 65,000 COP pp inc b/fast & a seafood lunch (or dinner). A guide to La Miel is inc in the room rate.

Cabañas Barracuda \ 824 3042. Budget travellers rave about this beachfront set of cabins on a backdrop of jungle & palms. Facilities are rustic with few frills & fuss – rates vary so be prepared to haggle.

Cabaña Narza Two comfortable twin rooms cost just 30,000 COP in this pleasant B&B where the owner can also arrange walking tours & fishing trips.

Cabañas Teonila. A large fan-cooled family-sized room can accommodate 4 people in this simple B&B at a cost of 15,000 COP pp.

Cabaña Tacarcuna Two cabañas each sleep 4 people in 2 dbl beds at a cost of 25,000 COP pp at this charming local home. Birding & snorkelling trips can also be arranged by the owners for 30,000 COP pp for a group of 5.

Casa del Monte \ 313 593 8265. Patron Guillermina Borrio has two guest rooms in her family-run B&B at 20,000 COP pp.

Cabaña Cabo Tiburon \ 314 632 4890. For 25,000 COP pp owner Yadiva Barrios offers 2 double fan-cooled rooms with an ample b/fast.

Donde De Mauro Seven rooms of various sizes and configurations cost 25,000 COP pp per night with discounts available for longer stays.

La Punta \ 314 666 5210. Without a doubt, this is one of Sapzurro's nicest places to stay, on account of its stunning location. Owner Mirium Serrano has a great eye for detail & each of her 4 guest rooms is beautifully decorated. Find La Punta 5 mins out of the town centre (reachable on foot or by boat).

Hotel Chileno \ 313 685 9862. This nice little hotel is located on Playa Diana with 2 rooms sleeping up to 8 people at 25,000 COP pp.

Donde Guille There are few sophisticated amenities on this family-run campsite, apart from washing facilities & a bathroom. However, it can accommodate 20 people & costs just 7,000 COP in high season (5,000 COP off-peak).

Nawaly There's sufficient room for 50 people on this decent-sized campsite. Onsite amenities include a shower block with prices from 5,000 COP.

Entertainment and nightlife It's fair to say that apart from a trio of bars and a couple of restaurants Sapzurro doesn't have much to offer once the sun sets. However, Martha Rubio (\ *314 622 3149*) organises 'meet the people' evenings to offer interaction with Sapzurro's elderly storytellers over local food and drink.

Shopping For a great selection of funky bags, jewellery, handicrafts, local produce, souvenirs, T-shirts, swimwear, flip-flops, sunhats, scarves, shorts, Kuna molas and carvings pop into **Tatuajes en Jagua** on the waterfront.

Other practicalities Sapzurro has an excellent COMCEL mobile signal, unlike many of Colombia's other remote jungle villages. An international telephone service is offered at the telephone Servicio shop next door to Tatuajes en Jagua on the waterfront. Generator-powered electricity runs from 09.00–02.00 so you may need a torch to be on the safe side. Snack shops (such as Los Almendros and Doña Marta on the waterfront) offer food supplies for jungle treks and camping trips. Muddy trails, high humidity and biting insects make boots, water, sun block and bug repellent essential items.

What to see and do

Coqueria de Agua Viva For a henna tattoo (using *jagun* ink) and a range of handicrafts ask a guide to direct you to this pretty private home. The owners are a couple of Argentine expatriates and welcome visitors – their home is near to the waterfall Cascada Agua Viva.

Kuna Indians in Carreto (45-minute trip to the north, more authentic) and in Calidonia (1½ hours to the north). Contact Martha Rubio (\ *314 622 3149*) – she makes the bookings with the *zaila* (chief) and is also the guide (some English) at 60,000 COP per person.

Local tour guide Martha Rubio (see *Tour guides*) is also involved in a local Turtle Protection Programme – *Protección, Monitoreo E Investigacíon Tortuga Caña* – led by local conservationist Emigdo Pertuz (e *emigdiopertuz@hotmail.com*). Aside from protecting nesting sites and breeding turtles, education initiatives include teaching local communities about conservation and dissuading against eating turtle meat and turtle eggs. Martha can organise volunteer placements and visits to the project, which remains in dire need of funding and resources.

LA MIEL La Miel means 'the honey' on account of its soft, sweet tranquillity, but a cluster of burnt-out buildings is testament to the fact that the town hasn't always been as peaceful as it is today. Local inhabitants fled their homes when 200 rebels from the Colombian Revolutionary Armed Forces (FARC) invaded in 1999. FARC activists had been hiding in Panama in the dense jungle in the hills above La Miel. Heavily forested mountains on the Panamanian side of the frontier have long provided perfect hiding places for drug labs and guerrilla camps and, in recent years, even coca plantations. More than 120 La Miel inhabitants fled to safer provinces, concerned that AUC paramilitaries would move into the area and kill villagers thought to be supporting FARC guerrillas.

Take a stroll through tiny La Miel to spot giggling toddlers and snoozing elders in porch-fronted homes of painted wood. At the end, coralline rocks form a craggy mass in the water by buildings destroyed to rubble in the troubles of the past. Thankfully, today, La Miel is peaceful and laid-back – even if a large proportion of the village's 142 population are children. Most villagers earn a living from coconut trading and fishing. However, when a tourist arrives in town a handful of enterprising housewives immediately set up a kitchen on the beach. Playa Blanca is a 25m curved stretch of white sand that is truly idyllic. If you have time, order a bowl of the dish of the day

CROSSING INTO PANAMA

A 45-minute gluey trail leads from the back of Sapzurro up 180 impossibly steep muddy steps to the Panamanian government checkpoint (a kind of pre-border border), called Cabo Tiburon. An obelisk bearing Panama's heraldic coat of arms marks a change in territory and from here the trip down into Panamanian soil is slippery, slidey and ungainly. Traversing this mud-fest eventually leads to the frontier settlement of La Miel – Panama's last (or first) town. Expect to arrive in an undignified sludge-like state, especially if it happens to be raining.

and find a spot on the beach and do nothing but soak up the views – pure bliss. Snorkel gear can also be rented at Playa Blanca where a boat to Puerto Obaldia (Panama's official border) costs US$65 and takes 20 minutes. This is also where you can pick up a boat back into Colombian waters, along a route that passes vast volcanic cliffs that signify the end of Panamanian territory in truly dramatic style.

Where to stay This is a pre-border frontier town, and tourists aren't permitted to stay overnight in La Miel. There are no hotels and camping is illegal, so head on to Puerto Obaldia.

Where to eat Many of La Miel's womenfolk offer meals for sale when they spot a tourist in town. Dishes tend to consist of shrimp, snail and fried fish with coconut and rice and are usually served on Playa Blanca. Expect to pay 6,000–7,000 COP (around US$3.50) for a bowl of caracol stew (*la cigua*) – with a generous portion usually part of the deal. Look out for the Atlas signs in the centre of town for a chance to sup one of Panama's finest beers.

PUERTO OBALDIA Panama's military checkpoint town of Puerto Obaldia is full of travellers keen to leave, so expect to encounter penniless backpackers frustrated by Panama's reams of red tape. Puerto Obaldia is a tatty transit town with few endearing qualities for travellers passing through. Hotels are shabby with the nicest accommodation available at the very basic Pensión Conde – expect to pay around 10,000 COP for little more than an airless, soulless box with its fair share of wildlife. A handful of mediocre restaurants offer a limited menu with a couple of bars that tend to get rowdy after dark. Pack plenty of patience ahead of a trip to Puerto Obaldia as immigration officials are slow, cheerless and woefully inefficient – and that's if they just happen to be awake.

Getting there Get an exit stamp at the DAS office in Capurgana by the harbour where a launch to Puerto Obaldia costs about 60,000 COP. This is a price for the whole boat, regardless of the number of passengers – so it makes sense to ask around to see if any fellow travellers are planning the journey. From La Miel, the price tends to be higher – in fact it can often double to around US$65. Head to Playa Blanca and ask around for a boatman prepared to do the trip. Officially, the immigration office stipulates that all travellers exiting Colombia to Panama require proof of yellow fever jabs and sufficient funds – but in practice this rarely happens. However, to be on the safe side, keep a credit card statement to hand – although it's likely that border staff will glimpse at it for a couple of seconds and decide it's good enough.

Getting around The four-times-a-week flight from Puerto Obaldia to Panama City on Wednesday, Thursday, Saturday and Sunday tends to be fully booked, so build in a contingency for making a reservation at the airline office in town or pre-arrange it via the internet or central booking system (*(507) 315 7500; www.aeroperlas.com*). Tickets cost around US$57 for the hour-long flight.

Other practicalities It's important to sort out US dollars before travelling into Panama. Although there are money changers in Puerto Obaldia the peso–US dollar exchange is truly pitiful. Credit cards aren't welcome anywhere in La Miel or Puerto Obaldia and nobody will touch Colombian currency. At the time of writing there isn't an ATM in either town. In La Miel there is no mains electricity or water supplies – so power and utilities can be iffy and bottled water recommended. Travellers can keep up to date via a local radio station to check what's going on – simply tune into 96.1 FM, 'Ecos del Darién'.

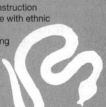

Appendix 1

AMAZON WILDLIFE GUIDE

taken from Amazon: The Bradt Travel Guide *and edited by Mike Unwin*

AMAZON PLANTS Warmth, constant sunlight and heavy rainfall speed up photosynthesis in rainforests, allowing prolific plant growth and at least 50,000 woody plants are recorded from the Amazon – around a fifth of all plant species known.

Trees Rainforest trees collectively take up and release so much water that they affect global weather patterns. Their trunks, stems, branches, leaves, fruits and roots also provide microhabitats for countless animals and smaller plants.

Rainforest layering The forest's vertical structure comprises four to six overlapping layers, differing in the amount of light and moisture they receive, and hence their species composition. The **emergent layer** comprises such giants as fig, teak, mahogany and kapok, which tower above the canopy, reaching 40m or more. The **middle (or closed-canopy) layer** consists of uniform-looking trees, 12–30m tall, with tall, narrow crowns; one tree never overlaps another of the same species. The **understorey (or shrub layer)** comprises typically a sparse growth of treelets and shrubs, from 1–6m, as well as small palms, tree-ferns and cycads. At **ground level** in mature forest, the closed canopy cuts off up to 98% of the light, allowing only shade-tolerant herbs, ferns, tree seedlings and fungi to grow. Many herbs have long, narrow, often variegated leaves; some are popular as houseplants.

Animal niches correspond to this layered structure. Birds and insects dominate emergent tree crowns, while the canopy has the greatest biodiversity, with birds, mammals and reptiles. Below the canopy, lianas and other parts of trees and shrubs are colonised by miniature ferns, mosses, lichens and other simple plants, creating a mini-forest for micro-animals, which break down dead plant matter and provide food for micro-predators such as centipedes and hunting spiders. On the forest floor, jaguar and other predators hunt a range of prey, while anteaters feast on ants and termites. Meanwhile in the soil and leaf litter invertebrates help fungi and microbes decompose organic matter to recycle the forest's nutrients.

Forest edges and gaps Numerous plants thrive where light is abundant. Acacias and mimosas are common beside water. Acacias often have elaborate red-orange flowers and large seedpods, like giant beans. Mimosas produce globular yellow or creamy-white flowers and have feathery leaves. Cecropia, with its large five-lobed leaves, is a common trees of river edges and is protected from insects and epiphytes by aggressive stinging ants. Heliconia has waxy red and yellow flowers that resemble crab-claws, and is pollinated by hummingbirds.

Epiphytes The treetops are ideal habitat for epiphytes. These 'plants on plants' perch on tree limbs, rooted in soil accumulated on branches or crevices and using their host tree to raise themselves to canopy height. The biggest are bromeliads and arum lilies. Others include orchids, philodendrons, peperomias, forest cacti and ferns. Velvet-green moss carpets every surface, and lichens and algae encrust branches and tree trunks.

Lianas and vines Lianas and vines are rooted on the ground, getting their nutrients from the thin forest soil. They hitch a ride upwards on new trees growing in forest gaps, or work their way into the canopy up the trunks of existing trees, connecting trees with one another and creating arboreal walkways for animals. There are over 15,000 liana species in the Amazon. *Ayahuasca*, also known as 'spirit vine' or 'vine of the soul', is widely used in religious ceremonies because of its powerful hallucinogenic properties. Vines tend to have spindly, often thorny stems and most are shorter-lived. They grow around forest edges and riverbanks, draping trees and shrubs with a mass of green. The delicate trumpet-shaped flowers of morning glories open early in the day to attract bees for a frenzy of nectar-feeding, but wither by the afternoon. Commercially important vines include *uña de gato,* or cat's claw, which has medicinal properties, while the passion vine has edible fruits used to make a soft drink..

Water plants Water plants form so-called 'floating meadows' that provide food for fish, arthropods and the manatee. Underwater roots and above-water vegetation shelter a community of small animals, including fish, amphibians and numerous invertebrates, which in turn provide sustenance for many predators. Water plants quickly colonise oxbow lakes and slow-flowing rivers, especially if manatee are absent. Most impressive is the Amazon or Victoria water lily, which grows pads up to 2m across that bristle underneath with large spines to deter manatees and herbivorous fish.

ANIMALS OF THE FOREST Rainforest harbours at least 50% of the planet's known animal species, a figure that would probably exceed 90% in the unlikely event that all the fauna were ever described.

Rainforest mammals Most rainforest mammals are very inconspicuous, being small, camouflaged, shy and nocturnal, and even larger creatures are mostly hidden by the dense vegetation. Many canopy mammals play a vital ecological role: nectar-feeding bats and rodents pollinate trees, while luscious fruit tempts monkeys who inadvertently disperse the seeds.

Pygmy marmoset

Primates Your expectation of seeing monkeys swinging from every branch quickly vanishes on entering the rainforest. Monkeys' activities rarely bring them within sight or sound of humans – especially in areas where they have been heavily hunted.

Some 30–35 lowland forest monkeys are known, with new ones still being discovered. South American monkeys, known as cebid monkeys, differ from Old World monkeys in having a prehensile tail, which acts as a fifth limb. The most commonly seen species is the squirrel monkey (*Saimiri sciureus*), although this one lacks a prehensile tail. Squirrel-sized and slender, it has a handsome gold-green coat with yellow-orange forelimbs. During the day, troops roam in search of fruiting trees. Often kept as pets, squirrel monkeys run free at the zoo in Leticia where their antics provide amusing entertainment.

Squirrel monkey

Marmosets and tamarins are not true monkeys. They are

smaller, with non-prehensile tails and, unlike monkeys, have claws instead of fingernails. The pygmy marmoset (*Callithrix pygmaea*) has a maximum body length of only 15cm, weighing no more than 141g. Its tawny colouring and mane around its face give rise to the local name *leoncito*, meaning 'little lion'. It is quite common and found throughout western Amazonia, where it prefers lowland flooded-forest areas. The saddle-back tamarin (*Saguinus fuscicollis*) is the primate most likely to be seen in the wild after the squirrel monkey, and gets its name from the large 'saddle' of dark red-brown fur on its shoulders.

Carnivores A variety of carnivores (order Carnivora) hunt both in the trees and on the ground, including members of the cats, dog, raccoon and weasel family.

Cats All South American cat species (family Felidae) are officially endangered and extremely unlikely to be seen in the wild on an average-length visit. They are rare, wary of humans and usually nocturnal, but you might spot evidence of activity, such as tracks by muddy rivers or claw marks on a tree. Largest, and top of the rainforest food chain, is the jaguar (*Panthera onca*), which is thinly distributed across the neo-tropics. Its name comes from the Indian word *yaguar* meaning 'he who kills with one leap',

Jaguar

and this powerful, spotted predator can take prey up to the size of a tapir. Next down is the puma (*Felis concolor*), which varies greatly in colour, but is generally a plain golden-brown. Smaller spotted cats include the ocelot and the similar but smaller margay,

Ocelot

Jaguarundi

both strictly nocturnal and seldom seen, though the plain-brown jaguarundi is sometimes encountered by day. These small cats prey on rodents, small reptiles, birds and reptiles.

Other carnivores Most common member of the raccoon family (Procyonidae) is the sociable coati, which has a ringed tail and long, flexible snout. Its omnivorous diet includes insects, small vertebrates, fruits, nuts and flowers. The rather less raccoon-like kinkajou wins the cutest rainforest animal contest, with its thick golden fur, wide brown eyes and docile manner. Uniquely among its family, it also has a prehensile tail. Among various rainforest members of the weasel family (Mustelidae) is the skunk-like grison, which eats small animals and sometimes fruit. The only two wild dogs (family Canidae) are the bush dog and the short-eared dog; both are small and exceedingly rare, with little known of their natural history.

Kinkajou

Coati

Sloths Sloths (family Bradypodidae) are the commonest large canopy mammals. They are also the world's slowest and, arguably, laziest land animals, moving along

Hoffman's two-toed sloth

branches at 4.5m a minute and spending up to 80% of their lives asleep or dozing. A slow metabolism enables them to survive on a low-energy diet of leaves, but they must eat lots to meet their nutritional needs. Sloths' excellent camouflage helps them evade predators. Their grooved fur encourages algae growth, creating a greenish hue, and grows in an opposite direction to that of other mammals so that rain runs off their inverted body. Sloths' main predators are eagles, though they may also fall prey to cats as they move across the forest floor to new feeding trees or make their weekly descent to ground level to defecate.

Anteaters and armadillos Anteaters belong to the same order (Pilosa) as sloths. The 2m-long giant anteater is among the largest rainforest animals. It searches the forest floor for ants and termites, using powerful claws to rip open their nests and a long sticky tongue to lap up the food. Armadillos (family Dasipodidae) are protected by their distinctive body armour. The nine-banded armadillo is the most widespread species, while the largest is the giant armadillo, which may weigh up to 60kg. Armadillos are shy, nocturnal and solitary. They feed on insects, small vertebrates, carrion, fungi and fruit.

Nine-banded armadillo

Bats These winged mammals are especially numerous and diverse in tropical rainforest. About 150–200 species are recorded from Amazonia, constituting 40% of the region's mammal species. The majority feed on flying insects. But there are also frog-eating bats, bird-eating bats and even bat-eating bats, while many are fruit- and nectar-feeders – the former dispersing seeds and the latter pollinating trees. Best-known of all are vampire bats. These will feed from cattle or wild mammals, but rarely humans. They do not suck blood, but cut a small flap of skin with their sharp incisors, from which they lap blood – anti-coagulant saliva preventing clotting. Another specialist is the greater bulldog or fishing bat, which plucks fish from the water like an osprey.

Ungulates Hoofed mammals of the rainforest are shy, retiring and seldom seen. They include the Brazilian tapir, which – at up to 250kg – is the biggest South American land mammal. Tapirs are related to horses, but have an elongated, highly mobile snout, useful for searching out fruits,

Brazilian tapir

Red brocket deer

berries, tubers, fungi and herbs. The smaller peccaries are related to pigs. The collared peccary, or *sajino*, is omnivorous and roams in groups of ten or more, often revealed by their pungent cheesy smell. It defends itself aggressively with its 8cm-long tusks. Both tapirs and peccaries are threatened due to intensive hunting. More common and widespread is the nocturnal red brocket deer, which often ventures into forest clearings or even to the edge of gardens and plantations.

Other mammals A great variety of rodents (order Rodentia) inhabits the rainforest, most of which are small, nocturnal and hard to see, let alone identify. Those found in the canopy include porcupines (family Erithizontidae) and squirrels (family Sciuridae), while ground-dwellers include the agouti and paca, which resemble giant-long-legged guinea pigs. The capybara is the world's largest rodent, reaching 113kg, and leads a semi-aquatic life beside river and swamps, where it browses water plants. Superficially rodent-like are the 40 species of opossum (Didelphidae) found in Amazonia, which range in size from a mouse to a raccoon. These marsupials sleep by day and forage at night.

Capybara

Rainforest birds Lowland Amazonia is home to at least 1,800–2,000 types of bird – about four times more than Europe, an area half as big again. The number fluctuates seasonally with migrants from Patagonia or North America. Many forest species, including the well-known toucans and macaws, remain largely hidden until they fly out across a river or clearing. But some perch more conspicuously in the open, including hawks, kingfishers, orioles and flycatchers. Many small birds are very hard to identify, with differences in song or behaviour often being the only clues.

Parrots and macaws Parrots (family Psittacidae) are the quintessential tropical birds, and often kept as pets in lodges, or jungle villages – though the pet trade has hastened the decline of many species. They use their powerful curved bill to break open hard nuts and seeds. Macaws are the largest. Nearly always seen in pairs, they have long tail-feathers and are easily identified by their colouring. Other parrots are smaller, with shorter tails, and generally fly in flocks. Most are difficult to distinguish in the field – especially since colour is hard to see as they fly overhead in silhouette.

Toucans Toucans (Ramphastidae) are rainforest icons and have the biggest bill, relative to body size, of any bird. As well as fruit, they also eat small animals and even the eggs and nestlings of other birds. One of the largest species is the white-throated toucan, which is black with a white chest, yellow rump and blue skin around the eye. Smaller toucans include araçaris and toucanets.

Harpy eagle

Hummingbirds Colombia is a hotspot for hummingbirds (family Trochilidae), with up to 132 species claimed by some authorities – more than any other country. These small nectar-feeding birds, hailed as messengers to the gods by pre-Columbian cultures, are rarely seen for long. They zip around between plants, and you will probably first hear the humming of their wing, which – at more than 80 beats per second in some species – are the fastest of any bird. The dazzling colours of hummingbirds have given rise to such evocative species names as glittering-throated emerald, golden-tailed sapphire and black-eared fairy. Hummingbirds are also ecologically essential as pollinators to many plants – notably of those with red, orange and yellow flowers.

Raptors The massive harpy eagle is the world's most powerful bird of prey, standing up to a metre in height, with huge yellow talons. This rare raptor is a major predator of monkeys and sloths, and may sometimes be glimpsed soaring

A1

above the canopy. Among a range of other raptors are the yellow-headed caracara, the black-collared hawk and the roadside hawk. The black vulture is abundant around settlements, especially around rubbish tips, while away from towns the turkey vulture and the greater yellow-headed vulture are more common.

Hoatzin

Hoatzin The hoatzin (*Opisthocomus hoazin*) is a pheasant-like bird with a 'mohican' crest, large blue eye-rings and bare facial skin. It is a poor flyer, with pectoral muscles reduced in size to allow space for its oversized crop, which stores its diet of 60% leaves. Gut bacteria ferment the material for up to four times longer than in most birds, which may explain the hoatzin's unpleasant smell, hence its nickname of 'stink bird'. Chicks, when threatened by a predator, fling themselves from the nest into the water below, before clambering back when the coast is clear, using their bill, feet and unique wing-claws. Hoatzins may be abundant in good habitat, forming surprisingly tame flocks of 25–30.

Night birds Several owls (families Strigidae, Tytonidae) are endemic to the Amazon. The tropical screech owl has a cooing whistle often heard just after nightfall or before dawn. Nighthawks and nightjars (family Caprimulidae) are seen flitting around at dusk, catching insects on the wing, and are often mistaken for bats. When perched, their eye-shine may be reflected in torchlight. Potoos hide during the day by mimicking a dead branch.

Other forest birds Numerous other birds inhabit the forest, from finches and flycatchers to antbirds and cotingas. It is impossible here to do justice to them all, but the following selection comprises some that the visitor might encounter. **Foliage-gleaners, horneros** and **spinetails** (*Furnariidae*) construct big, distinctive nests, ranging from the dome-shaped mud structures of horneros to the tangled stick nests of spinetails. **Honeycreepers** (*Thraupidae*), such as the bananaquit, feed on nectar, often piercing flower petals near the base. **Jacamars** (*Galbulidae*) are kingfisher-like birds with lance-like bills and glossy green plumage. **Manakins** (*Pipridae*) feed in the canopy on fruits and insects. Breeding males perform in groups called 'leks', clearing an area of forest floor for their courtship dance. **Motmots** (*Momotidae*) have a distinctive tail ending in two racquet-shaped tufts. **Oropendolas** (*Psarocolius* spp.) are common riverside birds, with a loud burbling call and woven nests that hang from branches like large pendulous fruits. **Pigeons** (*Columbidae*) are fruit-eating specialists. About a dozen species occur in lowland rainforest. **Puffbirds** (*Bucconidae*) have a tuft of bristles around the bill that may help them catch aerial insects. **Swallows and martins** (*Hirundinidae*) are recognised in flight by their forked tails and swept-back wings. **Swifts** (*Apodidae*) are supreme aerial insectivores, spending almost their entire life on the wing. **Tinamous** (*Tinamidae*) are poor flyers with loud calls that are heard more often than seen. **Tanagers** (*Thraupidae*) are colourful finch-like birds that feed mostly on fruit. **Trogons and quetzals** (*Trogonidae*) are elusive canopy birds with colourful plumage that feed on both fruit and insects. **Trumpeters** (*Psophiidae*) are ground birds with loud calls that enable them to communicate through thick undergrowth. **Woodcreepers** (*Furnariidae*) forage along branches, prising out insects from crevices. **Woodpeckers** (*Picidae*) are usually betrayed by their loud drumming, but are hard to glimpse among the branches, let alone identify. **Wrens** (*Trogolodytidae*) have beautiful, complex songs, and are more often heard than seen.

Aquatic birds The rivers, streams, lakes and swamps of the Amazon provide a haven for numerous aquatic and shore birds. Herons vary from the easily identified great and snowy egrets and little blue heron, to the white-necked heron, striated heron, and rufescent tiger heron, with the small zig-zag heron being a special rarity for birders. Nocturnal herons

include the black-crowned night heron and the boat-
billed heron, the latter's capacious bill being ideal for
capturing shrimps, fish and insects. The only
common stork species is the stately jabiru. Rarer
waterbirds include the sunbittern and the sungrebe, each
unusual enough to be classified in its own family.

*Amazon
kingfisher*

Along muddy banks, various species of sandpiper, ibis and rail are
also present, while birds hunting lakes for fish include the osprey, anhinga
and olivaceous cormorant. Kingfishers include the common ringed
kingfisher and Amazon kingfisher, which inhabit the edges of wide rivers and
open lakes. The wattled jacana inhabits quiet wetlands and backwaters, where
its long toes help it walk across floating vegetation. The horned screamer is a
goose-sized bird with a prominent quill or 'horn' projecting from its forehead and
a loud call that sounds a bit like 'Yoo-hoo!'

Rainforest reptiles Land reptiles, including snakes, lizards and tortoises, are all
represented in the Amazon. Aquatic reptiles are covered later in the chapter (see page 424).

Snakes The anaconda (see box, page 244) is the world's heaviest snake and may exceptionally
exceed 7m in length. This huge semi-aquatic constrictor asphyxiates prey within its powerful
coils. Other constrictors include the rainbow boa, which has an iridescent skin that reflects
all colours of the spectrum, the emerald tree boa which is nocturnal and hunts near water,
and the boa constrictor, which is diurnal and hunts mostly large rodents.

Few Amazonian snakes pose any threat to humans, with only five or six species considered
potentially dangerous. Of these, the fer-de-lance, common along trails, cultivated areas and
around dwellings, is the most feared – but not as deadly as its reputation suggests. More
imposing is the much rarer bushmaster, which – at 3m – is Amazonia's biggest poisonous
snake. Coral snakes have powerful venom, and a vivid banded pattern that varies between
species. They may be active day or night and are usually found under logs and rocks. Arboreal
snakes include the slender vine snakes and green tree-snakes, while spindle snakes are
adapted to burrowing in the forest floor.

Lizards The prehistoric-looking green iguana often basks on a branch overhanging water and
dives in at any hint of danger. Individuals may grow over 1.8m long, of which more than half
is tail. This species, also known as 'chicken of the forest', is a popular local food, and there
are even hopes that it can replace beef and so eliminate one cause of deforestation. Geckos
(Gekkonidae) are generally nocturnal and often seen prowling around lights on walls and
ceilings of hotels and lodges. They use adhesive toes to cling to the wall, and munch their
way through any insect they can capture.

Rainforest amphibians Frog and toad voices are an integral part of the rainforest chorus.
Come dusk, croaks, whistles, trills, burps and grunts prove their abundance as they prepare
for amorous encounters of the night. Expandable throat pouches greatly amplify the calls of
the males, allowing females to choose the most impressive. Different calls ensure species
remain separate and enable a skilled listener to identify them. Some species prey on others
and will even mimic their calls, so when a curious female arrives she is promptly eaten! Other
amphibians include salamanders, which sometimes turn up in damp leaf litter or tree holes,
and the legless, wormlike Caecilians.

Poison frogs So-called poison-dart frogs, properly called poison frogs, are day-glo coloured
to warn predators of their highly poisonous skin. However, only 55 of 135 known species is
actually toxic. Toxicity is diet-dependent: captive animals lose their poison after being fed
different food. Some species rank among the smallest terrestrial vertebrates.

A1

Other frogs and toads Tree frogs blend in with vegetation or mimic natural objects to escape predators, and use sucker pads on their feet to climb acrobatically. Glass frogs have colourless, virtually transparent skin and muscles, which reveal their heart, digestive system and bones underneath. The cane toad grows to around 30cm. Though native to Latin America, it is now established in the US and Australia and has become a serious pest in places.

Rainforest insects and other invertebrates
The rainforest hosts a staggering wealth of invertebrates (creatures without a backbone). Of these, the insects show the greatest number and diversity, with 34 different orders compared with 16 orders of mammal, and – according to recent studies of rainforest canopies – an estimated 30 million species. Without them, the rainforest would not function or even exist. They recycle nutrients, maintain soil structure and fertility, pollinate plants, disperse seeds, control populations of other organisms and are a major food source for birds, mammals, reptiles, amphibians, other invertebrates and even carnivorous plants.

Beetles Of the world's 1.75 million animal species so far described, a third are beetles. Notable rainforest beetles include the exquisite golden tortoise beetle, which resembles an Egyptian scarab carved in gold, as well as giants such as the Titan-longhorn, one of the world's largest insects, and the 12cm-long rhinoceros beetle, which sports impressive horns. Fire-flies, really beetles, are responsible for spectacular luminous displays along river edges and lowland areas at certain times of year, with each species using its own identification code of short and long flashes to attract a mate. The metallic green wing-cases of wood-boring beetles, also called jewel beetles because of their dazzling iridescence, are used locally in necklaces and other adornments. Weevils look like miniature tanks, armed with a nozzle-like proboscis and a rounded carapace. Locals harvest the thumb-sized grubs of the palm beetle for a handy, nutritious snack, called *suri*.

Wasps Wasps vary greatly in size, from the tiny to the worryingly large. Among the biggest is the tarantula hawk, which uses its sting to paralyse tarantulas, laying its eggs in the victim. Most wasps are communal, living in hives of from 5–10 individuals to many tens of thousands. Many are impressive architects: common wasps use chewed wood-pulp to build finger-shaped nests 2m long; potter wasps use clay to build compact globular nests. One Colombian species moulds a spherical clay nest about 10cm across, which has a covering of clay and sand cement that is virtually impenetrable, except via a small entrance hole.

Ants and termites Ants are the most abundant rainforest insects, comprising up to one tenth of the total animal biomass. Some consume the waste products of herbivorous insects, while others eat the insects themselves. Strictly speaking, even leaf-cutter ants are not herbivorous: the pieces of leaf that workers harvest and cut into neat shapes become compost for a fungus, which feeds every ant in the colony and is incessantly tended by workers.

Other ants include Azteca ants, which aggressively defend their host plant, the cecropia tree (see page 415), and honey ants, which 'farm' plant-sucking aphids. Army ants plunder other ant nests for eggs and larvae, and the flurry of activity caused by insects trying to escape draws insectivorous creatures, such as antbirds, to the scene. The glossy black bullet ant is the world's largest ant and has an excruciating sting. These ants are solitary by day, but at night they gather in small bands of a dozen or so and head out to collect their prey.

Termites, like ants, are master builders, but are more primitive insects that are closely related to cockroaches. The grey, pencil-wide tunnels that you see on the sides of trees are highways from the termites' food sources to their nests high above flood levels.

Butterflies and moths We do not know the precise number of butterfly and moth (Lepidoptera) species found in the lowland Amazon, though some 4,000 butterflies have been described from Peru alone. The trays of mounted butterflies and other insects sold by hawkers at tourist sites often include specimens imported from Asia, so are not representative of the local fauna. Do not encourage this destructive trade by buying them.

Morpho butterflies are distinguished by their large size and iridescent blue wings, which sport eye-spots on the underside that deter or confuse a predator. The caligo, like the morpho, has superb eye-spots – perfect replicas of owl eyes – while, to complete the deception, the rest of its wings and body mimic the bird's 'ears' and beak.

Many heliconiid butterflies are highly poisonous. They are thought to derive their toxins from the host plant, ingested by the caterpillar or butterfly and sequestered for later use. Different species of heliconiid have evolved to mimic one another, sharing similar wing patterns. This is known as Müllerian mimicry: a taste or two of a poisonous species leads a predator to associate its pattern with poison, thus all butterflies that share this pattern will benefit from being off the menu.

Hawkmoths resemble hummingbirds in form and size, and feed in a similar way by extracting nectar from flowers during their nocturnal forays. The rapid wing beats of the larger species create a 'hum' while hovering.

Spiders: a world of web sights Spiders and other arachnids are distinguished from insects by their eight legs, and a body divided into two, not three segments. Many rainforest species make distinctive webs. On jungle walks or canoe rides, look for the large, funnel-shaped webs woven by communal spiders, which are designed to catch prey that drops from the canopy. The elegant golden orb-weaver, which has long legs and an elongated black and silver body, spins a giant web of strong gold silk across forest gaps and trails, which is most disconcerting (though harmless) to walk into.

Tarantulas fit our preconception of a rainforest spider. These impressive creatures do not trap prey in webs but actively hunt it in swamp vegetation or other damp habitats. Most are harmless, with a bite no more painful than a bee sting. It is quite safe to let one walk across your arm, but you should not handle their hairy bodies, which may irritate the skin.

Some spiders are dangerous, with cytolytic venom that causes cells to break down, hindering the healing process. Among tens of thousands of species, however, only two or three are potentially life-threatening. One of these is considered the world's most venomous spider: the Brazilian wandering spider, which lives in the thatch or walls of jungle huts. The terrifying-looking tailless whip scorpion, by contrast, is all bluff, being completely harmless and lacking a sting.

Millipedes and centipedes These arthropods look like armoured caterpillars. Most millipedes (class Diplopoda) are cylindrical in cross-section, but one common rainforest species, greyish and up to 13cm long, has a flattened body with horizontal projections from each of its body segments. Centipedes (class Chilopoda), unlike the herbivorous millipedes, are hunters that prey on small insects and other invertebrates. They are flattened in cross-section and have only one pair of legs per segment. All centipedes have a venomous bite. Most are harmless to humans, but they should be avoided.

WATERWORLD The Amazon has the most diverse freshwater fauna on the planet. There are, for example, at least 2,000 fish species and perhaps a thousand more to be described, by contrast with a paltry 150 or so in Europe.

Aquatic mammals A number of specialised mammals have adapted to life in the waterways of the Amazon.

Freshwater dolphins Amazon dolphins are smaller than their marine relatives. They are most common at river mouths, where fish are abundant. Locals generally have taboos against eating dolphin. However, fishermen occasionally kill them by accident – or deliberately when they become entangled in nets. Some are also killed for medicinal or shamanistic purposes.

Size, colour and behaviour distinguish the two Amazon species. The pink dolphin is about 2.4m long, with a low dorsal ridge in place of a fin. It swims slowly, feeding on fish, crabs and small river turtles. Pink dolphins are active day and night, and you will often see a bachelor male, or sometimes a small family pod, swim by. Their body does not clear the water when they leap. The grey dolphin is smaller and shaped more like a marine dolphin, with a curved dorsal fin, and its body clears the water when jumping. It feeds mainly on fast-swimming fish close to the surface.

Manatee The Amazon manatee is a strictly freshwater species. Weighing up to 500kg, it is the largest Amazon mammal – though it wins no beauty contests. Nostrils positioned on top of its squarish muzzle enable it to breathe with its body and head submerged, while a paddle-like tail propels it ponderously through the water. Manatees are purely vegetarian, consuming over 45kg a day of waterweeds – which would otherwise quickly clog waterways. Unfortunately, unlike dolphins, no taboos protect the manatee, and hunting is virtually uncontrolled. Docile, slow-moving and conspicuous, it is easy prey, and high prices provide a strong incentive to a poor *ribereño*.

Otters Otters, which belong to the weasel family (Mustelidae), are supreme underwater fish catchers. The southern river otter is dark brown above and creamy below, while the Brazilian or giant otter is the world's largest freshwater otter. Unfortunately, otters' loud, playful antics do little to disguise their whereabouts from hunters. Formerly common and widespread, both species are now endangered.

Aquatic reptiles The Amazon's two main groups of aquatic reptiles are crocodilians and turtles. These are evolved from ancestors isolated when South America became an island continent.

Caiman Caiman are South American crocodilians. They eat mostly fish, but turtles, frogs and other reptiles also fall prey. The largest species is the black caiman, which can reach an impressive 5m. On night boat rides, you might see the red eye-shine of the common or spectacled caiman, which does not exceed 2.5m. Caiman make nests of vegetation in which they lay 30–60 eggs at a time, though just one or two individuals in a clutch survive. Their populations are under severe hunting pressure throughout the Amazon.

River turtles The 13 Amazon river turtle species are all side-necked turtles, so-called because they retract their head sideways into the shell. The giant river turtle is the largest, weighing up to 75kg. The matamata has a long neck, a tube-like snout that acts as a snorkel, and a carapace that resembles floating leaves to fool approaching prey. It feeds by opening its wide mouth suddenly to draw in small fish like a vacuum cleaner.

Fabulous fish Around 80% of the Amazon's fish species are Characins. This is the largest family of neo-tropical freshwater fish and includes such well-known groups as catfish, lungfish and piranhas.

Piranhas B-movies would have us believe that there is only one type of Amazon fish: the reputedly deadly piranha. In fact records show not a single human fatality, although fishermen have been known to lose toes and fingers. The best-known species is the red-bellied piranha, which has a silvery back, an orange-red underside and extremely sharp teeth that are serrated and triangular, like a tiny shark's. Piranhas' feeding habits depend on the season, with low water levels being likely to reduce food availability and thus increase competition – leading, on occasion, to the famous feeding frenzies. At this time they are easy to catch on a hook baited with raw meat, though their hundreds of tiny bones and rather greasy flesh make them rather an acquired taste. (See box, page 241.)

Electric eel A number of documented cases report fatalities caused by the infamous electric eel. It discharges a shock of up to 1,000 volts to knock out prey and defend itself against predators. The current is usually non-lethal for humans, but powerful enough to cause temporary paralysis – which can, on occasion, lead to drowning.

Other characins Jewel tetras, found in murky waters, are tiny living gems and among the most sought-after aquarium fish, their brilliant primary colours glowing under lights. Flying hatchet fish use their pectoral fins like wings to propel them through the air as a defence against predatory fish, and may even land in a speeding canoe. The more sedate headstanders spend the most of their lives with their tail up in the air, whereas pencil fish live mostly head-up.

Candirú The candirú family comprises a number of small, scaleless fish, one of which normally dwells within another fish's waste tract and is reputed to wriggle up the orifices of human swimmers. Apparently attracted by the warmth of urine, it zooms inside the opening, whereupon its sharp spines project into the tender flesh and it is removable only by surgery. Stay safe: wear a bathing suit and don't pee in the water while swimming. (See box, page 239.)

Catfishes Most of the hundred or more species of catfish are bottom-feeders, and use their long whiskers (barbels) to search the river mud for worms, crustaceans and snails. One of Amazonia's biggest fish, with a scientific name to match, is *Brachyplatystoma filamentosum*, up to 3m long. The more common dorado is a staple food for people along the river, and in fish markets you may also see the smaller suckermouth catfish, which has ornate horns on its heavy scales.

Arapaima and Arowana One of the world's largest freshwater fish, the predatory arapaima is shaped like a huge pike. Specimens over 4m long and weighing 250kg have been known, but this fish's huge size and tasty flesh have led to its demise. Its large greenish-bronze scales turn white when removed, and are used for decoration or jewellery. The closely related arowana, or water monkey, can leap out of the water to snatch unsuspecting meals from a branch, including birds, reptiles and even baby sloths.

Cichlids Many cichlids are commercially important, either as food or sport fish, or for the aquarium trade. The peacock bass grows to 30kg and is golden-yellow with black dorsal bars, and an eye spot on the tail to distract predators. Discus fish have a round, compressed body and their attractive markings make them popular in aquariums.

Other Amazon fishes The leaf fish mimics a dead leaf floating on water. Drifting around, pointing downward, it preys on unsuspecting fish that swim by. A transparent tail and pectoral fins allow it to move without being detected. Tiny killifish spend most of their lives as tough, drought-resistant eggs in shallow, ephemeral ponds. Some complete their entire life cycle in places where water lasts no more than three weeks. Sting rays, notably those of the strictly freshwater genus *Potamotrygon*, are the only freshwater cartilaginous fishes (although some sharks roam upriver from the ocean), and rest half-covered in sand on the beds of shallow rivers. The 'sting' is a venomous barbed fin at the base of the tail.

A1

Appendix 2

LANGUAGE

Of the more than 400 million people who speak Spanish (or Castilian) as their mother tongue, more than 300 million are in Latin America. Castillan Spanish is the official language of Colombia and there are close ties between the Spanish and Colombian language academies. Accents vary throughout the country and the dialect is full of local jargon and numerous Colombianisms, although in many ways it is similar to the style of Spanish observed in the southern parts of Spain.

The Caro y Cuervo Institute in Bogotá promotes the good use of the Spanish language in Colombia. Generally Spanish pronunciation and grammar are straightforward, with few irregularities. However, the singular second person pronoun *tú* is widely used in informal talk, while *usted* is used in formal talk. Most people in Bogotá use *tú* when addressing strangers. As a paradox, when talking with very close relatives such as parents, siblings or spouses the more formal *usted* is mostly used. Mixing formal pronouns and informal verbal forms is common, eg: '*Usted que piensas?*' (What do you [formal] think [informal]?). Another characteristic of Colombian Spanish is the use of diminutive forms -ico, -ica, used in words ending in 't', eg: *gato* (cat) . . . *gatico* (small cat), something that it shares with Costa Rican and Cuban Spanish. Words ending in a vowel, 'n' or 's' take the stress on the penultimate syllable; all words that end in other consonants take the stress on the last syllable. Irregular stresses are marked with an accent.

The strongest dialects in Colombia are found in Antioquía, Quindío, Risaralda and Caldas where people speak Spanish with a distinct Castilian-sounding 's'. In Bogotá, the city's clipped dialect is referred to as *cachaco* (meaning 'educated' or 'refined') while on the Caribbean the coastal (*costeño*) dialect is characterised by a suppressive drawl.

The Afro-Colombian communities in the department of Chocó have their own idioms and local terminology as do the population of the San Andrés Archipelago where on Isla Providencía English-patois is spoken. In addition to Spanish there are more than 180 indigenous languages and dialects belonging to such major linguistic groups as Arawakan, Chibchan, Cariban, Tupi-Guaraní, and Yuruman. Many tribes also use a form of communicative sign language wholly unique to their own communities.

PRONUNCIATION
Consonants

c	as in 'cat', before 'a', 'o', or 'u'; like 's' before 'e' or 'i'
d	as 'd' in 'dog', except between vowels, then like 'th' in 'that'
g	before 'e' or 'I', like the 'ch' in Scottish 'loch'; elsewhere like 'g' in 'get'
h	always silent
j	like the English 'h' in 'hotel', but stronger
ll	like the 'y' in 'yellow'
ñ	like the 'ni' in 'onion'
r	always pronounced as strong 'r'

rr	trilled 'rr'		
v	similar to the 'b' in 'boy' (not as English 'v')		
y	similar to English, but with a slight 'j' sound. When y stands alone it is pronounced like the 'e' in 'me'.		
z	like 's' in 'same'		

b, f, k, l, m, n, p, q, s, t, w, x as in English

Vowels

a	as in 'father' but shorter
e	as in 'hen'
i	as in 'machine'
o	as in 'phone'
u	usually as in 'rule'; when it follows a 'q' the 'u' is silent; when it follows an 'h' or 'g' it's pronounced like 'w', except when it comes between 'g' and 'e' or 'i', when it's also silent

USEFUL WORDS AND PHRASES with *Larissa Banting*
Essentials

Hello	*Hola*	I'm sorry	*Lo siento*
Good morning	*Buenos días*	Goodbye	*Adiós*
Good afternoon	*Buenas tardes*	See you later	*Hasta luego*
Good evening	*Buenas noches*	more	*más*
How are you?	*¿Cómo está?*	less	*menos*
Fine	*Muy bien*	better	*major*
And you?	*¿y Usted?* (formal) or *¿Y vos?* (informal)	much	*mucho*
		a little	*un poco*
Thank you	*Gracias*	large	*grande*
Thank you very much	*Muchas gracias*	small	*pequeño*
		quick	*rápido*
You are very kind	*Usted es muy amable*	slowly	*despacio*
You are welcome	*Con gusto*	good	*bueno*
Yes	*Sí*	bad	*malo*
No	*No*	difficult	*difícil*
I don't know	*Yo no sé*	easy	*fácil*
It's fine	*Está bien*	I don't speak Spanish	*No hablo español*
Please	*Por favor*		
Pleased to meet you	*Mucho gusto*	I don't understand	*No entiendo*
		Do you speak English?	*¿habla ingles?*
Excuse me	*Discúlpeme* (physically) *Perdóneme* (figuratively)		

Numbers

0	*cero*	10	*diez*
1	*uno* (masculine)	11	*once*
1	*una* (feminine)	12	*doce*
2	*dos*	13	*trece*
3	*tres*	14	*catorce*
4	*cuatro*	15	*quince*
5	*cinco*	16	*dieciséis*
6	*seis*	17	*diecisiete*
7	*siete*	18	*dieciocho*
8	*ocho*	19	*diecinueve*
9	*nueve*	20	*veinte*

30	*treinta*	500	*quinientos*
40	*cuarenta*	600	*seiscientos*
50	*cincuenta*	700	*setecientos*
60	*sesenta*	800	*ochocientos*
70	*setenta*	900	*novecientos*
80	*ochenta*	1,000	*mil*
90	*noventa*	2,000	*dos mil*
100	*cien*	3,000	*tres mil*
101	*ciento uno*	4,000	*cuatro mil*
200	*doscientos*	5,000	*cinco mil*
300	*trescientos*	10,000	*diez mil*
400	*cuatrocientos*	15,000	*quince mil*

Days of the week

Sunday	*domingo*	Thursday	*jueves*
Monday	*lunes*	Friday	*viernes*
Tuesday	*martes*	Saturday	*sábado*
Wednesday	*miércoles*		

Time

What time is it?	*¿Qué hora es?*	tomorrow,	*mañana*
one o'clock	*la una*	morning	*la mañana*
two o'clock	*las dos*	yesterday	*ayer*
at two o'clock	*a las dos*	week	*semana*
ten past three	*las tres y diez*	month	*mes*
06.00	*las seis de la mañana*	year	*año*
18.00	*las seis de la tarde*	last night	*anoche*
today	*hoy*	next day	*al día siguiente*

Terms of address

I	*yo*	Miss, young lady	*señorita*
you (formal)	*usted*	wife	*esposa*
you (informal)	*vos, tu*	husband	*esposo* or *marido*
he/him	*él*	friend	*amigo* (male)
she/her	*ella*		*amiga* (female)
we/us	*nosotros*	girlfriend	*novia*
you (plural)	*ustedes*	boyfriend	*novio*
they/them (males or mixed gender)	*ellos*	father	*padre*
		mother	*madre*
they/them (females)	*ellas*	son	*hijo*
		daughter	*hija*
Mr, Sir	*señor*	brother	*hermano*
Mrs, Ms, Madam	*señora*	sister	*hermana*

Getting around

Where is …?	*¿Dónde está …?*	north	*norte*
How far is …?	*¿Qué tan lejos está …?*	south	*sur*
From … to	*De … a*	west	*oeste*
highway	*la carretera*	east	*este*
road	*el camino*	straight ahead	*adelante*
street	*la calle*	to the right	*a la derecha*
block	*la cuadra*	to the left	*a la izquierda*
kilometre	*kilómetro*		

Accommodation

Can I see a room?	¿Puedo ver una habitación?	hot water	agua caliente
What is the rate?	¿Cuál es el precio?	cold water	agua fría
a single room	una habitación sencilla	towel	toalla
a double room	una habitación doble	soap	jabón
key	llave	toilet paper	papel higiénico
bathroom	baño	air conditioning	aire acondicionado
		blanket	cobija or manta

Public transport

bus stop	parada de bus	Here, please	Aquí, por favor
airport	aeropuerto	Where is this bus going?	¿Dónde va este bus?
ferry terminal	terminal de ferry		
I want a ticket to …	Quiero un pasaje/tiquete a…	round trip	ida y vuelta
		What do I owe?	¿Cuánto le debo?
I want to get off at …	Quiero bajar en…		

Food and drink

menu	menu	eggs	huevos
glass	vaso	bread	pan
mug	taza	watermelon	sandía
fork	tenedor	banana	banano
knife	cuchillo	apple	manzana
spoon	cuchara	orange	naranja
napkin	servilleta	meat (without)	(sin) carne
soft drink	gaseosa	chicken	pollo
coffee	café	fish	pescado
cream	crema	shellfish	camarones, mariscos
tea	té	fried	frito
sugar	azúcar	roasted	asado
drinking water	agua potable	barbecue	a la parilla
beer	cerveza	breakfast	desayuno
wine	vino	lunch	almuerzo
milk	leche	dinner	cena
juice	jugo	the bill	la cuenta

Making purchases

I need…	necesito…	I'm just looking	Estoy buscando
I want…	quiero…	Can I see…?	¿Puedo ver…?
I would like…	quisiera…	this one	ésto/ésta
How much does it cost?	¿Cuánto cuesta?	expensive	caro
		cheap	barato
What is the exchange rate?	¿Cuál es el tipo de cambio?	cheaper	más barato
		too much	demasiado

Health

Help me, please	Ayúdeme, por favor	diarrhoea	diarrea
I am ill	Estoy enfermo	chemist	farmacia
pain	dolor	medicine	medicina
fever	fiebre	pill, tablet	pastilla
stomach ache	dolor de estómago	birth control pills	pastillas anticonceptivas
vomiting	vomitar	condoms	preservativos

SLANG Colombia's street language is more colourful than its carnivals. Slang is widespread and has strong regional distinctions. It is particularly used in the Paisa region where it is known as 'Parlache'. Many of Colombia's slang expressions have been adopted by people living outside of their place of origin and are commonly understood countrywide.

Some of the most common slang terms with literal translation are listed below. Master a few and you'll significantly up your cred as a gringo on Colombian soil.

Slang	Meaning	Literal translation
abrirse	to leave	to open
Ala	Hey man	wing
almacén	shop	warehouse
andén	pavement, sidewalk	platform
armar videos	to lie	to do videos
atorarse	to choke	to get stuck
avión	a clever person	airplane
bacano	cool	good
balaca	headband	
barra	peso (currency unit)	bar
baúl	boot, trunk (of a car/automobile)	chest (furniture)
birra	beer	Italian for beer
bomba	baloon; also fuel pump	bomb
buzo	turtleneck sweater	diver
café	brown (colour)	coffee
camello	job, (heavy) work	camel
cana	gaol, jail	white hair
caneca	trash basket/waste bin	
cantaleta	repetitive scolding	
caña	bluff, bragging; also rhum	fishing rod
capar	to play truant	to castrate
carpeta	doily	folder
caspa	senseless speech	dandruff
catorce	favour	fourteen
chimba	excellent	
chino	kid, boy	Chinese
chupa	police officer	sucker
colorete	rouge	lipstick
cotejo	soccer/football match	comparison
culebra	debt	snake
duro	Skilful	hard
embarrarla	to make a grave mistake	to cover with mud
esfero	pen	sphere (masculine form)
Eye! Pilas!	be careful!	batteries!
filo	hunger	edge
gonorrea	vile person	gonorrhea
guayabo	hangover	guava tree
güevón	dude, bro	mispronunciation of 'huevón'
hacerse el gringo	to feign ignorance	to act as an American
hueco	pothole; also gaol, jail	hole
huevón	dude, bro	sluggish or idiot
jurgo	plethora, lot	
levantar	to seduce/to beat, thrash	to raise
ligar	to give money, bribe	to tie
listo	all right	ready

Slang	Meaning	Literal translation
llave	friend	key
lobo	bad taste	wolf
luca	a thousand	Colombian pesos
mamar	to bore	to suck
man	guy	man (English loanword)
marica	dude, bro	queer
marimba	marijuana	marimba
mono	blond(e), fair-haired	monkey
mosca (estar mosca)	be clever for a while; also annoyed	fly (as an adjective, 'be fly')
No joda!	Nuh-uh!/Get outta here!	Don't fuck
No me joda!	Don't bother me!	Don't fuck me!
Ojo!	Be careful!	Watch out!
olla	place where drugs are sold	saucepan
paila	bad luck	saucepan
paja	lie, falsehood; also masturbation	hay
parar bolas	to pay attention	to stand balls
parche	band	patch
pata	marijuana roach	leg
pedo	big problem	fart
perder el año	to die	to get an F (grade)
piedra	anger	stone
pilo	good student	battery (masculine form)
poner bolas	to pay attention	to put balls
poner los cachos	to cheat (relationships)	set the horns
puto	enraged	male prostitute
Qué boleta!	How embarrassing!	What a ticket!
Qué hubo? (Quiubo)	What's up?	What was there?
Qué mamera!	That's boring!	What a sucker!
Qué más?	What's up?	What else?
rascado	drunk	scratched
rata	robber	rat
sapo	meddler, snitch	frog
sobar	to disturb	to handle, touch
tinto	black coffee	red wine
tomba	the police/police officer	
vaina	thing	scabbard
Vientos o maletas?	How are you?	winds or suitcases

Appendix 3

FURTHER INFORMATION
BOOKS
Art

Basualdo, Carlos, Princenthal, Nancy and Huyssen, Andreas *Doris Salcedo* Phaidon Press, 2000. A collection of the Colombian sculptor's work, made from objects found in the abandoned homes of missing Colombians.

Botero, Werner Fernando *Spies* Prestel Verlag, 1997. An excellent overview of the broad range of works of this world-acclaimed Colombian figurative artist.

Calima and Malagana: Art and Archaeology in Southwestern Colombia Pro Calima Foundation, 2005. Based on 25 years of research by a multi-national team, this detailed chronicle centres on the cultural and artistic development from 8000BC to the early colonial period along with recent excavations of gold and pottery in the context of Colombia's social and political changes and indigenous belief systems.

Labbe, Amand J *Colombia Before Columbus: The People, Culture, and Ceramic Art of Pre-hispanic Colombia* Rizzoli International Publications 1986. Examines the ancient arts of Colombia's indigenous tribes, from gold deities to colourful pottery items.

Perez, Roberto, Botero, Clara and Londono, Santiago, *The Art of Gold* Skira Editore, 2007. Traces the legacy of gold in pre-Hispanic Colombia with 250 gold objects taken from the Gold Museum of Bogotá.

Saldarriaga, Alberto and Castenda Buragua, Antonio *Country Houses in Colombia* Villeghas Asociados SA, 2006. Explores how indigenous plants (such as guadua, a local bamboo) have influenced the Colombian architectural form.

Tellez, German *Casa De Hacienda: Architecture in the Colombian Countryside* Editores Villegas, Colombia, 1998. Coffee-table book that celebrates the rich architectural beauty of Colombia.

Villegas, Benjemin *Casa Republicana: Colombia's Belle Epoque*, Editores Villegas, 2000. Takes a look at Republican architecture and examines the era of ornate design.

Autobiographies/biographies

Betancourt, Ingrid *Until Death Do Us Part: My Struggle to Reclaim Colombia* Phoenix Press, 2003. A personal political memoir of a Colombian presidential candidate who was kidnapped by FARC after the publication of this international bestseller. She hasn't been seen since.

Bowden, Mark *Killing Pablo* Atlantic Books, 2002. An excellent read detailing the rise and fall of the infamous Colombian drug baron Pablo Escobar, who amassed a multi-million-dollar fortune before being killed after a massive man hunt.

Lynch, John *Simón Bolívar: A Life* Yale University Press, 2006. Bolívar was the very first president of Colombia, and known throughout South America as 'The Liberator'. This is his story.

Wepman, Denis *Simón Bolívar* Chelsea Harbour Publishers, 1985. The life and battles of Latin America's independence fighter.

Business

Buchelo, Marcelo *Bananas and Business: The United Fruit Company in Colombia 1899–2000* New York University Press, 2005. A critical analysis of the United Fruit Company's century-long presence in Colombia with a look at its widespread influence in the political, consumer, labour and historical arenas.

Colombia: A Tax Guide International Business Publications USA, updated edn, 2002.

Colombia Business Intelligence Report International Business Publications USA, 2nd edn, 2001

Colombia Investment & Business Guide International Business Publications USA, 3rd edn, 2000.

Colombian Government and Business Contacts Handbook International Business Publications Inc, 2004. Colombia's indispensable commercial bible.

Magnusson, Michael *Latin Glory: Airlines of Latin America* Motorbooks International Inc, 1995

Rippy, Fred J *The Capitalists and Colombia*, Ayer Co Publishing, repr. edn, 1976.

Cuisine

McCausland-Gallo, Patricia *Secrets of Colombian Cooking* Hippocrene Books, US, 2004. Over 175 tasty and authentic Colombian recipes. Contains dishes using fish from the Caribbean Sea, the Pacific Ocean and the Amazon, Magdalena and Cauca rivers and features the hearty stews of the Andes. Fleetwood, Jenni *South American Food & Cooking: Ingredients, Techniques and Signature Recipes from the Undiscovered Traditional Cuisines of Brazil, Argentina, Uruguay, Ecuador, Mexico, Colombia and Venezuela* Southwater, 2006

Montaña, Antonio *The Taste of Colombia* Villegas Editores Ltd, Colombia, 1997. Over 100 recipes and 199 tantalising photographs make up this illustrated tour of Colombian cuisine.

Drugs

Gugliotta, Guy *Kings of Cocaine* Harper Paperbacks, 1990. Background to the rise of the infamous drug ring, the Medellín cartel.

Kirk, Robin *More Terrible than Death: Drugs, Violence and America's War in Colombia* Publicaffairs Ltd, 2004. A personal, contemporary history of Colombia and the drug war, told by an employee of Human Rights Watch who was posted in Colombia for 12 years.

Molano, Alfredo *Loyal Soldiers in the Cocaine Kingdom: Tales of Drugs, Mules, and Gunmen* Colombia University Press, 2004. Testimonials of ordinary Colombian people who have become involved in smuggling in search of a better life, and the consequences that they have faced for their decisions. The translation has made this book confusing in parts, but it's worth a read.

Porter, Bruce Blow *How A Small-Town Boy Made $100 Million With the Medellín Cocaine Cartel and Lost it All* Saint Martín's Press, 2001. The true story of how George Jung introduced Cocaine to the US mass market. This was the basis of a successful film starring Johnny Depp in 2001.

Thoumi, Francisco E *Illegal Drugs, Economy and Society in the Andes* Johns Hopkins University Press, 2004. What leads some countries to develop illegal drugs industries?

Fiction

Issacs, Jorge *María* Losada, 2005. This famous novel represents the Colombian literary period known as Spanish-American Romanticism (Spanish).

Márquez, Gabriel García *One Hundred Years of Solitude* Penguin, new edn 1998. Tells the story of a poor Colombian family living through a century of extraordinary events in the Caribbean lowlands. Márquez was the winner of the 1982 Nobel Prize in literature, and is credited for developing the 'magical realism' style of writing.

Rainier, Peter W *The Bogotá Connection* Authorhouse, 2005. Espionage thriller based at an emerald mine in 1930s Colombia.

Silva, José Asunción *Obra Poetica Celest Ediciones Sa* Ed del centenario edn, 1996. A collection of the poet's modernismo work (Spanish).

Geography and natural history

Colombia Map International Travel Maps and Books, 2nd edn, 2007. By far the best map on the market.

Corwin, Jeff *Into Wild Amazon* Blackbirch Press 2004. A chronicled account of the flora and fauna found in the Amazon region.

Defler, Thomas Richard *Primates of Colombia* Conservation International, 2005. Illustrated field guide.

Eisenberg, John F *Mammals of the Neotropics: The Northern Neotropics – Panama, Colombia, Venezuela, Guyana, Surinam, French Guiana* University of Chicago Press, 1989.

Escobar, Rodrigo R, ed *Native Colombian Orchids* Editorial Colina, 1990.

Gentry, Alwyn H *A Field Guide to the Families and Genera of Woody Plants of Northwest South America (Colombia, Ecuador, Peru)* University of Chicago Press, 1996. A guide to identifying 250 types of woody plants.

Harris, Roger and Hutchinson, Peter *The Amazon*, Bradt Travel Guides, 3rd ed, 2007. The most comprehensive Amazon travel guide with detail information on the biodiversity of the region, expedition planning and jungle routes.

Hart Dyke, Tom and Winder, Paul *The Cloud Garden: A True Story of Adventure, Survival, and Extreme Horticulture* Lyons Press, 2004.

Hilty, Steven L and Brown, W A *A Guide to the Birds of Colombia*, Princeton University Press, 1986. The ultimate reference guide and handbook for twitchers.

Mejia Hernandez, Cecilia and Cobo-Borda, Juan Gustavo *Gardens of Colombia* Villegas Editores, 1997.

Mileti, Dennis S *The Eruption of Nevado Del Ruiz Volcano Colombia, South America, November 13, 1985* (Natural Disaster Studies), National Academy Press, 1991.

Ospina, Mariano *Orchids and Ecology in Colombia: To the Rescue of Paradise* Mariano Ospina, 1996.

Pollard, Michael *Great Rivers: The Amazon* Evans Brothers, 2003. Detailed look at the plants, terrain, birds and wildlife found in the Amazon watershed.

Shiva, Vandana, Vandermeer, John and Perfecto, Yvette, *Breakfast of Biodiversity: The Political Ecology of Rain Forest Destruction* Food First, 2005. Interesting insight into deforestation.

Von Humboldt, Alexander, *Personal Narrative of Travels to the Equinoctial Regions of America During the Years 1799–1804*, Indypublish.com, 2006. Three-volume studies and explorations of a German botanist.

Withner, Carl L *The South American Encyclia Species (Cattleyas)* Timber Press, 2000.

Guidebooks

Banting, Larissa *Costa Rica* Bradt, 2006
Hutchison, Peter & Harris, Roger *The Amazon* Bradt, 2007
Woods, Sarah *Panama* Bradt, 2006

Health

Schultes, Richard Evans *Vine of the Soul: Medicine Men, Their Plants and Rituals in the Colombian Amazonia* Synergetic Press Inc, 2004.

Duke, James A *The CRC Handbook of Alternative Cash Crops for the Tropics and the Amazonian Ethnobotanical Dictionary: The Green Pharmacy* US Aid for International Development, 2003.

These two excellent books provide a fascinating insight into traditional healing. Both explore roles of shaman in ancient medicine and the origins and potency of plants, while also examining the powers associated with the sacred ground of the Amazon region.

Winsor, Shane (ed) *Expedition Medicine* Profile Books, 2004. This essential guide to treating accidents and illnesses when travelling to remote areas includes how to handle remote medical emergencies and common infections. Lots of detail and advice comes with illustrations with tips for first aid kit items to pack and information on specific emergency procedures, including treatment of acute mountain sickness.

Young, Isabelle *Healthy Travel: Central and South America* Lonely Planet, 2000.

Lankester, Ted *Travellers' Good Health Guide* Sheldon Press, 2006.

Wilson-Howarth, Dr Jane, and Ellis, Dr Matthew *Your Child Abroad: A Travel Health Guide* Bradt Travel Guides, 2005

Wilson-Howarth, Dr Jane, *Bugs, Bites & Bowels* Cadogan, 2006

History

Bushnell, David *The Making of Modern Colombia: A Nation in Spite of Itself* University of California Press, 1993. This study looks beyond the drugs and the violence that frequently hit the headlines, to the achievements of Colombia: from its government and economic development to its impressive body of art and literature.

Dudley, Steven *Walking Ghosts: Murder and Guerrilla Politics in Colombia* Routledge, 2004. This powerful account details the political genocide that eliminated the Patriotic Unión party in the late 1980s and early '90s.

Hemming, John *The Search for El Dorado* Weidenfeld & Nicolson, 2001. Provides some useful background information on the colonisation of Colombia with plenty of pre-Columbian insight.

Rolddan, M *Blood and Fire: La Violencia in Antioquía*, Colombia, 1946–1953 Duke University Press, 2002. Examines the period of terror dubbed as 'La Violencia' that led to the death of over 200,000 Colombians.

Simons, Geoff *Colombia: A Brutal History* Saqi Books, 2004. A revealing insight into the violent drug cartels, foreign interference, corporate exploitation, paramilitary death squads and civil war of Colombia's past.

Taussig, Michael T *Law in a Lawless Land: Diary of a Limpieza in Colombia* University of Chicago Press, 2003. Anthropologist Michael Taussig's dramatic exposé of Colombia's paramilitary death squads is based on witness statements from friends and relatives of the victims of 'social cleansing', and his own experiences in a small Colombian village.

Language

Campbell, Lyle *American Indian Languages: The Historical Linguistics of Native America* Oxford University Press, USA, 2000. A useful examination of Native American languages, and the relationships between them.

Latin American Spanish Lonely Planet, 4th edn 2003.

Latin American Spanish Phrasebook Rough Guides, 2006. A decent phrasebook for everyday situations.

McVey Gill, Mary and Wegmann, Brenda *Streetwise Spanish: The User-Friendly Guide to Spanish Slang and Idioms* McGraw-Hill, 1998. An indispensable guide to the irregularities of Spanish language – including proper street-slang for gossip, swearing and undying love – and everything else you can imagine.

Strom, Clay *Studies in the Languages of Colombia* Summer Institute of Linguistics, 1993. A thorough look at the 60-plus languages and umpteen dialects of the Colombian peoples.

Literature

Aching, Gerard and Pupo-Walker, Enrique *The Politics of Spanish American Modernismo* Cambridge University Press, 1997. Debates the issues of modernity and the colonial/postcolonial condition in selected 19th-century Hispanic literatures.

Borda, Juan Gustavo *Historia de la Poesia Colombiana Siglo XX* Editores Villegas, Colombia, 2006. A compilation of significant Colombian works, selected by a prolific Colombian poet (Spanish).

Gonzalez, Anibal *A Companion to Spanish American Modernismo* Tamesis Books, 2007. Not published at time of writing.

Jrade, Cathy *Modernismo, Modernity and the Development of Spanish American Literature* University of Texas Press, 1998. Details the evolution of Spanish-language contemporary literature.

McKnight, Kathryn Joy *The Mystic of Tunja: Writings of Madre Castillo, 1671–1742,* University of Massachusetts Press, 1997. Pioneering nun Madre Castillo's struggle to balance her literary aspirations with the demands of religious service.

Suárez-Araúz, Nicomedes *Literary Amazonia: Modern Writing by Amazonian Authors* University Press of Florida, 2004. This remarkable selection of 20th-century Amazonian literature contains work from the Amazon's indigenous and mestizo people. Some 24 poets and 12 prose writers capture the spirit of the region and many of the community's forgotten voices, collected and translated into English for the first time.

Music

Ellingham, Mark, McConnachie, James and Broughton, Simón (eds) *World Music,* vol 2 (including Latin & North America, Caribbean, India, Asia and Pacific), Rough Guides, 2000. In particular, see pages 372–85.

List, George *Music and Poetry in a Colombian Village: A Tri-Cultural Heritage* Indiana University Press, 1983. Rural traditions in music and poetry explored.

Wade, Peter *Music, Race and Nation: Música Tropical in Colombia* University of Chicago Press, 2000. The rise of 'musica tropical', incorporating porro, 'cumbia and vallenato styles of music.

Waxer, Lise A *The City of Musical Memory: Salsa, Record Grooves and Popular Culture in Cali, Colombia* Wesleyan University Press, 2002. A thorough history of salsa and its importance to Cali's traditions and culture.

Xemina, Diego *Shakira: Woman Full of Grace* Simón & Schuster Ltd, 2001. Biography of Colombia's chart-topping singer/songwriter that chronicles the early days as a rising star and recent award-winning pop music success.

Older travellers

Gardener, Alison *Travel Unlimited: Uncommon Adventures for the Mature Traveler* Avalon Travel Publishing, 2000. Despite being in need of an update, this remains a valuable real first-of-its-kind, covering alternative worldwide travel options for adventurous older travellers. Detailed reviews explore ecological, cultural, and volunteer opportunities for people aged 50-plus who are still keen to indulge their irrepressible travel spirit.

Toland, James *Travel Tips & Trips for Seniors* Bridgeway Press, 2002. Humorous quips, anecdotes and insight make this an entertaining read for any 50-plus traveller looking for advice on great destinations that are ideal for an active older person keen to hit the ground running.

Photography

Hurtado García, Andrés *Secret Vistas of Colombia* Villegas Editores, 2005. A photographic collection focuses on panorama shots of Colombia's regional landscape and fine colonial cities.

Pulecio, Enrique and Salazar Aparicio, Miguel *Colombia Panoramica* Villegas Editores. A handsome coffee-table book containing colourful images of Colombia's most dramatic terrain.

Villegas, María *Bogotá from the Air* Villegas Asociados SA, 2002. A stunning photographic tour of Bogotá.

Von Rothkirch, Cristóbal *Bogotá Viva* Villegas Asociados SA, 2006. An anthology of urban photography, offering an honest reflection of both positive and negative aspects of city life.

Politics

Dáz Galindo, Félix *Monografá del Archipiélago de San Andrés* Ediciones Medio Pliego, 1978. Political examination of the conflict between Colombia and Nicaragua in relation to the San Andrés Archipelago (Spanish).

Kline, Harvey F *Chronicle of a Failure Foretold: The Peace Process of Colombian President Andrés Pastrana* University of Alabama Press, 2007. Not published at time of writing.

Lozano, Carlos *Guerra O Paz En Colombia?* Ocean Press, 2007. A historical perspective on the Colombian conflict, analysing the role of the US and the war on drugs, the right-wing paramilitaries and the left-wing guerrilla movements – and the real possibilities for achieving peace (Spanish).

Murillo, Mario A and Avirama, Jesús Rey *Colombia and the United States: War, Terrorism and Destabilization* Seven Stories Press, 2003. Discusses the origins of the Colombian conflict, the myths behind Colombian democracy, and how the involvement of the US has contributed to the problems.

San Andrés y Providencía: Tradiciones culturales y coyuntura política Uniandes 1989. A look at the political, social and cultural history of the San Andrés Archipelago.

Stokes, Doug *America's Other War: Terrorizing Colombia* Zed Books, 2004. A highly critical political analysis of US political involvement in Colombian policy.

Van-Cott, Donna Lee *From Movements to Parties in Latin America: The Evolution of Ethnic Politics* Cambridge University Press, 2005. Explores the surprising transformation of indigenous peoples' movements into viable political parties in the 1990s in four Latin American countries (Bolivia, Colombia, Ecuador, Venezuela) and their failure to succeed in two others (Argentina, Peru).

Van-Cott, Donna Lee *Enclave colonialista en Nicaragua: Diferendo de Nicaragua y Colombia: Plataforma Continental, Archipiélago San Andrés, Cayos, Luis Pasos Argüello* Cambridge University Press, 1978. A more detailed analysis of the dispute between Nicaragua and Colombia in relation to the contention of ownership of the San Andrés Archipelago (Spanish)

Religion

Brusco, Elizabeth C *The Reformation of Machismo: Evangelical Conversion and Gender in Colombia* University of Texas Press, 1995. Enlightening detail exploring the dramatic growth of evangelical conversion in Colombia with objective and comprehensive account of the historical failures of the Catholic Church to stem Pentacostalism.

Drury, Nevill *The Elements of Shamanism* Element Books, 1992. Concise explanation of the role of indigenous healing and spiritual rituals in tribal communities.

Eliade, Mircea *Shamanism: Archaic Techniques of Ecstasy* Arkana Publishing, 1989. A look at the hallucinogenic properties of traditional plants and their curative powers in indigenous groups.

Greco, David *Dios Sana Mi Nacion Colombia*Vida Publishing, 2002. A look at Colombian society from a healing perspective that examines God's provision for modern Christians and the nation's history of using the power of religion in a curative form.

Levine, Daniel H *Popular Voices in Latin American Catholicism* Princeton University Press, 1992. Combining interviews and community studies with analysis of broad ideological and institutional transformations, this is a fascinating look at religious and cultural change in Venezuela and Colombia.

Londono-Vega, Patricia *Religion, Society and Culture in Colombia: Medellín and Antioquía, 1850–1930* Clarendon Press, 2002. An exemplary debate about the role of the Catholic Church in the Antioquía department and its capital, Medellín.

Schultes, Richard Evans and Raffauf, Robert F *Vine of the Soul: Medicine Men, Their Plants and Rituals in the Colombian Amazonia* Synergetic Press, 2004. Over 12 years Evans Schultes and Raffauf collected 30,000 specimens, discovered 300 species and chronicled 2,000 novel medicinal plants to become two of the most important Amazonian plant explorers of the 20th century. This first hand photographic account of life in the Colombian Amazon takes an incredible journey through the use of plants in some of the most fascinating indigenous cultures on the planet.

Taussig, Michael T *Shamanism, Colonialism and the Wild Man: A Study in Terror and Healing* University of Chicago Press, 1991. Examines the role of the shaman and healing practices used in the Colombian jungles.

Society

Alfonso Florez, Jesús *Colombia's Pacific Coast: A Church Perspective* Catholic Institute for International Relations, 1996. Interesting report on the peoples of the Pacific region from a religious standpoint.

Atkins, Andy and Rey-Maquiera Palmer, Elena *Ethno-development: A Proposal to Save Colombia's Pacific Coast* Catholic Institute for International Relations 1997. Another Catholic Church report on the threat to the indigenous peoples of the Pacific coast.

Helen Kellogg Institute for International Studies *Peace, Democracy, and Human Rights in Colombia* University of Notre Dame Press, 2007. A scholarly collection of analyses and debate on the war in Colombia, the human rights of its people, the corruption and the political fragmentation.

Livingstone, Grace and Pearce, Jenny *Inside Colombia: Drugs, Democracy and War* Rutgers University Press, 2006. Intricate examination of the make-up of Colombia's conflict and the role of drugs and power in its turmoil.

Moody, Roger *The Indigenous Voice: Visions and Realities* International Books, 1993. A look at the world's indigenous tribes and the problems they face in modern societies.

Safford, Frank *Colombia: Fragmented Land, Divided Society* Oxford University Press, 2001. Background on the divisive issue of societal structure and classes in Colombia.

Salazar, Alonso *Born to Die in Medellín* Latin America Bureau, 1992. An insightful tour of the jails, hospitals and shanty towns of Colombia's second-largest city, exposing the violence of urban youth gangs.

Smith, A *Explorers of the Amazon* Penguin/Viking, 1990. An overview of the people of the Amazon region, from ancient tribes to Hispanic settlers.

Wade, Peter *Black Culture and Social Inequality in Colombia* Institute for Cultural Research, 2006.

Wade, Peter *Blackness and Race Mixture: Dynamics of Racial Identity in Colombia* John Hopkins University Press, 1995.

Sports

Hilton, Christopher *Juan Pablo Montoya* J H Haynes & Co Ltd, 2003. Story of former Formula One racing driver and current NASCAR professional, now a UN Goodwill Ambassador.

Josephs, Allen *Ritual and Sacrifice in the Corrida: The Saga of César Rincón* University Press of Florida, 2002. Demonstrates the importance of the bull fight in Colombian culture.

Rendel, Matt *Kings of the Mountains: How Colombia's Cycling Héroes Changed Their Nation's History* Aurum Press, June 2003. Part cycling history, part travelogue and part social analysis, captures the raw emotion perfectly. Rendel not only pays homage to Colombia's sporting heroes but links a passion for sport with nationalism in an almost religious understanding of cycling's pride, pain and glory.

Travel narratives

Heggstad, Glen *Two Wheels Through Terror: Diary of a South American Motorcycle Odyssey* Whitehorse Press, 2004. The shocking travelogue of adventure motorcyclist Heggstad's journey through the southern tip of South America, where he was captured by Colombia's rebel ELN army.

Kelly, B and London, M *Amazon* Harcourt 1983. A travelogue along the river by boat and plane during the pre-tourist era in the 1970s.

Mann, Mark *The Gringo Trail* Summersdale Publishers 2001. A terrifically raw, unglamorised account of backpacking around South America, including a harrowing experience in Colombia. A tumultuous read.

Nicholl, Charles *The Fruit Palace* Vintage, 1998. An amusing and eye-popping cutting-edge travelogue based on the author's amblings through Colombia in the 1980s.

Smith, Steven *Cocaine Train* Abacus, 2000. Captivating tale of Smith's journey from the UK to Colombia to trace the second family and history of his enigmatic grandfather, a railway pioneer.

Van Dyk, J *The Amazon* National Geographic, 1995. A full and descriptive travelogue of the author's trip along the length of the river.

Young readers

Cherry, Lynn *The Great Kapoc Tree: A Tale of the Amazon Rainforest* Harcourt Brace International, 2000. A good introduction to the issues of deforestation in the Amazon rainforest.

Harding, Colin *Colombia in Focus: A Guide to the People, Politics and Culture*, Latin America Bureau, 1996. Suitable for older children.

Jennings, Terry *Our World: Living in the Rainforest* 4Learning, 2002. Depicts the wildlife, birds and plants in the planet's rainforest regions, including the Amazon.

Streissguth, Thomas *Colombia in Pictures* Lerner Publications, 2004. A children's book of photographs aimed at readers aged 9–12.

WEBSITES

www.theotherlookofcolombia.com A cracking site dedicated to promoting the positive aspects of Colombia, from its sporting world champions to its pioneering physicists and peace campaigners

www.colombiaemb.org Colombian Embassy

www.visitcolombia.com Colombian tourist board

www.britain.gov.co British Embassy in Bogotá

www.travelhealth.co.uk Some useful health advice to bear in mind before you travel.

www.ethnologue.com An encyclopaedic reference cataloguing the world's 6,912 known languages

www.colombia.com Describes itself as the website of everything (Spanish)

pages.infinit.net/colombia/index.htm Some useful facts and stats on Colombia, with a rather alarming soundtrack

www.britishcouncil.org/colombia.htm (English/Spanish)

www.colombia.logtar.com Good Colombia blog from Medellín

www.juanvaldez.com Well-designed site containing news about the country's coffee industry, set up by Colombia's National Federation of Coffee Growers in order to honour the industry's rich coffee tradition and history and celebrate its iconic figurehead, Juan Valdez.

www.proexport.com.co Colombian government trade body

Bradt Travel Guides

www.bradtguides.com

Africa

Africa Overland	£15.99
Algeria	£15.99
Benin	£14.99
Botswana: Okavango, Chobe, Northern Kalahari	£15.99
Burkina Faso	£14.99
Cape Verde Islands	£13.99
Canary Islands	£13.95
Cameroon	£13.95
Congo	£14.99
Eritrea	£15.99
Ethiopia	£15.99
Gabon, São Tomé, Príncipe	£13.95
Gambia, The	£13.99
Ghana	£15.99
Johannesburg	£6.99
Kenya	£14.95
Madagascar	£15.99
Malawi	£13.99
Mali	£13.95
Mauritius, Rodrigues & Réunion	£13.99
Mozambique	£13.99
Namibia	£15.99
Niger	£14.99
Nigeria	£15.99
Rwanda	£14.99
São Tomé & Principe	£14.99
Seychelles	£14.99
Sudan	£13.95
Tanzania, Northern	£13.99
Tanzania	£16.99
Uganda	£15.99
Zambia	£17.99
Zanzibar	£12.99

Britain and Europe

Albania	£13.99
Armenia, Nagorno Karabagh	£14.99
Azores	£12.99
Baltic Capitals: Tallinn, Riga, Vilnius, Kaliningrad	£12.99
Belarus	£14.99
Belgrade	£6.99
Bosnia & Herzegovina	£13.99
Bratislava	£6.99
Budapest	£8.99
Bulgaria	£13.99
Cork	£6.99
Croatia	£13.99

Cyprus see North Cyprus	
Czech Republic	£13.99
Dresden	£7.99
Dubrovnik	£6.99
Estonia	£13.99
Faroe Islands	£13.95
Georgia	£14.99
Helsinki	£7.99
Hungary	£14.99
Iceland	£14.99
Kiev	£7.95
Kosovo	£14.99
Krakow	£7.99
Lapland	£13.99
Latvia	£13.99
Lille	£6.99
Lithuania	£13.99
Ljubljana	£7.99
Macedonia	£14.99
Montenegro	£13.99
North Cyprus	£12.99
Paris, Lille & Brussels	£11.95
Riga	£6.99
River Thames, In the Footsteps of the Famous	£10.95
Serbia	£14.99
Slovakia	£14.99
Slovenia	£12.99
Spitsbergen	£14.99
Switzerland: Rail, Road, Lake	£13.99
Tallinn	£6.99
Ukraine	£14.99
Vilnius	£6.99
Zagreb	£6.99

Middle East, Asia and Australasia

China: Yunnan Province	£13.99
Great Wall of China	£13.99
Iran	£14.99
Iraq	£14.95
Iraq: Then & Now	£15.99
Kyrgyzstan	£15.99
Maldives	£13.99
Mongolia	£14.95
North Korea	£13.95
Oman	£13.99
Sri Lanka	£13.99
Syria	£14.99
Tibet	£13.99
Turkmenistan	£14.99
Yemen	£14.99

The Americas and the Caribbean

Amazon, The	£14.99
Argentina	£15.99
Bolivia	£14.99
Cayman Islands	£14.99
Colombia	£15.99
Costa Rica	£13.99
Chile	£16.95
Dominica	£14.99
Falkland Islands	£13.95
Guyana	£14.99
Panama	£13.95
Peru & Bolivia: The Bradt Trekking Guide	£12.95
St Helena	£14.99
USA by Rail	£13.99

Wildlife

100 Animals to See Before They Die	£16.99
Antarctica: Guide to the Wildlife	£14.95
Arctic: Guide to the Wildlife	£15.99
Central & Eastern European Wildlife	£15.99
Chinese Wildlife	£16.99
East African Wildlife	£19.99
Galápagos Wildlife	£15.99
Madagascar Wildlife	£15.99
North Atlantic Wildlife	£16.99
Peruvian Wildlife	£15.99
Southern African Wildlife	£18.95
Sri Lankan Wildlife	£15.99

Eccentric Guides

Eccentric America	£13.95
Eccentric Australia	£12.99
Eccentric Britain	£13.99
Eccentric California	£13.99
Eccentric Cambridge	£6.99
Eccentric Edinburgh	£5.95
Eccentric France	£12.95
Eccentric London	£13.99
Eccentric Oxford	£5.95

Others

Your Child Abroad: A Travel Health Guide	£10.95
Something Different for the Weekend	£9.99

WIN £100 CASH!
READER QUESTIONNAIRE

Send in your completed questionnaire for the chance to win £100 cash in our regular draw

All respondents may order a Bradt guide at half the UK retail price – please complete the order form overleaf.

(Entries may be posted or faxed to us, or scanned and emailed.)

We are interested in getting feedback from our readers to help us plan future Bradt guides. Please answer ALL the questions below and return the form to us in order to qualify for an entry in our regular draw.

Have you used any other Bradt guides? If so, which titles? . . . .
. . . .

What other publishers' travel guides do you use regularly? . . . .
. . . .

Where did you buy this guidebook? . . . .

What was the main purpose of your trip to Colombia (or for what other reason did you read our guide)? eg: holiday/business/charity etc.. . . . .
. . . .

What other destinations would you like to see covered by a Bradt guide?
. . . .

Would you like to receive our catalogue/newsletters?

YES / NO (If yes, please complete details on reverse)

If yes – by post or email? . . . .

Age (circle relevant category) 16–25   26–45   46–60   60+

Male/Female (delete as appropriate)

Home country . . . .

Please send us any comments about our guide to Colombia or other Bradt Travel Guides. . . . .
. . . .
. . . .
. . . .

Bradt Travel Guides
23 High Street, Chalfont St Peter, Bucks SL9 9QE, UK
☏ +44 (0)1753 893444 f +44 (0)1753 892333
e info@bradtguides.com
www.bradtguides.com

CLAIM YOUR HALF-PRICE BRADT GUIDE!

Order Form

To order your half-price copy of a Bradt guide, and to enter our prize draw to win £100 (see overleaf), please fill in the order form below, complete the questionnaire overleaf, and send it to Bradt Travel Guides by post, fax or email.

Please send me one copy of the following guide at half the UK retail price

Title	Retail price	Half price
. . . .	. . . .	. . . .

Please send the following additional guides at full UK retail price

No	Title	Retail price	Total
. . .	....	. . . .	. . . .
. . .	....	. . . .	. . . .
. . .	....	. . . .	. . . .

Sub total . . . .
Post & packing . . . .
(£2 per book UK; £4 per book Europe; £6 per book rest of world)
Total . . . .

Name . . . .

Address . . . .

Tel . . . .   Email . . . .

☐ I enclose a cheque for £ . . . . made payable to Bradt Travel Guides Ltd

☐ I would like to pay by credit card. Number: . . . .

Expiry date: . . . / . . .   3-digit security code (on reverse of card) . . . . .

Issue no (debit cards only) . . . . .

☐ Please add my name to your catalogue mailing list.

☐ I would be happy for you to use my name and comments in Bradt marketing material.

Send your order on this form, with the completed questionnaire, to:

Bradt Travel Guides COL1
23 High Street, Chalfont St Peter, Bucks SL9 9QE
↘ +44 (0)1753 893444   f +44 (0)1753 892333
e info@bradtguides.com   www.bradtguides.com

Index

Page numbers in **bold** indicate major entries; those in *italics* indicate maps